Cancer in Women

3rd Edition

By

Suzanne Mahon, RN, DNSc, AOCN, AGN-BC

Upon successful completion of this course, continuing education hours will be awarded as follows:

Nurses: 30 Contact Hours*

*Western Schools is accredited as a provider of continuing nursing education by the American Nurses Credentialing Center's Commission on Accreditation.

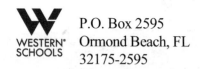

P.O. Box 2595
Ormond Beach, FL
32175-2595

ABOUT THE AUTHOR

Suzanne Mahon, RN, DNSc, AOCN, AGN-BC, has more than 35 years of oncology experience focusing primarily on cancer prevention, early detection, and genetics. She has authored more than 200 publications in peer-reviewed journals. Dr. Mahon is a frequent speaker for both the public and healthcare professionals on cancer-related topics.

Suzanne Mahon has disclosed that she has no significant financial or other conflicts of interest pertaining to this course book.

ABOUT THE PEER REVIEWER

Ellen Carr, RN, MSN, AOCN, is the Clinical Educator for the Multispecialty Clinic at the Moores Cancer Center (University of California, San Diego). She has been a healthcare writer for more than 30 years, specializing in clinical nursing, therapeutic and diagnostic technologies, and patient advocacy. As of July 2017, she is Editor of the *Clinical Journal of Oncology Nursing,* a peer-reviewed journal published by the Oncology Nursing Society (ONS).

Carr is a graduate of the University of Colorado, Boulder (BS in Journalism) and the MGH Institute of Health Professions, Boston, MA (MSN in Oncology Nursing). She holds advanced oncology nursing certification from the Oncology Nursing Certification Corporation and is a local and national member of the ONS.

Ellen Carr has disclosed that she has no significant financial or other conflicts of interest pertaining to this course book.

Nurse Planner: Patricia Hojnowski-Diaz, MS, MBA, RN

The planner who worked on this continuing education activity has disclosed that she has no significant financial or other conflicts of interest pertaining to this course book.

Copy Editor: Graphic World, Inc.

Indexer: Dianne L. Schneider

ISBN: 978-1-68041-377-9

COURSE INSTRUCTIONS
IMPORTANT: Read these instructions *BEFORE* proceeding!

HOW TO EARN CONTINUING EDUCATION CREDIT

To successfully complete this course you must:

1) Read the entire course
2) Pass the final exam with a score of 75% or higher*
3) Complete the course evaluation

You have three attempts to pass the exam. If you take the exam online, and fail to receive a passing grade, select "Retake Exam."
If you submit the exam by mail or fax and you fail to receive a passing grade, you will be notified by mail and receive an additional answer sheet.

Final exams must be received at Western Schools before the **Complete By** date located at the top of the FasTrax answer sheet enclosed with your course.

Note: The **Complete By** date is either 1 year from the date of purchase, or the expiration date assigned to the course, whichever date comes first.

HOW TO SUBMIT THE FINAL EXAM AND COURSE EVALUATION

ONLINE: BEST OPTION!

For instant grading, regardless of course format purchased, submit your exam online at **www.westernschools.com/my-courses**. Benefits of submitting exam answers online:

➢ Save time and postage
➢ Access grade results instantly and retake the exam immediately, if needed
➢ Identify and review questions answered incorrectly
➢ Access certificate of completion instantly

Note: If you have not yet registered on Western Schools' website, you will need to register and then call customer service at 800-618-1670 to request your courses be made available to you online.

Mail or Fax: To submit your exam and evaluation answers by mail or fax, fill out the FasTrax answer sheet, which is pre-printed with your name, address, and course title. If you are completing more than one course, be sure to record your answers on the correct corresponding answer sheet.

Complete the FasTrax Answer Sheet using blue or black ink only. If you make an error use correction fluid. If the exam has fewer than 100 questions, leave any remaining answer circles blank. Respond to the evaluation questions under the heading "Evaluation," found on the right-hand side of the FasTrax answer sheet. See the FasTrax Exam Grading & Certificate Issue Options enclosed with your course order for further instructions.

CHANGE OF ADDRESS?

Contact our customer service department at 800-618-1670, or customerservice@westernschools.com, if your postal or email address changes prior to completing this course.

WESTERN SCHOOLS GUARANTEES YOUR SATISFACTION

If any continuing education course fails to meet your expectations, or if you are not satisfied for any reason, you may return the course materials for an exchange or a refund (excluding shipping and handling) within 30 days, provided that you have not already received continuing education credit for the course. Software, video, and audio courses must be returned unopened. Textbooks must not be written in or marked up in any other way.

Thank you for using Western Schools to fulfill your continuing education needs!

WESTERN SCHOOLS
P.O. Box 2595
Ormond Beach, FL 32175-2595
www.westernschools.com

WESTERN SCHOOLS
COURSE EVALUATION

CANCER IN WOMEN

INSTRUCTIONS: Using the scale below, please respond to the following evaluation statements. All responses should be recorded in the right-hand column of the FasTrax answer sheet, in the section marked "Evaluation." Be sure to fill in each corresponding answer circle completely using blue or black ink. Leave any remaining answer circles blank.

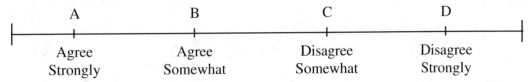

A	B	C	D
Agree Strongly	Agree Somewhat	Disagree Somewhat	Disagree Strongly

OUTCOMES: After completing this course, I am able to:

1. Describe cancer and cancer risk in women including trends, the impact of family history, and the genetic testing process.

2. Discuss the epidemiology, risk factors, prevention and detection strategies, common staging schemas, and treatment options for breast cancer.

3. Discuss the epidemiology, risk factors, prevention and detection strategies, common staging schemas, and treatment options for endometrial cancer.

4. Discuss the epidemiology, risk factors, prevention and detection strategies, common staging schemas, and treatment options for ovarian cancer.

5. Discuss the epidemiology, risk factors, prevention and detection strategies, common staging schemas, and treatment options for cervical cancer.

6. Discuss the epidemiology, risk factors, prevention and detection strategies, and treatment options for lung cancer in women.

7. Discuss the epidemiology, risk factors, prevention and detection strategies, and treatment options for colorectal cancer in women.

8. Discuss the epidemiology, risk factors, prevention and detection strategies, and treatment options for skin cancer in women.

9. Discuss the psychosocial issues that may accompany a diagnosis of cancer, including the nurse's role in and interventions for these issues.

10. Discuss psychologic, functional, and fertility issues associated with sexual activity and sexuality in women with cancer including interventions to address these issues.

11. Discuss complementary and alternative medicine options available.

12. Discuss ways for the nurse and interdisciplinary team to assist patients in evaluating and accessing credible educational resources.

COURSE CONTENT

13. The course content was presented in a well-organized and clearly written manner.

14. The course content was presented in a fair, unbiased, and balanced manner.

15. The course content presented current developments in the field.

16. The course was relevant to my professional practice or interests.

continued on next page

17. The final examination was at an appropriate level for the content of the course.

18. The course expanded my knowledge and enhanced my skills related to the subject matter.

19. I intend to apply the knowledge and skills I've learned to my practice.

A. Yes   B. Unsure   C. No   D. Not Applicable

CUSTOMER SERVICE

The following section addresses your experience in interacting with Western Schools. Use the scale below to respond to the statements in this section.

A. Yes   B. No   C. Not Applicable

20. Western Schools staff was responsive to my request for disability accommodations.

21. The Western Schools website was informative and easy to navigate.

22. The process of ordering was easy and efficient.

23. Western Schools staff was knowledgeable and helpful in addressing my questions or problems.

ATTESTATION

24. I certify that I have read the course materials and personally completed the final examination based on the material presented. Mark "A" for Agree and "B" for Disagree.

COURSE RATING

25. My overall rating for this course is

A. Poor   B. Below Average   C. Average   D. Good   E. Excellent

You may be contacted within 3 to 6 months of completing this course to participate in a brief survey to evaluate the impact of this course on your clinical practice and patient/client outcomes.

Note: To provide additional feedback regarding this course and Western Schools services, or to suggest new course topics, use the space provided on the Important Information form found on the back of the FasTrax instruction sheet included with your course.

CONTENTS

FIGURES, BOXES, AND TABLES

Chapter 7

Chapter 8

PRETEST

1. Begin this course by taking the pretest. Circle the answers to the questions on this page, or write the answers on a separate sheet of paper. Do not log answers to the pretest questions on the FasTrax test sheet included with the course.

2. Compare your answers to the pretest key located at the end of the pretest. The pretest key indicates the chapter where the content of that question is discussed. Make note of the questions you missed, so that you can focus on those areas as you complete the course.

3. Complete the course by reading the chapters and completing the exam questions at the end of each chapter. Answers to the exam questions should be logged on the FasTrax test sheet included with the course.

Note: Choose the one option that BEST answers each question.

1. Absolute risk is

   a. a characteristic associated with an increased risk of developing a disease.

   b. a comparison of the incidence of deaths among those with a particular risk factor compared with those without the risk factor.

   c. the amount of disease within the population that could be prevented by alteration of a risk factor.

   d. a measure of the occurrence of cancer, either incidence or mortality, in the general population.

2. What percentage of all diagnosed cancers are caused by hereditary factors?

   a. 5%

   b. 10%

   c. 15%

   d. 20%

3. A key indicator of hereditary cancer would be

   a. lung cancer in a 60-year-old woman with a history of smoking.

   b. colon cancer in a 40-year-old woman with a mother who had endometrial cancer at age 50 years.

   c. a woman with a maternal grandmother with breast cancer at age 62 years and a paternal aunt with breast cancer at age 55 years.

   d. a woman with cervical cancer at age 48 years.

4. Recommended strategies for the early detection of breast cancer in a woman of average risk would include

   a. mammography and magnetic resonance imaging (MRI).

   b. mammography.

   c. breast self-examination and mammography.

   d. breast self-examination, mammography, and MRI.

continued on next page

5. A malignant condition of the endometrium is

   a. fibroid tumors.

   b. endometriosis.

   c. adenocarcinoma.

   d. endometrial hyperplasia.

6. Ovarian cancer is a deadly cancer because

   a. the CA-125 gene is undetectable.

   b. pelvic exams never detect masses.

   c. there are no treatment options.

   d. there are few symptoms.

7. A Papanicolaou (Pap) test appointment should be scheduled preferably

   a. during the last half of the menstrual cycle following ovulation.

   b. 2 weeks after the first day of last period.

   c. less than 10 days after the first day of last period.

   d. at least 20 days after the last day of last period.

8. The leading cause of cancer deaths in women is

   a. breast cancer.

   b. colorectal cancer.

   c. lung cancer.

   d. skin cancer.

9. The most common type of lung cancer is

   a. mucinous.

   b. non-small cell lung cancer.

   c. carcinoid.

   d. small cell lung cancer.

10. For women in the United States, colorectal cancer is

   a. the main cause of death.

   b. the second leading cause of death.

   c. the third leading cause of death.

   d. equal to breast cancer as a cause of death.

11. A type of nonmelanoma skin cancer is

   a. actinic keratoses.

   b. squamous cell carcinoma.

   c. seborrheic keratoses.

   d. hemangiomas.

12. The minimum recommended sun protection factor (SPF) for sunscreen is

   a. 4.

   b. 15.

   c. 30.

   d. 40.

13. Studies about patient support indicate that one of the most supportive interventions a nurse can offer the patient with cancer is to

   a. ask a question.

   b. develop a plan of action.

   c. listen.

   d. document.

14. Younger women being treated for cancer may wish to preserve their reproductive options. Therefore, a first step in treatment planning is to

   a. immediately start tissue banking.

   b. choose to cryopreserve embryos.

   c. seek counseling about options.

   d. seek counseling about losing their ability to be mothers.

15. A strategy to discuss sexuality issues with a patient is the PLISSIT model. The PLISSIT model is an acronym for the levels of

    a. planning, limited information, specific suggestion, and idealism.

    b. permission, limited information, specific suggestion, and intensive therapy.

    c. prioritizing, limited ideas, some suggestions, and ideal timing.

    d. permission, levels of intervention, specific suggestions, ideas, and treatment.

16. An example of a complementary and alternative therapies category is

    a. chemotherapy.

    b. biotherapy.

    c. mind-body practices.

    d. immunotherapy.

17. A disadvantage of an Internet support group is

    a. the inability to assess body language.

    b. it is always available for a person to seek support.

    c. the time limitation.

    d. the limited geographical reach.

PRETEST KEY

1.	D	Chapter 1
2.	B	Chapter 2
3.	B	Chapter 3
4.	B	Chapter 3
5.	C	Chapter 4
6.	D	Chapter 5
7.	B	Chapter 6
8.	C	Chapter 7
9.	B	Chapter 7
10.	C	Chapter 8
11.	B	Chapter 9
12.	C	Chapter 9
13.	C	Chapter10
14.	C	Chapter 11
15.	B	Chapter 11
16.	C	Chapter 12
17.	A	Chapter 13

INTRODUCTION

LEARNING OUTCOMES

After completing this course, the learner will be able to:

1. Describe cancer and cancer risk in women including trends, the impact of family history, and the genetic testing process.

2. Discuss the epidemiology, risk factors, prevention and detection strategies, common staging schemas, and treatment options for breast cancer.

3. Discuss the epidemiology, risk factors, prevention and detection strategies, common staging schemas, and treatment options for endometrial cancer.

4. Discuss the epidemiology, risk factors, prevention and detection strategies, common staging schemas, and treatment options for ovarian cancer.

5. Discuss the epidemiology, risk factors, prevention and detection strategies, common staging schemas, and treatment options for cervical cancer.

6. Discuss the epidemiology, risk factors, prevention and detection strategies, and treatment options for lung cancer in women.

7. Discuss the epidemiology, risk factors, prevention and detection strategies, and treatment options for colorectal cancer in women.

8. Discuss the epidemiology, risk factors, prevention and detection strategies, and treatment options for skin cancer in women.

9. Discuss the psychosocial issues that may accompany a diagnosis of cancer, including the nurse's role in and interventions for these issues.

10. Discuss psychologic, functional, and fertility issues associated with sexual activity and sexuality in women with cancer including interventions to address these issues.

11. Discuss complementary and alternative medicine options available.

12. Discuss ways for the nurse and interdisciplinary team to assist patients in evaluating and accessing credible educational resources.

Cancer is a major public health problem. It is the second leading cause of death in women in the United States. An estimated 852,630 women are diagnosed annually with cancer, and 282,500 women die of the disease every year. Breast, lung, colorectal, and uterine cancers alone account for approximately 57% of newly diagnosed cancers each year. One in three women in the United States is at risk for developing cancer during her lifetime (American Cancer Society, 2017). This course will enable nurses to better understand the major cancers that affect women and the nursing care needs of these women and their families.

The experience of a woman diagnosed with cancer can be distinctive. Many cancers affect both males and females, but some are unique to women and impact women during childbearing years. The impact of a cancer diagnosis for either a man or a woman can be devastating and have a cascading impact on the immediate and extended family. Even though roles in society are evolving from what were historically female responsibilities, such as child care and household management, many women continue in these roles in addition to working outside the home and being head of households with financial responsibilities.

This course reviews many of the major concepts in nursing care when women are diagnosed with malignancies. The major cancers that affect women are addressed, including breast, ovarian, uterine, cervical, lung, colorectal, and skin cancers. Information about each of these cancers includes an overview of the epidemiology of the cancer, risk factors, risk assessment, prevention and detection strategies, diagnosis, staging, and treatment modalities. Chapters that address genetic risk, psychosocial concerns, sexuality, alternative and complementary medicine, and patient education considerations are also included.

Nurses have unique and privileged access to patients and families, which provides an opportunity to promote awareness of cancer prevention and early detection. Overall, the Healthy People 2020 goals seek to reduce the overall incidence of cancer from 163.2 to 161.3 per 100,000 population and to increase the number of persons living 5 or more years after a diagnosis of cancer from 62.5% to 71.7% by the year 2020 (U.S. Department of Health and Human Services, 2016). Specific goals are available for each of the major malignancies that affect women. These goals will only be met with the consistent application of cancer prevention and detection services combined with the most comprehensive and current treatments for malignancies, together with ongoing supportive care for the ever-growing population of cancer survivors. This course provides a foundation for nursing care to address the goals established by Healthy People 2020.

Nursing interventions are key in promoting the best possible outcomes no matter where a patient is on the cancer trajectory journey. Nurses with an interest in oncology will benefit from the resources provided for their own professional development and as information for patients and families. Case studies and commentaries are included throughout the course to illustrate content and to assist with concepts and knowledge acquisition for application in practice settings.

This course provides registered nurses and advanced practice nurses with evidence-based information to inform their practice when caring for women diagnosed with cancer. Its comprehensive content serves as a foundation for competent and state-of-the-art nursing practice.

References

American Cancer Society. (2017). *Cancer facts & figures – 2017.* Atlanta, GA: Author.

U.S. Department of Health and Human Services, Office of Disease Prevention and Health Promotion. (2016). *Healthy People 2020: Cancer.* Retrieved from https://www.healthypeople.gov/2020/data-search/Search-the-Data?&f[0]=field_topic_area%3A3513

CHAPTER 1

OVERVIEW OF CANCER IN WOMEN

LEARNING OUTCOME

After completing this chapter, the learner will be able to discuss cancer topics relevant to women with cancer, including epidemiology, prevention, and treatment.

CHAPTER OBJECTIVES

After completing this chapter, the learner will be able to:

1. Describe principles of cancer biology and epidemiology.

2. Identify assessment and prevention of cancer in women, including types of risk assessment, levels of prevention, and staging.

3. Explain the various treatment modalities available to women with cancer.

INTRODUCTION

Cancer remains a major public health problem. An estimated 852,630 women are diagnosed with cancer annually, and an estimated 282,500 women die of malignancy annually (American Cancer Society [ACS], 2017a). Women are most commonly diagnosed with cancers of the breast, lung, colon, uterus, cervix, ovary, and skin (malignant melanoma). Nurses will care for women at risk for these malignancies, women being treated for cancer, long-term survivors, and those receiving palliative and end-of-life care.

A woman recently diagnosed with cancer may feel helpless and believe that little can be done to change the course of cancer. This is an unfortunate myth. When nurses understand the basic concepts of cancer biology, genetics, and epidemiology, as well as how to prevent and detect cancer early, they can help women to understand how to play an important role in reducing the morbidity and mortality associated with a cancer diagnosis. Advances in treatments continue to improve outcomes after a diagnosis of cancer but require expert nursing care to educate and support patients and families, and to manage the side effects associated with malignancy and its treatments.

BIOLOGY AND EPIDEMIOLOGY OF CANCER

Women face both uniquely female-specific cancers and almost all other types of cancers with the exception of male-organ-specific types. Women diagnosed with cancer have specific and distinctive needs. Nurses have important roles in addressing the needs of women living with a cancer diagnosis, for example, as patient educators, advocates, and providers of direct patient care.

1

Biology

Cancer develops when cells grow and divide without control and consistency. Normal cells grow, divide, and die. Malignant cells continue to grow and form new abnormal cells and then can spread (metastasize) to other organs through the bloodstream or lymph system.

Normally, cell division and replication are a tightly organized process. Cancer cells proliferate because of genetic abnormalities and external changes (carcinogens) that cause damage to cellular DNA. When DNA is damaged, normal cells can repair themselves. However, malignant cells cannot repair themselves. Individuals can inherit damaged DNA, which accounts for inherited cancers (about 5% to 10% of all new cases); this is called a *germline mutation* (Weitzel, Blazer, MacDonald, Culver, & Offit, 2011). In most cancer cases, DNA becomes damaged by exposure to something in the environment (such as smoking, dietary consumption of carcinogens, or exposure to ultraviolet light; ACS, 2017b); these are known as somatic changes.

In most cases, malignancies develop over time in a multistep process. The genetic changes that contribute to cancer tend to affect three main types of genes known as proto-oncogenes, tumor suppressor genes, and DNA repair genes (Polek, 2017). Proto-oncogenes are involved in normal cell growth and division. However, when these genes are altered in certain ways or are more active than normal, they may become cancer-causing genes (or oncogenes), allowing cells to grow and survive when they should not. Tumor suppressor genes are also involved in controlling cell growth and division. Cells with certain alterations in tumor suppressor genes may divide in an uncontrolled manner. DNA repair genes are involved in fixing damaged DNA. Cells with mutations in these genes tend to develop additional mutations in other genes. Together, these mutations may cause the cells to become cancerous.

Cancer can result from abnormal proliferation of any of the different types of cells in the body; therefore, there are many types of cancer, which can vary substantially in their behavior and response to treatment. The most important issue in cancer pathology is the distinction between benign and malignant tumors. A tumor is any abnormal proliferation of cells, which may be either benign or malignant. A benign tumor, such as a common skin wart, remains confined to its original location, neither invading surrounding normal tissue nor spreading to distant body sites. A malignant tumor, however, is capable of both invading surrounding normal tissue and spreading throughout the body via the circulatory or lymphatic systems. This process is known as metastasis. It is important to detect malignancies early because malignant tumors have the ability to invade and metastasize throughout the body.

Epidemiology

Cancer is the second leading cause of death in the United States after cardiovascular disease. It affects three of every four families. According to the ACS, an estimated 852,630 women in the United States would be diagnosed with cancer during 2017, and 282,500 women would die from cancer (ACS, 2017a).

Clearly, cancer is a staggering public health concern. Approximately one of every two American men and one of every three American women will have some type of cancer at some point during their lifetime (ACS, 2017a). Anyone can get cancer at any age; however, about 86% of all cancers are diagnosed in people aged 50 years and older (ACS, 2017a). Although cancer occurs in Americans of all racial and ethnic groups, the rate of cancer occurrence (called the *incidence rate*) varies from group to group (ACS, 2015b,

2016a, 2017a). Incidence refers to the number of newly diagnosed cancers in a given time period in a specific population. The annual cost for treating cancer is estimated to be $74.8 billion (ACS, 2017a).

The 5-year relative survival rate for all cancers diagnosed between 2006-2012 is 66.9%, an improvement from 49% between 1975 and 1977 (ACS, 2017a). The survival statistics vary greatly by cancer type and stage at diagnosis. It is estimated that nearly 15.5 million people in the United States are living with cancer or have been cured of the disease (ACS, 2016b). When a cancer is detected and when treatment is initiated have a direct effect on the patient's odds for long-term survival: early detection and treatment lead to better long-term survival rates compared with later detection and treatment (ACS, 2017a).

Cancer epidemiology provided the foundation of cancer prevention and early detection recommendations. Figure 1-1 shows cancer incidence rates for all cancers (Howlader et al., 2016). Several professional organizations and reputable institutions offer general information about cancer for the layperson and healthcare provider. Some organizations provide detailed information about special populations and tumor types. Nurses need to obtain this information from valid and reliable resources and then direct patients to such information. See the Resources section at the end of this course for a listing of the organizations discussed later.

Each year the ACS publishes *Cancer Facts and Figures,* a reference that includes estimated incidence and mortality rates. The publication also is posted on the ACS website.

Another source of cancer data is the Surveillance, Epidemiology, and End Results Program database from the National Cancer Institute. Surveillance, Epidemiology, and End Results Program data include incidence, mortality, and survival data from 1973 to the present. Another commonly cited evidence-based resource is available from the National Comprehensive Cancer Network. This consortium of cancer centers updates evidence-based

FIGURE 1-1: NEW CANCER CASES AND DEATHS, 1992 TO 2013

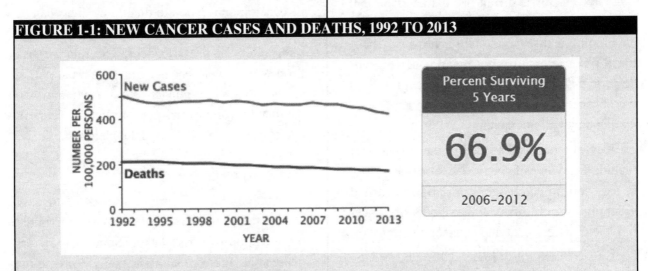

The number of new cases of cancer of any site was 448.7 per 100,000 men and women per year. The number of deaths was 168.5 per 100,000 men and women per year. These rates are age adjusted and are based on 2009 to 2013 cases and deaths. Approximately 39.0% of men and women will be diagnosed with cancer of any site at some point during their lifetime, based on 2011 to 2013 data.

Note. From Howlader, N., Noone, A. M., Krapcho, M., Miller, D., Bishop, K., Altekruse, S. F., ... Cronin, K. A. (Eds). (2016). *SEER cancer statistics review, 1975-2013, National Cancer Institute*. Bethesda, MD: National Cancer Institute. Retrieved from https://seer.cancer.gov/statfacts/html/all.html

cancer resources about prevention and screening, genetic assessment, management, and cancer treatment. This free resource provides specific cancer diagnosis summaries, which can be helpful when creating patient teaching plans.

Overall cancer mortality is decreasing. The total cancer mortality rate in the United States peaked in 1991 at 215 cancer deaths per 100,000 persons, largely because of widespread tobacco use (ACS, 2017a). From 1991 to 2012, the mortality rate dropped 25% because of reductions in smoking and improvements in early detection and treatment, resulting in more than 2.1 million fewer cancer deaths. Mortality rates have declined for lung, colorectal, and breast cancers (ACS, 2017a).

RISK ASSESSMENT, PREVENTION, AND DETECTION

Risk Assessment

A risk factor is a trait or characteristic that is associated with an increased likelihood of developing a disease. Notably, however, having a risk factor does not mean a person will develop a disease, such as malignancy, nor does the absence of a risk factor mean a disease or malignancy will not develop.

Key elements of a cancer risk assessment include a review of medical history, a history of exposure to carcinogens in daily living, and a detailed family history. The goals of cancer risk factor assessment and counseling are to: (a) provide accurate information about the genetic, biological, and environmental factors related to an individual's risk of developing cancer; (b) formulate appropriate recommendations for primary and secondary prevention; and (c) offer emotional and psychosocial support to facilitate adjustment to the information regarding risk,

and promote adherence to recommendations for prevention and early detection (Fagerlin, Zikmund-Fisher, & Ubel, 2011).

There are several types of risk. Absolute risk is a measure of the occurrence of cancer, either incidence (new cases) or mortality (deaths), in the general population. Absolute risk is helpful when a patient needs to understand what the odds are for all persons in a population of developing a particular disease. For example, women in the United States have a one in eight chance of developing breast cancer in their lifetime (ACS, 2015a).

The term relative risk refers to a comparison of the incidence or deaths among those with a particular risk factor compared with those without the risk factor. With the use of relative risk factors, individuals can determine their risk factors and thus better understand their personal odds of developing a specific cancer compared with an individual without such risk factors. If the risk of a person with no known risk factors is 1.0, one can evaluate the risk of those with risk factors in relation to this figure. This can be illustrated by considering several of the relative risk factors of breast cancer. The relative risk for a woman who has her first menstrual period at age 10 years compared with a woman who has her first menstrual period after 12 years of age is 1.3 (ACS, 2015a). This means she is 1.3 times more likely to have breast cancer than the woman with later menarche.

Attributable risk is the amount of disease within the population that could be prevented by alteration of a risk factor. Some risk factors that can be altered could potentially decrease the morbidity and mortality associated with malignancy in a large number of people. Smoking is an example of this. Since 1964, smoking has contributed to 20 million premature deaths (ACS, 2017b). Annually, tobacco use results in an estimated 480,000 premature deaths, of which

42,000 are attributed to secondhand smoke exposure (ACS, 2017a). Similarly, approximately one-quarter to one-third of the 1,688,780 cancer cases expected to occur annually can be attributed to poor nutrition, physical inactivity, overweight, and obesity; more attention needs to be given to these lifestyle factors and their role in carcinogenesis (ACS, 2017b; Kushi et al., 2012). Clearly, altering lifestyle risk factors could significantly change the morbidity and mortality associated with cancer in the future. Overall, the ACS estimates that at least half of all cancers could be prevented by embracing a healthier lifestyle, which includes quitting smoking, avoiding ultraviolet light exposure, eating healthier, exercising regularly, and maintaining an ideal body weight (ACS, 2017b).

The risk assessment drives the recommendations for screening. It is critical for patients and healthcare providers alike to understand the importance of an accurate assessment. The patient needs to understand that the more complete and accurate the data, the better the risk assessment and the more likely that appropriate screening and prevention strategies will be selected. If risk is underestimated, recommended general population screening maneuvers may not be adequate. If risk is overestimated, expensive and potentially unnecessary screening may be implemented.

An example of the importance of accurate risk assessment and recommendation of subsequent screening modalities would be the use of breast magnetic resonance imaging in women at increased risk for developing breast cancer (greater than 20%) or a documented genetic predisposition for developing breast cancer. The ACS recommends the use of breast magnetic resonance imaging with mammography starting at age 30 years in such women (ACS, 2015a).

Once all information is gathered, it must be communicated to the patient in understandable terms. Often this is accomplished by using various risk calculations such as absolute risk, relative risk, attributable risk, or specific risk models for various cancers (such as the Gail model for breast cancer risk). It is important for patients to understand that a general limitation of risk assessment is that no model completely and accurately explains an individual's risk for developing a particular cancer (Fagerlin et al., 2011).

Risk factor assessment is challenging to do and is not complete until the patient has an accurate understanding of her risk. Risk assessment can be confusing and frightening to patients. Not all risk factors are amenable to change. This is the case with many risk factors for breast cancer. Individuals cannot change their sex, age, family history, or age at menarche. If the risk factors are perceived as great in number, the individual may be too overwhelmed to engage in screening. If the risk factors can be modified or eliminated (such as tobacco and alcohol use or a high-fat diet), it is possible for an individual to actually decrease the risk of developing cancer. In such cases, it is important for the nurse to provide education and support to modify risk factors whenever possible.

Levels of Cancer Prevention

Cancer prevention has three levels: primary prevention, secondary prevention, and tertiary prevention. Primary prevention refers to the prevention of disease, such as immunization against childhood diseases, avoidance of tobacco products, or reduced exposure to ultraviolet rays. Lifestyle issues contribute significantly to cancers in women; poor diet, alcohol use, and physical inactivity account for more than 20% of all malignancies (ACS, 2017b). Recommended primary prevention measures are listed in Figure 1-2. Primary prevention can also include use of medications that prevent cancer from developing; this is termed chemoprevention.

FIGURE 1-2: PRIMARY CANCER PREVENTION STRATEGIES

- Achieve and maintain a healthy weight throughout life, avoiding excess weight gain at all ages.

- Limit consumption of high-calorie foods and beverages, especially those high in fat.

- Limit consumption of red and processed meat.

- Eat at least 2½ cups of vegetables and fruits each day.

- Choose whole grains instead of refined-grain products.

- Limit consumption of alcoholic beverages.

- Engage in regular physical activity; for adults, this means at least 150 minutes of moderate-intensity activity or 75 minutes of vigorous-intensity activity each week, or an equivalent combination. Children and adolescents should engage in at least 1 hour of moderate- or vigorous-intensity activity each day, with vigorous-intensity activity at least 3 days each week.

- Limit sedentary behavior, such as sitting, lying down, and engaging in screen-based entertainment.

- Avoid tobacco products of all types.

- Seek the shade when outdoors, especially between the hours of 10:00 a.m. and 4:00 p.m.

- Wear wide-brim hats that shade the face, ears, and neck.

- Choose clothing that adequately covers the arms, legs, and torso.

- Consistently wear ultraviolet-protective sunglasses to protect the eyes.

- Apply adequate amounts of broad-spectrum sunscreen lotion with a sun protection factor of 30 or higher to exposed skin.

- Avoid indoor tanning booths and sunlamps.

Note. Adapted from American Cancer Society. (2017a). *Cancer facts and figures – 2017.* Atlanta, GA: Author; American Cancer Society. (2017b). *Cancer prevention and early detection facts and figures 2017-2018.* Atlanta, GA: Author; Kushi, L. H., Doyle, C., McCullough, M., Rock, C. L., Demark-Wahnefried, W., Bandera, E. V., … Nutrition and Physical Activity Guidelines Advisory Committee. (2012). American Cancer Society guidelines on nutrition and physical activity for cancer prevention. *CA: A Cancer Journal for Clinicians, 62*(1), 30-67. doi:10.3322/caac.20140

Secondary prevention refers to early detection and/or screening and treatment of subclinical, asymptomatic, or early disease in persons without signs or symptoms of cancer. Forms of secondary cancer prevention include the use of the Papanicolaou (Pap) smear to detect cervical cancer and mammography to detect a nonpalpable breast cancer. Cancer screening is aimed at asymptomatic persons, with the goal of detecting disease when it is most easily treated.

Tertiary prevention is the third level of prevention, and it is becoming more and more important given the ever-growing number of cancer survivors. Tertiary prevention refers to the management of an illness such as cancer to prevent progression, recurrence, or other complications, such as second malignancies (ACS, 2017b).

Screening and Detection

Screening aims to find cancers in asymptomatic persons when treatment is most likely to be effective. Screening also offers the opportunity to detect some cancers early, when any treatment required is less extensive and more likely to be successful. For example, mammography can result in the detection of a breast cancer months to years before it might be symptomatic with palpation (ACS, 2017a). When a breast cancer is detected early, the woman often has the choice of having a less extensive surgery and avoiding chemotherapy. A breast cancer that is detected early that has not spread outside of the breast is associated with a 5-year survivorship rate of 99% (ACS, 2017a). Screening is effective for cancers of the breast, colon, rectum, cervix, skin, and lung (and in men for the prostate).

In some cases, cancers can be prevented during screening examinations. For example, screening can prevent colorectal and cervical cancers by allowing for the detection and removal of pre-cancerous lesions (ACS, 2017b, 2017c).

A screening protocol or recommendation defines how cancer screening tests should be used. Table 1-1 illustrates the current ACS recommendations for the early detection of cancer in asymptomatic women. This is an example of a screening protocol. Such recommendations can vary among organizations and practitioners. These recommendations are readily available for comparison from the U.S. Department of Health and Human Services, Agency for Healthcare Research and Quality (http://www.guidelines.gov). Recommendations are often modified for persons with many risk factors, especially for persons with a known hereditary risk for developing cancer.

The nurse working in a primary care, OB/GYN, clinic, or public health setting needs to be familiar with population- and age-specific screening recommendations to promote patient compliance and to provide education about the benefits of early detection of disease. After completing a comprehensive risk assessment that includes the woman's age and individual risk factors, the nurse can educate on the importance of screening and recommend an appropriate screening or protocol (Mahon, 2017). Oncology nurses and those who work with long-term survivors of malignancy also need to be familiar with recommendations for cancer prevention and early detection to decrease the risk for developing second malignancies.

Staging

Staging is the process of finding out how much cancer there is in the body and where it is located. This information is used to plan treatment and to predict prognosis. Cancers of the same stage usually have similar outlooks and are often treated the same way.

For most cancers, the stage is based on three main factors: tumor size, lymph node invasion, and spread to distant areas of the body. The American Joint Committee on Cancer developed the TNM classification system as a tool

TABLE 1-1: SUMMARY OF AMERICAN CANCER SOCIETY RECOMMENDATIONS FOR THE EARLY DETECTION OF CANCER IN WOMEN (1 OF 2)	
Cancer-Related Checkup	For individuals 20 years of age and older having periodic health examinations, a cancer-related checkup should include health counseling and might include examinations for cancers of the thyroid, oral cavity, skin, lymph nodes, and ovaries.
Breast Cancer	• All women aged 45 to 54 years should undergo annual screening mammography. • Women may choose to start annual mammography at age 40 years. • Women aged 55 years and older can choose biennial mammogram screening or choose to continue annual screening. • Women should continue mammography screening as long as overall health is good and life expectancy is estimated to be at least 10 years. • Women should be instructed on the signs and symptoms of breast cancer that should be evaluated immediately.

TABLE 1-1: SUMMARY OF AMERICAN CANCER SOCIETY RECOMMENDATIONS FOR THE EARLY DETECTION OF CANCER IN WOMEN (2 OF 2)	
Colorectal Cancer	Beginning at age 50 years, women at average risk for developing colorectal cancer should have one of the following screening tests. *Tests that find polyps and cancer* <ul><li>Flexible sigmoidoscopy every 5 years, followed by colonoscopy if positive</li><li>Colonoscopy every 10 years</li><li>Double-contrast barium enema every 5 years, followed by colonoscopy if positive</li><li>Computed tomographic colonography (virtual colonoscopy) every 5 years, followed by colonoscopy if positive</li></ul> *Tests that mainly find cancer (all to be followed by colonoscopy if positive)* <ul><li>Yearly fecal occult blood test</li><li>Yearly fecal immunochemical test</li><li>Stool DNA test, interval uncertain</li></ul> Persons of moderate or high risk should consult a healthcare provider for specific recommendations that consider risk factors and age of affected relatives.
Cervical Cancer	<ul><li>Women aged 21 to 29 years should have a Papanicolaou (Pap) test screening every 3 years with conventional or liquid-based Pap tests.</li><li>Women aged 30 to 65 years should have screening done every 5 years with both the human papillomavirus test and the Pap test, or every 3 years with the Pap test alone.</li><li>Women aged 66 years and older who have had three or more consecutive negative Pap tests or two or more consecutive negative human papillomavirus and Pap tests within the past 10 years, with the most recent test occurring in the past 5 years, should stop cervical cancer screening.</li><li>Women who have had a total hysterectomy should stop cervical cancer screening.</li></ul>
Endometrial Cancer	At menopause, all women should be informed about the risks and symptoms of endometrial cancer and strongly urged to report any unexpected bleeding or spotting.
Lung Cancer	<ul><li>All current smokers should be encouraged to quit and offered smoking cessation support.</li><li>Current or former smokers aged 55 to 74 years who are in good health with a pack-year history of smoking of 30 or more should be counseled about low-dose helical computed tomography. This should include a discussion of the potential harms and benefits of such screening.</li></ul>

Note. Adapted from American Cancer Society. (2017c). *Colorectal cancer facts and figures 2017-2019.* Atlanta, GA: Author.

for doctors to stage different types of cancer based on certain standards (Amin et al., 2017). In the TNM system, each cancer is assigned a T, N, and M category. The T category describes the original (primary) tumor in metric measurements. The N category describes whether the cancer has spread into nearby lymph nodes. The M category tells whether there are distant metastases (spread of cancer to other parts of body). Once the T, N, and M have been determined, they are combined, and an overall stage of 0, I, II, III, or IV is assigned.

Prognosis is also affected by the grade of the tumor. Tumor grade describes how different the cancer cells look compared with normal ones. Higher-grade cancers (4 on a scale of 1 to 4) usually have a poorer prognosis and sometimes need different treatments (Bossuyt & Symmans, 2016).

TREATMENT MODALITIES

Treatment for malignancy includes many modalities (ACS, 2017a). Surgery and radiation therapy are treatments that are used directly to remove or destroy the tumor that can be measured. Patients may have microscopic disease that is not easily measured or detectable on imaging. Often systemic therapies are used to directly treat the tumor, as well as microscopic cancers that may be throughout the body. Examples of systemic therapies include chemotherapy, immunotherapy, targeted therapy, and hormonal therapy.

Surgery is the oldest form of cancer treatment and in many cases can be curative. It also plays a key role in diagnosing and staging cancer. Advances in surgical techniques have allowed surgeons to successfully operate on a growing number of patients, often with less invasive procedures. Surgery can be used to debulk (remove as much tumor as possible), palliate (treat advanced complications of cancer), restore (reconstructive surgery), or prevent (prophylactic) cancer (Weitzel et al., 2011). Often, less invasive operations can be done to remove tumors while preserving as much normal tissue and function as possible.

Radiation therapy uses high-energy particles or waves, such as X-rays, gamma rays, electrons, or protons, to destroy or damage cancer cells (ACS, 2017a). Radiation therapy uses special equipment to deliver high doses of radiation to cancer cells, killing or damaging them so they cannot grow or spread. Radiation therapy works by breaking a strand of the DNA mol-

ecule inside the cancer cell, which prevents the cell from growing and dividing. Although some normal cells may be affected by radiation, most recover fully from the effects of the treatment.

Chemotherapy uses medications/agents or chemicals to kill cancer cells that have metastasized or spread to parts of the body far away from the primary tumor (ACS, 2017a). More than 100 chemotherapy agents are used in many different combinations. A single chemotherapy agent can be used to treat cancer; however, agents generally work better when used in certain combinations, called *combination chemotherapy.* A combination of chemotherapy agents with different actions can work together to kill more cancer cells and reduce the chance that the cancer may become resistant to any one chemotherapy medication. Chemotherapeutic agents may be administered in a number of ways, including intravenously or orally.

Researchers are developing newer medications, called *targeted-therapy drugs,* that focus on destroying cancer cells with specific biological characteristics (ACS, 2017a). Targeted-therapy drugs identify and attack certain parts of malignant cells that make them different from other cells, or they target other cells that help cancer cells grow.

Immunotherapy is a type of biological therapy that utilizes substances made from living organisms to treat cancer (ACS, 2017a). Monoclonal antibodies are a type of immunotherapy that is designed to bind to specific targets in the body. They can cause an immune response that destroys cancer cells.

Hormone therapy slows or halts the growth of cancers that depend on hormones to grow (ACS, 2015a). Hormone therapy works by blocking the body's ability to produce hormones or interfering with how hormones behave in the body. Hormone therapy can reduce the risk that cancer will recur, or stop or slow its growth.

An excellent resource for learning more about evidence-based recommendations for the treatment of malignancy is the National Comprehensive Cancer Network (see Resources).

CANCER IN WOMEN: TRENDS AND SPECIAL ISSUES

Epidemiologists take into account incidence and mortality rates together when making public health decisions. Figure 1-3 shows the incidence of the most common malignancies in females. Mortality, which is the number of people who die of a specific cancer during a particular time period, is presented in Figure 1-4.

Breast cancer, although sometimes diagnosed in men, is predominantly a female disease. Breast cancer is the most common new cancer diagnosed in women (followed by lung cancer); however, more women die of lung cancer each year (ACS, 2017a; see Figure 1-3). Breast cancer is the second leading cause of cancer deaths in women. Because of this, women are highly concerned with ways to prevent, diagnose, and treat breast cancer. For Black women, the interest is heightened because breast cancer is frequently diagnosed at a later stage than in White women, leading to a higher mortality rate (ACS, 2015a). See Figure 1-4 for

FIGURE 1-3: INCIDENCE OF 10 COMMON CANCERS DIAGNOSED IN FEMALES, 2017

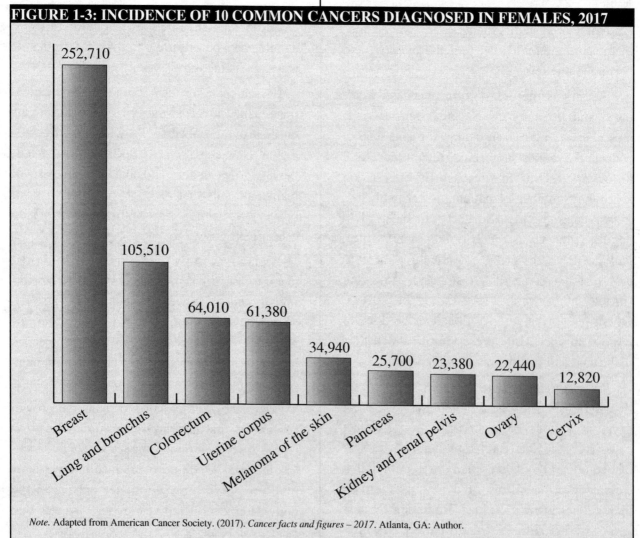

Note. Adapted from American Cancer Society. (2017). *Cancer facts and figures – 2017.* Atlanta, GA: Author.

FIGURE 1-4: MORTALITY FROM COMMON CANCERS DIAGNOSED IN FEMALES

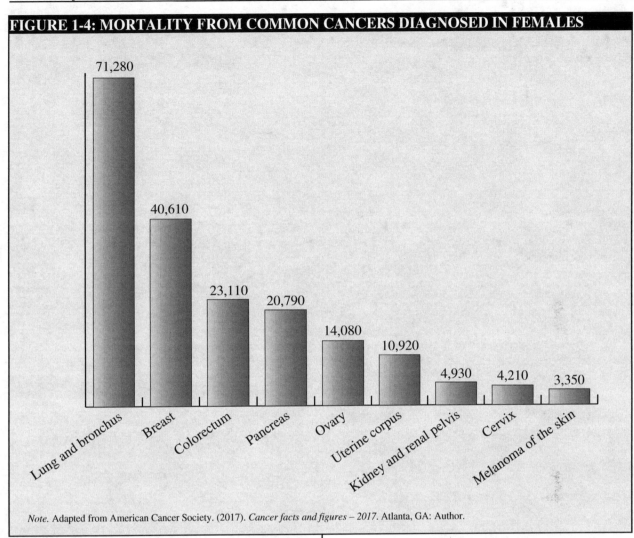

Note. Adapted from American Cancer Society. (2017). *Cancer facts and figures – 2017.* Atlanta, GA: Author.

the mortality rates from common cancers diagnosed in women.

Nurses work with women at risk for cancer to ensure they understand and engage in appropriate cancer prevention and early detection practices. (Table 1-1 reviews the ACS's recommendations for the early detection of cancer in women.) Nurses assist patients in navigating the healthcare maze during the detection and evaluation phase, provide specialized care during the workup and treatment phase, and provide supportive care throughout, whether long-term survival with ongoing checkups or when disease progresses to the terminal phase.

SUMMARY

This chapter provides an overview of cancer, including cancer biology, epidemiology, risk assessment, levels of prevention, screening, detection, staging, and treatment modalities. The highest mortality cancers specific to women are discussed. The information in this chapter is the platform for upcoming chapters that explore cancer in more depth, and inform the nurse about the specific cancers that affect women.

EXAM QUESTIONS

CHAPTER 1
Questions 1–5

Note: Choose the one option that BEST answers each question.

1. A comparison of the incidence or deaths among those with a particular risk factor compared with those without the risk factor is

   a. relative risk.
   b. absolute risk.
   c. mutation risk.
   d. attributable risk.

2. A primary prevention strategy is

   a. having an annual Papanicolua (Pap) smear.
   b. using a sunscreen with a sun protection factor of at least 30.
   c. having a cancer-related checkup.
   d. initiating mammography at age 45 years.

3. Nurses should educate a woman about a screening protocol that is appropriate for the woman based on

   a. mutation risk.
   b. age.
   c. comprehensive risk assessment.
   d. relative risk.

4. Examples of systemic therapies include

   a. surgery, radiation therapy, and chemotherapy.
   b. chemotherapy, radiation therapy, and targeted therapies.
   c. hormonal therapy, chemotherapy, and immunotherapy.
   d. surgery, hormonal therapy, and immunotherapy.

5. Which cancer produces the highest mortality rate among women each year?

   a. Breast cancer
   b. Lung cancer
   c. Skin cancer
   d. Colon cancer

REFERENCES

American Cancer Society. (2015a). *Breast cancer facts and figures 2015-2016*. Atlanta, GA: Author.

American Cancer Society. (2015b). *Cancer facts and figures for Hispanics/Latinos 2015-2017*. Atlanta, GA: Author.

American Cancer Society. (2016a). *Cancer facts and figures for African Americans 2016-2018*. Atlanta, GA: Author.

American Cancer Society. (2016b). *Cancer treatment and survivorship facts and figures 2016-2017*. Atlanta, GA: Author.

American Cancer Society. (2017a). *Cancer facts and figures – 2017*. Atlanta, GA: Author.

American Cancer Society. (2017b). *Cancer prevention and early detection facts and figures 2017-2018*. Atlanta, GA: Author.

American Cancer Society. (2017c). *Colorectal cancer facts and figures 2017-2019*. Atlanta, GA: Author.

Amin, M. B., Edge, S., Greene, F., Byrd, D. R., Brookland, R. K., Washington, M. K., ... Meyer, L. R. (Eds.). (2017). *AJCC cancer staging manual* (8th ed.). New York, NY: Springer.

Bossuyt, V., & Symmans, W. F. (2016). Standardizing of pathology in patients receiving neoadjuvant chemotherapy. *Annals of Surgical Oncology, 23*(10), 3153-3161. doi:10.1245/s10434-016-5317-x

Fagerlin, A., Zikmund-Fisher, B. J., & Ubel, P. A. (2011). Helping patients decide: Ten steps to better risk communication. *Journal of the National Cancer Institute, 103*(19), 1436-1443. doi:10.1093/jnci/djr318

Howlader, N., Noone, A. M., Krapcho, M., Miller, D., Bishop, K., Altekruse, S. F., ... Cronin, K. A. (Eds.). (2016). *SEER cancer statistics review, 1975–2013, National Cancer Institute*. Bethesda, MD: National Cancer Institute. Retrieved from http://seer.cancer.gov/csr/1975_2013/

Kushi, L. H., Doyle, C., McCullough, M., Rock, C. L., Demark-Wahnefried, W., Bandera, E. V., ... Nutrition and Physical Activity Guidelines Advisory Committee. (2012). American Cancer Society guidelines on nutrition and physical activity for cancer prevention. *CA: A Cancer Journal for Clinicians, 62*(1), 30-67. doi:10.3322/caac.20140

Mahon, S. M. (2017). Cancer epidemiology: Implications for prevention, early detection, and treatment. In S. Newton, M. Hickey, & J. M. Brant (Eds.), *Mosby's oncology nursing advisor: A comprehensive guide to clinical practice* (2nd ed., pp. 1-12). St. Louis, MO: Elsevier.

Polek, C. (2017). Cancer epidemiology: Implications for prevention, early detection, and treatment. In S. Newton, M. Hickey, & J. M. Brant (Eds.), *Mosby's oncology nursing advisor: A comprehensive guide to clinical practice* (2nd ed., pp. 12-24). St. Louis, MO: Elsevier.

Weitzel, J. N., Blazer, K. R., MacDonald, D. J., Culver, J. O., & Offit, K. (2011). Genetics, genomics and cancer risk assessment: State of the art and future directions in the era of personalized medicine. *CA: A Cancer Journal for Clinicians, 61*(5), 327-359. doi:10.3322/caac.20128

CHAPTER 2

GENETIC RISK FOR DEVELOPING OF CANCER

LEARNING OUTCOME

After completing this chapter, the learner will be able to describe how family history contributes to cancer risk for some cancer diagnoses in women, as well as the components of the genetic testing process.

CHAPTER OBJECTIVES

After completing this chapter, the learner will be able to:

1. Identify the genetic basis of hereditary risk and its key indicators.

2. Identify the components of a pedigree and how the pedigree is utilized to assess an individual's hereditary risk for cancer.

3. Describe what occurs during a genetic testing session with a credentialed genetics professional.

4. Describe possible outcomes of genetic testing and the implications of testing results for the individual and family members.

INTRODUCTION

Some families have multiple individuals with a history of malignancy, suggesting a hereditary risk beyond what would be expected by chance. Advances in genetic science and testing have made it possible to identify families at risk for developing malignancies because of mutated, absent, or defective genes. Hereditary risk accounts for approximately 10% of all malignancies (American Cancer Society, 2017). For some of these families, the risk for cancer can be as high as 80% to 90% over a lifetime (Weitzel, Blazer, MacDonald, Culver, & Offit, 2011). When genetic testing identifies a pathogenic mutation in a family, there is a possibility that family members who do not have a diagnosis of cancer can have genetic testing to clarify whether they have a high risk for developing malignancy. For those family members in whom a mutation that confers a high risk of developing malignancy is detected, tailored recommendations can be made to prevent or detect the early stages of cancer in those individuals. For those family members who test negative for a known family mutation, aggressive screening or preventative surgery is not needed, and it is appropriate for them to follow recommendations standard for the general population. For family members with a mutation, tailored recommendations can decrease the morbidity and mortality associated with certain cancers in these families (National Comprehensive Cancer Network [NCCN], 2016, 2017; Weitzel et al., 2011).

GENETIC BASIS OF CANCER AND TRANSMISSION OF HEREDITARY RISK

Genes provide the instructions for normal cell growth and development. A mutation is an error in the gene that prevents the gene from functioning correctly. Based on what is known about cancer and genetics, many malignancies are a result of acquired mutations that occur after conception because of exposure to carcinogens. Acquired mutations occur in one cell and then are passed on to new cells that arise from the divisions of the cell (Weitzel et al., 2011). They cannot be passed on to the next generation of offspring because they were acquired after conception. Acquired mutations, also called *sporadic,* or *somatic, mutations,* trigger a cell to become malignant.

The egg or sperm that forms the fetus carries an inherited gene mutation. After the egg is fertilized by the sperm, it creates a single cell called a *zygote* that then divides many times to create a human being. Because all cells in the body are from this first cell, this kind of mutation is in every cell in the body and can be passed on to the next generation (Gunder & Martin, 2011). This is also called a *germline mutation.*

Every human has 23 pairs of chromosomes, which contain thousands of genes. Every human has two copies of every gene, with one copy from each parent. Most genetic changes that cause a hereditary form of cancer are inherited as autosomal dominant disease and can be transmitted by either the father or the mother. If an individual inherits a susceptible gene from one parent, every cell in the body is affected with the mutated gene. Once the good copy in one cell from the other parent becomes damaged from the environment or other exposure, malignant cells begin to proliferate. Because persons with a hereditary cancer syndrome have a defective copy of the gene in every cell, they typically develop cancers more often than expected by chance and often at an early age.

Each parent gives one copy of each gene to each child. If a person has a dominant condition, there is a 50% chance of passing down the mutation to each of that person's children, male or female. The siblings of an individual with a mutation also have a 50% chance of having the same mutation if they share the same parent who carries the mutation because that parent has a working and a defective copy of the gene; at conception there is a 50% chance the parent will give the defective copy and a 50% chance the parent will give the normal, working copy (Gunder & Martin, 2011). The risk for other family members carrying the same mutations depends on how closely they are related to an affected individual (NCCN, 2016, 2017).

Incidence of Hereditary Cancer Syndromes

Cancer occurs when normal cells begin to grow uncontrollably, forming a malignant tumor. Most diagnoses of cancer are not hereditary. In about 10% of individuals diagnosed with cancer, malignancies are a result of a mutation (a harmful change in the genetic material) that increases the individual's risk to develop cancer compared with most individuals. In these families, the gene can be passed down from generation to generation (Weitzel et al., 2011). Genetic testing is now readily and commercially available for hereditary breast and ovarian cancer (HBOC), hereditary nonpolyposis colorectal cancer, familial adenomatous polyposis syndromes, and many less common hereditary cancer syndromes.

KEY INDICATORS OF HEREDITARY RISK

A focus on cancer genetics includes the identification of at-risk populations, referrals for hereditary cancer evaluation, assistance with the implementation of cancer prevention and detection measures, and management of the psychosocial ramifications of testing (Riley et al., 2012). An expectation of nursing practice is for any nurse to be able to identify individuals and families with suspected hereditary risk and refer them to a credentialed genetics professional (American Nurses Association, 2016).

The American College of Medical Genetics and Genomics and the National Society of Genetic Counselors have compiled extensive resources that outline conditions in which patients and families should be referred for genetic testing (Hampel et al., 2015). Figure 2-1

lists key indicators of hereditary risk to develop cancer. With proper assessment, referral for testing, and implementation of aggressive screening and prevention measures, nurses can significantly and positively affect the health of patients with increased risk and their families. Despite these extensive resources for indications for referral for genetic counseling, referrals remain low (Febbraro et al., 2015; Marcus et al., 2015).

A 2017 report in the *Journal of the American Medical Association* shows that despite 20 years since establishing the BRCA mutation test, routine screening for genetic abnormalities for those individuals at increased risk is inconsistent. This may be because the test is not offered, test results are not fully explained, or the test is not covered by insurance. As the report suggests, this is a missed opportunity to improve patient treatment and to detect breast, ovarian, and other cancers at early stages (Kurian et al., 2017).

FIGURE 2-1: KEY INDICATORS OF HEREDITARY RISK

- Cancer occurring at a younger age than expected in the general population (such as breast, endometrial, or colon cancer at age 50 years or younger)

- More than one primary cancer in one person or bilateral cancer in a paired organ

- Evidence of autosomal dominant inheritance (two or more generations affected, with both men and women affected)

- Any pattern of cancer associated with a known cancer syndrome (such as breast, ovarian, or pancreatic cancer or colon, endometrial, and ovarian cancer)

- Presence of premalignant conditions (20 colorectal adenomatous polyps)

- A diagnosis of a cancer associated with hereditary risk, such as male breast cancer, ovarian cancer, retinoblastoma, or a pheochromocytoma

- Specific clinical characteristics of a tumor associated with hereditary cancer syndromes, such as microsatellite instability in colon cancer or triple-negative breast cancer

- Individuals from families with a known mutation associated with increased cancer risk

Any of these characteristics in a patient or family is suggestive of hereditary risk, and consideration should be given to referring the patient and/or family to a credentialed genetics professional for further evaluation.

Note. Adapted from Hampel, H., Bennett, R. L., Buchanan, A., Pearlman, R., & Wiesner, G. L. (2015). A practice guideline from the American College of Medical Genetics and Genomics and the National Society of Genetic Counselors: Referral indications for cancer predisposition assessment. *Genetic Medicine, 17*(1), 70-87. doi:10.1038/gim.2014.147

GENETICS PROFESSIONALS

Genetics professionals provide genetic risk assessment services, construct and analyze pedigrees, and provide counseling before and after genetic testing. In addition, they can coordinate follow-up for other at-risk family members. Genetics professionals can include

- medical geneticists, who are physicians with board certification in genetics from the American Board of Medical Genetics;

- licensed genetics counselors, who have specialized graduate degrees in medical genetics and counseling, are certified by the American Board of Genetic Counseling, and hold a Certified Genetic Counselor credential; and

- credentialed genetic nurses, who have graduate degrees in nursing with specialized education and training in genetics. They are credentialed by the American Nurses Credentialing Commission and hold the advanced genetics nursing board-certified credential.

To locate genetics professionals, search the National Society of Genetic Counselors database (http://www.nsgc.org). To ensure that testing is covered and to reduce the risk for errors with testing, many insurance companies now require evaluation by and counseling with a genetics professional (Brierley et al., 2010; Riley et al., 2012). Errors may include incorrect, incomplete, or unnecessary testing; incorrect test interpretation; and inadequate counseling for both patients and other family members (Mahon, 2013c).

KEY COMPONENTS OF THE GENETIC TESTING PROCESS

Pedigree Construction

Cancer genetic counseling includes a number of steps. Every family that presents for genetic counseling should designate a spokesperson, or proband, for the family. The proband may or may not be diagnosed with cancer but serves as a point of reference when discussing risk.

Taking a detailed family history is the first step when identifying families with a possible hereditary predisposition to malignancy and other illnesses. A complete pedigree includes information about all relatives – both maternal and paternal – including children, siblings, parents, aunts, uncles, cousins, and grandparents (Mahon, 2016b). In Figure 2-2, the pedigree presents a three-generation family history; squares represent males, circles represent females, a slash represents a deceased person, and filled-in circles and squares represent diagnoses confirmed with pathology reports. The pedigree includes a key identifying those cancer diagnoses, with diagnoses verified, if possible, by pathology reports or death certificates. Also included are the family members' current age or age at death and the age at any cancer diagnosis. The arrow represents the proband, identified as III-1, the spokesperson for the family. Both maternal and paternal sides are shown, with each generation labeled with a Roman numeral. Also included is ethnicity. Guidelines call for pedigree updates annually, with the diagnosis of cancer, or when genetic testing occurs.

The credentialed genetics professional (see box on Genetic Professionals for more information on qualified providers) further investigates

FIGURE 2-2: PEDIGREE SUGGESTIVE OF HEREDITARY RISK

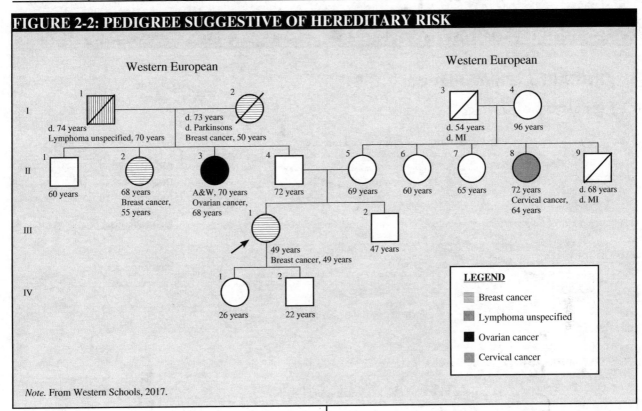

Note. From Western Schools, 2017.

ancestry because some ethnic groups are at higher risk for hereditary cancers. For example, persons of Ashkenazi Jewish ancestry are at increased risk for HBOC (Weitzel et al., 2011). The credentialed genetics professional examines the pedigree after it is constructed and considers whether it is reflective of hereditary predisposition for developing malignancy (see Figure 2-1). The pedigree should be updated whenever there is a change in family history or the results of genetic testing become available for family members.

The pedigree shows patterns of genetic transmission and possible genetic syndromes. In some families, pedigree information is incomplete, which affects its accuracy and completeness. Contact with biological family members may be interrupted or broken. Health histories among members or previous generations may be unknown. Those individuals who were adopted may have limited or no information about their family history. The genetics professional can discuss how missing information affects genetic testing.

Risk Calculations

Programs and models calculate statistical risks for developing cancer (Daly et al., 2017). As part of genetic counseling, the counselor reviews the incidence of cancer(s) in the general population, comparing that with the individual's personal risk and hereditary susceptibility mutation calculation (see Figure 2-3). These models have distinct strengths and limitations. If the family is small, these models can underestimate the risk of having a mutation (Riley et al., 2012; Wiseman, Dancyger, & Michie, 2010).

Once a genetics professional has detected a mutation in a family, it is possible to calculate the statistical risk based on Mendelian patterns of inheritance (Mahon, 2016b). In the case of autosomal dominance, first-degree relatives (children, siblings, and parents) have a 50% chance of having inherited the predisposition gene (Weitzel et al., 2011). Second-degree relatives (grandparents, aunts, and uncles) have a 25% chance of having the mutation (Weitzel et

FIGURE 2-3: MODELS OF CANCER RISK AND CHANCE OF HAVING A SUSCEPTIBILITY MUTATION (1 OF 2)

BRCAPro (BayesMendel 2.0-9)

Breast Cancer

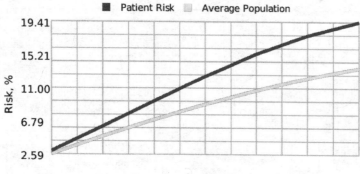

Carrier Probability

BRCA1   2.21%
BRCA2   12.45%
Any BRCA   14.66%

Calculated Risk

5-Year   3.01%
Lifetime   19.41%

Ovarian Cancer

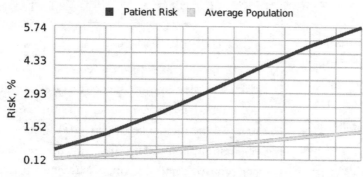

Carrier Probability

BRCA1   2.21%
BRCA2   12.45%
Any BRCA   14.66%

Calculated Risk

5-Year   0.50%
Lifetime   5.74%

Tyrer-Cuzick (IBIS Risk Evaluator v7.01)

Breast Cancer

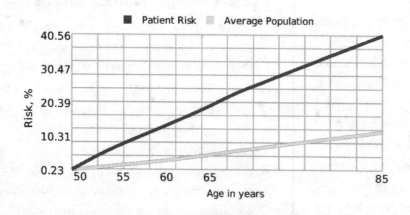

Carrier Probability

BRCA1   8.13%
BRCA2   2.27%
Any BRCA   10.40%

Calculated Risk

5-Year   6.74%
Lifetime   40.56%

FIGURE 2-3: MODELS OF CANCER RISK AND CHANCE OF HAVING A SUSCEPTIBILITY MUTATION (2 OF 2)

It is possible to calculate the risk for having cancer based on the family history. For the pedigree in Figure 2-2, it is possible to calculate the risk for development of breast and ovarian cancer based on the pedigree and other risk factors. For the proband, the BRCAPro model predicts the lifetime risk for development of breast cancer as 19.41%, and the Tyrer-Cuzick model predicts a lifetime risk of 40.56%. Both of these calculations suggest a lifetime risk for development of breast cancer that is much higher than the 12.28% risk in the general population. The BRCAPro model also suggests a higher lifetime risk for ovarian cancer. Different models consider different factors, so variability exists in risk values. A lifetime risk rate of greater than 20% for development of breast cancer is high enough to offer modified recommendations for cancer prevention and early detection.

It is also possible to use the pedigree to calculate the chance of having a BRCA mutation suggestive of hereditary breast and ovarian cancer. The BRCAPro suggests a 14.66% chance of having a mutation, and the Tyrer-Cuzick model suggests a 10.40% chance of having a mutation. In general, a calculated risk rate of 10% or greater suggests that it is appropriate to consider genetic testing.

Genetics professionals routinely make these calculations to help patients understand risk and guide decisions about testing and prevention and detection recommendations.

Note. This figure was created using Invitae Family History Tool, a pedigree drawing software. The risk calculations were created by the author.

---

al., 2011). If a mutation is not detected in the family, the calculation of the risks of developing cancer(s) can be helpful in selecting a plan of recommendation for cancer prevention and early detection (Hall et al., 2016).

Genetic Testing Process

Selection of the appropriate genetic test(s) depends on the risk factor assessment. If the chance of having a mutation exceeds 10% for some of the common hereditary cancer syndromes, such as HBOC or hereditary nonpolyposis colorectal cancer, or the patient satisfies criteria for testing, such as those from the NCCN or another recognized agency, the patient may be offered the option to consider genetic testing (Rich et al., 2015; Riley et al., 2012). Cancer susceptibility genetic testing has the potential to identify whether a person is at increased risk for particular cancer or cancers associated with a hereditary cancer syndrome. A limitation of these tests, however, is that they cannot predict when,

where, or if a cancer will be diagnosed (Thomas & Mohammed, 2016).

Cancer genetic counseling must be tailored to the individual needs and learning capabilities of each family member. This usually is a labor-intensive process, and families should anticipate at least one to three sessions lasting from 60 to 90 minutes before testing to ensure they truly have adequate information to provide informed consent and make a decision that is congruent with their own individual needs (Mahon, 2013a). Activities that typically occur in a cancer genetic counseling session are shown in Figure 2-4.

Historically, testing for germline hereditary predisposition syndromes has involved Sanger DNA sequencing with testing for one or two genes (Graffeo et al., 2016) The introduction of next-generation sequencing (NGS) panels that analyze less common cancer susceptibility genes has led to reduced cost and turnaround time with the simultaneous testing of multiple genes in the genetic testing process

FIGURE 2-4: EXAMPLE COMPONENTS OF CANCER GENETIC COUNSELING

(Session: 60 to 90 minutes)

- Collection of a detailed family history and pedigree construction occurs.

- Counseling discussion covers

  ○ risks for cancers in the population;

  ○ an individual's risk for a particular cancer;

  ○ potential genetic mutations and risk calculations linked to those mutations;

  ○ factors that limit the interpretation and calculation of risk, such as limited family history, adoption, or incomplete information about family members;

  ○ the rationale for ordering specific genetic test(s), including technical accuracy;

  ○ implications of a positive, negative, or noninformative test result;

  ○ prevention and early detection strategies – risks, benefits, and limitations, depending on the test outcome;

  ○ testing alternatives, including no testing;

  ○ risks to other family members;

  ○ options to enroll in variant or research studies, based on family history;

  ○ potential discrimination risks for insurance or employment and federal protection;

  ○ strategies to disclose results/information to other at-risk family members;

  ○ potential psychological risks and benefits of testing; and

  ○ fees for testing and counseling/education.

Note. From Western Schools, 2017.

(Rizzo & Buck, 2012). Many hereditary cancer syndromes have confusing clinical presentations, and it can be challenging to select the correct test (Mahon, 2013b; van Marcke, De Leener, Berlière, Vikkula, & Duhoux, 2016). Simultaneous testing for germline mutations associated with hereditary cancer syndromes using an NGS-targeted platform may be more efficient and cost-effective. NGS has made the detection of more mutations possible, especially in less common genes, but it has greatly increased the complexity of the genetic counseling and genetic testing process and the interpretation of test results (Stanislaw, Xue, & Wilcox, 2016). For example, multiple genes are associated with varying degrees of risk for developing multiple types of cancer (see Table 2-1).

If a patient decides to proceed with genetic testing, the patient needs information about the test(s) being ordered; potential management strategies; and the potential risks, benefits, and limitations of testing (American College of Medical Genetics and Genomics Board of Directors, 2013; Bernhardt et al., 2015). The patient signs a consent form to document that he or she understands the ramifications of testing and is not being coerced (see Figure 2-5). Testing requires a blood or saliva sample depending on the laboratory and the number of genes being tested.

Ideally, an affected family member will be the first one to be tested. A person who has been diagnosed with a cancer within the constellation of tumors that have been clearly linked to

TABLE 2-1: SELECTED GENETIC SYNDROMES

Gene	Associated Cancers
APC	Colon, small bowel, thyroid, pancreatic
ATM	Breast, colon, pancreatic
BARD1	Breast, ovarian
BMPR1A	Colon, gastric
BRCA1/BRCA2	Breast, ovarian, pancreatic, prostate, melanoma, endometrial
BRIP1	Breast, ovarian
CDH1	Gastric, breast, colon
CDK4	Melanoma, pancreatic, breast, skin
CDKN2A	Melanoma, pancreatic
CHEK2	Breast, prostate, colon, ovarian, thyroid
EPCAM/MLH1/MSH2/ MSH6/PMS2	Colon, endometrial, ovarian, gastric, pancreatic, biliary tract, urinary tract, small bowel, brain, sebaceous neoplasms
FANCC	Breast
MUTYH	Colon, small bowel, endometrial, ovarian
PALB2	Breast, pancreatic, colon
PTEN	Breast, thyroid, endometrial, colon, gastric, melanoma
RAD51D	Breast, ovarian
STK11	Breast, colon, pancreatic, gastric, small bowel, endometrial
TP53	Breast, sarcoma, brain, hematological malignancies, adrenocortical malignancies
XRCC2	Breast, pancreatic

Note. Adapted from Chan-Smutko, G. (2012). Genetic testing by cancer site: Urinary tract. *The Cancer Journal, 18*(4), 343-349. doi:10.1097/ PPO.0b013e31826246ac; Chun, N., & Ford, J. M. (2012). Genetic testing by cancer site: Stomach. *The Cancer Journal, 18*(4), 355-363. doi:10.1097/ PPO.0b013e31826246dc; Daniels, M. S. (2012). Genetic testing by cancer site: Uterus. *The Cancer Journal, 18*(4), 338-342. doi:10.1097/ PPO.0b013e3182610cc2; Gabree, M., & Seidel, M. (2012). Genetic testing by cancer site: Skin. *The Cancer Journal, 18*(4), 372-380. doi:10.1097/ PPO.0b013e3182624664; Jasperson, K. W. (2012). Genetic testing by cancer site: Colon (polyposis syndromes). *The Cancer Journal, 18*(4), 328-333. doi:10.1097/PPO.0b013e3182609300; Murray, A. J., & Davies, D. M. (2013). The genetics of breast cancer. *Surgery, 31*(1), 1-3. doi:10.1016/j. mpsur.2012.10.019; Senter, L. (2012). Genetic testing by cancer site: Colon (nonpolyposis syndromes). *The Cancer Journal, 18*(4), 334-337. doi:10.1097/ PPO.0b013e31826094b2; Shannon, K. M., & Chittenden, A. (2012). Genetic testing by cancer site: Breast. *The Cancer Journal, 18*(4), 310-319. doi:10.1097/ PPO.0b013e318260946f; Weissman, S. M., Burt, R., Church, J., Erdman, S., Hampel, H., Holter, S., … Senter, L. (2012). Identification of individuals at risk for Lynch syndrome using targeted evaluations and genetic testing: National Society of Genetic Counselors and the Collaborative Group of the Americas on Inherited Colorectal Cancer joint practice guideline. *Journal of Genetic Counseling, 21*(4), 484-493. doi:10.1007/s10897-011-9465-7.

particular cancer syndrome(s) will be the most informative for the rest of the family (Weitzel et al., 2011).

Because testing usually is expensive and insurance reimbursement is variable, providers seek preauthorization so that an individual understands his or her potential financial responsibilities (Mahon 2013a). The cost of genetic testing can range from about $300 (for a single-site test) to more than $6,000 (for a panel with many genes; Mahon 2013b). Many insurance companies, including Medicare and Medicaid, have specific criteria and prior authorization requirements for genetic testing as a covered benefit (Wang et al., 2011).

Results Disclosure

In most cases, testing results are available in 2 to 5 weeks, depending on the laboratory and the complexity of the test(s). Genetic testing can have multiple outcomes. These include the identification of a positive variant, a negative

FIGURE 2-5: EXAMPLE COMPONENTS OF INFORMED CONSENT FOR GENETIC TESTING

Before genetic testing, the individual will review and then sign a consent form. The consent form acknowledges that the individual undergoing testing has had the opportunity to explore all of the points of the consent (see below) and has the opportunity to ask questions.

- Consent includes review and discussion about

  ○ basic concepts of genetic transmission;

  ○ purpose of the genetic test, accuracy of the test, type of specimen required, and testing condition(s);

  ○ rationale for offering the test, chance of detecting a mutation, and ideal person in the family to initiate testing;

  ○ potential benefits, risks, and limitations of testing;

  ○ explanation of what test results mean – including positive and negative results – and the potential for uninformative results, including a variant of unknown significance;

  ○ screening options, based on test results;

  ○ available treatment options, depending on test results;

  ○ available counseling and support services for the entire family;

  ○ possible physical or emotional risks associated with the test;

  ○ how results might provide information about other family members' health, including the risk of developing a particular condition or the possibility of having affected children;

  ○ disclosure of results plan, that is, how, when, and to whom; and

  ○ test specimen storage after the test is complete.

With consent, the individual also

- acknowledges the opportunity provided to discuss the test with a knowledgeable genetics professional and

- acknowledges that he/she has the right to decline testing.

Note. From Western Schools, 2017.

variant, or a variant of unknown significance (Mahon, 2015a). Table 2-2 reviews the implications of genetic testing outcomes.

When results are disclosed depending on the outcome, additional counseling sessions may be scheduled to discuss recommendations, and management strategies, and provide coordination of care for other family members (Mahon, 2013a).

For example, some mutations are associated with a high risk of developing cancer.

For a woman diagnosed with a mutation in the *CHEK2* gene, her risk for breast, ovarian, endometrial, and colon cancers is greatly increased (Mahon, 2014a). Further discussion follows, including weighing treatment options, such as prophylactic mastectomies and total hysterectomy to reduce her risk of developing cancer. Colonoscopy might be recommended every 2 to 3 years beginning at age 35 years instead of every 10 years starting at age 50, which is the recommendation for persons with average risk.

TABLE 2-2: POTENTIAL OUTCOMES OF GENETIC TESTING (1 OF 2)			
Result	**Implications for Individual**	**Implications for Family**	**Other Implications**
Positive result	At increased risk for developing cancer(s)	First-degree relatives have a 50% chance of having the mutation. Single-site testing would clarify whether the family member has the mutation and associated increased risk. Single-site testing is less expensive.	Does not inform about what type of cancer will develop or when, only that the risk is greater. Enables individual to make decisions about prevention and early detection • Starting cancer screening tests for the cancers with higher risk earlier than usually recommended • Getting screened for the cancers with higher risk more often than generally recommended • Utilizing screening tests that are used only for people known to be at increased risk • Watching closely for signs or symptoms of cancer and getting any change checked out promptly • Considering utilizing prophylactic surgery or chemoprevention agents • Truly adopting a healthier lifestyle, including smoking cessation, eating healthier, exercising, limiting alcohol consumption, and reducing exposure to ultraviolet light

Direct-to-Consumer Testing

An additional concern about genetic testing is the developing market for direct-to-consumer (DTC) testing. Because test results may be flawed, incomplete, or difficult to interpret, providers caution individuals to proceed with this type of testing. Moreover, current DTC testing offers only a very small percentage of disease-causing variants, although some tests can indicate a BRCA mutation (Dohany, Gustafson, Ducaine, & Zakalik, 2012). At a minimum, DTC testing prompts some level of psychological stress and may lead to mistakes in decision making based on reported risk factors (Turrini & Prainsack, 2016).

Unfortunately, many individuals overestimate what they will learn from DTC testing and may be disappointed with the limited clinical

TABLE 2-2: POTENTIAL OUTCOMES OF GENETIC TESTING (2 OF 2)

Result	Implications for Individual	Implications for Family	Other Implications
True negative – no mutation detected in a person with a known mutation in family	Will not need screening more than that recommended for the general population Will not need to consider prophylactic surgery or chemoprevention	Offspring from this individual are not at risk. No further testing is necessary.	Provides a more accurate cancer risk assessment Provides psychological relief regarding risk for developing cancer and that offspring will not inherit the mutation
Negative result – no mutation identified in family	Usually occurs when the first individual in a family is tested. The cancer may be the result of a different mutation than the one tested, or the cancer seen in the family occurs because of nonhereditary reasons. Results are difficult to interpret and must be considered in conjunction with personal risk factors and family history.	Testing is not available to other unaffected members in the family because they will also test negative.	The best options for cancer prevention and early detection are not always clear. Individuals may consider participating in research studies or high-risk registries.
Variant of indeterminate significance	Test identifies a change in the genetic material; it is not clear if it is a harmless or harmful change. Results do not provide meaningful information.	Meaningful testing will not be available to other family members.	Creates uncertainty and anxiety about the usefulness of cancer risk-reduction strategies. Requires formulation of recommendations for cancer prevention and detection needs based on personal risk factors and family history with careful information about potential benefits and risks. Individuals may consider participation in a research study or hereditary cancer registry.

Note. Adapted from Mahon, S. M. (2015a). Management of patients with a genetic variant of unknown significance. *Oncology Nursing Forum, 42*(3), 316-318. doi:10.1188/15.ONF.316-318; Riley, B. D., Culver, J. O., Skrzynia, C., Senter, L. A., Peters, J. A., Costalas, J. W., ... Trepanier, A. M. (2012). Essential elements of genetic cancer risk assessment, counseling, and testing: Updated recommendations of the National Society of Genetic Counselors. *Journal of Genetic Counseling, 21*(2), 151-161. doi:10.1007/s10897-011-9462-x; and Rizzo, J. M., & Buck, M. J. (2012). Key principles and clinical applications of "next-generation" DNA sequencing. *Cancer Prevention Research, 5*(7), 887-900. doi:10.1158/1940-6207.capr-11-0432

significance of the results, lack of comprehensive testing, or inability to alter risk based on the findings (van der Wouden et al., 2016).

Advocates of DTC testing underscore that this type of testing supports the goal of self-care of patients (Covolo, Rubinelli, Ceretti, & Gelati, 2015). Until quality and process improves in the DTC marketplace, providers recommend testing and professional genetics counseling from reputable and reliable sources (American College of Medical Genetics and Genomics Board of Directors, 2016).

Nurses can advise patients that it is difficult, if not impossible, for patients to understand the potential lack of clinical utility from DTC genetic tests. Nurses can also explain that results can be difficult for patients to interpret without pretest and posttest genetic counseling, and may ultimately lead to psychological distress. If nurses and healthcare providers take the extra step to connect their patients with genetics professionals, they may not feel the need to undergo DTC genetic testing (Burke & Trinidad, 2016; Mahon, 2016a).

Implications for Other Family Members

Genetic testing for a hereditary cancer syndrome can have implications for other family members (Eijzenga, Hahn, Aaronson, Kluijt, & Bleiker, 2014). Once a family member is identified with a genetic mutation, the chance that another family member carries the same mutation can be made based on his or her position on the pedigree. When a positive result is identified, the genetics professional identifies which other family members should be offered testing that can determine whether they have increased risk. In this case, the possible outcomes of testing are a negative or positive test result. For this reason, before testing, communication issues, an important component of counseling and planning, are clarified: Just how

will other family members be informed of risk? By the proband? What is disclosed (Mahon, 2014b)? Guidelines recommend that minor children are not offered genetic testing unless medical management relies on test results (Eijzenga et al., 2014; NCCN, 2016, 2017).

Psychological Concerns

Many emotions surface when genetic testing results become known. Risks are also associated with the psychological and psychosocial effects of knowing one's genetic status (Eijzenga et al., 2014). Patients found to carry a cancer susceptibility mutation may experience anxiety, depression, anger, and feelings of vulnerability or guilt about possibly having passed the mutation to their children. It can be frightening to learn that an individual or someone else in the family is at increased risk for developing cancer. Sometimes individuals feel relief even if they test positive, because they can select a plan for cancer prevention and early detection that is more likely to be effective (Eijzenga et al., 2014).

Family members who test negative for a known mutation can feel relief that they did not inherit the risk and their offspring cannot inherit the mutation (Mahon, 2015b). Those who test negative for a known mutation in a family may also experience guilt, known as survivor guilt, especially if close family members are found to carry the mutation. Survivor guilt occurs when people who test negative question and feel guilty as to why they were fortunate enough to test negative when another sibling or relative tested positive (Mahon, 2014b). A genetics professional can help these individuals navigate these feelings and emotions (Mahon, 2013a).

Sometimes family members do not want to know if they might be at increased risk, especially if there is not much they can do about it or they are not willing to undergo more drastic prevention measures, such as preventative surgery. Family members should know they have the option to test, but each family member must decide individually if they want to test (Plutynski, 2012).

Some families are closer than others. If a mutation is detected, it will be the responsibility of the person tested to contact other family members and tell them they might be at risk and how to contact the genetics professional. This is important and can be difficult if family relationships are strained. Sometimes family secrets are revealed as a result of testing, such as learning about paternity, adoptions, or other difficult issues (Plutynski, 2012). Families need to realize that this can be a complication with genetic testing.

Risk of Discrimination

The Genetic Information Nondiscrimination Act of 2008, also referred to as GINA, is a federal law that protects most Americans from discrimination by health insurance companies and employers with more than 15 employees (U.S. Department of Health and Human Services, 2009). Unfortunately, it does not apply to military health plans, the Veterans Administration, or the Indian Health Service. This law prohibits health insurers from using genetic information when deciding whom to cover and how much to charge for insurance. GINA prohibits employers from discriminating on the basis of genetic information in hiring, firing or layoffs, salary, or other personnel actions, such as promotions, classifications, or assignments.

GINA does not restrict use of genetic information for life insurance, disability insurance, or long-term care insurance. If individuals want increased coverage for life, disability, or long-term care insurance, they should obtain this insurance before undergoing genetic testing.

NURSING IMPLICATIONS

Understanding issues related to hereditary cancer is an important component of nursing practice. All nurses, regardless of practice setting and roles, have a responsibility to refer patients to genetic healthcare providers, support patients and families, and understand the influence of genetics in health care (see Figure 2-6).

After undergoing genetic testing or consultation with a genetics professional, individuals will seek out nurses who can provide education, support, coordination of care, and assistance with the individual's prevention and/or risk-reduction plan (Weitzel et al., 2011).

CASE STUDY 2-1

At the request of her primary care physician, M.B. presented to a credentialed genetics professional for education and information about hereditary risk for cancer. She is a 32-year-old White woman with concerns about her personal risk for cancer. M.B. is recently married and wants to start a family. She is concerned not only about her personal risk for cancer, but also about potential risks to her offspring. In addition, M.B. reports that she had a child at age 24 years, whom she gave up for adoption.

M.B. has three sisters. Two are affected with premenopausal breast cancer; one of these sisters has bilateral breast cancer. A genetics counselor constructed a pedigree (see Figure 2-7). Maternal ethnicity is Scottish/Irish. M.B.'s mother is alive and reported to be healthy. Her only maternal uncle died in a motor vehicle accident. Her maternal grandparents did not have histories of malignancies. Paternal ethnicity is German/Ashkenazi Jewish. M.B.'s paternal family history is significant for ovarian cancer (paternal aunt), breast cancer (paternal

FIGURE 2-6: KEY NURSING ROLES IN CANCER GENETIC/GENOMIC CARE

Registered Nurses

- Perform risk assessments that include personal, medical, occupational, environmental, and family history risk factors.

- Refer families with a potential hereditary predisposition to a genetics professional.

- Assist to implement the genetics professionals' recommendations to prevent/early detect.

- Provide psychological support and encouragement to patients or families pursuing genetic testing.

Advanced Practice Nurse With Credential in Genetics

- Conduct in-depth assessments and pedigrees with individuals diagnosed with cancers, verified through medical records and death certificates.

- Calculate the individual's risk to develop cancer(s), based on personal and family history.

- Calculate the individual's mutation risk; evaluate patient's eligibility and appropriateness for genetic testing.

- Provide genetic counseling, as needed, including pretest and posttest counseling.

- Provide information to ensure informed consent regarding the strengths, risks, and limitations of testing.

- Identify the best person to initiate testing within the family.

- Select and order appropriate genetic test(s).

- Interpret test results and offer recommendations based on the personal health history, family history, and genetic testing results.

- Coordinate follow-up care, based on genetic testing results.

- Contribute to strategies to facilitate the individual's and family members' coping with any adverse psychological consequences about diagnosis or hereditary cancer syndrome.

- Assist enrolling families with unusual syndromes in research studies.

Note. Adapted from American Nurses Association. (2016). *Genetics/genomics nursing: Scope and standards of practice* (2nd ed.). Silver Spring, MD: Author; Mahon, S. M. (2013a). Allocation of work activities in a comprehensive cancer genetics program. *Clinical Journal of Oncology Nursing, 17*(4), 397-404. doi:10.1188/13.CJON.397-404

grandmother), and prostate cancer (father and paternal grandfather).

M.B.'s medical history includes menarche at age 12 years. She is gravida 1, para 1 (first complete pregnancy at age 24 years). She reports no hormonal therapy use but reports a history of more than 5 years of oral contraceptive use (from age 24 years to about 30). Her last Pap smear/pelvic examination was within the past 3 months and negative. She has never had a mammogram. During her last gynecological examination, she had a breast examination that was negative. She denies problems with depression or coping with difficult information. M.B. has had two breast biopsies for palpable masses, one at age 26 years and one at age 30. The first biopsy was a fibroadenoma; the second one indicated ductal hyperplasia with moderate atypia. Pathology reports confirmed both biopsies.

FIGURE 2-7: PEDIGREE FOR CASE STUDY 2-1

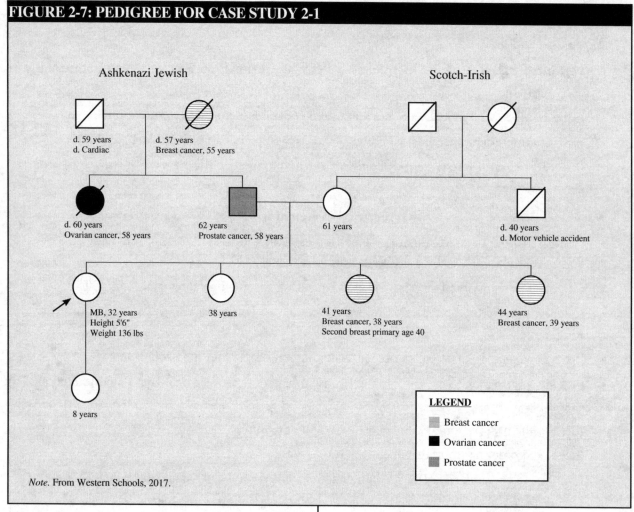

Ashkenazi Jewish

Scotch-Irish

d. 59 years
d. Cardiac

d. 57 years
Breast cancer, 55 years

d. 60 years
Ovarian cancer, 58 years

62 years
Prostate cancer, 58 years

61 years

d. 40 years
d. Motor vehicle accident

MB, 32 years
Height 5'6"
Weight 136 lbs

38 years

41 years
Breast cancer, 38 years
Second breast primary age 40

44 years
Breast cancer, 39 years

8 years

LEGEND

Breast cancer

Ovarian cancer

Prostate cancer

Note. From Western Schools, 2017.

M.B. works as an elementary school teacher. She denies use of tobacco or recreational drugs and states she occasionally drinks socially but has less than one or two drinks per month. She walks approximately 5 miles per day and consumes three to five servings of fruits and vegetables daily. Height is 5 foot 6 inches, and weight is 136 pounds. She has disclosed to her husband that she has given up a child for adoption. Figure 2-8 displays her risks for developing breast cancer.

M.B. reports concerns about her personal health and risks to potential offspring. She wants to consider prevention strategies and seeks recommendations for screening. Her primary care physician recommended that she consider genetic testing, and M.B. believes she will test positive because of her sisters' histories. She has not discussed her plan to be tested with her husband, even though a positive test could significantly affect their relationship and marriage. She has discussed testing with her affected sisters. They have not had testing or counseling for testing. M.B.'s risk of having a mutation in BRCA1/2 was calculated. She was provided a range of risk figures (see Figure 2-8), but almost all calculations showed risk of greater than 10%, suggesting she should be offered testing. The patient received copies of the pedigree and all risk calculations.

In this family, ideally, the person to test would be the youngest person in the family with cancer who is suspected to be part of a cancer syndrome. In M.B's family, her youngest sister with breast

FIGURE 2-8: RISK CALCULATIONS FOR CASE STUDY 2-1

BRCAPro (BayesMendel 2.0-9)

Breast Cancer

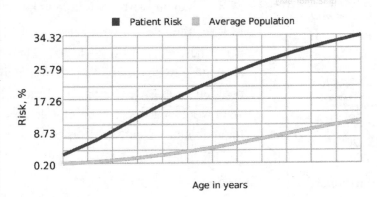

Carrier Probability

BRCA1   33.98%
BRCA2   13.23%
Any BRCA 47.21%

Calculated Risk

5-Year   2.48%
Lifetime   34.32%

Ovarian Cancer

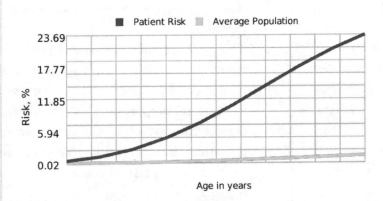

Carrier Probability

BRCA1   33.98%
BRCA2   13.23%
Any BRCA   47.21%

Calculated Risk

5-Year   0.43%
Lifetime   23.69%

Tyrer-Cuzick (IBIS Risk Evaluator v7.01)

Breast Cancer

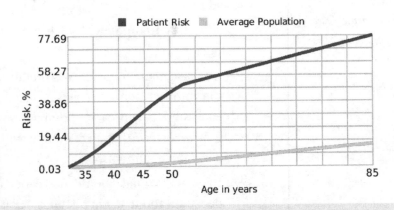

Carrier Probability

BRCA1   34.25%
BRCA2   13.14%
Any BRCA   47.40%

Calculated Risk

5-Year   9.95%
Lifetime   77.69%

Note. This figure was created using Invitae Family History Tool, a pedigree drawing software. The risk calculations were created by the author.

cancer should be tested. If she tests negative, then most likely this family would not have an identifiable hereditary syndrome, but family members could still be at risk for other, less common hereditary cancer syndromes. If the youngest sister tests positive and M.B. then tests negative, that would be considered a true negative, and her risk is that of the general population.

Following genetic counseling and discussion of the benefits and limitations of testing, M.B.'s sister with bilateral breast cancer decided to test. She tested positive for a mutation in BRCA1. Her other affected sister also tested positive. Both women had oophorectomies. Her sister with unilateral breast cancer completed a prophylactic mastectomy on the unaffected side. Then they both began formulating a plan on how to educate their daughters about risks.

M.B. was tested. She also tested positive. Recommendations followed, which included increased breast cancer screening, consultation with a breast surgeon, and breast magnetic resonance imaging. She eventually opted to have prophylactic mastectomies because of an estimated 85% lifetime risk of developing breast cancer. Twice a year she has pelvic examinations because of her risk for ovarian cancer, which is as high as 50%. She plans to have an oophorectomy between the age of 40 and 45 years. She is also seeing a dermatologist yearly because of the increased risk for melanoma. She received extensive information about reducing her risk for skin cancer.

She is exploring how to inform the adoption agency about the potential risk to her daughter. She reports that she is gradually adjusting to the changes in her life and is satisfied with her decisions.

Questions

1. Did M.B. follow a process to seek reliable testing and interpretation from a trained genetics professional?

2. M.B.'s youngest sister was tested first. Why?

3. M.B. communicated with her affected sisters about her decision to be tested. Then they also chose to be tested. As part of a communication strategy affecting family members, what would a genetics counselor discuss with the individual about her decision to be tested and the interpretation of test results?

Answers

1. Yes. M.B.'s primary care physician recommended testing. Then M.B. pursued testing from a reputable genetic laboratory at the recommendation of a genetic counselor, who provided consultation and professional interpretation of the results. Based on testing, M.B. had additional consultations and imaging as components of a comprehensive plan of care, which served as a foundation for further decision making. This is in keeping with NCCN (2017) guidelines.

2. Based on M.B.'s family's breast cancer history and confirmed diagnoses, her youngest sister diagnosed with cancer was suspected to be part of a cancer syndrome, so she was tested first.

3. Possible test findings and what they mean include:

   • Because there is a known mutation in the family, there is a 50% chance that each sibling will carry the mutation and a 50% chance that each sibling will not carry the mutation.

   • Each individual should make her own decision about testing after a balanced discussion of the potential benefits, risks, and limitations of testing.

- The alternative to testing is not testing.

- If the individual does relay test results to family members, what are their options as next steps?

SUMMARY

Cancer genetic testing is an emerging, powerful tool for certain individuals to reduce their risk for certain cancer diagnoses. With assistance and counseling from genetic professionals, patients and family members – with known or suspected cancer risk – can establish a foundation to understand the incidence of genetic cancer syndromes, risk indicators, the process of testing, and implications that the patient's test results have for the patient and other family members.

Equipped with knowledge about genetics, testing, and support for patients, nurses can help identify families at risk and mobilize referrals for these families to credentialed genetics professionals. Then after testing results are known, nurses can contribute to education, support, and coordination of care, which includes following recommendations for cancer prevention and early detection.

EXAM QUESTIONS

CHAPTER 2
Questions 6–9

Note: Choose the one option that BEST answers each question.

6. Based on what is known about cancer and genetics, many malignancies are a result of

    a. lifestyle issues.

    b. juvenile diabetes.

    c. acquired mutations that occur after conception because of exposure to carcinogens.

    d. acquired mutations that occur in utero.

7. The proband asks the nurse about genetic testing for hereditary cancer. The nurse responds with which of the following statements?

    a. "I can have that test ordered with your regular blood work."

    b. "It would probably be best to see a credentialed genetics nurse or genetics counselor for further evaluation."

    c. "You can get that answer with a direct-to-consumer genetic test."

    d. "The pedigree does not suggest hereditary risk."

8. The nurse looks at a pedigree. Which factor would be suggestive of hereditary risk?

    a. Both proband's mother and father have a history of skin cancer.

    b. Family history of colorectal cancer includes maternal grandmother at age 88 years and breast cancer in paternal aunt at age 65 years.

    c. Family is of Ashkenazi Jewish background.

    d. Family history of breast cancer includes mother at age 45 years and maternal grandmother with ovarian cancer at age 70 years.

9. During genetic counseling with the proband's daughter after a mutation was identified in the proband's mother, the genetics professional

    a. tells the daughter why she should have genetic testing.

    b. describes possible outcomes of genetic testing, including a positive or negative test result.

    c. tells the daughter that there is no risk of discrimination if she applies for life insurance after genetic testing.

    d. tells the daughter that she should not submit the costs of testing to her health insurance policy because she could lose coverage.

REFERENCES

American Cancer Society. (2017). *Cancer facts & figures – 2017.* Atlanta, GA; American Cancer Society

American College of Medical Genetics and Genomics Board of Directors. (2013). Points to consider for informed consent for genome/exome sequencing. *Genetic Medicine, 15*(9), 748-749. doi:10.1038/gim.2013.94

American College of Medical Genetics and Genomics Board of Directors. (2016). Direct-to-consumer genetic testing: A revised position statement of the American College of Medical Genetics and Genomics. *Genetic Medicine, 18*(2), 207-208. doi:10.1038/gim.2015.190

American Nurses Association. (2016). *Genetics/genomics nursing: Scope and standards of practice* (2nd ed.). Silver Spring, MD: Author.

Bernhardt, B. A., Roche, M. I., Perry, D. L., Scollon, S. R., Tomlinson, A. N., & Skinner, D. (2015). Experiences with obtaining informed consent for genomic sequencing. *American Journal of Medical Genetics Part A, 167*(11), 2635-2646. doi:10.1002/ajmg.a.37256

Brierley, K. L., Campfield, D., Ducaine, W., Dohany, L., Donenberg, T., Shannon, K., … Matloff, E. T. (2010). Errors in delivery of cancer genetics services: Implications for practice. *Connecticut Medicine, 74*(7), 413-423.

Burke, W., & Trinidad, S. (2016). The deceptive appeal of direct-to-consumer genetics. *Annals of Internal Medicine, 164*(8), 564-565. doi:10.7326/M16-0257

Chan-Smutko, G. (2012). Genetic testing by cancer site: Urinary tract. *The Cancer Journal, 18*(4), 343-349. doi:10.1097/PPO.0b013e31826246ac

Chun, N., & Ford, J. M. (2012). Genetic testing by cancer site: Stomach. *The Cancer Journal, 18*(4), 355-363. doi:10.1097/PPO.0b013e31826246dc

Covolo, L., Rubinelli, S., Ceretti, E., & Gelatti, U. (2015). Internet-based direct-to-consumer genetic testing: A systematic review. *Journal of Medical Internet Research, 17*(12), e279. doi:10.2196/jmir.4378

Daly, M. B., Pilarski, R., Berry, M., Buys, S. S., Farmer, M., Friedman, S., … Kohlmann, W. (2017). NCCN guidelines insights: Genetic/Familial high-risk assessment: Breast and ovarian, version 2.2017. *Journal of the National Comprehensive Cancer Network, 15*(1), 9-20.

Daniels, M. S. (2012). Genetic testing by cancer site: Uterus. *The Cancer Journal, 18*(4), 338-342. doi:10.1097/PPO.0b013e3182610cc2

Dohany, L., Gustafson, S., Ducaine, W., & Zakalik, D. (2012). Psychological distress with direct-to-consumer genetic testing: A case report of an unexpected BRCA positive test result. *Journal of Genetic Counseling, 21*(3), 399-401. doi:10.1007/s10897-011-9475-5

Eijzenga, W., Hahn, D., Aaronson, N., Kluijt, I., & Bleiker, E. (2014). Specific psychosocial issues of individuals undergoing genetic counseling for cancer – A literature review. *Journal of Genetic Counseling, 23*(2), 133-146. doi:10.1007/s10897-013-9649-4

Febbraro, T., Robison, K., Wilbur, J. S., Laprise, J., Bregar, A., Lopes, V., … Stuckey, A. (2015). Adherence patterns to National Comprehensive Cancer Network (NCCN) guidelines for referral to cancer genetic professionals. *Gynecologic Oncology, 138*(1), 109-114. doi:10.1016/j.ygyno.2015.04.029

Gabree, M., & Seidel, M. (2012). Genetic testing by cancer site: Skin. *The Cancer Journal, 18*(4), 372-380. doi:10.1097/PPO.0b013e3182624664

Graffeo, R., Livraghi, L., Pagani, O., Goldhirsch, A., Partridge, A. H., & Garber, J. E. (2016). Time to incorporate germline multigene panel testing into breast and ovarian cancer patient care. *Breast Cancer Research and Treatment, 160*(3), 393-410. doi:10.1007/s10549-016-4003-9

Gunder, L. M., & Martin, S. A. (2011). *Essentials of medical genetics for health professionals.* Sudbury, MA: Jones & Bartlett Learning.

Hall, M. J., Obeid, E. I., Schwartz, S. C., Mantia-Smaldone, G., Forman, A. D., & Daly, M. B. (2016). Genetic testing for hereditary cancer predisposition: BRCA1/2, Lynch syndrome, and beyond. *Gynecologic Oncology, 140*(3), 565-574. doi:10.1016/j.ygyno.2016.01.019

Hampel, H., Bennett, R. L., Buchanan, A., Pearlman, R., & Wiesner, G. L. (2015). A practice guideline from the American College of Medical Genetics and Genomics and the National Society of Genetic Counselors: Referral indications for cancer predisposition assessment. *Genetic Medicine, 17*(1), 70-87. doi:10.1038/gim.2014.147

Jasperson, K. W. (2012). Genetic testing by cancer site: Colon (polyposis syndromes). *The Cancer Journal, 18*(4), 328-333. doi:10.1097/PPO.0b013e3182609300

Kurian, A., Griffith, K., Hamilton, A., Ward, K. C., Morrow, M., Katz, S. J., & Jagsi, R. (2017). Genetic testing and counseling among patients with newly diagnosed breast cancer. *JAMA, 317*(5), 531-534. doi:10.1001/jama.2016.16918

Mahon, S. M. (2013a). Allocation of work activities in a comprehensive cancer genetics program. *Clinical Journal of Oncology Nursing, 17*(4), 397-404. doi:10.1188/13.CJON.397-404

Mahon, S. M. (2013b). Next-generation DNA sequencing: Implications for oncology care. *Oncology Nursing Forum, 40*(5), 437-439. doi:10.1188/13.ONF.437-439

Mahon, S. M. (2013c). Ordering the correct genetic test: Implications for oncology and primary care healthcare professionals. *Clinical Journal of Oncology Nursing, 17*(2), 128-131. doi:10.1188/13.CJON.128-131

Mahon, S. M. (2014a). Breast cancer risk associated with CHEK2 mutations. *Oncology Nursing Forum, 41*(6), 692-694. doi:10.1188/14.ONF.692-694

Mahon, S. M. (2014b). Providing care for previvors: Implications for oncology nurses. *Clinical Journal of Oncology Nursing, 18*(1), 21-24. doi:10.1188/14.CJON.21-24

Mahon, S. M. (2015a). Management of patients with a genetic variant of unknown significance. *Oncology Nursing Forum, 42*(3), 316-318. doi:10.1188/15.ONF.316-318

Mahon, S. M. (2015b). Risk assessment, prevention, and early detection: Challenges for the advanced practice nurse. *Seminars in Oncology Nursing, 31*(4), 306-326. doi:10.1016/j.soncn.2015.08.007

Mahon, S. M. (2016a). The deceptive appeal of direct-to-consumer genetics. *Annals of Internal Medicine, 165*(9), 675-676. doi:10.73 26/L16-0333

Mahon, S. M. (2016b). The three-generation pedigree: A critical tool in cancer genetics care. *Oncology Nursing Forum, 43*(5), 655-660. doi:10.1188/16.onf.655-660

Marcus, R. K., Geurts, J. L., Grzybowski, J. A., Turaga, K. K., Clark Gamblin, T., Strong, K. A., & Johnston, F. M. (2015). Challenges to clinical utilization of hereditary cancer gene panel testing: Perspectives from the front lines. *Familial Cancer, 14*(4), 641-649. doi:10.1007/s10689-015-9817-9

Murray, A. J., & Davies, D. M. (2013). The genetics of breast cancer. *Surgery, 31*(1), 1-3. doi:10.1016/j.mpsur.2012.10.019

National Comprehensive Cancer Network. (2016). *Genetic/familial high-risk assessment: Colorectal, version 2.2016.* Retrieved from http://www.nccn.org

National Comprehensive Cancer Network. (2017). *Genetic/familial high-risk assessment: Breast and ovarian, version 2.2017.* Retrieved from http://www.nccn.org

Plutynski, A. (2012). Ethical issues in cancer screening and prevention. *Journal of Medicine and Philosophy, 37*(3), 310-323. doi:10.1093/jmp/jhs017

Rich, T. A., Woodson, A. H., Litton, J., & Arun, B. (2015). Hereditary breast cancer syndromes and genetic testing. *Journal of Surgical Oncology, 111*(1), 66-80. doi:10.1002/jso.23791

Riley, B. D., Culver, J. O., Skrzynia, C., Senter, L. A., Peters, J. A., Costalas, J. W., … Trepanier, A. M. (2012). Essential elements of genetic cancer risk assessment, counseling, and testing: Updated recommendations of the National Society of Genetic Counselors. *Journal of Genetic Counseling, 21*(2), 151-161. doi:10.1007/s10897-011-9462-x

Rizzo, J. M., & Buck, M. J. (2012). Key principles and clinical applications of "next-generation" DNA sequencing. *Cancer Prevention Research, 5*(7), 887-900. doi:10.1158/1940-6207.capr-11-0432

Senter, L. (2012). Genetic testing by cancer site: Colon (nonpolyposis syndromes). *The Cancer Journal, 18*(4), 334-337. doi:10.1097/PPO.0b013e31826094b2

Shannon, K. M., & Chittenden, A. (2012). Genetic testing by cancer site: Breast. *The Cancer Journal, 18*(4), 310-319. doi:10.1097/PPO. 0b013e318260946f

Stanislaw, C., Xue, Y., & Wilcox, W. R. (2016). Genetic evaluation and testing for hereditary forms of cancer in the era of next-generation sequencing. *Cancer Biology & Medicine, 13*(1), 55-67. doi:10.28092/j. issn.2095-3941.2016.0002

Thomas, E., & Mohammed, S. (2016). Advances in genetic testing for hereditary cancer syndromes. *Recent Results in Cancer Research, 205*, 1-15. doi:10.1007/978-3-319-29998-3_1

Turrini, M., & Prainsack, B. (2016). Beyond clinical utility: The multiple values of DTC genetics. *Applied & Translational Genomics, 8,* 4-8. doi:10.1016/j.atg.2016.01.008

U.S. Department of Health and Human Services. (2009). "GINA": The Genetic Information Nondiscrimination Act of 2008: Information for researchers and health care professionals. Retrieved from http://www.genome.gov/Pages/PolicyEthics/GeneticDiscrimination/GINAInfoDoc.pdf

van der Wouden, C. H., Carere, D., Maitland-van der Zee, A. H., Ruffin, M. T., IV, Roberts, J. S., Green, R.C. (2016). Consumer perceptions of interactions with primary care providers after direct-to-consumer personal genomic testing. *Annals of Internal Medicine, 164*(8), 513-522. doi:10.7326/M15-0995

van Marcke, C., De Leener, A., Berlière, M., Vikkula, M., & Duhoux, F. P. (2016). Routine use of gene panel testing in hereditary breast cancer should be performed with caution. *Critical Reviews in Oncology/Hematology, 108,* 33-39. doi:10.1016/j.critrevonc.2016.10.008

Wang, G., Beattie, M. S., Ponce, N. A., & Phillips, K. A. (2011). Eligibility criteria in private and public coverage policies for BRCA genetic testing and genetic counseling. *Genetics in Medicine: Official Journal of the American College of Medical Genetics, 13*(12), 1045-1050. doi:10.1097/GIM.0b013e31822a8113

Weissman, S. M., Burt, R., Church, J., Erdman, S., Hampel, H., Holter, S., ... Senter, L. (2012). Identification of individuals at risk for Lynch syndrome using targeted evaluations and genetic testing: National Society of Genetic Counselors and the Collaborative Group of the Americas on Inherited Colorectal Cancer joint practice guideline. *Journal of Genetic Counseling, 21*(4), 484-493. doi:10.1007/s10897-011-9465-7

Weitzel, J. N., Blazer, K. R., MacDonald, D. J., Culver, J. O., & Offit, K. (2011). Genetics, genomics and cancer risk assessment: State of the art and future directions in the era of personalized medicine. *CA: A Cancer Journal for Clinicians, 61*(5), 327-359. doi:10.3322/caac.20128

Wiseman, M., Dancyger, C., & Michie, S. (2010). Communicating genetic risk information within families: A review. *Familial Cancer, 9*(4), 691-703. doi:10.1007/s10689-010-9380-3

CHAPTER 3

BREAST CANCER

LEARNING OUTCOME

After completing this chapter, the learner will be able to discuss breast cancer's epidemiology, risk factors, prevention and detection strategies, and common staging schemas and treatments.

CHAPTER OBJECTIVES

After completing this chapter, the learner will be able to:

1. Discuss the main risk factors for breast cancer.

2. Describe prevention and early detection strategies based on the American Cancer Society's guidelines.

3. Explain the diagnostic evaluation/workup for breast cancer.

4. Identify significant terminology in a pathology report.

5. Describe systemic treatment modalities for breast cancer.

6. Describe postoperative recovery options and rehabilitation strategies.

INTRODUCTION

Women understandably fear breast cancer. Breast cancer can also occur in men, although the diagnosis is most frequently associated with women. Most people know someone who has been affected by a diagnosis of breast cancer. Great strides have been made in the prevention, early detection, diagnosis, and treatment of breast cancer. An individualized approach to care that targets cell type, an individual's profile/risk, genetic components, and the stage at diagnosis can result in different therapy options among patients. Nurses play a key role informing patients on the advances, the importance of individualizing the approach to therapy, and offering support during each phase of the cancer diagnosis and care. With early detection and effective treatment, women who have been diagnosed with breast cancer can realistically expect to survive and live happy, productive lives.

EPIDEMIOLOGY

Breast cancer is the most common cancer among women in the United States and is a cause of significant fear for many women (American Cancer Society [ACS], 2017a). Box 3-1 lists statistics on breast cancer in the United States, showing the number of people affected and the severity of the diagnosis in terms of survival rates. Currently, approximately 2.5 million Americans are breast cancer survivors (this includes men and women). The absolute lifetime risk of developing invasive breast cancer is about 1 in 8 (in women), with the median age at diagnosis being 62 years (ACS, 2015). Breast cancer accounts for approximately 14% of all cancer deaths in women (ACS, 2017a).

BOX 3-1: BREAST CANCER FACTS

- 253,710 estimated new cases of invasive cancer annually in women

- Most frequently diagnosed cancer in women

- 63,410 new cases of in situ breast cancer annually

- 40,610 estimated deaths annually

- Second leading cause of cancer death in women

- 61% of breast cancers diagnosed in women are at the localized stage before it has spread to the lymph nodes

- 5-year survival rate for localized cancer is 99%

- 5-year survival rate for regional cancer is 85%

- 5-year survival rate for metastatic disease is 26%

- 10-year survival rate for all stages is 83%

Note. Adapted from American Cancer Society. (2017a). *Cancer facts and figures – 2017.* Atlanta, GA: Author.

Although breast cancer remains a major public health problem, there is an ever-increasing cohort of long-term survivors, and the mortality rate from breast cancer continues to decline. As of January 2014, more than 3.1 million women were living with a diagnosis of breast cancer (ACS, 2015). Much of this success can be attributed to improved cancer screening, use of mammography, and advances with multimodality, individualized treatment.

Figure 3-1 illustrates the lifetime risk of developing breast cancer at various ages for women with average risk. Although women have a cumulative lifetime risk of 12.4%, or 1 in 8 women, the risk is spread over time (ACS, 2017a). As a woman ages, she passes through different ranges of risk. Absolute risk figures for breast cancer are best explained in terms of a woman's current age. The risk of developing breast cancer differs in various ethnic groups (see Figure 3-2).

The median age of death from breast cancer is 68 years (ACS, 2015; see Figure 3-3). The significant disparities in death rates in some races may be attributable to difficulties with regular or timely access to screening or clinical evaluation and treatment. Advanced stages at diagnosis may be because of lack of health insurance. Breast cancer patients with lower incomes have lower 5-year relative survival rates than higher-income patients at every stage of diagnosis (ACS, 2015). Racial disparities in mortality are illustrated in Figure 3-4.

As of November 2016, the data on relative survival rates for women diagnosed with breast cancer are (ACS, 2017a)

- 90% at 5 years after diagnosis,

- 83% after 10 years, and

- 78% after 15 years.

BREAST ANATOMY

Breasts, the woman's milk-producing glands, are located on either side of the sternum, or breast bone, and are surrounded by and contain a fat layer (see Figure 3-5). Although these tear-shaped glands do not contain any actual muscle, they are positioned against the pectoralis major, a large chest muscle. Ligaments support and connect the breasts to the the chest wall.

A complex interplay of hormones causes breast tissue to develop, enlarge, and produce milk. The three major hormones affecting the glands and ducts that are just under the breast tissue are estrogen, progesterone, and prolactin. Estrogen and progesterone in particular cause glandular tissue in the breast and the uterus to change during the menstrual cycle.

FIGURE 3-1: PERCENTAGE OF NEW CASES BY AGE GROUP: FEMALE BREAST CANCER

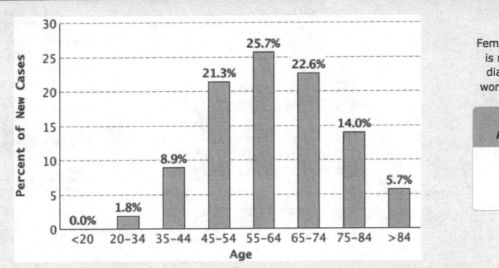

Female breast cancer is most frequently diagnosed among women aged 55-64.

Median Age At Diagnosis

62

SEER 18 2009-2013, All Races, Females

Female breast cancer is most common in middle-aged and older women. Although rare, men can have breast cancer as well. The number of new cases of female breast cancer is 125 per 100,000 women per year based on cases diagnosed from 2009 to 2013.

Note. From National Cancer Institute, Surveillance, Epidemiology, and End Results (SEER) Program. (n.d.). *SEER stat fact sheets: Female breast cancer.* Retrieved from http://seer.cancer.gov/statfacts/html/breast.html

FIGURE 3-2: NUMBER OF NEW CASES PER 100,000 PERSONS BY RACE/ETHNICITY: FEMALE BREAST CANCER

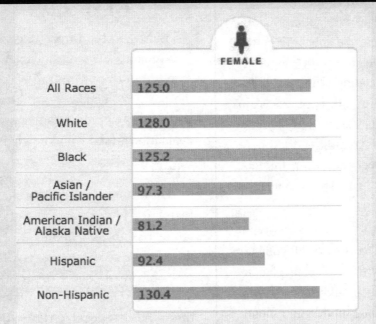

FEMALE

All Races	125.0
White	128.0
Black	125.2
Asian / Pacific Islander	97.3
American Indian / Alaska Native	81.2
Hispanic	92.4
Non-Hispanic	130.4

Number of new cases of breast cancer per 100,000 women in different ethnic groups.

Note. From National Cancer Institute, Surveillance, Epidemiology, and End Results (SEER) Program. (n.d.). *SEER stat fact sheets: Female breast cancer.* Retrieved from http://seer.cancer.gov/statfacts/html/breast.html

FIGURE 3-3: PERCENTAGE OF DEATHS BY AGE GROUP: FEMALE BREAST CANCER

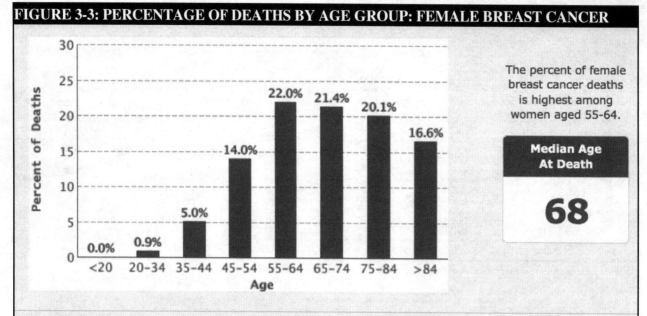

The percent of female breast cancer deaths is highest among women aged 55-64.

Median Age At Death

68

U.S. 2009-2013, All Races, Females

Overall, female breast cancer survival is good. However, women who are diagnosed at an advanced age are more likely than younger women to die of the disease. Female breast cancer is the fourth leading cause of cancer death in the United States. The number of deaths was 21.5 per 100,000 women per year based on data from 2009 to 2013.

Note. From National Cancer Institute, Surveillance, Epidemiology, and End Results (SEER) Program. (n.d.). *SEER stat fact sheets: Female breast cancer.* Retrieved from http://seer.cancer.gov/statfacts/html/breast.html

Each breast contains 15 to 20 lobes arranged in a circular fashion. The fat (subcutaneous adipose tissue) that covers the lobes gives the breast its size and shape. Each lobe is composed of many lobules, ending with tiny bulb-like glands, or sacs, where milk is produced in response to hormonal signals, especially by prolactin. Ducts, which deliver milk to the openings in the nipple, connect the lobes, lobules, and glands in nursing mothers. The areola is the darker pigmented area around the nipple.

A woman's breasts can change over the course of her lifetime. The breasts of younger women tend to have less fat and more glandular tissue. However, the glandular tissue in the breasts of women who have undergone menopause tends to disappear and be replaced with fat. The lower level of estrogen that occurs after menopause is one reason for this change (ACS, 2015).

RISK FACTORS

Clarity on the direct cause of breast cancer remains elusive; however, more is understood about contributing risk factors than in the past. Women who are aware of their own risk factors approach screening and healthcare evaluation armed with knowledge.

Age

Unfortunately, age is a nonmodifiable risk factor for breast cancer. Although all women are at risk for development of breast cancer – the lifetime risk is 12.4% (ACS, 2017a) – most cases of breast cancer occur after age 50 years. Therefore, older age is a major risk factor for this type of cancer (ACS, 2015). Figure 3-1 illustrates how women have different statistical risks for developing breast cancer at different ages. Women who have other risk factors in addition to age are at higher risk.

FIGURE 3-4: NUMBER OF DEATHS PER 100,000 PERSONS BY RACE/ETHNICITY: FEMALE BREAST CANCER

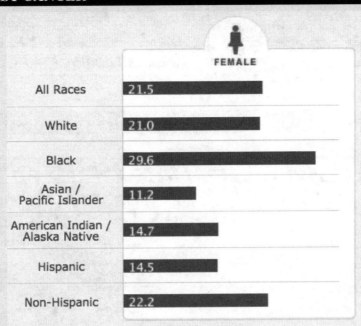

	FEMALE
All Races	21.5
White	21.0
Black	29.6
Asian / Pacific Islander	11.2
American Indian / Alaska Native	14.7
Hispanic	14.5
Non-Hispanic	22.2

A disparate number of African American women die from breast cancer. The number of deaths was 21.5 per 100,000 women per year based on 2009 to 2013 data.

Note. From National Cancer Institute, Surveillance, Epidemiology, and End Results (SEER) Program. (n.d.). *SEER stat fact sheets: Female breast cancer.* Retrieved from http://seer.cancer.gov/statfacts/html/breast.html

Reproductive Factors

A woman's hormone levels normally change throughout her life for a variety of reasons. These hormonal fluctuations can lead to changes in the breast tissue. Hormonal changes occur during puberty, pregnancy, and menopause. Multiple studies have linked start of menarche, menopause, and first live pregnancy to breast cancer risk (National Comprehensive Cancer Network [NCCN], 2017a). Collectively, the patterns of risk associated with reproductive history suggest that prolonged exposure to ovarian hormones increases breast cancer occurrence. The number of menstrual cycles during a lifetime may have a greater risk impact than the number of cycles until the first full-term pregnancy (Li et al., 2013). Thus, women who have experienced menarche before age 12 years or menopause after age 50 are considered at somewhat higher risk because of a total increased number of ovulatory cycles in a lifetime (ACS, 2015; NCCN, 2017a).

Breast tissue damage or aging starts at a constant rate at menarche continuing to a woman's first pregnancy, at which point there is a decrease in the rate of tissue aging. This continues to menopause, when there is an additional decrease, following which the rate is more constant but decreased (NCCN, 2017a). Thus, if the first full-term pregnancy is delayed, the proliferation attributable to pregnancy hormones would be acting on a more damaged or aged set of genetic components or profile, and thus carry a greater adverse effect.

Increasing parity is associated with a long-term risk reduction in breast cancer risk, presumably because of the interruption of estrogen cycling. Breast-feeding is also associated with a decreased risk for breast cancer (NCCN, 2016a).

History of Benign Breast Disease

Nonproliferative lesions (which account for more than 70% of all breast biopsies) include adenosis, fibrosis, cysts, mastitis, duct ectasia, fibroadenomas, and mild hyperplasia and con-fer no added risk for developing breast cancer. Pathology reports that suggest the presence of atypical hyperplasia or lobular carcinoma may indicate an increased risk for developing breast cancer (ACS, 2015).

FIGURE 3-5: ANATOMY OF THE BREAST: INTERNAL AND EXTERNAL STRUCTURES

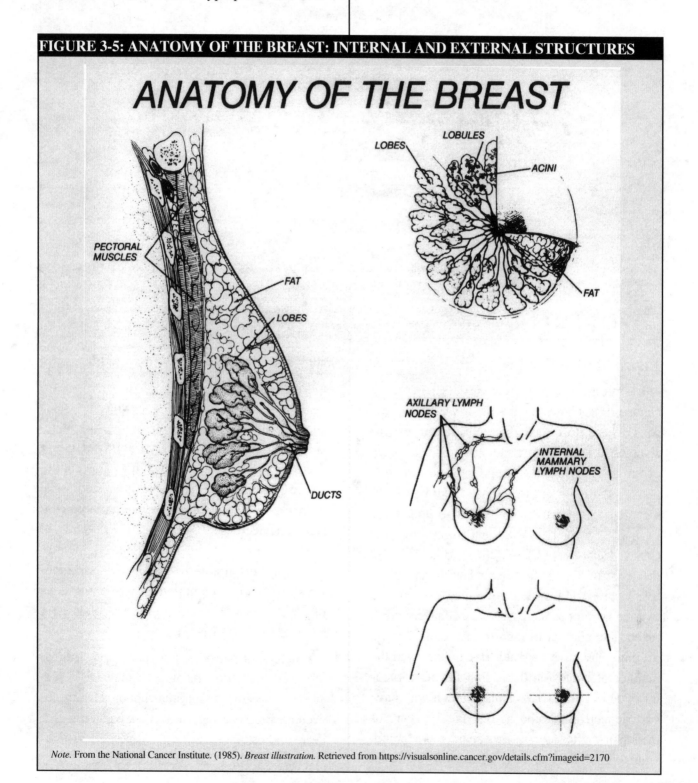

Note. From the National Cancer Institute. (1985). *Breast illustration.* Retrieved from https://visualsonline.cancer.gov/details.cfm?imageid=2170

Oral Contraceptive or Infertility Drug Use

The exact risk for breast cancer conferred by the use of oral contraceptives is controversial. The composition of oral contraceptives has changed greatly over time. Hormonal contraceptives that contain both estrogen and progesterone can slightly increase the risk for breast cancer, especially among women who have used hormonal contraceptives for 10 or more years (Beaber et al., 2014). Current and recent (less than 10 years since last use) users have a slightly increased risk compared with women who have never used hormonal contraceptives (Yang et al., 2011). Infertility treatment may increase the risk for development of breast cancer, although the exact risk is not clear; long-term prospective studies are needed to better characterize this risk (Brinton et al., 2014). This is a largely modifiable risk factor.

Hormone Therapy

Hormone therapy (HT) as a breast cancer risk factor is more fully documented than oral contraceptive use. Use of exogenous hormones (HT), especially estrogen-based therapy, after menopause increases the risk for breast cancer. Current or recent users of combined HT for 5 years or longer have an increased risk for breast cancer (Marjoribanks, Farquhar, Roberts, & Lethaby, 2012). Risk is also greater for women who start HT soon after the onset of menopause compared with those who begin use later (ACS, 2015).

Alcohol Consumption

Alcohol consumption, a modifiable risk factor, increases the risk of breast cancer. A woman who consumes alcohol on a daily basis increases her risk of developing breast cancer by about 7% to 10% for each drink of alcohol consumed regularly (ACS, 2015). The risk increases with the amount of alcohol consumed. Alcohol is associated with higher levels of estrogen (Chen, Rosner, Hankinson, Colditz, & Willett, 2011). Alcohol may also lower levels of some essential nutrients that protect against cell damage, such as folate (a type of B vitamin), vitamin A, and vitamin C (NCCN, 2016a).

Increased Body Mass

Increased body mass may be a more important risk factor in postmenopausal women compared with premenopausal women. Adipose tissue is an important source of extragonadal estrogens in postmenopausal women. The more tissue available, theoretically, the higher the circulating levels of these estrogens and the increased risk for developing breast cancer (ACS, 2015). Women with a body mass index of 31.1 or higher have a 2.5 times greater risk for development of breast cancer over a lifetime than those with a body mass index of 22.6 or lower (Emaus et al., 2014). A large meta-analysis of women who did not use HT suggests that for each 11 pounds gained during adulthood, the risk for postmenopausal breast cancer over a lifetime increases by 11% (Emaus et al., 2014).

Ionizing Radiation

Exposure of the breast to ionizing radiation is associated with an increased risk of developing breast cancer, especially when the exposure occurs between 10 and 30 years of age (ACS, 2017b). Women who have received radiation therapy to the chest, neck, and axilla area (called the *mantle radiation field*) have a higher risk of developing breast cancer. This increased risk has been particularly noted in women who received treatment to these areas for Hodgkin lymphoma before the age of 30 years (NCCN, 2017a).

Protective Factors

Women who engage in regular exercise may have a 10% to 25% lower risk of developing breast cancer compared with inactive women (ACS, 2015). This is especially true for postmenopausal women. Women who walk 7 or more hours per week have a 14% lower risk of developing breast cancer than women who walk 3 or fewer hours per week (ACS, 2017b). The protective benefit of physical activity may be because of decreased body mass, energy balance, and fewer ovulatory cycles (NCCN, 2017a).

The largest percentage of calories in the average American diet comes from foods high in fat, added sugar, and refined carbohydrates, as well as sugar-sweetened beverages that add little nutritional value to the diet and may contribute to increased amounts and distribution of body fat, insulin resistance, and increased concentrations of growth factors that promote the growth of cancers (ACS, 2017b). In addition to containing fewer calories, vegetables and fruits contain numerous vitamins, minerals, fiber, carotenoids, and other bioactive substances that may help prevent cancer (ACS, 2015). There is increasing evidence that consuming more nonstarchy vegetables (such as broccoli, green beans, lettuce, and squash) and fruits is associated with lower risk of developing estrogen-receptor-negative breast tumors (NCCN, 2017a). Increased vegetable intake may result in a healthier weight, which further reduces breast cancer risk. The ACS (2017a) recommends that women consume at least 2.5 cups of a variety of vegetables and fruits each day, and ideally half of a woman's plate would include fruits and vegetables for meals and snacks. Micronutrient intake, especially vitamin D and vitamin E, may also play a small role in preventing the development of breast cancer (ACS, 2015).

GENETIC RISK

Although risk factors for breast cancer are not yet clear or definitive, family history has emerged as an important risk factor for breast, ovarian, colon, pancreatic, and malignant melanoma cancers (NCCN, 2017b). For some women, after sex and age, a positive family history is the strongest known predictive risk factor for breast cancer. Overall, *BRCA1/2* mutation carriers have up to an 87% lifetime risk of developing at least one breast cancer, an approximate 50% risk for a second breast cancer, and about a 30% to 50% risk for development of ovarian cancer over a lifetime (NCCN, 2017b; Rich, Woodson, Litton, & Arun, 2015; Weitzel, Blazer, MacDonald, Culver, & Offit, 2011). For women with *BRCA1* or *BRCA2* mutations, approximately half of those women have had breast cancer by age 50 years (Daly et al., 2017). Family members of women with the *BRCA1* or *BRCA2* mutation who are aware of this risk can choose aggressive surveillance and adopt breast cancer prevention strategies.

Because most hereditary breast cancer syndromes are a result of autosomal-dominant transmission, approximately 50% of susceptible individuals inherit the predisposing genetic alteration that is associated with breast cancer (NCCN, 2017b). The susceptibility may be inherited through either the maternal or paternal side of the family.

Key indicators of hereditary breast cancer are shown in Figure 3-6. Women with such family histories should be referred to a credentialed genetics professional for counseling and evaluation for genetic testing.

As discussed in Chapter 2, the genetics professional usually begins a hereditary assessment by constructing a family tree or pedigree. Ethnic background also needs to be considered when deciding whether testing may be appropriate, and this information may alter testing strategies. For example, an estimated 2% of Ashkenazi Jews are estimated to carry one of three common *BRCA1* and *BRCA2* mutations associated with increased risk for breast, ovarian, and prostate cancers; 20% of Ashkenazi women with breast cancer before 40 years of age have one of

FIGURE 3-6: KEY INDICATORS OF HEREDITARY RISK FOR DEVELOPING BREAST CANCER

- Personal and/or family history of breast cancer diagnosed at 50 years or younger

- Multiple family members with breast cancer: The pedigree will often show two or more first-degree relatives on the same side of the family who experienced the same or related cancers. Usually the cancer is seen in more than one generation, and there is evidence of vertical transmission.

- Personal and/or family history of ovarian cancer diagnosed at any age

- Unique tumor-site combinations may be present, especially in families including breast, ovarian, pancreatic, melanoma, and prostate cancers

- Women of Ashkenazi Jewish ancestry diagnosed with breast and/or ovarian cancer at any age, regardless of family history

- Personal and/or family history of male breast cancer

- Triple-negative breast cancer diagnosed before the age of 60 years

- Bilateral breast cancer, especially if the diagnosis was at an early age

- Breast and ovarian cancer in the same woman

- Affected first-degree relatives with a known genetic mutation associated with increased risk for malignancy such as *BRCA1/2*

Note. Adapted from: American Cancer Society. (2015). Breast cancer facts and figures 2015-2016. Atlanta, GA: Author; National Comprehensive Cancer Network. (2016a). *Breast cancer screening and diagnosis: Version 1.2016.* Retrieved from http://www.nccn.org

Weitzel, J. N., Blazer, K. R., MacDonald, D. J., Culver, J. O., & Offit, K. (2011). Genetics, genomics and cancer risk assessment: State of the art and future directions in the era of personalized medicine. *CA: A Cancer Journal for Clinicians, 61*(5), 327-359. doi:10.3322/caac.20128

the three common mutations (Daly et al., 2017). This is attributable to a phenomenon referred to as the "founder effect," in which a population has descended from a relatively small number of people without the contribution of genetic material from other groups.

The commercial availability of genetic testing for the cancer susceptibility genes associated with hereditary breast/ovarian cancer syndromes has greatly changed oncology risk-assessment practices (Daly et al., 2016). Researchers have recently identified multiple genes associated with hereditary risk for developing breast cancer. Many are of lower penetrance than genes such as *BRCA1/2* (Daly et al., 2017). Different genes are associated with different risks for developing breast cancer (Rich et al., 2015; NCCN, 2017b). These tests, however, cannot predict

when, where, or if the individual will be diagnosed with breast cancer. One of the challenges in the communication of genetic risk information and genetic test results is the probabilities and uncertainties inherent in genetic information and testing (Rich et al., 2015).

Whether specific patients might benefit from predisposition genetic testing will depend on their degree of genetic risk, whether testing is likely to address their needs, their motivation to actively engage in prevention strategies, and the availability of an appropriate cancer predisposition test (Daly et al., 2017). For some genes, few evidence-based strategies exist for primary or secondary prevention, and the exact cancer risks conferred by these genes are not exactly clear (NCCN, 2017b). As of 2016, the estimated cost to a third-party insurance payer ranges from $2,760 to $4,100 for a panel of 20 to 30 genes covering a range of genes associated with a hereditary cancer syndrome (Foote et al., 2017). Because of the high cost of some genetic tests for full sequencing of a typical panel of breast cancer susceptibility genes, such as that listed in Table 3-1, reimbursement factors may need to be considered. Most insurers cover some or all of the cost of genetic testing in persons who meet eligibility criteria set by the insurer. The final testing decision, however, will depend on the patient understanding the potential risks and benefits and then deciding whether she wants to proceed.

Models for predicting risk of developing breast cancer or having a mutation are listed in Table 3-2. If an unaffected relative has been tested and found to carry a deleterious or pathogenic mutation known to be associated with increased cancer risk, then at-risk family members are likely to benefit from single-site testing for the same mutation (which is significantly less expensive, costing $250 to $450 in 2016; Foote et al., 2017).

If a woman tests negative for a known mutation, she has the same risk of developing breast cancer as any woman in the general population. If the woman tests negative and she is the first woman in her family to test, the family could

TABLE 3-1: SELECTED HEREDITARY BREAST CANCER SYNDROMES

Gene	Associated Cancers*
BRCA1/ BRCA2	Female breast (41% to 87%), ovarian (24% to 54%), prostate (20% to 34%), male breast (4% to 7%), pancreatic (5% to 10%), fallopian tube, primary peritoneal, endometrial (serous), melanoma
CDH1	Female breast (39% to 52%), diffuse gastric cancer (40% to 83%), colon (5% to 12%)
PTEN	Female breast (25% to 50%), thyroid (10%), endometrial (5% to 10%), colon, renal, melanoma
STK11	Female breast (32% to 54%), ovarian tumors (21%), colorectal (39%), pancreatic (11% to 36%), gastric (29%), lung (15%), small intestine (13%), cervical (10%), endometrial (9%), testicular tumors (9%)
ATM	Female breast (30% to 55%), colon (12% to 25%), pancreatic
TP53	Female breast, soft tissue sarcoma, osteosarcoma, brain, hematological malignancies, adrenocortical carcinoma overall risk for cancer: nearly 100% in females, 73% in males
CHEK2	Female breast, male breast, colon, prostate, thyroid, endometrial (serous), ovarian
BARD1	Female breast, ovarian
BRIP1	Female breast, ovarian
FANCC	Female breast
NBN	Female breast, melanoma, non-Hodgkin lymphoma
RAD51C	Female breast, ovarian
RAD51D	Female breast, ovarian
XRCC2	Female breast, ovarian, pancreatic

*If estimated risks are known, they are included in parentheses.

Note. Adapted from: Daly, M. B., Pilarski, R., Berry, M., Buys, S. S., Farmer, M., Friedman, S., … Kohlmann, W. (2017). NCCN guidelines insights: Genetic/familial high-risk assessment: Breast and ovarian, version 2.2017. *Journal of the National Comprehensive Cancer Network, 15*(1), 9-20; National Comprehensive Cancer Network. (2016a). *Breast cancer screening and diagnosis: Version 1.2016.* Retrieved from http://www.nccn.org

Weitzel, J. N., Blazer, K. R., MacDonald, D. J., Culver, J. O., & Offit, K. (2011). Genetics, genomics and cancer risk assessment: State of the art and future directions in the era of personalized medicine. *CA: A Cancer Journal for Clinicians, 61*(5), 327-359. doi:10.3322/caac.20128

still have a hereditary risk for developing breast cancer, but it might be an odd mutation for which testing is not available. With the advent of panel testing for multiple syndromes at one time, there is a greater chance of the identification of a vari-

ant of unknown significance because some of the newer genes are not as well categorized and understood (Mahon, 2013). In this case, the risk for developing cancer is not clear, and the patient is managed based on personal risk factors and

---

TABLE 3-2: SELECTED MODELS TO PREDICT RISK OF DEVELOPING BREAST CANCER

Selected Models to Predict Risk of Developing Breast Cancer

Gail model: Estimates breast cancer risk in women without a diagnosis of cancer. Considers woman's age, breast cancer history in mother and sisters, reproductive factors, and biopsy history.

Claus model: Estimates risk for development of breast cancer over time in 10-year increments in women with a family history of breast cancer. Considers age of onset of breast cancer.

National Cancer Institute breast risk tool: Estimates risk for development of breast cancer in 5 years and lifetime. Considers the woman's age, family history of breast cancer, reproductive factors, and biopsy history. Available at http://www.cancer.gov/bcrisktool.

Tyrer-Cuzick: Estimates risk for development of breast cancer in 5 years and lifetime. Considers woman's age, height, weight, reproductive history, biopsy history, and history of breast and ovarian cancer in offspring, siblings, aunts, and grandmothers (both maternal and paternal side). Available at http://www.ems-trials.org/riskevaluator.

Models to Predict Risk of Having a Mutation in *BRCA1* and/or *BRCA2*

Berry model: Estimates risk for carrying a *BRCA1* or *BRCA2* mutation.

Couch model: Estimates risk for carrying a *BRCA1* mutation.

Frank model (myriad tables): Estimates risk for carrying a *BRCA1* or *BRCA2* mutation.

Manchester model: Estimates risk for carrying a *BRCA1* or *BRCA2* mutation.

Pedigree Assessment Tool: Identifies women at increased risk for hereditary breast and ovarian cancer to offer genetic testing.

Shattuck-Eidens model: Estimates risk for carrying a *BRCA1* mutation.

Tyrer-Cuzick: Estimates risk for carrying a *BRCA1* or *BRCA2* mutation.

Note. Adapted from Claus, E. B., Schildkraut, J. M., Thompson, W. D., & Risch, N. (1996). The genetic attributable risk of breast and ovarian cancer. *Cancer, 77*(11), 2318-2324; Couch, F. J., DeShano, M. L., Blackwood, M. A., Calzone, K., Stopfer, J., Campeau, L., et al. (1997). BRCA1 mutations in women attending clinics that evaluate the risk of breast cancer. *New England Journal of Medicine, 336*(20), 1409-1415; Cuzick, J., Sestak, I., Bonanni, B., Costantino, J. P., Cummings, S., DeCensi, A., ... Wickerham, D. L. (2013). Selective oestrogen receptor modulators in prevention of breast cancer: An updated meta-analysis of individual participant data. *The Lancet, 381*(9880), 1827-1834; Decarli, A., Calza, S., Masala, G., Specchia, C., Palli, D., & Gail, M. H. (2006). Gail model for prediction of absolute risk of invasive breast cancer: Independent evaluation in the Florence-European Prospective Investigation into cancer and nutrition cohort. *Journal of the National Cancer Institute, 98*(23), 1686-1693; Evans, D. G., Eccles, D. M., Rahman, N., Young, K., Bulman, M., Amir, E., ... Lalloo, F. (2004). A new scoring system for the chances of identifying a *BRCA1/2* mutation outperforms existing models including BRCAPRO. *Journal of Medical Genetics, 41*(6), 474-480; Frank, T. S., Deffenbaugh, A. M., Reid, J. E., Hulick, M., Ward, B. E., Lingenfelter, B., ... Critchfield, G. C. (2002). Clinical characteristics of individuals with germline mutations in *BRCA1* and *BRCA2:* Analysis of 10,000 individuals. *Journal of Clinical Oncology, 20*(6), 1480-1490; Hoskins, K. F., Zwaagstra, A., & Ranz, M. (2006). Validation of a tool for identifying women at high risk for hereditary breast cancer in population-based screening. *Cancer, 107*(8), 1769-1776. doi:10.1002/cncr.22202; Parmigani, G., Chen, S., Iversen, E. S., Jr., Friebel, T. M., Finkelstein, D. M., Anton-Culver, H., ... Euhus, D. M. (2007). Validity of models for predicting *BRCA1* and *BRCA2* mutations. *Annals of Internal Medicine, 147*(7), 441-450; and Shattuck-Eidens, D., Oliphant, A., McClure, M., McBride, C., Gupte, J., Rubano, T., ... Thomas, A. (1997). *BRCA1* sequence analysis in women at high risk for susceptibility mutations. Risk factor analysis and implications for genetic testing. *Journal of the American Medical Association, 278*(15), 1242-1250.

family history; also, testing is not possible for unaffected family members.

For women who test positive, the risk of developing breast, ovarian, and other cancers is significant. They must make difficult decisions about how to manage the risk. One option is to screen more aggressively than what is recommended for the general population, but the woman might still develop breast cancer and will need some form of treatment. In some cases, hormonal manipulation with a drug such as tamoxifen may be used. Prevention of cancer in those with a known mutation is often best achieved with prophylactic mastectomy and oophorectomy (Daly et al., 2017).

HORMONE THERAPY AS PREVENTION

The U.S. Food and Drug Administration as of 2017 has approved two medications for the prevention of breast cancer in women with an increased risk (20% to 25% increased risk) for developing breast cancer: tamoxifen (Nolvadex) and raloxifene (Evista; Daly et al., 2017). These selective estrogen receptor modulators block estrogen in some tissues of the body, but they have an estrogen-like effect in others. A meta-analysis of more than 83,000 high-risk women from nine breast cancer prevention trials over a 10-year period found that women who take a selective estrogen receptor modulator reduced estrogen-receptor-positive breast cancer risk by 38% (NCCN, 2017a).

Tamoxifen (Nolvadex)

Tamoxifen is a hormone prescribed for women at high risk for breast cancer. It blocks the action of estrogen in breast tissue, thereby preventing estrogen from stimulating the proliferation of breast cells (ACS, 2015; NCCN, 2017a).

Studies show that tamoxifen decreases the risk for breast cancer in women with lobular carcinoma in situ (LCIS; NCCN, 2017a). For women responsive to hormone treatment, tamoxifen reduces the incidence of several benign breast diseases, including atypical hyperplasia, when noncancerous cells proliferate and can advance to invasive breast cancer (Daly et al., 2017). Tamoxifen is approved for both premenopausal and postmenopausal women.

Tamoxifen can contribute to or prompt weight gain, hot flashes, vaginal discharge or irritation, nausea, and irregular periods. When taking tamoxifen, women still menstruating or experiencing irregular periods may more easily become pregnant (Daly et al., 2017). Although rare, blood clots and cataracts can develop in individuals taking tamoxifen, which can be significant adverse effects. Some studies indicate that women taking tamoxifen have a slightly increased risk of developing endometrial cancer (ACS, 2015; NCCN, 2017a).

Raloxifene (Evista)

Raloxifene is another antiestrogen agent prescribed to prevent breast cancer in postmenopausal women. It has been shown to reduce the incidence of both breast and uterine cancers (NCCN, 2017a).

The Study of Tamoxifen and Raloxifene evaluated the efficacy of tamoxifen and raloxifene in postmenopausal women; the trial followed more than 20,000 women taking these agents for 5 to 10 years. The tamoxifen group had fewer cases of noninvasive breast cancer and uterine cancer than the raloxifene group (Cuzick et al., 2013). Those taking these hormone preventive agents did not have an increased incidence of other invasive cancer sites, ischemic heart disease events, or stroke.

However, women taking these hormonal agents can experience rare but significant side effects, including embolus and endometrial cancer. Women who opt to take a chemoprevention agent should do so only after a risk assessment validates that their cancer risk is increased and after they have had a discussion with their provider of the potential risks and benefits of taking a chemoprevention agent. They need to be monitored closely for negative side effects. Data are conflicting on when to start chemoprevention, and initiation of treatment depends on the family history and the length of time for which the patient will use the agent (usually 5 to 10 years; Cuzick et al., 2013).

SCREENING

Screening and genetic testing can decrease the morbidity and mortality associated with breast cancer (ACS, 2015; NCCN, 2016a). Screening is appropriate for asymptomatic women. For symptomatic women (see Figure 3-7), providers should directly refer them for a diagnostic evaluation, which may include an ultrasound, additional mammographic views, magnetic resonance imaging (MRI), and/or biopsy (ACS, 2015).

FIGURE 3-7: SIGNS AND SYMPTOMS OF BREAST CANCER

- Lump or mass in the breast
- Swelling in all or part of the breast
- Skin irritation or dimpling
- Breast pain
- Nipple pain or the nipple turning inward
- Redness, scaliness, or thickening of the nipple or breast skin
- Nipple discharge other than breast milk
- Lump in the underarm area

Note. Adapted from: American Cancer Society. (2015). *Breast cancer facts and figures 2015-2016.* Atlanta, GA: Author

National Comprehensive Cancer Network. (2016b). *Breast cancer: Version 2.2016.* Retrieved from http://www.nccn.org

Table 3-3 lists the ACS recommendations for the early detection of cancer. Reduction of breast cancer mortality rates is due in part to screening outreach and public awareness (ACS, 2017a). Government programs as well as many private organizations, such as Susan G. Komen for the Cure, promote and fund breast cancer screening. Notably, these programs have underwritten screening for underserved populations.

In 1990, the *Breast and Cervical Cancer Mortality Prevention Act* established the National Breast and Cervical Cancer Early Detection Program (NBCCEDP; Centers for Disease Control and Prevention, 2015). This program provides low-income, uninsured, and underserved women access to breast and cervical cancer screening and diagnostic services. It is estimated that 8% to 13% of U.S. women of screening age are eligible to receive NBCCEDP services (Centers for Disease Control and Prevention, 2015). Federal guidelines establish an eligibility baseline to direct services to uninsured and underinsured women at or below 250% of the federal poverty level; the guidelines cover women 18 to 64 years of age for cervical screening and 40 to 64 years of age for breast screening (Centers for Disease Control and Prevention, 2015). Services include clinical breast examinations (CBEs), mammograms, Papanicolaou (Pap) tests, diagnostic testing for women whose screening outcome is abnormal, surgical consultation, and referrals to treatment. Since 1991, the NBCCEDP has served more than 4.8 million women, provided more than 12.2 million screening examinations, and diagnosed 69,507 breast cancers (Centers for Disease Control and Prevention, 2015). At 65 years old, women become eligible for Medicare, which provides coverage for breast cancer screening, including annual mammography. Women who receive services under NBCCEDP who are diagnosed with breast cancer are eligible for the Breast and

TABLE 3-3: AMERICAN CANCER SOCIETY GUIDELINES FOR THE EARLY DETECTION OF BREAST CANCER

Guideline Component	Details
Date released	2015
Breast self-examination	Not recommended. Women should be instructed on changes and signs/symptoms that should be evaluated promptly.
Clinical breast examination	Not recommended.
Age to start mammography	45 years. Women should have the opportunity to begin annual screening between the ages of 40 and 44 years.
Interval to perform mammography	Women who are 45 to 54 years old should be screened annually. Women who are 55 years and older can transition to biennial screening or have the opportunity to continue screening annually.
Age to stop mammography	Women should continue screening mammography as long as their overall health is good and they have a life expectancy of 10 years or more.
Breast magnetic resonance imaging (MRI)	*Breast MRI is recommended for women with high lifetime risk, including* women with known *BRCA1/2* or other genetic susceptibility mutations; women who had radiation therapy to the chest when they were between 10 and 30 years of age; women who have a lifetime risk for breast cancer of 15% to 20%, according to risk-assessment tools that are based mainly on family history; and women who have a personal history of breast cancer, ductal carcinoma in situ, lobular carcinoma in situ, atypical ductal hyperplasia, or atypical lobular hyperplasia. Breast MRI can be instituted at age 30 years.

Note. Adapted from American Cancer Society. (2015). *Breast cancer facts and figures 2015-2016.* Atlanta, GA: Author.

Cervical Cancer Treatment Program (BCCTP), which assists with the costs of surgery, chemotherapy, hormonal therapy, and long-term follow-up.

Breast Self-Examination

Breast self-examination (BSE) enables women to actively participate, have control, and obtain early awareness of breast changes. BSE practice has prompted controversy about BSE as a component of optimal screening.

Although the ACS no longer recommends that all women perform monthly BSE, women should know the potential benefits and limitations associated with BSE or breast self-

awareness (ACS, 2017a). Studies indicate that structured BSE is less important than the woman's self-awareness about breast anatomy and breast examination changes (ACS, 2015). Women who detect their own breast tumors usually find them while bathing or getting dressed, outside of a structured BSE. For women who want to perform BSE, healthcare providers can instruct them and confirm technique (ACS, 2017a). Women performing BSE between professional examinations or mammography can detect tumors that develop between examinations or those undetected by mammography (NCCN, 2016a).

Clinical Breast Examination

CBE is a manual breast examination performed by a trained clinician. CBE is recommended especially for women who carry the *BRCA1, BRCA2,* or other high-risk mutation and usually at a more frequent interval (Daly et al., 2017). Women with a genetic mutation are typically managed by a breast surgeon who provides CBEs.

Mammography

Mammography is widely used to screen for breast disease in women who are asymptomatic. Mammograms can show masses, cysts, and small deposits of calcium in the breast. Although most calcium deposits are benign, microcalcifications may be an early sign of cancer. Some agencies, including the NCCN (2016a), recommend that women routinely begin having mammograms at 40 years of age.

Mammography is the single most effective method of early detection of breast cancer because it can identify cancer several years before physical symptoms, such as a nodule or lump, develop (ACS, 2017a). Mammography is a low-dose X-ray procedure that allows visualization of the internal structure of the breast, compressing tissue for better visualization. Standard screening views include the craniocaudal and the mediolateral oblique views. Typical views for a diagnostic mammogram may also include supplemental views tailored to better visualize the specific problem. Figure 3-8 shows a patient positioned for a craniocaudal view mammogram.

Mammography will detect about 87% to 90% of breast cancers in women who present without symptoms (ACS, 2015). Mammography is slightly more accurate in postmenopausal women than in premenopausal women because postmenopausal breast tissues tend to be less dense (NCCN, 2016b; see Figure 3-9). Factors that contribute to false-negative mammogram reports include increased breast density, faster tumor growth rate, inadequate positioning of the breast, or simply failing to see the small early signs of an abnormality. Each year approximately 5% to 10% of women have their mammogram interpreted as abnormal or inconclusive until further tests are done. In most instances, more testing, such as additional imaging studies and biopsy, lead to a final interpretation of normal breast tissue or benign changes (ACS, 2015).

As of 2015, the ACS had not recommended a specific upper age to discontinue mammography screening (ACS, 2015). The woman and her provider should determine discontinuing mammography screening based on several factors, including the potential benefits and risks of screening, the woman's overall health status, and estimated life span. That said, any woman whose health status allows her to be treated for breast cancer should continue mammography screening (NCCN, 2016a).

The routine use of mammography is partially responsible for the reduction in mortality rates for breast cancer (ACS, 2015). Mammography can detect breast cancers long before the tumor is palpable, as shown in Figure 3-10. All mammogram facilities should be certified by the American College of Radiology and use dedicated mammogram machines.

When a woman presents for a mammogram she should anticipate that she will be questioned about previous images, breast problems, hormone use, and breast surgery. If images have been done at another facility, access to those images is needed to compare studies. The patient can facilitate the transfer by obtaining the film or CD, or by signing a release requesting the digital images to be transmitted to the new provider. The woman should be instructed to avoid using deodorant or antiperspirant, lotions, powders, and creams to the axilla and the breast area on the day of the examination because some products

FIGURE 3-8: POSITIONING DURING THE MAMMOGRAM

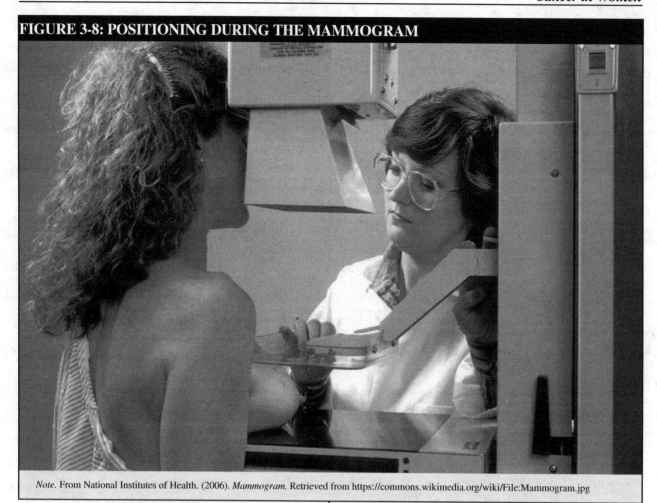

Note. From National Institutes of Health. (2006). *Mammogram.* Retrieved from https://commons.wikimedia.org/wiki/File:Mammogram.jpg

may contain substances that will interfere with mammogram interpretation by appearing on the mammographic images as white spots.

Ideally, the mammogram should be scheduled when the breasts are not tender or swollen to help reduce discomfort, which means avoiding the week before the menses. Federal law mandates that women receive a written summary of the findings. The woman must be instructed that if she does not receive a report in 7 to 10 days, she needs to contact the facility. Mammogram reports include information on whether the image is negative or more evaluation is needed. These categories, known as the BI-RADS reporting system, are shown in Table 3-4.

Additional Screening Imaging

Conventional screening with mammography is not adequate for some individuals (Daly et al., 2017). Some women have increased breast density. In young women (younger than 40 years), they may present with atypical imaging. These women have a higher lifetime risk of developing breast cancer.

Women whose risk profile increases because of hereditary breast cancer may need to start screening earlier than women at standard risk, or they may need more frequent or detailed screening (ACS, 2015). For women with a known genetic mutation or higher lifetime risk of developing breast cancer (>20%), screening recommendations differ (ACS, 2015; NCCN, 2016a). Recommendations for these women may include mammography beginning at 25 to 30 years of

FIGURE 3-9: FAT REPLACED AND DENSE BREAST ON MAMMOGRAPHY

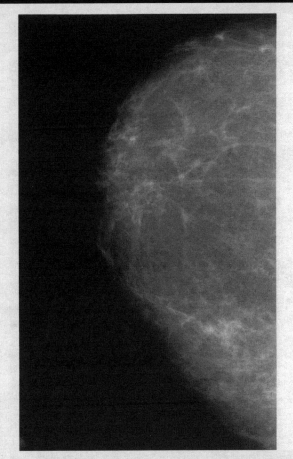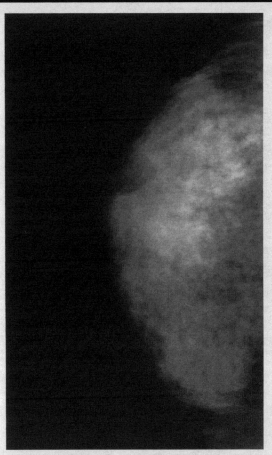

Note. From National Cancer Institute. (1994). *Mammogram showing dense and fatty breasts.* Retrieved from https://visualsonline.cancer.gov/ details.cfm?imageid=2699

age combined with bilateral breast MRI or MRI alone as screening imaging (Daly et al., 2017). The woman's plan of care should include genetics counseling (NCCN, 2017b).

MRI uses magnetic fields instead of X-rays to produce very detailed, cross-sectional images. Breast MRI examinations, performed on a dedicated breast MRI machine, are ordered with a contrast material (gadolinium DTPA) to enhance imaging; the patient is injected with the contrast material intravenously. Although an MRI is more sensitive than mammograms in detecting cancers, it also has a documented higher false-positive rate, prompting more recalls and biopsies (Daly et al., 2017; see Figure 3-11). MRI is also more expensive than mammography. Many

major insurance companies will likely pay for these screening tests if a woman is documented to be at high risk (NCCN, 2016a). For abnormalities detected on screening MRIs, MRI-guided breast biopsy should be performed then, using the screening MRI if the facility has that capability.

Digital breast tomosynthesis is a type of three-dimensional mammography that is emerging as the standard of care for breast cancer screening. Compared to standard two-dimensional digital mammography, it has a greater detection rate and lower recall rate. Digital breast tomosynthesis obtains multiple low-dose tomographic projections of the breast by moving the X-ray tube in an arc. The images are subsequently reconstructed and viewed on the work-

FIGURE 3-10: SMALL, NONPALPABLE LESION DETECTED ON MAMMOGRAPHY

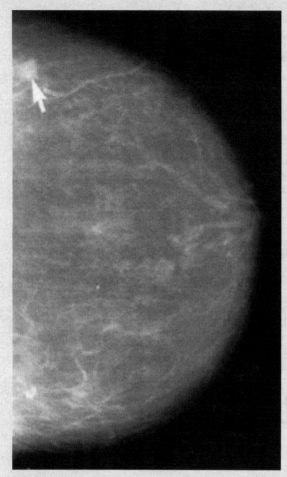 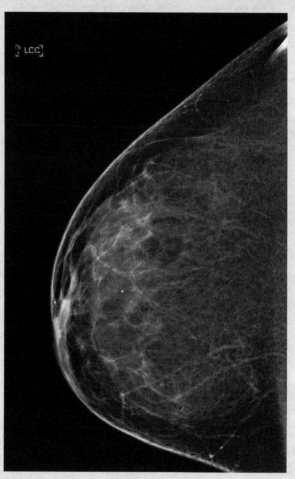

(A) Abnormal mammogram: The arrow on this mammogram points to a small cancerous lesion. A lesion is an area of abnormal tissue change.

(B) Normal mammogram: Breast tomosynthesis (three-dimensional mammography)

Note. National Institutes of Health. (2003). *Mammogram showing breast cancer.* Retrieved from https://commons.wikimedia.org/wiki/File:Mammogram_showing_breast_cancer.jpg; and (B) From National Cancer Institute. (2016). *Mammogram – Normal.* Retrieved from https://visuals online.cancer.gov/details.cfm?imageid=9405

station. Digital breast tomosynthesis overcomes the primary limitation of overlapping tissue inherent to standard two-dimensional mammography. Multiple studies have reported increased sensitivity and specificity of digital tomosynthesis in comparison with standard two-dimensional mammography (Gilbert, Tucker, & Young, 2016).

BREAST CANCER WORKUP

When suspicious masses are found on BSE, CBE, or mammography, providers will proceed with evaluating the findings by performing a diagnostic workup. The diagnostic workup can include a CBE by a surgeon, diagnostic mammogram, ultrasound, and/or a biopsy (NCCN, 2016b).

TABLE 3-4: BI-RADS MAMMOGRAM CLASSIFICATION

Assessment	Management
Category 0 – need additional imaging evaluation	Recall for additional imaging Likelihood of cancer is unknown
Category 1 – negative	Routine screening
Category 2 – benign	Routine screening
Category 3 – probably benign	Short-interval (6-month) follow-up or continued surveillance
Category 4 – suspicious Category 4A – low suspicion for malignancy Category 4B – moderate suspicion for malignancy Category 4C – high suspicion for malignancy	Biopsy indicated
Category 5 – highly suggestive of malignancy	Biopsy indicated
Category 6 – known biopsy-proven malignancy	Surgical excision when clinically appropriate

Note. Adapted from D'Orsi, C. J., Sickles, E. A., Mendelson, E. B., Morris, E. A., et al. (2013). *ACR BI-RADS® Atlas, Breast Imaging Reporting and Data System.* Reston, VA: American College of Radiology.

FIGURE 3-11: BREAST MAGNETIC RESONANCE IMAGING DETECTION OF AN OBSCURE IMAGE IN A DENSE BREAST

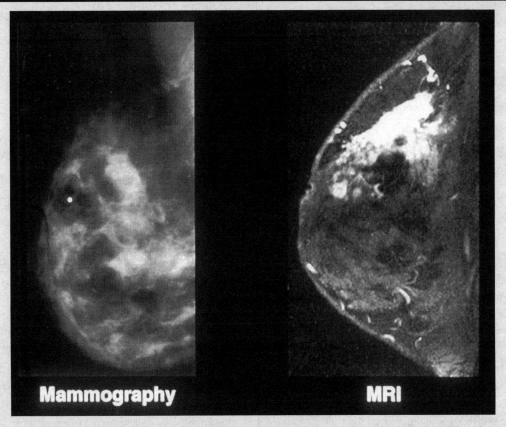

A mammography (left) and magnetic resonance imaging (MRI; right). Note the MRI's enhancement ability to confirm diagnosis, especially in a dense breast.

Note. From the National Cancer Institute. (1994b). *Mammogram vs. MRI.* Retrieved from https://visualsonline.cancer.gov/details.cfm?imageid=2705

As a component of the workup, diagnostic mammograms produce clearer, more detailed images of abnormal breast tissue areas, in comparison with the screening mammogram (ACS, 2015a; NCCN 2016b). Providers use these diagnostic mammograms to learn more about unusual breast changes, such as a lump, pain, thickening, nipple discharge, or alteration in breast size or shape. Diagnostic mammograms involve special imaging techniques and more views than screening mammograms.

Ultrasound imaging uses soundwaves to create the image (ACS, 2015). With ultrasound waves bouncing off tissue, the resulting image suggests whether a lump or abnormality is solid, filled with fluid, or a combination of solid and fluid (NCCN, 2016b). A cyst is a fluid-filled sac and is usually a benign finding. A solid mass requires further evaluation.

Breast MRI as a component of a diagnostic evaluation further characterizes suspicious tissue, lumps, or masses (NCCN, 2016b). During workup, additional diagnostic imaging may include digital mammography, MRI, and positron emission tomography. Further tests to determine possible spread of tumor cells include X-rays, bone scans, liver scans, and lung scans.

Proceeding with a biopsy, the provider will determine what type of biopsy is indicated. Biopsy options include fine needle, core biopsy (using a thick needle), or tissue biopsy (surgically removed). During a needle biopsy procedure, providers may use ultrasound or MRI as guidance.

In an excisional biopsy, the surgeon removes the entire lump or area. Excisional biopsies are seldom done because of the improved ability to perform a biopsy with mammography, ultrasound, and MRI (NCCN, 2016b).

During each type of biopsy, the radiologist or surgeon removes a sample of tissue. A pathologist checks the tissue for cancer cells. Once the patient knows whether the mammographic change or palpable mass is malignant, she can have further evaluation to determine the extent of disease before making a decision regarding what type of surgery she desires (NCCN, 2016b).

Sentinel Lymph Node Biopsy

Approximately 70% of women with early-stage breast cancer at the time of surgery will have no evidence of regional lymph node involvement (NCCN, 2016a, 2016b). Sentinel lymph node biopsy offers a means to sample the lymph nodes with a minimally invasive procedure that may also reduce the risk for lymphedema (see Figure 3-12). This is usually scheduled during the definitive breast surgery procedure, if surgery is part of the treatment plan. Sentinel lymph node biopsy may help determine which patients can avoid axillary node dissection and the removal of 10 to 30 lymph nodes. Most patients have only one to three sentinel lymph nodes under an arm (NCCN, 2016b).

Before performing a sentinel lymph node biopsy, the doctor injects a radioactive substance near the tumor. The injected contrast substance flows through the lymphatic system to the first lymph node or nodes where cancer cells are likely to have spread (the "sentinel" node or nodes). The doctor uses a scanner to locate the radioactive substance in the sentinel nodes. The surgeon can make a small incision and remove only the nodes with radioactive material – on average, only two sentinel lymph nodes (NCCN, 2016b). With limited need for extensive lymph node dissection, the woman has fewer postoperative complications and less lymphedema (ACS, 2015).

FIGURE 3-12: SENTINEL LYMPH NODE BIOPSY

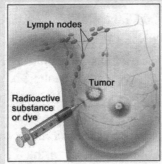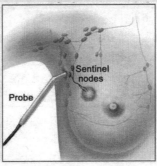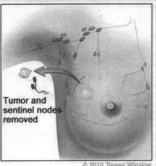

Sentinel lymph node biopsy of the breast. A radioactive substance and/or blue dye is injected near the tumor (left). The injected material is detected visually and/or with a probe that detects radioactivity (middle). The sentinel nodes (the first lymph nodes to take up the material) are removed and checked for cancer cells (right).

Note. From National Cancer Institute. (2015a). *Biopsy, sentinel lymph node, breast (3-panel).* Retrieved from https://visualsonline.cancer.gov/details.cfm?imageid=9094; © 2010 Terese Winslow, U.S. Govt has certain rights.

PATHOLOGY REPORT

Breast cancer is a heterogeneous disease with many different subtypes. Providers consider a number of factors, which a pathology report confirms. For example, the pathology report and further evaluation of the biopsy specimen may suggest that targeted therapies could provide optimal treatment for a specific biological subtype of the tumor. The pathology findings can indicate agents that would prompt the tumor cells to respond (see Table 3-5). Together with other data captured from the patient's workup, individualized treatment decisions follow (NCCN, 2016b).

The majority of primary breast cancers are adenocarcinomas, which can be divided into subtypes: ductal and lobular carcinomas. Based on microscopic findings, breast carcinomas are further classified as either in situ (noninvasive) or invasive (ACS, 2015).

In situ breast carcinomas have malignant epithelial cells within the ducts or lobules with no extension beyond the cell's basement membrane (see Figure 3-13). In situ carcinomas do not exhibit lymphovascular invasion and have not metastasized. They are noninvasive cancers, considered ductal carcinoma in situ (DCIS) or LCIS. Although DCIS is a noninvasive condition, it can progress to invasive cancer. However, the chance of that occurring is variable (NCCN, 2016b). DCIS incidence has increased markedly in the United States with broader use of screening mammography. In 1998 in the United States, DCIS was 18% of all newly diagnosed invasive and noninvasive breast tumors; in 2012, incidence of DCIS increased to more than 29% of newly diagnosed breast cancers (ACS, 2017a). Few cases of DCIS present as a palpable mass; 80% of cases are diagnosed by mammography alone.

The term *LCIS* is misleading; it is really lobular neoplasia. LCIS is a marker that identifies women at an increased risk for development of invasive breast cancer. This risk remains high even two decades after the initial diagnosis. In these cases, the cancer is ductal rather than lobular (NCCN, 2016b).

Invasive or infiltrating carcinomas extend beyond the basement membrane (see Figure 3-14). Extension may continue through the

continued on page 65

TABLE 3-5: COMPONENTS OF A PATHOLOGY REPORT (1 OF 2)

Component	Implications
Ductal or lobular	Breast cancer is divided into two main types: ductal and lobular. Cancer that originates in the ducts is the most common type. E-cadherin is a test that the pathologist may use to help determine whether the tumor is ductal or lobular. If the report does not mention E-cadherin, it means that this test was not needed to determine the type of cancer.
In situ or invasive	If the malignant cells are still confined to the breast ducts or lobules, without breaking out and growing into surrounding tissue, it is considered in situ carcinoma. Once the carcinoma cells have grown and broken out of the ducts or lobules, it is considered invasive.
Differentiation	Well-differentiated carcinomas have relatively normal-looking cells that do not appear to be growing rapidly and are arranged in small tubules for ductal cancer and cords in lobular cancer. These cancers tend to grow and spread slowly, and thus have a better prognosis. Poorly differentiated carcinomas lack normal features, tend to grow and spread faster, and have a worse prognosis. Moderately differentiated carcinomas have features and prognosis in between well-differentiated and poorly differentiated carcinomas.
Histological grade	This is sometimes called the *Nottingham* or *Elston grade*. Numbers are assigned to different features seen and then added up to assign the grade. • If the numbers add up to 3 to 5, then the cancer is grade 1 (well differentiated). • If they add up to 6 or 7, then the cancer is grade 2 (moderately differentiated). • If they add up to 8 or 9, then the cancer is grade 3 (poorly differentiated).
Ki-67	Measure of how fast the malignant cells are growing and dividing. Values greater than 30% suggest a poorer prognosis.
Tumor size	Smaller size usually means better prognosis.
Stage	The stage of a cancer is a measurement of the extent of the tumor and its spread; it is measured with TNM system, where T stands for tumor size, N for whether the malignancy has spread to the lymph nodes, and M for whether there is distant metastasis. Once the T, N, and M categories have been determined, this information is combined in a process called stage grouping. Stage is expressed in Roman numerals from stage I (the least advanced stage) to stage IV (the most advanced stage). Noninvasive (in situ) cancer is listed as stage 0.
Estrogen/ progesterone receptors	Receptors are proteins on the outside surfaces of breast cells. Normal breast cells and some breast cancer cells have receptors that attach to estrogen and progesterone. These two hormones often stimulate the growth of breast cancer cells. Results for estrogen receptors and progesterone receptors are reported separately and can be reported in different ways as follows: • Negative, weakly positive, positive • Percent positive • Percent positive and whether the staining is weak, moderate, or strong Hormone-receptor-positive cancers tend to have a better prognosis and are much more likely to respond to hormone therapy than cancers without these receptors.

TABLE 3-5: COMPONENTS OF A PATHOLOGY REPORT (2 OF 2)

Component	Implications
HER2/Neu	Approximately 20% of breast cancers have too much of a growth-promoting protein on the *HER2/Neu* gene, which is referred to as *HER2/Neu*-positive or amplified. These cancers tend to grow and spread more aggressively than other breast cancers and are much more likely to benefit from treatment with drugs that target the *HER2/Neu* protein, including trastuzumab (Herceptin) and lapatinib (Tykerb).
Oncotype DX assay (Genomic Health, Redwood, CA)	This is a 21-gene assay performed on the breast cancer tumor that estimates the chance of an in situ or stage I or II node-negative breast cancer recurring and provides an estimate of the potential benefit of additional treatment such as chemotherapy.

Note. Adapted from American Cancer Society. (2015). *Breast cancer facts and figures 2015-2016.* Atlanta, GA: Author; National Comprehensive Cancer Network. (2016b). *Breast cancer: Version 2.2016.* Retrieved from http://www.nccn.org

FIGURE 3-13: DUCTAL CARCINOMA IN SITU

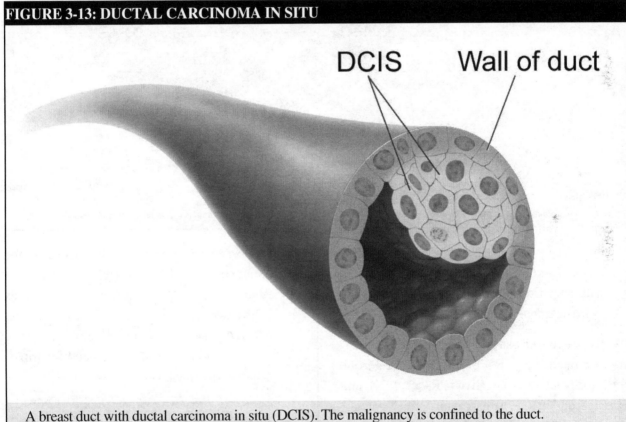

A breast duct with ductal carcinoma in situ (DCIS). The malignancy is confined to the duct.

Note. From National Cancer Institute. (2005a). *Breast cancer ductal carcinoma in situ.* Retrieved from https://visualsonline.cancer.gov/details.cfm?imageid=4353

breast parenchyma and into lymphovascular spaces and may metastasize to regional lymph nodes or distant sites.

After the initial pathology indicates breast cancer, special laboratory tests on the tissue follow. These tests further evaluate the tumor providing specific information that influences the treatment plan. Tests are as follows:

- *Hormone receptor test:* Indicates certain hormone receptors, which may be responsive to HT (estrogen or progesterone; NCCN, 2016b).

- *HER2 testing:* Indicates whether the tissue has the protein human epidermal growth factor receptor (EGFR-2 or HER2) or the *HER2/Neu* gene (NCCN, 2016b). Too much protein or too many copies of the gene in

FIGURE 3-14: INVASIVE BREAST CANCER

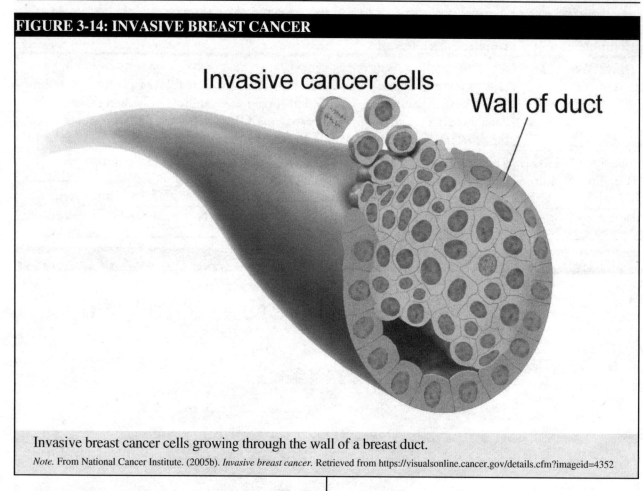

Invasive breast cancer cells growing through the wall of a breast duct.

Note. From National Cancer Institute. (2005b). *Invasive breast cancer.* Retrieved from https://visualsonline.cancer.gov/details.cfm?imageid=4352

the tissue may increase recurrence posttreatment. Tumors with this marker are treated with specific EGFR-responsive agents, such as trastuzumab (Herceptin; NCCN, 2016b).

Breast cancer can be estrogen receptor positive or negative (ER+ or ER-), progesterone receptor positive or negative (PR+ or PR-), and HER2+ or HER2-. Breast cancers are categorized as follows (ACS, 2015; NCCN, 2016b):

• *Luminal A (ER+PR+HER2−):* Approximately 74% of breast cancers are luminal A, which tend to be slow-growing and less aggressive than other subtypes. Luminal A tumors are associated with the most favorable prognosis in part because of the excellent response to hormonal therapy.

• *Triple negative (ER−PR−HER2−):* Triple negative, the breast cancer type with the poorest short-term prognosis, accounts for approximately 12% of all breast cancers. Black women are about twice as likely as White women to have it. Possessing the *BRCA1* gene mutation and being premenopausal also increase the likelihood for triple-negative breast cancer.

• *Luminal B (ER+PR+HER2+):* Overall, about 10% of breast cancers are Luminal B. They are highly positive for Ki67, which is an indicator of a large proportion of actively dividing cells. Luminal B breast cancers tend to be higher grade and more aggressive than Luminal A breast cancers.

• *HER2 enriched (ER−PR−HER2+):* About 4% of breast cancers produce excess HER2 and do not express hormone receptors. Although these cancers tend to grow and spread more aggressively than other breast cancers, the use of targeted therapies for HER2+ cancers has reversed much of the poor prognostic impact of HER2-enriched breast cancers.

TREATMENT

Staging emerges from the diagnostic workup and is based on the existence and size of a malignant tumor (T), whether malignant cells have spread to lymph nodes (L), and whether malignant cells have spread from the primary tumor (M = metastasis). Numbers are added to staging schemas to provide more specific information about the tumor and its behavior. For example, a stage IIB tumor can be a tumor 2 to 5 cm (T2) or greater than 5 cm (T3) with involvement in the axillary lymph node (N1) or no involvement (N0) and no metastasis (M0). Table 3-6 highlights staging criteria for breast cancer. When the tumor is localized, treatments are surgery and radiation therapy. Systemic treatments for tumors that have spread beyond the breast and axilla are HT, chemotherapy, and biological therapy.

Surgery

Multiple types of surgical approaches are used to treat breast cancer, from total mastectomy to breast-sparing surgeries including lumpectomy and segmental (partial) mastectomy (see Figure 3-15). During surgery, surgeons remove the axillary lymph nodes to determine cancer spread.

In breast-sparing surgery (lumpectomy), the surgeon removes the tumor in the breast and some tissue around it. The surgeon may also remove axillary lymph nodes and some of the lining over the chest muscles below the tumor. Lumpectomy is almost always followed by radiotherapy. The choice between breast-sparing surgery (followed by radiation therapy) and mastectomy depends on many factors (NCCN, 2016b), such as

TABLE 3-6: BREAST CANCER STAGE GROUPING

	T (Tumor)	N (Nodes)	M (Metastasis)
Stage 0	Tis	N0	M0
Stage IA	T1	N0	M0
Stage IB	T0	N1	M0
	T1	N1	M0
Stage IIA	T0	N1	M0
	T1	N1	M0
	T2	N0	M0
Stage IIB	T2	N1	M0
	T3	N0	M0
Stage IIIA	T0	N2	M0
	T1	N2	M0
	T2	N2	M0
	T3	N1	M0
	T3	N2	M0
Stage IIIB	T4	N0, N1, N2	M0
Stage IIIC	Any T	N3	M0
Stage IV	Any T	Any N	M1

Breast Cancer Survival by Stage	
Stage	**5-year relative survival rate**
0	98%
I	94%
IIA	86%
IIB	81%
IIIA	67%
IIIB	41%
IIIC	26%
IV	17%

Note. Adapted from: American Cancer Society. (2015). *Breast cancer facts and figures 2015-2016.* Atlanta, GA: Author; National Comprehensive Cancer Network. (2016b). B*reast cancer: Version 2.2016.* Retrieved from http://www.nccn.org

Amin, M. B., Edge, S., Greene, F., Byrd, D. R., Brookland, R. K., Washington, M. K., ... Meyer, L. R. (Eds.). (2017). *AJCC cancer staging manual* (8th ed.). New York, NY: Springer.

FIGURE 3-15: BREAST-CONSERVING SURGERY

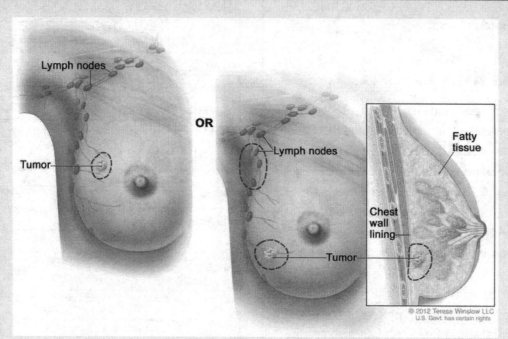

The left panel shows removal of the tumor and some of the normal tissue around it. The right panel shows removal of some of the lymph nodes under the arm and removal of the tumor and part of the chest wall lining near the tumor. Also shown is fatty tissue.

Note. From National Cancer Institute. (2015c). *Surgery, breast-conserving, female.* Retrieved from https://visualsonline.cancer.gov/details. cfm?imageid=7128; © 2012 Terese Winslow, U.S. Govt has certain rights.

- the size, location, and stage of the tumor;

- the size of the woman's breast;

- younger age at diagnosis and risk for a second primary cancer (especially if there is a genetic predisposition);

- certain features of the cancer including those with more aggressive breast cancers or diffuse, multiple clusters of calcifications;

- how the woman feels about saving her breast;

- the woman's perceptions and preferences related to radiation therapy; and

- the woman's ability to travel to a radiation treatment center.

During a total (simple) mastectomy, the surgeon removes the whole breast (see Figure 3-16). The surgeon also removes targeted axilla lymph nodes; this procedure is a sentinel lymph node biopsy (previously discussed).

In a modified radical mastectomy, the surgeon removes the whole breast and can remove many or all of the axillary lymph nodes and the lining over the chest muscles. The surgeon may remove a small amount of chest muscle so that lymph node removal is easier.

Radiation Therapy

Depending on the treatment plan, radiation therapy is a solo treatment or in combination with surgery (before or after breast-sparing surgery or mastectomy), and/or in combination with chemotherapy or HT. Radiation therapy destroys tumor cells with high-energy rays (NCCN, 2016b). Treatment depends on the size of the tumor and other factors, such as the woman's willingness to undergo daily radiation for 5 to 6 weeks and availability of radiation facilities a reasonable distance from her home (NCCN, 2016b).

FIGURE 3-16: TOTAL MASTECTOMY

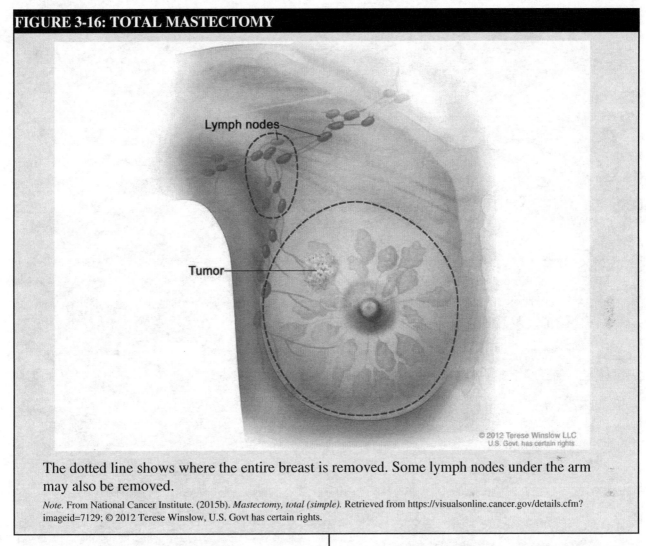

The dotted line shows where the entire breast is removed. Some lymph nodes under the arm may also be removed.

Note. From National Cancer Institute. (2015b). *Mastectomy, total (simple).* Retrieved from https://visualsonline.cancer.gov/details.cfm? imageid=7129; © 2012 Terese Winslow, U.S. Govt has certain rights.

External radiation targets cancer cells with external beams, which penetrate tissue. Treatments take place in a hospital or clinic and are usually 5 days a week for several weeks (see Figure 3-17).

Brachytherapy is radiation therapy targeted within the tissue via short-term implants. As breast cancer treatment, intracavitary brachy-therapy (MammoSite) is a small, deflated balloon attached to a thin tube, which is inserted into the space from the lumpectomy and is filled with a saline solution. The balloon and tube are left in place throughout treatment (with the end of the tube sticking out of the breast). Twice a day a source of radioactivity is placed into the middle of the balloon through the tube and then

removed. The outpatient procedure is for 5 days; then providers deflate and remove the balloon.

In interstitial brachytherapy, providers insert several small catheters into the breast around the area of the lumpectomy, enabling insertion of radioactive pellets for short periods each day for several days, then removing the catheters (see Figure 3-18).

Women experience some side effects, depending on the dose and type of radiation (external or brachytherapy). Frequently as a reaction to radiation therapy, the skin in the treated area becomes red, dry, tender, and itchy. Many women report that the breast feels heavy and tight. Some women experience moist des-quamation toward the end of therapy (ACS,

FIGURE 3-17: EXTERNAL RADIATION TO THE BREAST

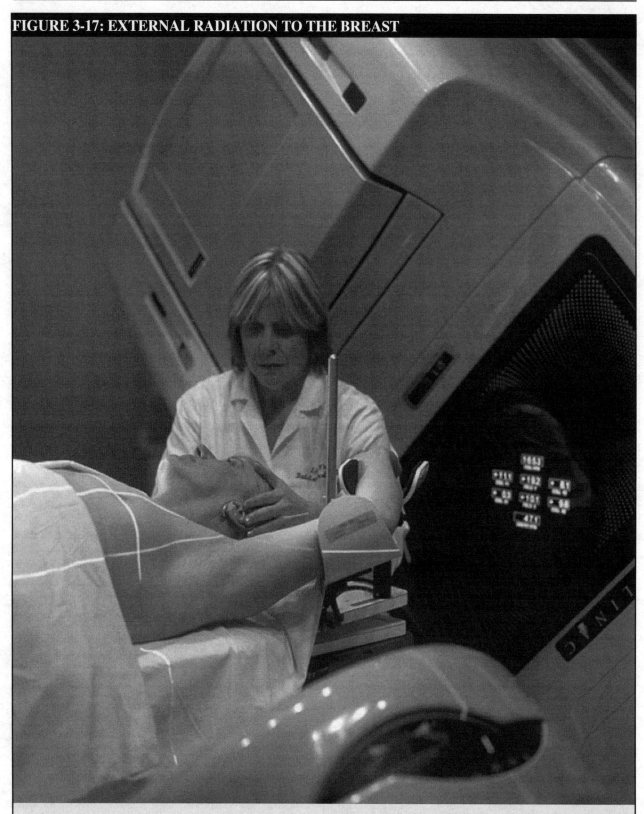

A radiation therapist is preparing a woman for radiation therapy by ensuring she is in the correct position to receive the proper dose of radiation to the tumor bed.

Note. From National Cancer Institute. (2007). *Woman prepared for radiation therapy.* Retrieved from https://Visualsonline.Cancer.Gov/Details. Cfm?Imageid=4469

FIGURE 3-18: BREAST BRACHYTHERAPY

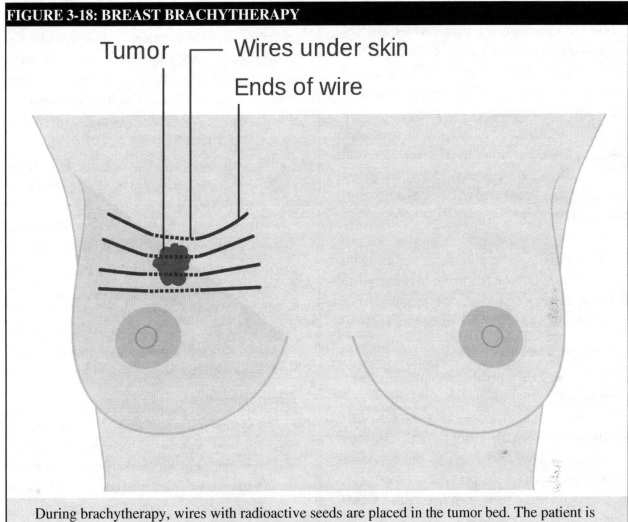

During brachytherapy, wires with radioactive seeds are placed in the tumor bed. The patient is on radiation precautions and limited contact when the seeds are intact.

Note. From Cancer Research UK/Wikimedia Commons. (2014). *Diagram showing how you have internal radiotherapy for breast cancer.* Retrieved from https://commons.wikimedia.org/wiki/File:Diagram_showing_how_you_have_internal_radiotherapy_for_breast_cancer_CRUK_159.svg

2015). Exposing this area to air as much as possible can help the skin heal (Feight, Baney, Bruce, & McQuestion, 2011). Skin in the treated area can become very sensitive.

Undergarments and clothing that come into contact with treated skin can cause soreness and discomfort. Nurses can be instrumental in assisting patients with skin care and advising women to wear loose-fitting cotton clothing during the treatment time and until healing takes place.

Providers may recommend topical preparations, such as urea of Aquaphor, to be applied to sensitive skin to lessen discomfort and pro-mote healing. Care must be taken to use only approved preparations during the treatment process. Products should not contain alcohol, perfumes, or other chemicals.

Skin reaction to radiation therapy resolves gradually with the end of treatment. However, skin color changes may continue (Feight et al., 2011). Fatigue is a major side effect of radiation therapy. Providers encourage patients to maintain adequate rest during and after treatment (Mitchell et al., 2014).

For the treatment of some invasive breast cancers, studies from 2007 to 2016 have shown that radiation therapy with lumpectomy is considered as effective a treatment as mastectomy and is associated with fewer complications (NCCN, 2016b). Radiation therapy with lumpectomy has been shown to improve survival when provided as an adjunct to breast-conserving surgery. For patients with more than four positive lymph nodes, studies have shown that with radiation therapy after surgery, local and regional recurrence can be reduced as much as 43% compared with surgery alone (NCCN, 2016b).

Radiation may be recommended as a strategy to manage pain from bone metastases with advanced disease (NCCN, 2016b). Providers may prescribe external beam radiation therapy and/or bisphosphonates to manage bone metastases.

Hormone Therapy

HT is an initial treatment option for any woman with newly diagnosed metastatic disease if the patient's tumor is ER+, PR+, or ER/PR-unknown (NCCN, 2016b). Table 3-7 lists breast cancer hormonal therapy options. As of 2017, most therapies are oral preparations, with the exception being fulvestrant (Faslodex), which is administered by an injection.

The side effects of HT depend on the specific agent or type of treatment. In general, the side effects of hormonal therapy are similar to those caused by menopause. The most common side effects of hormonal therapy are hot flashes, vaginal dryness, and vaginal discharge. Other side effects are headaches, fatigue, nausea, vomiting, vaginal itching, irritation of the skin around the vagina, and skin rash (NCCN, 2016b). Tamoxifen is the only agent approved for premenopausal women. For women who are known to be postmenopausal either because of bilateral oophorectomy, age 60 years or older, or documented menopause by hormone levels, other agents can be considered (NCCN, 2016b).

Targeted Therapy

More targeted therapies – monoclonal antibodies – have been approved as breast cancer treatments (see Table 3-8). For example, Herceptin targets tumors that have too much of the specific protein HER2; patients are classified as HER2-positive (NCCN, 2016b).

By blocking HER2, Herceptin slows or stops cancer cell proliferation (ACS, 2015). Providers can prescribe Herceptin alone or with chemotherapy. The first time a woman receives Herceptin, the most common side effects are fever and chills. Some women also have pain, weakness, nausea, vomiting, diarrhea, headaches, difficulty breathing, or rashes. Side effects usually become milder after the first treatment (NCCN, 2016b). Herceptin also may cause cardiac toxicity, which may lead to heart failure.

Chemotherapy

As systemic therapy for metastatic disease, chemotherapy protocols – neoadjuvant (before surgery) and adjuvant (after surgery) – boost the effectiveness of surgery and radiation. Table 3-9 lists common chemotherapy agents used in the treatment of breast cancer. As initial therapy, standard chemotherapy protocols include a combination of an anthracycline, an alkylating agent, and a taxane (NCCN, 2016b).

Treatment Strategies, Recommendations, and Decisions

Stage I, II, IIIA, and Operable IIIC

For stage I and II breast cancer, standard treatment protocols include breast-sparing surgery followed by radiation therapy or a mastectomy. For stage II or IIIA breast cancer, surgery may include axilla lymph node removal if the sentinel node is positive for malignancy (NCCN, 2016b). If cancer cells are found in one to three axilla lymph nodes or if the tumor in the breast is larger than 5 cm, providers rec-

TABLE 3-7: HORMONAL TREATMENT APPROACHES IN THE MANAGEMENT OF BREAST CANCER

Class	Action	Side Effects	Example(s)
Selective estrogen receptor modulators	Bind to estrogen receptors in breast cancer cells and block cancer cells	Side effects include • fatigue, • hot flashes, • vaginal dryness or discharge, and • mood swings. Serious but rare complications include embolism. Tamoxifen has been associated with an increased risk for development of endometrial cancer. Liver irregularities and chemical hepatitis are possible side effects. Tamoxifen is the only agent approved for premenopausal women.	tamoxifen (Nolvadex), toremifene (Fareston)
Estrogen blocker	Blocks the estrogen receptor and then also eliminates it temporarily Approved for use in postmenopausal women	Side effects include • hot flashes, • night sweats, • mild nausea, and • fatigue. Can lead to osteoporosis.	fulvestrant (Faslodex)
Aromatase inhibitors	Prevent production of estrogen in adrenal glands For use only in postmenopausal women (either natural, chemical, or surgical)	Side effects include • muscle pain and • joint stiffness. Can lead to osteoporosis.	exemestane (Aromasin), letrozole (Femara), anastrozole (Arimidex), megestrol (Megace)
Ovarian ablation (can include oophorectomy)	Leads to menopause	Side effects include • hot flashes, • night sweats, and • mood swings. Can lead to osteoporosis.	goserelin acetate (Zoladex), fulvestrant (Faslodex)

Note. Adapted from:

American Cancer Society. (2015). *Breast cancer facts and figures 2015-2016.* Atlanta, GA: Author.

National Comprehensive Cancer Network. (2016b). *Breast cancer: Version 2.2016.* Retrieved from http://www.nccn.org

TABLE 3-8: TARGETED THERAPY FOR BREAST CANCER (1 OF 2)			
Class	**Mechanism of Action**	**Side Effects**	**Examples**
Targeted therapy for *HER2*-positive breast cancer	It targets the *HER2/Neu* protein.	Left ejection fraction abnormalities can occur. Pertuzumab and lapatinib can cause severe diarrhea.	• **trastuzumab (Herceptin):** Trastuzumab is a monoclonal antibody that can be used to treat both early- and late-stage breast cancer with chemotherapy. When used to treat early breast cancer, this drug is usually given for a year. For advanced breast cancer, treatment is often given for as long as the drug is helpful. It is an intravenous (IV) infusion. • **pertuzumab (Perjeta):** This is also a monoclonal antibody that can be given with trastuzumab and chemotherapy to treat advanced breast cancer. It is also a neoadjuvant treatment. It is given by IV infusion. • **ado-trastuzumab emtansine (Kadcyla, also known as T-DM1):** This is a monoclonal antibody attached to a chemotherapy drug to treat advanced breast cancer in women who have already been treated with trastuzumab and chemotherapy. It is given intravenously. • **lapatinib (Tykerb):** Lapatinib is a kinase inhibitor that is taken daily as a pill. It is used to treat advanced breast cancer, most often when trastuzumab is no longer working.

ommend postmastectomy radiation therapy (NCCN, 2016b).

For stage II or IIIA breast cancers (large or difficult-to-remove tumors greater than 5 cm) when the tumors are triple negative (estrogen receptor negative, progesterone receptor negative, and HER2/Neu negative), neoadjuvant chemotherapy shrinks the tumor before surgery (NCCN, 2016b).

For women with stage II and III breast tumors, postsurgical adjuvant therapy follows. This can include radiation therapy, systemic treatment (chemotherapy or HT), or a combination (NCCN, 2016b).

TABLE 3-8: TARGETED THERAPY FOR BREAST CANCER (2 OF 2)			
Class	**Mechanism of Action**	**Side Effects**	**Examples**
Targeted therapy for hormone receptor-positive breast cancer	It can be used with hormone therapy in breast cancers that are estrogen receptor positive/progesterone receptor positive (ER+/PR+). Palbociclib blocks proteins in the cell called cyclin-dependent kinase (CDK) 4 and CDK6. Blocking these proteins in breast cancer cells that are hormone receptor positive helps stop the cells from dividing to make new cells. Everolimus is a targeted therapy drug that blocks mammalian target of rapamycin (mTOR), a protein in cells that normally promotes their growth and division. By blocking this protein, it can help stop cancer cells from growing and prevent tumors from developing new blood vessels, which can help limit their growth.	Palbociclib can cause anemia, fatigue, nausea, mouth sores, hair loss, and diarrhea. Everolimus can cause mouth sores, diarrhea, nausea, fatigue, anemia, shortness of breath, cough, and increased blood lipids.	• **palbociclib (IBRANCE):** Palbociclib is approved for postmenopausal women with advanced hormone receptor-positive, *HER2*-negative breast cancer. It is an oral agent that is taken once a day for 3 weeks at a time, with a week off before starting again. • **everolimus (Afinitor):** This is approved for postmenopausal women with advanced hormone receptor-positive, *HER2*-negative breast cancer. It is a daily pill.

Note. Adapted from:

American Cancer Society. (2015). *Breast cancer facts and figures 2015-2016*. Atlanta, GA: Author.

National Comprehensive Cancer Network. (2016b). *Breast cancer: Version 2.2016*. Retrieved from http://www.nccn.org

Stages IIIB and Inoperable IIIC

Providers prescribe systemic treatment (chemotherapy or targeted therapy) for stage IIIB (including inflammatory breast cancer) or inoperable stage IIIC breast cancer (NCCN, 2016b). Depending on the response to systemic treatment, providers may suggest further multimodality treatment, including surgery, radiation treatment, or both.

Stage IV

Stage IV breast cancer treatments include HT, chemotherapy, targeted therapies, or a combination of systemic therapies. The intent of stage IV systemic treatment is control of disease. For stage IV disease, a woman may choose a palliative plan of care, which focuses on pain management, symptom relief, comfort care, and strategies that support and optimize quality of life (NCCN, 2016b).

TABLE 3-9: CHEMOTHERAPY AGENTS USED IN THE TREATMENT OF BREAST CANCER

Class	Action	Side Effects	Examples
Anthracyclines	Alter DNA structure of cancer cells	• Decreased white blood cell count with increased risk for infection • Decreased platelet count with increased risk for bleeding • Loss of appetite • Darkening of nail beds and skin creases of hands • Hair loss • Nausea and vomiting • Mouth sores • Cardiotoxicity	doxorubicin (Adriamycin), epirubicin (Ellence)
Taxanes	Prevent cancer cells from dividing	• Decrease in white blood cells with increased risk for infection • Fever (often a warning sign of infection) • Fluid retention • Allergic reaction • Hair loss • Neuropathies • Liver function test abnormalities, chemical hepatitis • Nausea	paclitaxel (Taxol), docetaxel (Taxotere)
Alkylating agents	Target DNA of cancer cells	• Decreased white blood cell count with increased rate of infection • Hair loss • Nausea and vomiting • Loss of appetite • Sores in mouth or on lips • Diarrhea • Ceasing of menstrual periods	cyclophosphamide (Cytoxan)
Platinum agents	The platinum complexes bind to DNA, causing the DNA strands to cross-link, which ultimately triggers cells to die in a programmed way.	• Nephrotoxicity • Neurotoxicity • Ototoxicity • Nausea/Vomiting • Anemia • Allergic reactions	carboplatin (Paraplatin), cisplatin

Note. Adapted from:

American Cancer Society. (2015). *Breast cancer facts and figures 2015-2016.* Atlanta, GA: Author.

National Comprehensive Cancer Network. (2016b). *Breast cancer: Version 2.2016.* Retrieved from http://www.nccn.org

Recurrent Breast Cancer

Cancer can recur locally or distant from the primary breast site. Recurrence is different from a second primary breast cancer diagnosis – that is, a tumor diagnosed in the opposite breast or another part of the treated breast (ACS, 2015). Treatment for the recurrent disease depends on the location and extent of the recurred tumor and previous treatment. When a tumor recurs in the same breast after breast-sparing surgery, a treatment option is mastectomy.

If breast cancer recurs distant to the breast, treatments with the intent of control rather than cure are chemotherapy, HT, and/or targeted therapy. Chemotherapy protocols include various agents to offset tumor resistance to one chemotherapy agent (NCCN, 2016b). When tumor recurs in radiation-sensitive areas such as chest muscle, treatment can include radiation therapy.

POSTSURGERY REHABILITATION

A woman recovering from treatment for breast cancer faces some unique challenges. Among these are the need for postmastectomy or lumpectomy exercises to manage lymphedema. She may also have further surgery to reconstruct her breast. Surgery is usually scheduled a few weeks to months after the initial cancer surgery. Depending on the type of breast surgery and whether reconstruction will take place, a rehabilitation program after surgery is an important part of the healing and recovery process.

Exercises

For mastectomy or lumpectomy patients, exercising the arm and shoulder after surgery can help a woman regain motion, balance, and strength. Properly targeted and paced exercises reduce neck and back pain and stiffness (Fu, Deng, & Armer, 2014).

In general, surgeons recommend that a woman starts exercise after breast cancer surgery within 1 to 2 days. Often a physical therapist can suggest exercises. In time, exercising is gradually more active (depending on the surgery and timing of reconstruction) and becomes integrated in the woman's normal routine.

Lymphedema

Lymphedema causes swelling of the affected arm and hand because of lymph node removal during surgery. It can be a chronic condition, occurring almost immediately after surgery or years later. Lymphedema education for the patient and family includes strategies to monitor for early signs of lymphedema, prevention of lymphedema, and the importance of early intervention if lymphedema occurs (Fu et al., 2014).

To reduce and manage lymphedema, specially trained physical therapists perform massage and wrap the extremity with an elastic sleeve or cuff. Exercises protect the involved limb from injury or infection. Self-care and protection are part of lymphedema education (Fu et al., 2014). Education for women at risk for lymphedema includes instructions to

- avoid wearing tight clothing or jewelry on the affected arm;

- carry a purse or luggage with the other arm;

- use an electric razor to avoid cuts when shaving under the arm;

- have injections, blood tests, and blood pressure measurements on the other arm;

- wear gloves to protect the hands when gardening and when using strong detergents;

- have careful manicures and avoid cutting the cuticles; and

- avoid burns or sunburns to the affected arm and hand.

Breast Reconstruction

Women with total mastectomies may choose to have reconstructive surgery either at the time of the original mastectomy or later after healing. Although some women are not interested in breast reconstruction, many breast specialists support reconstructive surgery as an additional option of treatment. Women are encouraged to weigh both the advantages and disadvantages of breast reconstruction with their plastic surgeons and cancer treatment team. Then they can make an informed decision based on their own situation (ACS, 2015). The goal of breast reconstruction is to create breast symmetry when a woman is wearing a bra.

After cancer surgery, breast implants are inserted to expand the tissue as the first part of a two-part procedure (see Figure 3-19; NCCN, 2016b). The first surgery – installing the tissue expanders beneath the skin and chest muscle – requires a one-night stay in the hospital after the procedure. The tissue expander is similar to a balloon, and the surgeon will fill the expander with saline solution (usually once a week).

After the skin and muscle have sufficiently stretched, the surgeon will replace the tissue expander with a permanent implant. This is the second surgery, which usually occurs 3 to 4 months after the first implant surgery. Occasionally, a woman will not need a tissue expander. When this occurs, the surgeon proceeds directly to implant surgery. After 10 or 15 years, approximately 50% of implants need some type of modification or replacement (NCCN, 2016b).

Muscle flap procedures are longer than implant operations, lasting about 4 to 5 hours. Patients typically stay in the hospital for 3 to 4 days. Although recovery is slower, some women perceive that the breast looks and feels more natural (see Figures 3-20 and 3-21). Because muscle flap reconstruction involves the blood vessels, women who smoke or have diabetes, vascular disease, or connective tissue disease are not candidates for this type of breast reconstruction (NCCN, 2016b).

Because many breast cancers involve the nipple, the surgeon usually removes the nipple during mastectomy (ACS, 2015). After breast volume has been rebuilt with a tissue expander or muscle flap procedure, the surgeon re-creates the nipple. Surgeons schedule nipple re-creation approximately 2 to 6 months after the initial breast reconstruction to allow the new breast tissue ample time to heal. A skin graft from a woman's inner thigh or from the unaffected breast's areola (the pigmented region surrounding the nipple) becomes the new nipple. Occasionally after a skin graft, the skin of the newly created nipple turns white. Some surgeons prefer to tattoo the skin graft of the new nipple to ensure that the color matches the color of the nipple on the unaffected breast.

Breast Prosthesis

For women who do not choose reconstruction, they have the option of wearing a breast prosthesis to ensure adequate weight replacement and optimal appearance while wearing clothes (ACS, 2015).

An external breast prosthesis is an artificial breast form worn after the breast has been surgically removed (see Figure 3-22). Several types of prostheses exist: silicone gel, foam, fiberfill, or other materials that feel similar to natural tissue. Most prostheses are weighted so that they feel the same as the remaining breast (if only one breast has been removed). Some prostheses adhere to the chest area; others fit into pockets of postmastectomy bras. Prostheses may have different features, such as a mock nipple or special shape. Partial prostheses – equalizers or enhancers – are options for women who have parts of their breasts removed, such as a lumpectomy. A woman will be fitted for

FIGURE 3-19: BREAST RECONSTRUCTION USING A TISSUE EXPANDER

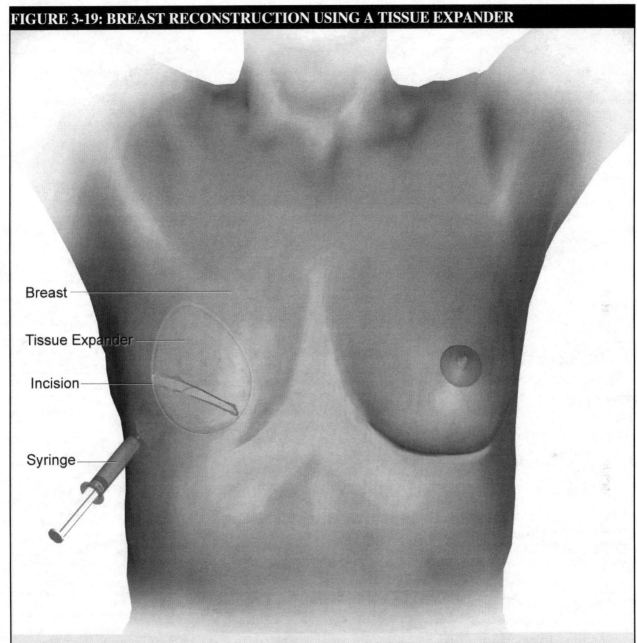

Breast

Tissue Expander

Incision

Syringe

An expander is placed behind the pectoralis muscle. A port is attached to the expander, and saline is injected over a period of weeks to stretch the muscle and make a pocket for the implant. When the space is created, the expander is removed during a second surgical procedure and the implant is placed. This is followed by creation of a nipple.

Note. From Blausen.com staff. Blausen gallery 2014. *Wikiversity Journal of Medicine.* doi:10.15347/wjm/2014.010. ISSN 20018762

a prosthesis so that it can be custom-made for her body; adjustments are made over time with assistance by a trained fitter. In addition to bras, swimsuits can be fitted with prostheses.

If a woman chooses to wear a breast prosthesis that does not adhere directly to her skin, she can wear a special postmastectomy bra or swimsuit with pockets for the breast form. Some women choose to wear special sleep or leisure bras overnight, with or without pockets for a prosthesis.

FIGURE 3-20: TRANSVERSE RECTUS ABDOMINIS MYOCUTANEOUS FLAP (TRAM)

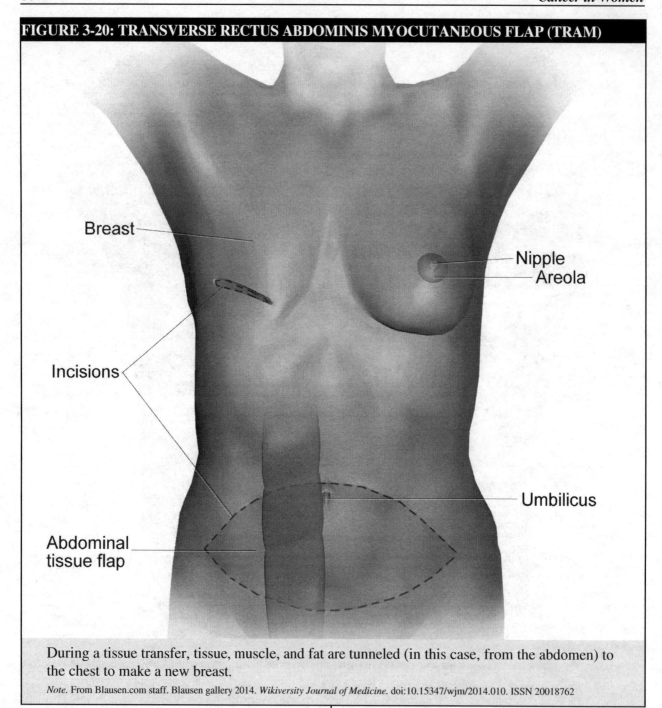

During a tissue transfer, tissue, muscle, and fat are tunneled (in this case, from the abdomen) to the chest to make a new breast.

Note. From Blausen.com staff. Blausen gallery 2014. *Wikiversity Journal of Medicine.* doi:10.15347/wjm/2014.010. ISSN 20018762

Sexuality

Breast cancer surgery and treatment affect the woman's sexuality. Researchers have studied postmastectomy patients, especially related to their sexuality. Body image can be a major concern for women. Learning to be comfortable with body image changes during and after breast cancer treatment is a personal journey that is different for every woman (ACS, 2015). Treatment affects women both physically and emotionally. For example, some women may experience a decline in sensation in the treated breast or have fluctuations in hormone levels due to such cancer treatments as chemotherapy. Others may feel less comfortable with their bodies. Breast cancer treatments, particularly surgery, may cause

FIGURE 3-21: BREAST RECONSTRUCTION TRANSVERSE RECTUS ABDOMINIS MYOCUTANEOUS FLAP (TRAM) – POSTOPERATIVE

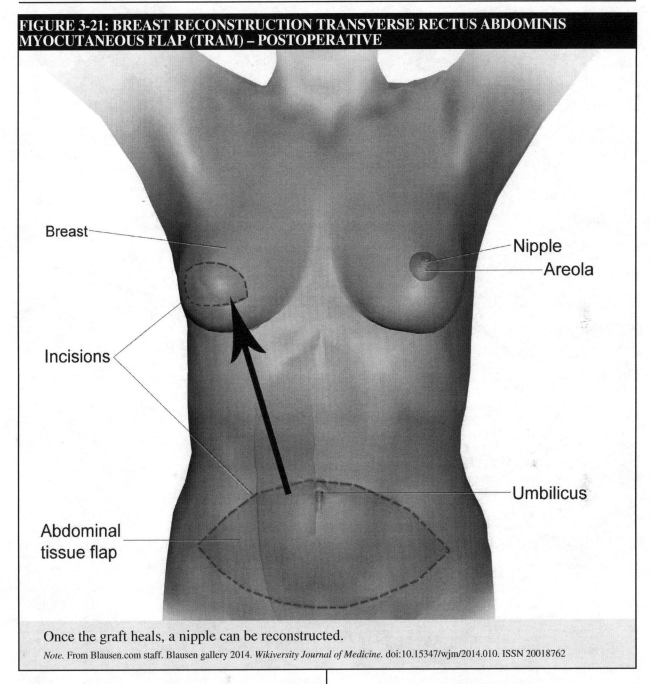

Breast

Nipple
Areola

Incisions

Umbilicus

Abdominal
tissue flap

Once the graft heals, a nipple can be reconstructed.

Note. From Blausen.com staff. Blausen gallery 2014. *Wikiversity Journal of Medicine.* doi:10.15347/wjm/2014.010. ISSN 20018762

a woman to be anxious about how to express physical and emotional love. These changes and feelings can influence sexual response and/or interest. Nurses should encourage women to speak about these concerns and direct them to resources as needed. Nurses, as key members of the healthcare team, can provide education and support as women evolve in accepting the new normal perceptions and feelings about their sexuality after any form of breast cancer treatment.

CASE STUDY 3-1

B.B. is a 61-year-old Hispanic woman who presented to her primary care physician with symptoms of the flu (fever and chills). The physician took a throat swab and sent it to cytology for evaluation. Before B.B. left, he asked her the date of her last mammogram. B.B. said she had not had a mammogram "for a while." The physician also ordered a mammogram.

FIGURE 3-22: BREAST RESTORATION WITH A PROSTHESIS

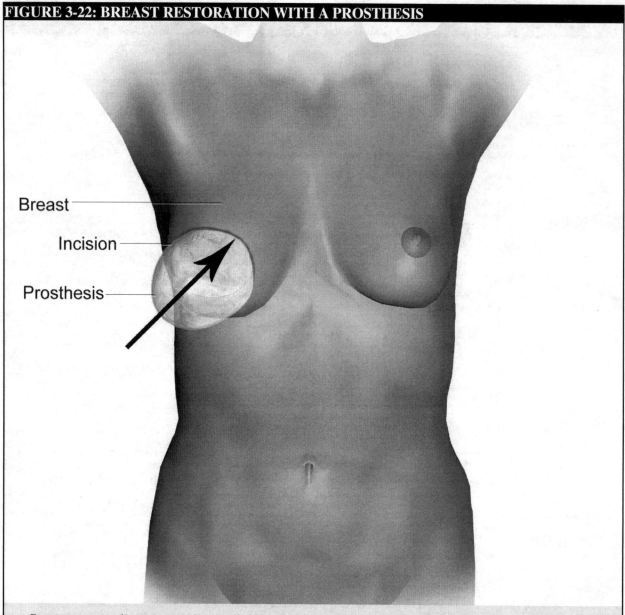

Breast
Incision
Prosthesis

Some women choose to replace weight and create symmetry using an external prosthesis which is placed over the mastectomy site. These can be worn in a pocketed bra, or some have rejuvenating silicone that adheres to the chest wall that should be supported with a bra.

Note. From Blausen.com staff. Blausen gallery 2014. *Wikiversity Journal of Medicine.* doi:10.15347/wjm/2014.010. ISSN 20018762

Mammogram results came back suspicious for an opaque, irregular mass on the outer right breast. B.B. was scheduled for an ultrasound-guided fine needle aspiration. Results indicated invasive ductal carcinoma that was ER+PR+HER2− (luminal A). Further workup included a bone scan, chest X-ray, and MRI, all of which were negative for metastatic disease.

After weighing her options with her primary physician, a breast surgeon, and radiation oncologist, B.B. opted to have a lumpectomy, followed by adjunctive radiation therapy. The lumpectomy procedure was unremarkable. (The excised nodule was 4 cm by 2 cm.) Based on sentinel node mapping, B.B. was found to have no positive nodes. B.B.'s breast cancer was staged at stage IIB (T2 N1 M0). She went home 4 hours after the procedure.

Postoperatively, B.B. experienced some pain that resolved within a few days. She also had some nausea because of the anesthesia, which resolved within 2 days of the procedure. She was instructed to reduce physical activity involving her right side for 7 to 10 days.

Radiation therapy began 4 weeks after surgery. The course was five treatments per week over 6 weeks. B.B. reported skin irritation from the radiation therapy, which started 2 weeks after her therapy began. She was counseled to manage her mild erythema by washing with gentle soap and water, avoiding heat, and using urea of Aquaphor cream on her breast. The erythema resolved about 2 weeks after her treatments ended.

At 3 months postradiation therapy, B.B. had another mammogram. The results were negative for any new masses. As part of her new vigilance about breast health, B.B. began to be more conscientious with observing her breast for changes and followed up with the breast surgeon for CBEs every 6 months.

Continued follow-up every 6 months has shown no new breast masses. Under a federally sponsored program, B.B. had a yearly mammogram.

Additional Information

B.B. started menopause at age 50 years. She believes she started menstruation at 13 years old. Her other health problems are obesity (50 pounds overweight), hypertension, and gout. There is more to B.B.'s experience with cancer than just during diagnosis and treatment.

B.B. loves to cook for her family. She makes traditional Mexican dishes that use oils, fat, and spices for flavor. She also uses medication that a local "herb" doctor in her neighborhood has recommended.

B.B. is a widow and the grandmother of seven. She splits her time between living with two of her daughters, who have families but work outside of the home. B.B. helps with housework and errands for her daughters, but she finds that her energy fades during the day, and she does not have the stamina she had before her lumpectomy and radiation therapy.

One of B.B.'s granddaughters has urged B.B. to ask her doctors about ovarian cancer, because the granddaughter says that she had heard that women with breast cancer "can get" ovarian cancer.

B.B. is pleased with her recovery, but states she has second thoughts about whether she should have had her breast removed as treatment. She says that some days she believes she should have had both breasts removed. Her physician has prescribed tamoxifen for her (because she was shown to be ER+), but she admits that she forgets to take her pills on some days. With the assistance of the social worker, B.B. was able to get continued coverage under the BCCTP, which is part of the NBCCEDP, to assist with the costs of tamoxifen and follow-up care.

Family and religion are extremely important to B.B. Since her diagnosis of breast cancer was made, she has attended religious services more frequently. She cries easily around her family. She says she has trouble sleeping, cannot concentrate, and feels low more days than not.

Questions

1. What are B.B.'s risk factors for breast cancer?

2. B.B. questions whether she should undergo an oophorectomy or bilateral mastectomy. What might be the nurse's response to her?

3. B.B. admits to forgetting to take her tamoxifen. What can the nurse do?

Answers

1. B.B. is obese and consumes a high-fat diet. She does not appear to exercise. Her age (61 years) is an additional risk factor. Like most women who experience development of breast cancer, she does not have other major risk factors for the disease.

2. In general, if a woman has an identified mutation in *BRCA1, BRCA2,* or another susceptibility gene, prophylactic bilateral mastectomy and oophorectomy are recommended. Because B.B. does not have this risk factor, she has received the standard of care. She is instructed to inform her breast oncology team if her family history changes.

3. Compliance with oral medication can be challenging. It is especially a problem in women who cannot afford the prescriptions or other follow-up care. B.B. was to be referred to a social worker who assured continued enrollment in the BCCTP to secure coverage for tamoxifen and other follow-up until B.B. is eligible for Medicare. The nurse needs to provide B.B. with support and education so she understands that tamoxifen is a very important part of her therapy because she has a hormonally sensitive tumor.

SUMMARY

Screening, early detection, and more effective treatments have led to a decline in the death rate for breast cancer. Ideally, all breast cancer can be detected in a noninvasive or preinvasive state, such as DCIS. Early detection is best accomplished with the use of mammography, which in some cases is supplemented by CBE and BSE or breast awareness. Definitive risk factors for breast cancer are elusive, but it is known that breast cancer is a disease of aging. Genetic predispositions to breast cancer have also been identified and can lead to true prevention in women with known genetic predisposition. Early-stage breast cancer is treated with surgery and radiation therapy. More advanced cancers follow multimodality protocols that also include chemotherapy, hormone therapies, targeted therapies, or combination of systemic therapies. With early detection and appropriate therapy, the long-term prognosis for breast cancer is good.

EXAM QUESTIONS

CHAPTER 3
Questions 10–17

Note: Choose the one option that BEST answers each question.

10. The main risk factors for breast cancer are

    a. sex, age, and breast trauma.

    b. sex, age, start of menarche, menopause, and first live pregnancy.

    c. sex, age, and excessive intake of vitamins.

    d. sex, age, and paternal history of colon cancer.

11. According to the American Cancer Society, breast cancer screening using mammography is routinely recommended for women beginning at age

    a. 30 years.

    b. 35 years.

    c. 45 years.

    d. 50 years.

12. A diagnostic workup for breast cancer might include

    a. clinical breast examination, mammography, ultrasound, and/or biopsy.

    b. positron emission tomography scan only.

    c. a CA-125 blood test.

    d. stereotactic needle biopsy.

13. If the pathology report states ductal carcinoma in situ, it indicates that

    a. there is involvement of the lymph nodes.

    b. the prognosis is poor.

    c. the malignancy has not metastasized.

    d. the malignant cells have extended beyond the basement membrane.

14. When staging cancer, factors that lead to appropriate treatment of early-stage breast cancer include

    a. the age of the woman.

    b. family members with breast cancer.

    c. whether the patient has smoked.

    d. the number of positive lymph nodes.

15. Neoadjuvant chemotherapy as a treatment for breast cancer is scheduled

    a. before surgery.

    b. during surgery.

    c. after surgery.

    d. as a sole modality.

16. Standard chemotherapy options as treatment for breast cancer include

    a. anthracycline, an alkylating agent, and taxane.

    b. progressive hormonal therapy.

    c. investigational drugs alone.

    d. watch-and-wait monitoring.

continued on next page

17. To reduce the risk for lymphedema after breast cancer surgery, women are advised to

   a. shower two times per day.

   b. apply cold to the affected area.

   c. sleep on the affected side.

   d. carry their purse or luggage with the other arm.

REFERENCES

American Cancer Society. (2015). *Breast cancer facts and figures 2015-2016.* Atlanta, GA: Author.

American Cancer Society. (2017a). *Cancer facts and figures – 2017.* Atlanta, GA: Author.

American Cancer Society. (2017b). *Cancer prevention and early detection facts and figures 2017-2018.* Atlanta, GA: Author.

Amin, M. B., Edge, S., Greene, F., Byrd, D. R., Brookland, R. K., Washington, M. K., ... Meyer, L. R. (Eds.). (2017). *AJCC cancer staging manual* (8th ed.). New York, NY: Springer.

Beaber, E. F., Malone, K. E., Tang, M.-T. C., Barlow, W. E., Porter, P. L., Daling, J. R., & Li, C. I. (2014). Oral contraceptives and breast cancer risk overall and by molecular subtype among young women. *Cancer Epidemiology Biomarkers & Prevention, 23*(5), 755-764. doi:10.1158/1055-9965.epi-13-0944

Brinton, L. A., Scoccia, B., Moghissi, K. S., Westhoff, C. L., Niwa, S., Ruggieri, D., ... Lamb, E. J. (2014). Long-term relationship of ovulation-stimulating drugs to breast cancer risk. *Cancer Epidemiology Biomarkers & Prevention, 23*(4), 584-593. doi:10.1158/1055-9965.epi-13-0996

Centers for Disease Control and Prevention. (2015). *National Breast and Cervical Cancer Early Detection Program (NBCCEDP).* Retrieved from http://www.cdc.gov/cancer/nbccedp/about.htm

Chen, W. Y., Rosner, B., Hankinson, S. E., Colditz, G. A., & Willett, W. C. (2011). Moderate alcohol consumption during adult life, drinking patterns, and breast cancer risk. *Journal of Antibiotics, 306*(17), 1884-1890. doi:10.1001/jama.2011.1590

Claus, E. B., Schildkraut, J. M., Thompson, W. D., & Risch, N. (1996). The genetic attributable risk of breast and ovarian cancer. *Cancer, 77*(11), 2318-2324.

Couch, F. J., DeShano, M. L., Blackwood, M. A., Calzone, K., Stopfer, J., Campeau, L., et al. (1997). BRCA1 mutations in women attending clinics that evaluate the risk of breast cancer. *New England Journal of Medicine, 336*(20), 1409-1415.

Cuzick, J., Sestak, I., Bonanni, B., Costantino, J. P., Cummings, S., DeCensi, A., ... Wickerham, D. L.; SERM Chemoprevention of Breast Cancer Overview Group. (2013). Selective oestrogen receptor modulators in prevention of breast cancer: An updated meta-analysis of individual participant data. *The Lancet, 381*(9880), 1827-1834. doi:10.1016/S0140-6736(13)60140-3

Daly, M. B., Pilarski, R., Axilbund, J. E., Berry, M., Buys, S. S., Crawford, B., ... Darlow, S. (2016). Genetic/familial high-risk assessment: Breast and ovarian, version 2.2015. *Journal of the National Comprehensive Cancer Network, 14*(2), 153-162.

Daly, M. B., Pilarski, R., Berry, M., Buys, S. S., Farmer, M., Friedman, S., ... Kohlmann, W. (2017). NCCN guidelines insights: Genetic/familial high-risk assessment: Breast and ovarian, Version 2.2017. *Journal of the National Comprehensive Cancer Network, 15*(1), 9-20.

Decarli, A., Calza, S., Masala, G., Specchia, C., Palli, D., & Gail, M. H. (2006). Gail model for prediction of absolute risk of invasive breast cancer: Independent evaluation in the Florence-European Prospective Investigation into cancer and nutrition cohort. *Journal of the National Cancer Institute, 98*(23), 1686-1693.

D'Orsi, C. J., Sickles, E. A., Mendelson, E. B., Morris, E. A., et al. (2013). *ACR BI-RADS® Atlas, Breast Imaging Reporting and Data System.* Reston, VA: American College of Radiology.

Emaus, M. J., van Gils, C. H., Bakker, M. F., Bisschop, C. N. S., Monninkhof, E. M., Bueno-de-Mesquita, H. B., ... May, A. M. (2014). Weight change in middle adulthood and breast cancer risk in the EPIC-PANACEA study. *International Journal of Cancer, 135*(12), 2887-2899. doi:10.1002/ijc.28926

Evans, D. G., Eccles, D. M., Rahman, N., Young, K., Bulman, M., Amir, E., ... Lalloo, F. (2004). A new scoring system for the chances of identifying a *BRCA1/2* mutation outperforms existing models including BRCAPRO. *Journal of Medical Genetics, 41*(6), 474-480.

Feight, D., Baney, T., Bruce, S., & McQuestion, M. (2011). Putting evidence into practice. *Clinical Journal of Oncology Nursing, 15*(5), 481-492. doi: 10.1188/11.cjon.481-492

Foote, J. R., Lopez-Acevedo, M., Buchanan, A. H., Alvarez Secord, A., Lee, P. S., Fountain, C., ... Havrilesky, L. J. (2017). Cost comparison of genetic testing strategies in women with epithelial ovarian cancer. *Journal of Oncology Practice, 13*(2), e120-e129. doi:10.1200/JOP.2016.011866

Frank, T. S., Deffenbaugh, A. M., Reid, J. E., Hulick, M., Ward, B. E., Lingenfelter, B., ... Critchfield, G. C. (2002). Clinical characteristics of individuals with germline mutations in *BRCA1* and *BRCA2:* Analysis of 10,000 individuals. *Journal of Clinical Oncology, 20*(6), 1480-1490.

Fu, M. R., Deng, J., & Armer, J. M. (2014). Putting evidence into practice: Cancer-related lymphedema. *Clinical Journal of Oncology Nursing, 18*(S6), 68-79. doi:10.1188/14.cjon.s3.68-79

Gilbert, F. J., Tucker, L., & Young, K. C. (2016). Digital breast tomosynthesis (DBT): A review of the evidence for use as a screening tool. *Clinical Radiology, 71,* 141-150. doi:10.1016/j.crad.2015.11.008

Hoskins, K. F., Zwaagstra, A., & Ranz, M. (2006). Validation of a tool for identifying women at high risk for hereditary breast cancer in population-based screening. *Cancer, 107*(8), 1769-1776. doi:10.1002/cncr.22202

Li, C. I., Beaber, E. F., Tang, M.-T. C., Porter, P. L., Daling, J. R., & Malone, K. E. (2013). Reproductive factors and risk of estrogen receptor positive, triple-negative, and HER2-neu overexpressing breast cancer among women 20-44 years of age. *Breast Cancer Research and Treatment, 137*(2), 579-587. doi:10.1007/s10549-012-2365-1

Mahon, S. M. (2013). Next-generation DNA sequencing: Implications for oncology care. *Oncology Nursing Forum, 40*(5), 437-439. doi:10.1188/13.ONF.437-439

Marjoribanks, J., Farquhar, C., Roberts, H., & Lethaby, A. (2012). Long term hormone therapy for perimenopausal and postmenopausal women. *Cochrane Database Systematic Review, 7,* CD004143. doi:10.1002/14651858. CD004143.pub4

Mitchell, S. A., Hoffman, A. J., Clark, J. C., Degennaro, R. M., Poirier, P., Robinson, C. B., & Weisbrod, B. L. (2014). Putting evidence into practice: An update of evidence-based interventions for cancer-related fatigue during and following treatment. *Clinical Journal of Oncology Nursing, 18*(S6), 38-58. doi:10.1188/14.cjon.s3.38-58

National Cancer Institute, Surveillance, Epidemiology, and End Results (SEER) Program. (n.d.). *SEER stat fact sheets: Female breast cancer.* Retrieved from http://seer.cancer.gov/statfacts/html/breast.html

National Comprehensive Cancer Network. (2016a). *Breast cancer screening and diagnosis: Version 1.2016.* Retrieved from http://www.nccn.org

National Comprehensive Cancer Network. (2016b). *Breast cancer: Version 2.2016.* Retrieved from http://www.nccn.org

National Comprehensive Cancer Network. (2017a). *Breast cancer risk reduction: Version 1.2017a.* Retrieved from http://www.nccn.org

National Comprehensive Cancer Network. (2017b). *Genetic/familial high risk assessment: Breast and ovarian: Version 2.2017.* Retrieved from http://www.nccn.org

Parmigani, G., Chen, S., Iversen, E. S., Jr., Friebel, T. M., Finkelstein, D. M., Anton-Culver, H., … Euhus, D. M. (2007). Validity of models for predicting *BRCA1* and *BRCA2* mutations. *Annals of Internal Medicine, 147*(7), 441-450.

Rich, T. A., Woodson, A. H., Litton, J., & Arun, B. (2015). Hereditary breast cancer syndromes and genetic testing. *Journal of Surgical Oncology, 111*(1), 66-80. doi:10.1002/jso.23791

Shattuck-Eidens, D., Oliphant, A., McClure, M., McBride, C., Gupte, J., Rubano, T., … Thomas, A. (1997). BRCA1 sequence analysis in women at high risk for susceptibility mutations. Risk factor analysis and implications for genetic testing. *Journal of the American Medical Association, 278*(15), 1242-1250.

Weitzel, J. N., Blazer, K. R., MacDonald, D. J., Culver, J. O., & Offit, K. (2011). Genetics, genomics and cancer risk assessment: State of the art and future directions in the era of personalized medicine. *CA: A Cancer Journal for Clinicians, 61*(5), 327-359. doi:10.3322/caac.20128

Yang, X. R., Chang-Claude, J., Goode, E. L., Couch, F. J., Nevanlinna, H., Milne, R. L., … Garcia-Closas, M. (2011). Associations of breast cancer risk factors with tumor subtypes: A pooled analysis from the Breast Cancer Association Consortium Studies. *Journal of the National Cancer Institute, 103*(3), 250-263. doi:10.1093/jnci/djq526

CHAPTER 4

ENDOMETRIAL CANCER

LEARNING OUTCOME

After completing this chapter, the learner will be able to discuss endometrial cancer epidemiology, risk factors, prevention and detection strategies, staging, and treatment modalities.

CHAPTER OBJECTIVES

After completing this chapter, the learner will be able to:

1. Identify risk factors for endometrial cancer.

2. Describe strategies to prevent endometrial cancer.

3. Discuss benign uterine conditions.

4. Identify detection methods and the diagnostic evaluation confirming endometrial cancer.

5. Explain the staging schema of endometrial cancer.

6. Describe treatment options and follow-up for endometrial cancer.

INTRODUCTION

Endometrial or uterine cancer is the most common gynecological cancer. It is highly curable if detected early. Treatment includes surgery, radiation, chemotherapy, or a combination of modalities. Multiple hereditary genes are associated with endometrial cancer and are the foundation for what is known about endometrial cancer risk factors.

EPIDEMIOLOGY

Cancer of the endometrium or the lining of the uterus accounts for 7% of incidents of cancer in women and 4% of deaths, or 10,470 deaths annually (American Cancer Society [ACS], 2017a). Box 4-1 and Figures 4-1 to 4-3 provide other epidemiological data about endometrial cancer.

ANATOMY

The uterus is a hollow organ about the size and shape of a medium-sized pear. It has two main components: The lower end of the uterus is the cervix, extending into the vagina; the upper part of the uterus, the corpus, is the body (see Figure 4-4).

The body of the uterus has two layers: the inner layer or lining, the endometrium, and the outer layer of muscle, the myometrium. During childbirth, the woman's thick layer of muscle contracts and pushes out the baby. The tissue coating the outside of the uterus is the serosa.

Hormones released during a woman's menstrual cycle prompt the endometrium to change. The ovaries produce estrogens during the early part of the cycle, before an egg releases (ovulation). During pregnancy, estrogen causes the endometrium to thicken so it can nourish the embryo. If there is no conception, and therefore no pregnancy, after ovulation, the level of estrogen decreases, whereas the hormone progester-

BOX 4-1: FACTS ABOUT ENDOMETRIAL CANCER

- Incidence rates have been increasing among women younger than 50 years by 1.3% per year since 1988 and among women 50 years and older by 1.9% per year since 2005.

- From 2004 to 2013, the incidence rate increased 1% per year for White women and 3% per year for Black women.

- From 2004 to 2013, mortality rates for cancer of the uterine corpus increased by 1.1% per year.

- The 5- and 10-year relative survival rates for uterine cancer are 82% and 79%, respectively.

- The 5-year survival rate is higher for White women (84%) than for Black women (62%).

- White women are more likely than Black women to be diagnosed with local stage disease (The percentage is 69% for White women versus 53% for Black women).

Note. Adapted from American Cancer Society. (2017a). *Cancer facts and figures – 2017.* Atlanta, GA: Author.

FIGURE 4-1: AGE DISTRIBUTION: ENDOMETRIAL CANCER, 2010 TO 2014

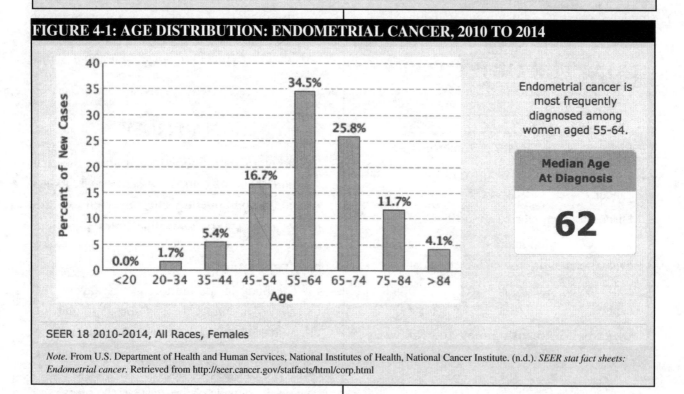

SEER 18 2010-2014, All Races, Females

Note. From U.S. Department of Health and Human Services, National Institutes of Health, National Cancer Institute. (n.d.). *SEER stat fact sheets: Endometrial cancer.* Retrieved from http://seer.cancer.gov/statfacts/html/corp.html

one level increases. This causes the innermost layer of the lining to begin shedding. At the end of the cycle, the endometrial lining sheds, initiating the woman's menstrual flow. This cycle repeats throughout a woman's life until menopause, unless interrupted by pregnancy.

RISK FACTORS

All women are at risk for endometrial cancer, and risk increases steadily with age. Table 4-1 reviews risk factors associated with endometrial cancer. Multiple risk factors combine to increase a woman's risk; however, genetic predisposition for some women is a solo risk for endometrial cancer.

FIGURE 4-2: NUMBER OF NEW CASES PER 100,000 WOMEN BY RACE/ETHNICITY: ENDOMETRIAL CANCER, 2010 TO 2014

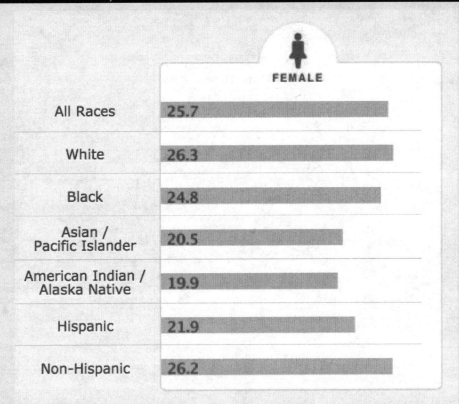

All Races	25.7
White	26.3
Black	24.8
Asian / Pacific Islander	20.5
American Indian / Alaska Native	19.9
Hispanic	21.9
Non-Hispanic	26.2

Surveillance, Epidemiology, and End Results (SEER) 18, 2010 to 2014, age-adjusted risk of developing endometrial cancer by ethnicity.

Note. From U.S. Department of Health and Human Services, National Institutes of Health, National Cancer Institute. (n.d.). *SEER stat fact sheets: Endometrial cancer.* Retrieved from http://seer.cancer.gov/statfacts/html/corp.html

FIGURE 4-3: AGE DISTRIBUTION: DEATH FROM ENDOMETRIAL CANCER, 2010 TO 2014

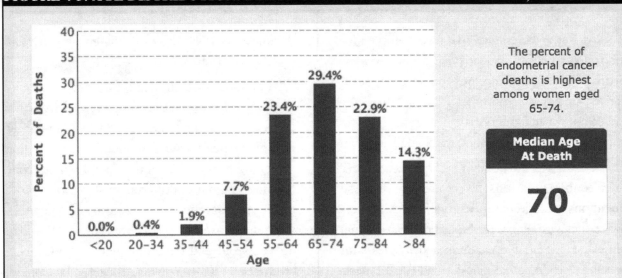

The percent of endometrial cancer deaths is highest among women aged 65-74.

Median Age At Death

70

U.S. 2010-2014, All Races, Females

Note. From U.S. Department of Health and Human Services, National Institutes of Health, National Cancer Institute. (n.d.). *SEER stat fact sheets: Endometrial cancer.* Retrieved from http://seer.cancer.gov/statfacts/html/corp.html

FIGURE 4-4: ANATOMY OF UTERUS AND NEARBY ORGANS

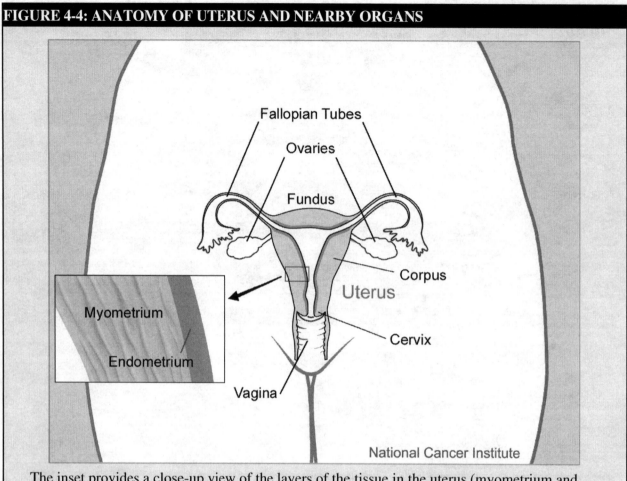

The inset provides a close-up view of the layers of the tissue in the uterus (myometrium and endometrium).

Note. From U.S. Department of Health and Human Services, National Institutes of Health, National Cancer Institute. (2007). *Visuals online: Uterus and nearby organs.* Retrieved from https://visualsonline.cancer.gov/details.cfm?imageid=4369

Women at hereditary risk to develop endometrial or ovarian cancer have a genetic syndrome: hereditary nonpolyposis colorectal cancer, or Lynch syndrome. Table 4-2 lists key indicators for hereditary risk. Table 4-3 lists the common genetic mutations associated with an increased risk for developing endometrial cancer.

Recommendations for women with these mutations include careful surveillance. Surveillance includes annual or semiannual transvaginal ultrasound of the endometrium and ovaries with concurrent endometrial biopsies and CA-125 testing. However, in premenopausal women, ultrasound evaluation cannot evaluate endometrial thickness well because of cyclic changes (Braun, Overbeek-Wager, & Grumbo, 2016).

For some women, healthcare providers may recommend preventative surgery. If a woman's risk to develop endometrial and ovarian cancer is high or healthcare providers determine that screening may be ineffective, these women may consider a total abdominal hysterectomy with bilateral salpingo-oophorectomy. In general, women who choose this treatment are 35 to 45 years old and have completed childbearing (Koh et al., 2014; Weitzel, Blazer, MacDonald, Culver, & Offit, 2011). This surgery prompts women to enter into premature menopause. Postoperative recovery is typically 4 to 8 weeks.

continued on page 97

TABLE 4-1: RISK FACTORS FOR ENDOMETRIAL CANCER

Risk Factor	Etiology
Hormonal factors	Risk for endometrial cancer increases with increased levels of circulating estrogen. Before menopause, the ovaries are the main source of estrogen and progesterone. A shift in the balance of these two hormones toward more estrogen increases a woman's risk for developing endometrial cancer. After menopause, the ovaries stop making these hormones, but a small amount of estrogen is still made naturally in fat tissue. This estrogen has a bigger impact after menopause than it does before menopause.
Estrogen stimulation	Hormone replacement therapy can reduce the hot flashes and vaginal dryness that can occur with menopause. Estrogen alone (without progesterone) can lead to endometrial cancer. Progesterone-like drugs must be given along with estrogen to avoid the increased risk for endometrial cancer. This approach is called *combination hormone therapy* and reduces endometrial cancer risk, but increases breast cancer risk. Usually this therapy is recommended for less than 5 years.
Total number of menstrual cycles	Having more menstrual cycles during a woman's lifetime increases her risk for endometrial cancer. Menarche before age 12 or going through menopause later in life increases the risk.
Obesity	Although most of a woman's estrogen is produced by her ovaries, fat tissue can change some other hormones into estrogens. Having more fat tissue can increase a woman's estrogen levels and, therefore, increase her endometrial cancer risk. In comparison with women who maintain a healthy weight, endometrial cancer is twice as common in overweight women and more than three times as common in obese women.
Tamoxifen therapy	Tamoxifen can be a very effective treatment for estrogen-receptor-positive breast cancer. Tamoxifen acts as an antiestrogen in breast tissue, but it acts like an estrogen in the uterus. It can cause the uterine lining to grow, which increases the risk for endometrial cancer. The risk for developing endometrial cancer from tamoxifen therapy is small – about 1 in 500. Women taking tamoxifen must balance this small risk against the value of this drug in treating breast cancer and reducing the odds of cancer developing in the other breast.
Age	Endometrial cancer risk increases with age, probably because cells are more sensitive to carcinogenic substances.
Polycystic ovary disease	Women with a condition called *polycystic ovary syndrome* have abnormal hormone levels, such as higher estrogen levels and lower levels of progesterone. The increase in estrogen relative to progesterone can increase a woman's odds of developing endometrial cancer.
Diabetes	Endometrial cancer may be as much as four times more common in women with diabetes. Although diabetes is more common in people who are overweight, even people with diabetes who are not overweight have a higher risk for endometrial cancer.
High-fat diet	A high-fat diet can increase the risk for several cancers, including endometrial cancer. Because fatty foods are also high-calorie foods, a high-fat diet can lead to obesity, which is a well-known endometrial cancer risk factor. High-fat foods may also have a direct effect on estrogen metabolism, which increases endometrial cancer risk.
Endometrial hyperplasia	Mild or simple hyperplasia, which is the most common type, has a very small risk of becoming malignant. It may resolve on its own or after treatment with hormone therapy. If the hyperplasia is called atypical, it has a higher chance of becoming a cancer. Simple atypical hyperplasia turns into cancer in about 8% of cases if it is not treated. Complex atypical hyperplasia has a risk of becoming malignant if not treated in up to 29% of cases.

Note. Adapted from Braun, M. M., Overbeek-Wager, E. A., & Grumbo, R. J. (2016). Diagnosis and management of endometrial cancer. *American Family Physician, 93*(6), 468-474; American Cancer Society. (2017a). *Cancer facts and figures – 2017.* Atlanta, GA: Author.; and Koh, W. J., Greer, B. E., Abu-Rustum, N. R., Apte, S. M., Campos, S. M., Chan, J., … Hughes, M. (2014). Uterine neoplasms, version 1.2014. *Journal of the National Comprehensive Cancer Network, 12*(2), 248-280.

TABLE 4-2: KEY INDICATORS OF HEREDITARY CANCER SYNDROMES ASSOCIATED WITH ENDOMETRIAL CANCER

- A personal history of colorectal or endometrial cancer diagnosed before 50 years of age

- A first-degree relative with colorectal cancer diagnosed before 50 years of age

- Two or more relatives with colorectal cancer or an HNPCC-associated cancer, which includes endometrial, ovarian, stomach, hepatobiliary, small-bowel, renal pelvis, or ureter cancer; one relative must be a first-degree relative of another

- Colorectal cancer occurring in two or more generations on the same side of the family

- A personal history of colorectal cancer and a first-degree relative with adenomas diagnosed before 40 years of age

- An affected relative with a known HNPCC or other susceptibility mutation

HNPCC = hereditary nonpolyposis colorectal cancer.

Note. Adapted from American Cancer Society. (2017a). *Cancer facts and figures – 2017.* Atlanta, GA: Author; Koh, W. J., Greer, B. E., Abu-Rustum, N. R., Apte, S. M., Campos, S. M., Chan, J., … Hughes, M. (2014). Uterine neoplasms, version 1.2014. *Journal of the National Comprehensive Cancer Network, 12*(2), 248-280; and Weitzel, J. N., Blazer, K. R., MacDonald, D. J., Culver, J. O., & Offit, K. (2011). Genetics, genomics and cancer risk assessment: State of the art and future directions in the era of personalized medicine. *CA: A Cancer Journal for Clinicians, 61*(5), 327-359. doi:10.3322/caac.20128

TABLE 4-3: HEREDITARY SYNDROMES ASSOCIATED WITH INCREASED RISK FOR DEVELOPING ENDOMETRIAL CANCER

Genes	Associated Cancer Risks
MSH1[a] *MSH2*[a] *MSH6*[a] *EPCAM*[a] *PMS2*[a]	Endometrial, colorectal, ovarian, gastric, pancreatic, biliary tract, urinary tract, small-bowel, brain, sebaceous neoplasms
BRCA1/ BRCA2	Female and male breast, ovarian, prostate, pancreatic, fallopian tube, primary peritoneal, endometrial, melanoma
PTEN	Endometrial, female breast, thyroid, colon, renal, melanoma
CHEK2	Female breast, male breast, colon, prostate, thyroid, endometrial, ovarian
TP53	Female breast, endometrial, soft tissue sarcoma, osteosarcoma, brain, hematological malignancies, adrenocortical carcinoma
MUTYH[b]	Colorectal (80%), duodenal (4%), endometrial
STK11	Female breast, colorectal, pancreatic, gastric, ovarian, lung, small intestine, cervical, endometrial, testicular tumors
POLE1	Colon, endometrial

[a]Genes associated with hereditary nonpolyposis colorectal cancer.

[b]Autosomal recessive syndrome; risk is higher in individuals with mutations in both copies.

Note. Adapted from Koh, W. J., Greer, B. E., Abu-Rustum, N. R., Apte, S. M., Campos, S. M., Chan, J., … Hughes, M. (2014). Uterine neoplasms, version 1.2014. *Journal of the National Cancer Network, 12*(2), 248-280; and Weitzel, J. N., Blazer, K. R., MacDonald, D. J., Culver, J. O., & Offit, K. (2011). Genetics, genomics and cancer risk assessment: State of the art and future directions in the era of personalized medicine. *CA: A Cancer Journal for Clinicians, 61*(5), 327-359. doi:10.3322/caac.20128

In addition to caring for the woman at risk, healthcare providers extend prevention, screening, and genetic counseling strategies to family members of the affected woman because of the hereditary cancer syndromes associated with increased endometrial cancer risk (Weitzel et al., 2011).

PREVENTION AND RISK REDUCTION

Historically, hysterectomy was the key strategy to prevent endometrial cancer. Currently, hysterectomy is reserved as a means of prevention for women with a known hereditary risk for developing endometrial cancer. However, reducing the risk of endometrial cancer is preferable. Prevention efforts target reduction of modifiable risk factors for endometrial cancer.

Nearly 70% of patients with early-stage endometrial cancer are obese (Braun et al., 2016). For this reason, efforts focus on reducing obesity, instructing women on the benefits of a low-fat diet, maintenance of an appropriate weight, and exercise (ACS, 2017b).

To reduce endometrial cancer risk, women taking hormone therapy (HT) should include a progestin and take HT for as short a time as necessary (Braun et al., 2016). Other prevention strategies include increased alertness to assessment and follow-through in treating symptoms of abnormal uterine bleeding.

Use of oral contraceptives reduces the risk for endometrial cancer. The risk is lowest in women who take oral contraceptives for more than 10 years, and the protection continues for at least 10 years after a woman stops taking it (ACS, 2017a). However, it is important to look at all of the risks and benefits when choosing a contraceptive method – endometrial cancer risk is only one factor to be considered. For example, the risk for breast cancer may be increased in women who use oral contraceptives.

BENIGN UTERINE CONDITIONS

The most common type of cancer of the uterus begins in the endometrium. (The terms *uterine cancer* and *endometrial cancer* frequently are used interchangeably.) Common benign conditions include fibroids, endometriosis, and endometrial hyperplasia. A diagnostic evaluation is indicated to rule out malignancy (Koh et al., 2014).

Fibroids

Benign tumors that form in the uterus are called *fibroids* or *leiomyomas*. They are a proliferation or abnormal growth of smooth muscle tissue. Uterine fibroids arise from the tissue in the muscle layer of the wall of the uterus – the myometrium. They are not malignant. The etiology of fibroids is not yet understood. Family history may play a role because fibroids can develop in women in the same family. Fibroids are two to three times more common in Black women compared with White women. Overweight women are at increased risk for fibroids (Wise et al., 2016).

Women with fibroids may not realize they have them because they may be asymptomatic. Healthcare providers detect them incidentally during diagnostic or therapeutic procedures. Fibroids are common; their estimated incidence rate is as high as 50% in women (Braun et al., 2016).

Women with fibroids can experience symptoms, depending on the fibroid size, location within the uterus, and how close the fibroid is to adjacent pelvic organs. Large fibroids can cause

- pelvic pressure;
- severe, localized pain, particularly when deteriorating;

- pressure on the bladder, with frequent or obstructed urination; or

- pressure on the rectum, with pain during defecation.

(Braun et al., 2016)

The most common fibroid symptom is abnormal uterine bleeding. If the tumors are near the uterine lining or interfere with the blood flow to the lining, they can cause heavy, painful, and prolonged periods or spotting between menses.

Endometriosis

Another benign condition of the uterus is endometriosis. Endometrial cells shed each month during menstruation. Endometriosis results when endometrial cells attach themselves to tissue outside the uterus. These endometrial implants most commonly occur in the ovaries, the fallopian tubes, the outer surfaces of the uterus or intestines, and the surface lining of the pelvic cavity, as well as in the vagina, cervix, and bladder (Koh et al., 2014).

Endometriosis prevalence cannot be confirmed because many women who have the condition do not experience symptoms. U.S. researchers estimate that endometriosis affects more than 1 million women (10% to 18% of women; Kvaskoff et al., 2015). It is a leading cause of pelvic pain, and if unresolved with medical management once diagnosed, attempts to obtain relief may lead to laparoscopic surgery or even hysterectomy.

Endometriosis affects women during their reproductive years, in general between 25 and 35 years of age. Endometriosis is rare in postmenopausal women. It more commonly occurs in White women than in Black and Asian women. Studies further suggest that endometriosis is most common in taller, thin women with a low body mass index. Delaying pregnancy until a woman is older is also believed to increase the risk of developing endometrio-

sis. The cause of endometriosis is unknown (Kvaskoff et al., 2015).

Theories suggest that during menstruation, endometrial tissue deposits outside the uterus, backing up into the fallopian tubes and the pelvic and abdominal cavities. Why this retrograde menstruation occurs is not clearly understood. Moreover, retrograde menstruation cannot be the sole cause of endometriosis because many women have retrograde menstruation in varying degrees, but not all of them develop endometriosis (Kvaskoff et al., 2015).

Most women with endometriosis are asymptomatic. When symptomatic, women report pain (usually pelvic pain) and can be infertile. Other symptoms related to endometriosis are

- lower abdominal pain,

- diarrhea and constipation,

- lower back pain,

- irregular or heavy menstrual bleeding, and

- blood in the urine.

A woman's pattern of symptoms or physical examination findings may prompt a healthcare provider to consider endometriosis as a differential diagnosis. Surgery (laparoscopy) with biopsy confirms an endometriosis diagnosis. Treatment of endometriosis includes medication and surgery for pain relief. If the woman with endometriosis wants to become pregnant, she also may need surgical treatment (Kvaskoff et al., 2015).

Endometrial Hyperplasia

Endometrial hyperplasia, a benign condition, occurs when the endometrium overproduces; it can be a precursor to cancer of the uterus. Abnormal vaginal bleeding is the most common symptom of endometrial hyperplasia. Additional endometrial hyperplasia risk factors that can accompany abnormal vaginal bleeding include (van Hanegem et al., 2016)

- being immediately premenopausal or postmenopausal,

- skipping menstrual periods or having no periods at all,

- being overweight,

- having diabetes,

- having polycystic ovary syndrome,

- taking estrogen without progesterone as an estrogen replacement (to relieve symptoms of menopause), and

- taking tamoxifen therapy.

When women present with vaginal bleeding or with vaginal bleeding and a combination of the above risk factors, healthcare providers proceed with a diagnostic evaluation, including a pelvic examination (see Figure 4-5), ultrasound (see Figure 4-6), dilatation and curettage (see Figure 4-7), and/or hysteroscopy with endometrial biopsy (see Figure 4-8; van Hanegem et al., 2016).

The treatment for endometrial hyperplasia includes the hormone progesterone, which prompts the endometrial lining to shed without building up. It can cause vaginal bleeding. For women who no longer want to bear children or are diagnosed with atypical hyperplasia, they may choose to undergo hysterectomy.

To reduce the risk for endometrial hyperplasia, healthcare providers advise women to take progesterone hormones (if taking hormones for menopausal symptoms) or lose weight (Wise et al., 2016).

DETECTION AND DIAGNOSTIC EVALUATION: SIGNS AND SYMPTOMS

The most common symptom of endometrial cancer is abnormal or unexpected vaginal bleeding, especially after menopause. One esti-

mate suggests that up to 20% of women who have abnormal bleeding after menopause are diagnosed with endometrial cancer (Braun et al., 2016).

For premenopausal women older than 35 years presenting with abnormal bleeding, healthcare providers may suspect endometrial cancer, although that diagnosis is less common. In rare cases, unexplained abnormal vaginal discharge may be an early endometrial cancer symptom.

Symptoms of advanced endometrial cancer include

- difficult or painful urination,

- pain in the pelvic area,

- a pelvic lump, and

- weight loss.

Other conditions with similar symptoms include cervical cancer and benign uterine conditions. For this reason, healthcare providers further evaluate any suspicious symptom or constellation of symptoms (ACS, 2016).

Diagnostic Evaluation

In most cases, being alert to any signs and symptoms of endometrial cancer, such as abnormal vaginal bleeding or discharge, and reporting them promptly, followed by an appropriate diagnostic evaluation, allows practitioners to diagnose the disease at an early stage. The ACS estimates that prompt evaluation of postmenopausal bleeding diagnoses 67% of cases at an early stage (ACS, 2017a).

At this time, there are no tests or examinations that can find endometrial cancer early in women who are at average endometrial cancer risk and have no symptoms. The ACS (2017) recommends that healthcare providers establish a plan of care with their patients, which includes regular, annual pelvic examinations (see Figure 4-5).

During the bimanual pelvic examination, the healthcare provider digitally palpates the

FIGURE 4-5: PELVIC EXAMINATION

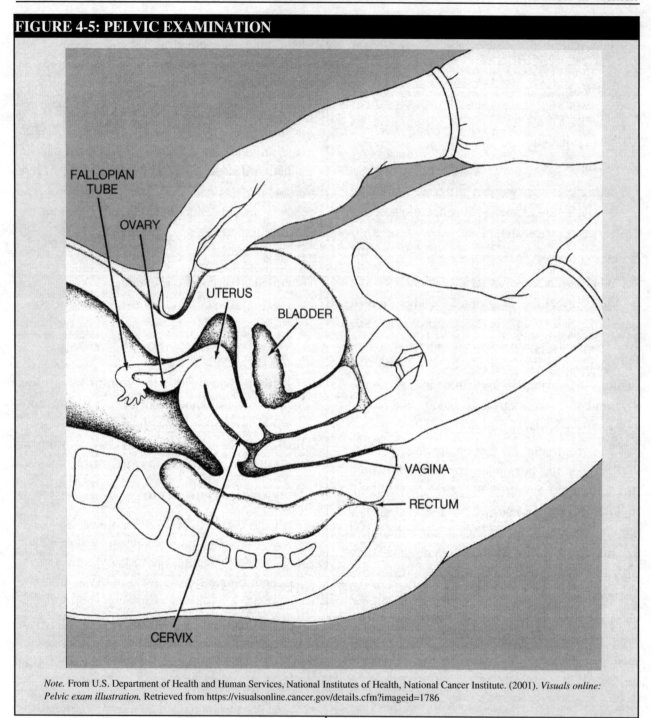

Note. From U.S. Department of Health and Human Services, National Institutes of Health, National Cancer Institute. (2001). *Visuals online: Pelvic exam illustration.* Retrieved from https://visualsonline.cancer.gov/details.cfm?imageid=1786

vagina and vaginal walls for any irregularities or tenderness; the cervix for shape, consistency, mobility, and any tenderness; and the adjacent pelvic organs and structures. Then the healthcare provider externally pushes the abdomen to assess the size and shape of the uterus and ovaries, and notes any tenderness or abnormal masses or lesions. The last part

of the pelvic examination is the rectovaginal examination. This allows the clinician to better examine the pelvic organs and structures. The examiner places an index finger into the vagina and a lubricated, gloved middle finger against the anus and asks the patient to bear down so that the anal sphincter will relax. As relaxation occurs, the examiner will insert the middle fin-

FIGURE 4-6: TRANSVAGINAL ULTRASOUND SHOWING UTERINE FLUID ACCUMULATION

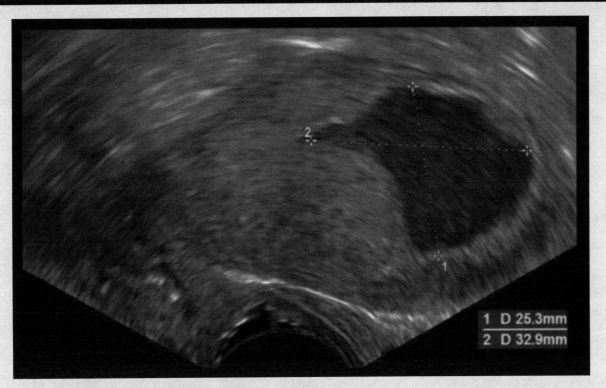

Transvaginal ultrasonography showing a uterine fluid accumulation in a postmenopausal woman seeking health care because of intermittent vaginal fluid discharge. Biopsy results showed endometrial adenocarcinoma.

Note. From Häggström, M. (2014). Medical gallery of Mikael Häggström 2014. *Wikiversity Journal of Medicine, 1*(2), 8. doi:10.15347/wjm/2014.008

FIGURE 4-7: DILATATION AND CURETTAGE

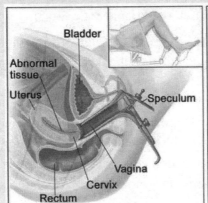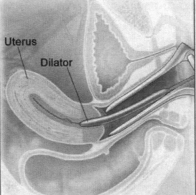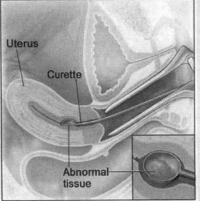

A speculum is inserted into the vagina to widen it to look at the cervix (left panel). A dilator is used to widen the cervix (middle panel). A curette is put through the cervix into the uterus to scrape out abnormal tissue (right panel).

Note. From U.S. Department of Health and Human Services, National Institutes of Health, National Cancer Institute. (2013). *Visuals online: Dilatation and curettage.* Retrieved from https://visualsonline.cancer.gov/details.cfm?imageid=9114; © 2010 Terese Winslow, U.S. Govt has certain rights.

FIGURE 4-8: HYSTEROSCOPY

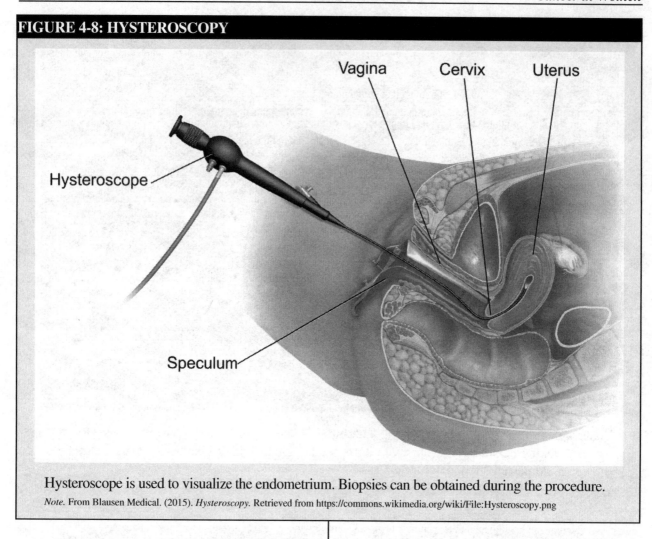

Vagina   Cervix   Uterus

Hysteroscope

Speculum

Hysteroscope is used to visualize the endometrium. Biopsies can be obtained during the procedure.

Note. From Blausen Medical. (2015). *Hysteroscopy.* Retrieved from https://commons.wikimedia.org/wiki/File:Hysteroscopy.png

ger into the rectum, enabling better assessment of the position and shape of the uterus. In addition, the examiner can evaluate any masses or tenderness at this point and examine the anal canal and rectum for polyps or other lesions.

The ACS also recommends healthcare providers educate their patients at menopause about the risks and symptoms of endometrial cancer and strongly encourage them to report any vaginal bleeding or spotting. Women should talk to their practitioners about getting regular pelvic examinations. Although the pelvic examination exposes some cancers, including some advanced uterine cancers, it is not very effective in finding early endometrial cancers. The Papanicolaou (Pap) test, effective to detect cervical cancer, is not effective in detecting endometrial cancer (ACS, 2017a; Lai, Hsu, Hang, & Li, 2015).

The ACS (2016) recommends that most women at increased risk should be informed of their risk, offered annual screening with endometrial biopsy beginning at age 35 years, and advised to see their doctors whenever there is any abnormal vaginal bleeding. This includes women whose risk for endometrial cancer is increased because of hereditary nonpolyposis colorectal cancer or other mutations that cause genetic susceptibility. Women receiving tamoxifen therapy need to evaluate whether the potential benefit in reducing breast cancer risk is greater than the slightly increased risk for developing endometrial cancer (ACS, 2016).

STAGING

Pathology

Endometrial cancers start in the cells that line the uterus and belong to the group of cancers called *carcinomas.* Most endometrial carcinomas are from the gland cells in the endometrium. These adenocarcinomas account for approximately 80% of endometrial cancers (ACS, 2017a).

Some endometrial cancers include squamous cells (flat, thin cells on the outer surface of the cervix) in addition to glandular cells. A cancer with both squamous and glandular cells is an adenocarcinoma with squamous differentiation. Pathologists may determine that endometrial glandular cells look cancerous, but the squamous cells do not, so the malignancy is reported as adenoacanthoma. If both the squamous cells and the glandular cells look malignant, these tumors are adenosquamous carcinomas. Other types of endometrial malignancies are secretory carcinoma, ciliated carcinoma, and mucinous adenocarcinoma. Less common forms of endometrial adenocarcinoma are clear cell carcinoma, serous carcinoma, and poorly differentiated carcinoma. These cancers are more aggressive than most endometrial cancers, spread rapidly, and may have already metastasized at the time of diagnosis.

Table 4-4 provides an overview of biopsy procedures used to obtain a tissue sample for the pathologist to review to make a diagnosis.

Staging System

The main system used to stage endometrial cancer is called the *FIGO* (International Federation of Gynecology and Obstetrics) *system.* This is a surgical staging system that evaluates tissue removed during a surgical procedure. The FIGO system classifies the tumor stages I through IV, with some stages subdivided. The American Joint Committee on Cancer (AJCC) TNM staging system for endometrial cancer matches the FIGO system (Amin et al., 2017).

An additional component of pathological staging is the cell grade, which determines differences between normal and abnormal cells. Grading the tumor indicates how quickly the cells are growing. Low-grade cancers typically grow slower than high-grade tumors.

The pathologist grades endometrial cancer on whether tumor cells from endometrial glandular tissue looks similar to normal, healthy endometrium tissue (Amin et al., 2017). The grades include:

GX: The grade cannot be evaluated.

G1: The cells are well differentiated and look more similar to normal tissue.

G2: The cells are moderately differentiated.

G3: The cells are poorly differentiated and are not similar to normal tissue.

When evaluating cells, the pathologist reports the grade, histology, and depth of myometrial invasion. Staging is based on the T (Tumor), N (Lymph Nodes), and M (Metastasis; Amin et al., 2017).

Additional diagnostic tests contribute to determining the stage of cancer including evaluation for metastasis through transvaginal ultrasound, magnetic resonance imaging, or computed tomography. Surgical staging follows, and together with the pathology and results from other diagnostic tests, the extent of disease is determined. Endometrial cancer can spread locally to other parts of the uterus and regionally to lymph nodes. The regional lymph nodes are located in the pelvis and distantly along the aorta. The lymph nodes along the aorta are called *para-aortic nodes.* Cancer can metastasize to distant lymph nodes and organs such as the lung, liver, bone, brain, and others.

TABLE 4-4: TESTS USED IN THE DIAGNOSTIC EVALUATION OF ENDOMETRIAL CANCER

Endometrial biopsy	An endometrial biopsy is the most commonly performed test for endometrial cancer. It can be done in the doctor's office. In this procedure, a very thin, flexible tube is inserted into the uterus through the cervix. Then, using suction, a small amount of endometrium is removed through the tube. The suctioning takes about a minute or less. The discomfort is similar to menstrual cramps and can be helped by taking a nonsteroidal anti-inflammatory drug such as ibuprofen before the procedure. Transvaginal ultrasound is often done before the biopsy. This helps the examiner locate any suspicious areas for which a biopsy should be done.
Hysteroscopy	For this technique, a tiny telescope (about 1/6 inch in diameter) is inserted into the uterus through the cervix. The uterus is filled with saline solution to get a better view of the inside of the uterus. This lets the examiner visualize and take a biopsy of anything that appears to be abnormal. This is usually done with the patient awake, using a local anesthetic. This is the most accurate way of directly examining for cancer.
Dilation and curettage (D&C)	If the endometrial biopsy sample does not provide enough tissue, or if the biopsy curettage (D&C) suggests cancer but the results are uncertain, a D&C must be done. The opening of the cervix is enlarged (dilated), and a curette is used to scrape tissue from inside the uterus. This may be done with or without a hysteroscopy. The procedure takes about an hour and may require general anesthesia or conscious sedation. A D&C is usually done in an outpatient surgery area. Most women have little discomfort after this procedure.

Note. Adapted from American Cancer Society. (2017a). *Cancer facts and figures – 2017.* Atlanta, GA: Author.; Braun, M. M., Overbeek-Wager, E. A., & Grumbo, R. J. (2016). Diagnosis and management of endometrial cancer. *American Family Physician, 93*(6), 468-474; and Van Hanegem, N., Prins, M. M. C., Bongers, M. Y., Opmeer, B. C., Sahota, D. S., Mol, B. W. J., & Timmermans, A. (2016). The accuracy of endometrial sampling in women with postmenopausal bleeding: A systematic review and meta-analysis. *European Journal of Obstetrics & Gynecology and Reproductive Biology, 197,* 147-155. doi:10.1016/j.ejogrb.2015.12.008

TREATMENT

Treatment options for endometrial cancer depend on the size of the tumor, the stage of the disease, whether female hormones affect tumor growth, and the tumor grade. The grade determines differences between normal and abnormal cells. Grading the tumor can also indicate how quickly the cells are growing. Low-grade cancers typically grow slower than high-grade tumors.

Staging is key to directing treatment decisions. Table 4-5 lists staging schema for endometrial cancer from two accepted sources: AJCC and FIGO. Staging also provides prognostic information (ACS, 2017a; Braun et al., 2016; Koh et al., 2014).

5-YEAR SURVIVAL RATES BY STAGE FOR ENDOMETRIAL ADENOCARCINOMA

- Stage 0: 90%
- Stage IA: 88%
- Stage IB: 78%
- Stage II: 74%
- Stage IIIA: 56%
- Stage IIIB: 57%
- Stage IIIC: 49%
- Stage IVA: 22%
- Stage IVB: 21%

Surgery

The main treatment for endometrial cancer, a hysterectomy, removes the woman's uterus and cervix (see Figure 4-9). When the sur-

TABLE 4-5: ENDOMETRIAL CANCER STAGING SUMMARY

- Stage IA – No or less than half myometrial invasion

- Stage IB – Invasion equal to or more than half of the myometrium

- Stage II – Tumor invades cervical stroma but does not extend beyond the uterus

- Stage III – Local and/or regional spread of the tumor

- Stage IIIA – Tumor invades the serosa of the corpus uteri and/or adnexa

- Stage IIIB – Vaginal metastasis and/or parametrial involvement

- Stage IIIC – Metastases to pelvic and/or para-aortic lymph nodes

- Stage IIIC1 – Positive pelvic nodes

- Stage IIIC2 – Positive para-aortic lymph nodes with or without positive pelvic nodes

- Stage IV – Tumor invasion of bladder and/or bowel mucosa and/or distant metastases

- Stage IVA – Tumor invasion of bladder and/or bowel mucosa

- Stage IVB – Distant metastases, including intra-abdominal and/or inguinal lymph node

Note. Adapted from Koh, W. J., Greer, B. E., Abu-Rustum, N. R., Apte, S. M., Campos, S. M., Chan, J., … Hughes, M. (2014). Uterine neoplasms, version 1.2014. *Journal of the National Comprehensive Cancer Network, 12*(2), 248-280; Edge, S. B., Byrd, D. R., Carducci, M., Compton, C. C., Fritz, A. G., Greene, F. L., & Trotti, A. (2010). *AJCC cancer staging manual* (7th ed.). New York, NY: Springer; and Creasman, W. T. (2009). Revised FIGO staging for carcinoma of the vulva, cervix and endometrium. *International Journal of Gynecology and Obstetrics, 105,* 103-104.

geon removes the uterus through an incision in the abdomen, it is a simple or total abdominal hysterectomy. When the surgical approach is removal of the uterus through the vagina, it is called a *vaginal hysterectomy.* Removal of the ovaries and fallopian tubes is not part of a hysterectomy. It is a separate procedure known as a bilateral salpingo-oophorectomy. Removal of the ovaries and tubes is performed during the hysterectomy procedure.

As a component of staging, the surgeon also will remove the lymph nodes (lymph node sampling) in the pelvis and around the aorta, either through the same incision as the abdominal hysterectomy or via laparoscopy during vaginal hysterectomy. Sentinel lymph node sampling removes a few of the lymph nodes to evaluate as representative of all lymph nodes in the area (Abu-Rustum, 2014). When removing most or all the lymph nodes, the procedure is a lymph node dissection or lymphadenectomy.

When endometrial cancer has spread to the cervix or the area around the cervix (the parametrium), the surgeon performs a radical hysterectomy. In this operation, the surgeon removes the entire uterus, both ovaries and fallopian tubes, the tissues next to the uterus (parametrium and uterosacral ligaments), and the upper part of the vagina (next to the cervix). The surgeon may perform a pelvic washing. The abdominal and pelvic cavities are rinsed using a saline solution wash, and the pathologist evaluates this fluid.

Proper surgical staging, the most important prognostic factor, provides information on the actual extent of disease and the grade, histology, and depth of myometrial invasion, which helps in planning adjuvant therapy.

Endometrial cancer surgery may also include an omentectomy. This procedure removes the omentum, the layer of fatty tissue that covers the internal abdominal organs like an apron, because tumor cells can spread to this tissue.

FIGURE 4-9: TYPES OF HYSTERECTOMY

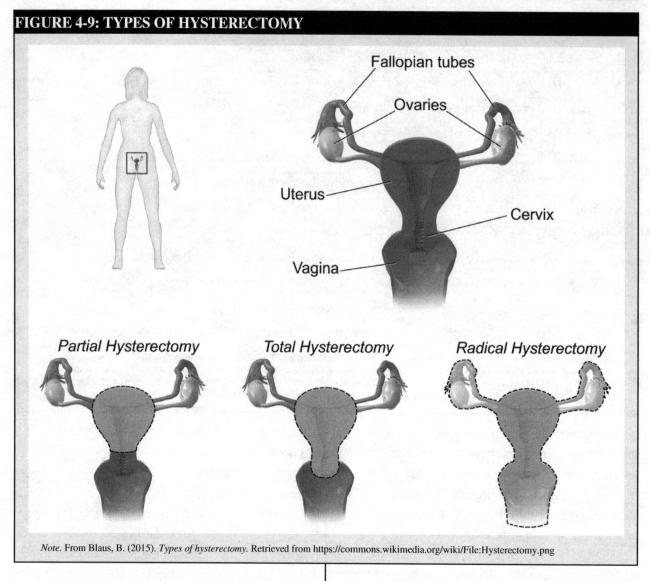

Partial Hysterectomy   Total Hysterectomy   Radical Hysterectomy

Note. From Blaus, B. (2015). *Types of hysterectomy.* Retrieved from https://commons.wikimedia.org/wiki/File:Hysterectomy.png

Preoperative teaching should include a review of postoperative care and what the woman should expect after surgery. Education and anticipatory guidance are warranted regarding perineal discomfort and pressure postoperatively from vaginal procedures associated with vaginal/rectal wound packing and care. Any hysterectomy creates infertility. For those who were premenopausal before surgery, removing the ovaries starts menopause. Women need to be alerted that, in addition to recovering from surgery, they will experience menopause and may have hot flashes, night sweats, and vaginal dryness (dyspareunia; National Comprehensive Cancer Network, 2017). Preoperative planning with the gyneco-logical oncologist or surgeon should include plans for addressing these symptoms based on adjuvant therapy.

Postoperative care after an abdominal or radical hysterectomy includes the same issues as after any major surgery: pain management, infection prevention, wound care to avoid excessive bleeding or infection, strategies to treat the woman's compromised urinary tract or gastric motility, and optimization of prompt ambulation to reduce deep vein thrombosis risk and build endurance. Hospital stays after radical surgery can be as long as 7 days, with at-home recovery lasting 4 to 8 weeks. If the woman undergoes a laparoscopic procedure, postoperative inpatient stays are much shorter, 1 to 2 days, with 3 to 4 weeks at home for recovery (Park, Yun, Kim, & Lee, 2016).

Radiation Therapy

Radiation therapy alone is a treatment option when the cancer is localized to cells in a specific area. Radiation therapy is also a treatment option for women who are poor surgical candidates because of pre-existing health problems.

For earlier-stage endometrial cancers when the cells are considered high grade, treatment protocols include surgery with radiation. These cancers can be staged at I, II, or III (Koh et al., 2014). Radiation therapy to the cancerous area can shrink the tumor before or after surgery.

Healthcare providers may recommend both external and internal radiation therapies when the tumor is large and fixed to the pelvic wall or other critical structures.

External Radiation

For external radiation treatment, the radiation source is outside of the body and targets the beam through the skin. A typical course of external beam radiation therapy is 5 days a week for 4 to 6 weeks. Although each treatment takes less than a half hour, the daily visits to the radiation center may be tiring.

As preparation to target the treatment field, the radiation team marks the field with permanent ink or injected dye. Additional preparation may include creating a customized mold of the pelvis and lower back. The mold immobilizing the targeted treatment area ensures consistent radiation beams to the targeted tumor cells during each treatment.

Internal Radiation

Internal radiation therapy or vaginal brachytherapy can be administered while the person is in the hospital or is an outpatient. The healthcare provider inserts a radiation-source cylinder into the woman's vagina. With this method, the radiation cylinder treats the area it contacts, such as the vaginal cuff. Adjacent structures to the cylinder, such as the bladder and rectum, receive less radiation exposure than the area in direct contact with the cylinder. Another internal radiation method is the insertion of a special applicator with radiation pellets into the woman's vagina. When this choice of treatment is indicated, the procedure is scheduled 4 to 6 weeks after the hysterectomy. Radiation safety and education are part of the treatment plan based on the modality of treatment selected.

Side Effects of Radiation Therapy

Negative side effects of radiation therapy can include fatigue, nausea, and diarrhea. Radiation treatment–prompted fatigue worsens over the radiation treatment period and lasts a few weeks beyond the end of treatment. Healthcare providers manage nausea, vomiting, and diarrhea with prescribed and over-the-counter medications (National Comprehensive Cancer Network, 2017). These side effects can be more intense when chemotherapy is combined with radiation.

Skin changes from external radiation beam therapy are also common, with the skin in the treated area turning red and/or sunburned (National Comprehensive Cancer Network, 2017). Damaged, irritated skin cells from treatment can be temporarily red or permanently discolored. Irritated skin can become infected and develop cellulitis. Nursing care includes teaching and interventions to clean and protect the radiation-exposed skin, and providing comfort including suggestions for adaptive clothing.

Additional negative side effects from radiation therapy can include bladder irritation (radiation cystitis), prompting urinary tract discomfort and urinary tract infection symptoms, such as an atypical urge to urinate, burning, and frequent urination. Radiation therapy can cause anemia (low red blood cells) and leukopenia (low white blood cells), resolving when radiation treatments end.

Pelvic radiation therapy may cause scar tissue to form in the vagina. The scar tissue can shorten and narrow the vagina, causing vaginal stenosis, which makes vaginal intercourse painful. Strategies to prevent vaginal stenosis include the woman intentionally stretches the walls of her vagina several times a week, by having sexual intercourse three to four times per week, or by using a vaginal dilator (a plastic or rubber tube that stretches out the vagina).

Hormone Therapy

HT is a treatment option for women who are not candidates for surgery or radiation therapy. Helathcare providers also prescribe HT for women with metastatic disease.

Progestins

HT used for endometrial cancer is progestins (Braun et al., 2016). The two common progestin treatments are medroxyprogesterone acetate (Provera) and megestrol acetate (Megace). Progestins slow endometrial cancer cell growth. Their side effects include increased blood sugar levels (notable for women with diabetes), hot flashes, night sweats, and weight gain. Blood clots are not associated with progestin treatment.

Tamoxifen

Tamoxifen, an antiestrogen treatment for breast cancer, is also a treatment for advanced or recurrent endometrial cancer (Koh et al., 2014). The goal of tamoxifen therapy is to prevent circulating estrogens from stimulating growth of the cancer cells. Even though tamoxifen may prevent estrogen from nourishing the cancer cells, it acts like a weak estrogen in other areas of the body. It does not cause bone loss, but it can prompt hot flashes and vaginal dryness.

Aromatase Inhibitors

When ovaries are removed (or are not functioning), estrogen is still made in fat tissue and to a lesser extent in the adrenal glands. This becomes the body's main source of estrogen. Aromatase inhibitors can stop estrogen from forming and reduce estrogen levels (Koh et al., 2014). Examples of aromatase inhibitors include letrozole (Femara), anastrozole (Arimidex), and exemestane (Aromasin). Aromatase inhibitor negative side effects include hot flashes and muscle pain. If a woman takes aromatase inhibitors for many years, she is at risk for weakened bones, sometimes advancing to osteoporosis.

Chemotherapy

Chemotherapy treatment options for endometrial cancer include combination protocols, consisting of doxorubicin (Adriamycin), cisplatin, carboplatin, paclitaxel (Taxol), topotecan (Hycamtin), bevacizumab (Avastin), and/or ifosfamide (Koh et al., 2014). Side effects of these systemic agents are discussed in Table 3-9.

CASE STUDY

C.C. is a 63-year-old Asian woman who presents to her primary care physician with intermittent vaginal bleeding for 3 months. She reports that the discharge occasionally was yellow and watery. She also reports pain on urination and has had problems with swelling in her abdomen, such that her skirts and pants are tight.

On pelvic examination, her clinician evaluated the size, shape, and consistency of her uterus and scheduled her for a hysteroscopy to obtain a sufficient endometrial biopsy. C.C. also underwent a vaginal probe ultrasonography with biopsy. The pathology report indicated that C.C. has endometrial adenocarcinoma.

C.C.'s surgeon performed a total abdominal hysterectomy, bilateral salpingo-oophorec-

tomy, and lymph node biopsy to stage her tumor. Pathological and staging results indicated T1c disease (AJCC staging) or stage 1C (FIGO staging). She discussed treatment options with her surgeon and oncologist, and opted to have her care team manage her with close observation, rather than add radiation therapy or chemotherapy.

After surgery, C.C. had periods of diarrhea and fatigue. She also experienced estrogen deficiency, manifested by vaginal dryness (dyspareunia). Her postoperative pain was controlled with hydrocodone with acetaminophen (Vicodin) accompanied with a stool softener. Her appetite and energy gradually returned, and she was back at work as a part-time sixth-grade teacher's aide 4 weeks after surgery.

Following surgery for the next 2 years, C.C. dutifully had follow-up checkups every 2 to 3 months. These checkups included a pelvic examination, complete blood count, and metabolic panel. Every 6 months for the first year posttreatment, she had a transvaginal ultrasound. She also underwent bone densitometry, which demonstrated osteopenia. During the third year postsurgery, checkups were scheduled every 6 months.

Additional Information

C.C.'s medical history is remarkable for the use of unopposed estrogens (estrogen without progesterone) for 10 years, no pregnancies (nulliparity), and menopause, which began after age 55 years. Estrogen withdrawal postsurgery prompted hot flashes, irritability, and osteoporosis. She and her physician discussed treatment options for these symptoms, which include evidence-based approaches to manage side effects.

C.C.'s social network is limited. She lives alone with her cats. She has a niece who lives nearby and looks in on her every 2 weeks. Her social support group is limited to a few neighbors and some teachers at her school. She plans to retire within the next 4 months and live on a

fixed income that is supplemented with social security checks. She fears that her medical bills will challenge her ability to stay healthy in her postretirement years.

She reveals that she takes Japanese herbs for her well-being and practices Reiki. In addition, C.C. has decided to boost her immune system with supplements that she has heard about on late-night television infomercials.

Questions

1. What classic symptom of endometrial cancer did C.C. have?

2. What risk factors for endometrial cancer does C.C. have?

3. Which of C.C.'s health practices might interfere with treatment?

Answers

1. Intermittent vaginal bleeding, especially in a postmenopausal woman, is an early sign of endometrial cancer. Later symptoms, not necessarily associated with early detection, are pain with urination, vaginal discharge, ascites, and lower-extremity swelling.

2. C.C. has a history of unopposed estrogen therapy (estrogen without progesterone to protect the uterus). She is nulliparous and experienced a later menopause. Regular screening might have resulted in the early detection of her endometrial cancer. Access to culturally sensitive healthcare providers may be limited in her geographic area. Awareness and health literacy are issues. Patients may be reluctant to engage in early detection or may not be fully informed of the importance of early detection.

3. C.C. uses Japanese herbs and supplements she ordered through a television infomercial. The purity of these substances is suspect. More importantly, these agents may interfere with other prescribed medications. The nurse needs to assess for these potential interac-

tions, explore and document use, and encourage C.C. to share the information with the prescribing healthcare providers.

SUMMARY

Endometrial cancer, the most common gynecological cancer, is a highly curable cancer when detected early. Atypical pain and/or uterine bleeding are early symptoms of this cancer. In addition to nonmodifiable genetic risk factors, additional risk factors include obesity, nulliparity, and smoking. The standard treatment for endometrial cancer remains surgery, although radiation therapy plays a therapeutic role alone or in combination with surgery and hormonal treatment. Treatment for advanced-stage endometrial cancers includes chemotherapy regimens.

EXAM QUESTIONS

CHAPTER 4
Questions 18–26

Note: Choose the one option that BEST answers each question.

18. The risk factors for endometrial cancer include

    a. hypotension, early menopause, and infertility.

    b. obesity (more than 20 lb overweight), no children, and history of breast or ovarian cancer.

    c. many children and early menopause.

    d. weight loss, early menopause, and productive cough.

19. Key indicators of hereditary nonpolyposis colorectal cancer include a family history of

    a. breast and endometrial cancer.

    b. endometrial, colon, ovarian, and stomach cancer.

    c. colorectal and liver cancer.

    d. pancreatic, ovarian, and stomach cancer.

20. Endometrial cancer prevention efforts target

    a. reduction of modifiable risk factors for endometrial cancer.

    b. the use of estrogen-only hormone therapy.

    c. obtaining annual Pap smears until age 70 years.

    d. obtaining routine CA-125 blood tests with annual checkups.

21. Two benign conditions of the uterus are

    a. human papillomavirus and postmenopausal bleeding.

    b. pelvic inflammatory disease and ectopic pregnancy.

    c. vaginal stenosis and chlamydia.

    d. endometriosis and fibroids.

22. The most common symptom of endometrial cancer that merits prompt evaluation is

    a. abnormal or unexpected vaginal bleeding.

    b. urinary frequency in a woman older than 35 years.

    c. pain during coitus.

    d. bowel irregularities.

23. The most frequent endometrial cancer cell type is

    a. adenocarcinoma.

    b. uterine papillary serous.

    c. squamous cell.

    d. clear cell.

24. In stage III endometrial cancer, the tumor

    a. has invaded the bladder.

    b. remains confined to the uterus.

    c. has spread outside the uterus, but not to the bladder.

    d. has spread only to the cervix.

continued on next page

25. Treatment for endometrial cancer can include

    a. surgery, radiation, and chemotherapy.

    b. surgery only.

    c. surgery and radiation only.

    d. surgery, radiation, and hormonal therapy.

26. Radiation therapy options for endometrial cancer

    a. can shrink the tumor only if it is administered before surgery.

    b. are the sole modality of therapy.

    c. can be delivered only with external beam radiation.

    d. can be administered by external beam and/or brachytherapy.

REFERENCES

Abu-Rustum, N. R. (2014). Sentinel lymph node mapping for endometrial cancer: A modern approach to surgical staging. *Journal of the National Comprehensive Cancer Network, 12*(2), 288-297.

American Cancer Society. (2016). *Cancer facts and figures for African Americans – 2016-2018*. Atlanta, GA: Author.

American Cancer Society. (2017a). *Cancer facts and figures – 2017*. Atlanta, GA: Author.

American Cancer Society. (2017b). *Cancer prevention and early detection facts and figures – 2017-2018*. Atlanta, GA: Author.

Amin, M. B., Edge, S., Greene, F., Byrd, D. R., Brookland, R. K., Washington, M. K., … Meyer, L. R. (Eds.). (2017). *AJCC cancer staging manual* (8th ed.). New York, NY: Springer.

Blaus, B. (2015). *Types of hysterectomy*. Retrieved from https://commons.wikimedia.org/wiki/File:Hysterectomy.png

Blausen Medical. (2015). *Hysteroscopy*. Retrieved from https://commons.wikimedia.org/wiki/File:Hysteroscopy.png

Braun, M. M., Overbeek-Wager, E. A., & Grumbo, R. J. (2016). Diagnosis and management of endometrial cancer. *American Family Physician, 93*(6), 468-474.

Creasman, W. T. (2009). Revised FIGO staging for carcinoma of the vulva, cervix and endometrium. *International Journal of Gynecology and Obstetrics, 105*, 103-104.

Edge, S. B., Byrd, D. R., Carducci, M., Compton, C. C., Fritz, A. G., Greene, F. L., & Trotti, A. (2010). *AJCC cancer staging manual* (7th ed.). New York, NY: Springer.

Häggström, M. (2014). Medical gallery of Mikael Häggström 2014. *Wikiversity Journal of Medicine, 1*(2), 8. doi:10.15347/wjm/2014.008

Koh, W. J., Greer, B. E., Abu-Rustum, N. R., Apte, S. M., Campos, S. M., Chan, J., … Hughes, M. (2014). Uterine neoplasms, version 1.2014. *Journal of the National Comprehensive Cancer Network, 12*(2), 248-280.

Kvaskoff, M., Mu, F., Terry, K. L., Harris, H. R., Poole, E. M., Farland, L., & Missmer, S. A. (2015). Endometriosis: A high-risk population for major chronic diseases? *Human Reproduction Update, 21*(4), 500-516. doi:10.1093/humupd/dmv013

Lai, C. R., Hsu, C. Y., Hang, J. F., & Li, A. F. Y. (2015). The diagnostic value of routine papanicolaou smears for detecting endometrial cancers: An update. *Acta Cytologica, 59*(4), 315-318.

National Comprehensive Cancer Network (2017). *Uterine Neoplasms Version 1.2017*. Available at nccn.org.

Park, D. A., Yun, J. E., Kim, S. W., & Lee, S. H. (2016). Surgical and clinical safety and effectiveness of robot-assisted laparoscopic hysterectomy compared to conventional laparoscopy and laparotomy for cervical cancer: A systematic review and meta-analysis. *European Journal of Surgical Oncology (EJSO)*. doi:http://dx.doi.org/10.1016/j.ejso.2016.07.017

U.S. Department of Health and Human Services, National Institutes of Health, National Cancer Institute. (n.d.). *SEER stat fact sheets: Endometrial cancer.* Retrieved from http://seer.cancer.gov/statfacts/html/corp.html

U.S. Department of Health and Human Services, National Institutes of Health, National Cancer Institute. (2001). *Visuals online: Pelvic exam illustration.* Retrieved from https://visualsonline.cancer.gov/details.cfm?imageid=1786

U.S. Department of Health and Human Services, National Institutes of Health, National Cancer Institute. (2007). *Visuals online: Uterus and nearby organs.* Retrieved from https://visualsonline.cancer.gov/details.cfm?imageid=4369

U.S. Department of Health and Human Services, National Institutes of Health, National Cancer Institute. (2013). *Visuals online: Dilatation and curettage.* Retrieved from https://visualsonline.cancer.gov/details.cfm?imageid=9114

van Hanegem, N., Prins, M. M. C., Bongers, M. Y., Opmeer, B. C., Sahota, D. S., Mol, B. W. J., & Timmermans, A. (2016). The accuracy of endometrial sampling in women with postmenopausal bleeding: A systematic review and meta-analysis. *European Journal of Obstetrics & Gynecology and Reproductive Biology, 197,* 147-155. doi:10.1016/j.ejogrb.2015.12.008

Weitzel, J. N., Blazer, K. R., MacDonald, D. J., Culver, J. O., & Offit, K. (2011). Genetics, genomics and cancer risk assessment: State of the art and future directions in the era of personalized medicine. *CA: A Cancer Journal for Clinicians, 61*(5), 327-359. doi:10.3322/caac.20128

Wise, M. R., Jordan, V., Lagas, A., Showell, M., Wong, N., Lensen, S., & Farquhar, C. M. (2016). Obesity and endometrial hyperplasia and cancer in premenopausal women: A systematic review. *American Journal of Obstetrics and Gynecology, 214*(6), 689. doi:e1-689.e17. doi:10.1016/j.ajog.2016.01.175

CHAPTER 5

OVARIAN CANCER

LEARNING OUTCOME

After completing this chapter, the learner will be able to identify the epidemiology, risk factors, detection strategies, staging, and treatment options for ovarian cancer.

CHAPTER OBJECTIVES

After completing this chapter, the learner will be able to:

1. Describe the epidemiology of ovarian cancer.

2. Identify the main risk factors for ovarian cancer.

3. Describe hereditary cancer syndromes associated with ovarian cancer.

4. Explain the diagnostic evaluation and staging for ovarian cancer.

5. Identify available treatment modalities for ovarian cancer.

INTRODUCTION

Ovarian cancer is one of the deadliest gynecological cancers. Unfortunately, there are few early signs and symptoms of ovarian cancer. In the majority of cases, when women present with ovarian cancer, it has progressed to a more advanced stage of malignancy. This chapter focuses on the known risks for ovarian cancer and the standard treatments. Because of the high morbidity of an ovarian cancer diagnosis, the initial workup and continuing follow-up after treatment are major nursing responsibilities.

EPIDEMIOLOGY

Ovarian cancer remains a treatment challenge in gynecological cancer. It is a deadly cancer because there are few symptoms, and most symptoms are vague (American Cancer Society [ACS], 2017a). See Box 5-1 for epidemiological facts about ovarian cancer.

In addition, tools for the early detection of ovarian cancer are limited. Thus, the disease is often identified when it is more advanced. Although strides have been made in ovarian cancer treatment, especially with chemotherapy, options for treatment still remain somewhat limited and have variable effectiveness. The median age of diagnosis is 63 years (see Figure 5-1). Survival depends on the stage at which the ovarian cancer is detected (see Figure 5-2). However, if ovarian cancer is detected early, approximately 9 of 10 women will live for at least 5 years with the disease. Ovarian cancer is slightly more common in White women (see Figure 5-3). The median age of death from ovarian cancer is 70 years (see Figure 5-4).

continued on page 118

BOX 5-1: EPIDEMIOLOGICAL FACTS REGARDING OVARIAN CANCER

- An estimated 22,440 new cases expected annually

- Accounts for about 3% of all cancers among women

- Second most frequently diagnosed gynecological cancer

- Since 1998, incidence rates have decreased by about 1% in White women and 0.4% in Black women

- An estimated 14,080 deaths are expected annually

- Causes more deaths than any other cancer of the female reproductive system (5% of all cancer deaths in women)

- Women younger than 45 years are more likely to survive 5 years (77%) after diagnosis compared with women 65 years and older (22%)

- Overall, the 5- and 10-year relative survival rate of ovarian cancer patients is 46% and 29%, respectively

- If diagnosed at the localized stage, the 5-year survival rate is 92%; however, only about 15% of all cases are detected at this stage

- If diagnosed with regional and distant disease, 5-year survival rates are 73% and 29%, respectively

- The 10-year relative survival rate for all stages combined is 46%

Note. Adapted from American Cancer Society. (2017a). *Cancer facts and figures – 2017.* Atlanta, GA: Author.

FIGURE 5-1: AGE DISTRIBUTION: OVARIAN CANCER

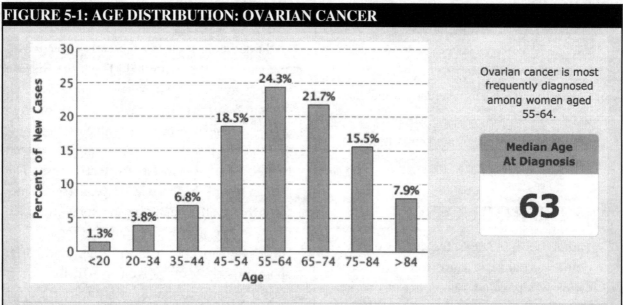

Ovarian cancer is most frequently diagnosed among women aged 55-64.

Median Age At Diagnosis

63

SEER 18 2010-2014, All Races, Females

Note. From U.S. Department of Health and Human Services, National Institutes of Health, National Cancer Institute. (n.d.b). *SEER stat fact sheets: Ovarian cancer.* Retrieved from http://seer.cancer.gov/statfacts/html/ovary.html

FIGURE 5-2: PERCENTAGE OF CASES AND 5-YEAR SURVIVAL BY STAGE AT DIAGNOSIS: OVARIAN CANCER, 2007 TO 2013

Percent of Cases by Stage

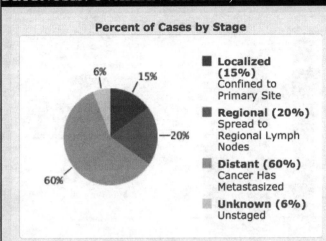

- **Localized (15%)** Confined to Primary Site
- **Regional (20%)** Spread to Regional Lymph Nodes
- **Distant (60%)** Cancer Has Metastasized
- **Unknown (6%)** Unstaged

5-Year Relative Survival

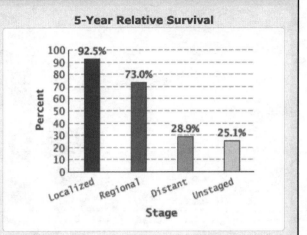

SEER 18 2007-2013, All Races, Females by SEER Summary Stage 2000

The earlier ovarian cancer is diagnosed, the better chance a woman has of surviving 5 years after diagnosis. For ovarian cancer, 14.8% of cases are diagnosed at the local stage. The 5-year survival rate for localized ovarian cancer is 92.5%.

Note. From U.S. Department of Health and Human Services, National Institutes of Health, National Cancer Institute. (n.d.b). *SEER stat fact sheets: Ovarian cancer.* Retrieved from http://seer.cancer.gov/statfacts/html/ovary.html

FIGURE 5-3: NUMBER OF NEW CASES PER 100,000 PERSONS BY RACE/ETHNICITY: OVARIAN CANCER, 2010 TO 2014

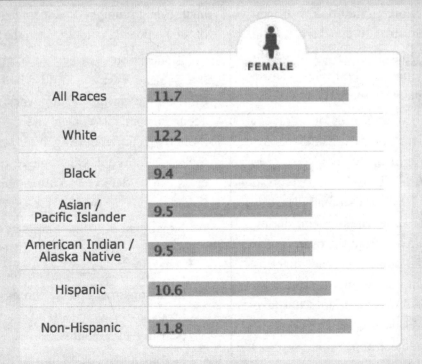

FEMALE

All Races	11.7
White	12.2
Black	9.4
Asian / Pacific Islander	9.5
American Indian / Alaska Native	9.5
Hispanic	10.6
Non-Hispanic	11.8

Note. From U.S. Department of Health and Human Services, National Institutes of Health, National Cancer Institute. (n.d.b). *SEER stat fact sheets: Ovarian cancer.* Retrieved from http://seer.cancer.gov/statfacts/html/ovary.html

FIGURE 5-4: PERCENTAGE OF DEATHS BY AGE GROUP: OVARIAN CANCER, 2010 TO 2014

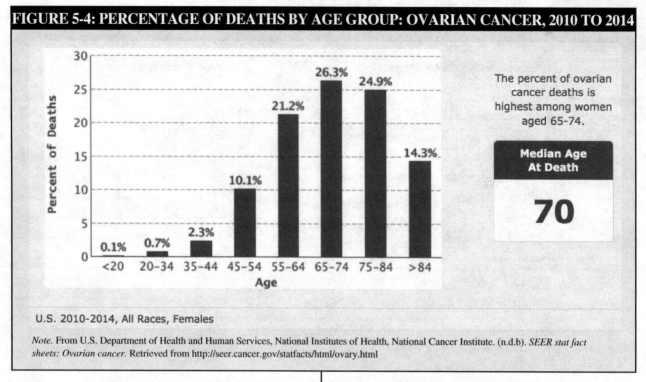

The percent of ovarian cancer deaths is highest among women aged 65-74.

Median Age At Death

70

U.S. 2010-2014, All Races, Females

Note. From U.S. Department of Health and Human Services, National Institutes of Health, National Cancer Institute. (n.d.b). *SEER stat fact sheets: Ovarian cancer.* Retrieved from http://seer.cancer.gov/statfacts/html/ovary.html

ANATOMY

A woman's ovaries have two roles: to produce eggs and to produce the female hormones estrogen and progesterone, which are integral to reproduction. In addition, estrogen and progesterone contribute to the characteristic changes that begin female puberty: development of breasts, body shape, and body hair. These hormones regulate the menstrual cycle.

Each of the two ovaries lies on adjacent sides of the uterus – the hollow organ that holds a growing embryo as it becomes a fetus (see Figure 5-5). Each ovary is about the size of an almond. Every month when a woman menstruates, one of the ovaries releases an egg during ovulation. The egg travels from the ovary to the uterus through the fallopian tube and, if fertilized, the egg implants in the uterus, where an embryo develops. If fertilization does not take place, menstruation results and the egg is part of the sluffing of the endometrium.

OVARIAN CYSTS

As with other cancer cell processes, ovarian cancer cells grow, divide, and produce more cells, creating tumors that are benign or malignant. Benign tumors do not spread to other parts of the body and do not threaten the woman's life.

A variation of a benign ovarian growth is the ovarian cyst – a fluid-filled sac that can form on the surface of the ovary. Cysts usually occur in younger women and can disappear on their own, not requiring intervention. If they remain, a surgeon can remove them. Ovarian cysts can be detected on ultrasound (Ackerman, Irshad, Lewis, & Anis, 2013; see Figure 5-6).

Functional cysts, or simple cysts, are part of the normal process of the menstrual cycle.

- Follicle cysts form when the sac does not break open to release the egg and the sac keeps growing. This type of cyst can disappear in 1 to 3 months.

- Corpus luteum cysts form if the sac does not dissolve. Instead, the sac seals off after the egg is released, followed by a fluid buildup

FIGURE 5-5: FEMALE REPRODUCTIVE ANATOMY

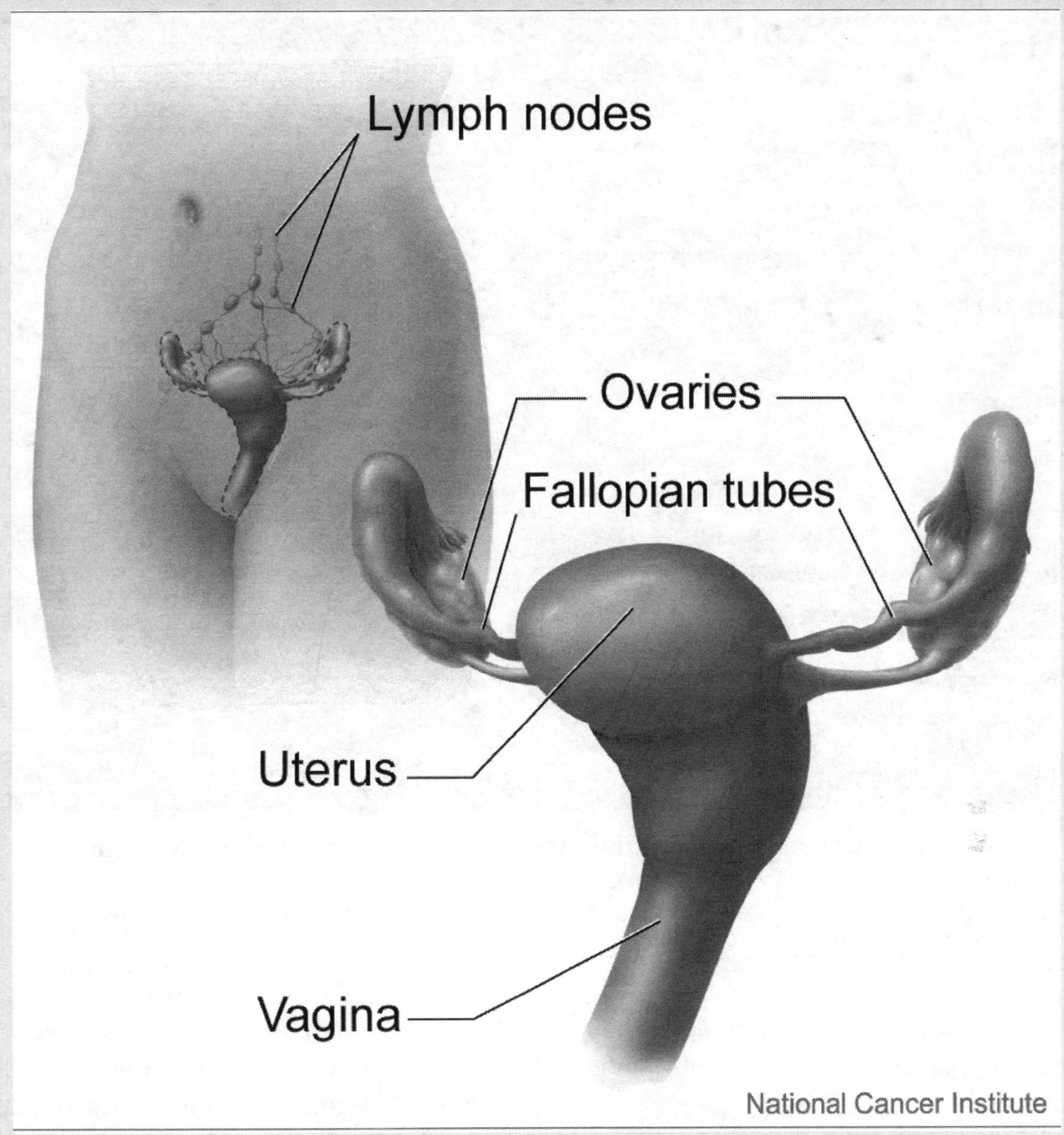

Lymph nodes located in the female reproductive area are shown, and an inset provides a close-up view of the ovaries, fallopian tubes, uterus, and vagina.

Note. From U.S. Department of Health and Human Services, National Institutes of Health, National Cancer Institute. (2006). *Female reproductive system (cervix, ovaries, uterus).* Retrieved from https://visualsonline.cancer.gov/details.cfm?imageid=4278

in the sac. Most of these cysts disappear after a few weeks, but they can grow to 8 to 10 cm. They may bleed or twist the ovary and cause pain. They are rarely malignant. Some drugs that prompt ovulation, such as Clomid or Serophene, can increase the risk for these cysts (Ackerman et al., 2013).

Other types of ovarian cysts include the following:

• Endometriomas form in women who have endometriosis. This problem occurs when tissue that looks and acts like the lining of the uterus grows outside the uterus. The tissue may attach to the ovary and form a

FIGURE 5-6: ULTRASONOGRAPHY OF OVARIAN CYST

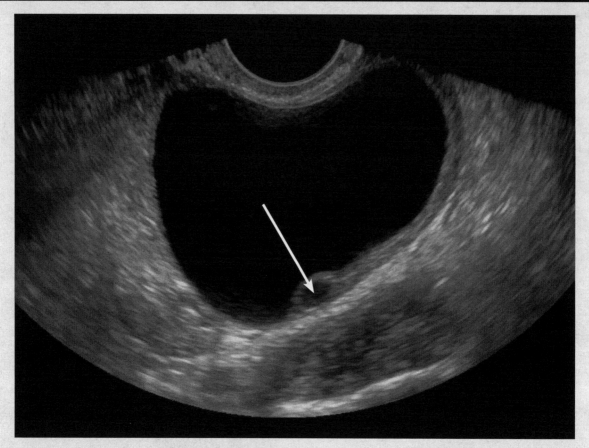

A left ovarian cyst (5 cm) pointed to with an arrow on this ultrasound. This is a benign follicular cyst.

Note. From Heilman, J. (2016). *A left ovarian cyst (5 cm) as seen on ultrasound.* Retrieved from https://commons.wikimedia.org/wiki/ File:LargeLeftOvCyst5cm.png

growth. These cysts can be painful during the menstrual cycle and occasionally during intercourse.

- Cystadenomas form from cells on the outer surface of the ovary. They can become large and cause pain.

- Dermoid cysts contain many types of cells. They may be filled with hair, teeth, and other tissues that become part of the cyst. They can become large and cause pain.

- Polycystic ovaries form cysts when eggs mature within the sacs but are not released. The cycle then repeats. The sacs continue to grow, and many cysts form.

Women may need surgery to remove the cyst or ovary to make sure that it is not ovarian cancer (Ackerman et al., 2013). Circumstances that are more likely to warrant surgery include

- complex ovarian cysts that do not go away,

- cysts that are causing symptoms and do not go away,

- simple ovarian cysts that are larger than 10 cm, and

- cysts in women who are near menopause or past menopause.

(Ackerman et al., 2013)

RISK FACTORS

Age, demographics, reproductive history, and lifestyle are risk factors for ovarian cancer. The risk of developing ovarian cancer increases with age; it is rare in women younger than 40 years, and most ovarian cancers develop after menopause. Half of all ovarian cancers diagnosed are found in women older than 63 years (see Figure 5-1).

Nulliparity increases the risk for ovarian cancer. Among the general population, parity decreases the risk for ovarian cancer compared with the risk of nulliparous women. After a woman has her first pregnancy, subsequent pregnancies appear to further decrease the risk for ovarian cancer. A 30% reduction in risk for ovarian cancer is associated with pregnancy at age 25 or earlier (National Comprehensive Cancer Network [NCCN], 2016b).

In addition to pregnancy, research has associated lactation and the use of oral contraceptives with a protective effect against ovarian cancer. Estimates show that the risk of developing ovarian cancer is 40% to 60% lower in women who use oral contraceptives, even if they stopped using them 10 to 30 years earlier (Doubeni, Doubeni, Myers, & Doubeni, 2016). In addition, women who undergo a bilateral salpingectomy or oophorectomy have a reduced risk of developing ovarian cancer (NCCN, 2016a).

Unfortunately, the most striking risk factors for ovarian cancer are linked to heredity and genetic syndromes that are out of the woman's control. Such syndromes may account for approximately 10% to 15% of all ovarian cancers (Weitzel, Blazer, MacDonald, Culver, & Offit, 2011). Current guidelines recommend that all women with a diagnosis of ovarian cancer, regardless of family history, be referred to a credentialed genetics healthcare provider for genetic evaluation (NCCN, 2016a, 2016b).

Research has linked the hereditary risk associated with ovarian cancer to multiple hereditary cancer syndromes, including hereditary breast and ovarian cancer in the *BRCA1/2* genes (lifetime risk of up to 50%; see Chapter 3), hereditary nonpolyposis colorectal cancer (HNPCC; lifetime risk of at least 12%; see Chapter 4), and multiple other syndromes (see Table 5-1; Helder-Woolderink et al., 2016). Women with ovarian cancers caused by some of these inherited gene mutations may have a better outlook than patients who do not have a family history of ovarian cancer. This may be because of aggressive screening and, most often, because of the implementation of primary prevention strategies (Mahon, 2014).

A diet high in animal fats increases the risk for developing ovarian cancer (ACS, 2017b). Recommendations include a diet rich in fruits and vegetables, which may have a small effect in preventing some ovarian cancers. Studies also advance the idea that supplementation with vitamins A, C, and E may decrease cancer risk, but no definitive guidelines have emerged (ACS, 2017b).

SIGNS AND SYMPTOMS

Signs and symptoms of ovarian cancer can be vague (ACS, 2017). In general, women report symptoms as the ovarian cancer tumor cells grow (Ebell, Culp, & Radke, 2016). These symptoms include

- abdominal swelling or abdominal pain;
- vaginal bleeding between periods or after menopause;
- bloating, gas, indigestion, or cramps;
- pelvic pain;
- loss of appetite;
- feeling full after a small meal, or feeling full quickly;

TABLE 5-1: HEREDITARY SYNDROMES ASSOCIATED WITH INCREASED RISK FOR DEVELOPING OVARIAN CANCER

Genes	Associated Cancer Risks
MSH1[a] *MSH2*[a] *MSH6*[a] *EPCAM*[a] *PMS2*[a]	Endometrial, colorectal, ovarian, gastric, pancreatic, biliary tract, urinary tract, small-bowel, brain, sebaceous neoplasms
BRCA1/ BRCA2	Female breast, male breast, ovarian, prostate, pancreatic, fallopian tube, primary peritoneal, endometrial, melanoma
PALB2	Female breast, male breast, pancreatic, ovarian
CHEK2	Female breast, male breast, colon, prostate, thyroid, endometrial, ovarian
TP53	Female breast, endometrial, soft tissue sarcoma, osteosarcoma, brain, hematological malignancies, adrenocortical carcinoma
BARD1	Female breast, ovarian
STK11	Female breast, colorectal, pancreatic, gastric, ovarian, lung, small intestine, cervical, endometrial, testicular tumors
BRIP1	Female breast, ovarian
RAD51C	Female breast, ovarian
RAD51D	Female breast, ovarian

[a]Genes associated with hereditary nonpolyposis colorectal cancer.

Note. Adapted from National Comprehensive Cancer Network. (2016b). *Ovarian cancer: Including fallopian tube and peritoneal cancer, version 1.2016;* National Comprehensive Cancer Network. (2016a). *Genetic/familial: High-risk assessment: Breast and ovarian, version 2.2016.* Weitzel, J. N., Blazer, K. R., MacDonald, D. J., Culver, J. O., & Offit, K. (2011). Genetics, genomics and cancer risk assessment: State of the art and future directions in the era of personalized medicine. *CA: A Cancer Journal for Clinicians, 61*(5), 327-359. doi:10.3322/caac.20128

- changes in bowel or bladder habits; and
- weight loss or weight gain.

PREVENTION, SCREENING, AND DIAGNOSTIC EVALUATION

Unfortunately, no definitive strategies for women to prevent ovarian cancer exist. General strategies to prevent ovarian cancer match those for other gynecological malignancies. They include having an annual pelvic examination to screen for symptoms, reducing dietary fat intake, increasing dietary intake of vitamin A, and using oral contraceptives for birth control in younger women (ACS, 2017a; Doubeni et al., 2016).

Women with a known mutation in *BRCA1/2*, a mutation associated with HNPCC, or other susceptibility mutations must give serious consideration to a prophylactic oophorectomy. Most often this is a laparoscopic procedure that is offered to patients between 35 and 45 years of age (NCCN, 2016b). With this surgery, risk reduces for over 95% in women with a known mutation (Weitzel et al., 2011). Genetic testing can clarify this risk and is often very helpful for women as they determine whether the benefits of an oophorectomy outweigh the risks (Weitzel et al., 2011). A small percentage of women may develop a primary peritoneal carcinoma (PPC), similar in appearance to ovarian cancer, after prophylactic oophorectomy (NCCN, 2016a).

At present, there is no evidenced-based effective screening recommendation for ovarian cancer (ACS, 2017a). Any woman with symptoms should have a prompt and thorough evaluation, which includes pelvic examination, imaging with ultrasound and other techniques, and blood work.

Pelvic Examination

For women of average risk (age and demographics), an annual bimanual rectovaginal examination (pelvic examination) is a consideration (Ebell, Culp, Lastinger, & Dasigi, 2015).

Standards for routine screening for women of average risk remain a dilemma with differing recommendations. The American College of Obstetricians and Gynecologists (2011) recommends an annual pelvic examination; the U.S. Preventive Services Task Force (2012) does not believe there is adequate evidence to justify an annual pelvic examination. The differences are due to the lack of a known effective means to screen for ovarian cancer (NCCN, 2016b). Risk assessment is important, and any woman with increased risk should be offered the option for a pelvic examination with or without ultrasound and/or CA-125 testing (ACS, 2017a; NCCN, 2016b). Any women with the vague symptoms associated with ovarian cancer should have a full diagnostic workup.

During a pelvic examination, the healthcare provider palpates the ovaries and uterus for size, shape, and consistency. Although a pelvic examination is an option for screening, most early ovarian tumors are difficult or impossible for even the most skilled examiner to detect. The most common reason for a healthcare provider to suspect ovarian cancer is if a mass is palpated during a pelvic examination.

A pelvic mass detected in a young girl or teenager who has not begun menstruating is likely malignant (usually a germ cell ovarian cancer). However, only 5% of masses felt on pelvic examination in menstruating women are malignancies. Certain characteristics of the mass suggest a cancerous tumor – solid, irregular, or fixed (Doubeni et al., 2016).

If a pelvic mass is detected or there are unexplained, vague symptoms associated with ovarian cancer, then additional evaluation is needed. This begins with a pelvic ultrasound and CA-125 testing. Other evaluation includes chest X-ray or computed tomography (CT), complete blood cell count with function tests, and gastrointestinal evaluation (NCCN, 2016b). Any unexplained abnormality should be further evaluated with a surgical laparotomy.

Imaging Procedures

Imaging such as CT scans, magnetic resonance imaging (MRI), and ultrasound studies can confirm whether a pelvic mass is present. Although imaging cannot confirm whether the mass is malignant without accompanying pathology, it can help assess whether tumor cells have spread to other tissues and organs.

Ultrasound

Because ovarian tumors and normal ovarian tissue often reflect sound waves differently, ultrasound determines whether a mass is solid or is a fluid-filled cyst.

Transvaginal sonography is an ultrasound test that places a small instrument (a tampon-like probe) in the vagina. It can help find a mass in the ovary, but it cannot diagnose the tumor without accompanying pathological findings (see Figure 5-6; Ackerman et al., 2013).

In studies of women at average risk for ovarian cancer, the screening tests of transvaginal sonography and CA-125 (reviewed later) did not lower the number of deaths caused by ovarian cancer (NCCN, 2016b). For this reason, transvaginal sonography and the CA-125 blood test are not recommended for routine ovarian cancer screening of women without known strong risk factors for ovarian cancer (ACS, 2017a). Although women at high risk undergo these tests, it is not known how effective they are in early detection.

Additional Imaging

When a mass is detected, additional radiological imaging will be ordered. This often includes one or more tests depending on the characteristics of the mass and blood work, as well as availability of imaging at the institution.

The CT scan can be utilized to determine whether the cancer has spread beyond the ovaries (NCCN, 2016b). An abdominal/pelvic CT shows the liver and other organs, such as the kidneys and bladder. CT scans show the size of the mass, invasion to other organs, and lymph node enlargement. Thoracic or chest CT shows whether a tumor is in the lungs; a CT scan of the chest shows more than a chest X-ray film.

In some cases, healthcare providers order an MRI scan to evaluate the brain and spinal cord for metastases (NCCN, 2016b). MRI can also be used to evaluate the bowel and rectum, urinary tract, peritoneum and mesentery, liver, lymph nodes, and uterus, as well as for the presence of ascites (NCCN, 2016b).

A positron emission tomography (PET) scan is nuclear medicine imaging that shows whether cancer cells have spread through body organs. Before the scan, the patient receives a glucose-based injection with a small amount of radioactive tracer. Because malignant cells are attracted to glucose (with the radioactive tracer), any organ with glucose lights up – the brain, the heart, and any organ with cancer cells. Coupled with a CT-targeted image, a PET-CT scan can provide a detailed image of metastatic spread of cancer cells (NCCN, 2016b).

To prepare the patient for any imaging study, the nurse advises the patient that she will be positioned, usually lying down, to best capture the image. The procedure can last a few minutes for an ultrasound to an hour or two for CT, MRI, or PET-CT scans.

Other Diagnostic Procedures

Colonoscopy

A colonoscopy provides a view of the colon ideally up to the small intestine, via a flexible tube with a tiny camera and light on its end, unless obstruction is present. The camera's view transmits to a monitor so the images can be evaluated. For patients with ovarian cancer, healthcare providers may schedule it when metastatic spread to the colon is suspected and to obtain a biopsy of colon polyps or tissue.

Nurses educate the patient before a colonoscopy; nurses focus the patient on clearing the colon with a reduced diet the day before the examination and taking a colon preparation solution at scheduled intervals the day and night before. Patients receive sedation during the procedure to manage anxiety and discomfort related to the insertion of air and the advancement of the colonoscope through the colon.

Laparoscopy

A surgeon schedules a laparoscopy using a laparoscope – another type of flexible tube with a camera on its tip – to view the ovaries and other pelvic organs and tissue, and to perform a biopsy of suspicious masses or tissue. The entry point of the laparoscope is through a small incision in the lower abdomen. During the procedure, the abdomen is inflated so that organs are visible. The camera's images are transmitted to a monitor that sends images of the pelvis or abdomen to a video monitor for review.

In addition to standard preoperative instruction (e.g., no oral intake at least 8 hours before the scheduled procedure and avoidance of blood thinners 7 to 10 days before the procedure), nurses should advise the patient that after the procedure she will experience uncomfortable abdominal pressure and possible shoulder pain (from the inflation of the abdomen during the procedure and absorption of gas through tissue) that dissipates with ambulation and when she passes gas.

Biopsy

Gynecological oncologists have the expertise to manage ovarian cancer and masses. Therefore, gynecological oncologists should manage the care of the patient at the time of laparotomy and going forward (NCCN, 2016b).

During laparoscopy or more extensive surgery, the surgeon performs a biopsy of the tissue specimens, which the pathologist evaluates for a definitive diagnosis. The surgeon uses ultrasound or CT scan to view the targeted area and captures the specimen either with a special needle that aspirates fluid (through the skin of the abdomen) or through direct extraction of tissue or a mass during surgery.

For patients with ascites (fluid buildup in the abdominal cavity), healthcare providers can extract the fluid via needle aspiration (paracentesis) for testing to identify the presence of cancer cells.

CA-125 Testing

CA-125 is a protein on the surface of ovarian cancer cells that is elevated when cancer cells are present (Doubeni et al., 2016). CA-125, released in the bloodstream, is a tumor marker that healthcare providers can trend over time to assess a woman's response to treatment or cancer status posttreatment. A CA-125 test result of greater than 35 U/mL is generally accepted as being elevated (NCCN, 2016b).

However, the CA-125 test returns a true-positive result in only about 50% of patients with stage I ovarian cancer, so it is not an adequate early-detection tool when used alone; an elevated level also can indicate the presence of other conditions, so it is not a unique marker specifically for ovarian cancer (NCCN, 2016b). For stage II, III, and IV ovarian cancer, CA-125 has an 80% chance of returning true-positive results. The other 20% of patients with ovarian cancer do not show any increase in CA-125 levels (Doubeni et al., 2016). Meanwhile, several reproductive disorders of women can cause a false-positive result. Endometriosis, benign ovarian cysts, first trimester of pregnancy, and pelvic inflammatory disease all produce higher levels of CA-125 (NCCN, 2016b).

Screening: Women at High Risk

Women who carry genetic markers (including *BRCA1/2* or mutations increasing risk of HNPCC) are at risk for ovarian cancer. Therefore, healthcare providers recommend an aggressive screening and follow-up schedule. Screening can include a thorough pelvic examination with further evaluation through ultrasound, usually on a biannual basis (NCCN, 2016b).

As a prophylactic approach, oophorectomy is performed, in which the surgeon removes the woman's ovaries before they become diseased. However, this procedure does not eliminate the woman's chances of developing ovarian cancer. Such a decision should be preceded by genetic testing and counseling (see Chapter 2; Weitzel et al., 2011).

TYPES OF OVARIAN TUMORS

Many types of tumors have their origin in the woman's ovary. Most of these are benign and never extend beyond the ovary. Benign tumors are usually treated successfully by removing either the ovary or the part of the ovary that contains the tumor. Ovarian tumors that are malignant can quickly metastasize to other parts of the body.

In general, ovarian tumors are defined and named according to the initial type of cells the tumor originated from and whether the tumor is benign or malignant. The three main categories of ovarian tumors are epithelial, germ cell, and stromal (Amin et al., 2017).

- Epithelial tumors start from the cells that cover the outer surface of the ovary. Most ovarian tumors are epithelial cell tumors.

- Germ cell tumors start from the cells that produce the ova (eggs).

- Stromal tumors start from connective tissue cells that hold the ovary together and produce the female hormones estrogen and progesterone.

Epithelial Ovarian Tumors

Benign Epithelial Tumors

Benign epithelial tumors include serous adenomas, mucinous adenomas, Brenner tumors, and serous papilloma tumors. Tumors of low malignant potential are also known as borderline epithelial ovarian cancer. These differ from typical ovarian cancers in that they do not grow into the supporting tissue of the ovary. These cancers can affect women at a younger age than the typical ovarian cancers, grow slowly, and are less life-threatening than most other ovarian cancers (NCCN, 2016b).

Malignant Epithelial Ovarian Tumors

About 85% to 90% of ovarian cancers are epithelial ovarian carcinomas (NCCN, 2016b). Epithelial ovarian cancers are classified into several types: serous, mucinous, endometrioid, and clear cell. The serous type is by far the most common. If the cells do not resemble or look like any of these subtypes, the tumor is called *undifferentiated*. Undifferentiated epithelial ovarian carcinomas tend to grow and spread more quickly than the other types. In addition to being classified by these subtypes, epithelial ovarian carcinomas are designated by a grade and a stage, as described later.

The grade classifies the tumor based on how much it looks like normal tissue on a scale of 1, 2, or 3. Grade 1 epithelial ovarian carcinomas look more like normal tissue and tend to have a better prognosis. Grade 3 epithelial ovarian carcinomas look less like normal tissue and usually have a poorer prognosis. The tumor stage is based on how far the tumor has spread (determined by imaging) from where it started in the ovary (NCCN, 2016b).

Primary Peritoneal Carcinoma

PPC is a rare cancer that is closely related to epithelial ovarian cancer (NCCN, 2016b). PPC develops in cells from the lining of the pelvis and abdomen (the peritoneum). These cells are very similar to the cells on the surface of the ovaries. Like ovarian cancer, PPC spreads along the surface of the pelvis and abdomen, so it is often difficult to determine its origin. This type of cancer can occur in women who still have their ovaries, but it is of more concern for women who have had their ovaries removed to prevent ovarian cancer. Symptoms of PPC are similar to those of ovarian cancer, including abdominal pain or bloating, nausea, vomiting, indigestion, and a change in bowel habits. Also, like ovarian cancer, PPC may elevate the blood level of CA-125.

Fallopian Tube Cancer

Fallopian tube cancer begins in the tube that carries an egg from the ovary to the uterus. Like PPC, fallopian tube cancer causes symptoms similar to those seen in women with ovarian cancer (NCCN, 2016b). The treatment and prognosis are similar to those for ovarian cancer.

Germ Cell Tumors

Germ cells are the cells that usually form the ova or eggs. Most germ cell tumors are benign, although some are cancerous and may be life-threatening. About 5% of ovarian cancers are germ cell tumors (NCCN, 2016b). There are several subtypes of germ cell tumors. The most common germ cell tumors are teratoma, dysgerminoma, endodermal sinus, and choriocarcinoma.

Stromal Tumors

Approximately 5% to 7% of ovarian cancers are ovarian stromal cell tumors. Most of these are granulosa cell tumors (Doubeni et al., 2016). More than half of stromal tumors are diagnosed in women older than 50 years; however, about 5% of stromal tumors occur in young girls. The most common symptom of these tumors is abnormal vaginal bleeding. This happens because many of these tumors produce female hormones (e.g., estrogen). These hormones can cause vaginal bleeding to start again after menopause or can cause menstrual periods and breast development in young girls. Less often, stromal tumors emit male hormones (e.g., testosterone). If male hormones are produced, the tumors can disrupt normal periods and cause facial and body hair to grow. Another symptom of stromal tumors can be sudden, severe abdominal pain when the tumor starts to bleed.

TREATMENT

Because ovarian cancer is a complicated and aggressive disease, a team of physicians may be involved in the woman's care – gynecological surgeon, medical oncologist, and radiation oncologist.

Surgery

Surgery for ovarian cancer has two main goals: to stage the cancer and to remove the ovarian tumors and any spread to adjacent organs.

Typically, the surgeon removes the uterus, both ovaries, and both fallopian tubes (a bilateral salpingo-oophorectomy). In addition, the surgeon removes the omentum (omentectomy). The surgeon also removes some lymph nodes in the pelvis and abdomen to determine whether the cancer has spread (see Figure 5-7).

If there is fluid in the pelvis or abdominal cavity, the surgeon will remove it for analysis. The surgeon may "wash" the abdominal cavity with saline solution and send that fluid for analysis. Staging is very important because ovarian cancers at different stages are treated differently. Figure 5-8 maps out staging criteria for ovarian cancer. The American Joint Commission on Cancer has established staging for ovarian cancer as follows (Amin et al., 2017):

Stage I – growth limited to the ovaries

Stage II – growth involving one or both ovaries, with pelvic extension

Stage III – tumor involving one or both ovaries, with peritoneal implants outside the pelvis and/or positive retroperitoneal or inguinal nodes; superficial liver metastases constitute stage III disease

Stage IV – distant metastases; pleural effusion with a positive cytology; parenchymal liver metastases

With debulking surgery, the surgeon removes all tumors larger than 1 cm. Patients who have had successful debulking surgery have a better prognosis after surgery than those with larger tumors remaining.

Gynecological oncologists are specialists who have training and experience in treating ovarian cancer and know how to stage and debulk ovarian cancer correctly. Women with ovarian cancer who do not have the correct or adequate surgery the first time may need to have additional surgery – performed by a gynecological surgeon – to stage and debulk the cancer.

FIGURE 5-7: FEMALE GENITAL SYSTEM

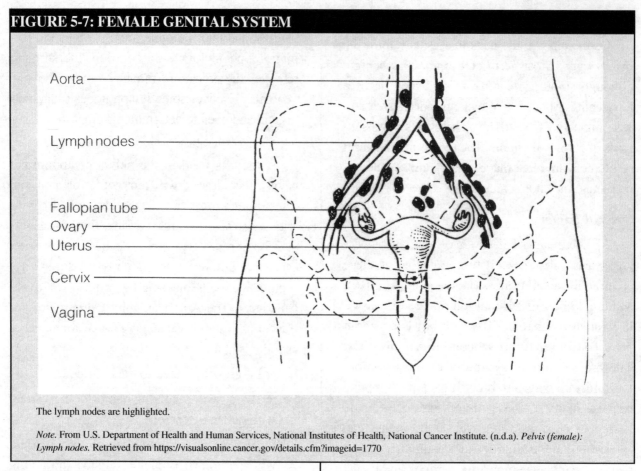

Aorta

Lymph nodes

Fallopian tube
Ovary
Uterus

Cervix

Vagina

The lymph nodes are highlighted.

Note. From U.S. Department of Health and Human Services, National Institutes of Health, National Cancer Institute. (n.d.a). *Pelvis (female): Lymph nodes.* Retrieved from https://visualsonline.cancer.gov/details.cfm?imageid=1770

Chemotherapy

After surgery, the risk for recurrence is high because microscopic cancer cells may remain or are particularly aggressive. Therefore, chemotherapy protocols are a major component of treatment. The most common combination chemotherapies that treat epithelial ovarian cancer include paclitaxel and either cisplatin or carboplatin. Table 5-2 lists selected ovarian cancer chemotherapies.

The two-drug combination of cisplatin plus paclitaxel is the current standard regimen for advanced ovarian cancer. Ovarian cancer is usually chemosensitive. These two classes of agents are often given both intravenously and by the intraperitoneal route.

Current treatment with combination chemotherapy results in a clinical complete remission rate in approximately 75% of all patients with advanced ovarian cancer (Jelovac & Armstrong, 2011). However, median progression-free survival ranges from 16 to 25 months, depending on the volume of disease present at the time of chemotherapy initiation.

Because most women with ovarian cancer who obtain a clinically complete remission will experience a relapse, numerous treatment strategies have been tested to prevent or delay recurrences. As of 2016, there was no maintenance therapy following initial therapy that improves survival rates in patients who achieve a clinically complete remission (NCCN, 2016b).

Intraperitoneal chemotherapy has been studied for more than two decades in patients with ovarian cancer. Intraperitoneal chemotherapy is delivered directly to the intraperitoneal cavity and dosed at a higher drug concentration to optimize its effect (Wright et al., 2016).

FIGURE 5-8: OVARIAN CANCER STAGING

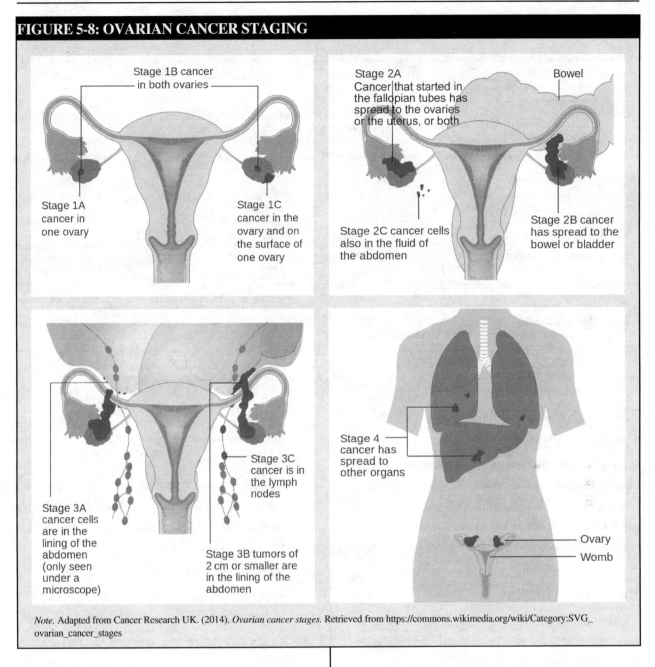

Note. Adapted from Cancer Research UK. (2014). *Ovarian cancer stages.* Retrieved from https://commons.wikimedia.org/wiki/Category:SVG_ovarian_cancer_stages

Recurrent ovarian cancer treatment focuses on control of symptoms. When women are diagnosed with ovarian cancer, the woman's CA-125 level has no prognostic significance. For patients whose elevated CA-125 normalizes with chemotherapy, an elevated CA-125 level that trends up is highly predictive of active disease. When this occurs, healthcare providers do not necessarily recommend immediate therapy (Ebell et al., 2016).

New biologic agents that target the poly (ADP-ribose) polymerase enzyme have been approved for women with ovarian cancer and known *BRCA1/2* mutations, and they have shown response to platinum-based chemotherapy (Matulonis et al., 2016; Yap, Sandhu, Carden, & de Bono, 2011). Olaparib (Lynparza) is approved for women with known *BRCA1/2* mutations as a second- and third-line therapy for ovarian cancer.

TABLE 5-2: SELECTED CHEMOTHERAPY TREATMENTS		
Agent, Trade Name (generic)	**Route**	**Side Effects**
Taxol (paclitaxel)	IV, IP	Nausea and vomiting, mucositis, hypersensitivity reactions, delayed myelosuppression
Platinol (cisplatin)	IV, IP	Nausea and vomiting, acute renal failure, peripheral neuropathy, ototoxicity, anorexia
Paraplatin (carboplatin)	IV	Hypersensitivity, nausea and vomiting, myelosuppression, alopecia, peripheral neuropathy
Adriamycin (doxorubicin)	IV	Nausea and vomiting, anorexia, mucositis, diarrhea, myelo-suppression, cardiotoxicity, fatigue
Avastin (bevacizumab)	IV	Hypertension, increased risk for bleeding
Eloxatin (oxaliplatin)	IV	Neurotoxicity, peripheral neuropathy, fatigue, nausea, vomiting, diarrhea, neutropenia, ototoxicity
Lynparza (olaparib)	Oral	Upper respiratory tract infection, anemia, nausea, vomiting, pharyngitis, increased serum creatinine, decreased hemoglobin

IP = intraperitoneal; IV = intravenous.

Note. Adapted from National Comprehensive Cancer Network. (2016b). *Ovarian cancer: Including fallopian tube and peritoneal cancer, version 1.2016*; Jelovac, D., & Armstrong, D. K. (2011). Recent progress in the diagnosis and treatment of ovarian cancer. *CA: A Cancer Journal for Clinicians, 61*(3), 183-203. doi:10.3322/caac.20113; and Wright, J. D., Hou, J. Y., Burke, W. M., Tergas, A. I., Ling, C., Hu, J. C., ... Chen, L. (2016). Utilization and toxicity of alternative delivery methods of adjuvant chemotherapy for ovarian cancer. *Obstetrics & Gynecology, 127*(6), 985-991. doi:10.1097/AOG.0000000000001436

Hormone Therapy

As an alternative to second- or third-line chemotherapy when further chemotherapy cannot be tolerated, hormone therapy is a short-term treatment when the cancer is in advanced stages. Hormone therapy options are tamoxifen or aromatase inhibitors (NCCN, 2016b).

Radiation Therapy

Radiation therapy as treatment for ovarian cancer is rare. It may be offered for palliation in focused areas of metastatic disease (NCCN, 2016b).

Ovarian Cancer Treatment Complications

Women treated for ovarian cancer may face additional complications from their treatments (i.e., surgery and chemotherapy) or from the cancer itself. These complications can include ascites, bowel obstruction, pain, pleural effusion, and malnutrition.

Due to anticipated complications, follow-up includes the following (NCCN, 2016b):

- Gynecological oncologist visits every 2 to 4 months for 2 years and then every 3 to 6 months for 3 years; annual visits after 5 years

- Physical examination including pelvic examination at each follow-up examination

- Testing for CA-125 or other tumor markers at every visit, if initially elevated

- Genetic counseling referral, if not previously done

- Complete blood cell count and metabolic panel

- Chest, abdominal, and pelvic CT, MRI, PET-CT, or PET as clinically indicated

- Chest radiography as clinically indicated

Early-Stage Ovarian Cancer Prognosis

Although ovarian cancer initial diagnosis usually occurs at a late stage, several factors can contribute to a more favorable prognosis overall. Among them are younger age, good performance status, cell type other than mucinous and clear cell, earlier stage, well-differentiated tumor, smaller disease volume before any surgical debulking, absence of ascites, and smaller residual tumor following primary cytoreductive surgery (Doubeni et al., 2016).

CASE STUDY 5-1

M.L. is a 55-year-old White woman who presents to her primary care physician with complaints of mild abdominal bloating for the past 5 months. On examination, her physician palpated a medium-size mass on her left ovary.

On ultrasound, the mass measured approximately 6 cm by 2.5 cm. (A normal ovary measures 2 cm by 3 cm.) A tubular cystic interface appeared to surround the ovary. The cyst borders appeared irregular. Doppler examination indicated large tortuous vessels within the left ovary. The right ovary was of normal size with no irregularities. These results are suggestive of a malignancy.

One week after her pelvic examination, M.L. had an exploratory laparotomy. During the procedure, M.L.'s surgeon performed a total abdominal hysterectomy, bilateral salpingo-oophorectomy, and lymph node biopsy. Combined with pathological results, including abdominal metastasis and positive lymph nodes, M.L.'s diagnosis is stage IIIC epithelial ovarian cancer. Postoperatively, the nurses caring for M.L. monitored her for signs of infection from her surgery. They managed her pain control, nutrition status, and provided psychosocial support.

After her surgery, M.L. received three aggressive courses of intraperitoneal chemotherapy – paclitaxel and cisplatin. As a supportive care intervention, M.L. required granulocyte colony-stimulating factor to increase her neutrophil count. Chemotherapy negative side effects included diarrhea, insomnia, nausea and vomiting, and sensory motor deficits.

After her third course of chemotherapy, M.L. had second-look surgery. Since her initial surgeries, M.L. had a follow-up appointment every 4 months, which included laboratory tests, a chest X-ray, and an abdominal CT scan.

At 16 months after ovarian cancer was diagnosed, repeat studies showed that her ovarian cancer had returned, spreading to her lungs and liver. As treatment, she received olaparib. After 5 months, her disease progressed.

With progression and no further treatment options, the decision was made by M.L., with the support of her family and oncology team, to engage the palliative care team. The team helped M.L. with care options to maximize her quality of life. She accepted community-based hospice services soon after care, which provided pain management and interventions for the final 4 months of her life.

Additional Information

M.L.'s medical history was remarkable for breast cancer (stage II, left breast) when she was 45 years old. Her breast cancer treatments were lumpectomy, followed by radiation therapy and adjuvant chemotherapy. Because she was estrogen-receptor-positive, she was also prescribed tamoxifen and took the medication until she was 50 years old. In the last 2 years, genetic testing determined that M.L. had the BRCA1/2 genetic factors.

Before her ovarian cancer diagnosis, M.L. was 20 lb overweight and was treated for hypertension. She dutifully had yearly follow-up physical examinations with her physician with clinical breast examinations, mammograms, and pelvic examinations. For the past 5 years, her pelvic and breast checks had been unremarkable. Although not diagnosed with diabetes herself, her father was a diabetic and died at the age of 78 years.

M.L. was divorced, the mother of two daughters, 21 and 25 years of age, and the grandmother of a 1-year-old boy. As a new mother, she breastfed both of her daughters until they were 6 months old. She started menstruation at age 12 years. Menopause was induced at age 46 years, when she received her chemotherapy for breast cancer.

M.L. was also a 20 pack-year smoker (if a person smokes one pack of cigarettes a day for 20 years, then she is a 20 pack-year smoker). She quit smoking when she was diagnosed with breast cancer.

From the time she was diagnosed with ovarian cancer, M.L. regularly self-medicated with complementary and alternative medicines to help her keep a sense of control and offset side effects from her chemotherapy regimen. She scheduled massages every 2 weeks and treated herself occasionally to aromatherapy to help her with her anxiety and nausea.

Throughout her illness and treatment, she was able to journal and practice meditation, which strengthened her spiritually. She was also a member of a cancer support group, which met biweekly at a local community center.

Questions

1. What was M.L.'s most outstanding risk factor for ovarian cancer?

2. What symptom of ovarian cancer did M.L. have?

Answers

1. Women with a mutation in *BRCA1* or *BRCA2* have an approximately 90% lifetime risk for developing breast cancer and up to a 50% lifetime risk for developing ovarian cancer. When M.L.'s *BRCA1/2* mutation was confirmed, she should have been counseled about options to reduce her ovarian cancer risk by having a prophylactic oophorectomy. Because she had a *BRCA1/2* muta-

tion, she was a candidate for olaparib.

2. Ovarian cancer has few early symptoms. Unfortunately, many women have vague gastrointestinal symptoms that are not directly linked to ovarian cancer. By the time women experience bloating or ascites, the ovarian tumor is large and at an advanced stage.

SUMMARY

Ovarian cancer usually is identified at more advanced stages. Presenting symptoms are vague or nonspecific, such as abdominal bloating or pain. Women at risk for ovarian cancer are usually older and can have a personal or family history of cancer. A woman at risk may also be obese and have never been pregnant. Screening methods include pelvic examinations with accompanying imaging. For women at high risk, regular pelvic examinations and surveillance are more frequent. To confirm an ovarian cancer diagnosis, a surgeon performs biopsies followed by the pathologist evaluation of the specimen. Once diagnosed, the patient's CA-125 level in the bloodstream is followed as a marker to evaluate treatment or cancer status. Standard treatments focus on surgery with adjuvant chemotherapy to eliminate micrometastases. Areas of study include better screening and diagnostic tools and targeted therapies that can boost the effectiveness of multimodality therapy.

EXAM QUESTIONS

CHAPTER 5
Questions 27–35

Note: Choose the one option that BEST answers each question.

27. The median age at diagnosis of ovarian cancer is

    a. 63 years.
    b. 50 years.
    c. 49 years.
    d. 70 years.

28. If ovarian cancer is detected early, approximately 9 of 10 women will live for

    a. at least 3 years with the disease.
    b. at least 5 years with the disease.
    c. at least 7 years with the disease.
    d. at least 10 years with the disease.

29. The most striking risk factors for ovarian cancer are linked to heredity and genetic syndromes that are out of the woman's control. Such syndromes may account for approximately

    a. 5% to 8% of all ovarian cancers.
    b. 10% to 15% of all ovarian cancers.
    c. 15% to 25% of all ovarian cancers.
    d. 20% to 35% of all ovarian cancers.

30. A woman has an increased risk for ovarian cancer if she

    a. is childless, had an early menarche, and is 40 years old.
    b. had a tubal ligation, had a late menarche, and is 65 years old.
    c. has a *BRCA1* mutation, is childless, and is 55 years old.
    d. had three children, had a late menarche, and is 50 years old.

31. The lifetime risk of developing ovarian cancer in a woman with a *BRCA1/2* mutation is

    a. 10%.
    b. 50%.
    c. 75%.
    d. 85%.

32. Signs of ovarian cancer include

    a. productive cough.
    b. headache.
    c. pronounced thirst.
    d. vague, nonspecific symptoms.

continued on next page

33. A diagnostic workup of ovarian cancer can include

    a. magnetic resonance imaging, transvaginal ultrasound, and surgery.

    b. bone scan, iron levels, and surgery.

    c. brain scan, gastric lavage, and surgery.

    d. oophorectomy, mammography, and sentinel node biopsy.

34. One of the goals of surgery for ovarian cancer is

    a. sterilization.

    b. reconstruction.

    c. debulking.

    d. removal of ova for future reproduction.

35. The most common combination chemotherapy agents used to treat epithelial ovarian cancer are

    a. paclitaxel and prednisone.

    b. carboplatin and paclitaxel.

    c. cisplatin and prednisone.

    d. doxorubicin (Adriamycin) and methotrexate.

REFERENCES

Ackerman, S., Irshad, A., Lewis, M., & Anis, M. (2013). Ovarian cystic lesions: A current approach to diagnosis and management. *Radiologic Clinics of North America, 51*(6), 1067-1085. doi:10.1016/j.rcl.2013.07.010

American Cancer Society. (2017a). *Cancer facts and figures – 2017.* Atlanta, GA: Author.

American Cancer Society. (2017b). *Cancer prevention and early detection facts and figures – 2017-2018.* Atlanta, GA: Author.

American College of Obstetricians and Gynecologists. (2011). The role of the obstetrician–gynecologist in the early detection of epithelial ovarian cancer. Committee Opinion No. 477. *Obstetrics and Gynecology, 117,* 742-746.

Amin, M. B., Edge, S., Greene, F., Byrd, D. R., Brookland, R. K., Washington, M. K., … Meyer, L. R. (Eds.). (2017). *AJCC cancer staging manual* (8th ed.). New York, NY: Springer.

Cancer Research UK. (2014). *Ovarian cancer stages.* Retrieved from https://commons.wikimedia.org/wiki/Category:SVG_ovarian_cancer_stages

Doubeni, C. A., Doubeni, A. R. B., Myers, A. E., & Doubeni, A. R. (2016). Diagnosis and management of ovarian cancer. *American Family Physician, 93*(11), 937-944.

Ebell, M. H., Culp, M., Lastinger, K., & Dasigi, T. (2015). A systematic review of the bimanual examination as a test for ovarian cancer. *American Journal of Preventive Medicine, 48*(3), 350-356. doi:10.1016/j.amepre.2014.10.007

Ebell, M. H., Culp, M. B., & Radke, T. J. (2016). A systematic review of symptoms for the diagnosis of ovarian cancer. *American Journal of Preventive Medicine, 50*(3), 384-394. doi:10.1016/j.amepre.2015.09.023

Heilman, J. (2016). *A left ovarian cyst (5 cm) as seen on ultrasound.* Retrieved from https://commons.wikimedia.org/wiki/File:LargeLeftOvCyst5cm.png

Helder-Woolderink, J. M., Blok, E. A., Vasen, H. F. A., Hollema, H., Mourits, M. J., & De Bock, G. H. (2016). Ovarian cancer in Lynch syndrome; a systematic review. *European Journal of Cancer, 55,* 65-73. doi:10.1016/j.ejca.2015.12.005

Jelovac, D., & Armstrong, D. K. (2011). Recent progress in the diagnosis and treatment of ovarian cancer. *CA: A Cancer Journal for Clinicians, 61*(3), 183-203. doi:10.3322/caac.20113

Mahon, S. M. (2014). Providing care for previvors: Implications for oncology nurses. *Clinical Journal of Oncology Nursing, 18*(1), 21-24. doi:10.1188/14.CJON.21-24

Matulonis, U. A., Harter, P., Gourley, C., Friedlander, M., Vergote, I., Rustin, G., … Ledermann, J. A. (2016). Olaparib maintenance therapy in patients with platinum-sensitive, relapsed serous ovarian cancer and a *BRCA* mutation: Overall survival adjusted for postprogression poly(adenosine diphosphate ribose) polymerase inhibitor therapy. *Cancer, 122*(12), 1844-1852. doi:10.1002/cncr.29995

National Comprehensive Cancer Network. (2016a). *Genetic/familial: High-risk assessment: Breast and ovarian, version 2.2017.*

National Comprehensive Cancer Network. (2016b). *Ovarian cancer: Including fallopian tube and peritoneal cancer, version 1.2016.*

U.S. Department of Health and Human Services, National Institutes of Health, National Cancer Institute. (n.d.a). *Pelvis (female): Lymph nodes.* Retrieved from https://visualsonline.cancer.gov/details.cfm?imageid=1770

U.S. Department of Health and Human Services, National Institutes of Health, National Cancer Institute. (n.d.b). *SEER stat fact sheets: Ovarian cancer.* Retrieved from http://seer.cancer.gov/statfacts/html/ovary.html

U.S. Department of Health and Human Services, National Institutes of Health, National Cancer Institute. (2006). *Female reproductive system (cervix, ovaries, uterus).* Retrieved from https://visualsonline.cancer.gov/details.cfm?imageid=4278

U.S. Preventive Services Task Force. (2012). Screening for ovarian cancer: U.S. Preventive Services Task Force reaffirmation recommendation statement. *Annals of Internal Medicine, 157*(12), 900-904.

Weitzel, J. N., Blazer, K. R., MacDonald, D. J., Culver, J. O., & Offit, K. (2011). Genetics, genomics, and cancer risk assessment: State of the art and future directions in the era of personalized medicine. *CA: A Cancer Journal for Clinicians, 61*(5), 327-359. doi:10.3322/caac.20128

Wright, J. D., Hou, J. Y., Burke, W. M., Tergas, A. I., Ling, C., Hu, J. C., … Chen, L. (2016). Utilization and toxicity of alternative delivery methods of adjuvant chemotherapy for ovarian cancer. *Obstetrics & Gynecology, 127*(6), 985-991. doi:10.1097/AOG.0000000000001436

Yap, T. A., Sandhu, S. K., Carden, C. P., & de Bono, J. S. (2011). Poly(ADP-ribose) polymerase (PARP) inhibitors: Exploiting a synthetic lethal strategy in the clinic. *CA: A Cancer Journal for Clinicians, 61*(1), 31-49. doi:10.3322/caac.20095

CHAPTER 6

CERVICAL CANCER

LEARNING OUTCOME

After completing this chapter, the learner will be able to identify the epidemiology, risk factors, prevention and detection strategies, common staging schemas, and treatments for cervical cancer.

CHAPTER OBJECTIVES

After completing this chapter, the learner will be able to:

1. Identify risk factors for cervical cancer.

2. Describe effective strategies to prevent cervical cancer.

3. Describe screening recommendations for cervical cancer.

4. Identify the diagnostic evaluation and staging for cervical cancer.

5. Describe the roles of various treatment modalities for cervical cancer.

INTRODUCTION

Despite the widespread use of the Papanicolaou (Pap) test and increasing availability of human papillomavirus vaccination, women continue to be diagnosed with cervical cancer (American Cancer Society [ACS], 2017a). Box 6-1 highlights the facts about cervical cancer. It is the fourth most common cancer among women worldwide, with significantly higher rates in developing countries, especially in Africa, the Caribbean, and Latin America (ACS, 2015). The diagnosis is also more common in minority women (ACS, 2016).

Strategies to prevent cervical cancer take into account risk reduction and appropriate screening with regular Pap testing (ACS, 2017a). The Pap test should detect abnormalities of the cervix before they progress to malignancy. To effectively detect premalignant cervical lesions in women, healthcare providers should follow appropriate, consistent screening recommendations, based on a woman's cervical cancer risk profile.

Current estimates suggest that 46% of women diagnosed with cervical cancer have never had a Pap test, and another 10% have not had a Pap test in the past 5 years (ACS, 2017a). Overall, only 82.8% of women aged 21 to 65 years have had a Pap test in the past 3 years; unfortunately, only 57.3% of uninsured women have had a Pap test in the past 3 years (ACS, 2017a).

EPIDEMIOLOGY

Cervical cancer remains a public health problem in the United States and worldwide; however, cervical cancer mortality rates have decreased in the United States (see Figure 6-1). Cervical cancer – once considered a highly deadly disease – has now dropped to 18th on the list of cancers that kill women in the United States (American Cancer Society [ACS], 2017a).

BOX 6-1: CERVICAL CANCER FACTS

- 12,820 estimated new cases annually

- Incidence rates are gradually decreasing in all races. From 2008 to 2013, incidence rates stabilized in women younger than 50 years and decreased by 3.0% per year in women 50 years or older

- Widespread utilization of the Pap smear results in more preinvasive lesions being detected

- 4,210 estimated deaths annually

- 5-year survival rate for localized disease is 91%

- Cervical cancer occurs more frequently in Black women (lifetime risk is 0.8 or 1 in 130) than in White women (lifetime risk is 0.6 or 1 in 176)

- Black women are more likely to die of cervical cancer (lifetime risk is 0.4 or 1 in 265) compared with White women (lifetime risk is 0.2 or 1 in 506)

Note. Adapted from:
American Cancer Society. (2016). *Cancer facts and figures for African Americans – 2016-2018.* Atlanta, GA: Author.
American Cancer Society. (2017a). *Cancer facts and figures – 2017.* Atlanta, GA: Author.

FIGURE 6-1: EPIDEMIOLOGY: CERVICAL CANCER, 2010 TO 2014

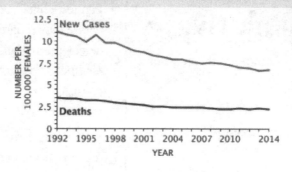

Estimated New Cases in 2017	12,820
% of All New Cancer Cases	0.8%
Estimated Deaths in 2017	4,210
% of All Cancer Deaths	0.7%

Percent Surviving 5 Years

67.1%

2007-2013

Number of New Cases and Deaths per 100,000: The number of new cases of cervix uteri cancer was 7.4 per 100,000 women per year. The number of deaths was 2.3 per 100,000 women per year. These rates are age-adjusted and based on 2010-2014 cases and deaths.

Lifetime Risk of Developing Cancer: Approximately 0.6 percent of women will be diagnosed with cervix uteri cancer at some point during their lifetime, based on 2012-2014 data.

Prevalence of This Cancer: In 2014, there were an estimated 256,078 women living with cervix uteri cancer in the United States.

Note. From U.S. Department of Health and Human Services, National Institutes of Health, National Cancer Institute. (n.d.). *SEER stat fact sheets: Cervix uteri cancer.* Retrieved from http://seer.cancer.gov/statfacts/html/cervix.html

Cervical cancer tends to occur in midlife. Most cases are found in women younger than 60 years, and it rarely develops in women younger than 20 years (see Figure 6-2; ACS, 2017). The 5-year relative survival rate for the earliest stage of invasive cervical cancer is 91.5%, and the 5-year survival rate overall for all stages combined is approximately 69% for white women and 57% for black women (ACS, 2017). Cervical cancer mortality is highest in middle-aged women (see Figure 6-3).

Cervical cancer is diagnosed at an early stage more often in White (49%) than in Black women (42%), and in women younger than 50 years (60%) than in women 50 years and older (34%; ACS, 2016a; see Figures 6-4 and 6-5).

FIGURE 6-2: AGE DISTRIBUTION OF CERVICAL CANCER, 2010 TO 2014

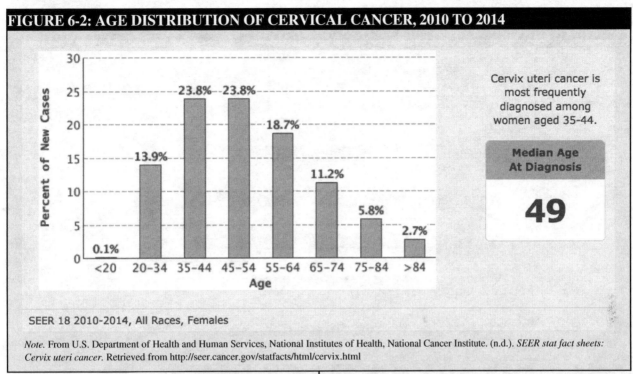

SEER 18 2010-2014, All Races, Females

Note. From U.S. Department of Health and Human Services, National Institutes of Health, National Cancer Institute. (n.d.). *SEER stat fact sheets: Cervix uteri cancer.* Retrieved from http://seer.cancer.gov/statfacts/html/cervix.html

FIGURE 6-3: PERCENTAGE OF DEATHS BY AGE GROUP: CERVICAL CANCER, 2010 TO 2014

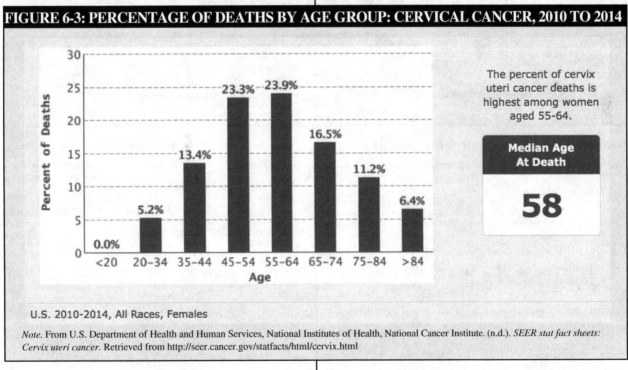

U.S. 2010-2014, All Races, Females

Note. From U.S. Department of Health and Human Services, National Institutes of Health, National Cancer Institute. (n.d.). *SEER stat fact sheets: Cervix uteri cancer.* Retrieved from http://seer.cancer.gov/statfacts/html/cervix.html

ANATOMY

The cervix is the lower part of the uterus. It is sometimes called the *uterine cervix.* The body of the uterus is where a fetus grows. The cervix connects the body of the uterus to the vagina (birth canal). The opening of the cervix, through which menstrual flow is released, is the os. The part of the cervix closest to the body of the uterus is called the *endocervix.* The part next to the vagina is the ectocervix. The place where these two parts meet is called the *transformation zone.* Most cervical cancers begin in the

FIGURE 6-4: NUMBER OF NEW CASES PER 100,000 PERSONS BY RACE/ETHNICITY: CERVICAL CANCER, 2010 TO 2014

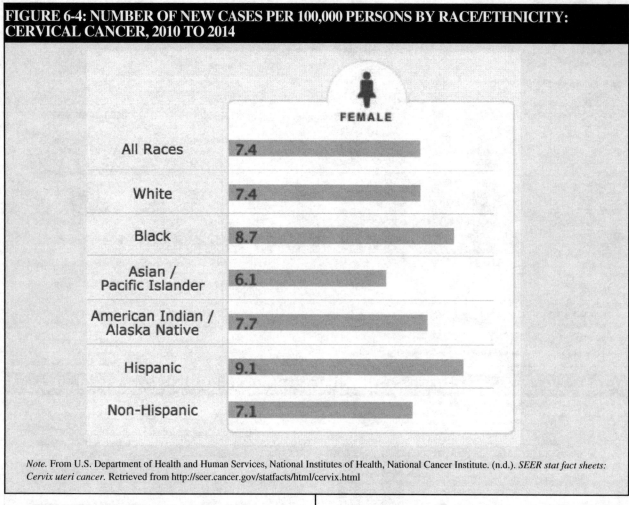

FEMALE

All Races	7.4
White	7.4
Black	8.7
Asian / Pacific Islander	6.1
American Indian / Alaska Native	7.7
Hispanic	9.1
Non-Hispanic	7.1

Note. From U.S. Department of Health and Human Services, National Institutes of Health, National Cancer Institute. (n.d.). *SEER stat fact sheets: Cervix uteri cancer.* Retrieved from http://seer.cancer.gov/statfacts/html/cervix.html

transformation zone. Figure 6-6 highlights these areas of the woman's anatomy.

RISK FACTORS

The etiology of cervical cancer is not known. However, studies suggest that the biggest risk factor for developing cervical cancer is related to persistent human papillomavirus (HPV) infection (ACS, 2017a). Women who start having sexual intercourse at an early age or who have had multiple sexual partners are at increased risk for developing an HPV infection. However, infection with HPV can occur with even one partner. HPV is a precursor to cervical cancer. Both persistence of HPV infection and progression to cancer are influenced by many factors, including a suppressed immune sys-

tem, a high number of childbirths, and cigarette smoking (ACS, 2017a). Table 6-1 lists risk factors for cervical cancer.

In the United States, HPV is the most common sexually transmitted infection. Annually, an estimated 14 million men and women become newly infected (ACS, 2017b). HPV infection is attributed to 11,771 cases of cervical carcinoma annually (7.4 per 100,000 females; Viens et al., 2016).

More than 100 different types of HPV exist. Fortunately, most are benign and resolve without treatment. Low-risk HPV types may cause visible warts known as condylomata acuminate. High-risk HPV types tend to persist and are associated with the development of precancerous lesions and cervical cancer. Approximately 15 high-risk HPV types are associated with

FIGURE 6-5: NUMBER OF DEATHS PER 100,000 PERSONS BY RACE/ETHNICITY: CERVICAL CANCER, 2010 TO 2014

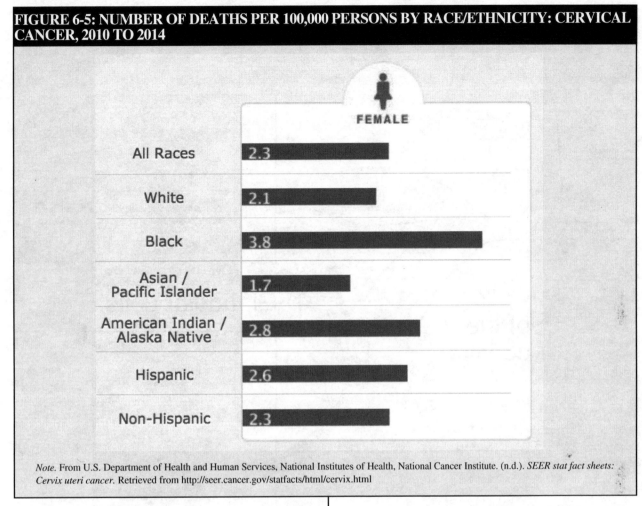

FEMALE

All Races	2.3
White	2.1
Black	3.8
Asian / Pacific Islander	1.7
American Indian / Alaska Native	2.8
Hispanic	2.6
Non-Hispanic	2.3

Note. From U.S. Department of Health and Human Services, National Institutes of Health, National Cancer Institute. (n.d.). *SEER stat fact sheets: Cervix uteri cancer.* Retrieved from http://seer.cancer.gov/statfacts/html/cervix.html

the development of cervical cancer, especially HPV types 16, 18, 31, 33, and 45 (ACS, 2017b). More than half of cervical cancers are caused by HPV 16 and 18, and these two types are associated with more than a 200-fold increased risk of developing invasive cervical cancer (ACS, 2017b) Transmission of HPV occurs by genital contact with an infected partner. The virus enters through a break in the squamous epithelium, where infection stimulates the replication of the epithelium. The time from exposure to infection may be 1 to 8 months (Koh et al., 2015).

The risk for acquiring HPV increases with the number of lifetime sexual partners and is not 100% preventable with condom use because the HPV infection can still be transmitted on body surfaces that are not covered by the condom (ACS, 2017b).

An additional risk factor is smoking. There is a direct link between smoking and cervical cancer (ACS, 2017b). Therefore, women who do smoke should engage in a smoking cessation program to reduce their risk (ACS, 2017b).

PREVENTION

The goal is that cervical cancer will be considered a preventable disease. Healthcare providers following standard screening protocols and implementing patient education strategies together with the participation of women are ways to reach this desired outcome. The strategies intend to prevent premalignant lesions and, if such lesions develop, to detect and treat the lesions before they become malignant. Although cervical cancer is potentially prevent-

FIGURE 6-6: CERVICAL CELLS

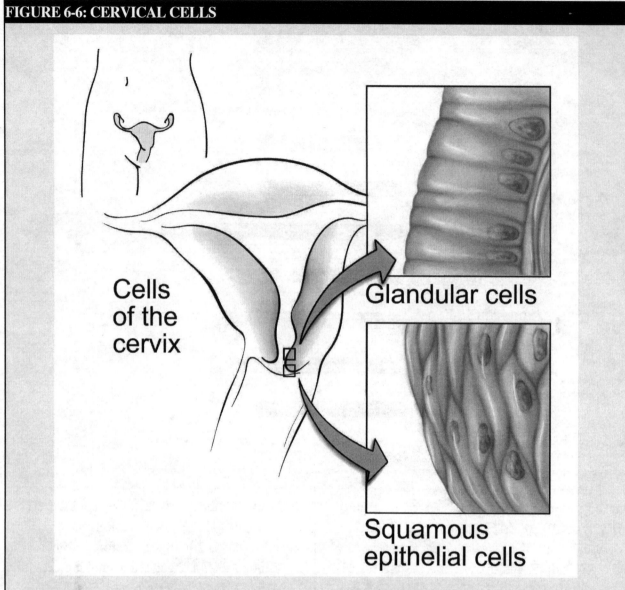

Cells
of the
cervix

Glandular cells

Squamous
epithelial cells

The location of the cervix in the body is shown along with a more detailed view of the cervix. The enlarged insets show the glandular and squamous epithelial cells found in the cervix.

Note. From U.S. Department of Health and Human Services, National Institutes of Health, National Cancer Institute. (2004). *Cells of the cervix.* Retrieved from https://visualsonline.cancer.gov/details.cfm?imageid=4349

able because the time between preinvasive and invasive stages usually is long and screening methods are effective, the rate of cervical cancer deaths remains high. Nurses play a pivotal role in providing and actively promoting patient and family education, emphasizing primary and secondary prevention approaches.

Women of all ages need to be informed; targeted populations include adolescents, women who test positive for HIV, and women with multiple sex partners. In addition to information about cervical cancer and safer sex practices, nurses can emphasize the importance of reducing modifiable risk factors that can contribute to cervical dysplasia and tumor development.

Avoiding exposure to HPV – a main risk factor for cervical cancer – requires particular emphasis. Most premalignant lesions of the cer-

TABLE 6-1: RISK FACTORS FOR CERVICAL CANCER	
Risk Factor	**Description**
HPV infection	Two HPV subtypes cause most genital warts and are associated with increased cervical cancer risk.
Sexual history	Women who begin having sexual intercourse at an early age and women who have had many sexual partners are at a greater risk for HPV infection and cervical cancer.
Reproductive history	Having three or more full-term pregnancies increases the risk for cervical cancer. The etiology of this risk factor is not clear.
Oral contraceptive use	Long-term use of oral contraceptives (5 or more years) may double cancer risk. There is evidence that taking OCs for more than 5 years increases the risk for cancer of the cervix. Research suggests that the risk for cervical cancer increases the longer a woman takes OCs, but the risk decreases again after the OCs are stopped.
Screening history	Women who are screened regularly are more likely to have lesions detected in a pre-malignant state. Abnormal changes can be treated before cancer develops. Women who are not screened are more likely to progress to cervical cancer.
Smoking	Cigarette smoking is associated with twofold increased risk. Nicotine deposits have been found in cervical tissue. Nicotine damages the DNA of cervix cells and may contribute to the development of cervical cancer. Smoking also makes the immune system less effective in fighting HPV infections.
Dietary factors	Women with diets low in fruits and vegetables may be at increased risk for cervical cancer. Also, overweight women are more likely to develop this cancer.
HIV	HIV damages the body's immune system and seems to make women at greater risk for HPV infections. In women with HIV, a cervical precancerous lesion might develop into an invasive cancer faster than it normally would.

HIV = human immunodeficiency virus; HPV = human papillomavirus; OC = oral contraceptive.

Note. Based on data from American Cancer Society. (2015a). *Global cancer facts and figures* (3rd ed.). Atlanta, GA: Author; American Cancer Society. (2017a). *Cancer facts and figures – 2017*. Atlanta, GA: Author; American Cancer Society. (2017b). *Cancer prevention and early detection facts and figures – 2017-2018*; and Viens, L. J., Henley, S. J., Watson, M., Markowitz, L. E., Thomas, C. C., Thompson, T. D., … Saraiya, M. (2016). Human papillomavirus-associated cancers – United States, 2008-2012. *MMWR: Morbidity & Mortality Weekly Report, 65*(26), 661-666. doi:10.15585/mmwr.mm6526a1

vix could be prevented by avoiding exposure to HPV (Viens et al., 2016). It is possible to have HPV for years yet be unaware of its presence because symptoms may not occur (ACS, 2017b). Therefore, an individual can have the virus and pass it on without knowing it. Certain types of sexual behavior increase a woman's risk for acquiring HPV infection, such as (National Comprehensive Cancer Network, 2016)

- having sex at a young age,
- having many sexual partners,
- having a partner who has had many sex partners, and
- having sex with uncircumcised males.

One of the most effective ways to prevent cervical cancer is to prevent HPV infection through vaccination (ACS, 2017b). Three vaccines have been approved by the U.S. Food and Drug Administration (FDA) for the prevention of HPV. HPV2 (Cervarix) protects against two HPV types (16 and 18) and is recommended for female use only. HPV4 (Gardasil) provides protection against four HPV types (6, 11, 16, and 18) and is recommended for use in both males and females. Currently HPV9 (Gardasil-9), for both males and females is the only vaccine offered in the United States; it protects against nine HPV types (6, 11, 16, 18, 31, 33, 45, 52, and 58; ACS, 2017b). All three HPV vaccines require three doses, administered over the course of 6 months. To be most effective, the vaccination series should be completed before a person becomes sexually active.

HPV vaccination among adolescents lags behind other recommended vaccines. As of 2015, 62.8% of girls and 49.8% of boys ages 13 to 17, initiated HPV vaccination (at least one dose; ACS, 2017b). Unfortunately only 41.9% of adolescent girls received at least three doses of the vaccine, which is an improvement from the 6% of girls who received the three-dose series in 2007, the first year the vaccine was recommended (ACS, 2017b). In 2015, among adolescent boys, only 28.1% received at least three doses of the vaccine which is a substantial increase from the 2% of boys who received three doses in 2011, the first year it was recommended for them (ACS, 2017b). The Centers for Disease Control and Prevention (CDC) has established the Vaccines for Preteens and Teens communication campaign to educate parents and clinicians about immunizations recommended for adolescents aged 11 to 18 years (CDC, 2015a). The ongoing goals of the CDC's adolescent vaccine campaign include efforts to: 1) inform parents about adolescent vaccines and the diseases they prevent; 2) educate healthcare providers about the adolescent immunization recommendations, including awareness of missed opportunities for HPV vaccination at the recommended ages of 11 or 12 years; and 3) provide communication tools and resources for public health professionals, immunization programs, and immunization healthcare providers to improve awareness.

The HPV vaccine has mild side effects (ACS, 2017b). The most common are short-term redness, swelling, and soreness at the injection site. This vaccine prevents HPV infection; it will not treat an already existing infection.

Recommendations state that the vaccine be given routinely to girls 11 to 12 years old. It can be given to younger girls (as young as 9 years old) at the discretion of their doctors (Viens et al., 2016). It is also recommended that females 13 to 26 years old who have not yet been vaccinated receive catch-up vaccinations if they have not been sexually active (ACS, 2017b).

The HPV vaccine is expensive. The vaccine series costs about $360 to $390 (not including any office visit fees or the cost of giving the injections; ACS, 2017b). As of 2017, the Affordable Care Act requires Medicaid (and other federally supported healthcare programs), in addition to all new and renewed private insurance plans, to cover HPV vaccination without deductible or copay for eligible adults and children. The HPV vaccine is also available through the federal Vaccines for Children program, which covers vaccine costs for children and teens who do not have insurance and for some children and teens who are underinsured or eligible for Medicaid (ACS, 2017b). Nurses in positions where vaccination is provided can inform parents and work with them to initiate and complete the series during regular physical examinations.

The vaccine does not protect against all cancer-causing types of HPV, so females who have been vaccinated should still follow the screening recommendations for their age group. One other benefit of the vaccine is that it protects against the viruses that cause 90% of genital warts.

SCREENING

Regular Pap testing can usually detect early stages of cervical cancer. Mortality rates from cervical cancer have decreased more than 40% since the late 1980s because of more widespread use of the Pap test (Practice Bulletin No. 157, 2016). With more women having regular Pap tests, preinvasive lesions (precancers) of the cervix are found more frequently than invasive cancers. The Pap test (Pap smear) is inexpensive and is considered cost-effective (Lees, Erickson, & Huh, 2016).

Pap Test

A Pap smear collects cells from the cervix during the pelvic examination, and the smear or collection of cells is tested in the laboratory (see Figure 6-7). Those cells are analyzed for abnor-mal cell changes that indicate precancerous conditions. During the pelvic examination, the healthcare provider also checks the woman's uterus, vagina, ovaries, fallopian tubes, bladder, and rectum and notes any abnormality in their shapes or sizes.

In 1943, Dr. George Papanicolaou introduced the Pap test as a cervical cancer screening test.

FIGURE 6-7: OBTAINING A PAP SMEAR FOR TESTING

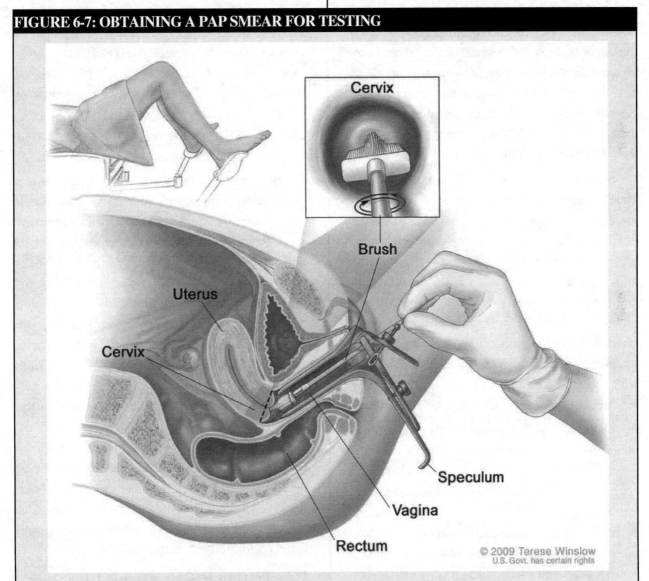

© 2009 Terese Winslow
U.S. Govt. has certain rights

Drawing shows a side view of the female reproductive anatomy when obtaining a Pap smear. A speculum is shown widening the opening of the vagina. A brush is shown inserted into the open vagina and touching the cervix at the base of the uterus. The rectum is also shown. One inset shows the brush touching the center of the cervix. The top image shows a woman in position for the exam, covered by a drape on an examination table with legs apart and feet in stirrups.

Note. From U.S. Department of Health and Human Services, National Institutes of Health, National Cancer Institute. (2013). *Pap test.* Retrieved from https://visualsonline.cancer.gov/details.cfm?imageid=8271; © 2009 Terese Winslow, U.S. Govt has certain rights.

In the United States, about 60 million Pap tests are performed each year, with approximately 3.7 million (11%) reported as abnormal and requiring medical follow-up (Lees et al., 2016). Annual Pap testing has been estimated to have reduced the cervical cancer mortality rate by 70% compared with the 1950s (Koh et al., 2015).

Since the development of the Pap smear, a variety of devices have been implemented to obtain cells for cytological evaluation. Most often the smear is taken with a smear device, which may be a cytobrush, swab, or broom instrument. These devices are inserted up through the vagina into the cervical opening, to the transformation zone, and are either rotated or left in place for a short period; then the devices are removed.

Sampling focus is in the transformation zone because that is where the majority of cervical cancers begin to develop. The cells on the device (or the device itself) are placed in a preservative solution or spread (smeared) on a slide and placed in or sprayed with a preservative and then sent to a laboratory. The liquid-based technologies may result in the transfer of more endocervical cells, which improves the possibility of detecting a cervical abnormality. This is why some organizations recommend screening less frequently with liquid-based technologies.

Unfortunately, 23% of cervical cancer diagnoses might have been made earlier or possibly prevented with early intervention as a result of errors in sampling and interpretation in previous Pap tests (Umana, Dunsmore, Herbert, Jokhan, & Kubba, 2013). These errors include incomplete sampling of the transformation zone, a poorly prepared slide with drying artifact or clumping of cells, and failure of the pathologist or cytotechnologist to detect abnormal cells. If the report shows the presence of endocervical cells, there is a much greater likelihood that the transformation zone was sampled. The overall false-negative rate of the Pap test for cervical cancer screening is estimated to be 15% to 25%; the overall sensitivity may range from 50% to 75% (Kim et al., 2016).

Liquid-based preparation systems help prevent poor sampling, uneven cell distribution, and improper fixation on the slide. With the liquid-based collections, the sample is not smeared directly onto a glass slide but placed in a small bottle containing fixative solution. At the laboratory, the sample is filtered and centrifuged to remove excess blood and debris, and a thin layer of cells is transferred to the slide. Liquid-based or thin-layer preparations improve the quality of the Pap smear, decrease unsatisfactory smears, and often increase the number of precancerous lesions detected (Umana et al., 2013).

Nurses play a key role in outpatient settings when they inform and educate women about several issues when scheduling and preparing for a Pap smear. The Pap smear should not be collected during a menstrual cycle. Two weeks after the first day of the last period is the optimal time to have the Pap test. Women should not douche or use vaginal creams during the 3 days before the Pap test. Finally, women should abstain from intercourse for 24 hours before the Pap smear because intercourse can cause inaccurate results. The nurse is often the point person in the medical practice, primary care setting, clinic, or gynecologist's office who follows up and communicates test results based on established protocols. When tests come back positive, the nurse is in the unique position to counsel, educate, and facilitate planning and interventions based on the findings.

Pap Testing Reimbursement

Many women do not schedule regular Pap tests for a variety of reasons, including an inability to pay for services, fatalistic attitudes, knowledge deficit, and lack of support (ACS, 2015b). Although many of these factors may not be easily addressed, women should consistently be offered education and support in finding appropriate resources. For example, the National Breast and Cervical Cancer Detection Program administered by the CDC provides free or low-cost cervical and breast cancer screening to qualified women through an extensive outreach program. Since 1991, National Breast and Cervical Cancer Detection Program–funded programs have served more than 4.8 million women, provided more than 12.2 million breast and cervical cancer screening examinations, and diagnosed more than 69,507 breast cancers, 3,771 invasive cervical cancers, and 173,582 premalignant cervical lesions, of which 40% were high-grade lesions (CDC, 2015b). In 2014 alone, this program screened 146,947 women for cervical cancer with the Pap test and diagnosed 194 cervical cancers and 6,491 premalignant cervical lesions, of which 39% were high-grade lesions. The widespread availability of this program makes cervical screening truly accessible to all women.

Signs and Symptoms

Regardless of when the last Pap test was completed, women who report any of the following symptoms need a diagnostic evaluation:

- Abnormal bleeding, including bleeding after sexual intercourse or between periods, heavier or longer-lasting menstrual bleeding, or bleeding after menopause

- Abnormal vaginal discharge (may be foul smelling)

- Pelvic or back pain

- Pain on urination

- Blood in the stool or urine

Screening Guidelines

Several guidelines for cervical screening have been published, with organizations issuing updates when new information warrants. Table 6-2 lists cervical screening guidelines from the

ACS, American College of Obstetricians and Gynecologists (ACOG), and U.S. Preventive Services Task Force (USPSTF).

Previously, there were substantial differences between the guidelines, but as of 2012, there are more commonalities among them. In the past, ACOG recommended against screening women younger than 21 years, regardless of age of sexual activity onset, whereas the ACC/American Society for Colposcopy and Cervical Pathology (ASCCP)/American Society for Clinical Pathology (ASCP) and the USPSTF recommended that screening begin by 21 years of age or at onset of sexual activity (whichever came first). Now, the ACS/ASCCP/ASCP and the USPSTF have joined the ACOG in recommending against screening women younger than 21 years (ACOG, 2016; Saslow et al., 2012).

For women aged 30 to 65 years, HPV-DNA testing is now approved by the FDA for adjunct screening *with* either conventional or liquid Pap testing (this is known as *cotesting*; Koh et al., 2015). Previously, the recommendation for women aged 30 to 65 who have had three consecutive normal Pap tests was to be screened every 3 years. Whereas the ACOG maintains this position (whether screening is done with Pap test alone or with Pap *plus* HPV testing), the ACS/ASCCP/ASCP and the USPSTF have changed their guidelines to include screening every 5 years with cotesting (ACOG, 2016; Moyer, 2012; Saslow et al., 2012).

Although having differed in the past, the recommendations on when to stop screening are now fairly consistent: Women who have had three consecutive negative Pap tests or two consecutive negative cotests within the 10 years before cessation of screening (with the most recent test occurring within the past 5 years), and who are not otherwise at high risk for cervical cancer, do not need to continue screening. Pap screening after hysterectomy is

TABLE 6-2: SCREENING RECOMMENDATIONS FOR THE EARLY DETECTION OF CERVICAL CANCER

	ACS, ASCCP, and ASCP, 2012	USPSTF, 2012	ACOG, 2016
When to start screening	Age 21 years Women younger than age 21 should not be screened	Age 21 years Recommend against screening women younger than 21	Age 21 years
Recommendation about annual screening	Women of any age should not be screened annually by any screening method	Individuals and clinicians can use the annual Pap test screening visit as an opportunity to discuss other health problems and preventive measures	Women of any age should not be screened annually by any screening method
Screening method and intervals			
Cytology (conventional or liquid based)	For 21 to 65 years of age, should be performed every 3 years	For 21 to 65 years of age, should be performed every 3 years	For 21 to 29 years of age, should be performed every 3 years; HPV testing is not recommended
HPV cotest (cytology + HPV test administered together)	HPV cotesting should not be used for women younger than 30 years; it is the preferred method in women 30 to 65 years old	HPV cotesting should not be used for women younger than 30 years; for women who want to extend their screening interval, HPV cotesting every 5 years is an option	Women 30 to 65 years of age should have Pap and HPV cotesting every 5 years; it is also acceptable to have a Pap smear every 3 years
When to stop screening	Age older than 65 years with adequate negative prior screening[a] and no history of CIN II or higher within the past 20 years	Age older than 65 years with adequate screening history[a] and not otherwise at high risk for cervical cancer	Age older than 65 years with adequate negative prior screening[a] results and no history of CIN II or higher

[a]Adequate negative prior screening results are defined as three consecutive negative cytology results or two consecutive negative cotest results within the previous 10 years, with the most recent test performed within the past 5 years.

ACOG = American College of Obstetricians and Gynecologists; ACS = American Cancer Society; ASCCP = American Society for Colposcopy and Cervical Pathology; ASCP = American Society for Clinical Pathology; CIN = cervical intraepithelial neoplasia; HPV = human papillomavirus; USPSTF = U.S. Preventive Services Task Force.

Note. Adapted from American Cancer Society. (2017a). *Cancer facts and figures – 2017*. Atlanta, GA: Author; American College of Obstetricians and Gynecologists. (2016). Practice Bulletin No. 168 Summary: Cervical Cancer Screening and Prevention. *Obstetrics & Gynecology, 128*(4), 923-925. doi:10.1097/AOG.0000000000001699; and Moyer, V. A. (2012). Screening for cervical cancer: U.S. Preventive Services Task Force recommendation statement. *Annals of Internal Medicine, 156*(12), 880-891. doi:10.7326/0003-4819-156-12-201206190-00424

generally not recommended if the cervix was removed and if the hysterectomy was performed for benign disease (ACOG, 2016; Moyer, 2012; Saslow et al., 2012).

DIAGNOSTIC EVALUATION AND STAGING

Pap Test Results

Scales to interpret Pap tests have evolved in their precision. Currently, the Bethesda system offers the most clarity in reporting cytological results. The 2014 Bethesda system correlates colposcopic, cytological, and histological data (Practice Bulletin No. 157, 2016; see Table 6-3).

The three main categories of the Bethesda system are

1. a statement of specimen adequacy,

2. a general categorization of normal or abnormal, and

3. descriptive diagnoses.

Epithelial cell abnormalities are divided into low- and high-grade groups. The Bethesda system also provides a means to evaluate hormonal state, infection, reactive and reparative changes, and glandular cell components (Saslow et al., 2012).

The Pap test is not only a screening test for cervical cancer, but also a screen that aids in the detection of benign and preinvasive cervical conditions.

Benign Conditions

Squamous intraepithelial lesions (SILs) are benign conditions. These tumors occur on the surface of the epithelial tissue. They include

- *low-grade SILs,* cells that are early in the process of changing in size, shape, and number on the surface of the cervix, and

- *high-grade SILs,* cells that are a large number of precancerous cells.

Treatment of SILs and warts includes cryosurgery (freezing the tissue to destroy the wart), laser treatment (destroying the wart with high-intensity light), loop electrosurgical excision procedure (the removal of tissue using a hot wire loop), and standard surgery (see Table 6-4; Saslow et al., 2012). Chemical treatments for SILs include applying podophyllin, bichloracetic acid, and trichloroacetic acid. By treating these benign conditions, healthcare providers can prevent or delay progression to premalignant or more invasive conditions (ACOG, 2013).

Inflammation contributes to mildly abnormal Pap tests. Table 6-5 reviews causes of inflammation affecting Pap test results. When cervical inflammation is treated and cleared, the tissue repairs itself. Then after several months, the woman has a repeat Pap test. Those test results are unaffected by inflammation, and frequently test results are then normal (ACOG, 2013).

Preinvasive Conditions

Premalignant changes of epithelial cells are referred to as dysplasia. The term *cervical intraepithelial neoplasia* (CIN) describes many intraepithelial changes that can occur before cells become invasive cervical cancer cells. Preinvasive disease does not penetrate the basement membrane (stroma) as does invasive disease.

Four degrees of classification grade the level of CIN (ACOG, 2013).

- CIN I: mild dysplasia; involvement of less than one-third of the thickness of the epithelium

- CIN II: moderate dysplasia; involvement of one-third to two-thirds of the thickness of the epithelium

- CIN III: severe dysplasia

- Carcinoma in situ: full-thickness involvement of the surface area

continued on page 151

TABLE 6-3: 2014 BETHESDA SYSTEM FOR THE CLASSIFICATION OF PAP SMEAR TESTING COMPONENTS

Specimen Type

Indicate: conventional test (Pap test), liquid-based preparation, or other

Specimen Adequacy

- Satisfactory for evaluation (describe presence or absence of endocervical/transformation zone component and any other quality indicators, e.g., partially obscuring blood, inflammation that might limit interpretation)

- Unsatisfactory for evaluation (specify reason)

  ○ Specimen rejected or not processed (specify reason)

  ○ Specimen processed and examined, but unsatisfactory for evaluation of epithelial abnormality (specify reason)

General Categorization

- Negative for intraepithelial lesion or malignancy

- Epithelial cell abnormality

- Other findings

Categorization section

Nonneoplastic findings (optional to report): might include atrophy, pregnancy-associated changes, inflammation, reactive changes (such as from an intrauterine device, *Trichomonas vaginalis* fungal organisms, shift in flora suggestive of bacterial vaginosis, cellular changes consistent with herpes simplex virus, cellular changes consistent with cytomegalovirus)

Epithelial cell abnormalities

- Squamous cell

  ○ Atypical squamous cells (ACSs)

    ▪ Of undetermined significance (ASC-US)

    ▪ Cannot exclude high-grade squamous intraepithelial lesion (HSIL; ASC-H)

  ○ Low-grade squamous intraepithelial lesion (LSIL) (encompassing human papillomavirus/mild dysplasia/cervical intraepithelial neoplasia [CIN] I)

  ○ High-grade squamous intraepithelial lesion (encompassing moderate and severe dysplasia, carcinoma in situ, CIN II and CIN III)

  ○ Squamous cell carcinoma

- Glandular cell

  ○ Atypical – favor benign or unable to classify

  ○ Atypical – endometrial or glandular cells, favor neoplastic

Endocervical adenocarcinoma in situ

Other malignant neoplasms (specify)

Note. Adapted from Practice Bulletin No. 157: Cervical cancer screening and prevention. (2016). *Obstetrics & Gynecology, 127*(1), e1-e20. doi:10.1097/AOG.0000000000001263; and Saslow, D., Solomon, D., Lawson, H. W., Killackey, M., Kulasingam, S. L., Cain, J., ... Myers, E. R. (2012). American Cancer Society, American Society for Colposcopy and Cervical Pathology, and American Society for Clinical Pathology screening guidelines for the prevention and early detection of cervical cancer. *CA: A Cancer Journal for Clinicians, 62*(3), 147-172. doi:10.3322/caac.21139

TABLE 6-4: TYPES OF CERVICAL BIOPSIES
Colposcopic Biopsy
The healthcare provider examines the cervix with a colposcope to find the abnormal areas. Using biopsy forceps, the healthcare provider will remove a small (about 1/8-inch) section of the abnormal area on the surface of the cervix. This may cause mild cramping or brief pain, and the woman may bleed lightly afterward. A local anesthetic is sometimes used to numb the cervix before the biopsy.
Endocervical Curettage (endocervical scraping)
Sometimes the transformation zone (the area at risk for human papillomavirus [HPV] infection and precancer) cannot be seen with the colposcope. A sample is obtained by inserting a narrow instrument (a curette) into the endocervical canal (the passage between the outer part of the cervix and the inner part of the uterus). The curette is used to scrape the inside of the canal to remove some of the tissue. After this procedure, patients may feel a cramping pain, and they may also have some light bleeding. This procedure is usually done at the same time as the colposcopic biopsy.
Cone Biopsy
In this procedure, also known as conization, a cone-shaped piece of tissue is removed from the cervix. The base of the cone is formed by the exocervix (outer part of the cervix), and the point or apex of the cone is from the endocervical canal. The transformation zone (the border between the exocervix and endocervix) is contained within the cone. This is the area of the cervix where precancers and cancers are most likely to develop. The cone biopsy can be used as a treatment to completely remove many precancers and some very early cancers. Having a cone biopsy will not keep most women from getting pregnant, but if the biopsy removes a large amount of tissue, these women may have a higher risk of giving birth prematurely. Two methods are commonly used for cone biopsies: the loop electrosurgical excision procedure (LEEP; also called *large loop excision of the transformation zone,* or LLETZ) and the cold knife cone biopsy.

- **Loop electrosurgical procedure (LEEP or LLETZ):** With this method, the tissue is removed with a thin wire loop that is heated by electrical current and acts as a scalpel. For this procedure, a local anesthetic is used, and it can be done in an office setting. It can take as little as 10 minutes. The woman may have mild cramping during and after the procedure and mild-to-moderate bleeding for several weeks.

- **Cold knife cone biopsy:** This method uses a surgical scalpel or a laser instead of a heated wire to remove tissue. It requires general anesthesia and is an outpatient procedure. After the procedure, cramping and some bleeding may persist for a few weeks.

Note. Adapted from Saslow, D., Solomon, D., Lawson, H. W., Killackey, M., Kulasingam, S. L., Cain, J., ... Myers, E. R. (2012). American Cancer Society, American Society for Colposcopy and Cervical Pathology, and American Society for Clinical Pathology screening guidelines for the prevention and early detection of cervical cancer. *CA: A Cancer Journal for Clinicians, 62*(3), 147-172. doi:10.3322/caac.21139; and American College of Obstetricians and Gynecologists. (2013). *Management of abnormal cervical cytology and histology* (ACOG Practice Bulletin No. 140). Washington, DC: Author.

Mild dysplasia and CIN I typically occur in younger women (25 to 35 years of age). Each year, an estimated 1.4 million women are diagnosed with SIL or CIN changes (Saslow et al., 2012).

When high-grade SILs invade deeper layers of the cervix, becoming severe dysplasia (CIN II or III) or carcinoma in situ, they can become invasive and spread. These lesions are more often identified in women between 30 and 40 years of age. Ultimately, when cervical cancer cells spread to other tissues or organs, the condition is invasive cervical cancer. Invasive cervical cancer is most often diagnosed in women older than 40 years (ACOG, 2013; Saslow et al., 2012).

Treatment strategies for CIN can range from observation to ablative therapies: electrocautery, cryotherapy, laser vaporization, excisional therapies, and hysterectomy.

TABLE 6-5: CAUSES OF INFLAMED CERVICAL TISSUE (AFFECTING THE RESULTS OF A PAP SMEAR)

- Viruses, especially herpes infections and condyloma acuminata (warts)

- Yeast or monilia infections

- *Trichomonas* infections

- Pregnancy, miscarriage, or abortion

- Immunosuppression from chemotherapy agents

- Chemicals (e.g., medications)

- Hormonal changes

Note. Adapted from Saslow, D., Solomon, D., Lawson, H. W., Killackey, M., Kulasingam, S. L., Cain, J., ... Myers, E. R. (2012). American Cancer Society, American Society for Colposcopy and Cervical Pathology, and American Society for Clinical Pathology screening guidelines for the prevention and early detection of cervical cancer. *CA: A Cancer Journal for Clinicians, 62*(3), 147-172. doi:10.3322/caac.21139; and American College of Obstetricians and Gynecologists. (2013). *Management of abnormal cervical cytology and histology* (ACOG Practice Bulletin No. 140). Washington, DC: Author.

If properly managed, dysplasias are nearly 100% curable. A small proportion of mild dysplasias (CIN I or low-grade SIL) will regress without treatment. However, for now, clinicians do not have methods to distinguish between dysplastic areas that will remain benign and those that will become malignant (ACOG, 2013; reaffirmed in 2016: http://www.acog.org/Resources-And-Publications/Practice-Bulletins-List).

The majority of cervical tumors are squamous cell carcinomas. The external surface of the cervix, or ectocervix, is lined with squamous epithelial cells. Most cervical cancers begin as an alteration of the transformation zone and originate from precursor lesions (Koh et al., 2015). Such lesions include atypical squamous cells of undetermined significance that do or do not exclude low-grade or high-grade SIL.

Low-grade SIL includes HPV, mild dysplasia, and CIN. High-grade SIL includes moderate-to-severe dysplasia and carcinoma in situ. Glandular cell changes from the cervix can also be atypical granular cells, which are more likely to become neoplastic or cancerous as adenocarcinoma of the endocervix in situ (Koh et al., 2015). To prevent progression to cervical cancer, healthcare providers schedule careful follow-up of an abnormal Pap test and initiate prompt treatment of the abnormality (Apgar, Kittendorf, Bettcher, Wong, & Kaufman, 2009). Pap test terms, recommendations for follow-up, and testing strategies are summarized in Table 6-6.

Further Diagnostic Evaluation and Staging

Cervical cancer cells are usually squamous cell in origin. As with other malignant tumors, cervical cancer cells can invade and damage tissues and organs near the tumor and can break away from a malignant tumor and move through the lymphatic system. Typical areas of spread are to the woman's rectum, bladder, bones of the spine, and lungs (ACS, 2017a). Therefore, healthcare providers order additional tests that explore those areas.

Table 6-7 lists components of diagnostic evaluation for cervical cancer. Treatment decisions are based on the staging information listed in Table 6-8 (Amin et al., 2017).

Cervical cancer is staged using the TNM system as follows:

- Tumor (T) describes the size of the original tumor.

- Lymph node (N) indicates whether the cancer is present in the lymph nodes.

- Metastasis (M) refers to whether cancer has spread to other parts of the body, usually the liver, bones, or brain.

Once the T, N, and M scores have been determined, an overall cervical cancer stage is assigned (Amin et al., 2017). Stage 0 cervical cancer means that the cancer cells are confined to the surface of the cervix. This stage is also called *carcinoma in situ* or CIN grade III (CIN III). In stage I cervical cancer, the cancer has grown deeper into the cer-

TABLE 6-6: PAP TEST TERMS, FOLLOW-UP, AND TESTING STRATEGIES

Pap Test Result	Abbreviation	Also Known as	Tests and Treatments May Include
Atypical squamous cells – undetermined significance	ASC-US		Human papillomavirus (HPV) testing with repeat Pap test Colposcopy and biopsy
Atypical squamous cells – cannot exclude high-grade squamous intraepithelial lesion	ASC-H		HPV testing with repeat Pap test Colposcopy and biopsy
Atypical glandular cells	AGC		HPV testing with repeat Pap test Colposcopy and biopsy and/or endocervical curettage
Endocervical adenocarcinoma in situ	AIS		Colposcopy and biopsy and/or endocervical curettage
Low-grade squamous intraepithelial lesion	LSIL	Mild dysplasia or cervical intraepithelial neoplasia grade I (CIN I)	HPV testing with repeat Pap test Colposcopy and biopsy
High-grade squamous intraepithelial lesion	HSIL	Moderate dysplasia, severe dysplasia, CIN II, CIN III, or carcinoma in situ (CIS)	Colposcopy and biopsy and/or endocervical curettage, further treatment with loop electrosurgical excision procedure, cryotherapy, laser therapy, conization, or hysterectomy

Note. Adapted from Apgar, B. S., Kittendorf, A. L., Bettcher, C. M., Wong, J., & Kaufman, A. J. (2009). Update on ASCCP consensus guidelines for abnormal cervical screening tests and cervical histology. *American Family Physician, 80*(2), 147-155; and American College of Obstetricians and Gynecologists. (2013). *Management of abnormal cervical cytology and histology* (ACOG Practice Bulletin No. 140). Washington, DC: Author.

vix but has not spread beyond it. Stage II cervical cancer means that the cancer has grown beyond the cervix and uterus, but has not reached the walls of the pelvis or the lower part of the vagina. Stage III cervical cancer means that the cancer has spread to the lower part of the vagina or the walls of the pelvis, but not to nearby lymph nodes or other parts of the body. In stage IV, the disease has spread to nearby organs or other parts of the body.

Based on the diagnostic workup, prognosis depends on

- the type of cervical cancer,

- the stage of the cancer (the size of the tumor and whether it affects part of the cervix or the whole cervix, or has spread to the lymph nodes or other places in the body),

- the patient's age and general health,

- whether the patient has a certain type HPV,

- whether the patient has HIV, and

- whether the cancer has just been diagnosed or has recurred.

TREATMENT

Healthcare providers recommend treatment options and base those options on

- the type of cancer,

- the stage of the cancer,

- the patient's desire to have children, and

- the patient's age.

TABLE 6-7: DIAGNOSTIC EVALUATION FOR CERVICAL CANCER
Cystoscopy: In cystoscopy, a slender tube with a lens and a light is placed into the bladder through the urethra to allow visualization of the bladder and urethra to see whether cancer is growing into these areas. Biopsy samples can be removed during cystoscopy for pathological (microscopic) testing. Cystoscopy can be done under a local anesthetic, but some patients may need general anesthesia.
Proctoscopy: Proctoscopy is a visual inspection of the rectum through a lighted tube to check for spread of cervical cancer into the rectum.
Chest X-ray: A chest X-ray scan is used to determine whether the malignancy has spread to the lungs.
Computed tomography (CT): CT scans are used to determine whether cancer has spread to the lymph nodes in the abdomen and pelvis. They can also be used to determine whether the cancer has spread to the liver, lungs, or elsewhere in the body.   CT scans are sometimes used to guide a biopsy needle precisely into an area of suspected cancer spread. For this procedure, called a CT-guided needle biopsy, the patient remains on the CT scanning table while a radiologist advances a biopsy needle toward the location of the mass. CT scans are repeated until the doctors are confident that the needle is within the mass. A fine-needle biopsy sample is removed and sent to pathology for evaluation.
Magnetic resonance imaging (MRI): MRI images are particularly useful in examining pelvic tumors. They are also helpful in detecting cancer that has spread to the brain or spinal cord.
Positron emission tomography (PET): PET scans are helpful to determine whether the cancer has spread to lymph nodes.
Note. Adapted from National Comprehensive Cancer Network. (2016). *Cervical cancer, version 1.2017.* Retrieved from nccn.org

Surgery

For early-stage cervical cancer, surgery is the treatment of choice. Surgeries can be simple hysterectomies or coupled with lymphadenectomies (removal of lymph nodes in the pelvis). Depending on the amount of disease, the surgeon may remove tissue around the uterus, part of the vagina, and the fallopian tubes (Koh et al., 2015).

As described in Chapter 4, a hysterectomy is a surgery that removes the woman's uterus and cervix. When the surgeon removes the uterus and cervix through an incision in the abdomen, it is a simple or total abdominal hysterectomy. The structures next to the uterus (parametria and uterosacral ligaments) are not removed. The vagina remains entirely intact, and pelvic lymph nodes are not removed. The ovaries and fallopian tubes are usually left in place unless there is some other reason to remove them (i.e., metastatic spread to the endometrium). When the surgeon removes the uterus and cervix through the vagina, it is a vaginal hysterectomy.

As a component of staging cervical cancer, as with other gynecological cancers, the surgeon will remove the lymph nodes (lymph node sampling) in the pelvis and around the aorta, either through the same incision as the abdominal hysterectomy or via laparoscopy during vaginal hysterectomy. Sentinel lymph node sampling removes a few of the lymph nodes to evaluate as representative of all lymph nodes in the area (Abu-Rustum, 2014). When removing most or all the lymph nodes, the procedure is a lymph node dissection or lymphadenectomy.

When cervical cancer has spread to the area around the cervix (the parametrium), the surgeon performs a radical hysterectomy. In this operation, the surgeon removes the entire uterus, both ovaries and fallopian tubes, the tissues next to the uterus (parametrium and

TABLE 6-8: CERVICAL CANCER STAGING

Stage	Description	5-Year Observed Survival Rate (%)
0	Carcinoma in situ: abnormal cells are found in the innermost lining of the cervix. These abnormal cells may become cancer and spread into nearby normal tissue.	93
IA	Stage IA1 and IA2 cervical cancer: In stage IA1, the cancer is not more than 3 mm deep and not more than 7 mm wide. In stage IA2, the cancer is more than 3 mm, but not more than 5 mm deep and not more than 7 mm wide.	93
IB	The cancer is more than 5 mm deep and more than 7 mm wide.	80
IIA	The cancer has spread beyond the cervix, but not to the pelvic wall or to the lower third of the vagina. In stages IIA1 and IIA2, cancer has spread beyond the cervix to the vagina. In stage IIA1, the tumor is 4 cm or smaller. In stage IIA2, the tumor is larger than 4 cm.	63
IIB	In stage IIB, cancer has spread beyond the cervix to the tissues around the uterus.	59
IIIA	The cancer has spread to the lower third of the vagina, but not to the pelvic wall.	35
IIIB	The cancer has spread to the pelvic wall and/or the tumor has become large enough to block the ureters.	32
IVA	The cancer has spread to nearby organs, such as the bladder or rectum.	16
IVB	The cancer has spread to other parts of the body, such as the lymph nodes, lung, liver, intestine, or bone.	15

Note. Adapted from American Cancer Society. (2017a). *Cancer facts and figures – 2017.* Atlanta, GA: Author; Koh, W. J., Greer, B. E., Abu-Rustum, N. R., Apte, S. M., Campos, S. M., Cho, K. R., … Scavone, J. L. (2015). Cervical cancer, version 2.2015. *Journal of the National Comprehensive Cancer Network, 13*(4), 395-404; and Amin, M. B., Edge, S., Greene, F., Byrd, D. R., Brookland, R. K., Washington, M. K., … Meyer, L. R. (Eds.). (2017). *AJCC cancer staging manual* (8th ed.), New York, NY: Springer.

uterosacral ligaments), and the upper part of the vagina (next to the cervix).

For an abdominal hysterectomy, a hospital stay of 3 to 5 days is common, and complete recovery takes about 4 to 6 weeks. Any type of hysterectomy results in infertility. Complications are unusual but could include excessive bleeding, wound infection, or damage to the urinary or intestinal systems (Koh et al., 2015).

A total hysterectomy is the treatment for stage IA cervical cancers (Koh et al., 2015). The operation is also used for some stage 0 cancers (carcinoma in situ) in cases where cancer cells are at the edges of the cone biopsy (positive margins).

More tissue is removed in a radical hysterectomy than in a simple one, so the hospital stay can be longer, usually about 5 to 7 days. The surgery results in infertility. Complications are unusual but could include excessive bleeding, wound infection, or damage to the urinary and intestinal systems. A radical hysterectomy and pelvic lymph node dissection are the usual treatment for stage IA2, stage IB, and less commonly, stage IIA cervical cancer, especially in young women.

Most women with stage IA2 and stage IB are treated with hysterectomy. Another procedure, known as a radical trachelectomy, allows some young women to be treated without losing their ability to have children. This procedure involves removing the cervix and the upper part of the vagina and placing a purse-string stitch to act as an artificial internal opening of the cervix os. The nearby lymph nodes are also removed using laparoscopy. The operation is done through either the vagina or the abdomen. After trachelectomy, some women are able to carry a pregnancy to term and deliver a healthy baby by cesarean section. In one study, the pregnancy rate after 5 years was more than 50%, but the risk for miscarriage after this surgery is higher than is seen in healthy women (Koh et al., 2015). The risk of the cancer coming back after this procedure is low (Koh et al., 2015).

A pelvic exenteration is a more extensive operation that may be used to treat recurrent cervical cancer. In this surgery, all of the organs and tissues, as in a radical hysterectomy with pelvic lymph node dissection, are removed. In addition, the bladder, vagina, rectum, and part of the colon may also be removed. This operation is used to treat recurrent cervical cancer.

If the bladder is removed, urostomy is needed. If the rectum and part of the colon are removed, a colostomy may be needed. If the vagina is removed, a new vagina can be surgically created out of skin, intestinal tissue, or myocutaneous (muscle and skin) grafts. Recovery from total pelvic exenteration takes up to 6 months after surgery and often a year or longer (Koh et al., 2015).

The advantages of surgery over radiation therapy include shorter treatment time, preserving the function of the ovaries, and limited sexual dysfunction. Surgery can also be the more appropriate treatment if the patient had previous radiation therapy, has inflammatory bowel or pelvic disease, or is pregnant (ACOG, 2013; Koh et al., 2015).

Cancer that starts in the cervix can spread to lymph nodes in the pelvis. To check for lymph node spread, the surgeon performs a lymph node dissection or lymph node sampling. It is done at the same time as a hysterectomy. Removal of lymph nodes can lead to fluid drainage problems in the legs. This can cause severe swelling in the legs, a condition called *lymphedema.*

Radiotherapy

Radiation therapy is an effective treatment for cervical cancer. Studies show that surgery and radiation are equivalent treatments for early-stage cervical cancers (Koh et al., 2015). Radiation therapy also is a treatment for advanced-stage disease. It can be targeted at the main malignant area and the lymph nodes. The advantage of radiation therapy is that the woman can avoid surgery if she is too ill or too high of a risk for surgical anesthesia.

A typical external beam radiation treatment dose is 4,500 centigray (cGy) over 5 weeks, scheduled 5 times per week. A cGy is a unit of absorbed ionizing radiation dose, equal to 1/100 of a gray, or 1 rad (The Free Dictionary, n.d.). An alternative to external beam radiation is intracavitary cesium radiotherapy, administered in the outpatient setting, as a few short-term high-dose treatments (Koh et al., 2015). For cervical cancer, this type of radiation therapy is often accompanied by low doses of chemotherapy, which is known as chemoradiotherapy. The chemotherapy sensitizes the cells to make the radiation more effective.

Brachytherapy for cervical cancer is another treatment option. The radioactive material is placed in a cylinder in the vagina. For some cancers, radioactive material may be placed in thin needles that are inserted directly in the tumor (Koh et al., 2015). Low-dose brachytherapy is completed in just a few days. During that time, the patient remains in the hospital, with instruments holding the radioactive material in place. Nurses caring for patients with radiation material in place for treatment need to be aware of radiation safety practices, wear monitors, and limit time and distance exposure while caring for patients. As an outpatient, the woman can receive high-dose-rate brachytherapy over several treatments. For each treatment, the radioactive material is inserted for a few minutes and then removed. The advantage of high-dose-rate brachytherapy is that it does not require the woman to be immobilized for a long time.

Common side effects of radiation therapy include tiredness, upset stomach, and diarrhea. Some women have problems with nausea and vomiting. These side effects tend to be worse when chemotherapy is given with radiation. Skin changes are also common.

Pelvic radiation therapy may cause scar tissue to form in the vagina (Koh et al., 2015). The scar tissue can make the vagina more narrow (vaginal stenosis) or shorter, which makes vaginal intercourse painful. Interventions for women who experience local and regional effects from radiation treatment were previously discussed in Chapter 4.

Pelvic radiation can damage the ovaries, causing premature menopause. Radiation can irritate the bladder, and problems with urination may occur. Radiation to the pelvis can also weaken the bones, leading to fractures. Hip fractures are the most common and may occur 2 to 4 years after radiation. Bone density studies are recommended (Koh et al., 2015).

Chemotherapy

Chemotherapy can be used as adjuvant treatment in cervical cancer to reduce the risk of recurrence from microscopic tumor cells; however, its role is limited.

Patients with stage IIA or higher cervical cancer who are in good medical condition and are candidates for radiation therapy will be offered chemotherapy to accompany radiation. Studies have shown that adding chemotherapy to radiation decreases mortality from cervical cancer (ACOG, 2013; Koh et al., 2015; Lapresa, Parma, Portuesi, & Colombo, 2015).

The most common chemotherapy regimens include

* cisplatin and paclitaxel;
* cisplatin, paclitaxel, and bevacizumab;
* cisplatin and topotecan;
* cisplatin and gemcitabine; or
* carboplatin and paclitaxel.

Table 6-9 presents the side effects of these commonly used regimens.

Recurrent Cervical Cancer

About one-third of patients with invasive cervical cancer will have a recurrence, and about two-thirds of these patients will present with the disease within 2 years after initial treatment (Koh et al., 2015). Recurrent disease presents as unexplained weight loss, excessive unilateral leg edema, vaginal discharge, and pelvic, thigh, and/or buttock pain.

Patients with recurrent disease have limited effective options. The patient may elect to have more surgery, such as a pelvic exenteration, and additional radiation therapy.

CASE STUDY 6-1

J.N. is a 37-year-old Vietnamese woman who over the years has not had annual pelvic examinations. At the community clinic, where J.N. receives her care, J.N. scheduled a clinical appointment because she has noted abnormal postcoital bleeding for the past year. She also complains of urinary urgency. Her nurse practitioner performs a pelvic examination and obtains a Pap smear. On examination, her clinician notes lesions in the perineal area that are suspicious for HPV.

TABLE 6-9: CHEMOTHERAPY AGENTS FOR CERVICAL CANCER (1 OF 2)		
Agent	**Administration**[a]	**Side Effects**
Cisplatin (Platinol)	IV The patient should be well-hydrated prior to administration of the drug. Poor hydration increases the likelihood of developing side effects. Use with extreme caution (if at all) in patients with kidney dysfunction, impaired hearing, pre-existing peripheral neuropathy, or history of an allergic reaction to this type of medication.	Nausea and vomiting Anaphylactic reactions (consisting of fast heart rate, wheezing, lowered blood pressure, and facial edema), kidney damage Nephrotoxicity Ototoxicity Bone marrow suppression with increased risk for bleeding and infection Electrolyte (sodium, potassium, and magnesium) disturbances Cardiac toxicity (manifested by electrocardiogram changes) may be seen.
Carboplatin (Paraplatin)	IV	The dose-limiting toxic effect is bone marrow suppression, particularly thrombocytopenia leading to increased risk for bleeding. Nausea and vomiting Nephrotoxicity Neurotoxicity, especially tingling and numbness of the hands and feet Ototoxicity
Paclitaxel (Taxol)	IV Anaphylactic-like (hypersensitivity) reactions have been seen with administration, characterized by wheezing, shortness of breath, facial flushing, facial swelling, and decreased blood pressure. Premedication with a steroid, Benadryl, and cimetidine will help minimize this adverse effect.	The dose-limiting side effect of Taxol is bone marrow suppression. Decreases in the white cell count are more predominant than platelet or red blood cell effects. Neuropathy, characterized by numbness, tingling, and pain, has also been seen. The neuropathy is typically reversible when the agent is discontinued. Symptom resolution usually occurs over several months. Cardiac side effects include lowering of the heart rate (bradycardia), but this is usually short-lived. Rarely, the slowing is progressive, leading to complete heart block. Other side effects include nausea and vomiting, diarrhea, mouth sores, hair loss, and flu-like symptoms consisting of joint and muscle aches (arthralgia and myalgia), fever, rash, headache, and fatigue.

TABLE 6-9: CHEMOTHERAPY AGENTS FOR CERVICAL CANCER (2 OF 2)		
Agent	**Administration**[a]	**Side Effects**
Topotecan (Hycamtin)	IV	The major side effect is the development of neutropenia. Lowered platelets and anemia have also been noted; 30% of patients experience nausea and vomiting. One-third of patients experience fever greater than 101°F. Microscopic blood in the urine has occurred in 10% to 12% of patients.
Gemcitabine (Gemzar)	IV	Bone marrow suppression is common. Other effects include a reversible skin rash, fever, nausea and vomiting, and the development of a flu-like syndrome.
Bevacizumab (Avastin)	IV Bevacizumab may cause severe bleeding that can be a life-threatening condition.	• Serious, life-threatening bleeding • Fainting • Loss of appetite • Heartburn • Change in ability to taste food • Diarrhea • Weight loss • Dry mouth • Sores on the skin or in the mouth • Voice changes

IV = intravenous.

[a]For the latest administration protocols, follow accepted and confirmed policies, procedures, guidelines, and Oncology Nursing Society and other professional organization recommendations.

Note. Adapted from Koh, W. J., Greer, B. E., Abu-Rustum, N. R., Apte, S. M., Campos, S. M., Cho, K. R., … Scavone, J. L. (2015). Cervical cancer, version 2.2015. *Journal of the National Comprehensive Cancer Network, 13*(4), 395-404; and Lapresa, M., Parma, G., Portuesi, R., & Colombo, N. (2015). Neoadjuvant chemotherapy in cervical cancer: An update. *Expert Review of Anticancer Therapy, 15*(10), 1171-1181. doi:10.1586/14737140.2015.1079777

The nurse practitioner sends J.N.'s Pap smear to a local laboratory for evaluation. J.N.'s Pap test results note HPV and dysplasia. On follow-up colposcopy, the nurse practitioner performed a biopsy on additional cervical tissue. The pathologist report indicates cervical cancer cells, CIN II.

J.N.'s risk factors include having multiple sex partners in her teens and 20s. She is married, but she and her husband are now separated. A relationship with him continues and they have intercourse intermittently when he is home from his deployments with the U.S. Navy.

To treat her CIN II, J.N. returns to the clinic for a scheduled cryosurgical procedure to remove the cervical lesions. Preprocedure, the nurse practitioner educates her about the procedure and advises her that she may experience some abdominal cramping and bleeding postprocedure that will gradually get better in a few days. Postprocedure, she does experience abdominal cramping and bleeding, which resolves within 48 hours. The nurse practitioner prescribes Tylenol #3 for her pain and instructs J.N. to return to the clinic for a follow-up pelvic examination in 6 months.

A year and a half later, J.N. presents as a walk-in to the clinic, reporting abnormal vaginal bleeding, dysuria, and hematuria for about 2 weeks. In comparison with her weight recorded 6 months ago, she has also lost 10 lb. As part of the diagnostic workup for her latest symptoms, the nurse practitioner performs additional tissue biopsies via curettage. The pathology report diagnoses J.N. with squamous cell cancer of the cervix. Based on clinical data, chest X-ray, and a CT scan of the colon and rectum, J.N. is staged at IIA disease (American Joint Committee on Cancer staging).

After discussion with her healthcare provider team, J.N. chooses to proceed with the recommended treatment: total abdominal hysterectomy followed by radiation therapy. Preoperative teaching included nursing care postsurgery, which focuses on preventing infection, postsurgical wound and packing management, and monitoring bleeding, pain management, and prompt ambulation. Postoperatively, J.N. experiences bleeding and pain. She also had surgical drains, which were removed on day 2 postoperatively. She was discharged from the hospital on day 3.

Five weeks after her surgery, J.N. started external beam radiotherapy (4,500 cGy over 5 weeks, five times per week) and intracavitary cesium radiotherapy (two applications). After completing the radiation treatment, J.N. complained of pain and dryness in her vagina. She also showed signs of vaginitis. Her healthcare provider prescribed a 10-day course of antibiotics and to address discomfort from treatment, and instructed her to use a water-soluble lubrication on her perineum.

During her first year posttreatment, J.N. was scheduled for follow-up at 3-month intervals. During the second year posttreatment, her follow-up examinations were scheduled every 3 to 4 months. Despite the recommended follow-up appointment schedule, J.N. rescheduled her follow-up examinations, which lapsed to every 5 to 6 months. Two years after surgery, J.N. continued to be disease-free on follow-up examination. Her follow-up examinations included chest X-ray, complete blood count, liver function tests, and an abdominal/pelvic computed tomography scan.

Additional Information

J.N. says that since her cancer diagnosis, she and her husband have decided to divorce. She has not seen him for the last year. She continues to work as a checkout clerk at the local retail store. She says she previously used a diaphragm as birth control, but she no longer requires birth control since her hysterectomy. She says she has had two sexual partners in the past 6 months.

On return visits to her nurse practitioner, J.N. is reluctant to discuss any additional screening strategies to maintain her health, including mammography and colonoscopy. Socially, she reveals that she also has isolated herself from friends and neighbors. Her sons (ages 4 and 10), although appearing to be clean and fed, act out when they are out with her. She appears distressed and tired.

J.N. does admit to regularly visiting her local Vietnamese market to purchase ingredients for her own "health" tea, which she says will prevent any future cancer.

Questions

1. What major risk factors does J.N. have for cervical cancer?

2. What side effect of radiation therapy should be addressed with J.N.?

Answers

1. J.N. has an HPV infection that is associated with higher risk for cervical cancer. J.N. has a history of having multiple sexual partners and started sexual activity at an early age. She did not have annual physicals through her 20s, which can often detect cervical tissue changes and with intervention prevent cervical cancer or identify a cervical cancer at a very early stage.

2. Radiation therapy to the cervix leads to significant vaginal stenosis, which is associated with vaginal dryness and painful intercourse or speculum examinations. J.N. might want to consider using a dilator to reduce vaginal stenosis. She may also consider using a vaginal moisturizer to decrease vaginal dryness. During intercourse, her nurse practitioner advises that she use a lubricant.

SUMMARY

Cervical cancer morbidity has decreased because of widely used detection methods – specifically, the Pap smear. Women at risk are usually younger, with risk factors of active or unprotected sexual activity and exposure to HPV or other viruses. Healthcare providers impact cervical cancer morbidity and mortality with targeted education about prevention – especially emphasizing sexual behavior and HPV vaccines, early detection, treating benign cervical tumors, and treating tumors at their earliest stage. Once diagnosed and staged, treatment options for cervical cancer include surgery, radiation, chemotherapy, or a combination of modalities.

EXAM QUESTIONS

CHAPTER 6
Questions 36–44

Note: Choose the one option that BEST answers each question.

36. A major risk factor of cervical cancer is

    a. sexual activity (at early age, multiple sex partners).
    b. colon cancer.
    c. estrogen-receptor-negative status.
    d. obesity.

37. Types of human papillomaviruses (HPVs) associated with cervical cancer include

    a. HPV6.
    b. HPV11.
    c. HPV16.
    d. HPV33.

38. The Gardasil-4 vaccine protects against which HPV types?

    a. 4, 12, 16, and 19
    b. 6, 11, 16, and 18
    c. 16, 18, 30, and 32
    d. 15, 16, 17, and 18

39. To be effective, the HPV vaccine

    a. requires a series of two vaccinations.
    b. should started at age 12 years.
    c. should be started after puberty.
    d. should be completed before the initiation of sexual activity.

40. A technique or strategy that is thought to improve the interpretation of Pap tests is

    a. immediate refrigeration of slides.
    b. air-drying the slide before transport.
    c. liquid-based thin-layer slide preparation.
    d. combing the smear with Betadine.

41. The Bethesda system for interpreting a Pap test includes

    a. cervical intraepithelial neoplasia (CIN) grading only.
    b. general categorization of normal or abnormal.
    c. categorization by class.
    d. HPV results.

42. When classifying cervical cellular changes, moderate dysplasia in one-third to two-thirds of the thickness of the epithelium would receive the classification grade of

    a. CIN I.
    b. CIN II.
    c. CIN III.
    d. carcinoma in situ.

43. The treatment for a woman with stage I cervical cancer is

    a. surgery.
    b. radiation.
    c. chemotherapy.
    d. hormonal manipulation.

continued on next page

44. Chemotherapy agents used as a treatment for cervical cancer include

    a. cisplatin and cyclophosphamide.
    b. cisplatin and paclitaxel.
    c. cisplatin and hydroxyurea.
    d. cisplatin and BCNU.

REFERENCES

Abu-Rustum, N. R. (2014). Sentinel lymph node mapping for endometrial cancer: a modern approach to surgical staging. *Journal of the National Comprehensive Cancer Network, 12,* 288-297.

American Cancer Society. (2015). *Global cancer facts and figures* (3rd ed.). Atlanta, GA: Author.

American Cancer Society. (2016). *Cancer facts and figures for African Americans – 2016-2018.* Atlanta, GA: Author.

American Cancer Society. (2017a). *Cancer facts and figures – 2017.* Atlanta, GA: Author.

American Cancer Society. (2017b). *Cancer prevention and early detection facts and figures – 2017-2018.* Atlanta, GA: Author.

American College of Obstetricians and Gynecologists. (2013). *Management of abnormal cervical cytology and histology* (ACOG Practice Bulletin No. 140). Washington, DC: Author.

American College of Obstetricians and Gynecologists. (2016). Practice Bulletin No. 168 summary: Cervical cancer screening and prevention. *Obstetrics & Gynecology, 128*(4), 923-925. doi:10.1097/AOG.0000 000000001699

Amin, M. B., Edge, S., Greene, F., Byrd, D. R., Brookland, R. K., Washington, M. K., ... Meyer, L. R. (Eds.). (2017). *AJCC cancer staging manual* (8th ed.), New York, NY: Springer.

Apgar, B. S., Kittendorf, A. L., Bettcher, C. M., Wong, J., & Kaufman, A. J. (2009). Update on ASCCP consensus guidelines for abnormal cervical screening tests and cervical histology. *American Family Physician, 80*(2), 147-155.

Centers for Disease Control and Prevention. (2015a). *HPV vaccine for preteens and teens.* Retrieved from https://www.cdc.gov/vaccines/parents/diseases/teen/hpv.html

Centers for Disease Control and Prevention. (2015b). *National Breast and Cervical Cancer Early Detection Program (NBCCEDP): About the program.* Retrieved from http://www.cdc.gov/cancer/nbccedp/about.htm

Kim, S. H., Lee, J. M., Yun, H. G., Park, U. S., Hwang, S. U., Pyo, J. S., & Sohn, J. H. (2016). Overall accuracy of cervical cytology and clinicopathological significance of LSIL cells in ASC-H cytology. *Cytopathology 28*(1), 16-23. doi:10.1111/cyt.12351

Koh, W. J., Greer, B. E., Abu-Rustum, N. R., Apte, S. M., Campos, S. M., Cho, K. R., ... Scavone, J. L. (2015). Cervical cancer, version 2.2015. *Journal of the National Comprehensive Cancer Network, 13*(4), 395-404.

Lapresa, M., Parma, G., Portuesi, R., & Colombo, N. (2015). Neoadjuvant chemotherapy in cervical cancer: An update. *Expert Review of Anticancer Therapy, 15*(10), 1171-1181. doi:10.1586/14737140.2015.1079777

Lees, B. F., Erickson, B. K., & Huh, W. K. (2016). Cervical cancer screening: Evidence behind the guidelines. *American Journal of Obstetrics & Gynecology, 214*(4), 438-443. doi:10.1016/j.ajog.2015.10.147

Moyer, V. A. (2012). Screening for cervical cancer: U.S. Preventive Services Task Force recommendation statement. *Annals of Internal Medicine, 156*(12), 880-891. doi:10.7326/0003-4819-156-12-201206190-00424

National Comprehensive Cancer Network. (2016). *Cervical cancer, version 1.2017.*

Practice Bulletin No. 157: Cervical cancer screening and prevention. (2016). *Obstetrics & Gynecology, 127*(1), e1-e20. doi:10.1097/AOG.0000000000001263

Saslow, D., Solomon, D., Lawson, H. W., Killackey, M., Kulasingam, S. L., Cain, J., … Myers, E. R. (2012). American Cancer Society, American Society for Colposcopy and Cervical Pathology, and American Society for Clinical Pathology screening guidelines for the prevention and early detection of cervical cancer. *CA: A Cancer Journal for Clinicians, 62*(3), 147-172. doi:10.3322/caac.21139

The Free Dictionary. (n.d.). *cGy.* Retrieved from http://medical-dictionary.thefreedictionary.com/cgy

Umana, A., Dunsmore, H., Herbert, A., Jokhan, A., & Kubba, A. (2013). Are significant numbers of abnormal cells lost on the discarded ThinPrep® broom when used for cervical cytology? *Cytopathology, 24*(4), 228-234. doi:10.1111/cyt.12029

U.S. Department of Health and Human Services, National Institutes of Health, National Cancer Institute. (n.d.). *SEER stat fact sheets: Cervix uteri cancer.* Retrieved from http://seer.cancer.gov/statfacts/html/cervix.html

U.S. Department of Health and Human Services, National Institutes of Health, National Cancer Institute. (2004). *Cells of the cervix.* Retrieved from https://visualsonline.cancer.gov/details.cfm?imageid=4349

U.S. Department of Health and Human Services, National Institutes of Health, National Cancer Institute. (2013). *Pap test.* Retrieved from https://visualsonline.cancer.gov/details.cfm?imageid=8271

Viens, L. J., Henley, S. J., Watson, M., Markowitz, L. E., Thomas, C. C., Thompson, T. D., … Saraiya, M. (2016). Human papillomavirus-associated cancers – United States, 2008-2012. *MMWR: Morbidity & Mortality Weekly Report, 65*(26), 661-666. doi:10.15585/mmwr.mm6526a1

CHAPTER 7

LUNG CANCER

LEARNING OUTCOME

After completing this chapter, the learner will be able to discuss the epidemiology, risk factors, prevention and detection strategies, and main treatments for lung cancer in women.

CHAPTER OBJECTIVES

After completing this chapter, the learner will be able to:

1. Describe the epidemiology of and risk factors for lung cancer.

2. Identify the signs and symptoms of lung cancer.

3. Explain detection and prevention strategies for lung cancer.

4. Explain the diagnostic evaluation and staging for lung cancer.

5. Describe the treatment modalities for small cell and non-small cell lung cancers.

INTRODUCTION

A review of cancer in women typically focuses on the gender-specific cancers unique to women. Yet, the second most prevalent cancer in women is lung cancer, a cancer that continues to evade prevention efforts and spurn hope promised by new treatments. Lung cancer accounts for 25% of all cancer deaths in women and is the number one cause of cancer-related deaths in women (American Cancer Society [ACS], 2017a). See Box 7-1 for lung cancer facts.

Unfortunately, the incidence and death rate of lung cancer in women, when compared to men, have not seen significant improvement in the last 20 years despite efforts to promote smoking cessation and increase awareness of the dangers of smoking (ACS, 2017a). Since the mid-1980s the incident rate in men has been declining; however, for women the decline only began in the mid-2000s. The lung cancer mortality rates have decreased 43% for men since 1990, but only 17% for women since 2002. From 2010 to 2014, men saw a death rate decrease of 3.5% per year while women saw a smaller reduction of 2% per year (ACS, 2017a). Tobacco use continues to be a primary cause of lung cancer, especially in women. Approaches to treatment have changed with the multidisciplinary approach to care; society's success in showing how deadly tobacco use can be and the development and evolution of novel targeted therapies have modestly extended the still-too-short survival rates. This chapter provides a review of the well-known challenges of lung cancer and the benefits associated with early detection and more strategic treatments.

EPIDEMIOLOGY

Most of the epidemiological data on lung cancer include small cell lung cancer (SCLC) and non-small cell lung cancer

BOX 7-1: LUNG CANCER FACTS

- There are 105,510 estimated new cases in women annually.

- The incidence rate in women has just begun to decrease after many years of increase; the current rate is 1 in 17 women.

- There are 71,280 estimated deaths among women annually.

- It is responsible for 12% of new cancers diagnosed in women annually.

- It is responsible for 25% of all cancer deaths in women.

- The mortality rate from lung cancer is slowly declining with fewer people who are smokers.

- The 1-year survival rate is 44%; the 5-year survival rate is 21%.

- Only 16% of cases are diagnosed at the localized stage, for which the 5-year survival rate is 55%.

Note. Based on data from American Cancer Society. (2017a). *Cancer facts & figures – 2017.* Atlanta, GA: Author.

(NSCLC). In general, SCLC accounts for about 13% of all lung cancers, and approximately 87% are NSCLCs (ACS, 2017a). Lung cancer is the second most common cancer in both men (after prostate cancer) and women (after breast cancer). It accounts for about 12% of all new cancers in women (ACS, 2017a).

Lung cancer incidence increases with aging; approximately two of every three people diagnosed with lung cancer are older than 65 years; fewer than 2% of all cases are found in people younger than 45 years (see Figures 7-1 and 7-2). The average age at the time of diagnosis is approximately 70 years. The mortality rate from lung cancer remains high; mean age at death is 72 years (see Figures 7-3 and 7-4). The prognosis for lung cancer is poor because few lung cancers are detected early (see Figure 7-5).

ANATOMY OF THE LUNGS

The lungs are two spongelike organs found in the chest (see Figure 7-6). The right lung is divided into three sections, called *lobes.* The left lung has two lobes. The left lung is smaller because the heart takes up more room on that side of the body. During inspira-

tion, air enters through the mouth or nose and goes into the lungs through the trachea. The trachea divides into tubes called the *bronchi,* which divide into smaller branches called *bronchioles.* At the end of the bronchioles are tiny air sacs known as alveoli.

Many tiny blood vessels run through the alveoli. They absorb oxygen from the inhaled air into the bloodstream and pass carbon dioxide from the body into the alveoli. This is expelled from the body during expiration.

A thin lining layer called the *pleura* surrounds the lungs. The pleura protects the lungs and helps them slide back and forth as they expand and contract during breathing.

Smoking and other risk factors contribute to the formation of lung cancer by damaging the cells that line the lungs. When cigarette smoke is inhaled, the carcinogens in cigarette smoke lead to changes in the lung tissue. Initially, the body may be able to repair this damage, but with repeated exposure, the normal cells that line the lungs are increasingly damaged. Over time, the damage causes cells to reproduce abnormally and eventually malignancy develops (ACS, 2017b).

continued on page 172

FIGURE 7-1: AGE DISTRIBUTION OF LUNG CANCER

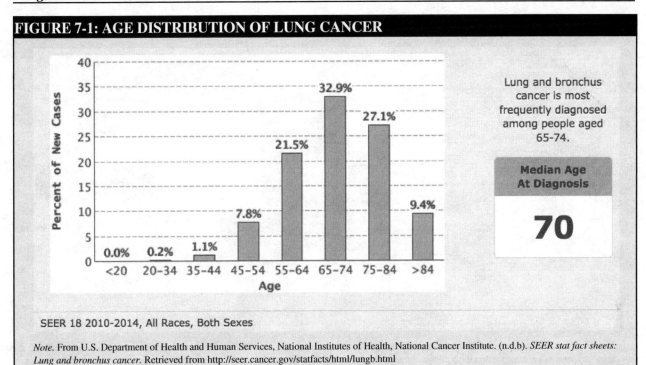

SEER 18 2010-2014, All Races, Both Sexes

Note. From U.S. Department of Health and Human Services, National Institutes of Health, National Cancer Institute. (n.d.b). *SEER stat fact sheets: Lung and bronchus cancer.* Retrieved from http://seer.cancer.gov/statfacts/html/lungb.html

FIGURE 7-2: NUMBER OF NEW CASES PER 100,00 PERSONS BY RACE/ETHNICITY AND SEX: LUNG CANCER

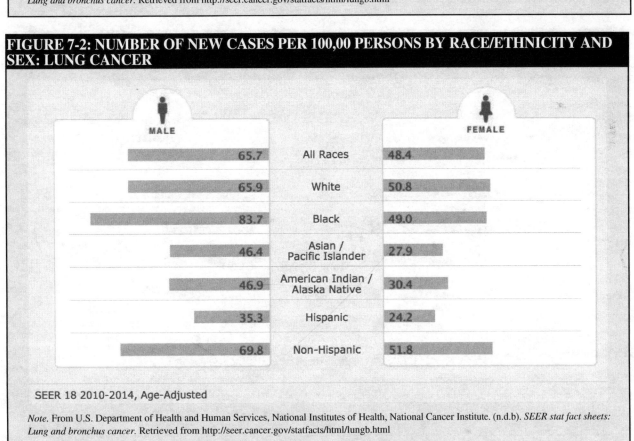

SEER 18 2010-2014, Age-Adjusted

Note. From U.S. Department of Health and Human Services, National Institutes of Health, National Cancer Institute. (n.d.b). *SEER stat fact sheets: Lung and bronchus cancer.* Retrieved from http://seer.cancer.gov/statfacts/html/lungb.html

FIGURE 7-3: AGE DISTRIBUTION OF DEATH FROM LUNG CANCER

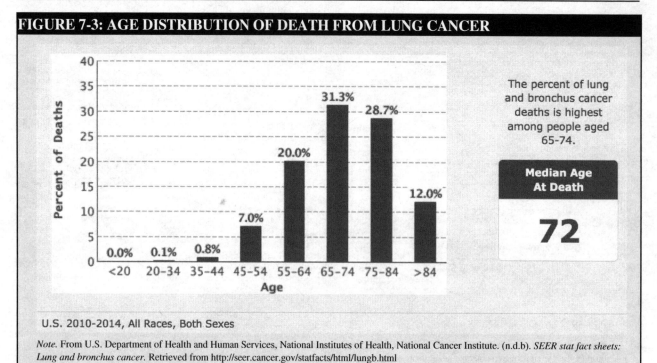

The percent of lung and bronchus cancer deaths is highest among people aged 65-74.

Median Age At Death

72

U.S. 2010-2014, All Races, Both Sexes

Note. From U.S. Department of Health and Human Services, National Institutes of Health, National Cancer Institute. (n.d.b). *SEER stat fact sheets: Lung and bronchus cancer.* Retrieved from http://seer.cancer.gov/statfacts/html/lungb.html

FIGURE 7-4: NUMBER OF DEATHS PER 100,000 PERSONS BY RACE/ETHNICITY AND SEX: LUNG CANCER

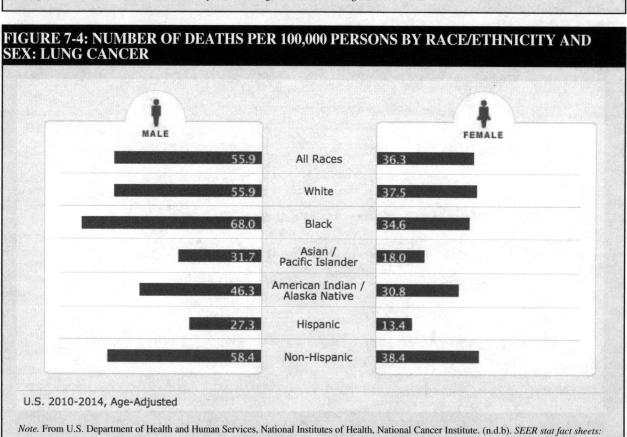

U.S. 2010-2014, Age-Adjusted

Note. From U.S. Department of Health and Human Services, National Institutes of Health, National Cancer Institute. (n.d.b). *SEER stat fact sheets: Lung and bronchus cancer.* Retrieved from http://seer.cancer.gov/statfacts/html/lungb.html

FIGURE 7-5: PERCENT OF CASES AND 5-YEAR SURVIVAL BY STAGE AT DIAGNOSIS: LUNG CANCER

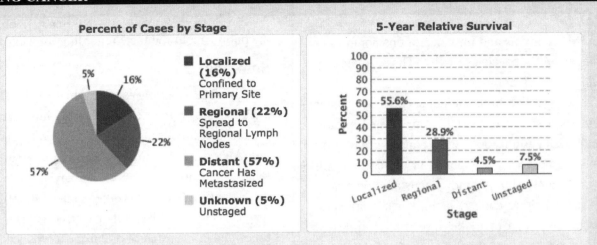

Percent of Cases by Stage

■ **Localized (16%)** Confined to Primary Site

■ **Regional (22%)** Spread to Regional Lymph Nodes

■ **Distant (57%)** Cancer Has Metastasized

■ **Unknown (5%)** Unstaged

5-Year Relative Survival

SEER 18 2007-2013, All Races, Both Sexes by SEER Summary Stage 2000

Note. From U.S. Department of Health and Human Services, National Institutes of Health, National Cancer Institute. (n.d.b). *SEER stat fact sheets: Lung and bronchus cancer.* Retrieved from http://seer.cancer.gov/statfacts/html/lungb.html

FIGURE 7-6: LUNG ANATOMY

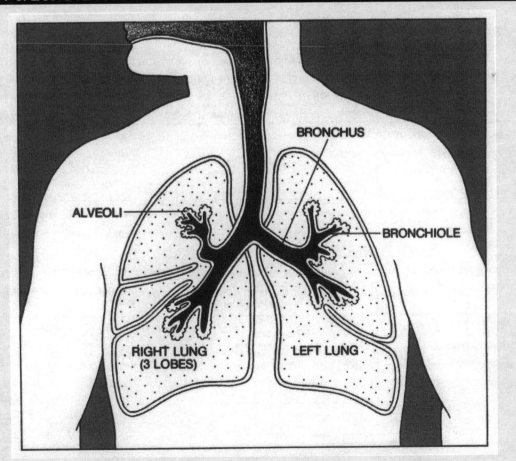

Note. From U.S. Department of Health and Human Services, National Institutes of Health, National Cancer Institute. (n.d.a). *Lungs.* Retrieved from https://visualsonline.cancer.gov/details.cfm?imageid=1775

RISK FACTORS

Myths

Many myths and misconceptions about lung cancer and tobacco use exist. These myths, as well as facts about tobacco use, are listed in Table 7-1. The high incidence of lung cancer and its associated mortality in women should make education about lung cancer prevention and the appropriate application of screening in women a priority. All individuals are potentially at risk for lung cancer, including nonsmokers, so nurses need to make sure that symptoms, especially fatigue and shortness of breath, are evaluated in both smokers and nonsmokers. Nurses have a major responsibility to educate the public about the facts regarding lung cancer.

Smoking

Cigarette smoking is the primary risk factor associated with the development of lung cancer – there is a direct causal effect of cigarette smoking. Although cigarette smoking and exposure to tobacco are not absolute causes of lung cancer, the patient's tobacco exposure is linked to 80% of lung cancers. A smoker's lung cancer risk is many times higher than that of a nonsmoker, depending

TABLE 7-1: MYTHS AND FACTS ABOUT TOBACCO USE (1 OF 2)	
Myths	**Facts**
Only smokers are at risk.	Most people diagnosed with lung cancer are not current smokers but are ex-smokers (some of whom have quit a decade or more ago). In addition, in 2017, approximately 21,000 Americans who never smoked learned that they have lung cancer.
	A smoker's lung cancer risk is many times higher than that of a nonsmoker, depending on how many cigarettes are smoked and how long the person has smoked, but nonsmokers who are exposed to secondhand smoke are also at risk. Tobacco use is linked to 80% of lung cancer cases.
Men and women are equally susceptible to the effects of lung carcinogens found in tobacco smoke.	Women may have a greater susceptibility to these carcinogens than men.
Once someone begins to smoke, the damage is done, so there is no point in quitting.	When smokers stop, the damage that leads to cancer may heal. Research shows that quitting helps those who already have lung cancer respond better to treatment.
Women need not worry about lung cancer.	Lung cancer is by far the leading cancer killer of women. According to the American Cancer Society, 71,280 American women will die of lung cancer in 2017, compared with 40,620 of breast cancer.
The first sign of lung cancer is coughing up blood.	Coughing up blood is a common symptom, but it usually appears later. The early signs are vague: fatigue and shortness of breath. The signs and symptoms of lung cancer may take years to appear and often are confused with symptoms of less serious conditions. They may not appear until the disease reaches an advanced stage. Depending on which organs are affected, the symptoms can include headaches, general weakness, pain, bone fractures, bleeding, or blood clots.
Nicotine replacement therapy (NRT) does not work.	NRT can double a smoker's chances of quitting smoking. The likelihood of not smoking for more than 6 months is increased when a smoker uses NRT according to the directions.

TABLE 7-1: MYTHS AND FACTS ABOUT TOBACCO USE (2 OF 2)	
Myths	**Facts**
The nicotine in cigarettes is the same as the nicotine found in NRT products, so it is just trading one addiction for another.	No, the products are different. The likelihood of long-term addiction to NRT is very low, and NRT products have a much lower risk for addiction than cigarettes. The nicotine found in NRT is regulated by the U.S. Food and Drug Administration. The amount of nicotine in NRT is less than in cigarettes and it is delivered more slowly.
With NRT, there are no withdrawal symptoms or cravings from quitting smoking.	NRT does reduce withdrawal symptoms associated with cigarette smoking; however, it may not completely eliminate them. The symptoms most helped by NRT include irritability, frustration, anger, craving, hunger, anxiety, difficulty concentrating, restlessness, and insomnia.
"Low-tar," "mild," "light," or "ultra-light" cigarettes are less harmful to health than "regular" cigarettes.	Although smoke from light cigarettes may feel smoother and lighter on the throat and chest, light cigarettes are not healthier than regular cigarettes. Light cigarettes do not reduce the health risks of smoking. The only way to reduce a smoker's risk, and the risk to others, is to stop smoking completely.
If a smoker fails to quit the first time, he or she will continue to be unsuccessful.	On average, it usually takes six attempts before a person actually succeeds in quitting smoking.
Electronic cigarettes are a safer form of smoking.	The health risks of electronic cigarettes are not known. They also may lead to the use of other tobacco products with known health risks.

Note. Adapted from:

American Cancer Society. (2015). *Global cancer facts and figures* (3rd ed.). Atlanta, GA: Author.

American Cancer Society. (2017a). *Cancer facts & figures – 2017*. Atlanta, GA: Author.

American Cancer Society. (2017b). *Cancer prevention and early detection facts and figures – 2016-2018*. Atlanta, GA: Author.

on how many cigarettes are smoked and how long the person has smoked (ACS, 2017a).

The risk of developing lung cancer as a result of smoking increases with

- the age at which smoking began,
- how long the person has smoked,
- the number of cigarettes smoked per day, and
- how deeply the smoker inhales.

Secondhand smoke also increases the risk for lung cancer. A nonsmoker who lives with a smoker has an approximately 20% to 30% greater risk of developing lung cancer (ACS, 2017a). Secondhand smoke is the attributed cause of more than 3,200 lung cancer deaths annually (ACS, 2017b).

Other Risk Factors

Table 7-2 lists risk factors for lung cancer. Most lung cancers develop from environmental exposures – carcinogens, viruses, and chemicals. Notable are the risks associated with exposure to asbestos, secondhand smoke, air pollutants, and radon (National Comprehensive Cancer Network [NCCN], 2017a).

Researchers have found that genetics plays a role in some families with a strong history of lung cancer. People who inherit certain DNA changes in particular genes are more likely to develop lung cancer, even if they smoke only a little. At this time, routine testing for these changes is not clinically available; genetic testing for lung cancer remains in development (ACS, 2017a).

TABLE 7-2: RISK FACTORS FOR LUNG CANCER

- Smoking cigarettes, cigars, and pipes (linked to 80% of lung cancers)

- Exposure to environmental tobacco smoke (secondhand smoke)

- Exposure to radon, the radioactive gas that occurs naturally in soil and rocks (second leading cause of lung cancer)

- Exposure to asbestos, naturally occurring minerals used in shipbuilding, asbestos mining and manufacturing, insulation work, and brake repair

- Inhaled chemicals or minerals such as arsenic, beryllium, cadmium, silica, vinyl chloride, nickel compounds, chromium compounds, coal products, mustard gas, and chloromethyl ethers

- Exposure to pollution and certain air pollutants, including by-products of the combustion of diesel and other fossil fuels, such as coal, coke, and soot; also, exposure to uranium, nickel, arsenic, and cadmium.

- Genetic predisposition may play a role in the development of lung cancer, especially in nonsmokers

- Personal history and previous lung cancer

Note. Adapted from American Cancer Society. (2017a). *Cancer facts & figures – 2017*. Atlanta, GA: Author.

It is not clear whether smoking marijuana increases lung cancer risk. Reasons to consider include that marijuana smoke contains tar, and many of the same carcinogens that are in tobacco smoke and marijuana are inhaled very deeply and the smoke is held in the lungs for a long time, which gives any cancer-causing substances more opportunity to deposit in the lungs. Those who use marijuana tend to smoke fewer marijuana cigarettes in a day or week than the amount of tobacco consumed by cigarette smokers. The lesser amount smoked would make it more difficult to identify an impact on lung cancer risk (Callaghan, Allebeck, & Sidorchuk, 2013). Results from pooled analyses provide little evidence for an increased risk for lung cancer among habitual or long-term cannabis smokers, although the possibility of potential adverse effects for heavy consumption cannot be excluded (Zhang et al., 2015).

SMOKING

In the United States, about 1 million people become new smokers each year. Of these, about half will eventually be killed by tobacco-induced illness if they do not stop smoking, and half of these deaths will be in middle age (35 to 69 years old). Approximately 1.5 million of the estimated 8 million cancer deaths in the world were caused by tobacco smoking (ACS, 2015). Worldwide, it is estimated that 30 million people start to smoke every year. It can be expected that the number of tobacco deaths in the world will exceed 10 million every year unless 20 million current smokers stop smoking (ACS, 2015).

Women and Smoking

According to the Centers for Disease Control and Prevention Office on Smoking and Health, about 24 million adult women and at least 1.9 million adolescent girls smoke cigarettes, despite what they know about death, disease, and addiction caused by smoking (Jamal et al., 2015).

Currently, estimates suggest that 21% of all American women smoke. Female smokers typically take up smoking during adolescence, usually before their senior year in high school, but often in middle school or junior high. The earlier a young woman begins smoking, the more likely she is to become a heavy smoker as an adult (ACS, 2017b).

Between 1965 and 1975, a sharp increase in smoking initiation occurred among women. This generation of women, born between 1950 and 1960, passed through adolescence and young adulthood at the time when cigarette brands such as Virginia Slims were introduced and were marketed intensively to women (Jamal et al., 2015).

Electronic Nicotine Delivery

Electronic nicotine delivery systems, known as electronic cigarettes, are battery-operated devices that allow the user to inhale a vapor produced from cartridges or tanks filled with a liquid that contains nicotine, propylene, other chemicals, and sometimes flavoring. Current estimates are that at least 2% of adults are utilizing electronic cigarettes (ACS, 2017b). Expenditures on electronic cigarette advertising have tripled in recent years. These products are advertised and promoted as a way to bypass smoke-free laws and as being a healthier alternative to traditional cigarettes. Unfortunately, little evidence exists to support these claims, and preliminary research suggests that the health risks of electronic cigarettes are not fully known and that these products lead to the use of other types of tobacco products with known health risks (Prokhorov, Calabro, & Tamí-Maury, 2016). Use of e-cigarettes is also increasing among youth. The prevalence of current e-cigarette use among high school students increased from 1.5% in 2011 to 4.5% in 2013 (ACS, 2017b).

Teenagers and Smoking

The overall decline in adult smoking has prompted the tobacco industry to recruit almost 1 million new smokers a year, most of them children and adolescents. Tobacco advertising targets younger smokers, which significantly increases an adolescent's likelihood to smoke (ACS, 2017b).

Many children start using tobacco by 11 years of age, and many become addicted by 14 years of age (ACS, 2017b). Studies show that a person who does not begin smoking as a child or adolescent is not likely to begin as an adult, with almost 90% of adult smokers having started smoking at or before 18 years of age (Prokhorov et al., 2016).

To reduce tobacco-related mortality, everything possible must be done to stop children and adolescents from starting to smoke. This will greatly affect the burden of tobacco-related deaths in the latter half of the 21st century. The major public health gain in the next 20 to 40 years will come from convincing smokers to stop smoking (Jones, Gardner, & Cleveland, 2014).

Health Policy and Marketing

State variations in smoking prevalence are influenced by several factors, including public awareness about the harmful health effects of tobacco use, social norms about tobacco use, educational levels within the state, racial and ethnic variations among the states, and tobacco-control activities at the state and local levels. Most Southern and Midwestern states continue to have a high prevalence of smoking and low excise tax, despite evidence that excise taxes and other components of comprehensive tobacco control can achieve substantial reductions in tobacco use (Jamal et al., 2015).

Research shows that the price of cigarettes is inversely and predictably related to tobacco use (ACS, 2017b). A 10% increase in price reduces overall cigarette use by 3% to 5% and youth use by 6% to 7%. The World Health Organization recommends that excise taxes account for at least 70% of the final consumer price (ACS, 2017a). This is especially important because youth are three times more likely to be dissuaded from tobacco use in the face of higher costs. In 2017, the federal excise tax was $1.01 (Campaign for Tobacco Free Kids, 2017). The average state cigarette excise tax rate was $1.69, with wide variation between states, ranging from 17 cents per pack in Missouri to $4.35 per pack in New York (Campaign for Tobacco Free Kids, 2017).

With young girls, the temptation to smoke is influenced by targeted marketing by cigarette companies and long-standing myths about cigarette use as a means to maintain or lose weight (Centers for Disease Control and Prevention, 2012). Many girls as young as those in the third and fourth grades are already concerned about their weight and body image, and many have already been on diets by the time they enter junior high school. Smoking is perceived as a means to lose weight and look sophisticated, which is a big concern of young women struggling with self-esteem and feeling like they do not belong. Research shows that smoking does not promote thinness, yet tobacco companies continue to utilize this marketing tactic to entice young women to smoke (Centers for Disease Control and Prevention, 2012).

SIGNS AND SYMPTOMS

Symptoms

Most lung cancers do not cause symptoms until the cancer has metastasized; however, symptoms may present in early stages of lung cancer (ACS, 2017a). As part of the differential diagnosis, symptoms may be identified as an infectious process and other pulmonary disease; therefore, once a symptom is detected, a full evaluation must be performed to determine the etiology of the symptom and to determine whether it is a malignancy. The most common symptoms of lung cancer are (ACS, 2017)

- a cough that does not go away;

- chest pain that is often worse with deep breathing, coughing, or laughing;

- hoarseness;

- weight loss and loss of appetite;

- bloody or rust-colored sputum;

- shortness of breath;

- recurring infections such as bronchitis and pneumonia; and

- new onset of wheezing.

When lung cancer spreads to distant organs, the tumor cells may cause (ACS, 2017a)

- bone pain;

- neurological changes (such as headache, weakness or numbness of a limb, dizziness, or recent seizure onset);

- jaundice; and

- lumps near the surface of the body as a result of cancer spreading to the skin or to the lymph nodes in the neck or above the collarbone.

Some lung cancers can cause a group of very specific symptoms. The group of symptoms is often described as syndromes.

Horner's Syndrome

Cancer of the top part of the lungs (sometimes called *Pancoast tumors*) may damage a nerve that passes from the upper chest into the neck. The most common symptom of these tumors is severe shoulder pain. The group of symptoms of Horner's syndrome include

- drooping or weakness of one eyelid (ptosis),

- having a smaller pupil in the same eye (pupil constriction), and

- reduced or absent sweating on the same side of the face.

Other conditions that cause Horner's syndrome involve the facial nerve where interruption to the sympathetic nerve supply to the eye occurs.

Paraneoplastic Syndromes

Some lung cancer cells can make hormone-like substances that enter the bloodstream and cause problems with distant tissues and organs, even though the cancer has not spread to those tissues or organs. These are called *paraneoplastic syndromes*. These syndromes are sometimes the first symptoms of early lung cancer. Because the symptoms affect other organs, patients and their doctors might first suspect that diseases other than lung cancer are causing them.

The most common paraneoplastic syndromes caused by NSCLC are

- hypercalcemia, which can cause frequent urination, constipation, weakness, dizziness, confusion, and other nervous system problems;

- excess growth of certain bones, especially those in the fingertips, which can be very painful;

- blood clots; and

- gynecomastia in males.

PREVENTION AND DETECTION STRATEGIES

In 2008, The Joint Commission received funding from the U.S. Department of Health and Human Services to develop and test standardized performance measures addressing tobacco screening and cessation counseling that now must be offered to all hospitalized inpatients, irrespective of their diagnosis/clinical condition (ACS, 2017b; Fiore & Adsit, 2016).

Highlights of these guidelines are as follows (ACS, 2017b, Fiore & Adsit, 2016):

- Clinicians must document the tobacco-use status of every patient.

- Every patient using tobacco should be offered one or more of the available effective smoking-cessation treatments.

- Tobacco dependence is a chronic disease that often requires repeated intervention and multiple attempts to quit. Effective treatments exist, and continued support and follow-up can significantly increase rates of long-term abstinence.

- Individual, group, and telephone counseling are effective, and their effectiveness increases with treatment intensity. Two components of counseling are especially effective, and clinicians should try to combine these when counseling patients who are making an attempt to quit.

Smoking Cessation

The longer an individual smokes, and the more packs per day smoked, the greater the risk for lung cancer. People who stop smoking before 50 years of age cut their risk of dying in the next 15 years in half compared with those who continue to smoke (ACS, 2017b). Individuals who are current smokers also should be informed that the more immediate preventive health priority is the elimination of tobacco use altogether because smoking cessation offers the most effective means of reducing the risk for premature mortality from lung cancer (ACS, 2017a). Smoking cessation also saves public health dollars; increasingly, health insurance plans are paying for smoking-cessation aids to save money long term (Athar et al., 2016). See Figure 7-7 for other benefits of smoking cessation.

Studies report that approximately 50% of those who smoke and want to quit have difficulty quitting because of the addictive nature of tobacco and nicotine products (Karam-Hage, Cinciripini, & Gritz, 2014). The Surgeon General's Report on Nicotine Addiction in 1988 was the first study that provided conclusive evi-

FIGURE 7-7: BENEFITS OF SMOKING CESSATION

Short-Term Benefits

- Blood pressure, pulse, and body temperature, which are abnormally elevated by nicotine, return to normal. Individuals who are taking blood pressure medication should continue to do so until told otherwise by their physicians.

- The body starts to heal itself. Carbon monoxide and oxygen levels in the blood return to normal.

- The risk of having a heart attack decreases.

- Nerve endings start to regenerate. The ability to taste and smell improves.

- Bronchial tubes relax, lung capacity increases, and breathing becomes easier.

- Circulation improves, and the lungs become stronger, making it easier to walk.

- Cilia in the lungs begin to regrow, increasing the ability of the lungs to handle mucus, clean themselves, and reduce infection. Coughing, sinus congestion, fatigue, and shortness of breath decrease.

- Overall energy level increases.

Long-Term Benefits

- The risk of dying of lung cancer is less than it would be if the individual continued to smoke.

- The risk of getting cancer of the throat, bladder, kidney, or pancreas also decreases.

- The risk of stroke or heart attack is reduced.

Note. Adapted from:

American Cancer Society. (2017b). *Cancer prevention and early detection facts and figures – 2016-2018.* Atlanta, GA: Author.

Sarna, L., & Bialous, S. A. (2016). Implementation of tobacco dependence treatment programs in oncology settings. *Seminars in Oncology Nursing, 32*(3), 187-196. doi:10.1016/j.soncn.2016.05.002

---

dence that cigarettes and other types of tobacco are addictive. The report underscored the fact that willpower alone could not eliminate smoking as a public health threat (ACS, 2017b).

Nicotine creates a physical dependence because nicotine receptors in the brain become saturated during exposure, creating an increased tolerance to nicotine. Studies have suggested that a person's genetic makeup may be a foundation for tobacco dependence. These early studies may lead to ways to target those individuals who are more susceptible to nicotine and smoking behaviors, so that early treatment or cessation interventions are effective (Shields, 2015).

Smoking behavior is also linked with psychological and social factors. Among those factors are being prone to anxiety and depression. In this area as well, researchers are studying methods to target interventions. Social support has been established as a method to help women quit smoking (Jones et al., 2014).

Once diagnosed, many of those with lung cancer continue to smoke because their tobacco addiction is well entrenched (NCCN, 2017f). Studies show that with acute illness, most lung cancer patients make attempts to quit (Mulshine & D'Amico, 2014). Nursing support to help patients quit is an important focus of care. Table 7-3 highlights some well-known strategies to help patients quit smoking.

TABLE 7-3: CONSIDERATIONS FOR SMOKING CESSATION (1 OF 2)

Preparing Yourself for Quitting

- Decide positively that you want to quit.

- List all the reasons you want to quit.

- Develop strong personal reasons, in addition to your health and obligations to others, for quitting. For example, think of all the time you waste taking cigarette breaks, rushing out to buy a pack, or hunting for a light.

- Begin to condition yourself physically: Start a modest exercise program, drink more fluids, get plenty of rest, and avoid fatigue.

- Set a firm target date for quitting – perhaps a special day such as your birthday, your anniversary, or the Great American Smokeout.

Knowing What to Expect

- Have realistic expectations.

- Understand that withdrawal symptoms are temporary. They usually last only 1 to 2 weeks.

- Know that most relapses occur in the first week after quitting, when withdrawal symptoms are strongest and your body is still dependent on nicotine.

- Mobilize all your personal resources – willpower, family, friends, and the tips – to get you through this critical period successfully.

- Know that most other relapses occur in the first 3 months after quitting, when situational triggers – such as a particularly stressful event – occur unexpectedly.

- Realize that most successful ex-smokers quit for good only after several attempts.

Involving Someone Else

- Ask your friend or spouse to quit with you.

- Tell your family and friends that you are quitting and when.

- Consider joining a smoking-cessation class or support group.

- Discuss cessation with your healthcare provider to see if he or she can provide additional support or assistance.

Quitting Tips

- Switch brands.

- Smoke only half of each cigarette.

- Decide beforehand how many cigarettes you will smoke during the day.

- Change your eating habits to help you cut down on smoking.

- Reach for a glass of juice instead of a cigarette for a pick-me-up.

- Do not empty your ashtrays.

- Make smoking inconvenient; stop buying cigarettes by the carton. Stop carrying cigarettes with you at home or at work.

Making Smoking Unpleasant

- Smoke only under circumstances that are not especially pleasurable for you. For example, if you like to smoke with others, smoke alone.

- Collect all your cigarette butts in one large glass container as a visual reminder of the filth made by smoking.

TABLE 7-3: CONSIDERATIONS FOR SMOKING CESSATION (2 OF 2)

Avoiding Temptation

• For the first 1 to 3 weeks, avoid situations you strongly associate with the pleasurable aspects of smoking.

• Limit your socializing to healthful, outdoor activities or situations where smoking is not allowed.

• Keep oral substitutes handy. Try carrots, pickles, sunflower seeds, apples, celery, raisins, or sugarless gum instead of a cigarette.

• Take 10 deep breaths and hold the last one while lighting a match.

• Never allow yourself to think that "one won't hurt" – it will.

• Recognize that the urge to smoke usually lasts only 3 to 5 minutes – try to wait it out.

Finding New Habits

• Change your habits to make smoking difficult, such as swimming, jogging, or playing tennis or handball.

• Do things that require you to use your hands.

• Find activities that you enjoy – without the need to smoke.

• Make things clean and fresh at home, work, and in the car.

• Use the money saved on cigarettes to buy something as a reward.

• Spend free time in places where smoking is not allowed.

• Drink water and juice. Do not drink alcohol because it can trigger a desire to smoke.

Using Medication and Pharmacology Methods

• Nicotine replacement treatments: gum, patch, lozenges, nasal spray, inhaler

• Bupropion (Zyban)

• Varenicline (Chantix)

Note. Adapted from:

American Cancer Society. (2015a). *Cancer prevention and early detection facts and figures – 2015-2016*. Atlanta, GA: Author.

National Comprehensive Cancer Network. (2015). *Smoking cessation, version 2.2015*. Retrieved from http://nccn.org

One simple way to talk to patients about smoking cessation is to use the START method before smoking cessation.

S = Set a quit date.

T = Tell family, friends, and coworkers that you plan to quit.

A = Anticipate and plan for the challenges you will face while quitting.

R = Remove cigarettes and other tobacco products from your home, car, and workplace.

T = Talk to your doctor about getting help to quit.

Many other helpful resources for smoking cessation are available at http://smokefree.gov.

Many patients will need additional help to stop smoking. Medications used to assist with smoking cessation are given in Table 7-4. Smoking cessation is more likely to be effective when coupled with a cessation aid; many health insurance plans will help cover the costs of these cessation aids (Athar et al., 2016; Stead et al., 2012).

Screening for Lung Cancer in Individuals at High Risk

Widespread, imaging-based screening for lung cancer is controversial. It is not included in recommendations for the early detection of cancer.

continued on page 183

	Prescription Needed?/Cost[a]	**Administration[a]**	**Benefits**	**Risks**
Agent				
Nicotine gum	No. Estimated cost is $275 per month.	Chew briefly. Park in mouth for 1 minute. Chew again. Repeat every 30 minutes. Use 2 to 4 mg, or no more than 20 pieces per day. Should take dose over 2 to 3 months. Not recommended for more than 6 months.	Easy to use. Delivers nicotine quickly.	Cannot eat or drink when chewing. Can cause dental problems or oral mucosa irritation.
Nicotine spray	Yes. Cost is about $300 per month.	Spray into each nostril and exhale through mouth. Use every 1 to 2 hours. Taper over 2 to 3 months. Not recommended for more than 6 months.	Very quick delivery of nicotine. Good for reducing sudden craving. May work well for heavy smokers.	Can lead to nasal and sinus irritation.
Nicotine patch	No. Cost is about $150 per month.	The nicotine patch is placed on the skin and supplies a small and steady amount of nicotine into the body. Nicotine patches contain varied concentrations of nicotine (21 mg, 14 mg, or 7 mg). Use over 2 to 3 months with gradual taper. Both 16- and 24-hour patches are available.	Very easy to use. Less expensive than some of the other methods.	Slower release of nicotine. Can cause skin irritation. Occasionally associated with tachycardia.
Nicotine inhaler	Yes. Cost is about $300 per month.	A nicotine inhaler consists of a cartridge attached to a mouthpiece. Inhaling through the mouthpiece delivers a specific amount of nicotine to the user. At least six cartridges are needed for the first 3 to 6 weeks. Taper at 2 to 3 months. Not recommended for more than 6 months.	Delivers nicotine very quickly.	May lead to throat irritation or coughing.

TABLE 7-4: AIDS FOR SMOKING CESSATION (1 OF 2)

TABLE 7-4: AIDS FOR SMOKING CESSATION (2 OF 2)

Agent	Prescription Needed?/Cost[a]	Administration[a]	Benefits	Risks
Nicotine lozenges	No. Estimated cost is $250 per month.	Nicotine lozenges look like hard candy and are placed between the cheek and gum tissue. The nicotine lozenge (2-mg or 4-mg dose) releases nicotine as it slowly dissolves in the mouth. Use every 1 to 2 hours over 2 to 3 months. Gradually taper at 3 months. Not recommended beyond 6 months.	Easy to use. Delivers nicotine very quickly.	Cannot eat or drink when using. Can cause dental problems or oral mucosa irritation.
Bupropion (Zyban)	Yes. Approximate cost is $120 per month depending on healthcare prescription coverage.	Bupropion helps to reduce nicotine withdrawal symptoms and the urge to smoke. Prescription taper is written by physician – usually taken for 7 to 12 weeks. Start taking 2 weeks before quitting.	Bupropion can be used safely with nicotine replacement products.	Contraindicated in persons with seizures or eating disorders. Not safe when pregnant or breastfeeding.
Varenicline (Chantix)	Yes. Approximate cost is $120 per month depending on healthcare prescription coverage.	Varenicline eases nicotine withdrawal symptoms and blocks the effects of nicotine from cigarettes if the user resumes smoking. Start taking 1 week before quitting. Dosage increases slowly during the first week. After day 8, the full dose can be taken for up to 12 weeks.	Eases withdrawal symptoms. Decreases pleasure from smoking.	Can cause nausea.

[a]Check with the manufacturer for current specific guidelines for administration and costs.

Note. Adapted from Athar, H., Chen, Z. A., Contreary, K., Xu, X., Dube, S. R., & Chang, M. H. (2016). Impact of increasing coverage for select smoking cessation therapies with no out-of-pocket cost among the Medicaid population in Alabama, Georgia, and Maine. *Journal of Public Health Management & Practice, 22*(1), 40-47. doi:10.1097/PHH.0000000000000302; National Comprehensive Cancer Network. (2015). *Smoking cessation, version 2.2015.* Retrieved from http://nccn.org; American Cancer Society. (2015a). *Cancer prevention and early detection facts and figures – 2015-2016.* Atlanta, GA: Author; and Stead, L. F., Perera, R., Bullen, C., Mant, D., Hartmann-Boyce, J., Cahill, K., & Lancaster, T. (2012). Nicotine replacement therapy for smoking cessation. *Cochrane Database of Systematic Reviews, 11.* doi:10.1002/14651858.CD000146.pub4

Routine screening with a chest radiograph is not effective because lesions are usually large by the time they are seen on a chest X-ray film, and treatment is not always effective (NCCN, 2017a).

The National Lung Screening Trial (NLST) is a large clinical trial that investigated the effectiveness of low-dose computed tomography (LDCT) of the chest to screen for lung cancer. LDCT of the chest uses lower amounts of radiation than a standard chest computed tomography (CT) and does not require contrast dye (National Lung Screening Trial Research Team et al., 2011). The NLST compared LDCT of the chest with chest X-rays in people at high risk for lung cancer to determine whether either of these tests could help reduce the mortality rate for lung cancer. The study included more than 50,000 people aged 55 to 74 years who were current or former smokers in reasonable health.

NLST inclusion criteria are as follows:

- At least a 30 pack-year history of smoking. A pack-year is the number of cigarette packs smoked each day multiplied by the number of years a person has smoked. For example, if a 50-year-old woman starting smoking one pack of cigarettes per day at age 15, her pack-year history would be 1 pack per day times 35 years equaling 35 pack-years.

- Former smokers could enter the study if they had quit within the past 15 years.

Exclusion criteria were as follows:

- Any history of lung cancer or lung cancer symptoms

- Removal of any part of the lung

- Regular oxygen use

- Other serious medical problems

Subjects in the NLST study received either three LDCTs or three chest X-ray scans, each a year apart, to look for abnormalities. The findings indicated that people who received LDCTs had a 16% lower chance of dying of lung cancer than those who received chest X-rays. They were also 7% less likely to die overall (from any cause) than those who received chest X-rays.

LDCT is not without risks. This test also detects abnormalities that require evaluation but are benign (false positives). The false-positive rate in the NLST was nearly 25%. Abnormalities are further evaluated with CT scans or more invasive tests such as needle biopsies or even surgery to remove a portion of lung. These tests can sometimes lead to complications, including pneumothorax and, rarely, death, even in people who do not have a malignancy (NCCN, 2017a).

Based largely on the NLST results, the U.S. Preventive Services Task Force recommends annual screening for lung cancer with LDCT. This should be offered to adults aged 55 to 80 years who have a 30-pack-year smoking history and currently smoke or have quit within the past 15 years. Screening with LDCT should be discontinued once a person has not smoked for 15 years, if the individual develops a health problem that substantially limits life expectancy, or if the person is unwilling to have curative lung surgery (Moyer, 2014). Both the NCCN (2017a) and the ACS (2017b) also recommend LDCT in high-risk individuals. All three agencies emphasize that LDCT is not a substitute for smoking cessation, and that smoking-cessation strategies should always be discussed with patients as the best option; the decision to use LDCT should be one of shared decision making with the healthcare provider (Mulshine & D'Amico, 2014)

Potential benefits of LDCT include earlier detection of lung cancer and improved quality of life. Potential risks include radiation exposure, costs, false-positive results, false-negative results, and unnecessary workups (NCCN, 2017a). The use of LDCT can decrease lung cancer mortality rate by more than 20% (NCCN, 2017a).

DIAGNOSIS AND STAGING

A number of imaging studies, a biopsy, and other tests are necessary to both diagnose and stage lung cancer.

Imaging Tests

Lung cancers are sometimes detected on chest X-ray films as masses or spots. The healthcare provider may order a chest radiograph as part of an evaluation for lung cancer or as part of an evaluation of a symptom. Next, the healthcare provider may order a CT scan (ACS, 2017a). Unlike a regular X-ray, a CT scan creates detailed images of the soft tissues in the body. A contrast agent can enhance the image. A CT scan can provide precise information about the size, shape, and position of tumors and can help find enlarged lymph nodes that might contain cancer that has spread from the lung. CT scans are more sensitive than routine chest X-rays in finding early lung cancers. This test can also help to locate masses in the adrenal glands, brain, and other internal organs that the spread of lung cancer may affect.

Like CT scans, magnetic resonance imaging (MRI) provides detailed images of soft tissues in the body; however, MRI uses radio waves and strong magnets instead of X-rays. Injection of a contrast material called *gadolinium* into a vein before the MRI may enhance details. MRIs are most often used to look for the possible spread of lung cancer to the brain or spinal cord (NCCN, 2017a).

Positron emission tomography (PET) scans involve injecting glucose that contains a radioactive tracer into the blood. Because cancer cells in the body are growing rapidly, they absorb large amounts of the radioactive glucose, which displays in a computer image. The picture is not finely detailed like a CT scan or MRI, but it provides helpful information about the whole body. A PET scan is also useful if metastasis is suspected, and it can reveal the spread of cancer to the liver, bones, adrenal glands, and some other organs (NCCN, 2017a). It is not as useful when looking at the brain because all brain cells metabolize large amounts of glucose. Some equipment offers a simultaneous PET and CT scan (PET/CT scan). This allows for a comparison of higher radioactivity on the PET scan with the appearance of that area on the CT scan.

A bone scan can help determine whether a cancer has metastasized to the bones (NCCN, 2017a). For this test, the radiology technician or technologist injects a small amount of low-level radioactive material intravenously. The substance settles in areas of bone turnover throughout the entire skeleton over the course of a couple of hours. An imaging procedure follows. Areas of active bone turnover appear as hot spots because they attract the radioactivity. These areas may suggest the presence of metastatic cancer; however, arthritis and other bone diseases can also cause the same pattern. To distinguish between these conditions and cancer, other imaging tests, such as simple X-rays or MRI, are utilized to better evaluate suspicious areas and guide a biopsy of the bone if indicated. Because PET scans can usually show the spread of cancer to the bones, it is not usually necessary to perform bone scans (NCCN, 2017a).

Biopsy Strategies

A pathology report that indicates a finding of malignant cells in a tissue sample establishes a diagnosis of lung cancer. There are many approaches to obtaining a tissue sample.

Sputum cytology is the least invasive of all methods for obtaining tissue samples. A sample of sputum is viewed under a microscope to detect whether cancer cells are present. The best way to do this is to get early-morning samples for 3 days in a row. Often, however, this test fails to provide adequate information (NCCN, 2017a).

The healthcare provider will often use fine-needle biopsy to get a small sample of cells from a suspicious area. For this test, the healthcare provider will numb the skin with local anesthesia where the needle is to be inserted and then advance a thin, hollow needle into the suspicious area while looking at the lungs with either fluoroscopy or CT scans. Unlike fluoroscopy, CT scanning does not give a continuous picture, so the healthcare provider inserts the needle in the direction of the mass, takes a CT image, and uses the image to guide the direction of the needle. This is repeated a few times until the needle is within the mass. The healthcare provider then withdraws a tiny sample of the target area into a syringe and examines it under a microscope to determine whether cancer cells are present.

A possible complication of CT scans and fluoroscopic procedures is that air may leak out of the lung at the biopsy site and into the space between the lung and the chest wall. This can cause part of the lung to collapse and can cause trouble breathing. In some cases, a pneumothorax will resolve without any treatment; often a chest tube is required to reinflate the lung.

During bronchoscopy, the healthcare provider passes a lighted, flexible, fiber-optic tube (bronchoscope) through the mouth or nose and down into the windpipe and bronchi after first spraying the mouth and throat with a local anesthetic. The patient usually undergoes intravenous sedation. Bronchoscopy can help the healthcare provider find some tumors or obstructions in the lungs. At the same time, the healthcare provider can pass small instruments down the bronchoscope to obtain biopsies. The healthcare provider can also insert a thin needle through the wall of the trachea or bronchus using a bronchoscope to sample nearby lymph nodes. This procedure, called *transtracheal* or *transbronchial fine-needle aspiration,* is effective for taking samples of lymph nodes near the trachea and bronchi (NCCN, 2017a).

In an endobronchial ultrasound, the healthcare provider passes a bronchoscope fitted with an ultrasound transducer at its tip into the trachea. The healthcare provider can point the transducer in different directions to look at the lymph nodes and other structures in the mediastinum. If the healthcare provider sees suspicious areas on the ultrasound, he or she can pass a hollow needle through the bronchoscope and, guided by ultrasound, into the abnormal structures to obtain a biopsy (NCCN, 2017a).

Mediastinoscopy and mediastinotomy allow for visualization and biopsy sampling of the structures in the mediastinum. The patient undergoes these procedures in an operating room under general anesthesia. The main differences between a mediastinoscopy and a mediastinotomy are the location and size of the incision (NCCN, 2017a).

During mediastinoscopy, the healthcare provider makes a small incision in the front of the neck above the sternum and inserts a thin, hollow, lighted tube behind the sternum. The healthcare provider can pass special instruments through this tube to obtain tissue samples from the lymph nodes along the windpipe and the major bronchial tube areas.

During mediastinotomy, the surgeon makes a slightly larger incision (usually about 2 inches long) between the left second and third ribs next to the breastbone. This allows the surgeon to reach lymph nodes that are not reached by mediastinoscopy (NCCN, 2017a).

Thoracentesis can determine whether a pleural effusion is the result of cancer spreading to the pleura (NCCN, 2017a). For this procedure, the healthcare provider numbs the skin and places a needle between the ribs to drain the fluid. The healthcare provider checks the fluid under a microscope to look for cancer cells. Chemical tests of the fluid are also sometimes useful in differentiating a malignant pleural effusion from a benign one. If a patient has a malignant pleural effusion, the healthcare provider may repeat thoracentesis to remove more fluid. Fluid buildup can prevent the lungs from filling with air, so thoracentesis can help the patient to breathe better.

Thoracoscopy can determine whether the cancer has spread to the space between the lungs and the chest wall and to the linings of these spaces. Most often, the patient undergoes this procedure in the operating room under general anesthesia. The healthcare provider inserts a lighted tube with a small video camera on the end through a small cut made in the chest wall to view the space between the lungs and the chest wall. During this procedure, it is possible for the healthcare provider to visualize potential cancer deposits on the lung or lining of the chest wall and remove small pieces of tissue for pathology. Thoracoscopy can be used to sample the lymph nodes and fluid for assessment of whether a tumor is growing into nearby tissues or organs (NCCN, 2017a).

Additional Diagnostic Tests

The healthcare provider sends the samples collected during biopsies or other tests to a pathology laboratory. Special tests may be needed to help classify the cancer. Cancers from other organs can spread to the lungs. It is very important to determine the primary site where the cancer originated because treatment is different for different types of cancer.

Immunohistochemistry can often differentiate the specific cell type of the cancer. In some cases, the healthcare provider may use molecular tests to look for specific gene changes in the cancer cells that might affect how they are best treated. This type of genetic testing is done

on the tumor and does not provide information about whether there is a hereditary risk for developing cancer. For example, epidermal growth factor receptor (EGFR) is a protein that sometimes appears in high amounts on the surface of cancer cells and helps them grow. Some anticancer drugs target EGFR; however, they only seem to work against certain cancers. Some healthcare providers may test for changes in genes, such as *EGFR* and *KRAS,* and other genetic markers to determine which specific treatments may be effective (NCCN, 2017a). The *KRAS* gene provides instructions for making a protein called K-Ras that is involved primarily in regulating cell division.

Blood tests are not used to diagnose lung cancer, but healthcare providers usually order these to assess an individual's overall health. Blood chemistry tests can help detect abnormalities in some organs. If cancer has spread to the liver or bones, it may cause abnormal levels of certain chemicals in the blood.

Pulmonary function tests are ordered and obtained from patients after a lung cancer diagnosis to determine how well the lungs function. This is especially important if the patient and healthcare provider are considering surgery. Because surgical removal of part or all of a lung results in lower lung capacity, it is important to know how well the lungs are functioning before surgery.

Classification and Patterns of Metastasis

Most lung cancers start in the bronchi, but they can also begin in other areas, such as the trachea, bronchioles, or alveoli. Research suggests that lung cancer tumors develop over many years (ACS, 2017a). They may start as areas of precancerous changes in the lung. The first changes occur within the cells themselves; however, at this point, the cells do not form a mass or tumor. They cannot be seen on an X-ray, and they do not cause symptoms. Over time, these precancerous changes may progress to cancer. As a cancer develops, the cancer cells may make chemicals that cause new blood vessels to form nearby. These new blood vessels nourish the cancer cells, which can continue to grow and form a tumor large enough to be seen on imaging tests such as radiographs. At some point, cells from the cancer may break away from the original tumor and spread, or metastasize, to other parts of the body. Lung cancer is a life-threatening disease because it often spreads in this way, even before it can be detected on an imaging test.

Lung cancer cells can enter lymphatic vessels and begin to grow in lymph nodes around the bronchi and in the mediastinum. When lung cancer cells have reached the lymph nodes, they are more likely to have spread to other organs of the body as well. The stage of the cancer and decisions about treatment are based on whether the cancer has spread to the nearby lymph nodes in the mediastinum (ACS, 2017a).

There are two major types of lung cancer: SCLC and NSCLC. If a lung cancer has characteristics of both types, it is called a *mixed small cell/large cell cancer.* This is uncommon. Some other rare types of lung cancer also exist, but most will be either SCLC or NSCLC.

Non-Small Cell Lung Cancer

About 85% to 90% of lung cancers are NSCLC. There are three subtypes of NSCLC: squamous cell carcinoma, adenocarcinoma, and large cell (undifferentiated) carcinoma. The cells in these subtypes differ in size, shape, and chemical makeup (NCCN, 2017c).

- *Squamous cell carcinoma:* About 25% to 30% of all lung cancers are squamous cell carcinomas. They are often linked to a history of smoking and tend to be found in the middle of the lungs, near a bronchus.

- *Adenocarcinoma:* This type accounts for about 40% of lung cancers. It is usually found in the outer region of the lung. People with one type of adenocarcinoma, sometimes called *bronchioloalveolar carcinoma,* tend to have a better outlook (prognosis) than those with other types of lung cancer.

- *Large cell (undifferentiated) carcinoma:* This type of cancer accounts for about 10% to 15% of lung cancers. It may appear in any part of the lung. It tends to grow and spread quickly, which can make it more difficult to treat effectively.

Small Cell Lung Cancer

About 10% to 15% of all lung cancers are SCLC (NCCN, 2017e). Other names for SCLC are oat cell cancer, oat cell carcinoma, and small cell undifferentiated carcinoma. SCLC often starts in the bronchi near the center of the chest, and it tends to spread throughout the body fairly early in the course of the disease (usually before it starts to cause symptoms). These cancer cells can multiply quickly, form large tumors, and spread to lymph nodes and other organs, such as the bones, brain, adrenal glands, and liver. SCLC is almost always caused by smoking. It is rare for someone who has never smoked to have SCLC (NCCN, 2017c).

In addition to the two main types of lung cancer, other tumors can occur in the lungs. Carcinoid tumors of the lung account for fewer than 5% of lung tumors. Most are slow-growing tumors that are called *typical carcinoid tumors.* They are generally cured by surgery. Although some typical carcinoid tumors can spread, they usually have a better prognosis than SCLC or NSCLC. Less common are atypical carcinoid tumors. The outlook for these tumors is somewhere between that for typical carcinoids and SCLC; the 5-year survival rate ranges from 93% for stage I to 57% for stage IV (NCCN, 2017c).

Other Types of Lung Cancer

Other types of lung tumors are even rarer, such as adenoid cystic carcinomas, hamartomas, lymphomas, and sarcomas. These tumors are treated with different chemotherapy agents than those used for the more common lung cancers; they may also be treated with radiotherapy and surgery (NCCN, 2017c).

Cancer that starts in other organs (such as the breast, pancreas, kidney, or skin) and metastasizes to the lungs is not the same as lung cancer. For example, cancer that starts in the breast and spreads to the lungs is still breast cancer, not lung cancer. Treatment for metastatic cancer to the lungs depends on the primary cancer site.

Like other cancers, lung cancer is staged using the tumor, nodes, metastasis (TNM) system. After the pathology of the tumor is determined, along with the stage, treatment can be planned. Staging of SCLC is typically reported as limited stage (cancer is confined to the lung and lymph nodes in the chest) or extensive stage (cancer has metastasized, usually to the brain, liver, or bone.)

Figure 7-8 provides a staging schema for lung cancer.

Prognosis

The prognosis of a patient diagnosed with NSCLC is determined by the following factors:

- Stage (extent of disease)

- Performance status (see Table 7-5)

- Weight loss

- Gender

(NCCN, 2017c, 2017e)

For patients with operable NSCLC, prognosis is adversely influenced by the presence of pulmonary symptoms, large tumor size (greater than 3 cm), and presence of the erbB-2 oncoprotein. Other adverse prognostic factors for some patients with NSCLC include mutation of the *KRAS* gene,

vascular invasion, and increased numbers of blood vessels in the tumor specimen (NCCN, 2017c). Based on ACS data (ACS, 2017a), stage as a basis for prognosis is as follows:

- For stage IA NSCLC, the 5-year survival rate is about 49%.

- For stage IB NSCLC, the 5-year survival rate is about 45%.

- For stage IIA cancer, the 5-year survival rate is about 30%.

- For stage IIB cancer, the survival rate is about 31%.

- For stage IIIA NSCLC, the 5-year survival rate is about 14%.

- For stage IIIB cancer, the survival rate is about 5%.

- Metastatic NSCLC that has spread to other parts of the body is often difficult to treat.

- Stage IV NSCLC has a 5-year survival rate of about 1%.

Without treatment, the median survival for patients with SCLC – from diagnosis to death – is only 2 to 4 months. At the time of diagnosis, approximately 30% of SCLC patients will have a tumor that is confined to the hemithorax of origin, the mediastinum, or the supraclavicular lymph nodes. Many lung cancers are diagnosed in later stages because vague symptoms go unnoticed, and easy and effective screening methods do not exist (NCCN, 2017e).

TREATMENT

Treatment depends on a number of factors, including the patient's general health, the type of lung cancer, and the size, location, and extent of the tumor. Many different treatments and combinations of treatments may be used to control lung cancer or to improve quality of life by reducing symptoms.

continued on page 190

FIGURE 7-8: LUNG CANCER STAGING

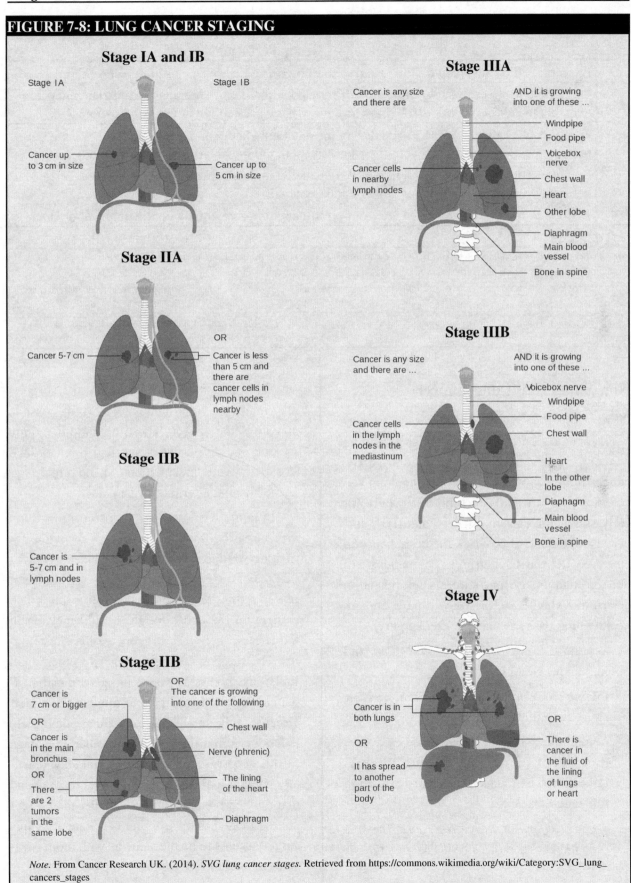

Note. From Cancer Research UK. (2014). *SVG lung cancer stages.* Retrieved from https://commons.wikimedia.org/wiki/Category:SVG_lung_cancers_stages

TABLE 7-5: EXAMPLE OF PERFORMANCE STATUS CRITERIA*	
Eastern Cooperative Oncology Group Performance Status Tool	
0	Asymptomatic (fully active, able to carry on all predisease activities without restriction)
1	Symptomatic but completely ambulatory (restricted in physically strenuous activity but ambulatory and able to carry out work of a light or sedentary nature, e.g., light housework, office work)
2	Symptomatic, less than 50% in bed during the day (ambulatory and capable of all self-care but unable to carry out any work activities; up and about more than 50% of waking hours)
3	Symptomatic, greater than 50% in bed, but not bedbound (capable of only limited self-care; confined to bed or chair 50% or more of waking hours)
4	Bedbound (completely disabled; cannot perform any self-care; totally confined to bed or chair)
5	Death

*Many scales and criteria are used by physicians, nurses, and researchers to assess how the disease affects the daily living abilities of the patient and to determine appropriate treatment and prognosis. This scale is one example that is commonly utilized.

Note. Adapted from American Cancer Society. (2017a). *Cancer facts & figures – 2017.* Atlanta, GA: Author; National Comprehensive Cancer Network. (2017b). *Non-small cell lung cancer, version 4.2016.* Retrieved from http://nccn.org; National Comprehensive Cancer Network. (2017d). *Small cell lung cancer screening, version 2.2016.* Retrieved from http://nccn.org; and Oken, M. M., Creech, R. H., Tormey, D. C., Horton, J., Davis, T. E., McFadden, E. T., & Carbone, P. P. (1982). Toxicity and response criteria of the Eastern Cooperative Oncology Group. *American Journal of Clinical Oncology, 5,* 649-655.

Non-Small Cell Lung Cancer

Surgery

Depending on the type and stage of a lung cancer, surgery may be used to remove the cancer along with some surrounding lung tissue. Surgery is usually recommended only for early-stage lung cancers (stages I and II). If surgery can be done, it provides the best chance to cure NSCLC (NCCN, 2017c). The patient will undergo pulmonary function tests beforehand to determine whether he or she will have enough healthy lung tissue remaining after surgery.

Several different operations can treat (and possibly cure) NSCLC:

• *Pneumonectomy:* The surgeon removes the entire lung in this surgery.

• *Lobectomy:* The surgeon removes a section (lobe) of the lung in this surgery. Lobectomy is a standard surgical resection for stage I disease.

• *Segmentectomy* or *wedge resection:* The surgeon removes part of a lobe in this surgery.

With any of these operations, the surgeon also removes lymph nodes to look for possible spread of the cancer. These operations require general anesthesia and a surgical thoracotomy. Postoperatively, most patients spend 5 to 7 days in the hospital after the surgery.

In some cases, a less invasive procedure, video-assisted thoracic surgery, is available for treating some early-stage lung cancers (NCCN, 2017c). During this operation, the surgeon places a thin, telescopic tube with a tiny video camera on the end through a small incision in the chest to help the surgeon see the chest cavity. The surgeon creates one or two other small incisions in the skin and passes long instruments through these holes to remove the tumor. Because only small incisions are needed, there is less pain after the surgery. Another advantage of this surgery is a shorter hospital stay – usually about 4 to 5 days. Most experts recommend that only early-stage tumors, smaller than 3 to 4 cm, be treated this way. The cure rate after this surgery seems to be the same as with more invasive techniques (NCCN, 2017c).

Possible complications depend on the extent of the surgery and a person's health beforehand. Serious complications can include excessive bleeding, wound infections, and pneumonia. Although it is rare, in some cases people may not survive the surgery, which is why it is important that surgeons select patients carefully and provide extensive information about the risks and potential complications (NCCN, 2017c). Because the surgeon must spread the ribs to get to the lung in patients undergoing a thoracotomy, the incision will be painful for some time after surgery and require significant pain management. Activity will be limited for at least 1 to 2 months.

If a pleural effusion occurs, the associated buildup of fluid can interfere with breathing. To remove the fluid and keep it from coming back, doctors sometimes perform a procedure called *pleurodesis* (Ettinger et al., 2014). The healthcare provider makes a small incision in the skin of the chest wall and places a chest tube into the chest to remove the fluid. The healthcare provider then instills either talc, a drug such as doxycycline, or a chemotherapy drug into the chest cavity. This causes the linings of the lung (visceral pleura) and chest wall (parietal pleural) to stick together, sealing the space and preventing further fluid buildup. The chest tube is generally left in for 1 to 2 days to drain any new fluid that might accumulate.

Radiation Therapy

After surgery, the patient may undergo radiation therapy (alone or with chemotherapy) to try to eliminate very small deposits of cancer that may have been missed by surgery (Ettinger et al., 2014). Radiation therapy can also relieve the symptoms of lung cancer, such as pain, bleeding, trouble swallowing, cough, and problems caused by brain metastases.

External beam radiation therapy uses radiation delivered from outside the body that is focused on the cancer. This is the type of radiation therapy most often used to treat a primary lung cancer or its metastases to other organs. Conventional external beam radiation therapy is used much less often than in the past (Ettinger et al., 2014). Newer techniques allow doctors to more accurately target the radiation to lung cancers while reducing the radiation exposure to nearby healthy tissues. These techniques may offer better odds of increasing the success rate and salvaging healthy adjacent tissue. New, more targeted techniques include the following:

- Three-dimensional conformal radiation therapy uses special computers to precisely map the location of the tumor (NCCN, 2017c). Radiation beams are shaped and aimed at the tumor from several directions, which makes it less likely that the radiation will damage normal tissues. Most doctors now recommend using three-dimensional conformal radiation therapy when it is available (ACS, 2017c).

- Intensity-modulated radiation therapy is an advanced form of three-dimensional therapy. It uses a computer-driven machine that moves around the patient as it delivers radiation (Ettinger et al., 2014). Along with shaping the beams and aiming them at the tumor from several angles, the intensity (strength) of the beams can be adjusted to minimize the dose reaching the most sensitive normal tissues. This technique is used most often if tumors are near important structures such as the spinal cord.

- Stereotactic radiation therapy is a newer form of treatment that is sometimes used to treat very early-stage lung cancers (NCCN, 2017c). Another type of stereotactic radiation therapy can sometimes be used instead of surgery for single tumors that have spread to the brain. Using a machine called a

Gamma Knife or CyberKnife, many beams of high-dose radiation are focused on the tumor from different angles over a few minutes to hours. The head is kept in the same position by placing it in a rigid frame.

- Brachytherapy is used most often to shrink tumors to relieve symptoms caused by the cancer, although in some cases it may be part of a larger treatment regimen aiming to cure the cancer. The healthcare provider places a small source of radioactive material (often in the form of pellets or seeds) directly into the cancer or into the airway next to the cancer. This is usually done through a bronchoscope, although it may also be done during surgery. The radiation travels only a short distance from the source, limiting the effects on surrounding healthy tissues. The radiation source is usually removed after a short time. Less often, small, radioactive "seeds" are left in place permanently, and the radiation gets weaker over several weeks. Depending on the dose, there may be restrictions on contact with family members for varying amounts of time (Stewart et al., 2016). When brachytherapy is utilized, nurses need to confirm what the exposure times and limits are and clearly communicate this to patients and their family members.

External beam radiation therapy is sometimes the main treatment of lung cancer (usually with chemotherapy), especially if the lung tumor cannot be removed by surgery because it is close to large blood vessels or the person's health is poor. Brachytherapy is most often used to help relieve blockage of large airways by cancer.

Negative side effects of external radiation therapy might include sunburn-like skin problems where the radiation enters the body, nausea, vomiting, and fatigue. Often, these side effects go away after treatment. Radiation might also make the side effects of chemotherapy more intense. Chest radiation therapy may damage the lungs and lead to problems with breathing and shortness of breath. Because the esophagus is located in the middle of the chest, it may be exposed to radiation, which could lead to trouble swallowing during treatment. Before radiation therapy that might include the esophagus, a referral to the dietician is appropriate for nutrition assessment, swallowing evaluation, and suggestions for maintaining nutrition. This evaluation should be repeated periodically during and after therapy as needed (Vickery, 2013). This usually improves after the treatment has ended.

Radiation therapy to large areas of the brain can sometimes cause changes in brain function (Ettinger et al., 2014). Some people notice memory loss, headache, trouble thinking, or reduced sexual desire. Usually these symptoms are minor compared with those caused by a brain tumor, but they can reduce quality of life. Side effects of radiation therapy to the brain usually become most serious 1 or 2 years after treatment. As part of the informed consent process for radiotherapy, patients and families should be educated on this potential long-term complication.

Nurses play a key role in providing education, guidance, and intervention strategies for patients who are experiencing negative side effects during and after receiving radiation therapy (see Table 7-6).

Chemotherapy

Depending on the type and stage of NSCLC, the patient may undergo chemotherapy as the main (primary) treatment or as an addition (adjuvant) to surgery or radiation therapy. Chemotherapy takes place in cycles, with each period of treatment followed by a rest period to allow the body time to recover. Chemotherapy cycles generally last about 3 to 4 weeks, and ini-

TABLE 7-6: RADIATION THERAPY SIDE EFFECTS: FOCUS OF NURSING CARE

Side Effects	Patient Teaching	Possible Interventions
Fatigue	• Cancer-related fatigue can be wearying and not alleviated with regular rest • Limit normal activities • Fatigue can be intermittent or lacking in patterns • Fatigue can begin a few weeks after starting radiation and continue until a few weeks after radiation therapy ends • If fatigue worsens or does not improve (cannot get out of bed for 24 hours; increased confusion), alert your care team	• Pace yourself; save energy • Prioritize activities • Reduce stress • Accept help from family and friends • Balance activities, do not spend all day in bed; rather, take frequent naps • Stay hydrated and well nourished • If the healthcare provider agrees, perform light exercise and physical activities

Skin changes	• Radiation dermatitis in treatment area may look red, irritated, swollen, blistered, sunburned, or tanned. After a few weeks, skin may become dry, flaky, or itchy, or it may peel
	• Expect hair loss to the treated area
		• Reduce itching and risk of infection:
		  ◦ No tight, irritating clothing
		  ◦ No tape on skin
		  ◦ No heat/cold directly on skin
		• Protect exposed skin with clothing and sun block
		• Use lukewarm water and only mild soap
		• Limit shaving to area (check with team first)
		• Use skin emollients/lotions as recommended by treatment team

Nutrition	• Treatment may cause throat irritation and loss of appetite	• Eat protein and high-calorie foods • Eat small, frequent meals and healthy snacks • If having problems swallowing regular food, consider powdered milk, yogurt, juice, or liquid nutrition • Maintain social contact and gather support from family and friends (company, purchasing food, preparing food)

Note. Adapted from:

American Cancer Society. (2017c). *Side effects from radiation therapy to the chest.* Retrieved from https://www.cancer.org/treatment/treatments-and-side-effects/treatment-types/radiation/radiation-therapy-guide/radiation-to-chest.html

National Cancer Institute. (2015). *Side effects.* Retrieved from https://www.cancer.gov/about-cancer/treatment/side-effects

tial treatment typically involves four to six cycles. Chemotherapy is often not recommended for patients in poor health; however, advanced age, by itself, is not a barrier to receiving chemotherapy. Most often, initial treatment for advanced NSCLC uses a combination of chemotherapy drugs.

The most common combinations of chemotherapy drugs include cisplatin or carboplatin plus one other drug, although some studies have found that using combinations is associated with more severe side effects. People who might not be able to tolerate combination chemotherapy, such as those in poor overall health, sometimes undergo single-drug chemotherapy. If the initial chemotherapy treatment is no longer working, second-line treatment may consist of a single drug or multidrug protocol with different agents (Ettinger et al., 2014). Chemotherapy agents used in NSLC include (NCCN, 2017c)

- cisplatin,
- carboplatin,
- paclitaxel (Taxol),
- albumin-bound paclitaxel (nab-paclitaxel, Abraxane),
- docetaxel (Taxotere),
- gemcitabine (Gemzar),
- vinorelbine (Navelbine),
- irinotecan (Camptosar),
- etoposide (VP-16),
- vinblastine, and
- pemetrexed (Alimta).

Targeted Therapy

For tumors to grow, they must form new blood vessels to keep them nourished. This process is called *angiogenesis*; it occurs in many malignancies and contributes to tumor growth in lung cancer (see Table 7-7).

Genetic profiling of the tumor sample often influences the decision whether to offer targeted therapy. Genetic profiling provides a foundation for understanding how tumor cells proliferate or when to consider targeted therapies as strategies for treatment. Factors to be considered are as follows (NCCN, 2017c, 2017e):

- Vascular endothelial growth factor (VEGF) is a protein that helps new blood vessels to form.

- EGFR is a protein that sometimes appears in high amounts on the surface of cancer cells and helps them grow. Some drugs that target EGFR seem to work best against lung cancers with certain changes in the *EGFR* gene, which

are more common in certain groups, such as nonsmokers, women, and Asian individuals.

- Some individuals have changes in the *KRAS* gene. These are treated with different agents.

- Approximately 5% of NSCLCs have a change in a gene called *ALK*. This change is most often seen in nonsmokers (or light smokers) who have the adenocarcinoma subtype of NSCLC. Different drugs target this change.

- Approximately 1% to 2% of NSCLCs have a rearrangement in the *ROS1* gene, which might make the tumor respond to certain targeted drugs.

- About 1% of NSCLCs also have a rearrangement in the *RET* gene. Certain drugs that target cells with *RET* gene changes might be options for treating these tumors.

Small Cell Lung Cancer

Because SCLC tends to be more widely disseminated at the time of diagnosis, aggressive chemotherapy is the standard treatment. Chemotherapy for SCLC generally uses a combination of chemotherapy agents, which typically include (NCCN, 2017e)

- cisplatin and etoposide,
- carboplatin and etoposide,
- cisplatin and irinotecan, or
- carboplatin and irinotecan.

If the cancer progresses during treatment or recurs after treatment is completed, different chemotherapy agents or combinations may be tried (NCCN, 2017e). The choice of drugs depends to some extent on how soon the cancer begins to grow again. The longer the disease-free interval, the more likely it is to respond to further treatment (NCCN, 2017e).

Complications

Complications specific to the treatment of lung cancer or the effects of spreading disease include

TABLE 7-7: SELECTED TARGETED THERAPIES FOR NON-SMALL CELL LUNG CANCER

Agent	Side Effects
VEGF-targeted agents – angiogenesis inhibitors • **Bevacizumab (Avastin)** is used to treat advanced NSCLC. It is a monoclonal antibody (a synthetic version of a specific immune system protein) that targets VEGF. Bevacizumab is often used with chemotherapy concurrently. If the cancer responds, the chemotherapy may be stopped and the bevacizumab given by itself until the cancer recurs. • **Ramucirumab (Cyramza)** is a monoclonal antibody that targets a VEGF receptor and works by stopping the formation of new blood vessels. It is usually a second-line therapy.	*Rare but serious adverse effects include bleeding or perforation – may be contraindicated in persons with squamous types.* • Fatigue • High blood pressure • Neutropenia • Headaches • Mouth sores • Loss of appetite • Diarrhea
EGFR inhibitors with EGFR gene mutations • Erlotinib (Tarceva) • Afatinib (Gilotrif) • Gefitinib (Iressa)	• Skin problems • Diarrhea • Mouth sores • Loss of appetite
EGFR inhibitors used for squamous cell NSCLC **Necitumumab (Portrazza)** is a monoclonal antibody that targets EGFR. It can be used along with chemotherapy as the first treatment in people with advanced squamous cell NSCLC.	• Skin problems • Diarrhea • Mouth sores • Loss of appetite
Drugs that target tumors with a mutation in the ALK gene • Crizotinib (Xalkori) • Ceritinib (Zykadia) • Alectinib (Alecensa) These are oral agents.	*Can cause severe neutropenia, lung inflammation, and cardiac arrhythmias.* • Nausea and vomiting • Diarrhea • Constipation • Fatigue • Changes in vision

EGFR = epidermal growth factor receptor; NSCLC = non-small cell lung cancer; VEGF = vascular endothelial growth factor.

Note. Adapted from:

National Comprehensive Cancer Network. (2016). *Non-small cell lung cancer, version 4.2016.* Retrieved from http://nccn.org

Ettinger, D. S., Wood, D. E., Akerley, W., Bazhenova, L. A., Borghaei, H., Camidge, D. R., ... Hughes, M. (2014). Non-small cell lung cancer, version 1.2015. *Journal of the National Comprehensive Cancer Network, 12*(12), 1738-1761. doi:10.6004/jnccn.2014.0176

pain, pleural effusions, anxiety, depression, and sleep disturbance. In addition to these complications, nurses also need to help patients with lung cancer manage fatigue, pain, loss of appetite, diarrhea, hemoptysis, mucositis, and weight loss.

Because many lung cancers are detected at a later stage, patients may be dealing with multiple symptoms. Supportive care should be introduced early to effectively manage symptoms and improve quality of life. Multiple evidence-based guidelines for symptom management and palliative care are available at www.nccn.org. The Oncology Nursing Society also provides evidenced-based reviews of many symptoms that occur in later stage disease at https://www.ons.org/practice-resources/pep.

CASE STUDY 7-1

T.M. is a 59-year-old African American woman who is a homemaker and was a part-time secretary for a manufacturing plant. She is a 30-pack-year smoker; she smoked about 1.5 packs a day for approximately 20 years and has attempted to quit at least twice. She says she now has about five cigarettes per week.

T.M. visited her primary care physician (PCP) because of a persistent cough (for 2 months), which kept her up at night. Occasionally she saw blood in phlegm from her cough. She tried to quit smoking again 6 weeks before her doctor's visit by using NicoDerm patches and keeping in contact with a friend who also was trying to quit smoking.

T.M.'s PCP ordered a chest radiograph. He also started her on a round of antibiotics because she has had bronchial infections in the past. During the office visit, auscultation of T.M.'s right lobe (middle) was muffled. Her PCP obtained a sputum sample and ordered laboratory tests, including a complete blood count and a standard metabolic panel.

Results from the chest X-ray film showed an opaque area in the right center of her chest. The following week, T.M. was scheduled for a CT-guided needle biopsy. Results came back as NSCLC (adenocarcinoma).

T.M.'s breathing status continued to worsen, with increasing dyspnea and swelling in her neck area. Of concern was the possibility of superior vena cava syndrome and developing pleural effusions. Lymph nodes were sampled with mediastinotomy. Staging indicated that T.M.'s adenocarcinoma was stage IIIA, T2, N2, M0, and she was referred to a medical oncolo-gist for further treatment. Because of her stage and the fact that she was not having hemoptysis or unusual bleeding, she was started on a course of paclitaxel, carboplatin, and bevacizumab (Avastin). She tolerated the first three cycles fairly well, except for significant fatigue.

After the latest chemotherapy treatment, she had a repeat chest CT that showed that the mass was back in her lung and appeared to be as large as before initiating chemotherapy. She was offered enrollment in a phase II clinical trial with agents she had not previously received, but she chose the option of palliative care.

Additional Information

T.M.'s health history is remarkable for two negative breast tissue fine-needle aspirations in the past 10 years, which were taken after she detected small masses in her left breast. She is 20 pounds over her ideal body weight and takes medication for hypertension (lisinopril 10 mg daily); however, in the last 3 months, she has lost 15 pounds.

T.M. has been married for 42 years. Her husband, a truck driver, plans to retire in 2 more years. She has two daughters and three sons who no longer live at home. T.M. started menopause at age 50 years. She keeps annual physical examination appointments and has a yearly mammogram. At age 55 years, she had a sigmoidoscopy, with no findings.

With her advancing disease, T.M. complains of dyspnea and profound fatigue. She has quit her job and receives continual humidified oxygen at 2.5 L from a nasal cannula. Her husband has cut down on his hours away from home. One of her daughters lives in the area and helps T.M. with her housekeeping and groceries.

T.M., a lifelong Baptist, has found comfort in reading the Bible and listening to inspirational tapes, which her pastor and fellow church members send to her. She says her out-

look is "sunny," but she states that she knows her good days are limited. Each week she finds herself staying in bed to rest longer. Her appetite has diminished, and she gets about 4 hours of fitful sleep a night.

T.M. has developed trust with her PCP's nurse and looks to her for help with her symptom management (dyspnea, fatigue, no appetite) and guidance on what is next in the progression of her illness. T.M. has said she wants to face the reality of her lung cancer but wants to spare her husband and children the stress of her illness. Her condition is deteriorating, and her energy to make decisions is waning. T.M. has expressed to the nurse that she has become profoundly sad about her condition and finds herself feeling defiant against her faith and family.

Questions

1. What early symptom of a lung cancer diagnosis did T.M. have?

2. What screening methods are recommended for T.M.?

3. What might be an important psychosocial intervention with T.M.?

Answers

1. There really are no early symptoms of lung cancer. Sometimes bloody sputum is associated with early lung cancer, but it can also be a later sign.

2. As a 30-pack-year smoker, she would be considered high risk. More and more, there are now LDCT chest surveillance programs for high-risk individuals. However, there are no routine, recommended screening methods for lung cancer. Efforts are usually directed toward smoking cessation.

3. Because T.M. finds comfort in reading the Bible, reinforcing a connection with her spiritual community and a visit from a chaplain are reasonable actions. Anger and sadness have been voiced by the patient and are her responses to dealing with a terminal diagnosis. The nurse could also offer to pray with the patient.

SUMMARY

The incidence and death rates for lung cancer are daunting, especially because the rate of smoking in young people continues to rise. Lung cancer in women is especially disturbing because some data indicate that women have particular susceptibilities to tobacco addiction and are influenced by myths that smoking promotes weight loss (Centers for Disease Control and Prevention, 2012). Every encounter for primary or wellness care should include assessment for tobacco use. For those patients who use tobacco, care should include assessment for readiness to stop, education about smoking-cessation strategies, evaluation for early symptoms of lung cancer, and a discussion of screening with LDCT for those with a smoking history of 30 or more pack-years. Risk assessment and the appropriate use of LDCT have the potential to detect lung cancer earlier in high-risk patients with the potential for successful treatment. Patients continue to ignore or be unaware of the signs and symptoms of lung cancer. The earlier that treatment is initiated, the more likely it is to be effective. Effective treatment is still based on surgery, with some modest gains when radiation and chemotherapy are added. Targeted therapy provides hope that a treatment tailored to the genetic makeup of the tumor will provide more effective treatment while minimizing damage to healthier cells. Symptom management, especially pain control, and palliative care are major nursing responsibilities for nurses caring for women with lung cancer.

EXAM QUESTIONS

CHAPTER 7
Questions 45–50

Note: Choose the one option that BEST answers each question.

45. In addition to smoking, risk factors for lung cancer include

    a. a high-fat diet, sedentary lifestyle, and exposure to secondhand smoke.

    b. exposure to secondhand smoke, air pollution, and radon.

    c. a previous history of colon, lung, or breast cancer.

    d. a well-defined genetic mutation, coupled with a history of tuberculosis.

46. The main signs and symptoms of lung cancer include

    a. a persistent cough that worsens over time, shortness of breath, and nausea.

    b. constant chest pain, especially radiating up the left arm, and a persistent cough that worsens over time.

    c. shortness of breath, a persistent cough that worsens over time, and bloody sputum.

    d. back pain, weight loss, and insomnia.

47. The smoking cessation strategy that does not require a prescription is

    a. bupropion.

    b. a nicotine inhaler.

    c. varenicline.

    d. a nicotine patch.

48. The U.S. Preventive Services Task Force recommends which strategy for the early detection of lung cancer?

    a. Chest X-ray

    b. Low-dose computed tomography

    c. Sputum cytology

    d. Positron emission tomography

49. Non-small cell lung cancer (NSCLC)

    a. is more common than small cell lung cancer.

    b. spreads more quickly than small cell lung cancer.

    c. is treated with chemotherapy in its early stages.

    d. has a better prognosis in elderly patients.

50. The primary modality to treat NSCLC (stage I) is

    a. surgery.

    b. 5-fluorouracil.

    c. immunotherapy.

    d. steroids.

REFERENCES

American Cancer Society. (2015). *Global cancer facts and figures* (3rd ed.). Atlanta, GA: Author.

American Cancer Society. (2017a). *Cancer facts & figures – 2017.* Atlanta, GA: Author.

American Cancer Society. (2017b). *Cancer prevention and early detection facts and figures – 2016-2018.* Atlanta, GA: Author.

American Cancer Society. (2017c). *Side effects from radiation therapy to the chest.*

Athar, H., Chen, Z. A., Contreary, K., Xu, X., Dube, S. R., & Chang, M. H. (2016). Impact of increasing coverage for select smoking cessation therapies with no out-of-pocket cost among the Medicaid population in Alabama, Georgia, and Maine. *Journal of Public Health Management & Practice, 22*(1), 40-47. doi:10.1097/PHH.0000000000000302

Callaghan, R. C., Allebeck, P., & Sidorchuk, A. (2013). Marijuana use and risk of lung cancer: A 40-year cohort study. *Cancer Causes & Control, 24*(10), 1811-1820. doi:10.1007/s10552-013-0259-0

Campaign for Tobacco Free Kids. (2017). *State cigarette excise tax rate and ranking.* Retrieved from https://www.tobaccofreekids.org/research/factsheets/pdf/0097.pdf

Cancer Research UK. (2014). *SVG lung cancer stages.* Retrieved from https://commons.wikimedia.org/wiki/Category:SVG_lung_cancers_stages

Centers for Disease Control and Prevention, Office on Smoking and Health. (2012). *A report of the Surgeon General. Preventing tobacco use among youth and young adults.* Retrieved from https://www.cdc.gov/tobacco/data_statistics/sgr/2012/consumer_booklet/pdfs/consumer.pdf

Ettinger, D. S., Wood, D. E., Akerley, W., Bazhenova, L. A., Borghaei, H., Camidge, D. R., ... Hughes, M. (2014). Non-small cell lung cancer, version 1.2015. *Journal of the National Comprehensive Cancer Network, 12*(12), 1738-1761. doi:10.6004/jnccn.2014.0176

Fiore, M. C., & Adsit, R. (2016). Will hospitals finally "do the right thing"? Providing evidence-based tobacco dependence treatments to hospitalized patients who smoke. *The Joint Commission Journal on Quality and Patient Safety, 42*(5), 207-208. doi:10.1016/s1553-7250(16)42026-x

Jamal, A., Homa, D. M., O'Connor, E., Babb, S. D., Caraballo, R. S., Singh, T., ... King, B. A. (2015). Current cigarette smoking among adults – United States, 2005-2014. *Morbidity and Mortality Weekly Report, 64*(44), 1233-1240. doi:10.15585/mmwr.mm6444a2

Jones, S. J., Gardner, C. L., & Cleveland, K. K. (2014). Development of a smoking cessation algorithm for primary care providers. *The Journal for Nurse Practitioners, 10*(2), 120-127. doi:10.1016/j.nurpra.2013.08.015

Karam-Hage, M., Cinciripini, P. M., & Gritz, E. R. (2014). Tobacco use and cessation for cancer survivors: An overview for clinicians. *CA: A Cancer Journal for Clinicians, 64*(4), 272-290. doi:10.3322/caac.21231

Moyer, V. A. (2014). Screening for lung cancer: U.S. Preventive Services Task Force Recommendation Statement. *Annals of Internal Medicine, 160*(5), 330-338. doi:10.7326/M13-2771

Mulshine, J. L., & D'Amico, T. A. (2014). Issues with implementing a high-quality lung cancer screening program. *CA: A Cancer Journal for Clinicians, 64*(5), 351-363. doi:10.3322/caac.21239

National Cancer Institute. (2015). *Side effects.* Retrieved from https://www.cancer.gov/about-cancer/treatment/side-effects

National Comprehensive Cancer Network. (2015). *Smoking cessation, version 2.2015.* Retrieved from http://nccn.org

National Comprehensive Cancer Network. (2016). *Non-small cell lung cancer, version 4.2016.* Retrieved from http://nccn.org

National Comprehensive Cancer Network. (2017a). *Lung cancer screening, version 1.2017.* Retrieved from http://nccn.org

National Comprehensive Cancer Network. (2017b). *Non-small cell lung cancer, version 4.2016.* Retrieved from http://nccn.org

National Comprehensive Cancer Network. (2017c). *Non-small cell lung cancer, version 5.2017.* Retrieved from http://nccn.org

National Comprehensive Cancer Network. (2017d). *Small cell lung cancer screening, version 2.2016.* Retrieved from http://nccn.org

National Comprehensive Cancer Network. (2017e). *Small cell lung cancer screening, version 3.2017.* Retrieved from http://nccn.org

National Comprehensive Cancer Network. (2017f). *Smoking cessation, version 1.2017.* Retrieved from http://nccn.org

National Lung Screening Trial Research Team; Aberle, D. R., Adams, A. M., Berg, C. D., Black, W. C., Clapp, J. D., Fagerstrom, R. M., ... Sicks, J. D. (2011). Reduced lung-cancer mortality with low-dose computed tomographic screening. *New England Journal of Medicine, 365*(5), 395-409. doi:10.1056/NEJMoa1102873

Oken, M. M., Creech, R. H., Tormey, D. C., Horton, J., Davis, T. E., McFadden, E. T., & Carbone, P. P. (1982). Toxicity and response criteria of the Eastern Cooperative Oncology Group. *American Journal of Clinical Oncology, 5,* 649-655.

Prokhorov, A. V., Calabro, K. S., & Tamí-Maury, I. (2016). Nicotine and tobacco use prevention among youth and families. *Seminars in Oncology Nursing, 32*(3), 197-205. doi:10.1016/j.soncn.2016.05.003

Sarna, L., & Bialous, S. A. (2016). Implementation of tobacco dependence treatment programs in oncology settings. *Seminars in Oncology Nursing, 32*(3), 187-196. doi:10.1016/j.soncn.2016.05.002

Shields, P. G. (2015). New NCCN guidelines: Smoking cessation for patients with cancer. *Journal of the National Comprehensive Cancer Network, 13*(5S), 643-645.

Stead, L. F., Perera, R., Bullen, C., Mant, D., Hartmann-Boyce, J., Cahill, K., & Lancaster, T. (2012). Nicotine replacement therapy for smoking cessation. *Cochrane Database of Systematic Reviews,* 11. doi:10.1002/14651858.CD000146.pub4

Stewart, A., Parashar, B., Patel, M., O'Farrell, D., Biagioli, M., Devlin, P., & Mutyala, S. (2016). American Brachytherapy Society consensus guidelines for thoracic brachytherapy for lung cancer. *Brachytherapy, 15*(1), 1-11. doi:10.1016/j.brachy.2015.09.006

U.S. Department of Health and Human Services, National Institutes of Health, National Cancer Institute. (n.d.a). *Lungs.* Retrieved from https://visualsonline.cancer.gov/details.cfm?imageid=1775

U.S. Department of Health and Human Services, National Institutes of Health, National Cancer Institute. (n.d.b). *SEER stat fact sheets: Lung and bronchus cancer.* Retrieved from http://seer.cancer.gov/statfacts/html/lungb.html

Vickery, C. (2013). Lung cancer. In C. Shaw (Ed.), *Nutrition and Cancer* (pp. 379-390). West Sussex, UK: John Wiley & Sons Ltd. doi:10.1002/9781118788707.ch19

Zhang, L. R., Morgenstern, H., Greenland, S., Chang, S.-C., Lazarus, P., Teare, M. D., Woll, P. J., Orlow, I., Cox, B., on behalf of the Cannabis and Respiratory Disease Research Group of New Zealand, Brhane, Y., Liu, G. & Hung, R. J. (2015), Cannabis smoking and lung cancer risk: Pooled analysis in the International Lung Cancer Consortium. *International Journal of Cancer, 136,* 894-903. doi:10.1002/ijc.29036

CHAPTER 8

COLORECTAL CANCER

LEARNING OUTCOME

After completing this chapter, the learner will be able to discuss the epidemiology, risk factors, prevention and detection strategies, and main treatments for colorectal cancer in women.

CHAPTER OBJECTIVES

After completing this chapter, the learner will be able to:

1. Describe the main risk factors for colorectal cancer.

2. Identify the signs and symptoms of colorectal cancer.

3. Describe current screening recommendations and the advantages and disadvantages of screening modalities.

4. Explain the components of a pathology report and staging for colorectal cancers.

5. Explain the various treatment modalities for colorectal cancer.

INTRODUCTION

This chapter provides an overview of colorectal cancer (CRC), with an emphasis on the disease in women. CRC remains a major public health challenge despite documented evidence that screening results in the prevention and early detection of the disease, ultimately reducing the morbidity and mortality associated with CRC. The lack of symptom recognition, symptom evaluation through follow-up care, and recommended screening are major barriers to detecting and diagnosing CRC.

Myths about CRC persist even in 2017. CRC is thought to be a disease of the elderly (it is not), a disease of men (women have nearly equal incidence rates), a disease of White individuals (CRC affects all races and ethnic groups), and that little can be done to prevent the disease (screening can remove polyps). The many widespread myths about CRC provide the nurse in all settings, but especially in primary care, with the challenge and opportunity to provide accurate information and educate patients by using methods that take into account language, culture, and value systems of diverse patient populations.

EPIDEMIOLOGY

Colorectal cancer (CRC) is a significant problem in the United States. In the United States, the cumulative lifetime risk of developing CRC is about 5% (American Cancer Society [ACS], 2017a). Early detection and removal of adenomatous polyps through regular screening have reduced the CRC mortality rate by 2.5% since 2002 (ACS, 2017b).

In the United States, CRC is the third leading cause of death in women and the second leading cause of cancer deaths in men (ACS, 2017a).

Worldwide, CRC is more prevalent in industrialized countries (ACS, 2015). Based on data gathered about cancer in women internationally, CRC has the second highest incidence worldwide (ACS, 2015).

The probability of developing CRC for men and women is similar (see Figure 8-1). CRC accounts for 8% of all new cancer cases in women and 8% of all cancer deaths in women, making it the third most common cancer diagnosed in women and the third leading cause of cancer death in women (ACS, 2017a). CRC affects men and women of all races equally, although there is a slightly higher risk in Black individuals (see Figure 8-1) and a slightly higher mortality rate in Black individuals (see Figure 8-2). A personal or family history of colorectal polyps, CRC, or inflammatory bowel disease leads to an increased risk greater than that of the general population.

The rate of CRC increases significantly in the sixth decade of life in individuals with average risk. Most frequently, CRC is diagnosed when people are older than 50 years of age (see Figure 8-3). The highest incidence rate for CRC is between 65 and 74 years of age. Nearly 50% of deaths from CRC occur after age 70 years (see Figure 8-4).

When detected early, the prognosis for CRC is favorable (see Figure 8-5); unfortunately, less than 40% of cases are detected at this stage (ACS, 2017b). Factors that contribute to disparities in CRC survival include differences in access to early detection tests, receipt of timely state-of-the-art treatment modalities, and the prevalence of other comorbid conditions (ACS, 2017b).

ANATOMY AND PHYSIOLOGY

The upper portion of the digestive system processes food for energy, whereas the lower portion (the colon and rectum) removes solid waste (fecal matter or stool) from the

FIGURE 8-1: NUMBER OF NEW CASES PER 100,000 PERSONS BY RACE/ETHNICITY AND SEX: COLON AND RECTAL CANCER

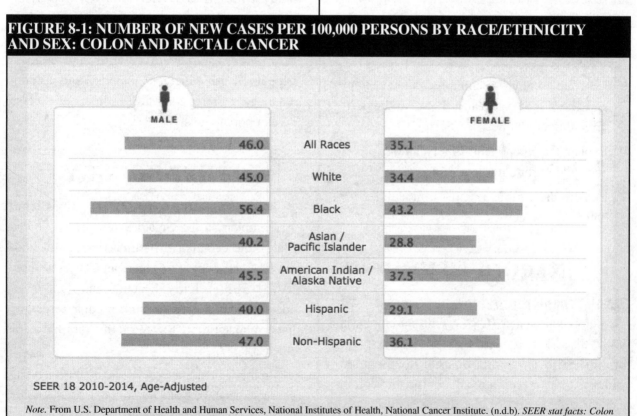

	MALE		FEMALE
All Races	46.0		35.1
White	45.0		34.4
Black	56.4		43.2
Asian / Pacific Islander	40.2		28.8
American Indian / Alaska Native	45.5		37.5
Hispanic	40.0		29.1
Non-Hispanic	47.0		36.1

SEER 18 2010-2014, Age-Adjusted

Note. From U.S. Department of Health and Human Services, National Institutes of Health, National Cancer Institute. (n.d.b). *SEER stat facts: Colon and rectum cancer.* Retrieved from http://seer.cancer.gov/statfacts/html/colorect.html

FIGURE 8-2: NUMBER OF DEATHS PER 100,000 PERSONS BY RACE/ETHNICITY AND SEX: COLON AND RECTAL CANCER

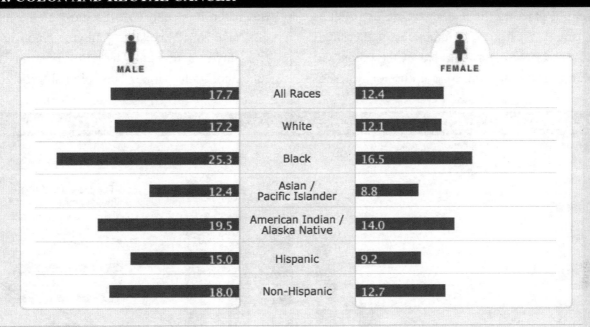

	MALE		FEMALE
All Races	17.7	12.4	
White	17.2	12.1	
Black	25.3	16.5	
Asian / Pacific Islander	12.4	8.8	
American Indian / Alaska Native	19.5	14.0	
Hispanic	15.0	9.2	
Non-Hispanic	18.0	12.7	

U.S. 2010-2014, Age-Adjusted

Note. From U.S. Department of Health and Human Services, National Institutes of Health, National Cancer Institute. (n.d.b). *SEER stat facts: Colon and rectum cancer.* Retrieved from http://seer.cancer.gov/statfacts/html/colorect.html

FIGURE 8-3: AGE DISTRIBUTION OF COLON AND RECTAL CANCER

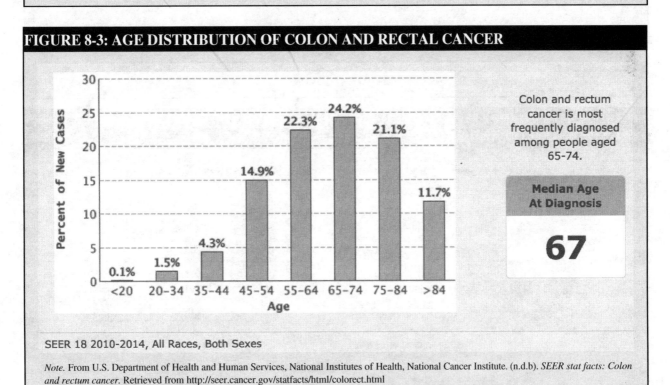

Colon and rectum cancer is most frequently diagnosed among people aged 65-74.

Median Age At Diagnosis

67

SEER 18 2010-2014, All Races, Both Sexes

Note. From U.S. Department of Health and Human Services, National Institutes of Health, National Cancer Institute. (n.d.b). *SEER stat facts: Colon and rectum cancer.* Retrieved from http://seer.cancer.gov/statfacts/html/colorect.html

body. After food is chewed and swallowed, it travels through the esophagus to the stomach. There, it is partly broken down and then sent to the small intestine. The diameter of the small intestine is narrower than that of the colon and rectum. The small intestine is the longest seg-

ment of the digestive system, measuring about 20 feet. The small intestine continues breaking down the food and absorbs most of the nutrients. The small intestine joins the colon in the right lower abdomen. The colon is a muscular tube about 5 feet long. The colon absorbs water

FIGURE 8-4: AGE DISTRIBUTION OF DEATH FROM COLON AND RECTAL CANCER

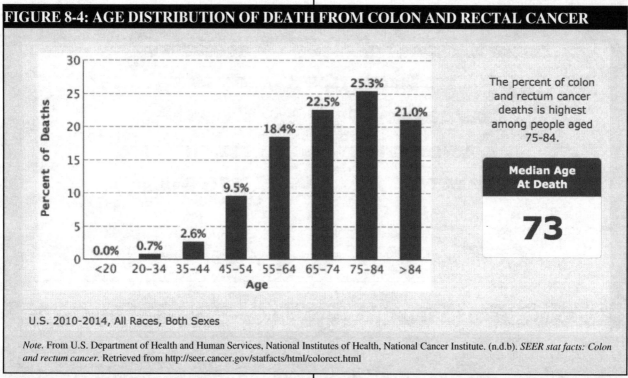

U.S. 2010-2014, All Races, Both Sexes

Note. From U.S. Department of Health and Human Services, National Institutes of Health, National Cancer Institute. (n.d.b). *SEER stat facts: Colon and rectum cancer.* Retrieved from http://seer.cancer.gov/statfacts/html/colorect.html

FIGURE 8-5: PERCENT OF CASES AND 5-YEAR RELATIVE SURVIVAL BY STAGE AT DIAGNOSIS: COLON AND RECTAL CANCER

SEER 18 2007-2013, All Races, Both Sexes by SEER Summary Stage 2000

Note. From U.S. Department of Health and Human Services, National Institutes of Health, National Cancer Institute. (n.d.b). *SEER stat facts: Colon and rectum cancer.* Retrieved from http://seer.cancer.gov/statfacts/html/colorect.html

and sodium from the food matter and serves as a storage place for waste matter. Figure 8-6 shows parts of the colon's anatomy.

The walls of the colon and rectum are made up of several layers of tissue. CRC starts in the innermost layer and can grow through some or all of the other layers. These layers, from the inner to the outer, are (ACS, 2017b)

- the inner lining (mucosa);

- a thin muscle layer (muscularis mucosa);

- the fibrous tissue beneath the muscle layer (submucosa);

FIGURE 8-6: ANATOMY OF THE COLON

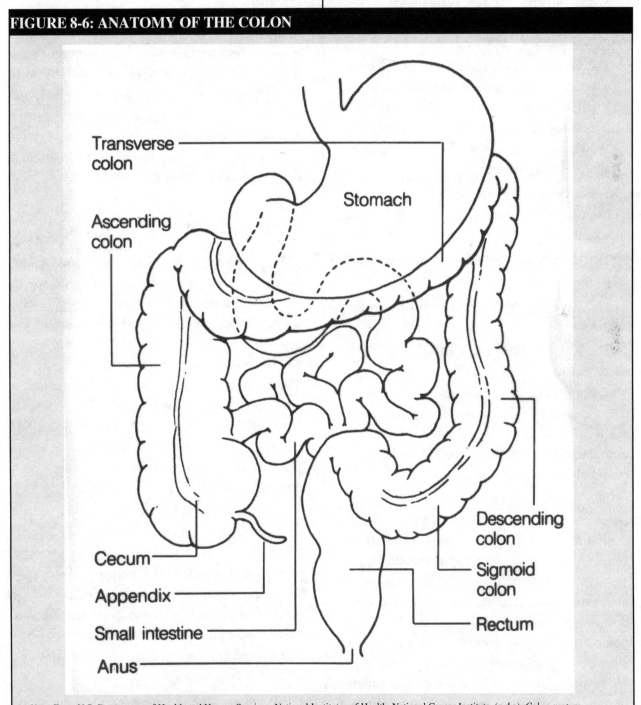

Note. From U.S. Department of Health and Human Services, National Institutes of Health, National Cancer Institute. (n.d.a). *Colon-rectum.* Retrieved from https://visualsonline.cancer.gov/details.cfm?imageid=1768

- a thick muscle layer (muscularis propria) that contracts to force the contents of the intestines along; and

- the thin, outermost layers of connective tissue (subserosa and serosa) that cover most of the colon, but not the rectum.

There are four different parts of the colon: ascending colon, transverse colon, descending colon, and sigmoid colon.

- The *ascending colon* starts with the cecum, which is a small pouch. This is where the small intestine attaches to the colon, and it extends upward on the right side of the abdomen. The cecum is where the appendix attaches to the colon.

- The *transverse colon* goes across the body, from the right to the left side, in the upper abdomen.

- The *descending colon* continues downward on the left side.

- The *sigmoid colon* is the final portion of the colon.

The waste matter that is left after material passes through the colon is known as feces or stool. It goes into the rectum, the final 6 inches of the digestive system. Approximately 30% of CRCs arise in the rectum (ACS, 2017b). From the rectum, the feces pass out of the body through the anus.

The colon plays an important role in fluid and electrolyte homeostasis, digestion of food, absorption of nutrients, propulsion of intestinal contents, and ultimately expulsion of waste products (Carrington & Scott, 2014). Digested food, known as chyme, enters the large intestine from the small intestine through the ileocecal sphincter. As chyme passes through the large intestine it is mixed with beneficial bacteria that have colonized the large intestine throughout a person's lifetime. Bacterial fermentation converts the chyme into feces and releases vita-

mins, including vitamins K, B_1, B_2, B_6, B_{12}, and biotin. Vitamin K is produced by the gut bacteria and is essential in coagulation. Gases such as carbon dioxide and methane are by-products of bacterial fermentation and are released from the body as flatulence. The absorption of water by the large intestine not only helps to condense and solidify feces, but also enables the body to retain water to be used in other metabolic processes. Ions and nutrients released by gut bacteria and dissolved in water are also absorbed in the large intestine and used by the body for metabolism. The dried, condensed fecal matter is finally stored in the rectum and sigmoid colon until it can be eliminated from the body through defecation (Carrington & Scott, 2014).

PATHOPHYSIOLOGY

CRC develops slowly over a period of several years. Before a cancer develops, a growth of tissue or tumor usually begins as a noncancerous polyp on the inner lining of the colon or rectum (see Figure 8-7). Some polyps can develop into cancer, but many never do. The probability of a polyp developing into a cancer depends on the kind of polyp (National Comprehensive Cancer Network [NCCN], 2016c). There are two general categories of polyps: adenomatous polyps and hyperplastic polyps (ACS, 2017b; NCCN, 2016c).

Adenomatous polyps (adenomas) are polyps that have the potential to develop into cancer. Because of this, adenomas are considered a precursor of cancer. Theoretically, removing the polyp prevents the cancer from developing. Adenomatous polyps develop on the mucous membrane that lines the large intestine. They are also called *adenomas* and are most often one of the following:

- Tubular polyp, which protrudes out in the center of the colon

FIGURE 8-7: COLON POLYP

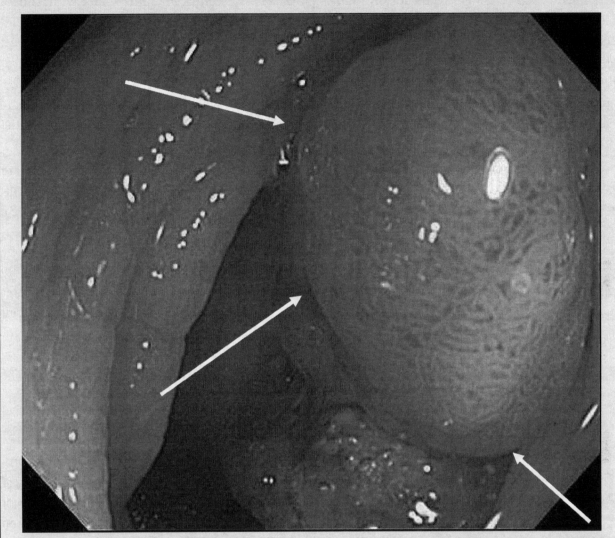

Some polyps have a stalk and others do not. The arrows in this image point to a polyp without a stalk.

Note. From Wikimedia. (2014). *Colon polyp.* Retrieved from https://commons.wikimedia.org/wiki/File:Colon-Polyp.jpg

- Villous adenoma, which is flat and spreading, and is more likely to become malignant

- Tubulovillous adenomas, which have a mixture of both tubular and villous growth patterns

When adenomas become malignant, they are known as adenocarcinomas, which originate in glandular tissue cells. Adenocarcinoma is the most common type of CRC.

Hyperplastic polyps in general are not premalignant and are considered a benign finding. Hyperplastic polyps can be associated with having a greater risk of developing adenomas and ultimately cancer if they are not removed, particularly when these polyps develop in the ascending colon.

In most cases, CRC arises from adenomatous polyps. This occurs during a multistep process involving the inactivation of multiple genes that suppress tumors and repair DNA and the simultaneous activation of oncogenes (ACS, 2017b). When gene function is altered, there can be a transformation from normal colonic epithelium, to an adenomatous polyp, to invasive CRC. This multistep process allows a window of time for screening to detect premalignant lesions and potentially prevent disease. In most sporadic cancers it takes 7 to 10 years for a polyp to develop and progress to CRC. These mutations are usually sporadic and nonhereditary; however, in approximately 10% of the cases, they are related to hereditary cancer syndromes (ACS, 2017b; NCCN, 2016c, 2016e).

If cancer forms within a polyp, it can eventually begin to grow into the wall of the colon or rectum. When cancer cells are in the wall, they can then grow into blood vessels or lymph vessels. Lymph vessels are thin, tiny channels that carry away waste and fluid. They first drain into nearby lymph nodes, which are bean-shaped structures that help fight against infections. When cancer cells spread into blood or lymph vessels, they can travel to distant parts of the body, such as the liver. This process of spread is called *metastasis* (ACS, 2017b).

RISK FACTORS

Table 8-1 reviews risk factors for CRC. Increasing age is the greatest risk factor for sporadic (not genetic) CRC. Statistics show that 90% of cases occur in people older than 50 years (ACS, 2017b). The much higher incidence of CRC in more affluent and industrialized countries, compared with less developed countries, is also associated with lifestyle factors, such as obesity and the consumption of processed meat, and an inverse relationship with physical activity and consumption of fruit and vegetables (ACS, 2015, 2017b, 2017c).

Genetic Factors

Approximately 10% to 20% of patients describe a family history of CRC, but the pattern of inheritance and clinical features are not consistent with an obvious hereditary cancer syndrome (Weitzel, Blazer, MacDonald, Culver, & Offit, 2011). Screening of individuals with known or suspected hereditary risk should begin at 40 years of age, or 10 years earlier than the youngest family member at the time of his or her cancer diagnosis (ACS, 2017b; NCCN, 2016c, 2016e). Individuals with this type of history would likely benefit from risk assessment to determine the best schedule for screening (NCCN, 2016e).

Approximately 10% of the mutations are germline (inherited) and associated with hereditary nonpolyposis colorectal cancer (HNPCC), familial adenomatous polyposis (FAP), and other unusual syndromes. HNPCC is characterized by early-onset CRC (before age 50 years) and endometrial, ovarian, small intestine, and renal cancers in the family (Senter, 2012). Persons with mutations in the HNPCC genes are at risk for multiple primary cancers in these sites. Usually, there is not an excessive number of polyps. The interval from polyp to cancer is very short, often 12 to 18 months (NCCN, 2016e).

FAP is characterized by the development of hundreds to thousands of adenomatous polyps in the colon and development of CRC and other cancers in the third and fourth decade of life. FAP and HNPCC are the most common of the familial cancer syndromes, but together these two syndromes account for fewer than 5% of cases of CRC (NCCN, 2016e). Screening for persons with HNPCC usually begins at 25 years of age with annual colonoscopy; for those with FAP, screening often begins at 10 years of age. Table 8-2 lists other hereditary CRC syndromes for which testing is available. The outcome of testing and the personal and family history determine the best interval for screening. Persons with known or suspected hereditary risk for developing CRC are also at risk for other gastrointestinal cancers and frequently have much more aggressive screening than individuals in the general population (NCCN, 2016e).

TABLE 8-1: RISK STRATIFICATION FOR COLORECTAL CANCER

Average Risk Factors

- *Age:* More than 90% of colorectal cancers (CRCs) occur after 50 years of age.
- *Ethnic background:* Risk may be higher in persons of Ashkenazi Jewish heritage.
- *Race:* Incidence and mortality is highest in Black individuals.
- *Diet:* Risk is increased in persons who consume a diet high in animal fat, red meat, and processed meats.
- *Lack of exercise:* Risk is increased in inactive persons.
- *Overweight:* Risk is increased in overweight and obese persons.
- *Smoking:* Smoking increases risk 30% to 40%.
- *Alcohol:* Risk is higher in those who drink more than one alcoholic beverage per day.
- *Diabetes:* Risk is increased by 30%.

Moderate Risk Factors

- *Personal history of CRC:* Even if completely resected, the risk of a second primary CRC is increased, especially if the diagnosis is before 60 years of age.
- *Personal history of polyps:* Risk is higher in persons with large dysplastic or hyperplastic polyps.
- *Personal history of bowel disease:* Risk is higher in persons with ulcerative colitis or Crohn's disease.
- *Family history of CRC:* Risk is higher if a first-degree relative has CRC.

High Risk Factors

- *Hereditary nonpolyposis CRC:* Risk is approximately 80%.
- *Familial adenomatous polyposis:* Risk is nearly 100%.
- Other hereditary cancer syndromes, including mutations in the following genes: *ATM, AXIN2, BMPR1A, CDH1, CHEK2, MUTYH, POLD1, POLE, PTEN, SCG5/GREM1, SMAD4, STK11,* and *TP53.* Risk can range from 35% to 75%.

Note. Adapted from:

Weitzel, J. N., Blazer, K. R., MacDonald, D. J., Culver, J. O., & Offit, K. (2011). Genetics, genomics and cancer risk assessment: State of the art and future directions in the era of personalized medicine. *CA: A Cancer Journal for Clinicians, 61*(5), 327-359. doi:10.3322/caac.20128

American Cancer Society. (2017b). *Colorectal cancer facts and figures – 2017-2019.* Atlanta, GA: Author.

National Comprehensive Cancer Network. (2016d). *Genetic/familial high-risk assessment: Colorectal, version 1.2016.* Retrieved from http://www.nccn.org

Persons with known or suspected colorectal hereditary cancer syndromes should have formal risk assessment and possible genetic testing with a credentialed genetics professional. These individuals will have recommendations for cancer prevention and early detection, which are generally much more aggressive than for those of the general population with average risk.

A family history of CRC involving a first-degree relative increases the risk of developing colon cancer 2- to 3-fold. The risk is higher when the relative was diagnosed before 50 years of age or if there are many family members who were diagnosed with CRC (Weissman et al., 2012).

The genetic syndromes HNPCC and FAP increase the risk of developing CRC by 80% and 100%, respectively (NCCN, 2016e). These syndromes create a condition whereby family members develop polyps that advance to adenomas and possible malignancies, and account for about 5% to 7% of all CRCs. Key indicators of these hereditary cancer syndromes are listed in Table 8-3.

TABLE 8-2: HEREDITARY SYNDROMES ASSOCIATED WITH INCREASED RISK FOR DEVELOPING COLORECTAL CANCER

Gene	Associated Cancer Risks
MSH1[a] *MSH2*[a] *MSH6*[a] *EPCAM*[a] *PMS2*[a]	Endometrial, colorectal, ovarian, gastric, pancreatic, biliary tract, urinary tract, small bowel, brain, sebaceous neoplasms
APC	Colorectal, duodenal or periampullary, gastric, thyroid, pancreatic, brain, liver
BMPR1A	Colorectal, gastric (especially if there are gastric polyps)
CHEK2	Breast, colorectal, prostate, thyroid, endometrial, ovarian
TP53	Breast, endometrial, soft tissue sarcoma, osteosarcoma, brain, hematological malignancies, adrenocortical carcinoma
MUYTH[b]	Colorectal, duodenal, endometrial
STK11	Breast, colorectal, pancreatic, gastric, ovarian, lung, small intestine, cervical, endometrial, testicular tumors
PTEN	Breast, thyroid, endometrial, colorectal, renal, melanoma
ATM	Breast, colorectal, pancreatic
SMAD4	Colorectal, gastric (especially if there are gastric polyps)
AXIN2	Colorectal
POLD1	Colorectal, endometrial
POLE	Colorectal
SCG5/ GREM1	Colorectal

[a]Genes associated with hereditary nonpolyposis colorectal cancer.

[b]Recessive syndrome; risk is much higher in individuals with two mutated copies.

Note. Adapted from:

National Comprehensive Cancer Network. (2016d). *Genetic/familial high-risk assessment: Colorectal, version 1.2016.* Retrieved from http://www.nccn.org

Weitzel, J. N., Blazer, K. R., MacDonald, D. J., Culver, J. O., & Offit, K. (2011). Genetics, genomics and cancer risk assessment: State of the art and future directions in the era of personalized medicine. *CA: A Cancer Journal for Clinicians, 61*(5), 327-359. doi:10.3322/caac.20128

Familial Adenomatous Polyposis

FAP is caused by mutations in the *APC* gene that a person inherits from his or her parents. About 1% of all CRCs are attributable to FAP (Jasperson, 2012).

People with this disease typically develop hundreds or thousands of polyps in their colons and rectums, usually in their teens or early adulthood (see Figure 8-8). Cancer usually develops in one or more of these polyps as early as 20 years of age. By 40 years of age, almost all people with this disorder will have developed cancer if a prophylactic colectomy is not done (NCCN, 2016e). FAP is sometimes associated with Gardner's syndrome, a condition that involves benign (noncancerous) tumors of the skin, soft connective tissue, and bones.

A less severe form of FAP, called *attenuated FAP,* is characterized by less than 100 polyps (usually about 20) at presentation and later onset of CRC (NCCN, 2016e). More than 850 mutations in the *APC* gene are asso-

TABLE 8-3: KEY INDICATORS OF HEREDITARY CANCER SYNDROMES

Nonpolyposis Cancer Syndromes

- Personal history of CRC diagnosed before 50 years of age
- Personal history of endometrial, ovarian, or breast cancer, especially if diagnosed before 50 years of age
- First-degree relative with CRC diagnosed before 50 years of age
- Two or more relatives with CRC or an HNPCC-associated cancer, including endometrial, ovarian, gastric, hepatobiliary, small bowel, renal pelvis, or ureter cancer; the first relative must be a first-degree relative of the others
- CRC occurring in two or more generations on the same side of the family
- A personal history of CRC and a first-degree relative with adenomas diagnosed before 40 years of age
- An affected relative with a known HNPCC or other susceptibility mutation associated with hereditary colorectal cancer syndromes

Polyposis Syndromes

- Patient has a clinical diagnosis of polyposis (20 or more polyps, lifetime count)
- Patient is a first-degree relative with multiple polyps
- Patient has an affected relative with a known FAP-associated gene, *MYH* mutation, or other susceptibility mutation associated with polyposis syndromes
- Personal or family history of CRC diagnosed before 50 years of age

CRC = colorectal cancer; FAP = familial adenomatous polyposis; HNPCC = hereditary nonpolyposis colorectal cancer.

Note. Adapted from American Cancer Society. (2017b). *Colorectal cancer facts and figures – 2017-2019.* Atlanta, GA: Author; National Comprehensive Cancer Network. (2016b). *Colorectal cancer screening, version 1.2016.* Retrieved from http://www.nccn.org; National Comprehensive Cancer Network. (2016d). *Genetic/familial high-risk assessment: Colorectal, version 1.2016.* Retrieved from http://www.nccn.org; and Weitzel, J. N., Blazer, K. R., MacDonald, D. J., Culver, J. O., & Offit, K. (2011). Genetics, genomics and cancer risk assessment: State of the art and future directions in the era of personalized medicine. *CA: A Cancer Journal for Clinicians, 61*(5), 327-359. doi:10.3322/caac.20128

ciated with FAP; some families have mutations that are unique to them (Jasperson, 2012). Approximately 30% of individuals with FAP are the first person in their family with the hereditary mutation for FAP (NCCN, 2016e). This is referred to as a de novo mutation. Future generations are at risk for inheriting the mutation. There is also an autosomal-recessive gene on chromosome 1, called *MYH,* that is associated with polyposis (NCCN, 2016e).

Hereditary Nonpolyposis Colorectal Cancer

HNPCC, also known as Lynch syndrome, is another clearly defined genetic colon syndrome. It accounts for about 3% to 5% of all CRCs (Senter, 2012). HNPCC can be caused by inherited changes in a number of different genes that normally help repair DNA damage. This syndrome also develops when people are relatively young.

People with HNPCC have polyps, but they have only a few, not hundreds as in FAP. The lifetime risk for CRC in people with this condition may be as high as 70% to 80% (Weitzel et al., 2011). The majority of mutations responsible for HNPCC occur in four mismatch repair genes: *MSH2, MLH1, PMS2,* and *MSH6.* Patients with a mutation in *MLH1* and *MSH2* have an 80% lifetime risk of developing CRC, compared with a 6% risk in the general population (NCCN, 2016e). Women with this condition also have a very high risk of developing cancer of the endometrium. Other cancers linked with HNPCC include cancer of the ovary, stomach, small bowel, pancreas, kidney, ureters, and bile duct. Women with mutations in these genes have a 70% lifetime risk for developing endometrial cancer and a 12% to 15% lifetime risk for developing ovarian cancer (NCCN, 2016e).

FIGURE 8-8: COLON OF AN INDIVIDUAL WITH FAMILIAL ADENOMATOUS POLYPOSIS

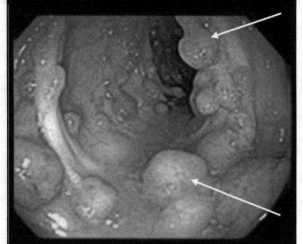

The endoscopic view looking into the interior lining of the colon. The multiple round, bulbous shapes and clusters noted in the lining are polyps.

Note. From U.S. Department of Health and Human Services, National Institutes of Health, National Cancer Institute. (2015). *FAP polyps – Endoscopic.* Retrieved from https://visualsonline. cancer.gov/details.cfm?imageid=10067

Although not associated with large numbers of polyps, persons with HNPCC who do form adenomatous polyps are more likely to do so at an earlier age, are more likely to develop right-sided colon cancer, and exhibit a very rapid progression to malignancy in 1 to 3 years instead of the 5- to 10-year pattern seen in the general population (ACS, 2017b; Weissman et al., 2012).

Taking an accurate family history is the key to identifying families with an HNPCC mutation. There are several considerations in identifying these patients, and any suspected family should be referred to a genetics professional to identify the most cost-effective and efficient strategy for genetic testing. About 90% of tumors from people who have HNPCC show instability in microsatellites, which are repeated sequences of DNA. Although the length of these microsatellites is highly variable from person to person, each individual has microsatellites of a set length. These repeated

sequences are common and normal. In cells with mutations in DNA repair genes, some of these sequences accumulate errors and become longer or shorter. The appearance of abnormally long or short microsatellites in an individual's DNA is referred to as microsatellite instability.

Tests are available that detect microsatellite instability in tumor cells, and finding numerous longer or shorter microsatellite regions in these cells suggests the presence of a mutated DNA mismatch repair gene with HNPCC. Thus, testing a tumor sample for microsatellite instability can often provide a helpful way to determine whether genetic testing for HNPCC is appropriate; it also provides valuable information about the tumor when making treatment decisions (NCCN, 2016e). If a patient's tumor cells show no evidence of microsatellite instability, it is unlikely that he or she has a mutated mismatch repair gene; the individual may, however, have a different susceptibility gene.

Identifying families with these inherited syndromes is important because it allows doctors to recommend specific steps, such as screening and other preventive measures, at an early age. Often, CRC screening begins in the teenage years for persons with a known mutation in FAP. When polyps begin to develop, a prophylactic colectomy is recommended. For persons with a known mutation in HNPCC, screening begins between 20 and 25 years of age and is done on an annual basis because polyps will often progress to CRC in 12 to 18 months. Women with a known HNPCC are usually advised to have their uterus and ovaries removed (total hysterectomy) at about 40 years of age because of their high risk for developing these cancers (60% lifetime risk for endometrial cancer and 12% risk for ovarian cancer). Because the testing and management strategies are complex for the patient with a hereditary cancer syndrome, he or she should be referred to a genetics professional.

History of Polyps

Polyps are precursors to CRC. They are most common as people age. Approximately 30% of individuals in their 50s are diagnosed with polyps, and approximately 50% of individuals in their 70s produce polyps (NCCN, 2016c).

Approximately 70% of polyps are adenomatous with malignant potential. Nevertheless, most polyps do not become cancerous (only 5% become malignant; NCCN, 2016c). Most polyps are pedunculated (stalked or tubular), rather than flat, or a combination of stalked and flat. Polyps that develop into cancerous cells develop over several years, starting with growing larger and then forming an adenoma that can become carcinoma in situ.

Polyps that are more likely to become cancerous are a higher grade and severely dysplastic. Patients who develop more than one polyp have a five to nine times greater likelihood of developing a malignancy (NCCN, 2016c). When detected, the smaller the polyp, the less likely it is that it will become malignant. For those who undergo regular polypectomy for recurring polyps, the incidence of developing CRC decreases by 90% (ACS, 2017b).

Personal History

A history of previous cancers increases the risk of developing CRC for some patients. Those who were previously diagnosed with CRC are at higher risk. This risk increases if the individual was diagnosed before age 50 years. Women with breast, endometrial, and ovarian cancer are at higher risk for developing CRCs. In most cases, these women will have more frequent and earlier CRCs than individuals in the general population.

Lifestyle Risk Factors

For those without a genetic predisposition, there are no specific and unique risks for CRC. However, together, many factors can put an individual at risk.

Epidemiological, experimental (animal), and clinical investigations suggest that diets high in total fat (saturated and monounsaturated), protein, calories, alcohol, and meat (both red and white) and low in calcium and folate (vegetables) are associated with an increased incidence of CRC (ACS, 2015c; Kushi et al., 2012). The risk is 2 to 2.5 times higher for those who follow a high-fat diet compared with those with low-fat diets (ACS, 2015c; Kushi et al., 2012). Regular physical activity of at least 150 intentional minutes of exercise weekly has been shown to reduce the risk of developing CRC (ACS, 2017b).

Colon cancer rates have been shown to be high in populations with high total fat intake and are lower in those populations where people consume less fat. This means that Western countries – with high-fat diets – have been shown to have more CRC cases (ACS, 2015, 2017c).

Inflammatory Bowel Disease

Inflammatory bowel disease, which includes ulcerative colitis and Crohn's disease, is a condition in which the colon is inflamed over a long period of time. For those with inflammatory bowel disease, the risk of developing CRC is increased (ACS, 2017b). These individuals need to be screened for CRC on a more frequent basis and earlier than the general population depending on the extent and severity of the ulcerative colitis and Crohn's disease. Often, the first sign that cancer may be developing is dysplasia found in areas of irritation. Inflammatory bowel disease is different from irritable bowel syndrome, which does not carry an increased risk for CRC.

SIGNS AND SYMPTOMS

Colon cancer may not produce symptoms until the tumor is well advanced. Signs and symptoms of CRC include

- rectal bleeding,

- blood in the stool,

- abdominal cramping or pain,

- change in bowel habits lasting more than a few days,

- narrowing of the stool,

- fatigue,

- urge to defecate after defecating, and

- unintended weight loss.

Unfortunately, these symptoms are also associated with many more benign gastrointestinal problems that necessitate a diagnostic evaluation. A change in bowel habits is a more common presenting symptom for left-sided cancers and is caused by a progressive narrowing of the bowel lumen, with diarrhea, a change in stool form, and eventually, intestinal obstruction (ACS, 2017b). About 10% of patients with iron deficiency have CRC, most commonly on the right side. Thus, iron deficiency in men and in women who are not menstruating is an indication for immediate evaluation to rule out CRC (NCCN, 2016e). The first symptom that is recognized by the patient is often blood in or on the stool.

Blood in or on the stool does not absolutely mean CRC is present; bleeding could be related to hemorrhoids, ulcers, a tear, or inflammatory bowel disease (ACS, 2017b). Bleeding, however, when related to CRC, is seldom associated with the early detection of CRC. Ideally, screening should begin before symptoms arise, if possible. When screening includes colonoscopy, polyps can be removed before they become malignant, essentially preventing the development of CRC. Although prompt evaluation of symptoms is important, ideally CRC is detected in the asymptomatic phase when treatment is most likely to be effective (ACS, 2017b).

PREVENTION

Behavior and Lifestyle Risk Factors

Direct efforts need to be made to prevent CRC. Evidence shows that 13% of CRC deaths are attributed to smoking (ACS, 2017b). The carcinogens found in tobacco increase cancer growth in the colon and rectum, and increase the risk of being diagnosed with this cancer. Efforts at smoking prevention and cessation should not be underestimated in terms of their impact on CRC.

Maintaining a healthy diet and being physically active are important components of CRC prevention. The amount of fat and fiber in the diet has been examined extensively as a risk factor associated with CRC. A diet high in fiber and low in fat, which for adults is 20 to 35 grams of fiber per day and about 30% or less of their total daily calories from fat, along with limited consumption of red meat, helps reduce the risk of CRC (ACS, 2017c). It is also recommended that men and women regularly eat fruits and cruciferous vegetables and consume calcium to decrease the risk of CRC (ACS, 2017b; Kushi et al., 2012).

Additionally, recent evidence indicates that inactivity can be associated with CRC (Kushi et al., 2012). The lack of physical activity in daily routines can also be attributed to the increased incidence of obesity in men and women, another factor associated with CRC (ACS, 2017c). Therefore, regular physical activity and a healthy diet can help decrease the risk for CRC.

Alcohol consumption is a factor in the diagnosis of CRC at a younger age and an increase of CRC in the distal colon. As with smoking, the regular consumption of alcohol causes a

2-fold increased risk for developing CRC, and limiting alcohol intake is recommended (ACS, 2017b, 2017c).

Chemoprevention

Nonrandomized studies have found that people who regularly use aspirin and other non-steroidal anti-inflammatory drugs (NSAIDs), such as ibuprofen (Motrin, Advil) and naproxen (Aleve), have a lower risk of CRC and adenomatous polyps (ACS, 2017b). Aspirin (600 mg daily) and COX-2 inhibitors may prevent the growth of polyps in people who were previously treated for early stages of CRC or who previously had polyps removed (NCCN, 2016c, 2016e). Because NSAIDs and COX-2 inhibitors can cause serious or life-threatening bleeding from stomach irritation, they are not recommended as a cancer prevention strategy for people at average risk for developing CRC.

Some individuals have a genetic predisposition for developing polyps, such as those with an FAP, SMAD4, BMPR1A, or MYUTH mutation. Because their risk for developing CRC is higher than in the general population, these individuals might want to consider taking a chemoprevention agent such as an NSAID or aspirin (NCCN, 2016e). The decision to use these in persons at increased risk should be made only after a careful discussion of the risks and benefits (NCCN, 2016e).

Polypectomy

Polypectomy is one of the most effective means for CRC prevention; it is routinely performed during screening colonoscopies (ACS, 2017b; NCCN, 2016c). Regular CRC screening is one of the most effective means in preventing CRC. From the time the first abnormal cells start to grow, it usually takes about 10 to 15 years for them to develop into CRC (ACS, 2017b). Regular CRC screening can, in many cases, prevent CRC altogether. This is because some polyps, or growths, can be found and removed before they have the chance to turn into cancer (NCCN, 2016c). CRC is a very preventable cancer. Detection and removal of adenomatous polyps, from which more than 95% of CRCs arise, reduce the risk of being diagnosed with or dying of this disease (NCCN, 2016c, 2016e). For this reason, nurses need to provide education about the importance of CRC screening as not only a means to detect CRC early, but more importantly, to prevent CRC. Polyps at highest risk for becoming malignant include those greater than 1 cm, those with high-grade dysplastic features on histology, and those that are removed in pieces (Levin et al., 2008; NCCN, 2016c). See Table 8-5 later in this chapter for recommendations for follow-up colonoscopy after polypectomy.

SCREENING AND DETECTION

Screening for CRC has changed five times since 2001 (Smith et al., 2016). Recommendations have included combinations of digital rectal examination, sigmoidoscopy, colonoscopy, barium enema, and fecal occult blood testing (FOBT). There are two categories of tests:

- *Tests that can find both colorectal polyps and cancer:* These tests look at the structure of the colon itself to find any abnormal areas. This is done either with a scope inserted into the rectum or with special imaging tests. Polyps found before they turn cancerous can be removed, so these tests may also prevent CRC. Because these tests offer the possibility of prevention in addition to early detection, they are preferred if they are available and the patient is willing to have them (ACS, 2017b; NCCN, 2016c).

- *Tests that mainly find cancer:* These tests involve testing the stool for signs that cancer may be present. These tests are less invasive, but they are less likely to detect polyps.

All guidelines for CRC screening require risk assessment as a first step. The approach to screening differs significantly based on risk category (average, increased, or high risk). The key element of a CRC screening recommendation is to suggest the right test beginning at the correct age for individuals at each risk level (ACS, 2017b). Screening should also be repeated at the proper interval, depending on risk level. For persons of average risk, screening should begin by 50 years of age because most CRC is diagnosed at 60 years of age (ACS, 2017b).

High-risk patients with hereditary CRC syndromes or inflammatory bowel disease should be referred to specialists when patients are young. Those with a suspected hereditary cancer syndrome need to be referred to a genetics expert for genetic testing to clarify risk. Those who test positive for a deleterious mutation should be managed by a clinician with expertise in these syndromes. Screening will likely be required on an annual basis beginning at a young age. Members of these families may also want to consider enrolling in chemoprevention trials. Refer to Chapter 2 for in-depth information about genetic risk and hereditary syndromes.

Regular screening for the average-risk person should begin by 50 years of age with FOBT annually, a sigmoidoscopy or double-contrast barium enema every 5 years, and a colonoscopy every 10 years (ACS, 2017a; NCCN, 2016c). Table 8-4 details screening tests used to identify CRC.

Fecal Occult Blood Testing

The goal of FOBT is to examine the stool for hidden blood that occasionally sheds from adenomatous polyps and cancer. One disadvantage of this screening method is that polyps often do not bleed. This test should be done every year by obtaining a three-sample card from a primary care provider; the patient takes the card home to obtain the stool samples for testing. Dietary guidelines must be followed before and during this test; if not done properly, the test can result in a false outcome. Additionally, negative FOBT results do not necessarily mean that no polyps or cancer is present, just that no blood was detected in the stool. Conversely, a positive FOBT does not indicate cancer, only that further screening should be administered to locate the bleeding. Any FOBT that was administered by a healthcare provider using a small stool sample on a single card is inadequate and not recommended as a CRC screening method (NCCN, 2016c).

Flexible Sigmoidoscopy

The flexible sigmoidoscopy is an inexpensive procedure that can be done in a physician's office and requires no sedation. The day before the procedure, the patient is placed on a clear liquid diet and given a prescription for a bowel preparation. According to guidelines based on age or at-risk individuals, a flexible sigmoidoscopy is recommended every 5 years along with an annual FOBT (ACS, 2017a). The primary disadvantage of flexible sigmoidoscopy is that only a portion of the distal colon can be examined. Using a 60-cm flexible sigmoidoscope, approximately 65% to 75% of adenomatous polyps and 40% to 65% of CRCs are within its reach, whereas with colonoscopy, the entire length of the colon can be visualized (NCCN, 2016c).

Colonoscopy

The colonoscopy is a more thorough examination and is becoming the preferred method of screening. Although utilization has increased in the past two decades, unfortunately less than 60% of adults aged 50 years and older in the United States have had a colonoscopy at the recommended 10-year interval (ACS, 2017b). This is especially unfortunate because Medicare

TABLE 8-4: SCREENING TESTS FOR COLORECTAL CANCER (1 OF 2)

Flexible Sigmoidoscopy

Interval: every 5 years

Preparation: partial bowel preparation with laxatives and enemas; sedation usually not used

Accuracy: 45% to 50% sensitivity

Risks/Limitations: evaluates only lower third of colon

Patient Teaching: a positive screen requires follow-up with colonoscopy; may cause some discomfort; very small risk of bleeding, infection, or perforation

Colonoscopy

Interval: every 10 years

Preparation: complete bowel preparation; requires conscious sedation

Accuracy: up to 95% sensitivity; can usually view entire colon, perform a biopsy, remove polyps, and diagnose other diseases

Risks/Limitations: perforation and bleeding; risk is increased with polypectomy

Patient Teaching: will need to miss a day of work and need someone to provide transportation to and from appointment

Double-Contrast Barium Enema

Interval: every 5 years

Preparation: complete bowel preparation; no sedation needed

Accuracy: 48% to 73% sensitivity

Risk/Limitations: rare cases of perforation; cannot perform biopsy of polyps

Patient Education: a positive screen requires follow-up with colonoscopy

Virtual Colonoscopy

Interval: every 5 years

Preparation: complete bowel preparation; no sedation

Accuracy: 55% to 59% sensitivity for large polyps

Risk/Limitations: rare cases of perforation

Patient Education: costly – may not be covered by insurance; a positive screen necessitates the need for colonoscopy; if not available on the same day, a second preparation will be required; may detect other problems outside of the colon that need evaluation

Fecal Occult Blood Testing

Interval: annually

Preparation: foods and medications to avoid 48 hours before and during collection include aspirin, nonsteroidal anti-inflammatory drugs, vitamin C, red meat, poultry, fish, and raw vegetables

Accuracy: 37% to 79% sensitivity

Patient Education: a positive screen requires further evaluation with colonoscopy

TABLE 8-4: SCREENING TESTS FOR COLORECTAL CANCER (2 OF 2)

Fecal Immunochemical Test

Interval: annually

Preparation: special sample collection instructions and transportation to laboratory

Accuracy: 29% to 94% sensitivity

Patient Education: one-time testing is likely to be ineffective; a positive screen requires follow-up with colonoscopy

Stool DNA

Interval: none specified

Preparation: requires collection of an adequate sample and proper preservation and shipping to laboratory

Accuracy: 26% to 59% sensitivity

Patient Education: a positive screen requires follow-up with colonoscopy

Note. Adapted from:

American Cancer Society. (2017b). *Colorectal cancer facts and figures – 2017-2019.* Atlanta, GA: Author.

National Comprehensive Cancer Network. (2016b). *Colorectal cancer screening, version 1.2016.* Retrieved from http://www.nccn.org

and most major insurers cover a significant portion of the costs. During a colonoscopy, the physician inserts a thin, lighted tube, which has a small camera attached, into the rectum. The physician guides the colonoscope through the rectum and colon; if any polyps are found, the physician can remove them for biopsy. For patients who cannot tolerate colonoscopy, barium enema is sometimes utilized. Colonoscopy has the unique advantage of being able to remove polyps. Figure 8-9 illustrates the colonoscopy procedure. Follow-up recommendations after polypectomy are listed in Table 8-5.

Virtual Colonoscopy

Virtual colonoscopy is a relatively new screening option to detect CRC (ACS, 2017b). In 2008, the ACS approved it as a technique to screen for early detection of CRC (ACS, 2017b; Levin et al., 2008). Virtual colonoscopy produces a dual or tridimensional colorectal image that is generated using data from a spiral computed tomography (CT) scan. This screening method is appealing to many people because it is non-invasive, requires no sedation, and provides a view of the entire colon and rectum. The preparation for this procedure does require the same

dietary restrictions and bowel cleansing as the colonoscopy, and air insufflation is needed for a clear view of the colon. Many people may prefer this screening method to flexible sigmoidoscopy or colonoscopy, but they need to be clearly informed that if any polyps are visible on the scan, the patient will then have to undergo a colonoscopy for further evaluation. If the facility cannot accommodate immediate colonoscopy, the patient will have to repeat the preparation at a later point (ACS, 2017b; Levin et al., 2008).

Stool DNA

Stool DNA tests do not look for blood in the stool. These tests look for specific abnormal sections of DNA from cancer or polyp cells (ACS, 2017b). CRC cells often contain DNA mutations in certain genes such as *APC, KRAS,* and *p53.* Cells from CRCs or polyps with these mutations are often shed into the stool, where tests may be able to detect them.

There is no specific interval for how often the test needs to be done (NCCN, 2016c). This test is also much more expensive than other forms of stool testing. It does not require any

FIGURE 8-9: COLONOSCOPY

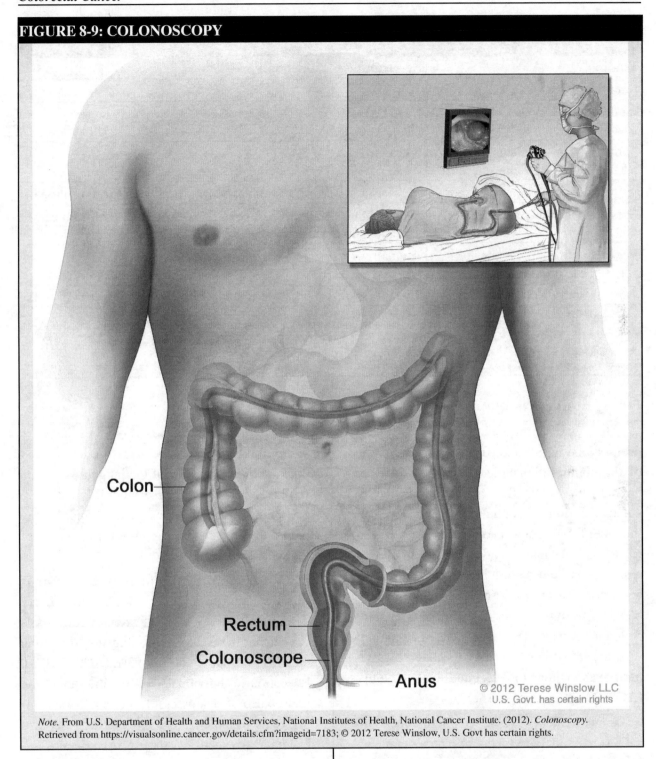

Colon

Rectum

Colonoscope

Anus

© 2012 Terese Winslow LLC
U.S. Govt. has certain rights

Note. From U.S. Department of Health and Human Services, National Institutes of Health, National Cancer Institute. (2012). *Colonoscopy.* Retrieved from https://visualsonline.cancer.gov/details.cfm?imageid=7183; © 2012 Terese Winslow, U.S. Govt has certain rights.

special preparation. If the results are positive, a colonoscopy is required to investigate further.

People who are having this test will receive a kit with detailed instructions from their doctor's office or clinic on how to collect the specimen. Stool DNA requires an entire stool sample. It is obtained using a special container that is placed in a bracket that stretches across the seat of the toilet. The specimen must be shipped to the laboratory within 24 hours of having the bowel movement in a special kit with ice.

TABLE 8-5: RECOMMENDATIONS FOR FOLLOW-UP SCREENING AFTER POLYPECTOMY

Finding	Screening Recommendations
Small hyperplastic rectal polyp	10 years
<2 tubular adenomas (<1 cm) with low-grade dysplasia	5 to 10 years
3 to 10 low-grade adenomas or any adenoma with high-grade dysplasia	5 years
≥10 adenomas on one examination	<3 years and referral for evaluation for hereditary cancer syndrome
Sessile adenomas removed in pieces	2 to 6 months to complete removal; when complete (both clinically and by pathology), at the discretion of the endoscopist
Persons with a known mutation for HNPCC or FAP	Annually – to also include upper endoscopy
Persons with CRC	1 year after resection; if normal, repeat in 3 years and then 5 years

CRC = colorectal cancer; FAP = familial adenomatous polyposis; HNPCC = hereditary nonpolyposis colorectal cancer.

Note. Adapted from:

American Cancer Society. (2017b). *Colorectal cancer facts and figures – 2017-2019.* Atlanta, GA: Author.

National Comprehensive Cancer Network. (2016b). *Colorectal cancer screening, version 1.2016.* Retrieved from http://www.nccn.org

Fecal Immunochemical Test

The fecal immunochemical test detects occult blood in the stool. This test reacts to part of the hemoglobin molecule, which is found on red blood cells. The fecal immunochemical test is done essentially the same way as the FOBT, but some people may find it easier to use because it has no drug or dietary restrictions, and sample collection may take less effort. This test is also less likely to react to bleeding from the upper digestive tract, such as from the stomach. This test is offered to patients who are unwilling or unable to undergo structural examinations to detect and remove polyps (ACS, 2017b; NCCN, 2016c).

As with the FOBT, the fecal immunochemical test may not detect a tumor that is not bleeding, so multiple stool samples should be tested. If the results are positive for hidden blood, a colonoscopy is required to investigate further (Levin et al., 2008). To be beneficial, the test must be repeated every year. It requires special mailing to the laboratory.

Patient Preparation

Examination of the bowel requires the colon to be empty in order to pass the scope and obtain a thorough view of the internal structure. Methods vary based on protocol, but usually oral preparations/laxatives administered the day before and enemas are required in advance of the scheduled procedure.

The diagnostic yield of the examination depends on adequate preparation. Early detection and removal of adenomatous polyps through regular screening could reduce the CRC mortality rate by 53% (ACS, 2017a). Education to individuals and families about the importance of risk assessment and CRC screening remains inadequate; more efforts need to be made toward developing organized CRC screening programs similar to breast centers and mammography programs (Verma, Sarfaty, Brooks, & Wender, 2015).

Prevention and Screening: Patient Education

Educating the public about the epidemiology, risk factors, symptoms, and screening options for CRC enables individuals to become advocates for their own health. Typically, individuals in the community setting have many misconceptions about CRC. For instance, many people do not know the difference between a sigmoidoscopy and a colonoscopy, or that FOBT should be done every year to increase the efficiency of sigmoidoscopy and help decrease the risk for CRC (ACS, 2017b). Many individuals believe that CRC inevitably ends in a colostomy. Many do not realize that polypectomy can prevent a colon cancer from developing. One of the most important things that healthcare providers can do is discuss the importance of regular colonoscopy to prevent colon cancer through polypectomy. Many people mistakenly believe that the goal of colonoscopy is to detect colon cancer; the goal is to prevent colon cancers (Ely et al., 2016). Efforts and education need to be expanded in this area (Barton, 2012). Correction of these misconceptions is critical to motivate individuals to engage in CRC screening. As health educators, nurses need to be aware of the latest recommendations and work to alter these perceptions, promote health literacy, and provide individuals with the correct information. The goal of health education is to promote healthy living and to encourage individuals to engage in practices and behaviors that are beneficial to long-term health and quality of life.

STAGING AND DIAGNOSIS

If colon cancer is suspected, diagnostic tests may include

- chest radiograph;
- CT scan of the abdomen or pelvis, with or without a needle biopsy;
- positron emission tomography scan;
- abdominal ultrasound;
- transrectal ultrasound;
- magnetic resonance imaging;
- blood tests (complete blood cell count [CBC], serum chemistry, and liver studies) and tests for serum carcinoembryonic antigen (CEA), a tumor-associated marker for cancer (normal, <2.5 ng/ml); and
- bone scan.

After all of the data are gathered, staging guides treatment decisions. The patient's CRC is staged based on the size of the tumor, presence or absence of lymph node involvement, and presence or absence of metastasis. Highlights of the staging schema for CRC are listed in Figure 8-10 (Edge et al., 2010).

Cancers develop from polyps that are benign changes. Over time, some polyps will develop dysplastic changes that eventually lead to malignant changes. Once the malignancy develops, it can spread into the wall of the colon or rectum. As the malignancy grows it can spread into blood or lymph vessels; they can metastasize to distant parts of the body, such as the liver, peritoneal cavity, lungs, bones, and adrenal glands. At diagnosis, approximately 41% of colon cancer cells and 50% to 60% of rectal cancer cells have metastasized to regional lymph nodes (ACS, 2017b).

Approximately 50% of colon cancer patients will be diagnosed with hepatic metastases, either at the time of initial presentation or as a result of disease recurrence. Although only a small proportion of patients with hepatic metastases are candidates for surgical resection, advances in tumor ablation techniques and in regional and systemic chemotherapy administration provide for a number of treatment options.

continued on page 229

FIGURE 8-10: COLON CANCER – PENETRATION AND PROLIFERATION AT EACH STAGE (1 OF 4)

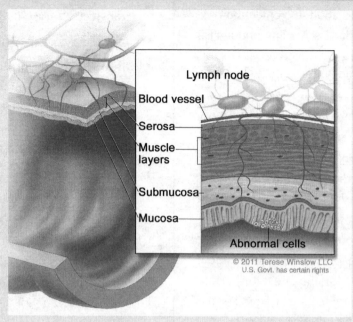

a. Stage 0

Stage 0 colorectal carcinoma in situ. A cross section of the colon/rectum is shown. An inset shows the layers of the colon/rectum wall with abnormal cells in the mucosa layer. Also shown are the submucosa, muscle layers, serosa, a blood vessel, and lymph nodes.

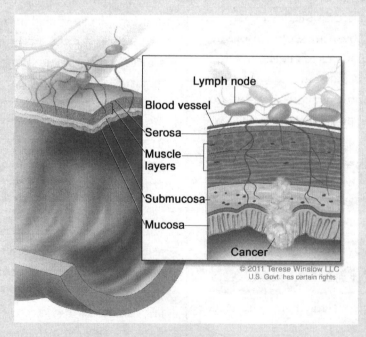

b. Stage I

Stage I colorectal cancer. A cross section of the colon/rectum is shown. An inset shows the layers of the colon/rectum wall with cancer in the mucosa, submucosa, and muscle layers. Also shown are the serosa, a blood vessel, and lymph nodes.

FIGURE 8-10: COLON CANCER – PENETRATION AND PROLIFERATION AT EACH STAGE (2 OF 4)

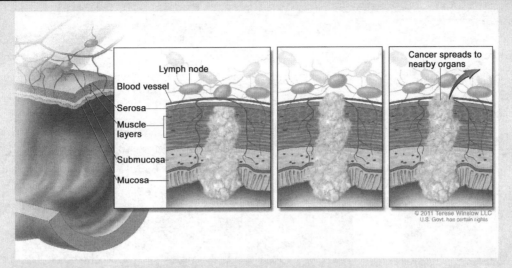

c. Stage IIA, IIB, and IIC colorectal cancer

A cross section of the colon/rectum and a three-panel inset are shown. Each panel shows the layers of the colon/rectum wall: mucosa, submucosa, muscle layers, and serosa. Also shown are a blood vessel and lymph nodes. The first panel shows stage IIA with cancer in the mucosa, submucosa, muscle layers, and serosa. The second panel shows stage IIB with cancer in all layers and spreading through the serosa. The third panel shows stage IIC with cancer spreading to nearby organs.

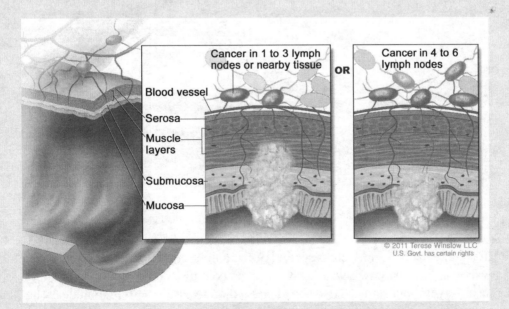

d. Stage IIIA

Stage IIIA colorectal cancer. A cross section of the colon/rectum and a two-panel inset are shown. Each panel shows the layers of the colon/rectum wall: mucosa, submucosa, muscle layers, and serosa. Also shown are a blood vessel and lymph nodes. The first panel shows cancer in the mucosa, submucosa, muscle layers, and two lymph nodes. The second panel shows cancer in the mucosa, submucosa, and five lymph nodes.

FIGURE 8-10: COLON CANCER – PENETRATION AND PROLIFERATION AT EACH STAGE (3 OF 4)

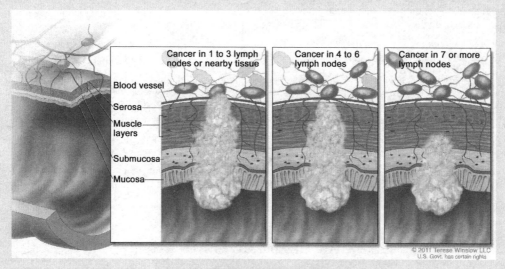

e. Stage IIIB

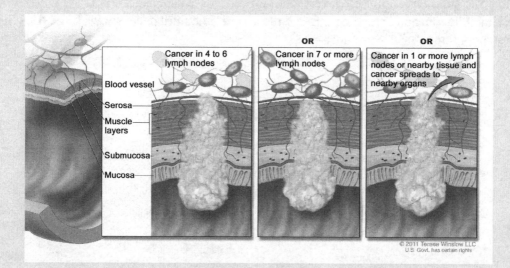

f. Stage IIIC

Stage IIIC colorectal cancer. A cross section of the colon/rectum wall and a three-panel inset are shown. Each panel shows the layers of the colon/rectum wall: mucosa, submucosa, muscle layers, and serosa. Also shown are a blood vessel and lymph nodes. The first panel shows cancer in all layers, spreading through the serosa, and in four lymph nodes. The second panel shows cancer in all layers and in seven lymph nodes. The third panel shows cancer in all layers, spreading through the serosa, in two lymph nodes, and spreading to nearby organs.

FIGURE 8-10: COLON CANCER – PENETRATION AND PROLIFERATION AT EACH STAGE (4 OF 4)

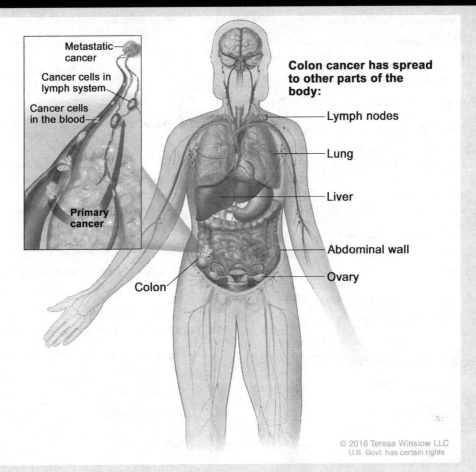

g. Stage IV

Stage IV colon cancer. Drawing shows other parts of the body where colon cancer may spread, including the lymph nodes, lung, liver, abdominal wall, and ovary. Inset shows cancer cells spreading from the colon, through the blood and lymph system, to another part of the body where metastatic cancer has formed.

Note. From U.S. Department of Health and Human Services, National Institutes of Health, National Cancer Institute. (a) (2011a). *Colon or rectal cancer stage 0*. Retrieved from https://visualsonline.cancer.gov/details.cfm?imageid=9147; (b) (2011b). *Colon or rectal cancer stage I*. Retrieved from https://visualsonline.cancer.gov/details.cfm?imageid=9148; (c) (2011c). *Colon or rectal cancer stage II*. Retrieved from https://visualsonline.cancer.gov/details.cfm?imageid=9149; (d) (2011d). *Colon or rectal cancer stage IIIA*. Retrieved from https://visualsonline.cancer.gov/details.cfm?imageid=9150; (e) (2011e). *Colon or rectal cancer stage IIIB*. Retrieved from https://visualsonline.cancer.gov/details.cfm?imageid=9151; (f) (2011f). *Colon or rectal cancer stage IIIC*. Retrieved from https://visualsonline.cancer.gov/details.cfm?imageid=9152; (g) (2016). *Colon or rectal cancer stage IV*. Retrieved from https://visualsonline.cancer.gov/details.cfm?imageid=9153; © 2011, 2016 Terese Winslow, U.S. Govt has certain rights.

For patients with a hepatic metastasis that is considered to be resectable (based on a limited number of lesions, intrahepatic locations of lesions, lack of major vascular involvement, absent or limited extrahepatic disease, and sufficient functional hepatic reserve), a negative margin resection has resulted in 5-year survival rates of 28% to 43% (NCCN, 2016c, 2016d). Patients with hepatic metastases that are deemed unresectable will occasionally become candidates for resection if they have a good response to chemotherapy. These patients have 5-year survival rates similar to those of patients who initially had resectable disease (NCCN, 2016c, 2016d).

There are several types of cancer of the colon and rectum, including the following:

- *Adenocarcinomas:* More than 95% of CRCs are a type of cancer known as adenocarcinomas. These are cancers that start in cells that form glands that make mucus to lubricate the inside of the colon and rectum (ACS, 2017b).

- *Carcinoid tumors:* These tumors develop from specialized hormone-producing cells of the intestine (ACS, 2017b).

- *Gastrointestinal stromal tumors:* These tumors develop from specialized cells in the wall of the colon called the *interstitial cells of Cajal.* Some are benign; others are malignant (ACS, 2017b).

- *Lymphomas:* These are cancers of immune system cells that typically develop in lymph nodes, but they may also start in the colon and rectum or other organs (ACS, 2017b).

As a component of the workup, the pathology report on cell type contributes to decisions about treatment.

PROGNOSIS

The 5-year relative survival by stage at diagnosis for CRC is demonstrated in Figure 8-5. Survival depends on the stage at diagnosis. Another factor that can affect the prognosis for CRC is the grade of the tumor (Amin et al., 2017; NCCN, 2017a, 2017b). Grade is a description of how closely the cancer resembles normal colorectal tissue microscopically. The scale used for grading CRC goes from G1 (where the cancer looks much like normal colorectal tissue) to G4 (where the cancer looks very abnormal). The grades G2 and G3 fall somewhere in between them. The grade is often simplified as either low grade (G1 or G2) or high grade (G3 or G4). In general, the prognosis is not as good for high-grade CRC as it is for low-grade CRC (NCCN, 2017a, 2017b). Grade is just one of many components evaluated when determining treatment options.

TREATMENTS

Treatment for CRC depends on the size, location, and extent of the tumor and on the patient's general health. Clinical staging of the tumor is one of the most important prognosticators (NCCN, 2017a, 2017b).

Most persons diagnosed with CRC will need care from a multidisciplinary team of healthcare professionals. Nursing and medical team members among the myriad of experts might include those working in endoscopy, surgery, radiation therapy, and medical oncology. Depending on the specific treatment plan developed, patients may also need dietary consults if nutrition is compromised, an enterostomal therapist to assist with wound and ostomy care, and psychosocial/sexual counseling as needed.

Surgery

Surgery is the main treatment for earlier-stage colon cancers (NCCN, 2017a). Surgery is usually the main treatment for rectal cancer, although radiation and chemotherapy will often be given before or after surgery (NCCN, 2017b). Several surgical methods are used for removing or destroying rectal cancers.

Colon Cancer

- *Polypectomy and local excision:* The surgeon can remove some early colon cancers (stage 0 and some early stage I tumors) or polyps with surgery through a colonoscope, avoiding an abdominal incision. For a polypectomy, the surgeon cuts out the cancer across the base of the polyp's stalk (see Figure 8-11). Local excision removes superficial cancers and a small amount of nearby tissue.

FIGURE 8-11: POLYPECTOMY

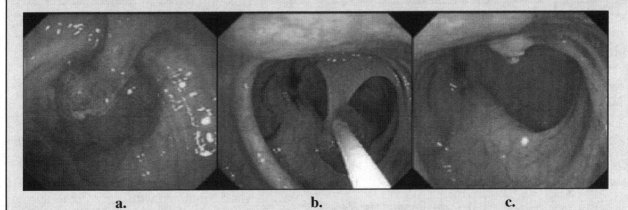

| a. | b. | c. |

a. Polyp is visualized with colonoscope. b. Snare from colonoscope is used to remove the polyp and cauterize to control bleeding. c. Postpolypectomy view to ensure hemostasis is achieved.

Note. From Wikimedia. (2009). *Polypectomy.* Retrieved from https://commons.wikimedia.org/wiki/File:Colon-Polyp.jpg

- *Colectomy:* A colectomy involves the surgeon removing part of the colon and nearby lymph nodes through an abdominal incision. Typically, the surgeon removes approximately one-fourth to one-third of the colon; however, the surgeon may remove more or less tissue, depending on the exact size and location of the tumor. The surgeon then reattaches the remaining segments of the colon.

- *Laparoscopic-assisted colectomy:* This approach removes part of the colon and nearby lymph nodes, which may be an option for some earlier-stage cancers. Instead of making one long incision in the abdomen, the surgeon makes several smaller incisions. The surgeon uses a laparoscope to remove part of the colon and lymph nodes. One of the instruments has a small video camera on the end, which allows the surgeon to see inside the abdomen. After the surgeon has freed the diseased part of the colon, one of the incisions is made larger to allow for its removal.

Because the incisions are smaller than with a standard colectomy, they usually heal faster. Patients may recover slightly faster and have less pain than they do after standard colon surgery (ACS, 2017b).

Laparoscopic-assisted surgery appears to be nearly as curative as the standard approach for earlier-stage cancers (NCCN, 2017a). Current recommendations from the NCCN state that this option should only be considered in patients with tumors that do not appear to be obstructed, and it must be carried out by surgeons with additional training and expertise in minimally invasive techniques.

Rectal Cancer

- *Polypectomy and local excision:* As in colon surgery, polypectomy can be used to remove superficial cancers or polyps. This is done with instruments inserted through the anus, without making a surgical opening in the skin of the abdomen.

- *Local transanal resection:* This is a full-thickness resection. A local transanal resection is done with instruments inserted through the anus, without making an opening in the skin of the abdomen. This operation involves cutting through all layers of the rectum to remove invasive cancer and some surrounding normal rectal tissue. This procedure can be used to remove some stage I rectal cancers that are relatively small and not too far from the anus.

- *Low anterior resection:* Some stage I rectal cancers and most stage II or III cancers in the upper two-thirds of the rectum can be removed with this procedure, in which the tumor is removed without affecting the anus. After low anterior resection, the colon will be attached to the anus and the waste will leave the body in the usual way through the anus. It requires an abdominal incision.

- *Abdominoperineal resection:* This operation can be used to treat some stage I cancers and most stage II or III rectal cancers in the lower third of the rectum, close to the sphincter muscle. There is one incision in the abdomen and another in the perineal area around the anus. This incision allows the surgeon to remove the anus and the tissues surrounding it, including the sphincter muscle. Because the anus is removed, a permanent colostomy is required to allow stool a path out of the body. Management of an ostomy requires much patient support and education (Colwell et al., 2016; Schreiber, 2016; see Table 8-6).

Chemotherapy

Chemotherapy may be given for two different reasons (Wolpin & Bass, 2014). Adjuvant chemotherapy is the use of chemotherapy after surgery with the intent to increase the survival rate for patients with colon cancer and rectal cancer. It is given when there is no pathological evidence of cancer, but there may be microscopic disease putting the patient at risk for recurrence. For some cancers, especially rectal cancers, chemotherapy is given (along with radiation) before surgery to try to shrink the tumor so that the tumor is entirely resectable

and makes surgery more effective (Berry et al., 2015). This is referred to as neoadjuvant treatment. Table 8-7 details chemotherapy agents used in the treatment of CRC.

Targeted Therapy

Drugs have been developed that specifically target the genetic and protein characteristics in cells that cause cancer. These targeted drugs work differently than standard chemotherapy drugs (Kirstein et al., 2014). In general, targeted therapies are combined with a chemotherapeutic agent or used as single agents if chemotherapy is no longer effective. Table 8-8 lists targeted therapies for the treatment of CRC.

Approximately 40% of CRCs have mutations in the *KRAS, NRAS,* and *BRAF* genes that make drugs targeting epidermal growth factor receptor ineffective. Tumors are routinely tested for these somatic gene changes before treatment, and epidermal growth factor receptor drugs are utilized only in persons who do not have these mutations (Kelley, Wang, & Venook, 2011).

Radiation Therapy

Radiation therapy in people with colon cancer is mainly used when the cancer has attached to an internal organ or the lining of the abdomen. Radiation therapy may also be used to kill any cancer cells that remain after surgery. Radiation therapy is seldom used to treat metastatic colon cancer because of side effects, which limit the dose that can be used (NCCN, 2017a, 2017b).

For rectal cancer, radiation therapy is usually given to help prevent the cancer from coming back in the pelvis. It may be given either before or after surgery. A treatment option for selected patients includes preoperative (neoadjuvant) treatment along with chemotherapy (NCCN, 2017b). If a rectal cancer's size or position makes surgery difficult, radiation may

TABLE 8-6: IMPORTANT ASPECTS OF OSTOMY MANAGEMENT

When educating a patient on ostomy management, keep in mind the following:

- Early participation in care is key to self-care after surgery. Teaching should begin as soon as possible before surgery.

- A one-piece system is placed immediately after surgery to allow healing; then the appliance is changed to a two-piece system.

- Initial drainage after surgery is liquid with blood. Then with increased diet, the discharge becomes solid. Final consistency depends on the placement of the stoma along the colon.

- Flatulence begins through the stoma, and occasional venting of appliance needs to be done throughout the day.

- Appliance choice depends on the location of the stoma.

- Appliance fit is key to prevent fecal leakage.

- Flange (faceplates) vary in size, shape, and adhesive, and are precut or customized.

- Skin barriers also vary.

- Pay attention to any early signs of infection or allergic reactions prompted by adhesive and appliance materials.

- Changing the appliance requires systematic cleaning, airing, and replacement of the bag. A routine schedule is encouraged.

- When adapting colostomy needs to lifestyle – returning to physical activities, work schedule, and sexual activities creates fear and apprehension – open discussion is essential for healthy coping.

Note. Adapted from Colwell, J. C., Kupsick, P. T., & McNichol, L. L. (2016). Outcome criteria for discharging the patient with a new ostomy from home health care: A WOCN Society consensus conference. *Journal of Wound, Ostomy, and Continence Nursing, 43*(3), 269-273. doi:10.1097/WON.0000000000000230

be used before surgery to shrink the tumor. Radiation therapy can also be given to help control rectal cancers in people who are not healthy enough for surgery.

Most side effects following radiation to the colon and/or rectum decrease after treatments are completed, but some problems may not resolve (ACS, 2017b; NCCN, 2017a, 2017b); for example,

- skin irritation, which can range from redness to blistering and peeling;

- nausea;

- rectal irritation, which can cause diarrhea, painful bowel movements, or blood in the stool;

- bowel incontinence;

- bladder irritation, including urgency frequency, burning/pain while urinating, or blood in the urine;

- fatigue; and

- vaginal irritation and dryness.

Radiation may also be used to palliate symptoms in people with advanced cancer that is causing intestinal blockage, bleeding, or pain.

Long-Term Follow-up

Once an individual has completed CRC treatment, regular endoscopy is very important (El-Shami et al., 2015). In addition to endos-

TABLE 8-7: CHEMOTHERAPY FOR COLORECTAL CANCER (1 OF 2)

Agent	Administration	Other Considerations and Indications	Side Effects
Fluorouracil (5-FU)	It may be given as an infusion over 2 hours. It may be given as IV push followed by continuous infusion over 1 or 2 days. For most chemotherapy regimens, treatment with 5-FU is repeated every 2 weeks, over a period of 6 months to 1 year.	It is often given together with another drug called leucovorin (or folinic acid), which increases its effectiveness.	Side effects such as nausea, anorexia, mouth sores, diarrhea, myelo-suppression, and photo-sensitivity are possible. A syndrome of hand and foot redness that is sometimes accompanied by blistering or skin peeling may also occur on the plantar and palmar surfaces.
Capecitabine (Xeloda)	Capecitabine is an oral chemotherapy agent that is usually taken twice a day for 2 weeks, followed by 1 week off.	Once in the body, it is changed to 5-FU when it enters the tumor site. Based on clinical trials, this drug appears as effective as giving continuous IV 5-FU with the advantage of being an oral agent.	The possible side effects are similar to those listed for 5-FU. Although most of the side effects seem to be less common with this drug than with 5-FU, problems with the hands and feet are more common and severe.
Irinotecan (Camptosar)	It is given as an IV infusion over 30 minutes to 2 hours.	Some people are unable to break down the drug, so it stays in the body and causes severe side effects. This is a result of an inherited genetic variation. The simplest test for this variation involves measuring the blood level of bilirubin. If it is slightly elevated, this can be a sign of the genetic variation that makes people sensitive to irinotecan. Most doctors do not routinely test for the genetic variant. In some cases it may be used as a single agent as a second-line treatment if other chemotherapy drugs are no longer effective. This drug is often combined with 5-FU and leucovorin (known as the FOLFIRI regimen) as a first-line treatment for advanced CRC.	Side effects such as severe diarrhea, myelo-suppression, and nausea are possible. A diarrhea prophylaxis regimen is recommended, and patients need to report any diarrhea promptly because it is a dose-limiting and potentially fatal side effect in compromised patients.

TABLE 8-7: CHEMOTHERAPY FOR COLORECTAL CANCER (2 OF 2)

Agent	Administration	Other Considerations and Indications	Side Effects
Oxaliplatin (Eloxatin)	Oxaliplatin is given as an IV infusion over 2 hours, usually once every 2 or 3 weeks.	This drug is usually combined with 5-FU and leucovorin (known as the FOLFOX regimen) or with capecitabine (known as the CapeOX regimen) as a first- or second-line treatment for advanced CRC.

It may also be used as adjuvant therapy after surgery for earlier-stage cancers. | Oxaliplatin can affect peripheral nerves, which can cause numbness, tingling, and intense sensitivity to temperature in the extremities, especially the hands and feet. This goes away after treatment has stopped in most patients, but in some cases it can cause long-lasting nerve damage. |
| Trifluridine and tipiracil (Lonsurf) | Taken orally twice daily within 1 hour of completion of morning and evening meals on days 1 through 5 and days 8 through 12 of each 28-day cycle until disease progression or unacceptable toxicity. | This drug is indicated for the treatment of patients with metastatic CRC who have been previously treated with fluoropyrimidine-, oxaliplatin-, and irinotecan-based chemotherapy, an anti-VEGF biological therapy, and if *RAS* wild-type, an anti-EGFR therapy. | Side effects include severe, life-threatening myelosuppression.

Other side effects include nausea, vomiting, diarrhea, abdominal pain, and loss of appetite. |

For up-to-date information about administration, refer to latest practice guidelines or manufacturer's recommendations.

CRC = colorectal cancer; EGFR = epidermal growth factor receptor; IV = intravenous; VEGF = vascular endothelial growth factor.

Note. Adapted from Berry, S. R., Cosby, R., Asmis, T., Chan, K., Hammad, N., Krzyzanowska, M. K., & Cancer Care Ontario's Gastrointestinal Disease Site Group. (2015). Continuous versus intermittent chemotherapy strategies in metastatic colorectal cancer: A systematic review and meta-analysis. *Annals of Oncology, 26*(3), 477-485. doi:10.1093/annonc/mdu272; Wolpin, B. M., & Bass, A. J. (2014). Managing advanced colorectal cancer: Have we reached the PEAK with current therapies? *Journal of Clinical Oncology, 32*(21), 2200-2202. doi:10.1200/jco.2014.55.6316; National Comprehensive Cancer Network. (2016a). *Colon cancer, version 2.2016.* Retrieved from http://www.nccn.org; and National Comprehensive Cancer Network. (2016f). *Rectal cancer, version 2.2016.* Retrieved from http://www.nccn.org

copy, surveillance includes regularly scheduled blood tests, imaging scans, and clinical evaluation, according to surveillance protocols (NCCN, 2017a, 2017b).

CASE STUDY 8-1

A.P. is a 62-year-old White woman who visited her physician for a complaint of cramping and bloating for 1 month. She noted that she thought she saw blood in her stool. She also complained of crushing fatigue, which seemed to have started a few months prior.

A.P. worked as a waitress for many years but retired from her job several years ago. She now provides child care for her grandchildren while her daughter works.

A.P. commented that her aunt had "cancer of the bowel." While waiting for the physician to see her, she revealed that she enjoys eating blue-plate specials with her husband of 40 years. She smoked until she was 50 years of age, but she quit with the help of a support group. She also said that she enjoys a mixed cocktail twice a week.

TABLE 8-8: TARGETED THERAPIES FOR COLORECTAL CANCER

Agents	Target	Administration	Side Effects
• Bevacizumab (Avastin) • Ramucirumab (Cyramza) • Ziv-aflibercept (Zaltrap)	VEGF is a protein that helps tumors form new blood vessels to get nutrients (a process known as *angiogenesis*). Drugs that stop VEGF from working can be used to treat some colon or rectal cancers.	These drugs are given as infusions into the vein (IV) every 2 or 3 weeks, typically along with chemotherapy.	Common side effects include hypertension, fatigue, myelosuppression, mouth sores, anorexia, and diarrhea. Rare but possibly serious side effects include blood clots, severe bleeding, colon perforations, cardiomyopathy, and protracted wound healing.
• Cetuximab (Erbitux) • Panitumumab (Vectibix)	EGFR is a protein that often appears in high amounts on the surface of cancer cells and helps them grow. Drugs that target EGFR can be used to treat some advanced colon or rectal cancers.	IV infusion, either once a week or every other week	The most common negative side effects include acne-like rash on the face and chest. The skin reactions with panitumumab can be more serious, leading to sloughing. Other side effects can include headache, fatigue, fever, and diarrhea. A rare but serious side effect of these drugs is an allergic reaction during the infusion.
• Regorafenib (Stivarga)	Kinase inhibitors attack proteins on or near the surface of a cell that are cellular transmitters that affect cellular proliferation. Regorafenib blocks several kinase proteins that either help tumor cells grow or help form new blood vessels to feed the tumor. Blocking these proteins can help stop the growth of cancer cells.	Oral agent	Common side effects include fatigue, anorexia, hand-foot syndrome, diarrhea, mouth sores, and hypertension. Less common but more serious side effects can include liver damage, severe bleeding, and perforations in the stomach or intestines.

EGFR = epidermal growth factor receptor; IV = intravenous; VEGF = vascular endothelial growth factor.

Note. Based on data from National Comprehensive Cancer Network. (2016a). *Colon cancer, version 2.2016.* Retrieved from http://www.nccn.org; National Comprehensive Cancer Network. (2016f). *Rectal cancer, version 2.2016.* Retrieved from http://www.nccn.org; Kirstein, M. M., Lange, A., Prenzler, A., Manns, M. P., Kubicka, S., & Vogel, A. (2014). Targeted therapies in metastatic colorectal cancer: A systematic review and assessment of currently available data. *The Oncologist, 19*(11), 1156-1168. doi:10.1634/theoncologist.2014-0032; and Kelley, R. K., Wang, G., & Venook, A. P. (2011). Biomarker use in colorectal cancer therapy. *Journal of the National Comprehensive Cancer Network, 9*(11), 1293-1302.

Two years ago, A.P.'s physician removed 15 benign polyps from her colon. However, because of a lapse in her insurance, she had not been to the physician for 2 years.

On digital rectal examination, A.P.'s physician did not note any masses but was concerned about her symptoms because of her past polypectomies. Her physician immediately scheduled her for a colonoscopy. Based on her symptoms and history, the physician also ordered a CBC to assess for anemia and the CEA test, which is a tumor marker that measures a protein that is sometimes elevated in persons with CRC.

During A.P.'s colonoscopy, biopsies were taken of three lesions found in her left and sigmoid colon. The biopsy results came back as adenocarcinoma in the sigmoid colon. Her CBC indicated anemia, and her CEA was 5.0 ng/ml (normal, <2.5 ng/ml).

A colectomy was scheduled to remove the cancerous area of her colon. Fortunately, because of the location of A.P.'s cancerous tumors, she did not need a colostomy. In preparation for her surgery, her physician ordered a chest radiograph, CT scan of the pelvis, and bone scan. A plan of care was shared with A.P. She was aware that depending on whether the cancer spread to regional lymph nodes, she might need postoperative chemotherapy.

Postoperatively, because her cancer had spread to regional lymph nodes, A.P. was referred to a medical oncologist for adjuvant chemotherapy. Three weeks after surgery, A.P. began a chemotherapy protocol that included 5-fluorouracil, leucovorin, and irinotecan (CPT-11; days 1, 8, 15, 22) every 6 weeks. Adverse effects from the chemotherapy included diarrhea, stomatitis, and leukopenia. The oncology nurses provided direction and support managing antidiarrheals, encouraging good hygiene, and monitoring for infection.

Six months after her surgery, a repeat CT scan, bone scan, and chest radiograph were ordered. All test results were negative. Her CEA level was unchanged.

While in the hospital after her surgery and during her chemotherapy treatments, A.P. had been made aware that her colon cancer may be associated with a hereditary syndrome. She was encouraged to proceed with genetic counseling and encourage family members to be checked regularly for polyp formation.

Additional Information

A.P. continues to do well after her colectomy and adjuvant chemotherapy treatments. She returns to her physician for checkups every 3 to 6 months. Because of a retirement benefit as part of her husband's job as a police dispatcher, her insurance remains intact.

Questions

1. What symptoms of CRC did A.P. display?

2. What risk factors does A.P. have for CRC?

3. What might have resulted in prevention of her CRC?

Answers

1. Blood in the stool, cramping, bloating, and abdominal pain are all typically late symptoms of CRC.

2. A.P. has an aunt with a history of CRC. She consumes a high-fat diet. She consumes some alcohol and has a history of smoking. She has a history of polyps.

3. Regular colonoscopy is probably the best means to prevent colon cancer. In this case with a positive history of polyps, colonoscopy determined by guidelines, and her physician's recommendations, colonoscopy is indicated. Polyps can be removed before they progress to CRC.

SUMMARY

Progress continues in the detection, screening, and treatment of CRC. Women and men have similar incidence and mortality rates for CRC. There are multiple screening protocols for CRC, and the screening protocol should be based on the risk assessment and, when indicated, genetic testing. Patients benefit from comprehensive education about the strengths and limitations of the various screening modalities, as well as what to expect with each modality. Polyp identification and removal are cornerstones in the successful early treatment of CRC and result in prevention of CRC.

Families with hereditary conditions, such as FAP and HNPCC, will require more vigilant screening, possibly prophylactic surgery, and will benefit from genetic testing and recommendations from a credentialed genetics professional. Persons with hereditary cancer syndromes are at risk for multiple primary malignancies.

Screening efforts include attention to signs, symptoms, and genetic histories; risk assessment to determine the appropriate screening protocol; and follow-up to detect precancerous conditions early, when treatment is most effective.

Surgery is the main treatment modality, although radiation therapy, targeted therapy, and chemotherapy play important roles in treating CRCs. When CRC has spread to the liver, treatment to control additional tumor spread focuses on surgery and ablative therapies. Depending on the treatment plan, persons with a diagnosis of CRC will typically receive care and side effect management support from a multidisciplinary team of oncology professionals.

With regular screening many CRCs could be prevented with polypectomy. With early detection, the 5-year survival rate for early-stage disease is 90% (ACS, 2017b). Early detection is best accomplished with regular screening. Nurses have a key role in promoting evidenced-based information when educating patients on the importance of prevention and early detection of colon cancer to decrease morbidity and mortality.

EXAM QUESTIONS

CHAPTER 8
Questions 51–59

Note: Choose the one option that BEST answers each question.

51. Genetic predisposition to colorectal cancer is associated with

    a. *BRCA1.*

    b. *BRAF.*

    c. *CA-125.*

    d. familial adenomatous polyposis.

52. Risk factors for colorectal cancer include

    a. being younger than 50 years.

    b. eating a low-fat, low-calorie, and low-fiber diet.

    c. polyp formation or history of polyps.

    d. history of thyroid or skin cancer.

53. The main signs and symptoms of colorectal cancer include

    a. a change in bowel habits, diarrhea, and blood in the stool.

    b. constipation and anxiety.

    c. weight gain and widening of the stool.

    d. shortness of breath, fatigue, and loss of appetite.

54. For persons at average risk for developing colorectal cancer, the American Cancer Society recommends colonoscopy, beginning at 50 years of age, every

    a. 3 years.

    b. 5 years.

    c. 7 years.

    d. 10 years.

55. The most accurate method to screen for colorectal cancer is

    a. colonoscopy.

    b. double-contrast barium enema.

    c. fecal occult blood test.

    d. sigmoidoscopy.

56. When colorectal cancer has spread to nearby lymph nodes, the cancer is staged as

    a. stage 0.

    b. stage I.

    c. stage II.

    d. stage III.

57. The main treatment of choice for early-stage colorectal cancer is

    a. radiation.

    b. surgery.

    c. targeted therapy.

    d. chemotherapy.

58. Teaching a colorectal patient about her ostomy care should begin

    a. as soon as possible before surgery.

    b. the day of surgery.

    c. postoperatively on day 2.

    d. 2 weeks after surgery.

continued on next page

59. An adjuvant chemotherapy regimen for colorectal cancer is

    a. Rituxan and interferon.

    b. bleomycin and etoposide.

    c. 5-fluorouracil and leucovorin.

    d. tamoxifen and docetaxel.

REFERENCES

American Cancer Society. (2015a). *Global cancer facts and figures* (3rd ed.). Atlanta, GA: Author.

American Cancer Society. (2017a). *Cancer facts and figures – 2017.* Atlanta, GA: Author.

American Cancer Society. (2017b). *Colorectal cancer facts and figures – 2017-2019.* Atlanta, GA: Author.

American Cancer Society. (2017c). *Cancer prevention and early detection facts and figures – 2017-2018.* Atlanta, GA: Author.

Amin, M. B., Edge, S., Greene, F., Byrd, D. R., Brookland, R. K., Washington, M. K., ... Meyer, L. R. (Eds.) (2017). *AJCC cancer staging manual* (8th ed.). New York, NY: Springer.

Barton, M. K. (2012). Physician-patient communication regarding colorectal cancer screening is lacking. *CA: A Cancer Journal for Clinicians, 62*(1), 1-2. doi:10.3322/caac.21130

Berry, S. R., Cosby, R., Asmis, T., Chan, K., Hammad, N., Krzyzanowska, M. K., & Cancer Care Ontario's Gastrointestinal Disease Site Group. (2015). Continuous versus intermittent chemotherapy strategies in metastatic colorectal cancer: A systematic review and meta-analysis. *Annals of Oncology, 26*(3), 477-485. doi:10.1093/annonc/mdu272

Carrington, E. V., & Scott, S. M. (2014). Physiology and function of the colon. In M. Lomer (Ed.), *Advanced nutrition and dietetics in gastroenterology* (pp. 28-32). Oxford, UK: John Wiley & Sons, Ltd. doi:10.1002/9781118872796.ch1.5

Colwell, J. C., Kupsick, P. T., & McNichol, L. L. (2016). Outcome criteria for discharging the patient with a new ostomy from home health care: A WOCN Society consensus conference. *Journal of Wound, Ostomy, and Continence Nursing, 43*(3), 269-273. doi:10.1097/WON.0000000000000230

Edge, S. B., Byrd, D. R., Carducci, M., Compton, C. C., Fritz, A. G., Greene, F. L., & Trotti, A. (2010). *AJCC cancer staging manual* (7th ed.). New York, NY: Springer.

El-Shami, K., Oeffinger, K. C., Erb, N. L., Willis, A., Bretsch, J. K., Pratt-Chapman, M. L., ... Cowens-Alvarado, R. L. (2015). American Cancer Society colorectal cancer survivorship care guidelines. *CA: A Cancer Journal for Clinicians, 65*(6), 427-455. doi:10.3322/caac.21286

Ely, J., Levy, B., Daly, J., Xu, Y., Ely, J. W., & Levy, B. T. (2016). Patient beliefs about colon cancer screening. *Journal of Cancer Education, 31*(1), 39-46. doi:10.1007/s13187-015-0792-5

Jasperson, K. W. (2012). Genetic testing by cancer site: Colon (polyposis syndromes). *The Cancer Journal, 18*(4), 328-333. doi:10.1097/PPO.0b013e3182609300

Kelley, R. K., Wang, G., & Venook, A. P. (2011). Biomarker use in colorectal cancer therapy. *Journal of the National Comprehensive Cancer Network, 9*(11), 1293-1302.

Kirstein, M. M., Lange, A., Prenzler, A., Manns, M. P., Kubicka, S., & Vogel, A. (2014). Targeted therapies in metastatic colorectal cancer: A systematic review and assessment of currently available data. *The Oncologist, 19*(11), 1156-1168. doi:10.1634/theoncologist.2014-0032

Kushi, L. H., Doyle, C., McCullough, M., Rock, C. L., Demark-Wahnefried, W., Bandera, E. V., ... American Cancer Society 2010 Nutrition and Physical Activity Guidelines Advisory Committee. (2012). American Cancer Society guidelines on nutrition and physical activity for cancer prevention. *CA: A Cancer Journal for Clinicians, 62*(1), 30-67. doi:10.3322/caac.20140

Levin, B., Lieberman, D. A., McFarland, B., Smith, R. A., Brooks, D., Andrews, K. S., ... American College of Radiology Colon Cancer Committee. (2008). Screening and surveillance for the early detection of colorectal cancer and adenomatous polyps, 2008: A joint guideline from the American Cancer Society, the US Multi-Society Task Force on Colorectal Cancer, and the American College of Radiology. *A Cancer Journal for Clinicians, 53*(3), 130-160. doi: 10.3322/CA.2007.0018

National Comprehensive Cancer Network. (2016a). *Colon cancer, version 2.2016.* Retrieved from http://www.nccn.org

National Comprehensive Cancer Network. (2016b). *Colorectal cancer screening, version 1.2016.* Retrieved from http://www.nccn.org

National Comprehensive Cancer Network. (2016c). *Colorectal cancer screening, version 2.2016.* Retrieved from http://www.nccn.org

National Comprehensive Cancer Network. (2016d). *Genetic/familial high-risk assessment: Colorectal, version 1.2016.* Retrieved from http://www.nccn.org

National Comprehensive Cancer Network. (2016e). *Genetic/familial high-risk assessment: Colorectal, version 2.2016.* Retrieved from http://www.nccn.org

National Comprehensive Cancer Network. (2016f). *Rectal cancer, version 2.2016.* Retrieved from http://www.nccn.org

National Comprehensive Cancer Network. (2017a). *Colon cancer, version 2.2017.* Retrieved from http://www.nccn.org

National Comprehensive Cancer Network. (2017b). *Rectal Cancer, version 3.2017.* Retrieved from http://www.nccn.org

Schreiber, M. L. (2016). Ostomies: Nursing care and management. *Medsurg Nursing, 25*(2), 127-130.

Senter, L. (2012). Genetic testing by cancer site: Colon (nonpolyposis syndromes). *The Cancer Journal, 18*(4), 334-337.

Smith, R. A., Andrews, K., Brooks, D., DeSantis, C. E., Fedewa, S. A., Lortet-Tieulent, J., ... Wender, R. C. (2016). Cancer screening in the United States, 2016: A review of current American Cancer Society guidelines and current issues in cancer screening. *CA: A Cancer Journal for Clinicians, 66*, 96-114. doi:10.3322/caac.21336

U.S. Department of Health and Human Services, National Institutes of Health, National Cancer Institute. (n.d.a). *Colon-rectum.* Retrieved from https://visualsonline.cancer.gov/details.cfm?imageid=1768

U.S. Department of Health and Human Services, National Institutes of Health, National Cancer Institute. (n.d.b). *SEER stat facts: Colon and rectum cancer.* Retrieved from http://seer.cancer.gov/statfacts/html/colorect.html

U.S. Department of Health and Human Services, National Institutes of Health, National Cancer Institute. (2011a). *Colon or rectal cancer stage 0.* Retrieved from https://visualsonline.cancer.gov/details.cfm?imageid=9147

U.S. Department of Health and Human Services, National Institutes of Health, National Cancer Institute. (2011b). *Colon or rectal cancer stage I.* Retrieved from https://visualsonline.cancer.gov/details.cfm?imageid=9148

U.S. Department of Health and Human Services, National Institutes of Health, National Cancer Institute. (2011c). *Colon or rectal cancer stage II.* Retrieved from https://visualsonline.cancer.gov/details.cfm?imageid=9149

U.S. Department of Health and Human Services, National Institutes of Health, National Cancer Institute. (2011d). *Colon or rectal cancer stage IIIA.* Retrieved from https://visualsonline.cancer.gov/details.cfm?imageid=9150

U.S. Department of Health and Human Services, National Institutes of Health, National Cancer Institute. (2011e). *Colon or rectal cancer stage IIIB.* Retrieved from https://visualsonline.cancer.gov/details.cfm?imageid=9151

U.S. Department of Health and Human Services, National Institutes of Health, National Cancer Institute. (2011f). *Colon or rectal cancer stage IIIC.* Retrieved from https://visualsonline.cancer.gov/details.cfm?imageid=9152

U.S. Department of Health and Human Services, National Institutes of Health, National Cancer Institute. (2012). *Colonoscopy.* Retrieved from https://visualsonline.cancer.gov/details.cfm?imageid=7183

U.S. Department of Health and Human Services, National Institutes of Health, National Cancer Institute. (2015). *FAP polyps – Endoscopic.* Retrieved from https://visualsonline.cancer.gov/details.cfm?imageid=10067

U.S. Department of Health and Human Services, National Institutes of Health, National Cancer Institute. (2016). *Colon or rectal cancer stage IV.* Retrieved from https://visualsonline.cancer.gov/details.cfm?imageid=9153

Verma, M., Sarfaty, M., Brooks, D., & Wender, R. C. (2015). Population-based programs for increasing colorectal cancer screening in the United States. *CA: A Cancer Journal for Clinicians, 65*(6), 496-510. doi:10.3322/caac.21295

Weissman, S. M., Burt, R., Church, J., Erdman, S., Hampel, H., Holter, S., ... Senter, L. (2012). Identification of individuals at risk for Lynch syndrome using targeted evaluations and genetic testing: National Society of Genetic Counselors and the Collaborative Group of the Americas on Inherited Colorectal Cancer joint practice guideline. *Journal of Genetic Counseling, 21*(4), 484-493.

Weitzel, J. N., Blazer, K. R., MacDonald, D. J., Culver, J. O., & Offit, K. (2011). Genetics, genomics and cancer risk assessment: State of the art and future directions in the era of personalized medicine. *CA: A Cancer Journal for Clinicians, 61*(5), 327-359. doi:10.3322/caac.20128

Wolpin, B. M., & Bass, A. J. (2014). Managing advanced colorectal cancer: Have we reached the PEAK with current therapies? *Journal of Clinical Oncology, 32*(21), 2200-2202. doi:10.1200/jco.2014.55.6316

CHAPTER 9

SKIN CANCER

LEARNING OUTCOME

After completing this chapter, the learner will be able to discuss the epidemiology, risk factors, prevention and detection strategies, staging and prognosis, and main treatments for skin cancer in women.

CHAPTER OBJECTIVES

After completing this chapter, the learner will be able to:

1. Describe the epidemiology of all types of skin cancer and risk factors for its development.

2. Explain strategies to prevent all types of skin cancer.

3. Describe the diagnostic workup and staging schemas for benign and malignant skin cancers.

4. Explain treatment modalities for benign and malignant skin cancers.

INTRODUCTION

Skin cancer describes many different types of malignancies that occur in the skin. Each type of skin cancer is associated with a different epidemiology, treatment, and prognosis. Skin cancer types include basal cell skin cancers, squamous cell skin cancers, Merkel cell skin cancers, dermatofibrosarcoma protuberans, cutaneous lymphoma, and malignant melanoma.

There are also many benign lesions of the skin, including actinic keratosis, Bowen's disease (squamous cell carcinoma in situ), seborrheic keratosis, hemangiomas, lipomas, and warts.

EPIDEMIOLOGY

Skin cancer is a major public health problem in both the United States and worldwide. Skin cancers account for approximately one-third of all diagnosed cancers. Box 9-1 provides facts about skin cancers. See Figure 9-1 for layers of the skin where the various skin cancers originate.

Basal cell skin cancers originate in the basal cell layer of the skin. Basal cell skin cancers are the most common skin cancer diagnosed in the United States (National Comprehensive Cancer Network [NCCN], 2017a). These cells are in the lower part of the epidermis and are constantly dividing to form new cells to replace the squamous cells that die and slough off the skin's surface. As these cells move up in the epidermis, they get flatter, eventually becoming squamous cells (NCCN, 2017a).

Squamous cell skin cancers are flat cells in the outer part of the epidermis that are constantly shed as new ones form (NCCN, 2017i). It is the second most common skin cancer diagnosed in the United States (NCCN, 2017i).

Merkel cell carcinoma is a rare type of skin cancer that usually appears as a flesh-colored or bluish red nodule, often on the face, head,

245

BOX 9-1: SKIN CANCER EPIDEMIOLOGY

- There are more than 5.4 million cases of basal cell skin cancer, squamous cell skin cancer, Merkel cell skin cancer, keratoacanthoma, dermatofibrosarcoma protuberans, and cutaneous lymphoma skin cancer annually.

- There are 39,940 new cases of malignant melanoma in women annually.

- The incidence rates of melanoma have been increasing for at least 30 years.

- Malignant melanoma primarily occurs in White individuals; rates are 10 times higher in White than in Black individuals.

- Annually, 3,350 women die of malignant melanoma.

- Annually, 990 women die of basal cell skin cancer, squamous cell skin cancer, Merkel cell skin cancers, keratoacanthomas, dermatofibrosarcoma protuberans, and cutaneous lymphoma.

- Most basal cell skin cancer, squamous cell skin cancer, Merkel cell skin cancers, keratoacanthomas, dermatofibrosarcoma protuberans, and cutaneous lymphoma skin cancers can be cured if the cancer is detected and treated early.

- The overall 5-year and 10-year relative survival rates for persons with malignant melanoma are 92% and 89%, respectively.

- For localized malignant melanoma, the 5-year survival rate is 98% (84% of malignant melanomas are detected at this stage).

- For regional stage malignant melanoma, the 5-year relative survival rate is 63%.

- For distant stage malignant melanoma, the 5-year relative survival rate is 17%.

Note. Adapted from American Cancer Society. (2017). *Cancer facts and figures – 2017.* Atlanta, GA: Author.

or neck (NCCN, 2017f). Merkel cells are in the layer of basal cells at the deepest part of the epidermis and are connected to nerves (McGrath & Uitto, 2016). Merkel cell carcinoma is sometimes referred to as neuroendocrine carcinoma of the skin (NCCN, 2017f). Merkel cell carcinoma tends to grow quickly and metastasize to other parts of the body (Erovic & Erovic, 2013).

Dermatofibrosarcoma protuberans is a rare skin cancer that begins in the dermis (NCCN, 2017b). It tends to grow slowly and seldom metastasizes to other parts of the body (Noujaim, Thway, Fisher, & Jones, 2015). The incidence of dermatofibrosarcoma protuberans is 4.2 per million persons (NCCN, 2017b).

Primary cutaneous lymphoma is another rare skin cancer; the incidence is 3.6 per million persons (NCCN, 2017g; Wilson, Hinds, & Yu, 2012). Risk factors for cutaneous lymphoma include body mass index equal to or larger than 30 kg/m^2, cigarette smoking for 40 years or more, eczema, family history of multiple myeloma, and also professions, such as crop and vegetable farmers, painters, woodworkers, and carpenters, that have exposure to chemical carcinogens (Sokołowska-Wojdyło, Olek-Hrab, & Ruckemann-Dziurdzińska, 2015).

Malignant melanoma has four subtypes: superficial spreading melanoma, nodular melanoma, lentigo maligna melanoma, and acral lentiginous melanoma (NCCN, 2017d). Table 9-1 provides characteristics of and prognostic information for these subtypes.

FIGURE 9-1: THE LAYERS OF THE SKIN

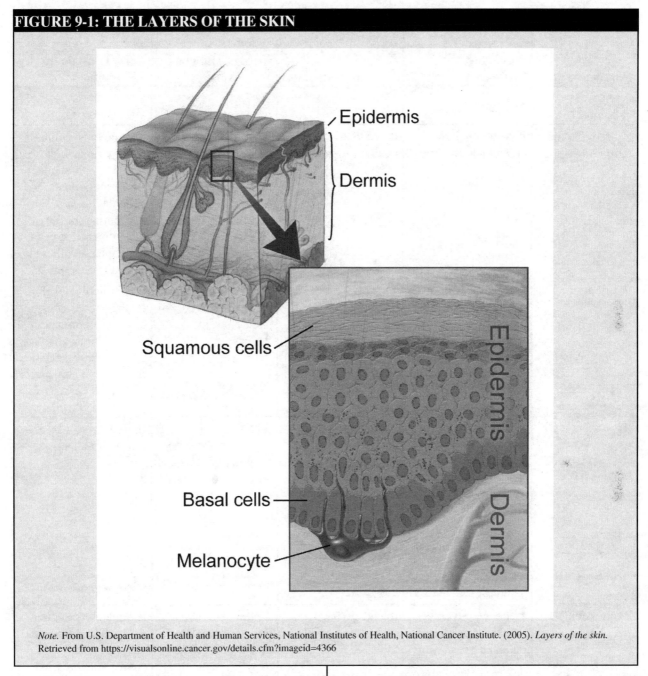

Note. From U.S. Department of Health and Human Services, National Institutes of Health, National Cancer Institute. (2005). *Layers of the skin.* Retrieved from https://visualsonline.cancer.gov/details.cfm?imageid=4366

Malignant melanoma can occur in all races and skin types. The risk for malignant melanoma is higher with age and in White individuals (see Figures 9-2 and 9-3; NCCN, 2017d). The lifetime risk of a woman developing malignant melanoma is 1 in 44 (American Cancer Society [ACS], 2017).

Melanoma is a deadly cancer (see Figures 9-4 and 9-5). Invasive malignant melanoma accounts for 1% of all new skin cancer cases but causes the majority of skin cancer deaths (ACS, 2017a). When detected early, the long-term survival for melanoma is good (see Figure 9-6).

Of great concern is the increasing incidence of malignant melanoma, which has been consistently increasing over the last 30 years (ACS, 2017a). Overall, the mortality rates have remained stable since 1980. This may be a result of improved earlier detection of malignant melanoma. Unfortunately, malignant melanoma

continued on page 251

TABLE 9-1: CHARACTERISTICS OF MALIGNANT MELANOMA SUBTYPES

Characteristics	Superficial Spreading Melanoma	Nodular Melanoma	Lentigo Maligna Melanoma	Acral Lentiginous Melanoma
Percent of melanoma cases	70%	15%	10%	5%
Male-to-female ratio	It is slightly more common in females.	It occurs more commonly in men.	It occurs most commonly in elderly people; equally in males and females.	It is the most common form of melanoma in Asian individuals, Black individuals, and people with dark skin, accounting for 50% of melanomas that occur in people with these skin types.
Distribution	In females, it most commonly appears on the legs. In males, it is more likely to develop between the neck and pelvis.	There is no specific distribution.	It typically occurs on sun-damaged skin, especially the face.	It commonly develops on the palms, soles, mucous membranes (such as those that line the mouth, nose, and female genitals), and underneath or near fingernails and toenails.
Appearance	It appears with irregular borders and various shades of black, brown, gray, blue, pink, red, or white. Within the lesion there can be a remarkable variation in color involving white, pink, brown, and black.	It is most often darkly pigmented; however, some lesions can be light brown or even colorless (nonpigmented). An ulcerated and bleeding lesion is common.	It begins as a spreading, flat patch with irregular borders and variable colors of brown.	It often looks like a bruise or nail streak.
Progression	It can progress quickly after a longer radial phase.	It tends to have a rapid radial phase, followed by a rapid vertical phase. Instead of arising from a pre-existing mole, it may appear in a spot where a lesion did not previously exist.	This spreading brownish patch may grow slowly for years.	It can appear to progress quickly. The lesion may have been present for a long period of time before being detected.
Age	It can occur in young persons. Mean age is 40 to 49 years.	The average age is 60 years.	The average age is 55 years.	There is no obvious age distribution.

Note. Adapted from Canavan, T., & Cantrell, W. (2016). Recognizing melanoma: Diagnosis and treatment options. *Nurse Practitioner, 41*(4), 24-30. doi:10.1097/01.NPR.0000481508.24736.81

FIGURE 9-2: PERCENT OF NEW CASES BY AGE GROUP: MELANOMA OF THE SKIN

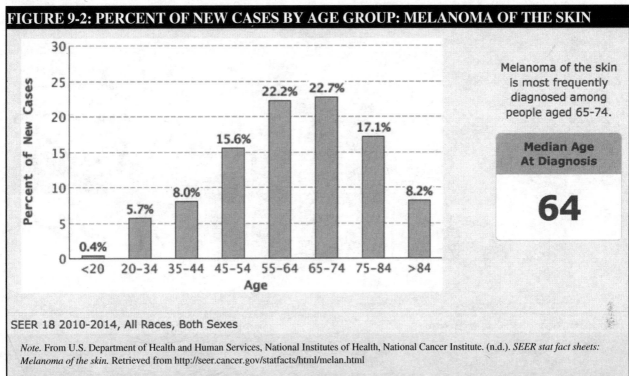

SEER 18 2010-2014, All Races, Both Sexes

Note. From U.S. Department of Health and Human Services, National Institutes of Health, National Cancer Institute. (n.d.). *SEER stat fact sheets: Melanoma of the skin.* Retrieved from http://seer.cancer.gov/statfacts/html/melan.html

FIGURE 9-3: NUMBER OF NEW CASES PER 100,000 PERSONS BY RACE/ETHNICITY AND SEX: MELANOMA OF THE SKIN

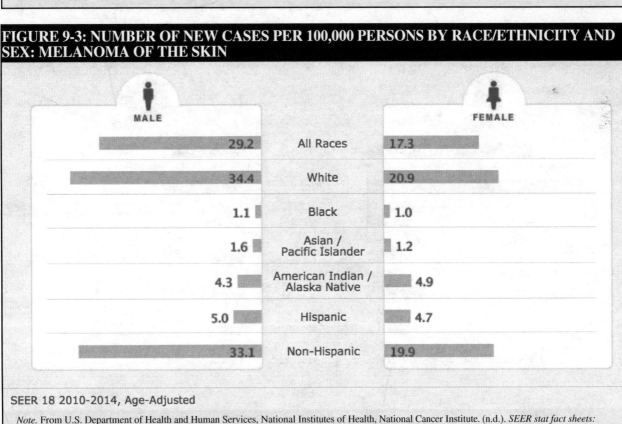

SEER 18 2010-2014, Age-Adjusted

Note. From U.S. Department of Health and Human Services, National Institutes of Health, National Cancer Institute. (n.d.). *SEER stat fact sheets: Melanoma of the skin.* Retrieved from http://seer.cancer.gov/statfacts/html/melan.html

FIGURE 9-4: PERCENT OF DEATHS BY AGE GROUP: MELANOMA OF THE SKIN

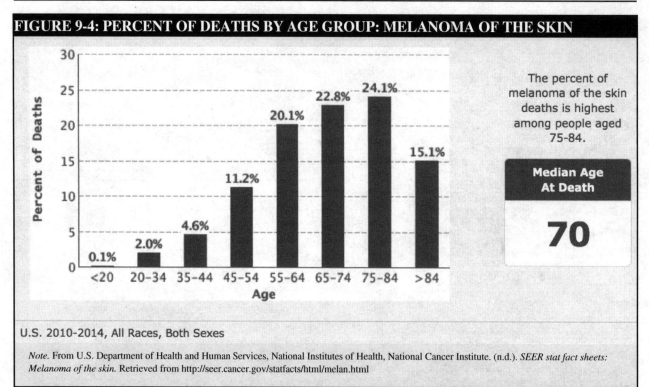

The percent of melanoma of the skin deaths is highest among people aged 75-84.

Median Age At Death

70

U.S. 2010-2014, All Races, Both Sexes

Note. From U.S. Department of Health and Human Services, National Institutes of Health, National Cancer Institute. (n.d.). *SEER stat fact sheets: Melanoma of the skin.* Retrieved from http://seer.cancer.gov/statfacts/html/melan.html

FIGURE 9-5: NUMBER OF DEATHS PER 100,000 PERSONS BY RACE/ETHNICITY & SEX: MELANOMA OF THE SKIN

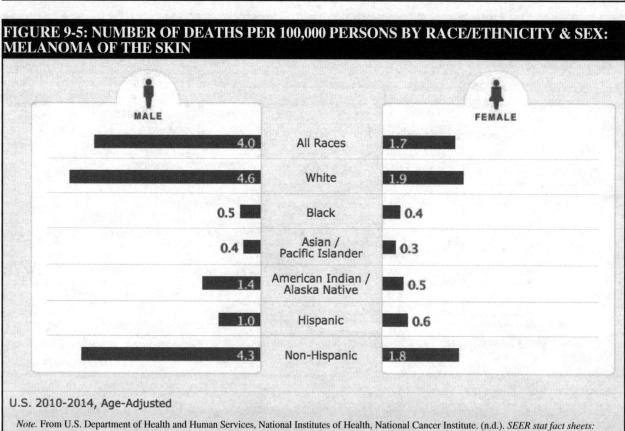

U.S. 2010-2014, Age-Adjusted

Note. From U.S. Department of Health and Human Services, National Institutes of Health, National Cancer Institute. (n.d.). *SEER stat fact sheets: Melanoma of the skin.* Retrieved from http://seer.cancer.gov/statfacts/html/melan.html

FIGURE 9-6: PERCENT OF CASES AND 5-YEAR RELATIVE SURVIVAL BY STAGE AT DIAGNOSIS: MELANOMA OF THE SKIN

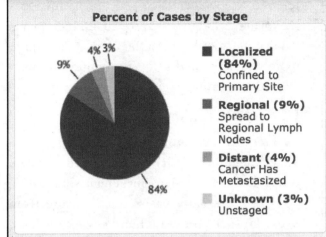

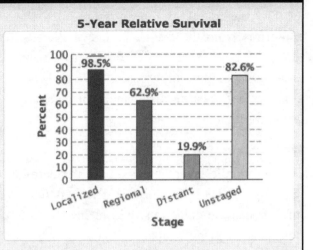

SEER 18 2007-2013, All Races, Both Sexes by SEER Summary Stage 2000

Note. From U.S. Department of Health and Human Services, National Institutes of Health, National Cancer Institute. (n.d.). *SEER stat fact sheets: Melanoma of the skin.* Retrieved from http://seer.cancer.gov/statfacts/html/melan.html

is associated with the highest risk for recurrence or metastasis compared with squamous cell or basal cell carcinoma.

ANATOMY

The skin is the largest organ in the body and serves several purposes, including (Mahon & McLaughlin, 2017)

- covering the internal organs and protecting them from injury,

- providing a barrier from sources of infection,

- preventing the loss of too much water and other fluids, and

- controlling body temperature.

The skin has three layers: the epidermis, dermis, and subcutis (see Figure 9-1).

Epidermis

The top layer of skin is the epidermis. Skin cancer typically begins in the epidermis (McGrath & Uitto, 2016). The epidermis is very thin, on average only 0.2 mm thick (about 1/100

of an inch). It protects the deeper layers of skin and the organs of the body from the environment.

Keratinocytes are the main cell type of the epidermis (McGrath & Uitto, 2016). These cells make keratin, an important protein that serves as a protective layer.

The outermost part of the epidermis is the stratum corneum or horny layer (McGrath & Uitto, 2016). It is composed of keratinocytes that are no longer living. The cells in this layer are squamous cells, which have a flat shape. These cells are continually shed as new cells form. Below the stratum corneum are living keratinocytes. These cells have moved there from the lowest part of the epidermis, the basal layer. The keratinocytes of the basal layer, called *basal cells,* continually divide to form new keratinocytes. These replace the older keratinocytes that wear off the skin's surface.

Melanocytes, the cells that can develop into melanoma, are also present in the epidermis (McGrath & Uitto, 2016). These skin cells make melanin, the protective brown pigment that makes skin tan or brown. Melanin protects the deeper layers of the skin from the harmful effects of the sun.

The basement membrane separates the epidermis from the deeper layers of the skin (McGrath & Uitto, 2016). The basement membrane is an important structure because when a cancer becomes more advanced, it generally grows through this barrier.

Dermis

The middle layer of the skin is the dermis (McGrath & Uitto, 2016). The dermis is much thicker than the epidermis. It contains hair follicles, sweat glands, blood vessels, and nerves that are held in place by collagen, a protein made by fibroblast cells. Collagen gives the skin its resilience and strength.

Subcutis

The last and deepest layer of the skin is the subcutis (McGrath & Uitto, 2016). It is also known as the subcutaneous layer. The subcutis and the lowest part of the dermis form a network of collagen and fat cells. The subcutis conserves heat and has a shock-absorbing effect that helps protect the body's organs from injury.

RISK FACTORS

Everyone has some risk for developing basal cell skin cancers, squamous cell skin cancers, Merkel cell skin cancers, dermatofibrosarcoma protuberans, cutaneous lymphoma, and malignant melanoma. Clearly, the risk is higher in individuals with lighter skin or a fair complexion. Table 9-2 shows risk factors for skin cancer.

Healthcare professionals should refer individuals with a significant family history of melanoma to a credentialed genetics professional for additional genetic testing, risk assessment, and education (Bressac-de Paillerets, Vabres, & Thomas, 2016). Patients with a personal or family history of basal cell nevus syndrome,

xeroderma pigmentosum, epidermolysis bullosa, or oculocutaneous albinism should also be referred to a credentialed genetics professional (Nikolaou, Stratigos, & Tsao, 2012). Individuals who come from high-risk families often require more extensive and frequent monitoring, usually from a dermatologist.

Ultraviolet Light Exposure

Frequent and prolonged exposure to ultraviolet radiation (UVR) over a period of years causes cellular changes in human skin (ACS, 2017b). On a daily basis, sun exposure from everyday activities, including walking back and forth from the car, adds up. Most individuals underestimate the cumulative effect of this exposure. Episodic high exposure resulting in sunburn, especially when it occurs in childhood, may be a critical risk factor (ACS, 2017b). Skin cancer risk begins at an early age. It is estimated that 80% of total lifetime UVR exposure occurs before 20 years of age. The risk is also higher in child athletes who repeatedly expose their skin to UVR (ACS, 2017b).

UVR leads to direct skin damage (ACS, 2017a). The effects of UVR are both acute and chronic. Acute changes include sunburn and discomfort. Chronic effects include photoaging, premalignant and malignant growths, and immunosuppression (ACS, 2017b).

Data suggest that basal cell and squamous skin cancers are associated with cumulative sun exposure, whereas malignant melanoma is associated with short, intense episodes of sun exposure, especially those involving sunburns (NCCN, 2017a, 2017d, 2017i). A history of severe and painful sunburn, especially repeated sunburn, is associated with upper extremity melanoma (NCCN, 2017d).

High sun exposure at certain times of life is associated with greater risk of developing different types of skin cancer, especially basal cell

TABLE 9-2: RISK FACTORS FOR SKIN CANCER

Risk Factor	Etiological Facts
History of basal cell skin cancers, squamous cell skin cancers, Merkel cell skin cancers, keratoacanthomas, dermatofibrosarcoma protuberans, cutaneous lymphoma, and malignant melanoma	A person who has already had a skin cancer is at much higher risk for another skin cancer because of lifetime exposure to UVR.
Sunlight (UVR) exposure	Risk comes from both natural and artificial sources, such as tanning booths.
Moles	Irregular, dysplastic, or multiple nevi increase the risk for malignant melanoma.
Fair skin	People with fair skin, freckles, or red or blond hair have a higher risk for basal cell skin cancers, squamous cell skin cancers, Merkel cell skin cancers, dermatofibrosarcoma protuberans, and malignant melanoma. Persons with red hair have the highest risk.
Family history	Approximately 10% of people with malignant melanoma have a first-degree relative with malignant melanoma.
Weakened immune system	Persons who have been treated with medicines that suppress the immune system, such as transplant patients, have an increased risk of developing basal cell skin cancers, squamous cell skin cancers, Merkel cell skin cancers, dermatofibrosarcoma protuberans, cutaneous lymphoma, and malignant melanoma.
Age	Risk is higher with aging, but malignant melanoma may occur in younger persons.
Gender	Men have a higher rate of malignant melanoma, basal cell skin cancers, and squamous cell skin cancers than women.

UVR = ultraviolet radiation.

Note. Adapted from American Cancer Society. (2017a). *Cancer facts and figures – 2017.* Atlanta, GA: Author; American Cancer Society. (2017b). *Cancer prevention and early detection facts and figures – 2017-2018.* Atlanta, GA: Author; Erovic, I., & Erovic, B. M. (2013). Merkel cell carcinoma: The past, the present, and the future. *Journal of Skin Cancer, 2013,* 929364. doi:10.1155/2013/929364; National Comprehensive Cancer Network. (2017a). *Basal cell skin cancer version 1.2017.* Retrieved from http://www.nccn.org; National Comprehensive Cancer Network. (2017b). *Dermatofibrosarcoma protuberans version 1.2017*; National Comprehensive Cancer Network. (2017e). *Melanoma version 3.2017.* Retrieved from http://www.nccn.org; National Comprehensive Cancer Network. (2017f). *Merkel cell carcinoma version 1.2017.* Retrieved from http://www.nccn.org; National Comprehensive Cancer Network. (2017h). *Primary cutaneous B-cell lymphoma version 2.2017.* Retrieved from http://www.nccn.org; and National Comprehensive Cancer Network. (2017i). *Squamous cell skin cancer version 1.2017.* Retrieved from http://www.nccn.org

skin cancers and squamous cell skin cancers (ACS, 2017b). Early sun exposure, particularly in childhood and adolescence, is associated with a much higher risk of developing basal cell carcinoma and is estimated to confer a 10-fold elevated risk for developing squamous cell carcinoma (NCCN, 2017a, 2017i). Sun exposure in the 10 years before diagnosis may be important in accounting for many cases of squamous cell carcinoma and is associated with a 2.5-fold increased risk compared with those without this exposure (ACS, 2017b).

Sun exposure during childhood and adolescence also seems to have a substantial influence on the risk of developing malignant melanoma (NCCN, 2017d). As noted earlier, approximately 80% of lifetime sun exposure occurs before 20 years of age. During this time, melanocytes may be more sensitive to the sun, resulting in an alteration of their DNA and possibly leading to the formation of unstable moles that have a greater potential to become malignant. Sunlight exposure and blistering sunburns during youth may be more intense than those incurred later in life because of the recreation patterns, including unprotected outdoor play of children (Tellez et al., 2016).

The eyes can also be negatively affected by UVR exposure (Strayer & Schub, 2016). Repeated and prolonged UVR exposure of the conjunctiva will lead to thickening and hypervascularity. There also appears to be a positive correlation between increased cataract formation, decreased latitude, increased ultraviolet B (UVB), and total sunlight exposure. UVR exposure to the eyes may be associated with an increased risk of developing ocular melanoma (NCCN, 2017g).

Genetic Risk Factors

Skin color is one of the most important genotypic features that place a person at risk for developing skin cancer. Malignant melanoma is rare in Black individuals (ACS, 2016). People with light skin or a fair complexion, those who have a tendency to freckle, and those who burn easily are at higher risk (NCCN, 2017a, 2017d, 2017i). The development of melanocytic nevi in childhood is strongly related to characteristics of pigmentation associated with poor sun tolerance (Roider & Fisher, 2016).

The epidermis of Black individuals has been shown to have a natural sun protection factor (SPF) of 13, with the melanin in the epidermis filtering twice as much UVB as the epidermis of White individuals (Strayer & Schub, 2016). This protection, however, is not complete, and basal cell skin cancer, squamous cell skin cancers, and malignant melanoma can develop in Black individuals (ACS, 2016). As many as

67% of malignant melanomas in the Black population arise in non-sun-exposed skin, such as on the palmar and plantar surfaces and even the mucous membranes (Strömberg et al., 2016).

Large congenital melanocytic nevi (moles) are a significant risk factor associated with the development of malignant melanoma; estimates suggest that they occur in 1% of newborns (Soura, Eliades, Shannon, Stratigos, & Tsao, 2016). Research reports increased risk ranging from 0.5% to 42%. The larger the nevus, the higher is the lifetime risk. Research suggests that surgical removal of these large nevi decreases the risk of developing malignant melanoma (NCCN, 2017d).

The number of moles is correlated with risk of developing malignant melanoma (NCCN, 2017d). The total number of moles is an indicator of risk; teenagers and adults with more than 100 nevi are seven times more likely to develop malignant melanoma compared with persons with 10 or fewer moles (Soura et al., 2016).

Dysplastic nevi may develop throughout life and show clinical features similar to those of normal moles and malignant melanomas (NCCN, 2017d). These features include a size greater than 6 to 8 mm, irregular borders, variable pigmentation, and irregular surface characteristics. Malignancy determination in dysplastic nevi can be difficult, thus clinically necessitating a biopsy in many cases to determine whether the lesion is a malignant melanoma (NCCN, 2017d).

Inherited Germline Predisposition to Developing Skin Cancer and Malignant Melanoma

Several inherited syndromes are associated with basal cell carcinoma and squamous cell carcinoma, including xeroderma pigmentosum, nevoid basal cell carcinoma syndrome, epidermodysplasia verruciformis, and albinism (Nikolaou et al., 2012). Persons with xeroderma pigmentosum have a 90% or greater risk of developing multiple squamous cell skin cancers (Griffin, Ali, & Lear, 2016; NCCN, 2017i). Most of these syndromes are associated with other physical abnormalities, and healthcare practitioners should refer these individuals to genetics and specialty clinics because of their high risk of developing malignancy and other complications (Nikolaou et al., 2012).

Approximately 10% of patients with malignant melanoma describe a history of an affected family member (Bressac-de Paillerets et al., 2016). People who have a family history of malignant melanoma or dysplastic nevi, or who have a large number of nevi themselves, are at a very high risk (an increase of greater than 100-fold) for developing malignant melanoma over their lifetime. Persons with a history of melanoma in a first-degree relative have twice the risk of developing malignant melanoma than those without a family history (NCCN, 2017d).

A hereditary predisposition to malignant melanoma is sometimes associated with an earlier age of diagnosis (especially before the age of 40 years; Soura et al., 2016). Sex distribution between males and females is usually about equal to those without a hereditary predisposition to malignant melanoma. Healthcare practitioners should suspect hereditary melanoma in patients with a family history of pancreatic cancer, breast cancer, or astrocytoma (NCCN, 2017c). Patients from these families are, however, often diagnosed with thinner lesions and generally have a better prognosis. This better outcome may be related to heightened awareness and increased surveillance (NCCN, 2017d). A second primary malignant melanoma will develop in 5% to 16% of patients from these families who survive their first malignant melanoma (Bressac-de Paillerets et al., 2016; NCCN, 2017d). See Table 9-3 for genes associated with increased risk for melanoma, as well as other skin cancers.

Personal Health History – A Risk Factor for Developing Skin Cancer

A personal history of basal cell carcinoma or squamous cell carcinoma is associated with a much higher risk for malignant melanoma (Griffin et al., 2016). A personal history of basal cell or squamous cell skin cancer is associated with a much higher risk of developing a second basal cell or squamous cell skin cancer, especially in persons with a history of significant sun exposure (NCCN, 2017a, 2017i). The overall risk of a subsequent primary melanoma can be as high as 28%, necessitating continued follow-up and screening for second melanomas in melanoma survivors (Caini et al., 2014). For these reasons, it is important that patients who have been diagnosed with any type of skin cancer have regular follow-up screenings to evaluate for additional skin cancers (ACS, 2017a).

Persons with chronic immunosuppression are at higher risk of developing malignant melanoma (Strayer & Schub, 2016). This includes renal transplant patients and persons with human papillomavirus and human immunodeficiency virus infections (NCCN, 2017c).

SIGNS AND SYMPTOMS

Basal cell carcinomas often appear as flat, firm, pale areas or small, raised, pink or red, translucent, shiny, waxy areas that may bleed after a minor injury (see Figure 9-7; NCCN, 2017a). They may have one or more visible abnormal blood vessels, a depressed area in the center, and/or blue, brown, or black areas (ACS, 2017a). A wide range of colors may be present, from pearly white to pink to red. Telangiectasias (small, dilated skin vessels near the surface of the skin) may or may not be present on the surface. Some lesions will have scaling plaques (NCCN, 2017a). As lesions progress, the center usually ulcerates, and the

TABLE 9-3: GENES ASSOCIATED WITH AN INCREASED RISK OF DEVELOPING BASAL CELL SKIN CANCER, SQUAMOUS CELL SKIN CANCER, SEBACEOUS SKIN CANCERS, AND MELANOMA

BRCA1/2	Breast, prostate, ovarian, pancreatic, melanoma, fallopian tube, primary peritoneal, endometrial
CDKN2A	Melanoma, pancreatic
MLH1, MSH2, MSH6, PMS2	Colorectal, endometrial, ovarian, gastric, pancreatic, biliary tract, urothelium, small bowel, brain, sebaceous neoplasms
PTEN	Female breast, thyroid, endometrial, colon, renal, melanoma
CDK4	Melanoma, squamous cell skin cancer, basal cell skin cancer, pancreatic
NBN	Breast, melanoma, non-Hodgkin lymphoma
PTCH1, PTCH2	Basal cell skin cancers
XPA-XPG, XPV	Xeroderma pigmentosum – squamous cell skin cancers
TYR, OCA2, MATP/ OCA4, TYRP1	Albinism – squamous cell skin cancers

Note. Adapted from Bressac-de Paillerets, B., Vabres, P., & Thomas, L. (2016). Genetic testing for melanoma – where are we with moderate-penetrance genes? *JAMA Dermatology, 152*(4), 375-376. doi:10.1001/jamadermatol.2015.4359; Griffin, L. L., Ali, F. R., & Lear, J. T. (2016). Nonmelanoma skin cancer. *Clinical Medicine, 16*(1), 62-65. doi:10.7861/clinmedicine.16-1-62; National Comprehensive Cancer Network. (2017a). *Basal cell skin cancer version 1.2017.* Retrieved from http://www.nccn.org; National Comprehensive Cancer Network. (2017c). *Genetic/familial high risk assessment: Breast and ovarian version 2.2017.* Retrieved from http://www.nccn.org; National Comprehensive Cancer Network. (2017d). *Melanoma version 1.2017.* Retrieved from http://www.nccn.org; National Comprehensive Cancer Network. (2017i). *Squamous cell skin cancer version 1.2017.* Retrieved from http://www.nccn.org; Nikolaou, V., Stratigos, A. J., & Tsao, H. (2012). Hereditary nonmelanoma skin cancer. *Seminars in Cutaneous Medicine and Surgery, 31*(4), 204-210. doi:10.1016/j.sder.2012.08.005; Soura, E., Eliades, P. J., Shannon, K., Stratigos, A. J., & Tsao, H. (2016). Hereditary melanoma: Update on syndromes and management: Genetics of familial atypical multiple mole melanoma syndrome. *Journal of the American Academy of Dermatology, 74*(3), 395-407, quiz 408-410. doi:10.1016/j.jaad.2015.08.038; and Strayer, D., & Schub, T. (2016). Melanoma: Risk factors and prevention. In D. Pravikoff (Ed.), *CINAHL nursing guide information sheets.* Glendale, CA: Cinahl Information Systems.

FIGURE 9-7: BASAL CELL CARCINOMA

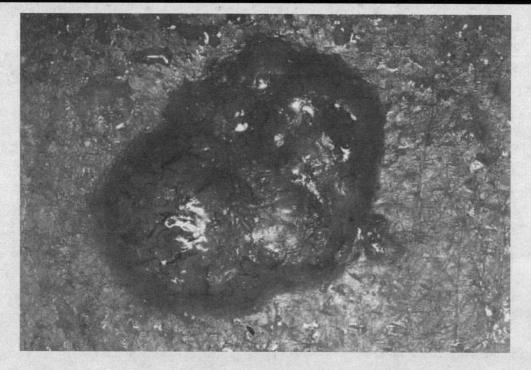

Note. From Wikimedia. (2006). *Basal cell carcinoma.* Retrieved http://commons.wikimedia.org/wiki/File:Basal_cell_carcinoma.jpg

borders develop a raised or rolled appearance. Large basal cell carcinomas may have oozing or crusted areas (NCCN, 2017a).

Squamous cell carcinomas may appear as growing lumps, often with a rough surface, or as flat, reddish patches in the skin that grow slowly (see Figure 9-8; NCCN, 2017i). They often begin as a red, raised, firm papule. Crusting and ulceration are often seen. It is not uncommon for the patient to report that the lesion is tender or painful.

Merkel cell carcinoma usually develops on sun-exposed skin as a painless, firm bump that can be red-purple or skin-colored (NCCN, 2017f). The lesion often grows rapidly. Malignant cells may invade surrounding tissues and can metastasize to other regions of the body via blood and the lymphatic system.

Dermatofibrosarcoma protuberans may initially appear as a small bump on the skin (NCCN, 2017b). It may resemble a deep, embedded pimple or a rough patch of skin. It can also look like a scar, and in children it sometimes resembles a birthmark.

Cutaneous lymphoma presents in multiple ways including papules (small, pimple-like lesions), red patches (flat lesions), plaques (thick, raised or lowered lesions), or pigmented nodules (NCCN, 2017g). The lesions are often itchy, scaly, and red to purple (Wilson et al., 2012). The lymphoma might show up as more than one type of lesion and on different parts of the skin (often in non-sun-exposed areas). Some skin lymphomas appear as a rash over some or most of the body (known as *erythroderma*; Sokołowska-Wojdyło et al., 2015). Sometimes larger lesions can ulcerate.

Malignant melanoma may appear with a wide range of clinical characteristics (see Figure 9-9). It is often difficult to distinguish a dysplas-

FIGURE 9-8: SQUAMOUS CELL SKIN CANCER

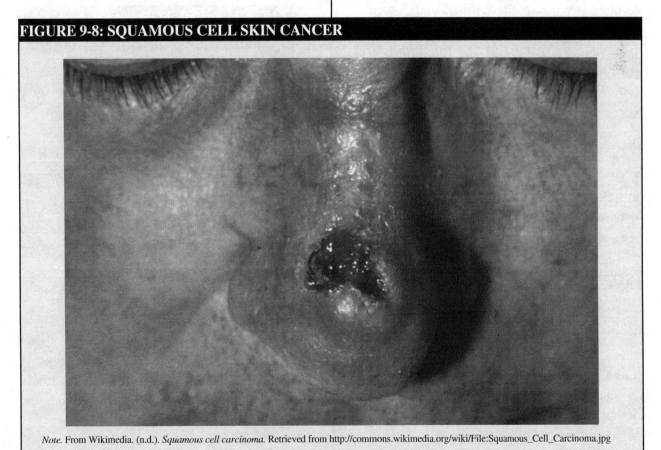

Note. From Wikimedia. (n.d.). *Squamous cell carcinoma.* Retrieved from http://commons.wikimedia.org/wiki/File:Squamous_Cell_Carcinoma.jpg

FIGURE 9-9: MALIGNANT MELANOMA

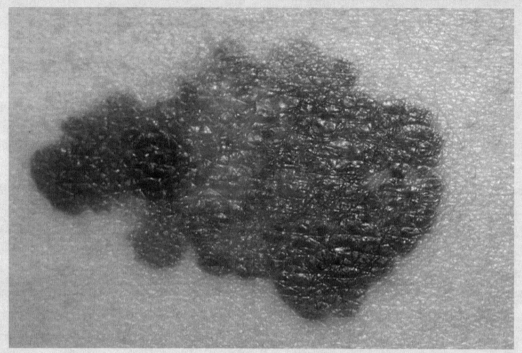

Note. From U.S. Department of Health and Human Services, National Institutes of Health, National Cancer Institute. (1985). *Melanoma.* Retrieved from https://visualsonline.cancer.gov/details.cfm?imageid=9186

tic nevus from a malignant melanoma. A good way to remember the physical characteristics of melanoma is the ABCDE rule (Abbasi et al., 2004; Friedman, Rigel, & Kopf, 1985; see Table 9-4).

PREVENTION

Prevention of skin cancer is a public health priority (ACS, 2017b). Efforts center around increasing awareness, reducing UVR exposure, and using evidence-based strategies to protect the skin against URV exposure (ACS, 2017b).

Ultraviolet Exposure

Children and infants younger than 6 months should be kept out of direct sunlight and protected from the sun using hats and protective clothing (ACS, 2017b). Sunscreen may be used on small areas of exposed skin only if adequate clothing and shade are not available (Ho et al., 2016). Infants' skin is thinner, with a thinner

TABLE 9-4: ABCDE FOR MALIGNANT MELANOMA

- **A**symmetrical

- **B**orders that are jagged or faded

- **C**olor characteristics of the lesion, such as two or more colors or a lesion that is a different color from the rest of the pigmented lesions on a patient

- **D**iameter greater than 5 mm

- **E**volution – a change in the appearance of the mole over time

Note. Adapted from American Cancer Society. (2017). *Cancer facts and figures – 2017.* Atlanta, GA: Author.

stratum corneum (Ho et al., 2016). The thinner stratum corneum protects the body less effectively against outside agents, and the chemicals in sunscreen penetrate deeper, making infants more vulnerable to contact dermatitis, allergies, or inflammation (Ho et al., 2016).

Children need constant attention to reduce UVR exposure (ACS, 2017b). They tend to spend more time outdoors, can burn more easily, and are not aware of the dangers of UVR exposure (Falk & Anderson, 2013). Parents and other caregivers should protect children from excess sun exposure by limiting exposure when UVR is strongest and consistently using sunscreen, protective clothing, and hats (ACS, 2017b). Parents should role-model behaviors to reduce UVR exposure (Ho et al., 2016). Children need to be taught about the dangers of UVR exposure as they become more independent (ACS, 2017b).

Time of Day

Approximately 60% of the total UVB exposure occurs between 10 a.m. and 2 p.m. (ACS, 2017b). When possible, avoiding prolonged exposure during this time is recommended. Shade from trees and canopies can help to reduce exposure (ACS, 2017b).

Geographic Location

Stratospheric ozone depletion allows more UVR to reach Earth's surface (ACS, 2017b). The depletion of the ozone layer during the past 50 years is a contributing factor to the increased incidence of basal cell, squamous cell, and malignant melanoma cancers (Norval et al., 2016).

The closer to the equator, the more intense the sun's rays become (ACS, 2017b). Higher altitudes are also associated with more intense exposure (Buller et al., 2017). The presence of snow and cold in higher altitudes does not decrease the intensity of the rays; reflection off of snow may actually increase intensity, so sunscreen and protective clothing are still important (Buller et al., 2017).

Ultraviolet Index

One way to gauge the intensity of and risk for UV exposure is to know the UV index for the geographic locale. The higher the sun is in the sky, the higher is the UVR level. UVR varies with time of day and time of year, with maximum levels occurring when the sun is at its maximum elevation, at around midday during the summer months. Latitude is also a factor because the highest UVR levels are at the equator; UVR levels decrease with increasing distance from the equator. UVR is reflected or scattered to varying extents by different surfaces. For example, snow can reflect as much as 80% of UVR, and dry beach sand reflects approximately 15% (Wei-Passanese et al., 2012). The UV index is a number from 0 to 10+ that indicates the amount of UVR reaching Earth's surface during the hour around noon. The higher the number, the greater is the exposure to UVR outdoors. The National Weather Service forecasts the UV index daily in 58 U.S. cities, based on local predicted conditions. The index covers a radius of approximately 30 miles from each city. The information can also be accessed through the local newspaper or TV and radio news broadcasts or online at http://www.cpc.noaa.gov/products/stratosphere/uv_index/uv_current.shtml.

Sunscreen

The primary goal of protecting the skin from UVR is not just to avoid sunburn. Studies demonstrate that incremental damage occurs with each exposure to UVR, regardless of whether there is clinical evidence of redness or burn (Rivas, Rojas, Araya, & Calaf, 2015). It is impractical and impossible to think that humans can avoid sun exposure completely; therefore, prevention with sunscreens and other protective clothing is necessary.

Epidemiological studies suggest that recent UVR exposure may be more important than cumulative UVR exposure (Strayer & Schub, 2015). Thus, even older individuals and those with a history of high cumulative sun exposure can benefit from sunscreen use by preventing the influence of recent sun exposure and by avoiding the initiation of new mutations. Sunscreen clearly reduces further actinic damage in patients with such damage when used consistently and adequately. These results can be evident in as soon as 2 years (ACS, 2017b).

There are two types of sunscreens: chemical and physical. Chemical sunscreens provide protection by absorbing UVR. Physical sunscreens block UVR from reaching the skin. Chemical sunscreens have been available since the 1920s with the introduction of sunscreens based on para-aminobenzoic acid. The importance of sunscreen should not be underestimated; research has clearly shown that it prevents sunburn, and regular use can retard or prevent the development of skin changes (ACS, 2017b). Educating the public about sunscreen is more complicated than it appears. Controversies continue regarding the labeling, application, and effectiveness of these agents. Figure 9-10 provides information for patient education regarding sunscreen.

Sunscreens previously were rated or classified by their SPF only, with the SPF numbers on a label solely referring to the product's ability to absorb, reflect, or scatter UVB rays. Until recently, guidelines on sunscreens failed to address UVA rays and their associated skin issues (i.e., early skin aging and skin cancer) because there was no acceptable standardized method to measure a sunscreen's ability to protect against UVA. However, in June 2011, the U.S. Food and Drug Administration (FDA) established a standard, broad-spectrum test procedure that measures UVA protection relative to UVB protection (Printz, 2012; see Figure 9-10). The guidelines allow sunscreen products that pass this test to be labeled "broad spectrum," meaning that these products protect against both UVB and UVA rays. As in the past, the SPFs

of these products indicate the amount (or level) of protection. Broad-spectrum sunscreens with SPF 30 or higher protect against skin cancer, early skin aging, and sunburn when used as directed and with other sun-protection measures (wearing protective clothing, limiting time in the sun, reapplying sunscreen at least every 2 hours). Sunscreens with SPF values listed but not labeled broad spectrum protect against sunburn only (FDA, 2011).

Chemical sunscreens are designed to be applied generously to all exposed skin 30 minutes before exposure. Depending on the chemicals used, a laboratory SPF can range from 2 to 50+. Higher SPFs are permitted, but in 2011 the FDA proposed new guidelines that would limit SPF values on labels to a maximum of "50+" because research has shown that SPF values greater than 50 do not seem to provide more protection than SPF 50 (FDA, 2011). Sunscreens are rated for their UVR absorption under strict and ideal laboratory conditions. In a laboratory, a sunscreen with an SPF of 15 will absorb 92% of UVB, an SPF of 30 will absorb 96.7% of UVB, and an SPF of 40 will absorb 97.5% of UVB (Printz, 2012). The effectiveness of a particular sunscreen agent is affected by an individual's body site of application, degree of normal skin color, thickness of the epidermis, time of day, time of year, cloud cover, ozone levels, reflection, and UVR scatter (Printz, 2012). A sunscreen of SPF 15 is adequate if it is applied in the amount of 2 mg/cm^2 (Printz, 2012). Because most individuals typically apply less sunscreen than is used in laboratories to establish the SPF number, the actual SPF protection is often 20% to 50% of the number on the label (FDA, 2011).

Protective Clothing and Hats

The effectiveness of hats and shirts as a primary prevention measure should not be underestimated. A brim size of 10 cm can lead to a reduction of 73% of UVR exposure to the

FIGURE 9-10: SUNSCREEN LABELING

Sunscreen Labeling According to 2011 Final Rule

If used as directed with other sun protection measures, this product reduces the risk of skin cancer and early skin aging, as well as helps prevent sunburn.

Only products labeled with both "Broad Spectrum" AND SPF15 or higher have been shown to provide all these benefits.

BRAND X
Sunscreen

BROAD SPECTRUM SPF 15

WATER RESISTANT (40 MINUTES)

Drug Facts

Active Ingredients	Purpose
Avobenzone 3%	
Homosalate 10%	Sunscreen
Octyl methoxycinnamate 7.5%	

Uses
• helps prevent sunburn
• if used as directed with other sun protection measures (see **Directions**), decreases the risk of skin cancer and early skin aging caused by the sun

Warnings

For external use only

Do not use on damaged or broken skin

When using this product keep out of eyes. Rinse with water to remove.

Stop use and ask a doctor if rash occurs

Keep out of reach of children. If product is swallowed, get medical help or contact a Poison Control Center right away.

Directions
• apply liberally 15 minutes before sun exposure
• reapply:
    • after 40 minutes of swimming or sweating
    • immediately after towel drying
    • at least every 2 hours
• **Sun Protection Measures.** Spending time in the sun increases your risk of skin cancer and early skin aging. To decrease this risk, regularly use a sunscreen with a broad spectrum SPF of 15 or higher and other sun protection measures including:
    • limit time in the sun, especially from 10 a.m. – 2 p.m.
    • wear long-sleeve shirts, pants, hats, and sunglasses
• children under 6 months: Ask a doctor

Inactive ingredients
aloe extract, barium sulfate, benzyl alcohol, carbomer, dimethicone, disodium EDTA, jojoba oil, methylparaben, octadecene/MA copolymer, polyglyceryl-3 distearate, phenethyl alcohol, propylparaben, sorbitan isostearate, sorbitol, stearic acid, tocopherol (vitamin E), triethanolamine, water

Other information
• protect this product from excessive heat and direct sun

Questions or comments?
Call toll free 1-800-XXX-XXXX

New U.S. Food and Drug Administration (FDA) labeling standards include separately delineating "broad spectrum" and sun protection factor (SPF) information in an equal font size. The claim "water resistant" must be specified with a time, either 40 or 80 minutes. The Drug Facts box on the back of the product must include usage directions, guidelines for sun protection, and other FDA-required statements.

Note. From U.S. Food and Drug Administration. (2017b). *Sunscreen and sun protection: More information about sunscreens.* Retrieved from https://www.fda.gov/Drugs/ResourcesForYou/Consumers/BuyingUsingMedicineSafely/UnderstandingOver-the-CounterMedicines/ucm239463.htm

head and neck (ACS, 2017b). For this reason, patients should be instructed that a wide-brim hat is the best choice to protect the face, neck, and shoulders.

The weave of the material used in hats and clothing is very important. Densely woven material provides a reflective barrier to UVR. Clothes designed to cover the most skin provide the most protection. Long-sleeved shirts with collars, long pants, and shoes and socks pro-

vide more coverage than tank tops, shorts, and sandals. In general, synthetic materials provide better protection against UVA than cotton materials (Aguilera, de Gálvez, Sánchez-Roldán, & Herrera-Ceballos, 2014). Darker materials also provide more protection. Most clothes, such as hats and summer wear, offer an SPF of 2 to 6.5, although sun-protective clothing is available that offers an SPF of up to 30 (ACS, 2017b).

Nurses can educate patients about ways to assess the effectiveness of fabric as a sun protectant. This is a very important method of reducing UVR exposure that is consistently underestimated. A simple test of efficacy is to hold the material up to strong light and see whether it casts a dense shadow or whether it is easy to distinguish objects through the shadow (Aguilera et al., 2014). Nurses should also educate patients that virtually all garments lose some of their sun-protective ability when wet; dry fabric is more protective than wet fabric (ACS, 2017b).

Eye Protection

Protection of the ocular structures from sun exposure is important. Some sunglasses offer protection against both UVA and UVB (Strayer & Schub, 2016). Consumers need to be instructed to read labels correctly and carefully before purchasing sunglasses to assure that they actually offer UVR protection (Mahon & McLaughlin, 2017). The label should state, "Blocks 99% of UVR." Some manufacturers state, "UVR up to 400 nm (nanometers)," which is equivalent to 100% UVR absorption. The color and degree of darkness do not provide any information about the ability of the lenses to block UVR (Strayer & Schub, 2016).

Indoor Tanning

Indoor tanning represents a relatively new area that public education programs need to target (Guy, Watson, Richardson, & Lushniak, 2016). Mounting evidence suggests that there is an increase in malignant melanoma risk for persons who regularly use artificial sources of UVA (Strayer & Schub, 2016).

Every day, more than 1 million Americans use tanning parlors, which are largely unregulated. The United States has an estimated 50,000 artificial tanning facilities, generating more than $5 billion in annual revenue (O'Leary, Diehl, & Levins, 2014). The FDA

and the Federal Trade Commission (FTC) share responsibilities in the regulation of sunlamps and tanning devices, but regulation of this industry is complicated and not well developed. The FDA enforces regulations concerning labels on the devices; the FTC investigates false, misleading, and deceptive advertising claims about the devices. When these agencies identify a violation, the FDA has the authority to remove products from the market. In May 2014, the FDA announced that a regulation was being implemented that requires user instructions and promotional materials for sunlamp products and UV lamps intended for use to include the following warnings: (a) the product is contraindicated for use by persons younger than 18 years, (b) the product must not be used if skin lesions or open wounds are present, (c) the product should not be used on people who have had skin cancer or who have a family history of skin cancer, and (d) people repeatedly exposed to UVR should be regularly evaluated for skin cancer (FDA, 2017a).

Indoor tanning beds typically emit approximately 95% UVA and 5% UVB, which the parlors market as a "safe tan" because sunburning seldom occurs (O'Leary et al., 2014). In reality, there is no known benefit from exposure to artificial UVA, and tanning actually represents the body's response to injury (Strayer & Schub, 2016). Exposure to artificial UVR before age 25 years increases the risk of developing nonmelanoma skin cancer by 40% to 100%, and currently more than 170,000 annual cases of such cancers are a result of indoor tanning, with risk being elevated in as few as 10 sessions (Colantonio, Bracken, & Beecker, 2014). Indoor tanning before age 35 years increases the risk of developing melanoma by 59% to 75% (O'Leary et al., 2014). Artificial tanning can substantially damage the skin, cause premature aging, and cause loss of elasticity, and it has been linked to ocular melanoma (ACS, 2017b). Table 9-5 provides patient education points regarding indoor tanning.

Public Health Initiatives

The *Healthy People 2020* guidelines are a government initiative that aims to decrease the U.S. mortality rate from malignant melanoma from 2.7 deaths per 100,000 persons to 2.4 deaths per 100,000 persons during the next 10 years (U.S. Department of Health and Human Services [USDHHS], 2016). The guidelines also seek to increase the proportion of people using skin cancer primary prevention strategies,

which include at least one of the following protective measures:

- Avoiding the sun between 10 a.m. and 4 p.m., when the UVR is most intense
- Wearing sun-protective clothing
- Using sunscreen with an SPF of 30 or higher
- Decreasing or avoiding UVR exposure

To reap the most benefits, public education programs need to be started early in a child's life, with the goal of having the individual adopt attitudes and practices that minimize UVR exposure. Such programs have demonstrated that even pre-

---

TABLE 9-5: PATIENT EDUCATION REGARDING INDOOR TANNING

- In 2013, approximately 4% of U.S. adults reported using an indoor tanning device in the past year; use was highest among women (7%), non-Hispanic White individuals (7%), and those aged 18 to 29 years (9%).

- The risk of melanoma is about 60% higher for people who began using indoor tanning devices before the age of 35 years, and melanoma risk increases with the number of total hours, sessions, or years that indoor tanning devices are used.

- Indoor tanning is a profitable industry, grossing more than $5 billion annually.

- 42 states in the United States have no tanning parlor regulations.

- Many facilities offer tanning packages, which encourage frequent tanning.

- Tanning may stimulate secretion of mood-boosting endorphins, which may have an addicting reinforcing effect.

- Any tan indicates that skin has undergone some cellular damage, which is what triggers the melanin production. No one knows how many times a person can tan before the damage becomes visible, but it is cumulative and largely irreversible.

- Long-term exposure to artificial sources of ultraviolet rays like tanning beds (or the sun's natural rays) increases the risk of developing skin cancer.

- Exposure to tanning salon rays increases damage caused by sunlight because ultraviolet light actually thins the skin, making it less able to heal.

- If an individual wants a tanned look, bronzers or spray tans are a safe alternative.

- Individuals should be educated on the importance of becoming involved in promoting more regulation of indoor tanning.

Note. Adapted from:

American Cancer Society. (2017b). *Cancer prevention and early detection facts and figures – 2017-2018.* Atlanta, GA: Author.

Watson, M., Holman, D. M., Fox, K. A., Guy, G. P., Jr., Seidenberg, A. B., Sampson, B. P., ... Lazovich, D. (2013). Preventing skin cancer through reduction of indoor tanning: Current evidence. *American Journal of Preventive Medicine, 44*(6), 682-689. doi:10.1001/jamadermatol.2015.3007

schoolers can learn and practice behaviors that reduce UVR exposure (ACS, 2017b). Evidence suggests that to get children to change their practices and attitudes, their parents must first adopt more healthy behaviors (USDHHS, 2016). Despite educational programs and knowledge about the dangers of exposure to UVR, many individuals fail to practice primary prevention strategies. Some believe that fear of skin cancer is not a deterrent to sun-seeking behaviors and that until it becomes more culturally acceptable to have untanned skin in the United States, there will not be a major decrease in malignant melanoma and nonmelanoma skin cancer incidence and mortality rates. Some groups advocate that public messages should try to change this social norm and emphasize the photoaging effects of excessive UVR exposure. As of January 1, 2017 only 13 states and the District of Columbia have a law prohibiting tanning for minors without exemptions; 37 states fail to fully protect minors under the age of 18 from the harms caused by indoor tanning devices (ACS, 2017b).

Since 2008, the ACS has been collaborating with the National Council on Skin Cancer Prevention (NCSCP) to promote prevention activities and improve national media relations efforts that raise public health awareness about the importance of skin cancer prevention (ACS, 2017b). The NCSCP and its partners have designated the Friday before Memorial Day as Don't Fry Day. This pre-Memorial Day awareness initiative uses key messages to ensure consistent communication about the individual steps people can take to prevent skin cancer (Borger, 2013). More information is available at The National Council on Skin Cancer Prevention website (http://www.skincancerprevention.org).

In 2014 *The Surgeon General's Call to Action to Prevent Skin Cancer* was released.

The goals are as follows (USDHHS, 2014):

- Increase opportunities for sun protection in outdoor settings, which includes efforts to increase shade in outdoor recreational settings, educational facilities, and for outdoor workers.

- Provide individuals with the information to make informed, healthy choices about UVR exposure including clear, effective messages, interventions for specific audiences, and skin cancer prevention education in schools.

- Promote policies that advance the national goal of preventing skin cancer.

- Support inclusion of sun protection in school policies, construction of school facilities, and school curricula.

- Reduce harms from indoor tanning by monitoring indoor tanning attitudes, beliefs, and behaviors, especially among indoor tanners, youth, and parents. Develop, disseminate, and evaluate tailored messages to reduce indoor tanning among populations at high risk. Enforce existing indoor tanning laws and consider adopting additional restrictions.

- Strengthen research, surveillance, monitoring, and evaluation related to skin cancer prevention.

EARLY DETECTION

The skin is a visible organ. This visibility facilitates early detection. All healthcare providers who assess skin should be aware of the signs and symptoms of skin cancer; any suspicious changes should be referred for further evaluation (ACS, 2017a).

The U.S. Preventive Services Task Force (2009) recommends the following:

1. Clinicians should be aware that fair-skinned men and women 65 years of age and older and people with atypical moles or more than 50 moles are at greater risk of developing melanoma.

2. Clinicians should remain alert for skin abnormalities when conducting physical examinations for other purposes.

The ACS (2017b) also recommends routine inspection of the skin as part of an annual cancer-related checkup. High-risk individuals may be encouraged to do skin self-examination to monitor for early changes. Special attention should be paid to all skin surfaces, not just the face or arms. This includes the area behind the ears, scalp, neck, entire torso (front and back), and palmar and plantar surfaces (ACS, 2017b).

The early detection of basal cell carcinoma and squamous cell carcinoma is important to prevent the disfiguring effects of these tumors and their treatment (NCCN, 2017a, 2017i). Basal cell and squamous cell cancers are most often found in areas that have repeated sun exposure, such as the head, neck, and arms, but they can also occur elsewhere (ACS, 2017b). Once diagnosed with a basal cell or squamous cell skin cancer, the risk of a subsequent basal cell and squamous cell skin cancer is increased (NCCN, 2017a, 2017i). These individuals need evaluation and screening on a regular basis to monitor for new lesions (NCCN, 2017a, 2017i).

Early detection of malignant melanoma is an approach that, if used effectively and consistently, can have a relatively rapid impact on decreasing the mortality rate from this disease (ACS, 2017b; Canavan & Cantrell, 2016). Melanomas can occur anywhere on the skin, but they are more likely to start in certain locations (ACS, 2017b). The trunk is the most common site in men. The legs are the most commonly affected site in women. The neck and face are other common sites (NCCN, 2017d). Persons with a personal history of melanoma, known genetic risk, or a family history of melanoma should have screening every 6 to 12 months by a dermatologist because the risk of developing melanoma is elevated (NCCN, 2017d).

DIAGNOSTIC EVALUATION

There are many benign and malignant tumors of the skin. Benign and malignant tumors can develop from different types of skin cells. The pathology results as part of the diagnostic evaluation to determine whether the suspicious lesion is benign or malignant and from what cell line it originates (Griffin et al., 2016).

Examples of benign lesions include the following:

- *Moles (nevi):* benign skin tumors that develop from melanocytes. Nearly all moles are benign, but some types may increase the risk of melanoma.

- *Seborrheic keratoses:* tan, brown, or black raised spots with a "waxy" texture or rough surface.

- *Hemangiomas:* benign blood vessel growths often called cherry spots, strawberry spots, or port-wine stains.

- *Lipomas:* soft growths of benign fat cells.

- *Warts:* rough-surfaced growths caused by a virus.

Examples of malignant lesions include the following:

- *Basal cell skin cancer:* malignant tumors that often appear as flat, firm, pale areas or small, raised, pink or red, translucent, shiny, waxy areas that may bleed after a minor injury. They may have one or more visible abnormal blood vessels, a depressed area in their center, and blue, brown, or black areas. Large basal cell carcinomas may have oozing or crusted areas.

- *Squamous cell carcinomas of the skin:* malignant tumors that may appear as a growing lump or bump. They often have a rough surface or appear as flat, reddish patches in the skin that grow slowly.

- *Melanoma:* malignant tumor arising from melanocyte cells that form a mole that changes in size, shape, or color or is larger than 5 mm.

History and Physical Examination

The first step in a diagnostic evaluation for skin cancer consists of taking a medical history and gathering information about changes in any skin lesions, as well as risk factors for the development of skin cancer. If genetic risk is suspected, the individual should be referred to a credentialed genetics professional for further evaluation (NCCN, 2017c). This is followed by a physical examination. During the physical examination, the healthcare provider will note the size, shape, color, and texture of the areas in question and whether there is bleeding or scaling. The entire body should be systematically checked for spots, moles, and other skin eruptions that may represent or be precursors to skin cancer. Nearby lymph nodes are also assessed. Suspicious findings should be referred for further evaluation and possible biopsy and/or removal (ACS, 2017a). General practitioners such as MDs and APRNs in primary care and specialty practice areas may refer patients with suspected skin cancer to dermatologists and APRNs who specialize in dermatology for further evaluation and, if needed, biopsies. These healthcare providers may perform procedures such as biopsies, aspirations, incisions, and excisions. More extensive excisions and procedures are usually performed by dermatological surgeons, plastic surgeons, or general surgeons, depending on the extent and location of the suspicious lesion or tumor.

Dermatoscopy

Along with a standard physical examination, or a dermatological examination performed by a dermatologist or APRN who specializes in this practice area, some healthcare providers use a technique called *dermatoscopy* (also called *epiluminescence microscopy*) to see spots on the skin more clearly. Dermatoscopy has been shown to increase the clinician's diagnostic accuracy when evaluating skin lesions (Marghoob, Usatine, & Jaimes, 2013). It is accomplished with a handheld instrument called a *dermatoscope,* which has a transilluminating light source and magnifying optics. The dermatoscope facilitates the visualization of subsurface skin structures not visible to the naked eye to help correctly identify lesions that have a high likelihood of being malignant and to assist in differentiating them from benign lesions clinically mimicking malignancies, thereby preventing unnecessary biopsies. Colors and structures visible with dermatoscopy are required for generating a correct diagnosis; extensive training is required to become proficient with using the dermatoscope. In systematic reviews, dermatoscopy has been shown to be more accurate than naked-eye examination for detecting melanoma in patients presenting with suspicious skin lesions (Schub & Caple, 2016). Estimates for sensitivity were 90% for dermatoscopy and 71% for naked-eye examination (Marghoob et al., 2013). The specificity estimate for dermatoscopy is 90% and for naked-eye examination is 81%.

Photography

Photography of lesions allows the clinician to accurately document the location and clinical characteristics for future reference. Total body photography with multiple photographs at regular intervals is an important tool used to assist in monitoring and identifying early skin changes in patients with dysplastic nevus syndrome (Hoorens et al., 2016). In some cases, measuring tapes may be placed on the skin before photography to assess for and document changes in size. Images require proper labeling and may need the patient's permission unless part of a visit consent to treat. Images must be protected as part of the patient's medical record. Nurses in some settings may take on the role of expert photographer who documents lesions and catalogs visits.

Biopsy

Skin Biopsy

Skin biopsy may be indicated to determine the diagnosis of a mole, lesion, or other skin eruption. Different methods can be used to perform a skin biopsy. The choice depends on the suspected type of skin cancer, the location on the body, the size of the affected area, and the judgment and expertise of the healthcare provider. Potential complications from biopsies include infection, bleeding, hyperpigmentation, hypopigmentation, adhesions, scarring, and problems with wound closure. These are reviewed with the patient by the healthcare provider, and consent is obtained per protocol. The nurse has a significant role in supporting the patient during the procedure, providing teaching about postbiopsy care, and may be responsible (based on the setting) for managing the surgical supplies, specimen handling, and documentation. Nurses should be familiar with the different types of skin biopsy so they can provide proper post-procedure care and patient education.

- A shave biopsy is one of the simplest ways to take a skin biopsy. After numbing the area with a local anesthetic, the healthcare provider "shaves" off the top layers of the skin (the epidermis and the most superficial part of the dermis) with a surgical blade. The specimen is placed in a labeled container and sent for evaluation to pathology. Suturing is not required.

- In a punch biopsy, the healthcare provider removes a deeper sample of skin. The punch biopsy tool is cylindrical, comes in a number of diameter sizes measured in millimeters, has a sharp-cutting edge, and the tip looks like a tiny, round cookie cutter. Once the skin is numbed with a local anesthetic, the healthcare provider places the punch biopsy tool's sharp edge on the surface of the skin in the area the healthcare provider wishes to obtain a sample, perpendicular to the skin's surface, and gently rotates the tool in a circular motion until it cuts through all the layers of the skin, including the dermis, epidermis, and upper parts of the subcutis. The tool is pulled out once it has penetrated the desired level, and the tissue sample is removed from the punch and placed in a labeled specimen container for evaluation to pathology. Pressure is placed on the site to manage any bleeding. If the punch site is tiny, just a small dressing is used to cover the site. Punch biopsy sites may be closed with a suture depending on the size of the tool used.

- If the physician has to examine and retrieve a tumor that may have grown into deeper layers of the skin, or completely remove a previously biopsied lesion, he or she will use an incisional or excisional biopsy technique.

An incisional biopsy involves removing only a portion of the tumor. Removal of the entire tumor is an excisional biopsy. The physician uses a surgical knife to cut through the full thickness of the skin. The surgeon removes a wedge or ellipse of skin for further examination and sutures the edges of the wound together. Both of these types of biopsies can be done in an office setting using local anesthesia. Specimens removed are placed in labeled containers and sent to pathology. For suspected melanoma, an excisional biopsy is preferred because it makes staging the depth of tumor invasion much more accurate (Amin et al., 2017; NCCN, 2017i).

Pathology

The tissue sample obtained from the biopsy is placed in a designated and labeled container and is sent to be examined by a pathologist. Many large academic centers employ dermatopathologists who are specially trained and exclusively examine and evaluate skin specimens. A dermatopathologist may be present in an operating suite during a procedure to examine specimens during the active part of the procedure in certain situations. Often this is done at the time of surgical resection to determine whether free margins have been obtained, decreasing the need for subsequent resections (ACS, 2017a; NCCN, 2017a, 2017i).

Lymph Node Biopsy

A lymph node biopsy may be done to determine whether cancer has spread from the skin to the lymph nodes. This may be indicated in larger basal cell and squamous cell cancers, especially if there are palpable lymph nodes (NCCN, 2017a). Sampling is typically accomplished with a biopsy.

- A fine-needle aspiration is the biopsy technique used by the healthcare provider when taking a syringe with a thin needle and inserting it into the node and pulling back or "aspirating" possible fluid and very small tissue fragments. The specimen is sent in a labeled container to pathology or the laboratory for evaluation. The healthcare provider uses a local anesthetic to numb the area. A fine-needle aspiration biopsy is not used to diagnose a suspicious skin tumor; however, it may be used when performing a biopsy of enlarged lymph nodes near a skin cancer to determine whether the cancer has spread to the lymph node.

- If the physician suspects spread of cancer to a lymph node, but the needle biopsy result is negative or is not clear, the healthcare provider may surgically remove the lymph node for examination. The physician can perform this procedure using local anesthesia in the office setting or in an outpatient surgical center. The procedure will leave a small scar.

Sentinel Lymph Node Mapping and Biopsy

Sentinel lymph node biopsy has become a common procedure to determine whether melanoma has spread to the lymph nodes (NCCN, 2017d). Surgeons use this procedure to find the lymph nodes that drain lymph fluid from the area of the skin where the melanoma started. If the melanoma has spread, these lymph nodes are the first place it will go.

To map the sentinel lymph node (or nodes), at some point before surgery, the surgeon injects a small amount of radioactive material and a blue dye into the area of the melanoma. By checking various lymph node areas with a radioactivity detector, the surgeon can see to what group of lymph nodes the melanoma is most likely to travel. The surgeon makes a small incision in the identified lymph node area and then checks the lymph nodes to find which ones turned blue or became radioactive. When the surgeon identifies the sentinel node, he or she removes it for examination under a microscope. If the sentinel node does not contain melanoma cells, no more lymph node surgery is needed because it is very unlikely that the melanoma would have spread beyond this point. If the sentinel node contains melanoma cells, the surgeon will remove the remaining lymph nodes in this area as well and examine them (Lee et al., 2016). This is known as a lymph node dissection. This more advanced procedure is usually performed in a surgical suite.

Additional Testing

In suspected metastatic basal cell or squamous cell skin cancer, additional imaging and evaluation may also be needed (NCCN, 2017a, 2017i). Additional imaging is also often indicated for Merkel cell skin cancers (NCCN, 2017f). Dermatofibrosarcoma protuberans skin cancers may require magnetic resonance imaging (MRI) evaluation and additional and immunological bloodwork (NCCN, 2017b). Cutaneous lymphomas require an extensive workup that includes imaging and bloodwork (NCCN, 2017g).

After the physician has diagnosed melanoma, tests are necessary to determine whether malignant cells have spread within the skin or to other parts of the body. These tests also are important in the staging process. Tests may include computed tomography scans, positron emission tomography scans, or MRI to evaluate the chest, abdomen, and pelvis for metastatic disease. Blood chemistry studies may be done to evaluate liver function or lactate dehydrogenase levels, which are often elevated in melanoma.

STAGING AND PROGNOSIS

Nonmelanoma skin cancer and malignant melanoma are staged using the TNM staging system from the American Joint Committee on Cancer (Amin et al., 2017). Table 9-6 shows the stage groupings. Figure 9-11 illustrates the depth of tumor invasion for melanoma.

Prognostic Indicators for Basal Cell Skin Cancer

Basal cell carcinoma is usually slow growing. Complete excision of a primary basal cell carcinoma results in a 95% cure rate (ACS, 2017a). Primary lesions that are large and involve underlying structures, although rare, are more likely to have metastasized, in which case the prognosis is poorer. Extensive local invasion from basal cell carcinoma may cause significant cosmetic defects depending on the anatomical location of the lesion. For metastatic lesions, the 1-year survival rate is less than 20%; the 5-year survival rate is 10% (ACS, 2017a).

Prognostic Indicators for Squamous Cell Carcinoma

The course of squamous cell carcinoma is variable and ranges along a continuum from slow-growing, locally invasive tumors, to rapidly growing, widely invasive ones. Overall, the 5-year survival rate for squamous cell carcinoma is 90%, and its metastatic rate is 3% to 6% (ACS, 2017a). Dermal invasion and vertical tumor thickness are important prognostic indicators.

Prognostic Indicators for Merkel Cell Cancer

Overall, the 5-year survival rate for Merkel cell cancer is about 60% (NCCN, 2017f). The 5-year survival rate for localized disease is 80%; for metastatic disease, the 5-year survival rate is 20% (NCCN, 2017f).

Prognostic Indicators for Dermatofibrosarcoma Protuberans

The general prognosis for dermatofibrosarcoma protuberans is excellent. If properly excised, the 5-year cure rate is 98% (NCCN, 2017b). A poor prognosis of less than 20% is associated with metastasis (NCCN, 2017b).

Prognostic Indicators for Malignant Melanoma

Some special staging considerations are warranted with malignant melanoma. The pathologist analyzing the skin biopsy determines the Breslow measurement by measuring the thickness of the melanoma under the microscope with a device called a *micrometer* (NCCN, 2017d). The thinner the melanoma, the better the prognosis. In general, melanomas less than 1 mm in depth (approximately 1/25 inch, or the diameter of a period or a comma) have a very small chance of spreading. As the melanoma becomes thicker, it has a greater chance of spreading (NCCN, 2017d).

TABLE 9-6: STAGE GROUPING FOR MELANOMA

Stage 0 – The melanoma is in situ, meaning that it involves the epidermis but has not spread to the dermis (lower layer). This is also called Clark level I.

Stage I

Stage IA: Tumor is not more than 1 mm thick, with no ulceration (Clark level II or III).

Stage IB: Clark level III or IV

Tumor is either

- not more than 1 mm thick and it has ulceration; or
- more than 1 mm thick but not more than 2 mm thick, with no ulceration.

Stage II – There is no lymph node involvement.

Stage IIA: Tumor is either

- more than 1 mm thick but not more than 2 mm thick, with ulceration; or
- more than 2 mm thick but not more than 4 mm thick, with no ulceration.

Stage IIB: Tumor is either

- more than 2 mm thick but not more than 4 mm thick, with ulceration; or
- more than 4 mm thick, with no ulceration.

Stage IIC: Tumor is more than 4 mm thick, with ulceration.

Stage III – The tumor may be any thickness, with or without ulceration, with one or more of the following:

- The cancer has spread to one or more lymph nodes.
- Lymph nodes are matted together.
- Very small tumors are found on or under the skin, not more than 2 cm away from the primary tumor.

Stage IV – The cancer has spread to other places in the body, such as the lungs, liver, brain, bone, soft tissue, or gastrointestinal tract.

Note. Adapted from Amin, M. B., Edge, S., Greene, F., Byrd, D. R., Brookland, R. K., Washington, M. K., … Meyer, L. R. (Eds.). (2017). *AJCC cancer staging manual* (8th ed.). New York, NY: Springer.

Another technique, called the *Clark level,* describes how far a melanoma has penetrated into the skin instead of actually measuring it (NCCN, 2017d). The Clark level of a melanoma uses a scale of I to V (with higher numbers indicating a deeper melanoma) to describe the following characteristics:

- Whether the cancer stays in the epidermis (Clark level I)

- Whether the cancer has begun to invade the upper dermis (Clark level II)

- Whether the cancer involves most of the upper dermis (Clark level III)

- Whether the cancer has reached the lower dermis (Clark level IV)

- Whether the cancer has invaded to the subcutis (Clark level V)

(NCCN, 2017d)

FIGURE 9-11: TUMOR STAGING OF MELANOMA

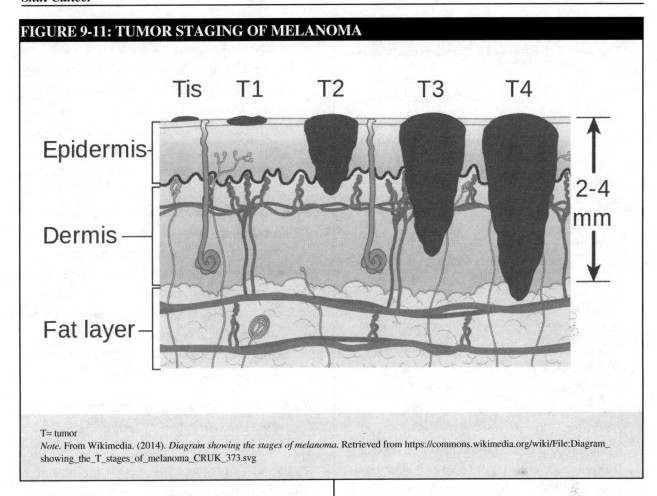

T= tumor

Note. From Wikimedia. (2014). *Diagram showing the stages of melanoma.* Retrieved from https://commons.wikimedia.org/wiki/File:Diagram_ showing_the_T_stages_of_melanoma_CRUK_373.svg

Research suggests that the Breslow measurement of thickness is generally more useful than the Clark level of penetration in determining a patient's prognosis (NCCN, 2017i). The thickness is easier to measure and depends less on the pathologist's judgment, and the Clark level sometimes shows that a melanoma is more advanced than physicians may think it is from the Breslow measurement. The Clark level is, however, more useful in staging thin melanomas.

The 5- and 10-year relative survival rates for melanoma are 92% and 89%, respectively (ACS, 2017a). The 5-year survival rate is 98% for localized melanoma (84% of cases), but it declines to 63% for regional disease and only 17% for distant-stage disease (ACS, 2017a).

TREATMENT

Basal Skin Cancers

In most cases, basal cell skin cancer can be completely cured by surgical removal (ACS, 2017a). Selection of surgical technique or approach for these cancers depends on the size and location of the basal cell skin cancer (NCCN, 2017a). Complete removal of the lesion, including tumor-free margins, is the goal of treatment (NCCN, 2017a). Extensive or recurrent skin cancer, however, may require complex surgical or radiation therapy, may be more expensive and difficult to treat, and has a less certain outcome (NCCN, 2017a).

Surgery

The surgical options for basal skin cancers are as follows:

- A simple excision is similar to an excisional biopsy; however, in this case, the diagnosis is already known (often this follows a shave or punch biopsy). For this procedure, the surgeon first numbs the skin with a local anesthetic. The surgeon then uses a surgical knife to cut out the tumor along with some surrounding normal skin. The surgeon then carefully stitches the remaining skin back together, leaving a small scar. This is typically performed as an outpatient procedure.

- In the curettage and electrodessication technique, the surgeon removes the cancer by scraping it with a curette, then treating the area where the tumor was located with an electrode to destroy any remaining cancer cells. This process is often repeated. Curettage and electrodessication is an option for treatment with small basal cell skin cancers. It will leave a scar.

- In laser removal, which is indicated for small tumors, the physician uses lasers to destroy the tumors.

- Similarly, cryosurgery is the use of freezing temperatures to destroy tissue. The physician may swab or spray the cryogen on the lesion or may use a cryoprobe. The physician will apply the swab or cooled cryoprobe to the lesion for seconds or minutes. The deepest part of the tumor must reach at least −50°C during freezing. More than one freeze-thaw cycle may be required, and the physician must take care to destroy subclinical diseased areas (NCCN, 2017a).

- Mohs micrographic surgery (see Figure 9-12) is indicated for tumors that carry a high risk of recurrence or metastasis, have indistinct margins, or were incompletely excised and are in a location where excision with wide margins of healthy skin removal would be surgically or cosmetically unacceptable (NCCN, 2017a). The surgeon excises the tumor under local anesthesia using horizontal frozen sections that are microscopically examined during the surgery. This allows the surgeon to selectively excise any margins of areas with residual tumor while normal tissues are preserved, with the process continuing until clear margins are obtained. This process is slow, but it means that more normal skin near the tumor can be saved. Mohs technique provides better cosmetic outcome, so it is the surgical treatment of choice for scalp and facial tumors. This is a highly specialized technique that requires specialized surgical training.

Radiation Therapy and Topical Chemotherapy

Radiation therapy and chemotherapy are reserved for extensive metastatic disease. Radiation and topical *imiquimod* are effective for patients who are poor surgical candidates (NCCN, 2017a).

Squamous Cell Skin Cancers

In most cases, squamous cell skin cancer is also completely cured by surgical removal (ACS, 2017a). Complete removal of the lesion, including tumor-free margins, is the goal of treatment (NCCN, 2017i). The risk for more extensive or recurrent squamous cell skin cancer is higher than with basal cell skin cancers, so complete removal is important and may require radiation therapy or topical therapies as well (NCCN, 2017i).

Surgery

The surgical options for squamous cell skin cancers are as follows:

- A simple excision
- Curettage and electrodessication

FIGURE 9-12: MOHS SURGERY

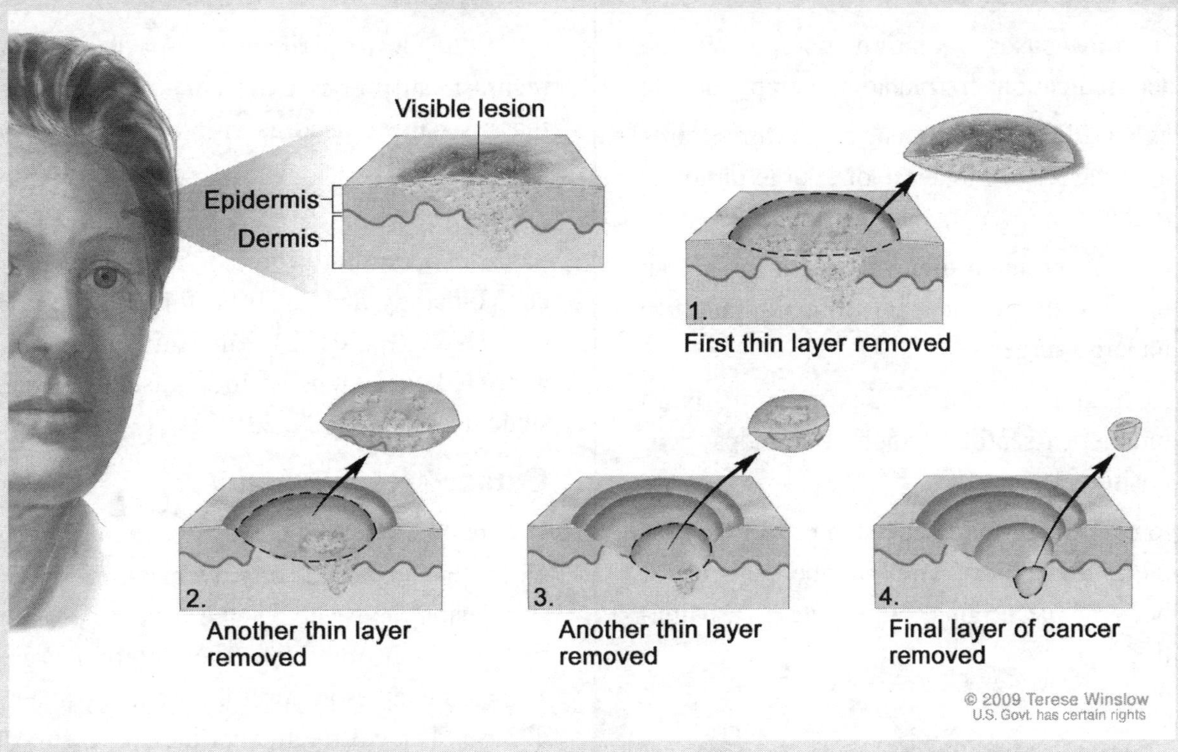

Visible lesion

Epidermis
Dermis

1.
First thin layer removed

2.
Another thin layer removed

3.
Another thin layer removed

4.
Final layer of cancer removed

© 2009 Terese Winslow
U.S. Govt. has certain rights

Drawing shows a patient with skin cancer on the face. The pullout shows a block of skin with cancer in the epidermis (outer layer of the skin) and the dermis (inner layer of the skin). A visible lesion is shown on the skin's surface. Four numbered blocks show the removal of thin layers of the skin one at a time until all of the cancer is removed.

Note. From U.S. Department of Health and Human Services, National Institutes of Health, National Cancer Institute. (2013). *Surgery, Mohs – skin cancer.* Retrieved from https://visualsonline.cancer.gov/details.cfm?imageid=8261. © 2009 Terese Winslow, U.S. Govt. has certain rights.

- Cryosurgery

- Mohs micrographic surgery

(NCCN, 2017i)

Radiation Therapy and Topical Chemotherapy

Radiation therapy and chemotherapy are reserved for extensive metastatic disease (NCCN, 2017i). Radiation therapy can also be effective for patients who are poor surgical candidates (NCCN, 2017i).

Topical and intralesional fluorouracil (5-FU) have been used to treat squamous cell cancer. The physician will usually prescribe topical applications to be used twice a day for several weeks for small, superficial tumors in patients who are unable to tolerate other treatments. Severe irrita-

tion may occur with topical 5-FU. Patients should apply the chemotherapy with a cotton-tipped applicator or latex glove to avoid contact with other skin surfaces. In general, a dressing is not necessary. If the physician requests a dressing, it should be gauze with tape rather than an adherent-type dressing. Because topical 5-FU can lead to a significant photosensitizing reaction, patients must be instructed to avoid UVR exposure.

Merkel Cell Skin Cancer

The initial therapy for Merkel cell skin cancer is surgery. Surgical approaches depending on the size and location of the lesion include a wide excision or Mohs micrographic surgery (NCCN, 2017f). A sentinel lymph node biopsy is usually performed to stage the Merkel cell skin cancer (NCCN, 2017f).

In some cases, radiation therapy may be needed. Indications for radiation therapy include

- as an adjuvant treatment to the tumor area after surgery in the case of a large tumor or if clean tumor margins were not achieved;

- to treat the main tumor if surgery is not an option if the person is unwilling or unable to undergo surgery;

- to treat the lymph nodes near the main tumor if a sentinel lymph node biopsy was positive; and

- to help treat Merkel cell skin cancer that has metastasized or recurred in other parts of the body or the original tumor site as a palliative measure.

(NCCN, 2017f)

Metastatic Merkel cell skin cancer may also be treated with chemotherapy (NCCN, 2017f). Commonly utilized agents include

- cisplatin,

- carboplatin,

- etoposide, and

- topotecan.

(NCCN, 2017f)

Other systemic therapies include immunotherapy for metastatic Merkel cell skin cancer (NCCN, 2017f). Commonly utilized agents include

- avelumab (Bavencio), and

- pembrolizumab (Keytruda).

(NCCN, 2017f)

Dermatofibrosarcoma Protuberans

The initial therapy for dermatofibrosarcoma protuberans cell skin cancer is surgery. Surgical approaches depending on the size and location of the lesion include a wide excision or Mohs micrographic surgery (NCCN, 2017b).

If the dermatofibrosarcoma protuberans recurs locally or is extremely deep, radiation therapy can be used as an adjuvant treatment (NCCN, 2017b).

For recurrent cases or in the rare case of metastatic dermatofibrosarcoma protuberans, chemotherapy has not been found to be effective (NCCN, 2017b). Imatinib mesylate is approved for extensive local disease or metastatic disease (NCCN, 2017b).

Cutaneous Lymphoma

Treatment for cutaneous lymphoma depends on the extent of skin involvement, the type of skin lesion, and whether the cancer has spread to the lymph nodes or other internal organs. Topical therapies are useful for small patches of disease. Topical treatments include corticosteroids, retinoids, or imiquimod (NCCN, 2017g).

Systemic therapies for more advanced disease are usually deferred until patients have not responded well to topical therapies. Systemic therapies include

- bortezomib (Velcade),

- denileukin diftitox (Ontak),

- pralatrexate (Folotyn),

- romidepsin (Istodax), or

- vorinostat (Zolinza).

(NCCN, 2017g)

Combination chemotherapy regimens are usually reserved for when patients have not responded well to several single-agent therapies. Options for refractory disease include alemtuzumab (Campath), liposomal doxorubicin (Doxil), and gemcitabine (Gemzar; NCCN, 2017g).

Melanoma Skin Cancers

The treatment of melanoma is based on the location, appearance, and extent of disease and the condition of the patient. Initial treatment consists of complete excision of the primary lesion with disease-free margins. The surgeon bases decisions regarding lymph node sampling on the size of the primary lesion and clinical staging information. Lymph node sampling is rarely warranted for patients with nonulcerated, thin (1 mm) melanomas. For those with primary lesions larger than 1 mm, ulcerated lesions, or lesions with poor prognostic features, sentinel lymph node biopsy is recommended (NCCN, 2017d).

Recommendations for treatment of metastatic melanoma are based on the number of metastases and the location of metastases. Solitary lesions or those of a limited number may be amenable to surgical excision that can result in significant palliation and even long-term survival. For patients with multiple metastatic sites in multiple organs, chemotherapy, radiation therapy, and immunotherapy may be utilized (NCCN, 2017d).

Surgical Excision

Complete surgical excision should be wide and should include disease-free margins. The surgeon can usually repair the defects with primary closure, although skin flaps may be necessary. The surgical margin size has been the subject of much controversy. In the past, margins of 3 to 5 mm were advocated for lesions of all sizes. Margin size has been the subject of several studies, and practice standards currently allow for smaller margins with smaller tumors, although discussion continues in this area (NCCN, 2017d). Surgical excision is the primary treatment for melanoma. The NCCN's (2017d) Principles of Surgical Margins for Wide Excision of Primary Melanoma recommend the following:

- For melanomas less than or equal to 1 mm in thickness, a 1-cm surgical margin

- For melanomas 1.01 to 2 mm in thickness, a 1- to 2-cm surgical margin

- For melanomas 2.01 to 4 mm in thickness, a 2-cm surgical margin

- For melanomas greater than 4 mm in thickness, a 2-cm surgical margin

The NCCN also notes that margins may be modified to accommodate individual anatomic or functional considerations (NCCN, 2017d).

The NCCN (2017d) recommends that practitioners discuss sentinel lymph node biopsy with all patients with a melanoma greater than 1 mm. Although the prognostic value of sentinel lymph node biopsy is clear, the potential therapeutic benefit remains uncertain. The rationale for performing an elective lymph node dissection includes improved staging, better local control, and the capacity to perform a procedure at detection of microscopic disease, which reduces the risk of procedure-related morbidity.

Complete lymph node dissection is indicated when the physician has determined that lymph nodes are positive by physical examination or by sentinel lymph node biopsy (Plitas & Ariyan, 2012). Infection, seroma, and nerve dysfunction are all potential side effects of lymphadenectomy. Lymphedema may also occur.

Chemotherapy

For patients with in situ or node-negative primary melanoma (stage IA, ≤1 mm thick or without adverse features), no standard adjuvant therapy is recommended by the NCCN (2017d). For patients with node-negative early-stage melanoma who are at risk for recurrence (stage IB or II, ≤1.0 mm thick with ulceration, or Clark level IV to V, ≥1.0 mm thick), adjuvant treatment options include a clinical trial or observation (NCCN, 2017d). For patients with node-negative stage IIB or IIC disease, adjuvant treatment options include clinical trial, interferon (IFN)-alpha, and observation (NCCN, 2017d).

For patients with stage III melanoma, adjuvant treatment options include clinical trial (https://www.cancer.gov/about-cancer/treatment/clinical-trials), IFN-alpha, and observation; for those with positive lymph nodes, consideration can be given to radiation to the nodal basin (NCCN, 2017d). For those with unresectable metastatic stage IV melanoma, considerations include clinical trial, systemic therapy, radiation therapy to palliate symptoms, and best practice supportive care (NCCN, 2017d).

Chemotherapy agents may be given as single agents or in combination and include the following:

- Dacarbazine (DTIC): DTIC has been the standard of comparison for all other antineoplastic agents used to treat malignant melanoma. In patients with soft tissue metastases, overall response rates up to 20% have been documented with single-agent DTIC (NCCN, 2017d). Side effects of DTIC vary with the dose and may include mild hematological toxicity, nausea and vomiting, photosensitivity, and liver toxicity (Wilkes & Barton-Burke, 2017).

- Temozolomide: This agent can cross the blood-brain barrier and is therefore indicated in the treatment of brain metastases. A phase II study of temozolomide noted regression of brain lesions in 20% of patients (NCCN, 2017d).

- Paclitaxel: Alone or in combination with carboplatin, paclitaxel may provide clinical benefit to some patients with metastatic melanoma; however, the duration of clinical benefit is short (2 to 7 months; NCCN, 2017d).

Radiation Therapy

Radiation therapy may be of use in the treatment of melanoma, although it is rarely the primary mode of therapy for this disease. For some patients, healthcare providers may recommend radiation used for adjuvant or palliative treatment (or as a component of multimodality treatment) for metastases to other parts of the body. Some retrospective data support the use of adjuvant radiation after lymphadenectomy in patients at high risk for local recurrence (Plitas & Ariyan, 2012). High-risk factors include more than three involved lymph nodes, lymph node with tumor deposit larger than 3 cm, extracapsular extension in the setting of palpable lymphadenopathy, and recurrent disease (NCCN, 2017d). In such cases, radiation therapy would follow surgical excision. This therapy may also be useful for palliation of symptoms of metastases, such as bone pain, obstruction, and spinal cord compression.

Immunotherapy

Immunotherapy is another systemic treatment for melanoma. These therapies include targeted therapies (monoclonal antibody may be broadly classified as either specific or nonspecific). Specific immunotherapy agents target the tumor; monoclonal antibody therapy is an example. Nonspecific immunotherapy agents (e.g., IFN) stimulate the immune system as a whole.

Interferon. Research suggests that IFN both directly affects malignant cells and indirectly affects them by augmenting and stimulating the host immune response (Bhatia & Thompson, 2012). High-dose IFN therapy is associated with significant toxicities (Bhatia & Thompson, 2012; Saranga-Perry, Ambe, Zager, & Kudchadkar, 2014).

Patient and family education, consistent assessment, early intervention, and supportive care are important strategies the nurse utilizes when involved with the care of this patient population. Patients may experience flu-like symptoms, including fever, chills, malaise, anorexia, and fatigue. Symptoms may range along a continuum from mild to life-threatening.

Myelosuppression and liver toxicity are also seen with high-dose IFN regimens.

Interleukin-2. In 1988, the FDA approved interleukin-2 (IL-2) for the treatment of metastatic melanoma. High-dose intravenous bolus IL-2 treatment resulted in overall objective response rates of approximately 12% to 21%. The therapeutic effect of IL-2 is brought about by stimulation of the immune system rather than direct cytotoxicity to melanoma cells. In the presence of IL-2, natural killer cells are activated to form lymphokine-activated killer cells, which destroy melanoma cells. IL-2 may also cause damage to cells by generating nitric oxide. High-dose IL-2 therapy may cause significant, life-threatening toxicities, including capillary leak syndrome, respiratory distress, and hypotension, necessitating intensive monitoring and administration by expert clinicians (Eriksson et al., 2014). Because of the significant toxicities of this agent, which can result in hypotension, arrhythmias, and liver and renal toxicities, IL-2 is recommended only in patients with few comorbidities and an excellent performance status. There is a 1% to 2% risk of mortality with IL-2, which highlights the importance of choosing a patient well-suited for this treatment modality (Bhatia & Thompson, 2012).

BRAF Inhibitors. Mutations in *BRAF* result in constitutive activation of downstream signaling in the mitogen-activated protein kinase (MAPK) pathway, leading to cell proliferation and the prevention of apoptosis. A recent study detected a *BRAF* somatic missense mutation in 66% of patients with malignant melanoma, 80% of whom had a single substitution of glutamic acid (E) for valine (V) in codon 600. *BRAF V600* mutations are most commonly noted in melanomas originating from sun-exposed skin sites (Saranga-Perry et al., 2014). *BRAF* mutations occur more commonly in younger patients. Accurate determination of the *BRAF* muta-

tion status in melanoma tumor samples is critical because the efficacy of targeted therapy is restricted to patients whose tumors harbor activating *BRAF* mutations (Bhatia & Thompson, 2012). Specific inhibitors of *BRAF* include vemurafenib and dabrafenib (NCCN, 2017d).

Toxicities of single-agent *BRAF* inhibitor therapy are fairly consistent among the agents. The most common toxicities of *BRAF* inhibitors include arthralgias, rash, photosensitivity, fatigue, alopecia, pyrexia, and cutaneous squamous cell carcinomas (keratoacanthoma type). Cutaneous squamous cell carcinomas occur in approximately 25% of treated patients (Saranga-Perry et al., 2014).

MEK Inhibitors. Clinical studies using single-agent *BRAF* inhibitors have shown short-term responses, which suggests that nearly all patients develop acquired resistance to *BRAF* inhibitors. In an attempt to overcome this resistance, scientists have investigated ways to inhibit the activated MAPK pathway downstream of *BRAF* (Shah & Dronca, 2014). Trametinib has been the most studied and is an oral, small-molecule, selective inhibitor of MEK1 and MEK2.

Trametinib also can cause a rash, but the rash tends to be acneiform rather than the hyperkeratotic rash of agents such as vemurafenib (Shah & Dronca, 2014). Peripheral edema and diarrhea were also more common with this agent, whereas squamous cell carcinomas were not reported. More rare but serious events included decreased ejection fraction and blurred vision secondary to serous retinopathy (Bhatia & Thompson, 2012).

CTLA-4 Blocker. Ipilimumab received FDA approval in March 2011 (Saranga-Perry et al., 2014). Ipilimumab is a monoclonal antibody that prevents downregulation of T-cell activation, thus allowing sustained immune responses to tumor antigens on malignant melanocytes (Saranga-Perry et al., 2014; Shah & Dronca,

2014). The recommended dose of ipilimumab is 10 mg/kg administered intravenously over 90 minutes every 3 weeks for four doses followed by 10 mg/kg every 12 weeks for up to 3 years (NCCN, 2017d).

C-Kit Changes. Approximately 15% to 20% of acral and mucosal melanomas have been found to express mutations in c-*KIT*, a transmembrane tyrosine kinase receptor, and may have a response to imatinib (Gleevec) and nilotinib (Tasigna).

NRAS. Mutations in *NRAS* have been found in approximately 20% of cases of malignant melanoma (Shah & Dronca, 2014). Tumors expressing *NRAS* mutations rarely coexpress *BRAF* mutations; therefore, these patients represent a distinct population that could benefit from targeted therapy. Investigational agents include trametinib (Saranga-Perry et al., 2014).

Clearly, there is more and more interest in targeted therapy of metastatic melanoma because of the early promise of ipilimumab and vemurafenib. The optimal timing and sequence of the currently available therapies, the mechanisms of resistance development, and the identification of new predictive biomarkers warrant more research. Until curative therapies are available for malignant melanomas, the NCCN recommends participation in well-designed clinical trials because these should be considered the standard of care (https://www.cancer.gov/about-cancer/treatment/clinical-trials; Bhatia & Thompson, 2012; NCCN, 2017d).

CASE STUDY 9-1

*M*rs. S. is a 70-year-old woman who presented to her primary care physician for a routine follow-up examination for essential hypertension. She has never had major surgery. She had two pregnancies and vaginal deliveries without complications. She has been treated eight times for basal cell carcinoma. On routine assessment of her blood pressure, a 4-mm, pearly, shiny lesion was noted on her nose. The center of the pearly lesion had telangiectasias.

Mrs. S. is a retired school teacher. Hobbies include gardening, fishing, and reading. She is married and enjoys spending time with her four grandchildren.

Mrs. S. is at risk for skin cancer in that she is fair, freckled, and redheaded. She experienced many sunburns in her youth and young adult years. She used "suntan lotion" years ago for protection but still suffered numerous blistering sunburns.

Mrs. S. was first diagnosed with basal cell carcinoma in 1978. The first basal cell carcinoma presented as a sore on her arm, and the physician did a shave biopsy. She frequently verbalizes frustration that she now has red skin, scars from the excisional biopsies, blotchy spots, and areas of less pigment. She states, "I'm always concerned with the look of my skin. I usually wear long-sleeved shirts and long pants whenever possible."

Because of the location of the lesion on the nose, Mrs. S. was referred for Mohs surgery. The diagnosis, confirmed by the dermatopathologist, is basal cell carcinoma. The procedure took over 6 hours because a total of five resections were needed to ensure clear margins. She followed the specific instructions she was given for postoperative care by the procedure nurse. Her recovery was uneventful, and after 3 months, the scar was barely visible.

Mrs. S. now faithfully uses sunscreen with an SPF of 30 and wears protective clothing and eyewear. She is also vigilant about these measures with her grandchildren. She realizes that these measures may offer her some benefit in reducing or delaying the development of another basal cell carcinoma. She is also aware that she will need to have continued follow-up with a dermatologist, initially every few months after skin cancer treatment ends. Then, based on her status, risk factors, and healthcare provider recommendations, visits will be yearly or more often if a suspicious lesion occurs.

Questions

1. What classic symptom of basal cell skin cancer does Mrs. S. have?

2. What risk factors for skin cancer does Mrs. S. have?

3. What follow-up will be recommended for Mrs. S.?

4. What prevention measures might benefit Mrs. S.?

Answers

1. A white, pearly-colored lesion with telangiectasia is one of the most classic presentations of basal cell skin cancer. Typically, it occurs on the face or sun-exposed areas, as is the case with Mrs. S.

2. Mrs. S. is at risk for skin cancer because she is fair, freckled, and redheaded. She has a long history of ultraviolet light exposure and sunburns. She has previously been treated for skin cancer.

3. Mrs. S. will need lifetime follow-up with a dermatologist. This will probably include a full-body examination every 3 to 6 months for 2 years, then every 6 to 12 months for 3 years, and then at least annually for life with prophylactic removal of suspicious lesions. Her risk for additional skin cancers is substantial.

4. Mrs. S. needs to be sure that she regularly uses sunscreen with an SPF of 30 or higher and wears protective clothing and eyewear.

SUMMARY

The management of patients with skin cancer provides many challenges for oncology and primary care nurses. Patients may delay seeking treatment because they fail to recognize the early signs of skin cancer. Others may have a misconception that all cancer is uniformly fatal, despite the excellent prognosis for basal cell and squamous cell skin cancer (Husein-Elahmed, Gutierrez-Salmeron, Naranjo-Sintes, & Aneiros-Cachaza, 2013). When detected early, the prognosis for malignant melanoma is also excellent.

Clearly, more efforts need to be made to prevent skin cancer. Reducing UVR exposure from both natural and artificial sources is a key prevention measure. If individuals cannot avoid direct exposure, they should wear protective clothing and eyewear, seek shade, and use sunscreen appropriately. Prevention efforts are the key to reducing the morbidity and mortality associated with skin cancer.

The skin is a readily accessible organ. Nurses should be aware of the signs and symptoms of skin cancer and when changes are noted, refer patients for further evaluation. Awareness of skin changes and the possible implications of those changes is the responsibility of all nurses, not just those who specialize in dermatology. Not all nurses are involved in physical examinations or total body skin examinations, but educating patients on the need for such an examination as part of annual physicals is a key opportunity for nurses to promote early detection and prevention of skin cancer.

When a patient has increased risk because of personal or family history, regular screening examinations by dermatologists can help decrease the morbidity and mortality associated with all skin cancer through early detection and prompt treatment of lesions. Multiple surgical options exist for the treatment of basal cell and squamous cell skin cancer. Malignant melanoma requires accurate staging and comprehensive evaluation to select the best therapy or therapies. In most cases, malignant melanoma is initially treated with surgical resection. Depending on the stage and other characteristics of the malignant melanoma, systemic therapies may be needed. The emerging use of targeted therapies offers more hope for effective treatment of melanoma. Nurses need to be aware of risk factors for skin cancer, including the importance of a patient's personal and family histories, early exposure to damaging UVR, and the signs and symptoms of skin changes. Nurses can effectively educate the public and provide support to patients and families who have a skin cancer diagnosis if they used evidence-based interventions that promote prevention and if they understand the scope of treatment options and follow-up care needed should disease occur.

EXAM QUESTIONS

CHAPTER 9
Questions 60–69

Note: Choose the one option that BEST answers each question.

60. The subtype of malignant melanoma that has a rapid radial phase, followed by a rapid vertical phase is

    a. superficial spreading melanoma.

    b. nodular melanoma.

    c. lentigo maligna melanoma.

    d. acral lentiginous melanoma.

61. The skin cancer with the highest risk of recurrence or metastasis is

    a. basal cell.

    b. malignant melanoma.

    c. Merkel cell.

    d. squamous cell.

62. Which one of the following people would have the highest risk for developing skin cancer?

    a. A 15-year-old Black student

    b. A 30-year-old Asian teacher

    c. A 70-year-old Hispanic factory worker

    d. A 75-year-old White wheat farmer

63. Most of the sun exposure that results in later development of skin cancer occurs

    a. before age 5 years.

    b. before age 10 years.

    c. before age 15 years.

    d. before age 20 years.

64. Chemical sunscreen's ability to protect against both ultraviolet A and B rays is indicated by which product label?

    a. Broad spectrum

    b. Wide spectrum

    c. SPF 30

    d. SPF 50+

65. Which of the following can reduce ultraviolet radiation exposure to the face and neck by more than 70%?

    a. Baseball cap

    b. Sunglasses and collared shirt

    c. Wide-brimmed hat

    d. Loosely woven shirt

66. Public education programs to reduce the mortality rate from malignant melanoma have demonstrated to be effective if initiated in

    a. early childhood so that children can adopt attitudes and practices that minimize ultraviolet radiation (UVR) exposure.

    b. the middle years, before individuals have had too much sun exposure and suffered irreversible effects.

    c. adulthood, to prevent the effects of cumulative skin damage from unprotected skin.

    d. older adulthood, because older adults have a greater risk for skin cancer as a result of repeated UVR exposure.

continued on next page

281

67. Which of the following has been determined to be most helpful in predicting the prognosis of malignant melanoma?

    a. Age of the patient

    b. Clark level

    c. Breslow measurement

    d. Location of the lesion

68. The treatment for most cases of nonmelanoma skin cancer is

    a. surgery.

    b. radiation.

    c. chemotherapy.

    d. immunotherapy.

69. Immunotherapy agents used in the treatment of advanced malignant melanoma include interferon-alpha and

    a. adriamycin.

    b. 5-fluorouracil.

    c. cytoxan.

    d. vemurafenib.

REFERENCES

Abbasi, N. R., Shaw, H. M., Rigel, D. S., Friedman, R. J., McCarthy, W. H., Osman I., ... Polsky D. (2004). Early diagnosis of cutaneous melanoma: Revisiting the ABCD criteria. *JAMA, 292*(22), 2771-2776. doi:10.1001/jama.292.22.2771

Aguilera, J., de Gálvez, M. V., Sánchez-Roldán, C., & Herrera-Ceballos, E. (2014). New advances in protection against solar ultraviolet radiation in textiles for summer clothing. *Photochemistry and Photobiology, 90*(5), 1199-1206. doi:10.1111/php.12292

American Cancer Society. (2016). *Cancer facts & figures for African Americans 2016-2018.* Atlanta, GA: Author.

American Cancer Society. (2017a). *Cancer facts and figures – 2017.* Atlanta, GA: Author.

American Cancer Society. (2017b). *Cancer prevention and early detection facts and figures – 2017-2018.* Atlanta, GA: Author.

Amin, M. B., Edge, S., Greene, F., Byrd, D. R., Brookland, R. K., Washington, M. K., ... Meyer, L. R. (Eds.). (2017). *AJCC cancer staging manual* (8th ed.). New York, NY: Springer.

Bhatia, S., & Thompson, J. A. (2012). Systemic therapy for metastatic melanoma in 2012: Dawn of a new era. *Journal of the National Comprehensive Cancer Network, 10*(3), 403-412.

Borger, A. L. (2013). Protect your skin today and every day. *Journal of the Dermatology Nurses' Association, 5*(2), 66-70. doi:10.1097/jdn.0b013e318288d18a

Bressac-de Paillerets, B., Vabres, P., & Thomas, L. (2016). Genetic testing for melanoma – where are we with moderate-penetrance genes? *JAMA Dermatology, 152*(4), 375-376. doi:10.1001/jamadermatol.2015.4359

Buller, D. B., Andersen, P. A., Walkosz, B. J., Scott, M. D., Beck, L., & Cutter, G. R. (2017). Effect of an intervention on observed sun protection by vacationers in a randomized controlled trial at North American resorts. *Preventive Medicine, 99,* 29-36. doi:10.1016/j.ypmed.2017.01.014

Caini, S., Boniol, M., Botteri, E., Tosti, G., Bazolli, B., Russell-Edu, W., ... Gandini, S. (2014). The risk of developing a second primary cancer in melanoma patients: A comprehensive review of the literature and meta-analysis. *Journal of Dermatological Science, 75*(1), 3-9.

Canavan, T., & Cantrell, W. (2016). Recognizing melanoma: Diagnosis and treatment options. *Nurse Practitioner, 41*(4), 24-30. doi:10.1097/01.NPR.0000481508.24736.81

Colantonio, S., Bracken, M. B., & Beecker, J. (2014). The association of indoor tanning and melanoma in adults: Systematic review and meta-analysis. *Journal of the American Academy of Dermatology, 70*(5), 847-857.

Eriksson, H., Frohm-Nilsson, M., Järås, J., Kanter-Lewensohn, L., Kjellman, P., Månsson-Brahme, E., ... Hansson, J. (2014). Prognostic factors in localized invasive primary cutaneous malignant melanoma—results of a large population-based study. *British Journal of Dermatology, 172*(1), 175-186. doi:10.1111/bjd.13171

Erovic, I., & Erovic, B. M. (2013). Merkel cell carcinoma: The past, the present, and the future. *Journal of Skin Cancer, 2013,* 929364. doi:10.1155/2013/929364

Falk, M., & Anderson, C. (2013). Influence of age, gender, educational level and self-estimation of skin type on sun exposure habits and readiness to increase sun protection. *Cancer Epidemiology, 37*(2), 127-132. doi:10.1016/j.canep.2012.12.006

Friedman, R. J., Rigel, D. S., & Kopf, A. W. (1985). Early detection of malignant melanoma: The role of physician examination and self-examination of the skin. *CA Cancer Journal of Clinicians, 35*(3), 130-151.

Griffin, L. L., Ali, F. R., & Lear, J. T. (2016). Nonmelanoma skin cancer. *Clinical Medicine, 16*(1), 62-65. doi:10.7861/clinmedicine.16-1-62

Guy, G. P., Jr, Watson, M., Richardson, L. C., & Lushniak, B. D. (2016). Reducing indoor tanning – An opportunity for melanoma prevention. *JAMA Dermatology, 152*(3), 257-259. doi:10.1001/jamadermatol.2015.3007

Ho, B. K., Reidy, K., Huerta, I., Dilley, K., Crawford, S., Hultgren, B. A., ... Robinson, J. K. (2016). Effectiveness of a multicomponent sun protection program for young children. *JAMA Pediatrics, 170*(4), 334-342. doi:10.1001/jamapediatrics.2015.4373

Hoorens, I., Vossaert, K., Pil, L., Boone, B., De Schepper, S., Ongenae, K., ... Brochez, L. (2016). Total-body examination vs lesion-directed skin cancer screening. *JAMA Dermatology, 152*(1), 27-34. doi:10.1001/jamadermatol.2015.2680

Husein-Elahmed, H., Gutierrez-Salmeron, M.-T., Naranjo-Sintes, R., & Aneiros-Cachaza, J. (2013). Factors related to delay in the diagnosis of basal cell carcinoma. *Journal of Cutaneous Medicine and Surgery, 17*(1), 27-32. doi:10.2310/7750.2012.12030

Lee, D. Y., Lau, B. J., Huynh, K. T., Flaherty, D. C., Lee, J.-H., Stern, S. L., ... O'Day, S. J. (2016). Impact of completion lymph node dissection on patients with positive sentinel lymph node biopsy in melanoma. *Journal of the American College of Surgeons, 223*(1), 9-18. doi:10.1016/j.jamcollsurg.2016.01.045

Mahon, S. M., & McLaughlin, L. (2017). Skin cancer. In C. H. Yarbro, D. Wujcik, & B. H. Gobel (Eds.), *Cancer nursing principles and practice* (8th ed., pp. 1897-1935). Burlington, MA: Jones & Bartlett Learning.

Marghoob, A. A., Usatine, R. P., & Jaimes, N. (2013). Dermoscopy for the family physician. *American Family Physician, 88*(7), 441-450.

McGrath, J. A., & Uitto, J. (2016). Anatomy and organization of human skin. In C. Griffiths, J. Barker, T. Bleiker, R. Chalmers, & D. Creamer (Eds.), *Rook's textbook of dermatology* (4 vols., 9th ed., pp. 3.1-3.54). Hoboken, NJ: Wiley Blackwell.

National Comprehensive Cancer Network. (2017a). *Basal cell skin cancer version 1.2017.* Retrieved from http://www.nccn.org

National Comprehensive Cancer Network. (2017b). *Dermatofibrosarcoma protuberans version 1.2017.* Retrieved from http://www.nccn.org

National Comprehensive Cancer Network. (2017c). *Genetic/familial high risk assessment: Breast and ovarian version 2.2017.* Retrieved from http://www.nccn.org

National Comprehensive Cancer Network. (2017d). *Melanoma version 1.2017.* Retrieved from http://www.nccn.org

National Comprehensive Cancer Network. (2017e). *Melanoma version 3.2017.* Retrieved from http://www.nccn.org

National Comprehensive Cancer Network. (2017f). *Merkel cell carcinoma version 1.2017.* Retrieved from http://www.nccn.org

National Comprehensive Cancer Network. (2017g). *Primary cutaneous B-cell lymphoma version 1.2017.* Retrieved from http://www.nccn.org

National Comprehensive Cancer Network. (2017h). *Primary cutaneous B-cell lymphoma version 2.2017.* Retrieved from http://www.nccn.org

National Comprehensive Cancer Network. (2017i). *Squamous cell skin cancer version 1.2017.* Retrieved from http://www.nccn.org

Nikolaou, V., Stratigos, A. J., & Tsao, H. (2012). Hereditary nonmelanoma skin cancer. *Seminars in Cutaneous Medicine and Surgery, 31*(4), 204-210. doi:10.1016/j.sder.2012.08.005

Norval, M., Lucas, R. M., Cullen, A. P., de Gruijl, F. R., Longstreth, J., Takizawa, Y., & van der Leun, J. C. (2016). Environmental effects of ozone depletion and its interactions with climate change: Progress report, 2015. *Photochemistry & Photobiology Science, 15*(2), 141-174. doi:10.1039/c6pp90004f

Noujaim, J., Thway, K., Fisher, C., & Jones, R. L. (2015). Dermatofibrosarcoma protuberans: From translocation to targeted therapy. *Cancer Biology & Medicine, 12*(4), 375-384. doi:10.7497/j.issn.2095-3941.2015.0067

O'Leary, R. E., Diehl, J., & Levins, P. C. (2014). Update on tanning: More risks, fewer benefits. *Journal of the American Academy of Dermatology, 70*(3), 562-568. doi:10.1016/j.jaad.2013.11.004

Plitas, G., & Ariyan, C. E. (2012). Controversies in the management of regional nodes in melanoma. *Journal of the National Comprehensive Cancer Network, 10*(3), 414-421.

Printz, C. (2012). Dermatology community applauds new FDA sunscreen regulations: Labeling requirements aim to make it easier for consumers to select a sunscreen. *Cancer, 118*(1), 1-3. doi:10.1002/cncr.27368

Rivas, M., Rojas, E., Araya, M. C., & Calaf, G. M. (2015). Ultraviolet light exposure, skin cancer risk and vitamin D production. *Oncology Letters, 10*(4), 2259-2264. doi:10.3892/ol.2015.3519

Roider, E. M., & Fisher, D. E. (2016). Red hair, light skin, and UV-independent risk for melanoma development in humans. *JAMA Dermatology, 152*(7), 751-753. doi:10.1001/jamadermatol.2016.0524

Saranga-Perry, V., Ambe, C., Zager, J. S., & Kudchadkar, R. R. (2014). Recent developments in the medical and surgical treatment of melanoma. *CA: A Cancer Journal for Clinicians, 64*(3), 171-185. doi:10.3322/caac.21224

Schub, T., & Caple C. (2016). Melanoma: Early detection through screening. In D. Pravikoff (Ed.), *CINAHL nursing guide information sheets.* Glendale, CA: Cinahl Information Systems.

Shah, D. J., & Dronca, R. S. (2014). Latest advances in chemotherapeutic, targeted, and immune approaches in the treatment of metastatic melanoma. *Mayo Clinic Proceedings, 89*(4), 504-519. doi:10.1016/j.mayocp.2014.02.002

Sokołowska-Wojdyło, M., Olek-Hrab, K., & Ruckemann-Dziurdzińska, K. (2015). Primary cutaneous lymphomas: Diagnosis and treatment. *Postępy Dermatologii I Alergologii, 32*(5), 368-383. doi:10.5114/pdia.2015.54749

Soura, E., Eliades, P. J., Shannon, K., Stratigos, A. J., & Tsao, H. (2016). Hereditary melanoma: Update on syndromes and management: Genetics of familial atypical multiple mole melanoma syndrome. *Journal of the American Academy of Dermatology, 74*(3), 395-407, quiz 408-410. doi:10.1016/j.jaad.2015.08.038

Strayer, D., & Schub, T. (2015). Melanoma: Sunscreen use. In D. Pravikoff (Ed.), *CINAHL nursing guide information sheets.* Glendale, CA: Cinahl Information Systems.

Strayer, D., & Schub, T. (2016). Melanoma: Risk factors and prevention. In D. Pravikoff (Ed.), *CINAHL nursing guide information sheets.* Glendale, CA: Cinahl Information Systems.

Strömberg, U., Peterson, S., Holmberg, E., Holmén, A., Persson, B., Sandberg, C., & Nilbert, M. (2016). Cutaneous malignant melanoma show geographic and socioeconomic disparities in stage at diagnosis and excess mortality. *Acta Oncologica, 55*(8), 993-1000. doi:10.3109/0284186X.2016.1144934

Tellez, A., Rueda, S., Conic, R. Z., Powers, K., Galdyn, I., Mesinkovska, N. A., & Gastman, B. (2016). Risk factors and outcomes of cutaneous melanoma in women less than 50 years of age. *Journal of the American Academy of Dermatology, 74*(4), 731-738. doi:10.1016/j.jaad.2015.11.014

U.S. Department of Health and Human Services. (2014). *The Surgeon General's call to action to prevent skin cancer.* Washington, DC: U.S. Department of Health and Human Services, Office of the Surgeon General.

U.S. Department of Health and Human Services. (2016). *Cancer.* Retrieved from https://www.healthypeople.gov/2020/topics-objectives/topic/cancer

U.S. Department of Health and Human Services, National Institutes of Health, National Cancer Institute. (n.d.). *SEER stat fact sheets: Melanoma of the skin.* Retrieved from http://seer.cancer.gov/statfacts/html/melan.html

U.S. Department of Health and Human Services, National Institutes of Health, National Cancer Institute. (1985). *Melanoma.* Retrieved from https://visualsonline.cancer.gov/details.cfm?imageid=9186

U.S. Department of Health and Human Services, National Institutes of Health, National Cancer Institute. (2005). *Layers of the skin.* Retrieved from https://visualsonline.cancer.gov/details.cfm?imageid=4366

U.S. Department of Health and Human Services, National Institutes of Health, National Cancer Institute. (2013). *Surgery, Mohs – skin cancer.* Retrieved from https://visualsonline.cancer.gov/details.cfm?imageid=8261

U.S. Food and Drug Administration. (2011, June 17). Revised effectiveness determination; sunscreen drug products for over-the counter human use. *Federal Register, 76*(117), 35672-35678. Retrieved from https://www.fda.gov/downloads/drugs/developmentapprovalprocess/developmentresources/over-the-counterotcdrugs/statusofotcrulemakings/ucm313542.pdf

U.S. Food and Drug Administration. (2017a). *FDA proposes new safety measures for indoor tanning devices: The facts.* Retrieved from https://www.fda.gov/ForConsumers/ConsumerUpdates/ucm350790.htm

U.S. Food and Drug Administration. (2017b). *Sunscreen and sun protection: More information about sunscreens.* Retrieved from https://www.fda.gov/Drugs/ResourcesForYou/Consumers/BuyingUsingMedicineSafely/UnderstandingOver-the-CounterMedicines/ucm239463.htm

U.S. Preventive Services Task Force. (2009). Screening for skin cancer: U.S. Preventive Services Task Force Recommendation Statement. *Annals of Internal Medicine, 150*(3), 188-193.

Watson, M., Holman, D. M., Fox, K. A., Guy, G. P., Jr., Seidenberg, A. B., Sampson, B. P., ... Lazovich, D. (2013). Preventing skin cancer through reduction of indoor tanning: Current evidence. *American Journal of Preventive Medicine, 44*(6), 682-689. doi:10.1016/j.amepre.2013.02.015

Wei-Passanese, E. X., Han, J., Lin, W., Li, T., Laden, F., & Qureshi, A. A. (2012). Geographical variation in residence and risk of multiple nonmelanoma skin cancers in US women and men. *Photochemistry and Photobiology, 88*(2), 483-489. doi:10.1111/j.1751-1097.2012.01077.x

Wikimedia. (n.d.). *Squamous cell carcinoma.* Retrieved from http://commons.wikimedia.org/wiki/File:Squamous_Cell_Carcinoma.jpg

Wikimedia. (2006). *Basal cell carcinoma.* Retrieved http://commons.wikimedia.org/wiki/File:Basal_cell_carcinoma.jpg

Wikimedia. (2014). *Diagram showing the stages of melanoma.* Retrieved from https://commons.wikimedia.org/wiki/File:Diagram_showing_the_T_stages_of_melanoma_CRUK_373.svg

Wilkes, G. M., & Barton-Burke, M. (2017). *Oncology nursing drug handbook 2017.* Burlington, MA: Jones & Bartlett Learning.

Wilson, L. D., Hinds, G. A., & Yu, J. B. (2012). Age, race, sex, stage, and incidence of cutaneous lymphoma. *Clinical Lymphoma, Myeloma & Leukemia, 12*(5), 291-296. doi:10.1016/j.clml.2012.06.010

CHAPTER 10

PSYCHOSOCIAL ISSUES

LEARNING OUTCOME

After completing this chapter, the learner will be able to discuss the psychosocial concerns that may accompany a diagnosis of cancer in women.

CHAPTER OBJECTIVES

After completing this chapter, the learner will be able to:

1. Define *distress.*

2. Describe common psychosocial responses to a diagnosis of cancer, including anxiety and depression.

3. Identify psychosocial distress at various stages of the cancer trajectory.

4. Describe the identification, nursing assessment, and management of various psychosocial problems.

5. Explain approaches and nursing interventions that promote psychosocial well-being.

INTRODUCTION

Adjusting to the many physical changes associated with cancer and its treatment is a complex process. The diagnosis of cancer and its treatment are also associated with changes in the patient's emotional state, body image, and life roles. This chapter identifies areas of concern and explores effective strategies the nurse and the healthcare team can use to support the woman with cancer, her family, and her significant others.

PSYCHOSOCIAL DISTRESS

Definitions

A diagnosis of cancer is a stressful event and is often accompanied by increasing anxiety and depression (National Comprehensive Cancer Network [NCCN], 2017c). Not only is the diagnosis period stressful, but treatment and follow-up also have potential psychological consequences (Andersen et al., 2014). By possessing knowledge of the salient psychosocial stressors that patients face at any of the stages of their cancer experience – from diagnosis, treatment, posttreatment surveillance, to survival status – nurses can better support patients and their family members (Piet, Würtzen, & Zachariae, 2012).

Psychosocial distress is commonly associated with a diagnosis of cancer (Johns et al., 2016). *Distress* is a broad term defined as an unpleasant emotional experience that might affect psychological, social, or spiritual aspects of well-being (NCCN, 2017c). Distress exists on a continuum that ranges from "normal" reactions to the diagnosis and its associated treatment to severe, disabling psychiatric problems (Andersen et al., 2014). Approximately 30% of women with cancer show significant distress at some point during the illness and its treatment (NCCN, 2017c). Everyone reacts to a cancer diagnosis differently (Fish, Ettridge, Sharplin, Hancock, & Knott,, 2014). Despite the diversity of reactions, a diagnosis of cancer has some common themes and psychosocial reactions, such as those presented in Table 10-1.

Management of distress should be a priority in cancer care (NCCN, 2017c). According to the NCCN, all individuals should be assessed for psychosocial distress and have access to competent multidisciplinary psychosocial care. Surveys have found that 20% to 47% of patients show a significant level of distress at some point during their cancer experience; however, less than 10% of distressed patients are actually identified and referred for psychosocial care (NCCN, 2017c). The NCCN has established standards of care so that all patients experiencing psychosocial distress will be accurately and routinely identified, assessed, and treated. These guidelines include recommendations for screening, triage, and initial evaluation and referral, as well as treatment guidelines for each participating profession: mental health (psychology and psychiatry), social work, palliative care, and pastoral care (NCCN, 2017c). Screening methods and assessment are the foundation for proper identification and treatment of the patient (NCCN, 2017c).

TABLE 10-1: PSYCHOSOCIAL CONCERNS ASSOCIATED WITH A CANCER DIAGNOSIS

The possible psychosocial reactions to a cancer diagnosis may include:

- Physical symptoms, including fatigue, sleep disturbances, nausea, and pain

- Body image changes, including those related to surgery, weight, skin, and hair

- Sexual dysfunction (painful intercourse, vaginal dryness, early menopause, decreased libido)

- Fear of recurrence

- Stress

- Informational needs regarding treatment

- Treatment-related anxieties

- Emotional distress (cognitive dysfunction, anxiety, depression, grief, helplessness, anger, low self-esteem)

- Persistent anxiety or intrusive, distressing thoughts about body and illness

- Marital or partner communication issues

- Concerns regarding minor children and/or aging parents

- Social isolation or difficulty communicating with friends

- Fears of vulnerability

- Difficulties completing duties associated with career or other roles

- Financial and insurance concerns

- Existential and related fears of death

Note. Adapted from Boerger-Knowles, K., & Ridley, T. (2014). Chronic cancer: Counseling the individual. *Social Work in Health Care, 53*(1), 11-30. doi:10.1080/00981389.2013.840355; Holland, J. C. (2013). Distress screening and the integration of psychosocial care into routine oncologic care. *Journal of the National Comprehensive Cancer Network, 11*(5S), 687-689. doi:10.6004/jnccn.2013.0202; National Comprehensive Cancer Network. (2016). *Distress management, version 2.2016.* Retrieved from http://www.nccn.org; U.S. Department of Health and Human Services, National Institutes of Health, National Cancer Institute. (2016a). *Psychological stress and cancer.* Retrieved from https://www.cancer.gov/about-cancer/coping/feelings/stress-fact-sheet; and U.S. Department of Health and Human Services, National Institutes of Health, National Cancer Institute. (2016b). *Support for caregivers of cancer patients.* Retrieved fromhttps://www.cancer.gov/about-cancer/coping/caregiver-support

Physiological Response

An individual's response to stress mobilizes a neuroendocrine response that is specific to the individual (Würtzen et al., 2013). The response depends on the stressor, perception of the stressor, and other variables (Garland, Tamagawa, Todd, Speca, & Carlson, 2013). Variables that can affect the response are the person's mood, coping styles, and personality, in addition to her reaction to social support (NCCN, 2017c).

Researchers have identified a wide range of stressors that can induce maladaptive psychoneuroimmune responses (Casault, Savard, Ivers, & Savard, 2015; Guo et al., 2013). These stressors move along pathways that involve the hypothalamus, the pituitary gland, and the sympathetic nervous system (NCCN, 2017c). Moreover, physiological responses differ depending on whether the stressor is acute or chronic in nature and the way in which the person copes with or adapts to the stressor (NCCN, 2017c). Physiological responses to the stress that occurs in a cancer diagnosis are not unique to women.

If a patient's exposure to the stressor becomes more long term, the physiological responses can change from being an acute response to one of habituation (O'Toole, Zachariae, Renna, Mennin, & Applebaum, 2017). For example, initial increased pulse and blood pressure rates may gradually resolve and be replaced by increased basal muscle tension (O'Toole et al., 2017). When responding to a stressor during an acute period, individuals may respond in an exaggerated way and have difficulty returning to the prestress state of relaxation (Holland, 2013). Over time, these individuals may exhibit higher blood pressures, increased sweating, and increased respiratory rates and epinephrine levels compared with nonstressed individuals (NCCN, 2017c). Also, they may develop mood changes, such as anxiety, depression, and more serious reactions (NCCN, 2017c). Because stress can have a negative effect on the body and healing, healthcare providers and patients need to make direct efforts to decrease stress. For this reason, the NCCN (2017c) has made the assessment and management of distress a priority in oncology care.

PSYCHOSOCIAL RESPONSES TO A CANCER DIAGNOSIS

Psychologically, a significant proportion of individuals will experience some degree of depression and anxiety (Holland, 2013). These symptoms may be brief adjustment reactions, which decrease as the patient receives more information about the diagnosis and treatment, or they may be present intermittently or long term throughout the cancer continuum. The diagnosis is almost always a threat to one's security and order in life (Holland, 2013).

Healthcare practitioners should address the psychological functioning of patients throughout all phases of the cancer trajectory (NCCN, 2017c). Psychosocial health impacts quality of life and treatment outcomes (Groarke, Curtis, & Kerin, 2013). Research has documented better disease status and longer survival in patients with fewer psychosocial disturbances (Sarfati, Koczwara, & Jackson, 2016).

Distress extends along a continuum ranging from common, normal feelings of vulnerability, sadness, and fear to problems that become disabilities, such as depression, anxiety, panic, social isolation, and existential and spiritual crises (Wagner, Spiegel, & Pearman, 2013). Distress affects family life, employment, and psychosocial functioning (Chambers et al., 2014). Distress can occur at any phase of the cancer trajectory; however, each phase of the trajectory is associated with specific stressors (Branstrom, Kvillemo, & Moskowitz, 2012; Chi, Demiris, Lewis, Walker, & Langer, 2016; Groh, Vyhnalek, Feddersen, Führer, & Borasio, 2013; Matthews et al., 2014; NCCN, 2017c).

Anxiety

During a stressful illness such as cancer, female patients and family members often become anxious (Johannsen et al., 2016). They may be afraid of what the future will bring or worry about the illness (Lengacher et al., 2014). These are normal reactions that may last from a few days to a few weeks (Jassim, Whitford, Hickey, & Carter, 2015; Lengacher et al., 2014). Anxiety occurs in varying degrees and may increase as the disease progresses or as treatment becomes more aggressive or more debilitating (NCCN, 2017c). As many as 44% of cancer patients (rate represents both men and women) report having some form of anxiety, and 23% report significant anxiety (Smith, Cope, Sherner, & Walker, 2014). A more intense anxiety, beyond ordinary worry, can develop over time and prevents individuals from doing things that are important to them. Symptoms of anxiety include the following (Smith et al., 2014):

- Tiring easily, yet having trouble sleeping
- Constant body tension
- Racing thoughts
- The inability to control how much time is spent worrying
- Frequent aches and pains that cannot be traced to physical illness
- Being irritable most of the time
- Trembling or shaking
- A racing heart, dry mouth, excess sweating, or shortness of breath
- An overwhelming belief that the worst will happen

For individuals who experience symptoms that also may interfere with their life, a mental health evaluation may be helpful (NCCN, 2017c). Therapy can often help, in addition to interventions such as the following (O'Sullivan & Mansour, 2015):

- Encourage the woman to talk about her fears and feelings.
- Listen carefully to what the woman is saying.
- Promote discussion of feelings and fears by performing active listening, offering support, responding to questions, and not denying or discounting feelings.
- Provide assurance that it is normal to feel sad, angry, and frustrated at times.
- Encourage regular exercise.
- Offer music therapy.
- Provide education on breathing and relaxation exercises.
- Encourage the use of prayer or other types of spiritual support, especially if the woman has found it helpful in the past.
- Provide a referral for a cancer support group.
- Provide referral to a cognitive-behavioral therapy program and local support groups.
- Suggest the use of massage or aromatherapy massage.
- Provide a referral to a psychiatrist to discuss the use of antianxiety agents or antidepressants.

(Fulcher, Kim, Smith, & Sherner, 2014; Smith et al., 2014)

Nurses can promote quality of life by assessing for anxiety and suggesting interventions (Gatto, Thomas, & Berger, 2016). Patients may be reluctant to talk with oncologists or family members about personal fears and anxiety related to a diagnosis of cancer (Smith et al., 2014).

Depression

It is normal to grieve over the changes that cancer brings to a person's life. The future is suddenly uncertain (Cohen & White, 2016). Some dreams and plans may be lost forever (Greer et al., 2012). Reactive depression commonly occurs when the diagnosis is initially made (Belgacem et al., 2013). For some, the depression lasts longer (NCCN, 2017c). The exact prevalence of depression in women with cancer is not fully understood. It may be as high as twice the incidence seen in the general population (Fulcher et al., 2014). Estimates suggest that approximately 1 in 4 individuals with cancer has clinical depression (Fulcher et al., 2014). These data represent both men and women. Clinical depression causes great distress, impairs functioning, and may make the woman with cancer less able to follow her cancer treatment plan (NCCN, 2017c). Nurses need to emphasize that, even though depression is a common reaction to a diagnosis of cancer, clinical depression can be treated (Griffin et al., 2013).

Signs of depression include the following (Fulcher et al., 2014):

- Feelings of helplessness and hopelessness

- Loss of interest in family, friends, and activities

- Loss of appetite

- Changes in energy level, such as extreme fatigue or loss of energy

- Ongoing sad or "empty" mood for most of the day

- Major weight loss (when not dieting) or weight gain

- Trouble sleeping, such as early waking, sleeping too much, or not being able to sleep

- Trouble focusing thoughts, remembering, or making decisions

- Feeling guilty or worthless

The observation or report of the presence of five or more of these symptoms nearly every day for 2 weeks or longer may indicate the need for a referral to a psychologist, psychiatric clinical nurse specialist, or social worker for professional help (NCCN, 2017c). If the symptoms are severe enough to interfere with normal activities, an evaluation for clinical depression by a qualified clinician or mental health professional is indicated (Fulcher et al., 2014). Depending on the seriousness of depression and the length of obvious symptoms, short- or long-term intervention may be indicated (NCCN, 2017c). Women and their families need to be advised that these interventions are not offered because the person is "weak," but to improve quality of life and to help them cope with their situation.

Evidence-based strategies that are effective in managing depression include the following:

- Antidepressant medication

- Cognitive-behavioral interventions or approaches

- Mindfulness-based stress reduction

- Psychoeducation and psychoeducational interventions

- Individual psychotherapy

- Peer counseling

- Relaxation therapy

- Exercise

(Fulcher et al., 2014)

Any indication of suicidal thoughts requires immediate intervention (NCCN, 2017c). The patient and family should be instructed on this point to seek immediate care. Indications of suicidal thoughts are listed in Table 10-2. Because the signs of suicidal thoughts are often vague or difficult to discern from depression, it is often necessary for the nurse to ask the patient directly whether she is having suicidal thoughts (NCCN, 2017c).

TABLE 10-2: INDICATORS OF SUICIDE IDEATION	
Behavioral Symptoms	• Giving away prized possessions
	• Talking about death/dying and dying
	• Using phrases such as "When I'm gone…" or "I'm going to kill myself"
	• Getting affairs in order
	• Saying goodbye to loved ones
	• Obtaining items needed for suicide attempt
	• Decreased social contact
	• Increasing drug and alcohol usage
	• Withdrawing from activities that were once pleasurable
	• Increasing risky behaviors
Physical Symptoms	• Scars or injuries from past suicide attempts
	• Changes in eating or sleeping habits
	• Chronic and/or terminal illness
	• Trouble breathing
	• Sweating
	• Severe restlessness
Cognitive Symptoms	• Preoccupation with death and dying
	• Belief that dying by suicide is the only way to end emotional pain
	• Confusion

Note. Adapted from Burke, T. A., Hamilton, J. L., Cohen, J. N., Stange, J. P., & Alloy, L. B. (2016). Identifying a physical indicator of suicide risk: Non-suicidal self-injury scars predict suicidal ideation and suicide attempts. *Comprehensive Psychiatry, 65,* 79-87. doi:10.1016/j.comppsych.2015.10.008; Chu, C., Klein, K. M., Buchman-Schmitt, J. M., Hom, M. A., Hagan, C. R., & Joiner, T. E. (2015). Routinized assessment of suicide risk in clinical practice: An empirically informed update. *Journal of Clinical Psychology, 71,* 1186-1200. doi:10.1002/jclp.22210; National Comprehensive Cancer Network. (2016). *Distress management, version 2.2016.* Retrieved from http://www.nccn.org; and Spokas, M., Wenzel, A., Brown, G. K., & Beck, A. T. (2012). Characteristics of individuals who make impulsive suicide attempts. *Journal of Affective Disorders, 136*(3), 1121-1125. doi:10.1016/j.jad.2011.10.034

Antidepressants may help patients (both women and men) who feel extreme sadness, hopelessness, or a lack of interest in activities (NCCN, 2017c). Medications may also be used to help patients sleep, relax, and begin to cope with the diagnosis (Eyles et al., 2015; Langford, Lee, & Miaskowski, 2012). As with any medication, it is important to discuss potential side effects and interactions that may occur with current medications and medical treatments (Heise & van Servellen, 2014). Common side effects of antidepressants and antianxiety medications include the following (Heise & van Servellen, 2014; NCCN, 2017c):

• Nausea

• Weight gain

• Sexual dysfunction

• Fatigue or insomnia

• Dry mouth

• Blurred vision

• Constipation

• Dizziness

• Mental slowing

Table 10-3 provides examples of antidepressants. Additional interventions include the following:

• Encourage the depressed woman to continue treatment until symptoms improve or to talk with the physician or advanced practice nurse prescriber about a different treatment if there is no improvement after 4 to 6 weeks.

TABLE 10-3: COMMON ANTIDEPRESSANTS

Tricyclic Antidepressants

Examples of tricyclic antidepressants include:

- Amitriptyline (Elavil)
- Clomipramine (Anafranil)
- Desipramine (Norpramin)
- Doxepin (Sinequan)
- Imipramine (Tofranil)
- Nortriptyline (Pamelor)

Selective Serotonin Reuptake Inhibitors

Examples of SSRIs include:

- Citalopram (Celexa)
- Fluoxetine (Prozac)
- Fluvoxamine (Luvox)
- Paroxetine (Paxil)

- Sertraline (Zoloft)

Monoamine Oxidase Inhibitors

Examples of MAOIs include:

- Tranylcypromine (Parnate)
- Phenelzine (Nardil)

Atypical Antidepressants

Examples of atypical antidepressants include:

- Bupropion (Wellbutrin)
- Trazodone (Desyrel)
- Nefazodone (Serzone)
- Mirtazapine (Remeron)
- Maprotiline (Ludiomil)
- Venlafaxine (Effexor)

Note. Adapted from Andersen, B. L., DeRubeis, R. J., Berman, B. S., Gruman, J., Champion, V. L., Massie, M. J., … American Society of Clinical Oncology. (2014). Screening, assessment, and care of anxiety and depressive symptoms in adults with cancer: An American Society of Clinical Oncology guideline adaptation. *Journal of Clinical Oncology, 32,* 1605-1619. doi:10.1200/JCO.2013.52.4611; Carvalho, A. F., Hyphantis, T., Sales, P. M., Soeiro-de-Souza, M. G., Macedo, D. S., Cha, D. S., … Pavlidis, N. (2014). Major depressive disorder in breast cancer: A critical systematic review of pharmacological and psychotherapeutic clinical trials. *Cancer Treatment Reviews, 40,* 349-355. doi: 10.1016/j.ctrv.2013.09.009; Li, M., Kennedy, E. B., Byrne, N., Gerin-Lajoie, C., Katz, M. R., Keshavarz, H., … Green, E. (2016). Management of depression in patients with cancer: A clinical practice guideline. *Journal of Oncology Practice, 12,* 747-756. doi:10.1200/JOP.2016.011072; Lloyd-Williams, M., Payne, S., Reeve, J., & Kolamunnage Dona, R. (2013). Antidepressant medication in patients with advanced cancer – An observational study. *QJM, 106,* 995-1001. doi:10.1093/qjmed/hct133; and National Comprehensive Cancer Network. (2017c). *Distress management, version 1.2017.* Retrieved from http://www.nccn.org

- Promote any form of physical activity, especially mild exercise such as daily walks.
- Help the woman make appointments for mental health treatment, if needed.
- Provide assistance or arrange for transportation for treatment, if needed.
- Keep in mind that caregivers and family members can also become depressed. Encourage family members to take time to get the help and support they need.

(Belgacem et al., 2013)

PSYCHOSOCIAL DISTRESS AT VARIOUS STAGES OF THE CANCER TRAJECTORY

The diagnostic period can be an extremely anxiety-provoking time for the patient (Gibbons, Groarke, & Sweeney, 2016). Depending on the clinical presentation of the cancer, a woman may or may not be surprised or unprepared for a diagnosis of cancer (Dempster, Howell, & McCorry, 2015).

With increased screening, especially for breast and colorectal cancer, many women will experience an abnormal screen that results in additional diagnostic procedures and biopsies (American Cancer Society [ACS], 2017b). An estimated 10% to 20% of breast biopsies are positive, which means that more than 2 million women annually will undergo a procedure to evaluate whether the breast change is malignant, most of which will prove to be negative (ACS, 2015). The psychosocial needs of the group of women in this phase of the cancer trajectory should not be overlooked (Siu & U.S. Preventive Services Task Force, 2016). Finding a lump or other symptom of cancer can be a frightening experience, as can an undefined or suspicious finding on a routine screening examination such as a mammogram (NCCN, 2017c). This leads to additional appointments for more radiological studies and, often, a biopsy (ACS, 2017a). Often a period of days to a week or more can separate each phase of the diagnostic process. This can be a period of great anxiety and fear for women (Kashani, Vaziri, Akbari, Jamshidifar, & Sanaei, 2014).

Patients (both men and women) who are undergoing any type of biopsy may have escalated feelings of uncertainty and anxiety because of the potential diagnosis and its implications for relationships, sexuality, ability to earn income, and ultimately, mortality (Miller et al., 2014). This may be the first significant experience a woman has with health care or surgical procedures (Miller et al., 2014). Care during this time can be very fragmented; a woman may be seen by a radiologist, surgeons, oncologists, nurses, and a myriad of technicians. Specific psychosocial care services may be very limited during this phase or the need overshadowed during the period before confirming a diagnosis (Wardle, Robb, Vernon, & Waller, 2014). Patients are encouraged to seek support from previously established sources of psychosocial support (i.e., therapists) when in the process of being diagnosed or undergoing treatment (Hoffman et al., 2012; NCCN, 2017c).

Some worries fall into what is considered normal for persons with a diagnosis of cancer, and it is not uncommon for individuals to experience one or two of the symptoms for a short time (i.e., less than 2 weeks; NCCN, 2017c). It is important for the individual to be instructed to seek professional care if anxious feelings are strong, if there are fearful thoughts, or if the individual becomes so preoccupied or overwhelmed that she cannot accomplish ordinary daily activities (McCarter et al., 2015).

Waiting for the results of a pathological diagnosis can be extremely difficult (Meijer et al., 2013). It often takes nearly a week for a final report to become available, during which time a woman often feels that her life is "on hold." Although a great many patients eventually receive the good news that their biopsy was benign, a portion of patients will receive a diagnosis of malignancy (ACS, 2015). Assisting women to find a supportive environment and supportive individual during this phase is critical, especially when the diagnosis is malignancy (NCCN, 2017c).

Stress can be increased with scheduling problems and the long waits for appointments and test results. For this reason, all efforts should be made to reduce wait times and provide continuity of care with an identified healthcare provider who can answer questions and provide guidance along each step of the way (Smith et al., 2016).

Reactions to the Diagnosis

Although most individuals fear a diagnosis of cancer, the patient's initial response when the diagnosis is confirmed and disclosed is often one of shock and disbelief (Holland, 2013). Despite the fact that patients may have been given information about risk and are undergoing screening examinations, a diagnosis of cancer is perceived as a shock for most individuals and for their families and/or significant others (NCCN, 2017c).

A cancer diagnosis at any point in a woman's life can be very stressful, very sudden, and unexpected (Carlson, Waller, & Mitchell, 2012). Without warning or choice, a woman is forced to abandon her current identified life to attend healthcare appointments and undergo tests, which usually involve unfamiliar and uncomfortable procedures (U.S. Department of Health and Human Services [HHS], 2016a). Often, a woman feels she has lost control of her life after she receives a diagnosis of malignancy (Mehta & Roth, 2015). A woman diagnosed with cancer may experience any combination of the following emotions and thoughts:

- Uncertainty

- Anger

- A feeling of lack of control

- Sadness

- Fear

- Frustration

- Guilt

- Mood swings

- Much stronger and intense feelings

- A sense of being disconnected or isolated from others

- Loneliness

- Resentment

A woman might also experience positive reactions at the time of diagnosis, including the following:

- A greater sense of resilience or strength

- Peace, or a feeling of being at ease

- A clearer idea of her priorities in life

- More appreciation for her quality of life and the people she loves

(Fulcher et al., 2014; Smith et al., 2014)

Informing women that these can be common reactions is the first step in facilitating adjustment to the diagnosis and its treatment (Jassim et al., 2015).

Denial is a common reaction (Aggarwal & Rowe, 2013). The disbelief that the diagnosis has been made is actually psychologically protective unless it persists for an extended period or impairs the patient's decision making regarding care or engagement in appropriate treatment (Perry, Metzger, & Sigal, 2015). Short-term denial can be helpful because it provides time for the woman and her family to adjust to the diagnosis (Williams, Olfson, & Galanter, 2015). Most patients work through the denial fairly quickly and have some acceptance of the fact that they have cancer by the time treatment begins (Williams et al., 2015).

Guilt is another common reaction to the diagnosis of cancer (NCCN, 2017c). Some women feel guilt related to prior use of hormone replacement therapy or birth control pills (ACS, 2015). Others feel guilty if they believe they have a hereditary predisposition for developing breast cancer and fear they have passed the susceptibility gene to a child (NCCN, 2017d). Women with cervical cancer may think prior sexual practices, which resulted in a human papillomavirus infection, caused the cancer (Kwan et al., 2011). Others with later-detected cancers may feel guilty for ignoring symptoms or failing to engage in regular screening (ACS, 2017a). Individuals with lung cancer may feel guilty because of years of tobacco usage (Dirkse, Lamont, Li, Simonič, Bebb, & Giese-Davis, 2014). Women with skin cancer may feel guilty for failing to utilize practices that reduce ultraviolet light exposure (ACS, 2017b). Others may feel guilty because they perceive themselves to be a burden to others (Hendrix et al., 2015). Acknowledging that these feelings are common and encouraging patients to discuss them can be helpful (Mehta & Roth, 2015).

Anger is another reaction that must be acknowledged and dealt with (NCCN, 2017c). Patients and families may be angry about the diagnosis or specific incidents involving healthcare providers, family stressors or friends, and sometimes they are angry with an existential power (Pan et al., 2013). Encouraging individuals to discuss their feelings of anger is often an effective tool for dealing with this emotion (NCCN, 2017c).

The diagnosis of cancer can be accompanied by a wide range of fears and concerns. Patients and families most often are initially fearful of existential concerns and mortality (NCCN, 2017c). As the reality of the diagnosis surfaces, fears may center on pain, alopecia, nausea and vomiting, surgery, unknown healthcare procedures, fatigue, managing day-to-day activities for the family, paying for the costs of treatment, and keeping a job (Mehta & Roth, 2015). There may also be fears and concerns about how to discuss the diagnosis with friends and others (Lengacher et al., 2012). Assisting the patient to identify specific fears and develop concrete strategies to manage each specific problem can be very effective in reducing stress (NCCN, 2017c).

Distress During Disease Workup and Decisions Related to Treatment

Once the diagnosis of cancer has been made, the patient, family, physicians, and nurses will begin to discuss the next steps, such as staging, required consultations, and treatment options. Most women are unprepared for the diagnosis and even less prepared for the array of medical consultants they will see and the number of treatment decisions they will have to make (Harding,

2014). Lives and work schedules are usually abruptly interrupted for the woman and those supporting her during the decision-making and treatment process (Zhu et al., 2015).

The first few days and weeks after the biopsy or primary surgical procedure typically involve more diagnostic workups, which can be a frightening and unfamiliar experience for the woman (Harding, 2014). Such workups are necessary to determine the stage of disease and other prognostic factors so that an effective treatment plan can be formulated (ACS, 2017a). This information can be technically complex (Harding, 2014). Healthcare providers often struggle to explain the details of the pathology reports using terminology that the patient is familiar with, and patients can have significant difficulty understanding the findings (Carlsson, Pettersson, Hydén, Öhlén, & Friberg, 2013; Epstein, 2010). This can lead to more anxiety and distress for the woman and those supporting her (NCCN, 2017c). Providing patients with a copy of the pathology report and explaining each term, such as *stage, grade,* and *tumor prognostic markers,* can be very helpful to some patients (ACS, 2015). Nurses need to be familiar with the components of the pathology report to reinforce education and should provide educational resources for patients to review at home (Kaltenbaugh et al., 2015).

Following presentation of the pathological findings, the next step is discussion of treatment, which can be a very overwhelming experience (NCCN, 2017c). The discussion often includes more than one treatment option, which may require the patient to make a decision that may lead to associated worry about making the "right" choice (Lamb, Green, Vincent, & Sevdalis, 2011). In some cases, few choices are available; in other cases, such as with breast cancer, there are multiple options to consider (Lamb et al., 2011). Women with breast cancer are frequently asked to decide about the type of treatment (e.g., mastectomy with or without reconstruction, or lumpectomy with radiation) and adjuvant treatment (standard or investigational; ACS, 2017a).

Essentially, the woman is being asked to make decisions about lifesaving treatments for which she usually has little knowledge and background (Lamb et al., 2011). Whereas some patients find that this decision-making process restores a sense of control, others find it very stressful (NCCN, 2017c). The ability to make informed decisions may be influenced by the patient's education level, stress level, family and social support systems, and previous experiences with the healthcare system (Légaré & Witteman, 2013). Family and friends may offer opinions, some of which are based on both negative and positive personal experiences (Livaudais, Franco, Fei, & Bickell, 2013). Nurses need to point out that there are many different types and subtypes of malignancy and treatment options, and that the experience of others will not necessarily be that of the patient. Nurses need to provide women with factual information that directly pertains to their diagnosis to facilitate decision making (Yun et al., 2011). Women need to be reminded that although a decision is needed, they should not be too hasty, because this can result in decisions that are later regretted (Mehta & Roth, 2015). Women may benefit from a second opinion with another group of specialists to ensure that treatment decisions are appropriate (Lamb et al., 2011).

Communication and patient education can be challenging because of the shock of the diagnosis. Shock and anxiety can limit the woman's ability to comprehend information (Smith et al., 2014). For this reason, it is recommended that women bring a supportive person to appointments who is also learning about the options (Mahon, 2012). The woman should also be encouraged to write down questions when they occur (Mahon, 2012). Keeping a journal or notes can be helpful in organizing questions so she can bring them up for discussion when seeing the healthcare provider (Mahon, 2012). Acceptance of the disease and its treatment comes at different rates for different individuals (NCCN, 2017c). Lack of information increases anxiety, and information can provide individuals with a sense of control (Slev et al., 2016). Striking a balance is important.

The decision for treatment lies with the patient but must be made based on information from the physician, nurse, and other resources (Yun et al., 2011). Some treatment alternatives are based on the size or location of the tumor, prognostic markers, and pre-existing or comorbid conditions (ACS, 2017a).

Psychosocial distress may also be increased during this time because women may need to deal with multiple specialists (Harding, 2014). Although these healthcare providers are ideally seen as a team, usually women must go from office to office or different departments. Fragmentation of care can be a source of additional psychosocial distress (NCCN, 2017c).

Distress During Active Treatment

After the treatment plan is determined, a woman may feel some sense of relief because there is a plan; however, new fears and concerns usually surface related to the treatment (Smith et al., 2014).

The shift toward outpatient and short-stay surgical procedures adds to the psychosocial distress for some families. If a surgical procedure was required, women may be discharged with drains and dressings, and initially have limited mobility (ACS, 2015). This means someone must be available to help with household responsibilities and the management of drains and an incision (Berg, Årestedt, &

Kjellgren, 2013). Careful assessment of the support system available to the woman is necessary for successful care (Berg et al., 2013). Often, those who are close to the woman may need help in addressing their own psychosocial concerns (Slev et al., 2016).

Following the initial adjustment to the diagnosis of cancer, as well as the comprehensive workup, the patient begins the journey of treatment (NCCN, 2017c). Treatment may include any combination of surgery, chemotherapy, radiation therapy, hormonal therapy, targeted therapy, or close follow-up, depending on the tumor type, stage at diagnosis, and other factors (Drageset, Lindstrøm, Giske, & Underlid, 2011). Treatment almost always results in a change in physical health, which also affects the psychosocial health of the patient. Side effects of these changes can be related to the actual therapy, household responsibilities, alteration in independence, financial instability, and body image alterations (NCCN, 2017c).

Depression and anxiety can increase as side effects worsen, which in turn can intensify the physical symptoms (HHS, 2016a). Depression can lead to an increase in anxiety and pain, can cause difficulty with concentration, and can result in insomnia (NCCN, 2017c). Early identification of anxiety and depression is important so interventions can be delivered (NCCN, 2017c). If depression or anxiety becomes too severe, there can be delays in treatment of the tumor, which can ultimately decrease long-term survival (Smith et al., 2014).

Reactions to Treatment Completion and Long-Term Survival

The end of treatment can be a time of mixed emotions for many women (ACS, 2016). The stress associated with the transition is often underestimated (NCCN, 2017g). There is joy in completing treatment, but there is also the fear of leaving the close monitoring of the healthcare team (ACS, 2016). Some patients experience a sense of comfort in having chemotherapy or radiation therapy that will fight the cancer (NCCN, 2017g). For some patients, when treatment is over, the sense of control over the cancer is also taken away. Talking with others who have completed treatment may help to normalize these feelings. A strong bond with caregivers may have formed during treatment (NCCN, 2017g). Once treatment is completed, the routine exposure to team members and the consistent support will now be absent (ACS, 2016; NCCN, 2017g).

Many survivors are unprepared for the lingering effects of therapy, including fatigue, cognitive dysfunction, and premature menopause (Meisel et al., 2012). Although much time is spent preparing patients for the acute toxicities of treatment (such as nausea, vomiting, fatigue, or alopecia), much less time is devoted on what to expect in the pattern of recovery and adjustment following active treatment (Alfano, Ganz, Rowland, & Hahn, 2012). Appropriately, in many cases, nurses may tell patients it takes as much time to recover as it did to complete the therapy, although little specifically is known about how this recovery takes place (NCCN, 2017g).

Throughout the diagnosis and treatment period, it is common for a woman to identify herself as a patient with cancer (ACS, 2016). Other roles, such as wife, mother, or career woman, are put on hold, and cancer becomes the main focus (Alfano et al., 2012). Although often difficult, it is important for women with cancer to learn to integrate the cancer and related treatments into their lives (NCCN, 2017g). Some patients may find strength in groups where women discuss how they have returned to "new normal" (without cancer) lives, whereas others may prefer individual counseling to help them understand the meaning of the illness and return to a normal life (Weis & Giesler, 2014). The ultimate goal is to understand the effects of the cancer on the individual and the best ways to move forward with life (NCCN, 2017g). For some, this may mean a change in career, which may pose financial hardship, whereas others may find they have a different perspective on life after having experienced a serious illness (Alfano et al., 2012).

Following the end of treatment, some women may find the possibility of a recurrence frightening and almost paralyzing (McCabe, Faithfull, Makin, & Wengstrom, 2013). For some, this fear is manifested as an increased dependence on the healthcare team (McCabe et al., 2013). Fears of recurrence are a well-documented concern among long-term survivors (Dunn et al., 2015). Acknowledging that this is a common response and can be exacerbated at follow-up visits and examinations can be helpful for some women (Mehta & Roth, 2015).

Long-term survivorship can be influenced by healthy living habits following diagnosis and treatment for cancer (ACS, 2016). Exercise has been associated with higher quality of life at least 10 years after cancer diagnosis (Ma, Rosas, & Lv, 2016) and a decrease in long-term fatigue, which is often felt following treatment for cancer (ACS, 2017a). Encouraging a healthy lifestyle may help reduce or prevent distress during this phase of the trajectory (ACS, 2016, 2017b).

Reactions to Recurrent or Advanced Disease

Although the overall prognosis for cancer may be good, especially for those who have early detection, many women will experience a recurrence of cancer or never really have a response to initial treatment, especially if their cancer was diagnosed at a later stage (ACS, 2017a). Recurrence is defined as the return of the disease after an initial course of treat-

ment with a disease-free period (Simard et al., 2013). Although recurrence does not necessarily lead to terminal illness, patients with recurrent disease are usually much more aware of the reality and potential mortality of their diagnosis (Simard et al., 2013). Often, this event occurs years or decades after the initial diagnosis (ACS, 2016). For many it is considered a failure by both the patient and the treatment team (Koch, Jansen, Brenner, & Arndt, 2013). Because recurrence is frequently associated with clinical symptoms from the cancer, including increased pain, cough, headaches, or other changes, the woman has a tangible, constant reminder that her condition is serious and perhaps life-limiting (Faller et al., 2013). This can lead to enormous stress for the patient and her family (Dunn et al., 2015).

Recurrent disease may be treated with the same, similar, or completely new treatments than the primary treatment. Women may feel overwhelmed by the treatment and their potential mortality (NCCN, 2017c). Women with recurrent cancer may have more anxiety about treatment because of previous experiences, and they may have more symptom distress, including fatigue and pain (Kim et al., 2012; NCCN, 2017a). Patients may also have anger, self-blame, and regret about prior treatment choices (Mehta & Roth, 2015). Women may be less hopeful about outcomes because the first treatment did not completely eradicate the disease (ACS, 2016).

As the disease progresses, attention to symptom and pain relief becomes paramount (NCCN, 2017a). This phase of the illness is also often accompanied by concerns related to spiritual and existential matters that should be addressed (Lim et al., 2015). There are many fears in the terminal phases of disease, including fear of the unknown, pain, suffering, abandonment, loss of control, loss of identity, loss of body image, loss of loved ones, and loss of hope (NCCN, 2017c). Acknowledgment of these fears and stressors and that they are a common reaction is often the first step in helping patients to cope with these overwhelming feelings (Mehta & Roth, 2015). Open communication with family and significant others may decrease some distress and offer an opportunity for closure for the patient and those involved in her care (Lim et al., 2015).

At many different times during treatment and recovery, women with cancer may be fearful and anxious (NCCN, 2017c, 2017f). For most people with cancer, diagnosis and recurrence cause the most anxiety and fear. Fear of treatment, doctor visits, and tests may also cause apprehension (NCCN, 2017f). Women may be afraid of uncontrolled pain, dying, or what happens after death, including what may happen to loved ones. Sometimes, despite having the symptoms, the person may deny having these feelings (NCCN, 2017f).

PSYCHOSOCIAL SEQUELAE OF PHYSICAL SYMPTOMS

Persons with a diagnosis of cancer who have physical symptoms, such as pain or fatigue, also are more likely to have emotional distress (NCCN, 2017c). In some cases, these physical symptoms can be controlled with medications; however, it may take more than one attempt to find the right drug or combination of drugs (NCCN, 2017c).

Psychological responses to cancer can be very unpredictable. Someone with cancer can feel good one day and terrible the next (NCCN, 2017c). Learning to live with uncertainty is part of learning to live with cancer, for both the patient and her significant others (O'Sullivan & Mansour, 2015). There may be times when the uncertainty and fear cause the person with cancer to seem angry, depressed, or withdrawn (NCCN, 2017c). This is normal and is a part of the process of grieving and adjusting to the diagnosis. Over time, most people are able to adjust to the new reality in their lives and move forward (NCCN, 2017c). Many patients, families, and caregivers face some degree of depression, anxiety, and fear when cancer becomes part of their lives (Emanuel, Johnson, & Taromino, 2016). These feelings are normal responses to such a life-changing experience (Emanuel et al., 2016).

Fatigue

The fatigue associated with cancer is different from the fatigue of everyday life (Mitchell et al., 2014). Everyday normal fatigue is most often a short-term problem that gets better with rest (NCCN, 2017b). Cancer-related fatigue is worse, and it causes more distress (NCCN, 2017b, 2017c). Rest does not necessarily make it go away (NCCN, 2017b). For some people, this kind of fatigue can cause even more distress than pain, nausea, vomiting, or depression (Borneman, 2016). Cancer-related fatigue can be overwhelming and greatly affects quality of life and relationships with family and friends (Borneman, 2016). Severe and persistent fatigue can impact the patient's ability to follow a treatment plan, sustain a precancer lifestyle, or maintain a schedule (NCCN, 2017b).

Cancer-related fatigue is the most common side effect of cancer and cancer treatment. Research suggests that approximately 70% to 100% of cancer patients receiving treatment experience fatigue (NCCN, 2017b). In addition, about 30% to 50% of cancer survivors have reported fatigue that lasts for months or even years after they finish treatment (NCCN, 2017b). Signs of fatigue include the following (Mitchell et al., 2014; NCCN, 2017b):

- Feelings of tiredness that are recurrent or become severe

- Feeling more tired than usual during or after an activity

- Feeling tired when it is not related to an activity

- Fatigue not getting better with rest or sleep

- Sleeping more than usual

- Feeling confused or being unable to concentrate or focus thoughts

- Complaining of complete lack of energy

- Being unable to get out of bed for more than 24 hours

- Experiencing disruptions in work, social life, or daily routine

- Feeling a lack of desire to do the things one would normally do

- Feeling negative, sad, or irritable

Cancer can cause fatigue directly, by spreading to the bone marrow and causing anemia, or indirectly, by forming toxic substances in the body that change the way normal cells function (NCCN, 2017b). Fatigue is also very common with many cancer treatments, such as chemotherapy, radiation therapy, and immunotherapy (NCCN, 2017b). Cancer treatments often kill fast-growing healthy cells, especially the red blood cells, resulting in anemia (NCCN, 2017b). Treatments can kill normal cells and cancer cells, which leads to a buildup of cell waste (Saligan et al., 2015). The body needs extra energy to clean up this waste and repair damaged tissue (Saligan et al., 2015). Fatigue may be a presenting symptom of an endocrine disorder secondary to immunotherapy, such as a thyroid or pituitary disorder (NCCN, 2017b). Immune-related endocrine disorders can occur relatively late in treatment and take months to resolve or potentially be irreversible (Mitchell et al., 2014; NCCN, 2017b). However, some can be easily corrected with prompt interventions (Linardou & Gogas, 2016).

Medications utilized in the treatment of cancer symptoms can contribute to fatigue (NCCN, 2017b). In particular, opioids and antidepressants can have fatigue as a side effect (NCCN, 2017b). A consult with a pharmacologist or palliative care specialist may be helpful to evaluate whether there is a better choice or combination of medications that will treat the symptom while minimizing fatigue (Mitchell et al., 2014).

Other factors that can worsen fatigue should be considered in an assessment of fatigue, including the following (Mitchell et al., 2014; NCCN, 2017b):

- Anemia

- Pain

- Emotional distress (including depression and anxiety)

- Sleep problems

- Medications that worsen symptoms (including antidepressants)

- Other medical problems (e.g., infection, low thyroid function, or heart, lung, liver, kidney, or nervous system disease)

- Nutrition problems

- Low level of physical activity

Fatigue can have a negative effect on quality of life and self-esteem if the woman is too tired to take part in daily household activities, employment, relationships, social events, and community activities (NCCN, 2017b). Fatigue can lead to mental fatigue and mood changes resulting in difficulty paying attention and problems with memory and clear thinking (Mitchell et al., 2014). The impact of fatigue should not be minimized (Mitchell et al., 2014). Nurses can provide support and education about fatigue (e.g., that it can be a common symptom associated with malignancy and a side effect of some treatments) and suggest evidence-based interventions to mitigate fatigue (Mitchell et al., 2014).

Managing these factors can greatly help reduce fatigue (Mitchell et al., 2014). However, fatigue is often caused by more than one problem, and the treatment of any underlying cause is very important (Mitchell et al., 2014). Nurses should educate patients that many fatigued patients will benefit from any of several non-pharmacological interventions, including cognitive-behavioral interventions, exercise, hypnosis, yoga, relaxation, support groups, distraction, and prayer (Campos, Hassan, Riechelmann, & Del Giglio, 2011; Mitchell et al., 2014).

Nurses should educate patients and families about energy conservation as an effective nonpharmacological means of managing fatigue (Mitchell et al., 2014). Energy conservation is the deliberate and planned management of one's personal energy resources to prevent their depletion; strategies include planning, delegating, setting priorities, pacing, resting, and scheduling activities that require high-energy use at times of peak energy (Greenlee et al., 2014). Balancing rest and activity during times of high fatigue allows for maintaining adequate energy to perform valued activities and reach important goals (Greenlee et al., 2014).

In addition, the following strategies can help patients cope with fatigue in their daily routines:

* Asking for help and having other people assist with tasks when possible

* Placing things that are frequently used within easy reach

* Setting up and following a structured daily routine, keeping as normal a level of activity as possible

* Balancing rest and activity

* Scheduling activities around rest periods (shorter rest periods are reported to be better than long ones)

(Greenlee et al., 2014; Mitchell et al., 2014)

Pain

Cancer pain is a significant source of distress, and most patients with cancer experience pain at some point during the trajectory of the disease (NCCN, 2017a). Accurate assessment of pain is important because the experience is unique for each individual (Paice, 2016). Management of this symptom is critical to improve quality of life and decrease distress. Unfortunately, cancer pain frequently is assessed and treated inadequately (Greco et al., 2014).

Pain is a very individual sensation and personal experience; pain is what the patient reports the pain to be (NCCN, 2017a). It is interpreted and reported by patients differently depending on multiple variables, including gender, ethnicity, and age differences (Wandner, Scipio, Hirsh, Torres, & Robinson, 2012).

Pain may be caused by the cancer, diagnostic procedures, cancer treatment (including surgery and radiation), or pre-existing conditions (NCCN, 2017a). Neuropathic pain is associated with surgical procedures, such as radical neck dissection, mastectomy, thoracotomy, nephrectomy, and limb amputation, and with chemotherapy, including vinca alkaloids, taxanes, platinum compounds, and thalidomide (NCCN, 2017a).

At the time of diagnosis, 20% to 75% of patients with cancer report having pain (NCCN, 2017a). Pain can be categorized as acute, chronic, breakthrough, or refractory, and it is caused by injury to body tissues (nociceptive) or damage to the peripheral or central nervous system (neuropathic; NCCN, 2017a).

Acute pain is typically related to diagnostic procedures and cancer treatment, and it is generally defined as lasting no longer than 3 months (NCCN, 2017a). The most common types of acute pain related to cancer treatment are postoperative pain and the pain of oral mucositis (NCCN, 2017a). The acute pain of some patients with cancer may be caused by arthralgia or myalgia, which can be side effects of some chemotherapy drugs and biological therapy (NCCN, 2017a; Paice, 2016).

Breakthrough pain is sudden, brief pain that occurs during a period when chronic pain is generally well controlled (typically with opioids; Daeninck et al., 2016). Breakthrough pain may happen when the patient is at rest or may be related to activity or a change of position (NCCN, 2017a).

Pain is considered chronic when it persists 3 months or longer (NCCN, 2017a). The most frequent cause of cancer-related chronic pain is bone metastasis (NCCN, 2017a). Chronic pain may also be a result of cancer treatment, including surgery, chemotherapy, and radiation therapy (Cuomo et al., 2014).

Intractable pain or refractory pain occurs when pain cannot be adequately controlled despite aggressive measures (Kurita et al., 2015; NCCN, 2016d). Pain can also result from adhesion formation postsurgery and based on the location of the adhesion(s) impose discomfort locally at the site or if attached to organs such as the bowel or bladder (NCCN, 2017a; Paice, 2016).

There are many ways to assess pain. Patients should be asked to describe the location, sensation, and aggravating and relieving factors (Paice, 2016). Patients can rate their pain intensity on a scale of 0 to 10, with 0 being no pain and 10 the worst pain (see Table 10-4; Paice, 2016). This rating provides a baseline that facilitates evaluation of the effectiveness of an intervention (Ham, Kang, Teng, Lee, & Im, 2015).

Excellent pain management is almost always the result of the thoughtful development of a pain management treatment plan (NCCN, 2017a). Patients and healthcare professionals should work together to develop this plan, which forms the cornerstone of effective pain

management (Paice, 2016). Pharmacological management of pain should be given on an around-the-clock basis, with additional agents for breakthrough pain (NCCN, 2017a). Table 10-5 lists suggested pharmacological agents that aid in pain management.

Nonpharmacological and complementary methods are often useful adjuncts for pain management. For some patients, a consult from the supportive or palliative care team can result in a more comprehensive plan for pain management (NCCN, 2017a). Nonpharmacological methods often utilized in the management of pain include (NCCN, 2017a)

- acupuncture;
- biofeedback, hypnosis, and guided imagery;
- distraction;
- emotional support and counseling;
- relaxation;
- massage;
- meditation;
- reflexology;
- aromatherapy; or
- music or art therapy.

IDENTIFICATION AND ASSESSMENT OF PSYCHOSOCIAL FUNCTIONING

The assessment of psychosocial distress is important because an estimated one-third to one-half of women diagnosed with breast cancer experience significant levels of distress (Holland, 2013). Predictors of increased psychosocial stress and problems in women with cancer include younger age at diagnosis and poor prior psychosocial functioning (NCCN, 2016a). Weak social support systems and lower socioeconomic status are also risk factors for significant psychosocial

TABLE 10-4: PAIN ASSESSMENT

Pain assessment should include:

- A description of the location

- A description of what the pain feels like – for instance, sharp, dull, throbbing, gnawing, burning, shooting, steady

- Intensity (using the following 0-10 pain scale)

- Duration

- Relieving factors

- Exacerbating factors

- Impact of pain on daily life

- Current medications for pain and the effectiveness of those medications

- Presence of breakthrough pain between analgesia doses

- Patient goals for pain management and satisfaction with pain relief

- Consideration of the cause, pathophysiology, and specific pain syndrome

Using a pain scale is helpful in describing the intensity of pain. To use the following pain intensity scale, the patient should be instructed to try to assign a number from 0 to 10 to the pain level. If there is no pain, use a 0. As the numbers increase, they represent worsening pain. A 10 means it is the worst pain one can imagine.

```
0     1     2     3     4     5     6     7     8     9     10
no pain                                              worst pain
```

The rating scale can be used to describe

- how bad the pain is at its worst,

- how bad the pain is most of the time,

- how bad the pain is at its least, and

- how the pain changes with treatment or medication.

Note. Adapted from:

Greco, M. T., Roberto, A., Corli, O., Deandrea, S., Bandieri, E., Cavuto, S., & Apolone, G. (2014). Quality of cancer pain management: An update of a systematic review of undertreatment of patients with cancer. *Journal of Clinical Oncology, 32*(36), 4149-4154. doi:10.1200/jco.2014.56.0383

Ham, O.-K., Kang, Y., Teng, H., Lee, Y., & Im, E.-O. (2015). Consistency and accuracy of multiple pain scales measured in cancer patients from multiple ethnic groups. *Cancer Nursing, 38*(4), 305-311. doi:10.1097/NCC.0000000000000179

National Comprehensive Cancer Network. (2017a). *Adult cancer pain, version 2.2017.* Retrieved from http://www.nccn.org

distress (Ahmad, Fergus, & McCarthy, 2015; Evans et al., 2016). Nurse should be aware of individuals who might be at higher risk for psychosocial distress (Zhang et al., 2015).

Psychosocial Providers

Psychosocial services should be provided by oncology caregivers as part of total medi-cal care (NCCN, 2016a). This responsibility initially rests with oncologists and oncology nurses (Sheldon, Harris, & Arcieri, 2012). Often, referrals to specialists in psycho-oncology are indicated (Mehta & Roth, 2015). Table 10-6 provides an overview of healthcare providers who contribute to promoting psychosocial health in oncology patients and their families.

continued on page 310

TABLE 10-5: PHARMACOLOGICAL MANAGEMENT OF PAIN (1 OF 2)

For management of mild-to-moderate pain

Nonopioids (no prescription is needed)

- Acetaminophen (Tylenol)
- Nonsteroidal anti-inflammatory drugs, such as aspirin and ibuprofen

For management of moderate-to-severe pain

Opioids (a prescription is required) – may be combined with nonopioids

- Morphine
- Fentanyl
- Hydromorphone
- Hydrocodone
- Oxycodone
- Codeine

For management of breakthrough pain

Rapid-onset opioids (prescription is required)

- Fast-acting oral morphine
- Fentanyl
- A short-acting opioid, which relieves breakthrough pain quickly and is often used with a long-acting opioid for chronic pain

For management of tingling and burning pain

Antidepressants (prescription is required)

- Amitriptyline (Elavil)
- Nortriptyline (Pamelor)
- Duloxetine (Cymbalta)
- Venlafaxine (Effexor)

Anticonvulsants (prescription is required)

- Carbamazepine (Tegretol)
- Gabapentin (Neurontin)
- Phenytoin (Dilantin)
- Pregabalin (Lyrica)
- Clonazepam (Klonopin)

TABLE 10-5: PHARMACOLOGICAL MANAGEMENT OF PAIN (2 OF 2)

For management of pain caused by swelling or pressure

Steroids (prescription is required)

- Prednisone

- Dexamethasone

Note. Adapted from:

Greco, M. T., Roberto, A., Corli, O., Deandrea, S., Bandieri, E., Cavuto, S., & Apolone, G. (2014). Quality of cancer pain management: An update of a systematic review of undertreatment of patients with cancer. *Journal of Clinical Oncology, 32*(36), 4149-4154. doi:10.1200/jco.2014.56.0383

National Comprehensive Cancer Network. (2017a). *Adult cancer pain, version 2.2017.* Retrieved from http://www.nccn.org

TABLE 10-6: ONCOLOGY TEAM MEMBERS WHO CONTRIBUTE TO PSYCHOSOCIAL CARE (1 OF 2)

- **Medical oncologist:** The oncologist directs care related to chemotherapy and targeted therapy. The oncologist may take responsibility for referrals for psychosocial care. Often the oncologist will prescribe pharmacological agents to help manage psychological problems and other symptoms that cause psychosocial distress.

- **Nurse:** Oncology nurses provide ongoing assessment, and they deliver and coordinate care and psychosocial support for patients undergoing active treatment, patients with stable disease or in remission, and long-term survivors. They may recommend interventions to facilitate psychosocial adjustment, facilitate referrals, and collaborate with other members of the oncology team. They typically work with medical oncologists, radiation oncologists, surgeons, and plastic surgeons. Nurses offer the patient and family a holistic approach to care, provide education on the disease process and self-care issues, and may administer chemotherapy according to the medical oncologist's prescription. Advanced practice nurses work in all areas of oncology, providing ongoing care to patients with a variety of cancer diagnoses.

- **Radiation oncologist:** The radiation oncologist plans all treatment with radiation therapy.

- **Radiation oncology technologist:** The radiation oncology technologist delivers the radiation dose as prescribed by the radiation oncologist. The technologist sees the patient on a daily basis and assesses for complications and tolerance of therapy.

- **Surgical oncologist:** The surgeon provides surgical care, including removal of the tumor, and often assists with the placement of implanted ports and other infusion devices.

- **Plastic surgeon:** The plastic surgeon provides all plastic and reconstructive surgery and services.

- **Pharmacist:** Pharmacists fill prescriptions, dispense drugs, and are also a great source of information. They educate healthcare professionals and patients about the expected effects and side effects of pharmacological agents.

- **Dietician:** Dieticians work with patients who are having difficulty eating and help other patients to establish appropriate dietary programs. They can help long-term survivors develop healthy habits and promote good nutrition for healing and recovery.

- **Social worker:** Oncology social workers can have diverse job responsibilities that may include helping individuals to find support groups, dealing directly with financial issues, providing guidance for how to deal with workplace issues, and assisting with paperwork, such as advance directives or living wills. They also provide direct support through counseling and by finding ways to assist with transportation to office visits, nutritional supplements, wigs, or prosthetics.

TABLE 10-6: ONCOLOGY TEAM MEMBERS WHO CONTRIBUTE TO PSYCHOSOCIAL CARE (2 OF 2)

- **Psychologist:** Psychologists can help patients and families by talking with them and identifying specific psychosocial problems. They can help develop a concrete plan for how to deal with any identified psychosocial problems.

- **Psychiatrist:** Psychiatrists can be particularly helpful with patients and families who have underlying mental illness concerns that may have existed prior to the diagnosis of cancer or have been exacerbated by the diagnosis and treatment. They can provide supportive therapy and prescribe medications for these disorders.

- **Patient educator:** Many institutions and medical practices have nurses who serve as patient educators. Their primary responsibility is to provide individual and group education on cancer and its treatment. They often work in information centers and help patients select other appropriate materials, such as videos, pamphlets, Internet sites, and other educational tools. They may offer regular classes on cancer-related topics. They often provide individualized education and facilitate support groups.

- **Prosthetics fitter:** Prosthetics fitters are certified and trained to assist with fitting bras and other prosthetics for women undergoing breast surgery, such as mastectomy, lumpectomy, and reconstruction. They provide extensive psychosocial support and assist women with adapting to the body image changes associated with breast surgery.

- **Enterostomal therapist:** Enterostomal therapists are nurses with specialized training in managing ostomies. They often provide extensive psychosocial and psychosexual care to patients and their partners to assist them in managing an ostomy.

- **Genetics counselor:** Families with a hereditary susceptibility for developing cancer should be referred to genetics counselors, nurses with specialized genetic education, or advanced practice nurses who are credentialed in genetics to explore the risks and benefits of genetic testing for their particular families.

- **Home care nurse:** Some patients may need assistance with healthcare needs at home, including wound care or infusion services. While in the home setting, home care nurses often identify psychosocial issues and can either manage these issues or refer the patient to other members of the healthcare team.

- **Occupational therapist:** Occupational therapists can help patients regain, develop, or relearn skills needed for independent living. Many breast cancer patients with lymphedema utilize the services of these professionals.

- **Physical therapist:** Physical therapists often work with occupational therapists to help patients learn exercises and instruct on ways to regain strength and mobility. They may also help with lymphedema services.

- **Nurse navigator:** Navigators serve as a point of contact for patients and families. They are readily available to answer questions, assist with care coordination, and follow patients from diagnosis through survivorship. They can assist the patient move through a continuum of care to obtain the appropriate services based on the various stages of treatment and recovery. They ensure that patients receive services that improve their quality of life and adjustment to the diagnosis of cancer.

- **Hospice workers:** Hospice workers provide care to the patient and family in the terminal phase of the illness. This includes a team of nurses, aides, volunteers, and other members.

- **Chaplain:** Chaplains assist patients and families with the spiritual aspects of their care. They may pray with the patient, discuss existential concerns, and provide supportive counseling. They may be based in the institution, or patients may know them from their own religious institutions.

Note. Adapted from National Comprehensive Cancer Network. (2017c). *Distress management, version 1.2017.* Retrieved from http://www.nccn.org

Younger Women

A diagnosis of cancer in women younger than 40 years can be particularly challenging and puts these women at increased risk for psychosocial distress (Mehta & Roth, 2015). If the diagnosis is made during pregnancy or shortly after delivery, a woman must not only confront the diagnosis but also manage the demands of a young family and infant (Keyser, Staat, Fausett, & Shields, 2012). The threat of early menopause, or infertility, is also associated with increased psychological distress (ACS, 2015). Additionally, younger women are challenged by trying to juggle work and early career development as many are trying to establish themselves (Raque-Bogdan et al., 2015). Protection of fertility is a significant concern that cannot be underestimated (Waimey, Smith, Confino, Jeruss, & Pavone, 2015). Supporting partners, friends, and children will ultimately build a better support system for the patient (Chou, Stewart, Wild, & Bloom, 2012).

Lesbian, Gay, Bisexual, and Transgender Individuals

Studies have found that lesbian, gay, bisexual, and transgender (LGBT) women get less routine health care than other women, including colon, breast, and cervical cancer screening tests (Landry, 2017; Quinn et al., 2015). Many LGBT women have poor or no health insurance because many health insurance policies do not cover unmarried partners, which makes it more difficult for many lesbians and bisexual women to obtain quality health care (Quinn et al., 2015). Many LGBT women do not tell their healthcare providers about their sexual orientation because they do not want discrimination to affect the quality of health care they receive, making it more difficult to have a comfortable relationship with a healthcare provider (Quinn et al., 2015; Unger, 2014). Fear of having a negative experience with a healthcare provider can lead some women to delay or avoid medical care, especially routine care including cancer screening early detection tests, which can lead to cancer being diagnosed at a later stage, when it is more difficult to treat (Quinn et al., 2015). Many LGBT people want to retain their identity and remain "out" throughout the cancer trajectory; these patients need care services that will support their full identity without stigma, bias, or discrimination (Burkhalter et al., 2016).

Elderly Women

In the United States, cancer is a disease of aging (ACS, 2017a). The average 65-year-old patient has an anticipated life expectancy of 20 years, and clinicians should take this into account when making cancer screening and management decisions (NCCN, 2017e). However, older persons with a diagnosis of cancer can present with wide variations in health status and comorbidities, and treatment in older persons needs to include a careful evaluation of comorbidities, physical function, polypharmacy, and other issues that could potentially impact a patient's ability to undergo chemotherapy and other treatments without excessive risk (Karuturi, VanderWalde, & Muss, 2016). Standard chemotherapy regimens are just as effective in older patients as they are in the younger population, and they can substantially prolong life expectancy when used in the appropriate patients (NCCN, 2017e). Elderly women with a diagnosis of cancer may benefit from an evaluation and consultation with a geriatrician to assist with balancing cancer treatment with comorbidities (NCCN, 2017e).

Prior Psychosocial Functioning

It is beneficial to assess the patient's psychosocial history (Sarfati et al., 2016). The diagnosis and treatment of cancer are stressful and could potentially exacerbate pre-existing conditions that have been under control (Grassi,

Caruso, Hammelef, Nanni, & Riba, 2014). For instance, a patient with a longstanding history of clinical depression may find that the diagnosis of cancer increases the depression, and she may require more intensive interventions (NCCN, 2017c). Assessment and understanding of past effective coping strategies may provide insight into how to manage the multiple stressors that accompany a diagnosis of cancer (NCCN, 2017c).

Assessment of Family Support

Supporting the patient also means supporting the family (Belgacem et al., 2013). It is helpful to assess the needs of the family at the time of diagnosis (Matsuda, Yamaoka, Tango, Matsuda, & Nishimoto, 2014). Issues such as intimacy and sexuality, femininity, role changes, childcare needs, and ways to talk to a partner or children about the diagnosis are areas that require assessment and, frequently, intervention (Fiszer, Dolbeault, Sultan, & Brédart, 2014).

Family and friends also play a critical role in a patient's decisions regarding treatment (Zhu et al., 2015). As part of the initial assessment, it is important for the healthcare team to determine whether the patient has any preconceived beliefs or ideas from family members or friends (Laidsaar-Powell, Butow, Bu, Fisher, & Juraskova, 2016). This will present an opportunity for the healthcare team to dispel any misconceptions regarding the patient's diagnosis, offer an estimate of the baseline information the woman and her family have about the diagnosis and its treatment, and provide appropriate resources to better understand the diagnosis and treatment options (Wittenberg, Goldsmith, Ferrell, & Ragan, 2016).

Caring for an individual with cancer can be very stressful. In addition to normal daily tasks, such as preparing meals, cleaning up, and running errands, caregivers can become intri-cately involved with the cancer treatment team (Hendrix, Landerman, & Abernethy, 2013). This may include talking to the healthcare team, dealing with the insurance company, giving medicines, and helping to decide whether a treatment is working (Chambers et al., 2014). Many caregivers fail to meet their own needs, including not getting enough sleep and exercise, eating poorly, and neglecting personal health needs (Porter et al., 2011). Caregivers should not feel guilty or selfish for taking time for themselves so they will have the energy needed to provide care. Some caregivers will need time off from work and may need to take unpaid time off under the Family and Medical Leave Act (Chi et al., 2016).

The diagnosis of cancer in mothers with children living at home is disruptive to the routines in the home, and especially to the accessibility and availability of mothers to children (Strickland, Wells, & Porr, 2015). Ultimately, this often results in negative effects on overall tension in the home and marriage (Watson et al., 2016).

Cancer brings change to any family, whether it is a young couple, a couple with children, an older couple, a single person, a widowed person, or an individual living in a nontraditional relationship (Campbell-Enns & Woodgate, 2016). Healthcare providers need to assess the impact of the diagnosis and its subsequent change in each specific situation (Sheldon et al., 2012). This includes an assessment of finances (including whether the patient can work during treatment), living arrangements (so there is someone available to assist the patient), and how daily activities will be managed (this can be especially important in families with children; Fenn et al., 2014). A clear and thorough assessment may help identify potential problems so that interventions can be delivered early (Fiszer et al., 2014).

Assessment Instruments

The NCCN (2017c) recommends using the Distress Thermometer to assess for psychosocial distress. The Distress Thermometer is an evidence-based screening tool (score of 0 to 10) accompanied by a problem list (NCCN, 2017c). The problem list asks patients about practical problems that cause distress (e.g., child care, housing, transportation, or insurance), family problems (e.g., dealing with children or partner), emotional problems (e.g., depression, fears, nervousness, sadness, worry, or loss of interest in usual activities), spiritual or religious concerns, and physical problems (e.g., breathing problems, constipation, fatigue, or fever). Patients can complete the form while in a waiting room, and those who have a score of 4 or more (moderate or severe distress) should be evaluated further by a nurse or physician. NCCN (2017c) recommends regular evaluation of distress. The American College of Surgeons Commission on Cancer developed an accreditation standard, implemented in 2015, that requires the psychosocial domain to be a component of routine care; this component includes use of the Distress Thermometer to document the regular assessment of distress in all oncology patients (Watson et al., 2016). A score of 4 or more may alert the nurse or physician to perform a more in-depth assessment and possibly the need for specific referrals to mental health professionals (NCCN, 2017c). Repeated use of the tool helps the practitioner to evaluate improvements and discover new problems with distress (NCCN, 2017c).

The NCCN (2017a) recommends that all patients be screened for pain at each contact. Evidence-based scales for assessment of pain include scoring of 0 (no pain) to 10 (worst pain imaginable) or a series of faces that show increasing grimaces in which the patient points to the face that represents her pain. The NCCN (2017a) also recommends that pain be assessed to describe the qualities of the pain, the effectiveness of pain-management interventions, and the satisfaction with pain-management strategies.

Fatigue can also be assessed with a similar scale of 0 representing no fatigue and 10 representing the worst fatigue possible (NCCN, 2017b). The NCCN (2017b) recommends using this scale on a regular basis for assessment. Those patients who score a 4 or higher should have a more extensive evaluation to try to determine the underlying cause and to implement interventions to reduce fatigue (NCCN, 2017b).

INTERVENTIONS TO PROMOTE PSYCHOSOCIAL WELL-BEING

Communication in Families With Children

Parents with children can experience particular psychosocial challenges with a diagnosis of cancer (Sheldon et al., 2012). It is important to discuss the cancer diagnosis with children in developmentally appropriate ways (Rashi, Wittman, Tsimicalis, & Loiselle, 2015). Young children may believe a parent's illness is a result of their behaviors and that they are being punished (Krattenmacher et al., 2012). Children may also have questions about how an individual contracts cancer or whether they can "catch" cancer, or they may be curious about why mom is losing her hair (Krattenmacher et al., 2012). It is important to create an environment where children are able to ask questions and receive age-appropriate answers (Ernst, Beierlein, et al., 2013). In many communities, there are support groups that target the psychological needs of young children, teenagers, and partners (Sheldon et al., 2012).

Families with childrearing concerns or children with concerns often benefit from services that are tailored to these needs (Bultmann et al., 2014). Mutual disclosure of fears, anxieties, and hopes between mothers, significant others, and children appears to have benefits for both the woman and her family (Asbury, Lalayiannis & Walshe, 2014). Teenage children can have particular challenges and difficulty accepting and adjusting to the diagnosis of cancer in a mother (Krattenmacher et al., 2013). Verbalizing their feelings and concerns with their parents, significant others, and perhaps another trusted adult may be very helpful (Krattenmacher et al., 2013).

Children and teens should be encouraged to go to school, complete homework, and continue to participate in extracurricular activities and sports (Ernst, Götze, et al., 2013). Parents may need to rely on the assistance of others from time to time to enable children to continue to participate in these activities (Ernst, Götze, et al., 2013). If a woman is unable to attend an activity with a child, she should make every effort to discuss the activity when the child comes home (Bultmann et al., 2014). It may be possible to videotape a sports event or other activity to enable the parent to share in the activity with the child at a later point. Helpful interventions include preparing the children for what is going to happen in the immediate future and what the more distant future holds (Bultmann et al., 2014).

For some, relationships are strengthened by the challenges imposed by cancer and its treatment (Rashi et al., 2015). Open communication with children and honest, age-appropriate answers to emotionally laden questions, including questions about death, are important. Parents may need coaching and assistance with these issues (Sheldon et al., 2012). Open communication helps the parents to understand the child's worries and thoughts, and can lead to increased understanding (Bultmann et al., 2014). Support should provide concrete, child-appropriate, and child-oriented strategies (Bultmann et al., 2014; see Table 10-7).

Family Relationships and Support

Relationships are tested and challenged throughout the diagnosis, treatment, and survival of cancer (Sheldon et al., 2012). Relationships that are already fraught with conflict may experience an exacerbation of problems with the diagnosis (Belgacem et al., 2013). Even caring, committed relationships will be stressed by the diagnosis (NCCN, 2017c). Emotional distance may surface because of the inability to discuss feelings about grief, loss, change, and potential loss; because of significant changes in body image or a sense of loss of femininity; and because partners may want to protect a woman from other distressing situations or information (Venetis, Magsamen-Conrad, Checton, & Greene, 2014). Women without a partner, supportive friends, or family may have significant distress because of a lack of support (Kroenke et al., 2013).

Strategies that might be helpful with families include the following (Kroenke et al., 2013, Traa, De Vries, Bodenmann, & Den Oudsten, 2015; Venetis et al., 2014):

- Clarify the diagnosis, treatment options, and side effects. Take time to ensure that the patient understands each issue.

- Explain that cancer has a trajectory and that needs change over time. Assure the patient and the family that support is available during each phase as needed.

- Remind the patient that psychosocial health is just as important as physical health. Explain that this is why psychosocial assessment is conducted regularly.

- Acknowledge that distress is common, note expected times that distress might increase,

TABLE 10-7: TALKING WITH CHILDREN ABOUT CANCER AND ITS TREATMENT

Use these specific suggestions for talking with children about cancer and its treatment.

- Always be honest and open with children. If they ask a difficult question, think first and then reply in an honest manner. Try to phrase the response so that it is as nonthreatening as possible.

- Assure children that they will be cared for, no matter what happens during or as a result of the cancer treatment.

- Remind children that cancer is not universally fatal, and try to give them concrete examples of people they know and can relate to who are long-term survivors of the disease with good prognostic factors.

- Assure children of all ages that there is nothing they could have said, done, or thought that led to the development of the cancer.

- Assure children that it is quite normal to be angry, scared, or sad when someone they love is diagnosed with cancer.

- Assure children that even though the appearance of the person with cancer (e.g., mother, grandmother, sister, brother, aunt, family friend, teacher, babysitter) may change during treatment, cancer is not contagious and they cannot "catch" it.

- It is sometimes helpful for children to participate in a support group with other children so they realize they are not the only family experiencing a diagnosis of cancer.

- Help children to understand how and to what extent they should discuss with others what is happening in their family.

- Inform children that others may be reluctant to talk with them or, conversely, seem like they are overly kind and generous. Tell them this is a normal reaction because they might not be sure what to do or they may be really sad about the diagnosis as well.

- Be honest that home routines will probably be disrupted and that they may need to assume some extra responsibilities for a period of time and possibly permanently.

- Remind children that even if a parent cannot attend a sports event or other activity, it does not mean that the parent is not interested. Remind children that it usually saddens parents as well when they have to miss those types of events. Try to have someone else attend the event if the parent cannot be present.

- Remind children that they are still expected to keep up with their schoolwork and to participate in extracurricular activities. The diagnosis is not an excuse to not study.

Note. Adapted from:

Asbury, N., Lalayiannis, L., & Walshe, A. (2014). How do I tell the children? Women's experiences of sharing information about breast cancer diagnosis and treatment. *European Journal of Oncology Nursing, 18,* 564-570. doi:10.1016/j.ejon.2014.07.003

Bultmann, J. C., Beierlein, V., Romer, G., Möller, B., Koch, U., & Bergelt, C. (2014). Parental cancer: Health-related quality of life and current psychosocial support needs of cancer survivors and their children. *International Journal of Cancer, 135,* 2668-2677. doi:10.1002/ijc.28905

Rashi, C., Wittman, T., Tsimicalis, A., & Loiselle, C. G. (2015). Balancing Illness and parental demands: Coping with cancer while raising minor children. *Oncology Nursing Forum, 42*(4), 337-344. doi:10.1188/15.ONF.337-344

and explain that the patient needs to communicate feelings of distress in addition to the healthcare provider assessing for distress.

- Suggest concrete recommendations for coping with distress, including journaling, speaking with a trained counselor (psychologist, nurse, psychiatric nurse clinical specialist, chaplain, social worker, mental health counselor, etc.), and joining a support group.

- Coordinate resources and make referrals as indicated.

- Manage symptoms promptly.

- Assess the effectiveness of interventions.

Financial, Employment, and Legal Concerns

All women, regardless of their socioeconomic situation, may eventually have financial, employment, and legal issues that are related to the diagnosis of cancer (NCCN, 2017c). Addressing these issues often improves quality of life for these women (NCCN, 2017c). The costs associated with cancer treatment can be staggering (Zafar & Abernethy, 2013). In addition to healthcare costs for surgery, chemotherapy, and radiotherapy, there are many hidden costs (Zafar & Abernethy, 2013). These include copayments, transportation costs when going to treatment, parking costs at treatment, time away from work for the patient and perhaps a significant other, increased childcare costs, and other nonreimbursable charges (Kale & Carroll, 2016). Unemployment or time away from work can result in an inability to meet regular living expenses (Kale & Carroll, 2016). These costs can quickly deplete savings. In many cases, agencies and social service resources can assist families with these needs, and patients are often unaware of these resources (Kircher et al., 2016). Ongoing assessment in this area is essential, with prompt referral when problems become evident (Ehmke et al., 2015). Table 10-8 lists some resources that patients may or may not be aware of related to meeting the costs of cancer care.

Some women face multiple issues in the workplace, whereas others do not (Ehmke et al., 2015). Some women benefit from coaching and anticipatory preparation of what to expect when returning to work (Yin et al., 2017). Coworkers may not know how to approach a person who is newly diagnosed or returning to work after an absence (Robinson, Kocum, Loughlin, Bryson, & Dimoff, 2015). Employers may be unsure of how much a patient can or cannot do (Yin et al., 2017). They may not be aware of lingering fatigue, even after treatment is complete. Women with cancer need to anticipate what problems may occur and be prepared to address these issues (Yin et al., 2017).

Survivorship

Long-term survivors continue to need support as they move forward with their lives (ACS, 2016). Although there is a tendency to assume that individuals will not have psychosocial concerns when they are disease-free, this is not necessarily the case (De Moor et al., 2013). Table 10-9 provides interventions that are helpful with this population.

Beginning in 2015, the American College of Surgeons set a standard in its accreditation program requiring that cancer survivors receive a care plan that outlines their treatment and follow-up plan (Stricker & O'Brien, 2014). This was a consensus-based recommendation to facilitate coordination of cancer care between specialists and primary care providers (Mayer, 2014).

End-of-Life Care

Some women will present with metastatic disease, and unfortunately for some, despite treatment the disease continues to progress. These women eventually will be faced with decisions about whether to decline or discontinue treatment. For women to make decisions,

continued on page 319

TABLE 10-8: TIPS AND RESOURCES FOR MANAGING FINANCIAL CONCERNS (1 OF 2)

Instruct the patient to keep records of the following:

- Medical bills from all healthcare providers

- Claims filed

- Reimbursements (payments from insurance companies) received and explanations of benefits

- Dates, names, and outcomes of contacts made with insurers and others

- Nonreimbursed or outstanding medical and related costs

- Meals and lodging expenses

- Travel to appointments (including gas and parking)

- Admissions, clinic visits, laboratory work, diagnostic tests, procedures, and treatments

- Drugs given and prescriptions filled

Instruct the patient on legislation for insurance coverage and employment:

- *Consolidated Omnibus Budget and Reconciliation Act of 1986 (COBRA)* – COBRA gives people the right to temporarily continue health insurance coverage at the employer's group rates, but these rates are usually much higher than those paid when employed. This coverage is available when coverage is lost as a result of certain "qualifying events," such as stopping work, reducing work hours, divorce or legal separation, the covered person becoming entitled to Medicare, a dependent child no longer considered to be dependent according to the terms of the plan, or the death of the employee. COBRA allows people to continue coverage of their group medical insurance for a certain period, depending on the qualifying event.

- *Health Insurance Portability and Accountability Act of 1996 (HIPAA)* – HIPAA allows a person who has had health insurance for at least 12 months with no long loss of coverage (usually more than 63 days) to change jobs and be guaranteed other coverage with a new employer that also offers group insurance. In this situation there may be no waiting period, and the pre-existing condition exclusion may be reduced or not applied. The act also guarantees the availability of group insurance coverage for employers of small businesses of 2 to 50 people.

- *Family and Medical Leave Act of 1993 (FMLA)* – This act requires employers (with at least 50 employees) to provide up to 12 weeks of unpaid, job-protected leave to eligible employees for certain family and medical reasons. Employees are eligible if they have worked for a covered employer for at least 1,250 hours in the previous 12 months. For the period of the FMLA leave, the employer must maintain the employee's medical insurance coverage under the company group health plan.

- *Americans with Disabilities Act of 1990 (ADA)* – This act offers protection against discrimination in the workplace to anyone who has, or has had, certain disabilities, including any diagnosis of cancer. It requires private employers that employ 15 or more people, labor unions, employment agencies, and government agencies to treat employees equally, including the benefits offered to them, without regard to their disabling condition or medical history.

TABLE 10-8: TIPS AND RESOURCES FOR MANAGING FINANCIAL CONCERNS (2 OF 2)

- *Genetic Information Nondiscrimination Act of 2008 (GINA)* – GINA prohibits discrimination in health coverage and employment on the basis of genetic information. GINA, together with already existing nondiscrimination provisions of HIPAA, generally prohibits health insurers or health plan administrators from requesting or requiring the genetic information of an individual or the individual's family members and the use of such information for decisions regarding coverage, rates, or pre-existing conditions. The law also prohibits most employers from using genetic information for hiring, firing, or promotion decisions and for any decisions regarding terms of employment.

Note. Adapted from Ehmke, N., Hunnicutt, B., Hoverman, B., Irvin, J., Biddle, H., & Heral, L. (2015). Seasons: A prospective study assessing the physical, psychosocial, spiritual and financial needs of breast and prostate cancer patients. *Oncology Nursing Forum, 42*(2), E146. doi:10.1200/jco.2016.34.3_suppl.4; Fenn, K. M., Evans, S. B., McCorkle, R., DiGiovanna, M. P., Pusztai, L., Sanft, T., … Abu-Khalaf, M. (2014). Impact of financial burden of cancer on survivors' quality of life. *Journal of Oncology Practice, 10*(5), 332-338. doi:10.1200/JOP.2013.001322; Kale, H. P., & Carroll, N. V. (2016). Self reported financial burden of cancer care and its effect on physical and mental health related quality of life among US cancer survivors. *Cancer, 122*(8), 283-289. doi:10.1002/cncr.29808; Kircher, S. M., Rutsohn, J. P., Yarber, J. L., Guevara, Y., Lyleroehr, M. M., Nimeiri, H. S., … De Souza, J. A. (2016). Predictors of financial burden at a comprehensive cancer center. *Journal of Clinical Oncology, 34*(Suppl. 15), e18263. doi:10.1200/JCO.2016.34.15_suppl.e18263; and Zafar, S. Y., & Abernethy, A. P. (2013). Financial toxicity, part I: A new name for a growing problem. *Oncology (Williston Park), 27*(2), 80-81, 149.

TABLE 10-9: STRATEGIES AND INTERVENTIONS TO PREPARE INDIVIDUALS AND FAMILIES FOR LONG-TERM SURVIVORSHIP (1 OF 2)

- Give patients and families a range of what to expect in terms of prognosis, physical symptoms, emotional concerns, and sexual function.

- Women, especially those who have premature menopause because of the effects of treatment, may have problems with hot flashes and vaginal dryness. They should receive education and support that there are measures to help reduce these symptoms, which can be very bothersome.

- Remind patients and significant others that they may never return to their previous "normal" state and that they may need to establish a new normalcy.

- Specifically define those symptoms that should promptly be reported for further evaluation.

- Describe the anticipated follow-up schedule for office visits, scans, and laboratory work with the rationale for the proposed schedule.

- Teach the patient what tertiary prevention is and what specific tertiary screening measures will be recommended, for example, colon screening, bone densitometry, and gynecological screening.

- Develop a wellness plan that includes a specific strategy for exercise, diet, skin cancer prevention, and smoking cessation when indicated.

- Remind the patient and significant others that it is not uncommon to have "trigger" events that are upsetting, such as the anniversary of diagnosis, the diagnosis of a loved one with a similar disease, or feelings of anxiety surrounding things that remind the patient of unpleasant aspects of treatment.

- Discuss that recovery from treatment is a gradual process, and it may take a year or more before full energy returns.

TABLE 10-9: STRATEGIES AND INTERVENTIONS TO PREPARE INDIVIDUALS AND FAMILIES FOR LONG-TERM SURVIVORSHIP (2 OF 2)

- Assess the patient for mental health problems, and manage depression and anxiety early. Remind patients and family members that even though treatment is completed, it may not be uncommon to have some feelings of depression, anxiety, or being overwhelmed. Discuss that there are treatments to manage these symptoms and that it is important for the patient to bring these concerns to the attention of the healthcare provider to explore the best means to improve this aspect of quality of life.

- Acknowledge that the patient may need to adopt a new self-image in terms of energy, physical appearance, and sexuality. For many, staying active and exploring new hobbies and activities help in developing a new self-image.

- Assess for financial problems. Survivors may be paying for the costs of care long after care is complete. If appropriate, remind the patient that social services may be able to assist.

- Discuss the need to try to maintain healthcare coverage. If the patient or family member carrying the insurance wants to switch jobs or make a change that would lead to a lapse in coverage, it is important to consider a referral to social services.

- The patient and significant others may want to consider becoming advocates for others with cancer or volunteering in some other way. Some individuals find benefit from continued participation in a support group.

- Some patients experience problems or changes with memory or concentration after chemotherapy. Instruct patients to let their healthcare providers know about this because certain strategies can decrease the impact of these problems.

- If the family history suggests hereditary susceptibility for developing the cancer and the family has not yet received counseling about genetic testing, it is appropriate for the family to consider learning more about genetic risk.

- When meeting new people or dating, it can be awkward to know when to disclose that the individual has completed cancer treatment. Talking with other survivors can help make survivors more comfortable with how and when to disclose. Survivors should be instructed that they may need to plan what to disclose, how to disclose it, and how much to disclose.

- Recognize that there may still be challenges in the workplace related to follow-up care, energy levels, or other health-related concerns. Encourage the patient to discuss these needs with her employer. If problems cannot be resolved, a referral to social services, local cancer advocacy services, or legal resources may be indicated.

- Provide patients with a long-term survivorship care plan that includes treatment received, pathology information, and schedule for follow-up; the patient can share this plan with other healthcare providers.

Note. Adapted from American Cancer Society. (2016). *Cancer treatment and survivorship facts and figures – 2016-2017.* Atlanta, GA: Author; Mayer, D. K. (2014). Survivorship care plans: Necessary but not sufficient? *Clinical Journal of Oncology Nursing, 18*(Suppl.), 7-8. doi:10.1188/14.CJON.S1.7-8; National Comprehensive Cancer Network. (2017g). *Survivorship, version 1.2017.* Retrieved from http://www.nccn.org; and Stricker, C. T., & O'Brien, M. (2014). Implementing the Commission on Cancer standards for survivorship care plans. *Clinical Journal of Oncology Nursing, 18*(Suppl.), 15-22. doi:10.1188/14.CJON.S1.15-22

they need information about whether the proposed treatment is likely to be curative or palliative (NCCN, 2017f). This requires that the oncology team be honest with the patient and provide enough accurate information so the patient can make an informed decision. When the decision is made, the patient and family need to feel that they are being supported in their decision and that all efforts will be made to maximize quality of life.

The NCCN (2017f) recommends that when life expectancy is estimated to be months to weeks, patients need education about the incurability of the disease. Ideally, hospice and palliative care are discussed at this time so that patients can focus on symptom management and comfort (NCCN, 2017f). Based on availability and the actual diagnosis, palliative care can be incorporated into care even earlier to maximize quality of life and to assist the woman with decision making and treatment options. Although it is difficult to initiate this discussion, it allows patients the opportunity to discontinue treatment, which might have serious side effects and improve quality of life for what time is left. It is important for nurses to communicate to patients and the family that transitioning care to palliative or hospice care does not mean they are giving up or abandoning the patient, but trying to maximize quality for the time left (NCCN, 2017f).

Interventions to Promote Adjustment Across the Trajectory

Hope is important throughout the cancer trajectory. Hope may change throughout the trajectory, but there is a need to continually help patients and families identify hope in different situations (Oosterveld-Vlug, Francke, Pasman, & Onwuteaka-Philipsen, 2016). For the newly diagnosed, it might mean hope that the therapy will be effective (Ripamonti, Miccinesi, Pessi, Di Pede, & Ferrari, 2016). For the sur-

vivor, it might mean hope for a new normalcy in her life (NCCN, 2017g). For someone in the terminal phases, it might mean hope for achieving good symptom management, finishing projects, or experiencing closure with loved ones (Goldzweig, Baider, Andritsch, Pfeffer, & Rottenberg, 2016; Solano, da Silva, Soares, Ashmawi, & Vieira, 2016).

Quality of life is also improved when problems are assessed and confronted directly (Jassim et al., 2015). Nurses need to assess for symptoms that can be managed, such as pain, psychosocial distress, and fatigue. Nurses can assist by explaining to the patient why the symptom is occurring, whether it is a common symptom, and what concrete steps will be taken to decrease the negative effects of the symptoms. When symptoms are decreased, quality of life usually is improved (Jassim et al., 2105).

Support groups often help individuals to realize that many others share similar feelings and concerns (Kaltenbaugh et al., 2015). Support groups can also be an excellent and efficient way to provide patient education. Before referring a patient to a support group, it is important to understand the focus of the support group, the ground rules, the biases of the facilitator, and how acute emotional distress is managed. If the group's philosophy is congruent with the value system of the patient and the healthcare team, participation may be a useful adjunct to improve quality of life (Johns et al., 2016). Cancer support groups are often another place where people can receive education. Support groups can have a number of purposes and approaches. They offer a way for people with cancer and their significant others to come together and talk with others facing similar problems and challenges (Oosterveld-Vlug et al., 2016). Support groups often have an educational component in addition to sharing. When the educational component is delivered by a professional with expertise on the subject, it can be a very effective means to communicate about and educate persons on issues related to cancer treatment (Kroenke et al., 2013).

A referral to a cancer information or resource center can also be a therapeutic strategy (ACS, 2017a). An information center is usually staffed by a registered nurse who provides education and support. Resource centers often distribute brochures, videos, educational models, wigs, head coverings, and temporary prostheses, all of which help facilitate psychosocial adjustment. Nurses can often provide guidance on Internet searches and answer specific questions. The continuity of the same nurses in all service settings (e.g., chemotherapy, surgery, and radiotherapy) can be very helpful, providing continuity and consistency, and decreasing the sense of fragmentation in care. Many institutions now offer such services, and healthcare providers should encourage and refer patients to utilize such services where available (ACS, 2017a; Zimmermann-Schlegel, Hartmann, Sklenarova, Herzog, & Haun, 2017).

Barriers to Providing Comprehensive Psychosocial Care

Several barriers can prevent women from receiving adequate psychosocial care (Stricker & O'Brien, 2014; Zimmermann-Schlegel et al., 2017). Care has gradually shifted from inpatient to outpatient settings. Outpatient clinics may lack a full complement of specialists in psychosocial care (Zebrack & Kayser, 2016). Furthermore, mental health services are often limited in insurance coverage, and many women lack the financial means to afford such specialty care (Zebrack et al., 2016). Busy clinical settings also discourage women from discussing psychosocial concerns because they may have stigmas attached or be perceived as unnecessary extras (Lawrence, McLoone, Wakefield, & Cohn, 2016). Table 10-10 provides an overview of the barriers to

assessing and promoting psychosocial care. When such barriers are identified in a care setting, the nurse must take direct action to address and remove the barriers (Cohen & White, 2016; Recklitis & Syrjala, 2017).

CASE STUDY

*M*s. W. is a 33-year-old mother of a girl aged 9 years and a boy aged 11 years. She is recently divorced. Ms. W. and her ex-husband have an amicable arrangement, and although she has physical custody of the children, the couple shares legal custody with regularly scheduled visitation. Ms. W. has not dated since the divorce. Although she receives modest child support, and her children have health insurance from her ex-husband, finances are tight and she currently has no health insurance. Self-employed, she has a small in-home childcare service.

During a self-breast examination in the shower, Ms. W. detected a small lump in her left breast. She sought care in a local clinic that serves uninsured and underinsured women. The advanced practice registered nurse who examined Ms. W. immediately referred her to the local breast center for an evaluation, which included a mammogram, confirming a possible malignancy. The lump was determined to be malignant following an ultrasound-guided needle biopsy. Ms. W. was referred to a social worker, who assisted her with completing paperwork for Medicaid assistance and referred her to the affiliated oncology center for care.

On her first visit to the oncology center the nurse performed an initial assessment that included a distress screening. Her score on the 0 to 10 scale (10 being the most severe) was an 8. The oncology nurse inquired in more detail about Ms. W.'s level of distress based on the screening results. Ms. W. revealed she was worried about losing her in-home daycare busi-

TABLE 10-10: BARRIERS TO USE OF PSYCHOSOCIAL SERVICES

- Poor access to services because of the lack of readily available healthcare providers in some settings

- Healthcare providers lack awareness of community services

- Reluctance of the patient and family to ask for help

- Lack of communication between the healthcare provider and patient about psychosocial concerns

- Poor health insurance coverage for psychosocial services

- Expense of cancer care is staggering; many lack financial resources for additional services such as psychosocial care

- Fragmentation among care providers

- Lack of a systematic method to routinely assess for psychosocial distress

- Lack of time to assess for difficulties

- Lack of widespread adoption of clinical practice guidelines to promote psychosocial functioning

- Perception that psychosocial services are secondary to treatment needs

- General misconceptions about mental health care and psychological functioning

- Inadequate quality assurance and accountability for psychosocial care

Note. Adapted from:Ahmad, S., Fergus, K., & McCarthy, M. (2015). Psychosocial issues experienced by young women with breast cancer. *Current Opinion in Supportive and Palliative Care, 9*(3), 271-278. doi:10.1097/spc.0000000000000162; Campbell Enns, H. J., & Woodgate, R. L. (2016). The psychosocial experiences of women with breast cancer across the lifespan: A systematic review. *Psychooncology,* doi:10.1002/pon.4281; Légaré, F., & Witteman, H. O. (2013). Shared decision making: examining key elements and barriers to adoption into routine clinical practice. *Health Affairs, 32*(2), 276-284. doi:10.1377/hlthaff.2012.1078; Recklitis, C. J., & Syrjala, K. L. (2017). Provision of integrated psychosocial services for cancer survivors post-treatment. *The Lancet Oncology, 18*(1), e39-e50. doi:10.1016/S1470-2045(16)30659-3; Sheldon, L. K., Harris, D., & Arcieri, C. (2012). Psychosocial concerns in cancer care: The role of the oncology nurse. *Clinical Journal of Oncology Nursing, 16*(3), 316-319. doi:10.1188/12.cjon.316-319; and Zebrack, B., Kayser, K., Padgett, L., Sundstrom, L., Jobin, C., Nelson, K., & Fineberg, I. C. (2016). Institutional capacity to provide psychosocial oncology support services: A report from the Association of Oncology Social Work. *Cancer, 122*(12), 1937-1945.

ness, paying bills if she could not work because she had minimal savings, and taking care of her children. She was also worried about her prognosis because her paternal aunt and grandmother had both died of breast cancer before the age of 50 years.

The nurse and breast surgeon met with Ms. W. as a team. They explained that more information was needed to determine the extent of her disease. She was sent for a breast magnetic resonance imaging, which did not show any additional malignancy in her left breast or her right breast. A chest computed tomography scan was performed, and the results confirmed there was no evidence of disease outside of the left breast.

Ms. W. was referred for genetic testing based on her presentation and family history. There was a lengthy discussion of her treatment options with the breast surgeon, medical oncologist, and radiation therapist. Her tumor was 4 cm. Neoadjuvant chemotherapy was recommended. The breast surgeon felt she was a candidate for a lumpectomy with radiation therapy if the tumor shrunk with the chemotherapy and if the genetic testing was negative. If the genetic testing showed hereditary predisposition, bilateral mastectomies would be recommended.

After the lengthy discussion with her physician and team, Ms. W. showed signs of being overwhelmed, which included periods of anxi-

ety, as well as a focus on covering her medical bills, an inability to concentrate and make decisions, and moments of being teary, especially when anticipating care of her children during her treatment. The nurse encouraged her to verbalize her concerns and fears. The social worker was consulted to determine whether programs were available to assist with the finances. Ms. W. was eligible for assistance with paying her rent and utilities, enabling her to keep her apartment if she could not work during treatment.

Ms. W. was very worried about chemotherapy and side effects. The nurses caring for her provided her with information about what to expect in terms of side effects and reassured her that although she might experience side effects associated with the chemotherapy, most could be managed or minimized. Because of her high distress level, Ms. W. was also referred to the cancer center's psychologist for counseling and support. The nursing team helped her to obtain a wig. They referred her to the ACS Look Good Feel Better program, where she learned about managing her image, tying scarves, and applying makeup as her physical appearance changed secondary to treatment.

Ms. W. was referred to a support group with younger women who have a diagnosis of breast cancer who had successfully completed treatment and were willing to share how they had adjusted to their situation.

Following her first round of chemotherapy she learned she had a CHEK2 mutation. Bilateral mastectomies were recommended by the treatment team when chemotherapy was completed.

When Ms. W. received confirmation of the CHEK2 mutation, another distress assessment was performed by the nurse and her distress score was a 5. Ms. W. continued to express feelings of being overwhelmed. She voiced concern about her self-image and fears about recon-

structive surgery. Ms. W. verbalized that she understood having a double mastectomy is a life-saving strategy based on her diagnosis and genetic testing, but that she was concerned about the added limitations having this surgery will place on her and how to discuss all of this with her children.

Ms. W. reconnected with the program psychologist who offered her behavioral interventions that included relaxation methods to use when she felt overwhelmed. The psychologist determined Ms. W. was depressed and a recommendation was made to her physician to prescribe antidepressant therapy, which she started immediately. Ms. W. also engaged a music therapist at the cancer center, who helped her compile a program of music therapy. The program was designed to distract and relax Ms. W. when needed.

At the end of the fourth chemotherapy treatment, Ms. W. reported her distress score at a level 3. The behavioral interventions and antidepressant therapy continued. The music therapist continued music therapy sessions with Ms. W. The nurse continued to assess for side effects and provide support and education. Seven months after her initial diagnosis, Ms. W. had completed chemotherapy, surgery for bilateral mastectomies, and began a regular schedule of surveillance. Ms. W. had not yet made a decision about reconstructive surgery. A distress assessment will continue to be performed and monitored by the nursing staff at each follow-up visit.

Questions

1. In addition to referrals for support groups, what other suggestions could the nurse recommend based on Ms. W.'s current marital situation and family support as a way to obtain additional assistance during treatment?

2. With bilateral mastectomy surgery in a young woman, what concerns does Ms. W. have and how can the nurse assist and support her?

3. How does the nurse guide Ms. W. in talking to her children about what is going on?

Answers

1. The nurse can encourage Ms. W. to reach out to her local support system, including her spiritual community, but specifically to her parents and two close friends who live in the area. If the marital situation can include involvement of her ex-husband, having him increase assistance with child-related issues may be an option for her to explore. The nurse informs her she can bring family/friends to visits and to chemotherapy treatments, not only to provide support but to listen and advocate for her throughout the process. Asking for help is an important part of getting through the entire course of treatment and the required aftercare. Continuing visits with the psychologist is encouraged.

2. Ms. W. was hoping her genetic testing was negative. Because the results were positive, she is upset at hearing about the oncology team's recommended treatment plan, which includes a double mastectomy. She shares her fears about reconstructive surgery with the nurse. The nurse can assist Ms. W. by working together with the treatment team to reinforce her options, review the steps to be taken if she chooses reconstruction, and encourage her to stay connected with her psychologist to assist her through the decision-making process. Listening and validating the feelings of fear, loss, anger, and grief that Ms. W. expresses about her situation are key. Explaining that these are expected and normal responses to the situation can help Ms. W. to not feel alone. Encouraging Ms. W. to focus on her health and well-being during treatment by connecting to survivor groups and engaging in stress-reduction practices, along with maintaining a connection to her care team, can help direct interventions. The

nurse should also reassess Ms. W.'s distress level during follow-up visits.

3. Talking to one's children about a potentially terminal diagnosis is very difficult. If the situation with the children's father is stable and amicable, Ms. W. may want to include him, and as parents they can reassure the children that they will be cared for, safe, and have minimal disruption in their routine. If it is not feasible to include her ex-husband in these discussions, she may wish to involve a close family member whom the children have a relationship with and trust. It is important that the nurse encourages Ms. W. to seek and obtain guidance about how to approach the topic, is clear, concise, and responds to the children's questions in a simple, honest, and developmentally appropriate way. A social worker or the psychologist can help Ms. W. script and prepare for discussions with her children. Too much detail can be overwhelming and frightening for children. Love, reassurance, and anticipatory guidance about what to expect can help the children cope with their fears about their mother's diagnosis and treatment.

SUMMARY

Psychosocial issues are important components of the cancer experience for a woman; they can have a large impact on her outlook and ability to cope with her diagnosis and treatment. In addition to a diagnosis of cancer, women experience other stressors, including varying degrees of family and social support, baseline problems with psychosocial functioning, other comorbidities, and stressors related to age. Psychosocial distress, including anxiety and depression, may occur at any point of the cancer trajectory. Nurses perform a key role in the provision of comprehensive care that includes psychosocial assessment, includes implementation of evidence-based interventions that promote adjustment to a diagnosis of cancer and associated treatment, and ultimately results in improved quality of life.

EXAM QUESTIONS

CHAPTER 10
Questions 70–82

Note: Choose the one option that BEST answers each question.

70. Distress is a term defined as

    a. an unpleasant emotional experience that may affect psychological, social, or spiritual aspects of well-being.

    b. an abnormal reaction to the diagnosis of cancer.

    c. an unpleasant emotional experience that is associated with chronic mental illness.

    d. an abnormal reaction that is more common in younger and elderly women.

71. Anxiety occurs in varying degrees and may

    a. increase as the disease progresses.

    b. cause constipation.

    c. not affect the patient.

    d. trigger delusions.

72. Therapy for anxiety can often help patients. In addition to therapy, interventions the nurse can engage in include

    a. promoting discussion of feelings and fears by performing active listening, offering support, responding to questions, and not denying or discounting feelings.

    b. disregarding the patient's anxious feelings.

    c. ignoring patient complaints that she feels afraid and nervous.

    d. not acknowledging fears voiced by the patient during a visit.

73. For women with cancer, clinical depression may cause

    a. anemia and elevated potassium levels.

    b. aggressive behavior and hallucinations.

    c. sweating and enhanced awareness.

    d. great distress and impaired functioning.

74. In general, women with five or more depressive symptoms may need professional help when their symptoms have lasted

    a. 4 days.

    b. 2 weeks.

    c. 4 months.

    d. 2 years.

75. Women undergoing a biopsy may be having their first significant experience with health care or surgical procedures and may experience escalated feelings of

    a. euphoria.

    b. uncertainty and anxiety.

    c. denial.

    d. paranoia and anger.

76. Although most individuals fear a diagnosis of cancer, the patient's initial response when the diagnosis is confirmed and disclosed is often

    a. relief.

    b. reassurance.

    c. shock and disbelief.

    d. associated with a fear of death.

325

continued on next page

77. Cancer-related fatigue is the most common side effect of cancer and cancer treatment. Severe and persistent fatigue can

   a. impact the patient's ability to follow a treatment plan.

   b. fade quickly once treatment is over.

   c. dissipate and enable the patient to have periods of very high energy.

   d. indicate a lack of response to treatment.

78. Excellent pain management is almost always the result of a thoughtful pain management treatment plan. Pharmacological and nonpharmacological approaches to pain control should be considered. If a pharmacological approach to pain management is instituted,

   a. medication should be given on an around-the-clock basis, with additional agents for breakthrough pain.

   b. medication should be offered only when patients request it.

   c. medication should be offered only on a strict schedule, with additional agents for breakthrough pain.

   d. medication should be avoided to prevent addiction.

79. The American College of Surgeons Commission on Cancer's accreditation requirement that the psychosocial domain to be a component of routine care includes use of the

   a. Vanderbilt Assessment Scale.

   b. Braden scale.

   c. Distress Thermometer.

   d. Rankin scale.

80. The assessment instrument that can be used to evaluate distress, pain, and fatigue is the

   a. Brief Symptom Inventory.

   b. Karnofsky scale.

   c. 0 to 10 scale.

   d. Facing Cancer Symptoms Scale.

81. When the nurse is asked by a woman how to begin discussing her cancer diagnosis with her school-age children, it is important for the nurse to recommend

   a. telling the children, "There's nothing to worry about."

   b. allowing the children to miss school whenever they feel upset about their mother's cancer diagnosis.

   c. a rule that the children are not allowed to discuss their mother's cancer diagnosis with other people such as teachers because cancer is a family secret.

   d. open communication with children, and honest, age-appropriate answers to emotionally laden questions, including questions about death.

82. For someone in the *terminal phases* of the cancer trajectory, the word *hope* can mean many things, but as discussed in this chapter, it might refer specifically to hope

   a. for achieving good symptom management, finishing projects, or experiencing closure with loved ones.

   b. for a spontaneous remission.

   c. for a new cure.

   d. that lost hair grows back a different color after chemotherapy.

REFERENCES

Aggarwal, N., & Rowe, M. (2013). Denial in patient–physician communication among patients with cancer. In *New challenges in communication with cancer patients* (pp. 15-25). New York, NY: Springer US.

Ahmad, S., Fergus, K., & McCarthy, M. (2015). Psychosocial issues experienced by young women with breast cancer. *Current Opinion in Supportive and Palliative Care, 9*(3), 271-278. doi:10.1097/spc.0000000000000162

Alfano, C. M., Ganz, P. A., Rowland, J. H., & Hahn, E. E. (2012). Cancer survivorship and cancer rehabilitation: Revitalizing the link. *Journal of Clinical Oncology, 30*(9), 904-906. doi: 10.1200/JCO.2011.37.1674

American Cancer Society. (2015). *Breast cancer facts and figures – 2015-2016.* Atlanta, GA: Author.

American Cancer Society. (2016). *Cancer treatment and survivorship facts and figures – 2016-2017.* Atlanta, GA: Author.

American Cancer Society. (2017a). *Cancer facts and figures – 2017* Atlanta, GA: American Cancer Society.

American Cancer Society. (2017b). *Cancer prevention and early detection facts and figures – 2017-2018.* Atlanta, GA: Author.

Andersen, B. L., DeRubeis, R. J., Berman, B. S., Gruman, J., Champion, V. L., Massie, M. J., ... American Society of Clinical Oncology. (2014). Screening, assessment, and care of anxiety and depressive symptoms in adults with cancer: An American Society of Clinical Oncology guideline adaptation. *Journal of Clinical Oncology, 32,* 1605-1619. doi:10.1200/JCO.2013.52.4611

Asbury, N., Lalayiannis, L., & Walshe, A. (2014). How do I tell the children? Women's experiences of sharing information about breast cancer diagnosis and treatment. *European Journal of Oncology Nursing, 18,* 564-570. doi:10.1016/j.ejon.2014.07.003

Belgacem, B., Auclair, C., Fedor, M.-C., Brugnon, D., Blanquet, M., Tournilhac, O., & Gerbaud, L. (2013). A caregiver educational program improves quality of life and burden for cancer patients and their caregivers: A randomised clinical trial. *European Journal of Oncology Nursing, 17*(6), 870-876. doi:10.1016/j.ejon.2013.04.006

Berg, K., Årestedt, K., & Kjellgren, K. (2013). Postoperative recovery from the perspective of day surgery patients: A phenomenographic study. *International Journal of Nursing Studies, 50*(12), 1630-1638. doi:10.1016/j.ijnurstu.2013.05.002

Boerger-Knowles, K., & Ridley, T. (2014). Chronic cancer: Counseling the individual. *Social Work in Health Care, 53*(1), 11-30. doi:10.1080/00981389.2013.840355

Borneman, T. (2016). Fatigue. In C. Dahlin, P. Coyle, & B. Ferrell (Eds.), *Advanced Practice Palliative Nursing* (pp. 279-288). New York, NY: Oxford University Press.

Branstrom, R., Kvillemo, P., & Moskowitz, J. T. (2012). A randomized study of the effects of mindfulness training on psychological well-being and symptoms of stress in patients treated for cancer at 6-month follow-up. *International Journal of Behavioral Medicine, 19,* 535-542. doi:10.1007/s12529-011-9192-3

Bultmann, J. C., Beierlein, V., Romer, G., Möller, B., Koch, U., & Bergelt, C. (2014). Parental cancer: Health-related quality of life and current psychosocial support needs of cancer survivors and their children. *International Journal of Cancer, 135,* 2668-2677. doi:10.1002/ijc.28905

Burke, T. A., Hamilton, J. L., Cohen, J. N., Stange, J. P., & Alloy, L. B. (2016). Identifying a physical indicator of suicide risk: Non-suicidal self-injury scars predict suicidal ideation and suicide attempts. *Comprehensive Psychiatry, 65,* 79-87. doi:10.1016/j.comppsych.2015.10.008

Burkhalter, J. E., Margolies, L., Sigurdsson, H. O., Walland, J., Radix, A., Rice, D., ... Maingi, S. (2016). The National LGBT Cancer Action Plan: A White Paper of the 2014 National Summit on Cancer in the LGBT Communities. *LGBT Health,* 3(1), 19-31. doi:10.1089/lgbt.2015.0118

Campbell-Enns, H. J., & Woodgate, R. L. (2016). The psychosocial experiences of women with breast cancer across the lifespan: A systematic review. *Psycho-Oncology.* doi:10.1002/pon.4281

Campos, M. P., Hassan, B. J., Riechelmann, R., & Del Giglio, A. (2011). Cancer-related fatigue: A practical review. *Annals of Oncology, 22,* 1273-1279. doi:10.1093/annonc/mdq458

Carlson, L. E., Waller, A., & Mitchell, A. J. (2012). Screening for distress and unmet needs in patients with cancer: Review and recommendations. *Journal of Clinical Oncology, 30,* 1160-1177. doi:10.1200/JCO.2011.39.5509

Carlsson, E., Pettersson, M., Hydén, L., Öhlén, J., & Friberg, F. (2013). Structure and content in consultations with patients undergoing surgery for colorectal cancer. *European Journal of Oncology Nursing, 17*(6), 820-826. doi:10.1016/j.ejon.2013.07.002

Carvalho, A. F., Hyphantis, T., Sales, P. M., Soeiro-de-Souza, M. G., Macedo, D. S., Cha, D. S., ... Pavlidis, N. (2014). Major depressive disorder in breast cancer: A critical systematic review of pharmacological and psychotherapeutic clinical trials. *Cancer Treatment Reviews, 40,* 349-355. doi:10.1016/j.ctrv.2013.09.009

Casault, L., Savard, J., Ivers, H., & Savard, M. H. (2015). A randomized-controlled trial of an early minimal cognitive-behavioural therapy for insomnia comorbid with cancer. *Behavior Research and Therapy, 67,* 45-54. doi:10.1016/j.brat.2015.02.003

Chambers, S. K., Girgis, A., Occhipinti, S., Hutchison, S., Turner, J., McDowell, M., ... Dunn, J. C. (2014). A randomized trial comparing two low-intensity psychological interventions for distressed patients with cancer and their caregivers. *Oncology Nursing Forum, 41*(4), E256-E266. doi:10.1188/14.ONF.E256-E266

Chi, N., Demiris, G., Lewis, F. M., Walker, A. J., & Langer, S. L. (2016). Behavioral and educational interventions to support family caregivers in end-of-life care: A systematic review. *American Journal of Hospice and Palliative Medicine, 33,* 894-908. doi:10.1177/1049909115593938

Chou, A. F., Stewart, S. L., Wild, R. C., & Bloom, J. R. (2012). Social support and survival in young women with breast carcinoma. *Psychooncology, 21*(2), 125-133. doi:10.1002/pon.1863

Chu, C., Klein, K. M., Buchman-Schmitt, J. M., Hom, M. A., Hagan, C. R., & Joiner, T. E. (2015). Routinized assessment of suicide risk in clinical practice: An empirically informed update. *Journal of Clinical Psychology, 71,* 1186-1200. doi:10.1002/jclp.22210

Cohen, M., & White, L. (2016). Cancer-related distress. In C. Yarbro, D. Wujcik, & B. Gobel (Eds.), *Cancer nursing: Principles and practice* (8th ed., pp. 759-779). Sudbury, MA: Jones & Bartlett.

Cuomo, A., Russo, G., Esposito, G., Forte, C. A., Connola, M., & Marcassa, C. (2014). Efficacy and gastrointestinal tolerability of oral oxycodone/naloxone combination for chronic pain in outpatients with cancer: An observational study. *American Journal of Hospice and Palliative Medicine, 31,* 867-876. doi:10.1177/1049909113510058

Daeninck, P., Gagnon, B., Gallagher, R., Henderson, J. D., Shir, Y., Zimmermann, C., & Lapointe, B. (2016). Canadian recommendations for the management of breakthrough cancer pain. *Current Oncology, 23,* 96-108. doi:10.3747/co.23.2865

De Moor, J. S., Mariotto, A. B., Parry, C., Alfano, C. M., Padgett, L., Kent, E. E., ... & Rowland, J. H. (2013). Cancer survivors in the United States: Prevalence across the survivorship trajectory and implications for care. *Cancer Epidemiology and Prevention Biomarkers, 22*(4), 561-570. doi:10.1158/1055-9965.EPI-12-1356

Dempster, M., Howell, D., & McCorry, N. K. (2015). Illness perceptions and coping in physical health conditions: A meta-analysis. *Journal of Psychosomatic Research, 79*(6), 506-513. doi:10.1016/j.jpsychores.2015.10.006

Dirkse, D., Lamont, L., Li, Y., Simonič, A., Bebb, G., & Giese-Davis, J. (2014). Shame, guilt, and communication in lung cancer patients and their partners. *Current Oncology, 21*(5), e718-e722. doi:10.3747/co.21.2034

Drageset, S., Lindstrøm, T. C., Giske, T., & Underlid, K. (2011). Being in suspense: Women's experiences awaiting breast cancer surgery. *Journal of Advanced Nursing, 67*(9), 1941-1951. doi:10.1111/j.1365-2648.2011.05638.x

Dunn, L. B., Langford, D. J., Paul, S. M., Berman, M. B., Shumay, D. M., Kober, K., ... Miaskowski, C. (2015). Trajectories of fear of recurrence in women with breast cancer. *Supportive Care in Cancer, 23*(7), 2033-2043. doi:10.1007/s00520-014-2513-8

Ehmke, N., Hunnicutt, B., Hoverman, B., Irvin, J., Biddle, H., & Heral, L. (2015). Seasons: A prospective study assessing the physical, psychosocial, spiritual and financial needs of breast and prostate cancer patients. *Oncology Nursing Forum, 42*(2), E146. doi:10.1200/jco.2016.34.3_suppl.4

Emanuel, L., Johnson, R., & Taromino, C. (2016). Adjusting to a diagnosis of cancer: Processes for building patient capacity for decision-making. *Journal of Cancer Education,* 1-5. doi:10.1007/s13187-016-1008-3

Epstein, J. I. (2010). The FAQ initiative explaining pathology reports to patients. *American Journal of Surgical Pathology, 34*(7), 1058-1060. doi:10.1097/pas.0b013e3181d7b01c

Ernst, J., Götze, H., Krauel, K., Romer, G., Bergelt, C., Flechtner, H. H., ... von Klitzing, K. (2013). Psychological distress in cancer patients with underage children: Gender-specific differences. *Psychooncology, 22,* 823-828. doi:10.1002/pon.3070

Ernst, J. C., Beierlein, V., Romer, G., Möller, B., Koch, U., & Bergelt, C. (2013). Use and need for psychosocial support in cancer patients: A population-based sample of patients with minor children. *Cancer, 119,* 2333-2341. doi:10.1002/cncr.28021

Evans, C., Hamilton, R. J., Tercyak, K. P., Peshkin, B. N., Rabemananjara, K., Isaacs, C., & O'Neill, S. C. (2016). Understanding the needs of young women regarding breast cancer risk assessment and genetic testing: Convergence and divergence among patient-counselor perceptions and the promise of peer support. *Healthcare (Basel), 4*(3), 35. doi:10.3390/healthcare4030035

Eyles, C., Leydon, G. M., Hoffman, C. J., Copson, E. R., Prescott, P., Chorozoglou, M., & Lewith, G. (2015). Mindfulness for the self-management of fatigue, anxiety, and depression in women with metastatic breast cancer: A mixed methods feasibility study. *Integrative Cancer Therapies, 14,* 42-56. doi:10.1177/1534735414546567

Faller, H., Schuler, M., Richard, M., Heckl, U., Weis, J., & Küffner, R. (2013). Effects of psycho-oncologic interventions on emotional distress and quality of life in adult patients with cancer: Systematic review and meta-analysis. *Journal of Clinical Oncology, 31*(6), 782-793. doi:10.1200/JCO.2011.40.8922

Fenn, K. M., Evans, S. B., McCorkle, R., DiGiovanna, M. P., Pusztai, L., Sanft, T., ... Abu-Khalaf, M. (2014). Impact of financial burden of cancer on survivors' quality of life. *Journal of Oncology Practice, 10*(5), 332-338. doi:10.1200/JOP.2013.001322

Fish, J. A., Ettridge, K., Sharplin, G. R., Hancock, B., & Knott, V. E. (2014). Mindfulness-based cancer stress management: Impact of a mindfulness-based programme on psychological distress and quality of life. *European Journal of Cancer Care, 23,* 413-421. doi:10.1111/ecc.12136

Fiszer, C., Dolbeault, S., Sultan, S., & Brédart, A. (2014). Prevalence, intensity, and predictors of the supportive care needs of women diagnosed with breast cancer: A systematic review. *Psychooncology, 23*(4), 361-374. doi:10.1002/pon.3432

Fulcher, C. D., Kim, H. J., Smith, P. R., & Sherner, T. L. (2014). Putting evidence into practice: Evidence-based interventions for depression. *Clinical Journal of Oncology Nursing, 18*(Suppl.), 26-37. doi:10.1188/14.CJON.S3.26-37

Garland, S. N., Tamagawa, R., Todd, S. C., Speca, M., & Carlson, L. E. (2013). Increased mindfulness is related to improved stress and mood following participation in a mindfulness-based stress reduction program in individuals with cancer. *Integrative Cancer Therapies, 12,* 31-40. doi:10.1177/1534735412442370

Gatto, M., Thomas, P., & Berger, A. (2016). Anxiety. In C. Dahlin, P. Coyle, & B. Ferrell (Eds.), *Advanced practice palliative nursing* (pp. 301-310). New York, NY: Oxford University Press.

Gibbons, A., Groarke, A., & Sweeney, K. (2016). Predicting general and cancer-related distress in women with newly diagnosed breast cancer. *BMC Cancer, 16,* 935. doi:10.1186/s12885-016-2964-z

Goldzweig, G., Baider, L., Andritsch, E., Pfeffer, R., & Rottenberg, Y. (2016). A dialogue of depression and hope: Elderly patients diagnosed with cancer and their spousal caregivers. *Journal of Cancer Education,* 1-7. doi: 10.1007/s13187-015-0975-0

Grassi, L., Caruso, R., Hammelef, K., Nanni, M. G., & Riba, M. (2014). Efficacy and safety of pharmacotherapy in cancer-related psychiatric disorders across the trajectory of cancer care: A review. *International Review of Psychiatry, 26*(1), 44-62. doi: 10.3109/09540261.2013.842542

Greco, M. T., Roberto, A., Corli, O., Deandrea, S., Bandieri, E., Cavuto, S., & Apolone, G. (2014). Quality of cancer pain management: An update of a systematic review of undertreatment of patients with cancer. *Journal of Clinical Oncology, 32*(36), 4149-4154. doi:10.1200/jco.2014.56.0383

Greenlee, H., Balneaves, L. G., Carlson, L. E., Cohen, M., Deng, G., Hershman, D., ... Society for Integrative Oncology. (2014). Clinical practice guidelines on the use of integrative therapies as supportive care in patients treated for breast cancer. *Journal of the National Cancer Institute. Monographs, 2014,* 346-358. doi:10.1093/jncimonographs/lgu041

Greer, J. A., Traeger, L., Bemis, H., Solis, J., Hendriksen, E. S., Park, E. R., ... Safren, S. A. (2012). A pilot randomized controlled trial of brief cognitive-behavioral therapy for anxiety in patients with terminal cancer. *Oncologist, 17,* 1337-1345. doi:10.1634/theoncologist.2012-0041

Griffin, J. M., Meis, L., Carlyle, M., Greer, N., Jensen, A., MacDonald, R., & Rutks, I. (2013). Effectiveness of family and caregiver interventions on patient outcomes among adults with cancer or memory-related disorders: A systematic review. VA-ESP Project #09-009. Washington, DC: U.S. Department of Veterans Affairs. Retrieved from http://www.hsrd.research.va.gov/publications/esp/caregiver-interventions.pdf

Groarke, A., Curtis, R., & Kerin, M. (2013). Cognitive-behavioural stress management enhances adjustment in women with breast cancer. *British Journal of Health Psychology, 18,* 623-641. doi:10.1111/bjhp.12009

Groh, G., Vyhnalek, B., Feddersen, B., Führer, M., & Borasio, G. D. (2013). Effectiveness of a specialized outpatient palliative care service as experienced by patients and caregivers. *Journal of Palliative Medicine, 16*(8), 848-856. doi:10.1089/jpm.2012.0491

Guo, Z., Tang, H. Y., Li, H., Tan, S. K., Feng, K. H., Huang, Y. C., ... Jiang, W. (2013). The benefits of psychosocial interventions for cancer patients undergoing radiotherapy. *Health and Quality of Life Outcomes, 11,* 121. doi:10.1186/1477-7525-11-121

Ham, O.-K., Kang, Y., Teng, H., Lee, Y., & Im, E.-O. (2015). Consistency and accuracy of multiple pain scales measured in cancer patients from multiple ethnic groups. *Cancer Nursing, 38*(4), 305-311. doi:10.1097/NCC.0000000000000179

Harding, M. M. (2014). Incidence of distress and associated factors in women undergoing breast diagnostic evaluation. *Western Journal of Nursing Research, 36*(4), 475-494. doi:10.1177/0193945913506795

Heise, B., & van Servellen, G. (2014). The nurse's role in primary care antidepressant medication adherence. *Journal of Psychosocial Nursing and Mental Health Services, 52*(4), 48-57. doi:10.3928/02793695-20131126-08

Hendrix, C. C., Bailey, D. E., Jr., Steinhauser, K. E., Olsen, M. K., Stechuchak, K. M., Lowman, S. G., ... Tulsky, J. A. (2015). Effects of enhanced caregiver training program on cancer caregiver's self-efficacy, preparedness, and psychological well-being. *Supportive Care in Cancer, 24,* 327-336. doi:10.1007/s00520-015-2797-3

Hendrix, C. C., Landerman, R., & Abernethy, A. P. (2013). Effects of an individualized caregiver training intervention on self-efficacy of cancer caregivers. *Western Journal of Nursing Research, 35,* 590-610. doi:10.1177/0193945911420742

Hoffman, C. J., Ersser, S. J., Hopkinson, J. B., Nicholls, P. G., Harrington, J. E., & Thomas, P. W. (2012). Effectiveness of mindfulness-based stress reduction in mood, breast- and endocrine-related quality of life, and well-being in stage 0 to III breast cancer: A randomized, controlled trial. *Journal of Clinical Oncology, 30,* 1335-1342. doi:10.1200/JCO.2010.34.0331

Holland, J. C. (2013). Distress screening and the integration of psychosocial care into routine oncologic care. *Journal of the National Comprehensive Cancer Network, 11*(5S), 687-689. doi:10.6004/jnccn.2013.0202

Jassim, G. A., Whitford, D. L., Hickey, A., & Carter, B. (2015). Psychological interventions for women with non-metastatic breast cancer. *Cochrane Database of Systematic Reviews, 5,* CD008729. doi:10.1002/14651858.CD008729.pub2

Johannsen, M., O'Connor, M., O'Toole, M. S., Jensen, A. B., Hojris, I., & Zachariae, R. (2016). Efficacy of mindfulness-based cognitive therapy on late post-treatment pain in women treated for primary breast cancer: A randomized controlled trial. *Journal of Clinical Oncology, 34,* 3390-3399. doi:10.1200/JCO.2015.65.0770

Johns, S. A., Brown, L. F., Beck-Coon, K., Talib, T. L., Monahan, P. O., Giesler, R. B., ... Kroenke, K. (2016). Randomized controlled pilot trial of mindfulness-based stress reduction compared to psychoeducational support for persistently fatigued breast and colorectal cancer survivors. *Supportive Care in Cancer, 24,* 4085-4096. doi:10.1007/s00520-016-3220-4

Kale, H. P., & Carroll, N. V. (2016). Self-reported financial burden of cancer care and its effect on physical and mental health-related quality of life among US cancer survivors. *Cancer, 122*(8), 283-289. doi:10.1002/cncr.29808

Kaltenbaugh, D. J., Klem, M. L., Hu, L., Turi, E., Haines, A. J., & Hagerty Lingler, J. (2015). Using web-based interventions to support caregivers of patients with cancer: A systematic review. *Oncology Nursing Forum, 42,* 156-164. doi:10.1188/15.ONF.156-164

Karuturi, M., VanderWalde, N., & Muss, H. (2016). Approach and management of breast cancer in the elderly. *Clinics in Geriatric Medicine, 32*(1), 133-153. doi:10.1016/j.cger.2015.08.011

Kashani, F. L., Vaziri, S., Akbari, M. E., Jamshidifar, Z., & Sanaei, H. (2014). Stress coping skills training and distress in women with breast cancer. *Procedia - Social and Behavioral Sciences, 159,* 192-196. doi:10.1016/j.sbspro.2014.12.355

Keyser, E. A., Staat, B. C., Fausett, M. B., & Shields, A. D. (2012). Pregnancy-associated breast cancer. *Reviews in Obstetrics and Gynecology, 5*(2), 94-99. doi:10.3909/riog0172

Kim, Y., Carver, C. S., Spillers, R. L., Love-Ghaffari, M., & Kaw, C. K. (2012). Dyadic effects of fear of recurrence on the quality of life of cancer survivors and their caregivers. *Quality of Life Research, 21*(3), 517-525. doi:10.1007/s11136-011-9953-0

Kircher, S. M., Rutsohn, J. P., Yarber, J. L., Guevara, Y., Lyleroehr, M. M., Nimeiri, H. S., … De Souza, J. A. (2016). Predictors of financial burden at a comprehensive cancer center. *Journal of Clinical Oncology, 34*(Suppl. 15), e18263. doi:10.1200/JCO.2016.34.15_suppl.e18263

Koch, L., Jansen, L., Brenner, H., & Arndt, V. (2013). Fear of recurrence and disease progression in long-term (≥ 5 years) cancer survivors – A systematic review of quantitative studies. *Psychooncology, 22*(1), 1-11. doi:10.1002/pon.3022

Krattenmacher, T., Kühne, F., Ernst, J., Bergelt, C., Romer, G., & Möller, B. (2012). Parental cancer: Factors associated with children's psychosocial adjustment – A systematic review. *Journal of Psychosomatic Research, 72,* 344-356. doi:10.1016/j.jpsychores.2012.01.011

Krattenmacher, T., Kühne, F., Führer, D., Beierlein, V., Brähler, E., Resch, F., … Möller, B. (2013). Coping and psychological functioning in adolescents when a parent has cancer: A multi-centre and multi-perspective study. *Journal of Psychosomatic Research, 74,* 252-259. doi:10.1016/j.jpsychores.2012.10.003

Kroenke, C. H., Quesenberry, C., Kwan, M. L., Sweeney, C., Castillo, A., & Caan, B. J. (2013). Social networks, social support, and burden in relationships, and mortality after breast cancer diagnosis in the Life After Breast Cancer Epidemiology (LACE) study. *Breast Cancer Research and Treatment, 137*(1), 261-271. doi:10.1007/s10549-012-2253-8

Kurita, G. P., Benthien, K. S., Nordly, M., Mercadante, S., Klepstad, P., Sjogren, P., & European Palliative Care Research Collaborative (EPCRC). (2015). The evidence of neuraxial administration of analgesics for cancer-related pain: A systematic review. *Acta Anaesthesiologica Scandinavica, 59,* 1103-1115. doi:10.1111/aas.12485

Kwan, T. T. C., Cheung, A. N. Y., Lo, S. S. T., Lee, P. W. H., Tam, K.-F., Chan, K. K. L., and Ngan, H. Y. S. (2011), Psychological burden of testing positive for high-risk human papillomavirus on women with atypical cervical cytology: A prospective study. *Acta Obstetricia et Gynecologica Scandinavica, 90,* 445-451. doi:10.1111/j.1600-0412.2011.01092.x

Laidsaar-Powell, R., Butow, P., Bu, S., Fisher, A., & Juraskova, I. (2016). Oncologists' and oncology nurses' attitudes and practices towards family involvement in cancer consultations. *European Journal of Cancer Care, 26,* e12470. doi:10.1111/ecc.12470

Lamb, B., Green, J. S. A., Vincent, C., & Sevdalis, N. (2011). Decision making in surgical oncology. *Surgical Oncology, 20*(3), 163-168. doi:10.1016/j.suronc.2010.07.007

Landry, J. (2017). Delivering culturally sensitive care to LGBTQI patients. *The Journal for Nurse Practitioners, 13*(5), 342-347. doi:10.1016/j.nurpra.2016.12.015

Langford, D. J., Lee, K., & Miaskowski, C. (2012). Sleep disturbance interventions in oncology patients and family caregivers: A comprehensive review and meta-analysis. *Sleep Medicine Reviews, 16,* 397-414. doi:10.1016/j.smrv.2011.07.002

Lawrence, R. A., McLoone, J. K., Wakefield, C. E., & Cohn, R. J. (2016). Primary care physicians' perspectives of their role in cancer care: A systematic review. *Journal of General Internal Medicine, 31*(10), 1222-1236. doi:10.1007/s11606-016-3746-7

Légaré, F., & Witteman, H. O. (2013). Shared decision making: Examining key elements and barriers to adoption into routine clinical practice. *Health Affairs, 32*(2), 276-284. doi:10.1377/hlthaff.2012.1078

Lengacher, C. A., Reich, R. R., Post-White, J., Moscoso, M., Shelton, M. M., Barta, M., … Budhrani, P. (2012). Mindfulness based stress reduction in post-treatment breast cancer patients: An examination of symptoms and symptom clusters. *Journal of Behavioral Medicine, 35,* 86-94.

Lengacher, C. A., Shelton, M. M., Reich, R. R., Barta, M. K., Johnson-Mallard, V., Moscoso, M. S., … Kip, K. E. (2014). Mindfulness based stress reduction (MBSR [BC]) in breast cancer: Evaluating fear of recurrence (FOR) as a mediator of psychological and physical symptoms in a randomized control trial (RCT). *Journal of Behavioral Medicine, 37,* 185-195. doi:10.1007/s10865-011-9346-4

Li, M., Kennedy, E. B., Byrne, N., Gerin-Lajoie, C., Katz, M. R., Keshavarz, H., … Green, E. (2016). Management of depression in patients with cancer: A clinical practice guideline. *Journal of Oncology Practice, 12,* 747-756. doi:10.1200/JOP.2016.011072

Lim, H. A., Griva, K., Yoong, R. K., Chua, J., Leow, M. Q., Chan, M. F., … Mahendran, R. (2015). Do caregivers of cancer patients receiving care in home hospice services have better quality of life? An exploratory investigation in Singapore. *Psychooncology, 25,* 471-474. doi:10.1002/pon.3876

Linardou, H., & Gogas, H. (2016). Toxicity management of immunotherapy for patients with metastatic melanoma. *Annals of Translational Medicine, 4,* 272. doi:10.21037/atm.2016.07.10

Livaudais, J. C., Franco, R., Fei, K., & Bickell, N. A. (2013). Breast cancer treatment decision-making: Are we asking too much of patients? *Journal of General Internal Medicine, 28*(5), 630-636. doi:10.1007/s11606-012-2274-3

Lloyd-Williams, M., Payne, S., Reeve, J., & Kolamunnage Dona, R. (2013). Antidepressant medication in patients with advanced cancer – An observational study. *QJM, 106,* 995-1001. doi:10.1093/qjmed/hct133

Ma, J., Rosas, L. G., & Lv, N. (2016). Precision lifestyle medicine: A new frontier in the science of behavior change and population health. *American Journal of Preventive Medicine, 50*(3), 395-397. doi:10.1016/j.amepre.2015.09.035

Mahon, S. M. (2012). Complexities of genetic care: Implications for advanced practice nurses. *Journal for Nurse Practitioners, 8*(8), e23-e27. doi:10.1016/j.nurpra.2012.04.020

Matsuda, A., Yamaoka, K., Tango, T., Matsuda, T., & Nishimoto, H. (2014). Effectiveness of psychoeducational support on quality of life in early-stage breast cancer patients: A systematic review and meta-analysis of randomized controlled trials. *Quality of Life Research, 23*(1), 21-30. doi:10.1007/s11136-013-0460-3

Matthews, E. E., Berger, A. M., Schmiege, S. J., Cook, P. F., McCarthy, M. S., Moore, C. M., & Aloia, M. S. (2014). Cognitive behavioral therapy for insomnia outcomes in women after primary breast cancer treatment: A randomized, controlled trial. *Oncology Nursing Forum, 41,* 241-253. doi:10.1188/14.ONF.41-03AP

Mayer, D. K. (2014). Survivorship care plans: Necessary but not sufficient? *Clinical Journal of Oncology Nursing, 18*(Suppl.), 7-8. doi:10.1188/14.CJON.S1.7-8

McCabe, M. S., Faithfull, S., Makin, W., & Wengstrom, Y. (2013). Survivorship programs and care planning. *Cancer, 119*(Suppl. 11), 2179-2186. doi:10.1002/cncr.28068

McCarter, K., Britton, B., Baker, A., Halpin, S., Beck, A., Carter, G., ... Wolfenden, L. (2015). Interventions to improve screening and appropriate referral of patients with cancer for distress: Systematic review protocol. *British Medical Journal, 5,* e008277. doi:10.1136/bmjopen-2015-008277

Mehta, R. D., & Roth, A. J. (2015). Psychiatric considerations in the oncology setting. *CA: A Cancer Journal for Clinicians, 65,* 300-314. doi:10.3322/caac.21285

Meijer, A., Roseman, M., Delisle, V. C., Milette, K., Levis, B., Syamchandra, A., ... Thombs, B. D. (2013). Effects of screening for psychological distress on patient outcomes in cancer: A systematic review. *Journal of Psychosomatic Research, 75,* 1-17. doi:10.1016/j.jpsychores.2013.01.012

Meisel, J. L., Domchek, S. M., Vonderheide, R. H., Giobbie-Hurder, A., Lin, N. U., Winer, E. P., & Partridge, A. H. (2012). Quality of life in long-term survivors of metastatic breast cancer. *Clinical Breast Cancer, 12*(2), 119-126.

Miller, S. J., Sohl, S. J., Schnur, J. B., Margolies, L., Bolno J., Szabo J., ... Montgomery, G. H. (2014). Pre-biopsy psychological factors predict patient biopsy experience. *International Journal of Behavioral Medicine, 21,* 144-148. doi:10.1007/s12529-012-9274-x.

Mitchell, S. A., Hoffman, A. J., Clark, J. C., DeGennaro, R. M., Poirier, P., Robinson, C. B., & Weisbrod, B. L. (2014). Putting evidence into practice: An update of evidence-based interventions for cancer-related fatigue during and following treatment. *Clinical Journal of Oncology Nursing, 18*(Suppl.), 38-58. doi:10.1188/14.CJON.S3.38-58

National Comprehensive Cancer Network. (2017a). *Adult cancer pain, version 2.2017.* Retrieved from http://www.nccn.org

National Comprehensive Cancer Network. (2017b). *Cancer-related fatigue, version 2.2017.* Retrieved from http://www.nccn.org

National Comprehensive Cancer Network. (2017c). *Distress management, version 1.2017.* Retrieved from http://www.nccn.org

National Comprehensive Cancer Network. (2017d). *Genetic/familial high risk assessment: Breast and ovarian, version 2.2017.* Retrieved from http://www.nccn.org

National Comprehensive Cancer Network. (2017e). *Older adult oncology, version 2.2017.* Retrieved from http://www.nccn.org

National Comprehensive Cancer Network. (2017f). *Palliative care, version 1.2017.* Retrieved from http://www.nccn.org

National Comprehensive Cancer Network. (2017g). *Survivorship, version 1.2017.* Retrieved from http://www.nccn.org

Oosterveld-Vlug, M. G., Francke, A. L., Pasman, H. R. W., & Onwuteaka-Philipsen, B. D. (2016). How should realism and hope be combined in physician-patient communication at the end of life? An online focus-group study among participants with and without a Muslim background. *Palliative & Supportive Care, 15,* 359-368. doi:10.1017/ S1478951516000833

O'Sullivan, D., & Mansour, M. (2015). The nurse's role in managing the psychological and emotional impact on women diagnosed with breast cancer. *Clinical Nursing Studies, 3*(4), 29-33.

O'Toole, M. S., Zachariae, R., Renna, M. E., Mennin, D. S., & Applebaum, A. (2017). Cognitive behavioral therapies for informal caregivers of patients with cancer and cancer survivors: A systematic review and meta-analysis. *Psychooncology, 26,* 428-437. doi:10.1002/pon.4144

Paice, J. (2016). Pain. In C. Dahlin, P. Coyle, & B. Ferrell (Eds.), *Advanced Practice Palliative Nursing* (pp. 219-232). New York, NY: Oxford University Press.

Pan, X. F., Fei, M. D., Zhang, K. Y., Fan, Z. L., Fu, F. H., & Fan, J. H. (2013). Psychopathological profile of women with breast cancer based on the symptom checklist-90-R. *Asian Pacific Journal of Cancer Prevention, 14*(11), 6579-6584. doi:10.7314/ APJCP.2013.14.11.6579

Perry, J. C., Metzger, J., & Sigal, J. J. (2015). Defensive functioning among women with breast cancer and matched community controls. *Psychiatry, 78*(2), 156-169. doi:10.108 0/00332747.2015.1051445

Piet, J., Würtzen, H., & Zachariae, R. (2012). The effect of mindfulness-based therapy on symptoms of anxiety and depression in adult cancer patients and survivors: A systematic review and meta-analysis. *Journal of Consulting and Clinical Psychology, 80,* 1007-1020. doi:10.1037/a0028329

Porter, L. S., Keefe, F. J., Garst, J., Baucom, D. H., McBride, C. M., McKee, D. C., ... Scipio, C. (2011). Caregiver-assisted coping skills training for lung cancer: Results of a randomized clinical trial. *Journal of Pain and Symptom Management, 41,* 1-13. doi:10.1016/j.jpainsymman.2010.04.014

Quinn, G. P., Sanchez, J. A., Sutton, S. K., Vadaparampil, S. T., Nguyen, G. T., Green, B. L., ... Schabath, M. B. (2015). Cancer and lesbian, gay, bisexual, transgender/transsexual, and queer/questioning (LGBTQ) populations. *CA: A Cancer Journal for Clinicians, 65,* 384-400. doi:10.3322/caac.21288

Raque-Bogdan, T. L., Hoffman, M. A., Ginter, A. C., Piontkowski, S., Schexnayder, K., & White, R. (2015). The work life and career development of young breast cancer survivors. *Journal of Counseling Psychology, 62*(4), 655-669. doi:10.1037/cou0000068

Rashi, C., Wittman, T., Tsimicalis, A., & Loiselle, C. G. (2015). Balancing illness and parental demands: Coping with cancer while raising minor children. *Oncology Nursing Forum, 42*(4), 337-344. doi:10.1188/15. ONF.337-344

Recklitis, C. J., & Syrjala, K. L. (2017). Provision of integrated psychosocial services for cancer survivors post-treatment. *The Lancet Oncology, 18*(1), e39-e50. doi:10.1016/S1470-2045(16)30659-3

Ripamonti, C. I., Miccinesi, G., Pessi, M. A., Di Pede, P., & Ferrari, M. (2016). Is it possible to encourage hope in non-advanced cancer patients? We must try. *Annals of Oncology, 27*(3), 513-519. doi:10.1093/annonc/mdv614

Robinson, L., Kocum, L., Loughlin, C., Bryson, L., & Dimoff, J. K. (2015). I wanted you to know: Breast cancer survivors' control of workplace communication about cancer. *Journal of Occupational Health Psychology, 20*(4), 446-456. doi:10.1037/a0039142

Saligan, L. N., Olson, K., Filler, K., Larkin, D., Cramp, F., Sriram, Y., … Multinational Association of Supportive Care in Cancer Fatigue Study Group – Biomarker Working Group. (2015). The biology of cancer-related fatigue: A review of the literature. *Supportive Care in Cancer, 23*(8), 2461-2478. doi:10.1007/s00520-015-2763-0

Sarfati, D., Koczwara, B., & Jackson, C. (2016). The impact of comorbidity on cancer and its treatment. *CA: A Cancer Journal for Clinicians, 66*(4), 337-350. doi:10.3322/caac.21342

Sheldon, L. K., Harris, D., & Arcieri, C. (2012). Psychosocial concerns in cancer care: The role of the oncology nurse. *Clinical Journal of Oncology Nursing, 16*(3), 316-319. doi:10.1188/12.cjon.316-319

Simard, S., Thewes, B., Humphris, G., Dixon, M., Hayden, C., Mireskandari, S., & Ozakinci, G. (2013). Fear of cancer recurrence in adult cancer survivors: A systematic review of quantitative studies. *Journal of Cancer Survivorship, 7*(3), 300-322. doi:10.1007/s11764-013-0272-z

Siu, A. L., & U.S. Preventive Services Task Force. (2016). Screening for breast cancer: U.S. Preventive Services Task Force Recommendation Statement. *Annals of Internal Medicine, 164*(4), 279-296. doi:10.7326/M15-2886

Slev, V. N., Mistiaen, P., Pasman, H. R., Verdonck-de Leeuw, I. M., Uden-Kraan, C. F., & Francke, A. L. (2016). Effects of eHealth for patients and informal caregivers confronted with cancer: A meta-review. *International Journal of Medical Informatics, 87,* 54-67. doi:10.1016/j.ijmedinf.2015.12.013

Smith, P. R., Cope, D., Sherner, T. L., & Walker, D. K. (2014). Update on research-based interventions for anxiety in patients with cancer. *Clinical Journal of Oncology Nursing, 18*(Suppl.), 5-16. doi:10.1188/14.CJON.S3.5-16

Smith, R. A., Andrews, K., Brooks, D., DeSantis, C. E., Fedewa, S. A., Lortet-Tieulent, J., … Wender, R. C. (2016). Cancer screening in the United States, 2016: A review of current American Cancer Society guidelines and current issues in cancer screening. *CA: A Cancer Journal for Clinicians, 66*(2), 95-114. doi:10.3322/caac.21336

Solano, J. P. C., da Silva, A. G., Soares, I. A., Ashmawi, H. A., & Vieira, J. E. (2016). Resilience and hope during advanced disease: A pilot study with metastatic colorectal cancer patients. *BMC Palliative Care, 15*(1), 70. doi:10.1186/s12904-016-0139-y

Spokas, M., Wenzel, A., Brown, G. K., & Beck, A. T. (2012). Characteristics of individuals who make impulsive suicide attempts. *Journal of Affective Disorders, 136*(3), 1121-1125. doi:10.1016/j.jad.2011.10.034

Stricker, C. T., & O'Brien, M. (2014). Implementing the Commission on Cancer standards for survivorship care plans. *Clinical Journal of Oncology Nursing, 18* (Suppl.), 15-22. doi:10.1188/14.CJON.S1.15-22

Strickland, J. T., Wells, C. F., & Porr, C. (2015). Safeguarding the children: The cancer journey of young mothers. *Oncology Nursing Forum, 42*(5), 534-541. doi:10.1188/15.ONF.534-541

Traa, M. J., De Vries, J., Bodenmann, G., & Den Oudsten, B. L. (2015). Dyadic coping and relationship functioning in couples coping with cancer: A systematic review. *British Journal of Health Psychology, 20*(1), 85-114. doi:10.1111/bjhp.12094

Unger, C. A. (2014). Care of the transgender patient: The role of the gynecologist. *American Journal of Obstetrics and Gynecology, 210*(1), 16-26. doi:10.1016/j.ajog.2013.05.035

U.S. Department of Health and Human Services, National Institutes of Health, National Cancer Institute. (2016a). *Psychological stress and cancer.* Retrieved from https://www.cancer.gov/about-cancer/coping/feelings/stress-fact-sheet

U.S. Department of Health and Human Services, National Institutes of Health, National Cancer Institute. (2016b). *Support for caregivers of cancer patients.* Retrieved from https://www.cancer.gov/about-cancer/coping/caregiver-support

Venetis, M. K., Magsamen-Conrad, K., Checton, M. G., & Greene, K. (2014). Cancer communication and partner burden: An exploratory study. *Journal of Communication, 64*(1), 82-102. DOI:10.1111/jcom.12069

Wagner, L. I., Spiegel, D., & Pearman, T. (2013). Using the science of psychosocial care to implement the New American College of Surgeons Commission on Cancer distress screening standard. *Journal of the National Comprehensive Cancer Network, 11*(2), 214-221. doi:10.6004/jnccn.2013.0028

Waimey, K. E., Smith, B. M., Confino, R., Jeruss, J. S., & Pavone, M. E. (2015). Understanding fertility in young female cancer patients. *Journal of Women's Health, 24*(10), 812-818. doi:10.1089/jwh.2015.5194

Wandner, L. D., Scipio, C. D., Hirsh, A. T., Torres, C. A., & Robinson, M. E. (2012). The perception of pain in others: How gender, race, and age influence pain expectations. *The Journal of Pain, 13*(3), 220-227. doi:10.1016/j.jpain.2011.10.014

Wardle, J., Robb, K., Vernon, S., & Waller, J. (2014). Screening for prevention and early diagnosis of cancer. *American Psychologist, 70,* 119-129. doi:10.1037/a0037357

Watson, L., Groff, S., Tamagawa, R., Looyis, J., Farkas, S., Schaitel, B., … Bultz, B. D. (2016). Evaluating the impact of provincial implementation of screening for distress on quality of life, symptom reports, and psychosocial well-being in patients with cancer. *Journal of the National Comprehensive Cancer Network, 14*(2), 164-172.

Weis, J., & Giesler, J. M. (2014). Rehabilitation for cancer patients. In *Psycho-Oncology* (pp. 87-101). Heidelberg, Germany: Springer-Verlag Berlin Heidelberg.

Williams, A. R., Olfson, M., & Galanter, M. (2015) Assessing and improving clinical insight among patients "in denial". *JAMA Psychiatry, 72*(4), 303-304.

Wittenberg, E., Goldsmith, J., Ferrell, B., & Ragan, S. L. (2016). Promoting improved family caregiver health literacy: Evaluation of caregiver communication resources. *Psycho-Oncology, 26*(7), 935-942. doi:10.1002/pon.4117

Würtzen, H., Dalton, S. O., Elsass, P., Sumbundu, A. D., Steding-Jensen, M., Karlsen, R. V., … Johansen, C. (2013). Mindfulness significantly reduces self-reported levels of anxiety and depression: Results of a randomised controlled trial among 336 Danish women treated for stage I-III breast cancer. *European Journal of Cancer, 49,* 1365-1373. doi:10.1016/j.ejca.2012.10.030

Yin, W., Horblyuk, R., Perkins, J. J., Sison, S., Smith, G., Snider, J. T., … & Philipson, T. J. (2017). Association between breast cancer disease progression and workplace productivity in the United States. *Journal of Occupational and Environmental Medicine, 59*(2), 198-204. doi:10.1097/JOM.0000000000000936

Yun, Y. H., Lee, M. K., Park, S., Lee, J. L., Park, J., Choi, Y. S., … Hong, Y. S. (2011). Use of a decision aid to help caregivers discuss terminal disease status with a family member with cancer: A randomized controlled trial. *Journal of Clinical Oncology, 29,* 4811-4819.

Zafar, S. Y., & Abernethy, A. P. (2013). Financial toxicity, part I: A new name for a growing problem. *Oncology (Williston Park), 27*(2), 80-81, 149.

Zebrack, B., & Kayser, K. (2016). Assuring quality psychosocial care for all patients: An analysis of institutional capacity to deliver services to minority patients. *Psycho-oncology, 25,* 33.

Zebrack, B., Kayser, K., Padgett, L., Sundstrom, L., Jobin, C., Nelson, K., & Fineberg, I. C. (2016). Institutional capacity to provide psychosocial oncology support services: A report from the Association of Oncology Social Work. *Cancer, 122*(12), 1937-1945.

Zhang, M. F., Wen, Y. S., Liu, W. Y., Peng, L. F., Wu, X. D., & Liu, Q. W. (2015). Effectiveness of mindfulness-based therapy for reducing anxiety and depression in patients with cancer: A meta-analysis. *Medicine, 94,* e0897-0. doi:10.1097/MD.0000000000000897

Zhu, L., Ranchor, A. V., van der Lee, M., Garssen, B., Sanderman, R., & Schroevers, M. J. (2015). The role of goal adjustment in symptoms of depression, anxiety and fatigue in cancer patients receiving psychosocial care: A longitudinal study. *Psychology & Health, 30*(3), 268-283. doi:10.1080/08870446.2014.969263

Zimmermann-Schlegel, V., Hartmann, M., Sklenarova, H., Herzog, W., & Haun, M. W. (2017). Accessibility, availability, and potential benefits of psycho-oncology services: The perspective of community-based physicians providing cancer survivorship care. *Oncologist, 22*(6), 719-727. doi:10.1634/theoncologist.2016-0245

CHAPTER 11

SEXUALITY: WOMEN WITH CANCER

LEARNING OUTCOME

After completing this chapter, the learner will be able to discuss psychological functioning, fertility, and sexuality-related issues associated with a cancer diagnosis in women and interventions used to address those issues.

CHAPTER OBJECTIVES

After completing this chapter, the learner will be able to:

1. Describe physical and psychological changes that affect the sexuality of a woman who is diagnosed with cancer.

2. Discuss the effect of cancer treatment modalities on a woman's sexual functioning and fertility.

3. Identify components of a sexual history and assessment.

4. Identify strategies to promote sexual integrity.

INTRODUCTION

Sex and sexuality are important components of everyday life. The difference between sex and sexuality is that sex or sexual intercourse is an activity, whereas sexuality is more about the way an individual feels and is linked to human needs for caring, closeness, and touch (Clayton & Harsh, 2016). Each patient and partner define sexuality within a context of gender, age, per-

sonal attitudes, and religious and cultural values (Falk & Dizon, 2013). Sexuality affects quality of life, including feelings of pleasure, intimacy, and self-image. Alterations in sexuality impact reproductive processes. Sexuality also influences relationships with others, roles, and sexual orientation (Falk & Dizon, 2013). When a woman faces a serious illness such as cancer, her sexuality is affected in many ways, and the experience of each woman is unique.

Patients and healthcare providers routinely exchange information about how treatment will affect nutrition, pain, and ability to return to work, but despite the profound impact of sexuality on daily life, it is often overlooked or not discussed as a woman receives treatment for cancer (Dow & Kennedy Sheldon, 2015). Many patients and healthcare providers feel uncomfortable discussing sexuality. Others feel it is less important than other aspects of cancer treatment. One study of survivors of gynecological cancer found that less than 7% received information about managing sexual dysfunction or other issues related to sexuality, yet more than 40% stated they would like to have such information and did not know how to begin the discussion with their healthcare provider (Minkin, 2016).

It is normal for individuals to be interested in sex and have sexual feelings throughout their lives (Minkin, 2016). Many cancers occur more commonly in people older than 50 years. Popular culture and media often suggest that sex and sexuality are only concerns or needs for the young, and that older people universally experience decreased libido and sexual dysfunction. These beliefs are largely myths.

Many women and men stay sexually active until the end of their lives. However, it is true that sexual response and function may change with aging (Minkin, 2016). These changes may occur before a diagnosis of cancer, but they are often exacerbated by the stressors and effects of the treatment (Schover et al., 2014). As with any issue that patients face, nurses can support patients by approaching sexual assessment in a competent, open, and caring manner. This chapter reviews strategies for assessment and reviews interventions that can help patients who face sexuality issues.

PHYSIOLOGICAL INFLUENCES ON THE SEXUAL RESPONSE

Sexual Response

The sexual response has four phases (Clayton & Harsh, 2016): desire, excitement, orgasm, and resolution. A person may go through the phases in the same order; however, the sexual response can end at any phase (Falk & Dizon, 2013). Table 11-1 outlines these phases. Cancer and cancer treatments can influence the sexual response during any or all of the four phases.

Menopause

The ovaries usually stop producing eggs and greatly reduce their hormone output when a woman reaches approximately 50 years of age, although the age for menopause varies among women (Thorley, 2016). Many women fear that menopause will result in a lack of sexual desire; however, for many women, the decline in ovarian hormones does not decrease sexual desire (Samouei & Valiani, 2017).

Estrogens and androgens are the hormones that help a woman feel desire (Roberts & Hickey, 2016). Androgens are considered male hormones, but women also produce a minimal level. The adrenal gland makes about half of the androgens in women, and the ovaries make the rest (Roberts & Hickey, 2016). When a woman goes through menopause, the adrenal glands continue to secrete hormones. Thus, enough androgens are usually produced, even after the ovaries stop making them, to facilitate sexual desire (Roberts & Hickey, 2016).

The Role of Estrogen

Estrogen helps keep the vagina moist, flexible, and responsive to sexual arousal (Roberts & Hickey, 2016). When a woman is not sexually aroused, her vagina is not an open cavity. The vaginal walls are relaxed and folded so they are touching, but the vagina lengthens and widens as the woman begins to experience arousal. It becomes slippery as the cells lining it begin to "sweat" droplets of fluid. Estrogen is the cause of these changes. A drop in estrogen levels may slow down these changes, which is often seen after menopause (Minkin, 2016). The drop in estrogen level with menopause results in the following changes:

- Thinning of the vaginal lining
- Decreased elasticity of the vaginal walls
- Vaginal atrophy

Overall Impact of Cancer Treatment

Lack of Desire

Both men and women often lose interest in sexual intercourse during cancer treatment, at least for a time (Anderson, 2013). At first, concern for survival from a cancer diagnosis is so great that sexual issues are often lower on the hierarchy of needs. When women are in active treatment, loss of desire may be because of worry, uncertainty, depression, grief, nausea,

TABLE 11-1: FOUR PHASES OF THE SEXUAL RESPONSE

- **Desire** is an interest in sex. This might include thoughts about sex or attractions to another individual. The desire phase includes physiological, cognitive, and behavioral components leading to the wish to participate in sexual activity and initiation of sexual activity or receptivity in the partner. Sexual desire is a normal part of life from the teenage years onward.

- **Excitement** is the phase when arousal occurs. This phase is affected by interpersonal factors such as psychological or relationship issues, partner availability, aging, pregnancy or infertility concerns, and a history of sexual abuse or trauma. Touching and stroking feel much more intense when an individual is aroused. Excitement also results from sexual fantasies and sensual sights, sounds, scents, and tastes. Physically, excitement can cause increased pulse and heart rate, increased blood pressure, increased vaginal lubrication, and increased body temperature.

- **Orgasm** is the sexual climax. The nervous system creates intense pleasure in the genitals. The muscles around the genitals contract in rhythm, sending waves of feeling through the body. This is associated with feelings of pleasure and satisfaction.

- **Resolution** occurs within a few minutes after an orgasm. The body returns to its unexcited state. Heartbeat and breathing slow down, the extra blood drains out of the genital area, and mental excitement subsides.

Note. Adapted from:

Clayton, A. H., & Harsh, V. (2016). Sexual function across aging. *Current Psychiatry Reports, 18*(3), 28. doi:10.1007/s11920-016-0661-x

Falk, S. J., & Dizon, D. S. (2013). Sexual dysfunction in women with cancer. *Fertility & Sterility, 100*(4), 916-921. doi:10.1016/j.fertnstert.2013.08.018

---

pain, or fatigue. Any emotion or thought that keeps a woman from feeling aroused can interfere with desire for sex. Distracting thoughts can prevent a woman from becoming aroused (Sanchez Varela, Zhou, & Bober, 2013).

A woman who has cancer may worry that a partner will find her unattractive because of changes in her body or other stressors. These worries can also affect desire (Rhoten, 2016).

Pain

Pain during intercourse is a common problem for women in active cancer treatment. It is often related to changes in the vagina's size or moistness. These changes can occur following pelvic surgery or radiation therapy, because of menopause, or because treatment has affected a woman's hormones (Goldfarb et al., 2013).

Pain during intercourse may be because of vaginismus. If a woman has vaginismus, the muscles around the opening of the vagina become tense without the woman being aware of it (Simonelli, Eleuteri, Petruccelli, & Rossi, 2014). Her partner cannot penetrate the vagina. Pushing harder increases the woman's pain because her vaginal muscles are clenched in a spasm. Counseling and special relaxation training are treatments for vaginismus.

Premature Menopause

Premature menopause resulting from treatment (e.g., hysterectomy or chemotherapy) can affect sexual response. Symptoms are often more severe than the slow changes that happen during natural menopause, including increased and more severe mood swings, increased hot flashes, and vaginal dryness (Marino et al., 2014). Presently, most women without a diagnosis of cancer can expect to live at least one-third of their lives in the postmenopausal state. For younger women treated aggressively for cancer, the duration of a postmenopausal state can be significantly longer. The risk of premature menopause for women receiving chemotherapy is significant for women between 35 and 45 years of age (Roberts & Hickey, 2016; Taylor, Harley, Absolom, Brown, & Velikova, 2016).

Vaginal Dryness

Vaginal dryness is an often overlooked concern that is related to both premature menopause and some of the therapies used to treat cancer (Falk & Dizon, 2013). Cancer treatments and menopause commonly reduce the amount of moisture that the vagina produces during sexual arousal.

Women may need extra lubrication during intercourse to optimize comfort and pleasure. Initially, they can be instructed to use a water-based vaginal lubricant that has no perfumes, coloring, spermicide, or flavors added because these chemicals can irritate genital tissues (Tersigni et al., 2015). Lubricants are usually located near the birth control or feminine hygiene products in drugstores or grocery stores. These lubricants are typically applied at the time of intercourse or as part of foreplay. Warming gels can cause burning in some women, so they should be advised to avoid using them.

For some women, lubricants are not enough to replace vaginal moisture. Vaginal moisturizers are agents that women can use two or three times a week to help keep the vagina moist and at a more normal acid balance (pH). The effects of these products last longer than those of lubricants, and they are available over the counter. Nurses can encourage women to try different products to determine which is most effective (Roberts & Hickey, 2016).

Some women benefit from the use of local vaginal hormones to help vaginal dryness; these hormones are applied to and absorbed into the genital area, rather than taken by mouth (Roberts & Hickey, 2016). They come in gel, cream, ring, and tablet forms. Most are put into the vagina, although some creams can be applied to the vulva. A healthcare provider must prescribe local vaginal hormones. The use of these agents is sometimes controversial and may be contraindicated in women with hormonally based breast cancers (Taylor et al., 2016).

Petroleum jelly, skin lotions, and other oil-based lubricants are not appropriate choices for vaginal lubrication. In some women, they may increase the risk for a yeast or other vaginal infection (Roberts & Hickey, 2016). Latex condoms can be damaged by petroleum products and lotions, which reduces or eliminates their effectiveness. Condoms or gels that contain nonoxynol-9 can irritate the vagina, especially if the tissues are already dry or fragile (Damast et al., 2012).

Nurses should instruct women to put lubricant around and inside the entrance of the vagina before intercourse. Lubricant can also be spread on the partner's penis or fingers. This helps get the lubricant inside the vagina. Many couples treat this as a part of foreplay. Depending on how long intercourse lasts and the severity of the vaginal dryness, it may be necessary to pause briefly during intercourse and smooth on extra lubricant. Even if a woman uses vaginal moisturizers every few days, it may still be necessary to use gel lubricant before and during intercourse (Simonelli et al., 2014).

Hot Flashes

Hot flashes are a commonly occurring symptom in menopause. They may be more pronounced in women with premature menopause, which results from chemotherapy, radiation, or surgical interventions for cancer (Kaplan & Mahon, 2014). Hot flashes seem to be an especially common problem for women being treated for breast cancer, but they can occur in any woman who experiences premature menopause (Dow & Kennedy Sheldon, 2015; Kaplan & Mahon, 2014). Hot flashes may be more troublesome to younger women diagnosed with breast cancer; they are estimated to occur in 78% of women being treated for malignancy (Kaplan & Mahon, 2014).

In some women, hormone therapy (HT) can reduce the intensity of hot flashes and may be utilized short-term (3 to 5 years; Thorley, 2016). Women with intolerable menopausal symptoms should be educated on the benefits of symptom relief against the small absolute risk of harm arising from short-term use of low-dose HT (Marjoribanks, Farquhar, Roberts, Lethaby, & Lee, 2017). Low-dose HT is contraindicated in women at increased risk for cardiovascular disease, thromboembolic disease (such as those with obesity or a history of venous thrombosis), or some types of cancer (including breast and uterine cancers; Marjoribanks et al., 2017). This therapy is reserved for short-term use only in women who do not have a hormonally based malignancy.

For many women, especially women being treated for breast cancer, the use of HT may be contraindicated (Kaplan & Mahon, 2014). In fact, most postmenopausal women taking HT at the time of their breast cancer diagnosis are immediately taken off of HT and experience significant hot flashes (Goldfarb et al., 2013). Because HT is not an option for most breast cancer patients, these women must consider other options to manage symptoms.

Such stimuli as spicy food, hair dryers, and anxiety may trigger hot flashes. Some women find it helpful to dress in layers so that clothes can easily be removed during hot flashes, to wear clothing made of natural fibers, and to use cold packs intermittently. Individual women might use a hot-flash diary to identify potential triggers for hot flashes that may help in modify-

ing future symptoms. Lifestyle modifications, such as exercise, achieving a healthy weight, and smoking cessation, will sometimes improve hot flashes. Behavioral measures that are sometimes effective in managing hot flashes include (Kaplan & Mahon, 2014) the following:

- Acupuncture
- Cognitive behavioral interventions
- Exercise
- Hypnosis/hypnotherapy
- Peer counseling
- Relaxation therapy
- Yoga

Hot flashes can also be treated in other ways, such as with medicines that control the nervous system's reaction to a lack of estrogen. The only two evidence-based nonhormonal medications demonstrated to be effective in decreasing hot flashes are gabapentin and venlafaxine (Kaplan & Mahon, 2014).

Skin Changes

Some patients may experience skin changes from treatment. Radiation therapy can cause redness and irritation of the skin. Redness may occur early in the treatment, whereas dry or moist desquamation occurs nearer to the end of the scheduled treatment series. Both may continue following treatment (Feight, Baney, Bruce, & McQuestion, 2011). Hyperpigmentation may also occur during radiation therapy, and the darker pigmentation may remain following treatment (Feight et al., 2011). Radiated skin is more sensitive to exposure to ultraviolet light, and skin protection must continue indefinitely (Feight et al., 2011).

Skin changes can be very distressing to women and are another reminder of the malignancy and its treatment. These changes can adversely affect body image and lead to feelings of being unattractive. Encouraging women to share their feelings about these changes can be helpful. Changes in pigmentation can sometimes be addressed with makeup. Resources such as the Look Good Feel Better program, discussed later in this chapter, can often help women address these issues. For women experiencing skin reactions from targeted therapy, early intervention is important.

Fatigue

A common side effect associated with radiation therapy and chemotherapy is fatigue (Mitchell et al., 2014). Fatigue can be especially bothersome in the later weeks of treatment. Nurses should instruct women who experience fatigue to get plenty of rest and to try to maintain an active lifestyle. Although many patients can still work and participate in normal activities during radiation therapy, some patients find it necessary to limit their work or activities until treatment is complete. Fatigue can also decrease libido (Sanchez Varela et al., 2013). Some women need to rest before sexual intercourse. Open communication with a partner about fatigue is important. Evidence-based interventions to help mitigate fatigue include regular exercise (Mitchell et al., 2014). Other measures that are likely to be effective include the following:

- Cognitive behavioral interventions for sleep
- Energy conservation and activity management
- Management of concurrent symptoms
- Massage/aromatherapy massage
- Mindfulness-based stress reduction
- Psychoeducation/psychoeducational interventions
- Yoga

(Mitchell et al., 2014)

Concerns of the Partner

The woman's partner brings his or her own issues of concern, including fear of losing the partner to cancer, ability to help the partner cope with physical changes, loss of interest in sex, and attitude toward the changes that a cancer diagnosis brings to the situation (e.g., family roles, income). Strained relations before the woman is diagnosed are often exacerbated following a cancer diagnosis, which will affect the patient's sexual health (Taylor et al., 2016).

Patient and partner misconceptions, such as the mistaken belief that the partner can get cancer from the woman during intercourse, can also affect sexual response (Taylor et al., 2016). Some patients and partners may believe, although incorrectly, that past sexual activity, an extramarital affair, a sexually transmitted disease, or an abortion caused the cancer. Some may believe, again incorrectly, that sexual activity will promote a recurrence of the cancer (Taylor et al., 2016). This misconception is especially common in individuals with a malignancy of the pelvic or genital area. For example, women with squamous cell carcinoma of the cervix may have read or been told that this cancer is associated with the sexually transmitted human papillomavirus. Nurses can provide accurate information about cause and effect. In this case, the nurse should provide accurate information, because the virus, not the cancer, is transmittable through sexual contact (Chesson, Dunne, Hariri, & Markowitz, 2014).

Depression

Depression can be prevalent in cancer patients; researchers estimate that it occurs at some point in at least 50% of all persons diagnosed with cancer (Fulcher, Kim, Smith, & Sherner, 2014). With depression, a common presenting symptom is a loss of sexual desire (Fulcher et al., 2014). In some cases, patients will identify sexual dysfunction as the problem when it is a secondary effect of depression. Thus, appropriate assessment and treatment of the patient's condition should follow; if it is depression, the patient and healthcare team can explore interventions that address the depression (Fulcher et al., 2014).

THE IMPACT OF SPECIFIC INTERVENTIONS OR ASSOCIATED SEQUELAE ON THE SEXUAL RESPONSE

Chemotherapy

Some chemotherapy drugs irritate all mucous membranes in the body. This includes the lining of the vagina, which may become dry and inflamed. Yeast infections are common during chemotherapy, especially in women who are taking steroids or antibiotics to treat or prevent bacterial infections (Simonelli et al., 2014). Chemotherapy can also lead to an exacerbation of genital herpes or genital warts if a woman has had them in the past (Simonelli et al., 2014).

Any infection can lead to serious problems because of immune suppression (Koehler & Cornely, 2016). Yeast infections can often be prevented by not wearing panty hose, nylon panties, or tight pants. Nurses should encourage women to wear loose clothing and cotton undergarments to avoid trapping moisture in the vaginal area. It is also important to remind the woman to wipe front to back after emptying the bladder and to discourage the use of douches.

Women who are receiving chemotherapy often notice decreased libido (Melisko & Narus, 2016). Physical side effects, such as upset stomach, nausea, tiredness, and weakness, may leave little energy for relationships. Sexual desire often returns when a woman feels better. If a woman is getting chemotherapy every 2 to 3 weeks, her sexual interest might only come back a few days before she is due for her next treatment.

Women undergoing chemotherapy also tend to feel unattractive (Melisko & Narus, 2016). Hair loss, weight loss or gain, and infusion catheters or ports can make it challenging to have a positive sexual image.

Alopecia

For women with cancer, alopecia is a side effect that can cause great distress during treatment. Although some women embrace hair loss as a symbol of their fight against the disease, most feel self-conscious. The loss of hair can be a traumatic event, and preparing a patient for this occurrence may help ease the adjustment (Choi et al., 2014). Some women want to keep their own hair for as long as possible, preferring to let it fall out gradually. Other patients adjust better to cutting the hair short before the time they will begin to lose it. Both of these choices can help the patient to gain a little control over what feels like, and basically is, an uncontrollable event.

Wigs, scarves, and hats are some of the many options for hair covering. A patient may find it hard to see herself without hair, and some women will wear a head covering even while alone. Many resources are available to help women adjust to the hair loss resulting from cancer therapy and some of the other physical changes they may experience. Look Good Feel Better is a free program sponsored by the Personal Care Products Council Foundation in partnership with the American Cancer Society (ACS) and the Professional Beauty Association (2016). The Look Good Feel Better website (www.lookgoodfeelbetter.org) offers helpful tips for hair and makeup during cancer treatment and features a program finder for classes where women can learn more. The information is available in English and Spanish, and specific information is available for teens.

Weight Changes

For most people, food is a source of joy and comfort. However, for the patient experiencing nausea, vomiting, and diarrhea, food can become a source of frustration. The question "What did you eat today?" can become a source of stress for the patient, the family, and the healthcare team. When weight loss occurs, it serves as a visual reminder of the stress of eating and the resulting changes in body image, which can contribute to feelings of anxiety, depression, and decreased libido (Carroll, Baron, & Carroll, 2016). Nutritional supplements are available to improve calorie and protein intake for patients who are having difficulties with eating. A nutritional consultation may be helpful for women experiencing difficulty eating and subsequent weight loss. Correction of nutritional imbalances can improve quality of life and eliminate or reduce psychosocial and sexual problems (Tonorezos & Jones, 2013).

Weight gain can also occur as a result of treatment and can have a negative impact on body image (Carroll et al., 2016). Medications, such as steroids used as part of a chemotherapy regimen, can cause increased hunger and weight gain. Hormonal manipulation, especially in breast cancer treatment, can lead to weight gain (Baumgart, Nilsson, Evers, Kallak, & Poromaa, 2013). For example, researchers have documented an average weight gain of 5 to 14 pounds in women being treated for breast cancer (Paterson, Lengacher, Donovan, Kip, & Tofthagen, 2016). At a time when the patient may already have difficulty with body image because of the diagnosis of cancer, and related surgery or treatments, weight gain may add more stress and lead to sexual distress (Male, Fergus, & Cullen, 2016).

Radiation Therapy

Radiation to the pelvic area often affects a woman's sexuality (Welsh & Taylor, 2014).

If the ovaries get a large radiation dose, they probably will cease functioning. Women who receive radiation to the pelvis often become infertile. No matter what the radiation dose, women younger than 50 years should talk with their doctors before stopping birth control because it may be possible to become pregnant, which could be harmful to fetal development (Sanchez Varela et al., 2013).

With larger doses of radiation therapy, such as those used for cervical cancer, the woman's reproductive organs no longer function; the damage is almost always permanent (Damast et al., 2012). If the woman is younger and desires children, options for fertility preservation should be explored before beginning radiation therapy (Moawad, Santamaria, Rhoton-Vlasak, & Lightsey, 2017).

If a woman has already gone through menopause, she may notice little or no change because her ovaries have already stopped making hormones. However, if she has not reached menopause, the radiation may cause an abrupt menopause, followed by significant hot flashes and vaginal dryness (Sanchez Varela et al., 2013).

During radiation, tissues in the treatment area get pink and inflamed, and they may look sunburned (Damast et al., 2012). A woman's vagina may feel tender during radiation treatment and for several weeks after therapy. The vaginal walls, which are usually thick and elastic, can become tough and fibrous. This may inhibit the vagina's ability to stretch during arousal and intercourse. The lining of the vagina can also become thin and fragile as a result of radiation damage. Women often feel no pain during intercourse but may find that they experience light bleeding afterward. In a few cases, ulcers or open sores in the vagina can occur. These can take several months to heal after the conclusion of radiation therapy. As the irritation heals, scarring may occur (Miles & Johnson, 2014).

The scarring that normally occurs after pelvic radiation can shorten or narrow the vagina and decrease the elasticity of the tissue (Damast et al., 2012). A woman can often keep tight scar tissue from forming by stretching the walls of her vagina with sexual intercourse at least three or four times a week or by using a vaginal dilator on a regular basis (Miles & Johnson, 2014). A vaginal dilator is a plastic or rubber tube used to stretch out the vagina (Morris, Do, Chard, & Brand, 2017). It feels much like putting a large tampon inside the vagina for a few minutes. Even if a woman is not interested in staying sexually active, keeping her vagina normal in size allows for more comfortable gynecological examinations, which is an important and frequent component of long-term follow-up (Miles & Johnson, 2014).

Pelvic radiation therapy usually does not hinder a woman's ability to have sexual intercourse, unless she is bleeding heavily from a tumor in her vagina, cervix, uterus, bladder, or rectum. Radiation therapy does not affect the sensitivity of the outer or inner vagina, and orgasm can still be reached as long as no pain occurs during touching or intercourse (Krychman & Millheiser, 2013).

A woman should receive education about intercourse during radiation therapy (Krychman & Millheiser, 2013). External radiation does not leave any radiation in the body, so a partner will not come in contact with it. Generally, unless there is bleeding or skin irritation that would make intercourse painful, there are no restrictions. Some women are treated with an implant, a form of internal radiation therapy. An implant is a radiation source put inside the bladder, uterus, or vagina for a few days. Intercourse will not be allowed while the implant is in place (Damast et al., 2012). Women treated with this type of radiation do not transmit radiation after the implant is removed and unless there is bleeding or skin irritation that would make intercourse painful, there are no restrictions.

Surgery

Breast Surgery

Restoration of the breast is an important aspect in the care and rehabilitation of women with breast cancer. For women diagnosed with breast cancer, breast reconstruction may be offered as an option after mastectomy (for primary cancer treatment). Many of these women may choose breast restoration to improve body image and to prevent physical problems.

The decision to use a prosthesis or have reconstructive surgery is a personal one. There is not a right or wrong answer for any one woman (Ashraf et al., 2013). The woman needs to feel supported in her decision about the type of breast restoration she chooses so she feels confident and satisfied with her decision (Ashraf et al., 2013). Research suggests that women who explore their options carefully before surgery, are well educated about all options, and feel they have a major role in all aspects of the decision-making process tend to be more satisfied with whatever choice they make for breast restoration (Cohen et al., 2016). Some women will decide they do not want breast restoration (Flitcroft et al., 2016).

Breast restoration might include surgical procedures to reconstruct a breast and the use of prosthetics. Prostheses and expertly fitted bras are also extremely useful in correcting breast disparities that result from extensive or multiple surgical biopsies and long-term atrophy after lumpectomy and radiation. In some cases, they are used to improve the outcome of reconstructive surgery.

Unlike in the past, many different options are now available for women who will need breast restoration. Although a prosthesis or breast reconstruction will never completely replace what was lost with surgery, it can make an enormous difference in how a woman ultimately adjusts to the diagnosis of cancer and the changes in her body image. This is also an important step in helping the woman to reintegrate her body image with a healthy sexual identity (Paterson et al., 2016).

Breast restoration can be central to restoring and improving body image after the surgical management of breast cancer (Kim et al., 2015). After a woman has been diagnosed with breast cancer, adjusting to alterations in body image can contribute to her quality of life. By providing her with information and education on breast restoration, a nurse can help improve the survivor's quality of life. Breast restoration helps reduce or remove the constant reminder that a woman has faced a life-threatening diagnosis. It can allow a woman to wear attractive clothes comfortably, which ultimately results in improved self-image and sexual function.

Breast prosthetics are an excellent option for breast restoration for many women. The nurse should refer women considering this option to a reputable fitter. It takes a tremendous amount of courage for a woman to have a breast prosthesis fitted; women need support and encouragement as they go through the fitting process. Although research is extremely limited, some women are dissatisfied with the external prosthetic for which they have been fitted (Liang & Xu, 2015). Women often feel dissatisfaction linked to the fitting experience, including insufficient time, lack of privacy, fitting by a man, incorrect fit, and attitude of the fitter (Liang & Xu, 2015). Women also feel dissatisfaction when the prosthesis is uncomfortable to wear or when clothing and lingerie choices are extremely limited. For this reason, before referring a woman for a fitting, the nurse should be familiar with the fitter and provide the woman with information about what to expect during the fitting.

A temporary prosthesis may be given to a woman through the Reach to Recovery program of the ACS, which also typically includes a visit from a breast cancer survivor and provision of literature (ACS, 2015). A temporary prosthesis is a lightweight fiber-filled prosthesis that can be worn immediately after surgery. Most women are ready to be fit for a permanent prosthesis 4 to 6 weeks after a mastectomy. Waiting for this period of time allows for postoperative swelling and skin sensitivity to resolve.

Permanent prostheses come in a variety of shapes and sizes. These include nonattachable prostheses that are traditionally used in the pocket of a bra. Traditional prostheses are made from silicone, which is encased in polyurethane. They are available in various shapes, densities, weights, and sizes (Liang & Xu, 2015). An attachable prosthesis is a breast form with a rejuvenating silicone on the back of the prosthesis. The silicone sticks directly to the chest wall. The woman must be willing to care for this prosthesis on a daily basis. It does not work well for women with a lot of perspiration or those experiencing hot flashes. It cannot be worn while swimming.

Partial prostheses are also available for women who have had lumpectomies, reconstruction, or multiple biopsies and those with congenital disparities (Fitch et al., 2012). These come in varying shapes, thicknesses, and sizes. Some fitters will even custom-design the prosthesis with fiber-filled pads or foam breast cups. Many times, a well-fitting, supportive bra can disguise the disparity and is all that is needed. These principles are also helpful for women undergoing reconstruction using expanders, during which time the prosthesis needs change. Occasionally after surgical reconstruction, some disparity or asymmetry is still evident, which can be camouflaged with a well-fitting bra or a partial prosthesis. Table 11-2 describes patient education considerations related to breast prosthetics.

TABLE 11-2: PATIENT EDUCATION POINTS FOR A PROSTHETIC FITTING

- In most cases, there is insurance coverage for breast prosthetics and bras at designated intervals.

- Fitting a permanent prosthesis usually takes at least 1 to 2 hours. The bra is fit first, followed by a variety of types of prosthetics.

- As a woman's body changes because of treatment or the normal effects of aging, different prostheses or bras might be needed. The fit of the prosthesis should be assessed on a regular (usually annual) basis.

- There are many different types of prosthetics, and women should be open to trying different options.

- It may be helpful for the woman to bring a supportive person with her to the fitting.

- The woman should wear a tightly fitted solid top to the prosthetic fitting. She may also want to bring articles of clothing she likes if she is concerned that she may not be able to wear them with the prosthesis. Often, adjustments can be made so women can continue to wear favorite items of clothing.

- In some cases, a woman may be able to continue to wear the same bras she wore preoperatively. She should bring these bras to the fitting.

Note. Adapted from:

Fitch, M. I., McAndrew, A., Harris, A., Anderson, J., Kubon, T., & McClennen, J. (2012). Perspectives of women about external breast prostheses. *Canadian Oncology Nursing Journal, 22*(3), 162-174. doi:10.5737/1181912x223162167

Liang, Y.-N., & Xu, B. (2015). Factors influencing utilization and satisfaction with external breast prosthesis in patients with mastectomy: A systematic review. *International Journal of Nursing Sciences, 2*(2), 218-224. doi:10.1016/j.ijnss.2015.04.005

Breast Reconstruction

The most common method of reconstructive breast surgery in the United States is the use of expanders and breast implants. This is a two-stage procedure. First, the physician places an expander behind the pectoralis muscle. The expander is used to stretch the skin and is ultimately replaced by a permanent breast implant (saline or silicone) during a separate procedure several months later. Tissue transfer is another option for breast restoration.

For some patients, implant reconstruction is the best choice. However, if part of a patient's cancer treatment included or will include radiation therapy, there is a heightened chance of potential long-term complications. These complications include capsular contracture, pain, and deformity. Further surgery may even be required as a result of such complications. Most implants will last approximately 10 to 15 years, so over time, a younger woman will need to have an implant replaced (Cohen et al., 2016).

The latissimus procedure uses muscle from the back of the shoulder blade, which is brought around to the breast mound to help create a new breast. During the procedure, a section of skin, fat, and muscle is detached from the back and brought to the breast area. Patients will have a scar on the back shoulder region that can sometimes be seen when wearing a tank top, swimsuit, or sundress (Cohen et al., 2016). Women who are very active in sports should know that this procedure can reduce the ability to participate in activities such as golf, climbing, swimming, or tennis.

Transverse rectus abdominis myocutaneous flap surgery is a common breast reconstruction technique that utilizes skin, fat, and rectus abdominis muscle from the lower abdomen. The tissue (or flap) is then relocated to the chest to create the new breast (Cohen et al., 2016). This procedure also results in a tightening of the lower abdomen, or a "tummy tuck."

The decision to undergo breast reconstruction is a major one. Women should be instructed to get at least two opinions and to ask many questions (Cohen et al., 2016). Table 11-3 includes a list of sample questions.

Adjusting to Changes After Breast Surgery

Research has linked mastectomy and lumpectomy to sexual problems. Losing a breast can be very distressing. The most common side effect from these procedures that affects sexuality is feeling less attractive (Dow & Kennedy Sheldon, 2015). A woman may feel insecure following breast removal because of our culture's view that breasts are an important component of beauty and womanhood. She may worry about how it will affect both her and her partner emotionally and sexually, and in some cases she may even fear that her partner will not find her attractive anymore. Foreplay and intercourse often include touching of breasts and nipples, which adds to sexual excitement for many women. Some women may even find they can reach orgasm simply through having their breasts stroked (Dow & Kennedy Sheldon, 2015).

Surgery for breast cancer can interfere with pleasure from breast caressing (Slatman,

---

TABLE 11-3: QUESTIONS TO ASK WHEN CONSIDERING RECONSTRUCTIVE SURGERY

Questions that a woman may ask when considering reconstructive surgery include:

- What are the possible surgical options?
- What are the benefits of the recommended procedure?
- What are the risks of the recommended procedure?
- What are the limitations of the recommended procedure?
- How many times has the surgeon done this particular procedure?
- Does the surgeon have pictures showing the results of this procedure for other patients?
- What type of anesthesia will be used?
- How long will the surgery take?
- What follow-up procedures will be needed?
- Where will the incisions be placed?
- What is the anticipated recovery?
- What are the restrictions during recovery?
- When is it recommended that reconstruction begin?
- What are the estimated costs, and how much will insurance cover?

Note. Adapted from:

Cohen, W. A., Ballard, T. N., Hamill, J. B., Kim, H. M., Chen, X., Klassen, A., ... Pusic, A. L. (2016). Understanding and optimizing the patient experience in breast reconstruction. *Annals of Plastic Surgery, 77*(2), 237-241. doi:10.1097/SAP.0000000000000550

Liang, Y.-N., & Xu, B. (2015). Factors influencing utilization and satisfaction with external breast prosthesis in patients with mastectomy: A systematic review. *International Journal of Nursing Sciences, 2*(2), 218-224. doi:10.1016/j.ijnss.2015.04.005

Paterson, C. L., Lengacher, C. A., Donovan, K. A., Kip, K. E., & Tofthagen, C. S. (2016). Body image in younger breast cancer survivors: A systematic review. *Cancer Nursing, 39*(1), E39-E58. doi:10.1097/NCC.0000000000000251

Halsema, & Meershoek, 2016). Some women still enjoy being stroked around the area of the healed scar, whereas others dislike being touched there and may no longer enjoy having the remaining breast and nipple touched. Communication about what is and is not pleasurable may help women to adjust to surgical changes (Krychman & Millheiser, 2013).

After a mastectomy, some women feel self-conscious in certain sexual positions in which they are "on top" because their chests are more visible to their partners. Some women mitigate this anxiety by wearing a nightgown, a camisole, or a bra and prosthesis to keep the breast area covered during sexual activity (Slatman et al., 2016). Other women find the breast prosthesis awkward or in the way during intercourse. Nurses should encourage women to communicate with their partners about preferences (Dow & Kennedy Sheldon, 2015).

Some women have long-term pain in their chests and shoulders after radical mastectomy (Slatman et al., 2016). It may help to support the chest and shoulder with pillows during sex. It may also help if the woman avoids positions where weight rests on the chest or arm (Boquiren et al., 2016; Dow & Kennedy Sheldon, 2015).

Hysterectomy

A hysterectomy does not usually change a woman's ability to feel sexual pleasure. The vagina is shortened, but there are generally no changes in the sensitivity in the area around the clitoris and the lining of the vagina. Some women feel less feminine after a hysterectomy (Lonnée-Hoffmann & Pinas, 2014). They may view themselves as an "empty shell" or not feel like a "real" woman (Thakar, 2015). Such negative thoughts can keep women from thinking about the sexual function that they still have (Brito, Pouwels, & Einarsson, 2014). For women who do not undergo radiation therapy,

the risk of sexual dysfunction is much lower (Welsh & Taylor, 2014).

If cancer is causing pain or bleeding with intercourse, a hysterectomy can help stop those symptoms and improve a woman's sex life (Brito et al., 2014). Although the vagina may be shorter after surgery, couples usually adjust to this change. Extra time spent on caressing and other forms of foreplay can help ensure that the vagina has lengthened enough to allow intercourse (Welsh & Taylor, 2014).

Abdominoperineal Resection

An abdominoperineal (AP) resection for colon cancer includes removal of the lower colon and rectum. It also creates a colostomy so that stool can pass out of the body. An AP resection does not damage the nerves that control the feeling in a woman's genitals and allow orgasm (Konanz, Herrle, Weiss, Post, & Kienle, 2013). Some women may notice vaginal dryness, especially if their ovaries were removed (Faubion, Kuhle, Shuster, & Rocca, 2015). If so, a water-based gel can help make intercourse more comfortable.

Intercourse in some positions may be uncomfortable or even painful (Konanz et al., 2013). Without a rectum to cushion the vagina, the vagina may move more during intercourse. When this happens, it may pull on the tissues that hold the vagina and uterus in place inside the pelvis. A couple may need to try different positions to find one that works for them (McIntosh, Pardoe, & Brown, 2013).

Having a colostomy requires much communication between couples and often some changes, but sexual satisfaction can be achieved (McIntosh et al., 2013). The appliance needs to fit correctly. It is best to empty the ostomy appliance and ensure it is secured before sexual intercourse. This will reduce the chance of a major leak. In the case of a leak, the patient can be encouraged to jump into the shower with her partner and then try again. Some women like to use a pouch to cover the stoma and to make the pouch appear less "medical." Depending on the ostomy, it may be possible to wear a special small-sized ostomy pouch during sexual activity. Some women wear a wide sash around the waist to keep the pouch out of the way. Others tape the pouch to the body to keep it from moving around. Still others wear a T-shirt to cover the appliance (McIntosh et al., 2013).

To reduce rubbing against the appliance, the couple should choose positions for sexual activity that keep the partner's weight off the ostomy (McIntosh et al., 2013). Some women like to be on the bottom during intercourse and find that it helps to put a small pillow above the ostomy faceplate. With this approach, the partner can lie on the pillow rather than on the appliance.

Because elimination is periodic, a colostomy is not active at all times. An approach may be to plan sexual activity for a time of day when the ostomy is usually not active (Vural et al., 2016). Women who irrigate the colostomy may be able to wear just a stoma cover or a small safety pouch during intercourse. Nurses can provide guidance about dietary considerations and advise women to avoid eating foods that produce gas on days when they are likely to have intercourse (Göttgens & Breukink, 2017).

FERTILITY

Both radiation therapy and chemotherapy are associated with increased risk of infertility. Sterility from these therapies may be temporary or permanent. Contributing factors to fertility issues caused by cancer treatments include the individual's gender, age at the time of treatment, type of therapeutic agent, radiation field, total dose, single versus multiple agents, and length of time since treatment (Kort, Eisenberg, Millheiser, & Westphal, 2014).

An estimated 9.2% of women diagnosed with cancer in the United States are younger than 45 years. Given that 5-year survival rates are greater than 75% for these patients, reproductive issues are increasingly important. Many treatment modalities negatively impact fertility (ACS, 2016). An acknowledgment and discussion of these risks are essential to providing comprehensive quality care for women (Kort et al., 2014). This discussion should occur during the decision-making treatment planning phase so a woman can explore fertility preservation options if she desires before initiating therapy (or therapies) that might negatively affect fertility (Kort et al., 2014). The American Society for Reproductive Medicine and the American Society of Clinical Oncology both advocate for a discussion of fertility preservation options with all patients before starting cancer treatment (Loren et al., 2013).

With chemotherapy, the effect on the patient's fertility status depends on the agent(s) administered, the doses received, and the patient's age at the time of treatment. Age of the woman when treated is an important factor, as are the treatment medications, the radiation treatment fields and doses, the scope of surgery affecting reproductive organs, and the duration of therapy. Baseline ovarian reserve before treatment is one of the most important factors in estimating posttreatment fertility (Kort et al., 2014). Older patients typically begin treatments with less ovarian reserve compared with younger persons. The cessation of menstrual cycles after gonadotoxic treatment is estimated to be more than 50% among patients diagnosed and treated in their forties (Koga et al., 2017).

Many chemotherapy agents damage the woman's eggs. Alkylating agents are associated with damage to the ovarian vasculature and fibrosis of the ovarian cortex, suggesting that there may be additional mechanisms of chemotherapy-induced ovarian dysfunction (Kort et al.,

2014). Bevacizumab, a monoclonal antibody that targets vascular endothelial growth factor, can induce amenorrhea; similar risks may be associated with other monoclonal antibodies, but more research is needed to confirm effect. Predicting the outcome for any individual patient is difficult because ovarian function following chemotherapy varies. Older age, higher doses, and longer duration of treatment all increase the toxic effects of chemotherapy on the ovary.

Women older than 40 years have a smaller pool of remaining oocytes in the ovaries. When radiation therapy is given, it takes only 5 to 6 Gy (Gray is the radiation dose expressed in terms of absorbed energy per unit mass of tissue) to produce permanent ovarian failure, whereas a dose of 20 Gy is needed to produce permanent ovarian failure in women younger than 40 years (Schover et al., 2014).

In the treatment of cervical or rectal cancers, strategies to minimize the effect of radiation on reproductive organs include shielding the gonads or adjusting the radiation field. Surgical strategies to preserve reproductive function in cases where pelvic radiation is required include oophoropexy, which reduces the risk of infertility by surgically relocating the ovaries from the irradiated field and affixing them to a safer area of the abdomen (Kort et al., 2014). This technique is useful for women with adequate baseline ovarian reserve who are anticipating pelvic radiation and are not expected to undergo other systemic treatments such as chemotherapy (Kort et al., 2014). Although oophoropexy does not completely mitigate the risk of ovarian radiation exposure, it does increase the likelihood of preserving ovarian function (Kort et al., 2014).

As part of the informed consent process, oncology professionals should discuss reproductive cell and tissue banking with patients at risk for gonadal failure. If the patient is concerned about fertility, it is necessary to refer the patient to a reproductive endocrinologist before chemotherapy or radiation is initiated. The technique of oocyte cryopreservation has had some success, but with significant limitations and only a small number of reported pregnancies (Kort et al., 2014). In this technique, reproductive cells and/or tissues are cryopreserved for future use in artificial insemination for patients who wish to protect their reproductive capacity. Removal of the entire ovary for freezing is also a technique with a promising ability to preserve fertility (Kort et al., 2014). After treatment, the embryos may be implanted in the woman, who may then be able to carry a pregnancy to term. Overall current survival rates for the freeze-thaw process range from 90% to 95%, with approximately 50% to 65% fertilization rates, but clinical pregnancy rates are often less than 15% (Kort et al., 2014).

Counseling is an important part of the decision-making process for patients (Loren et al., 2013). Thinking through options and making decisions at a time when women are struggling with issues of a potentially deadly disease and toxic therapy are very difficult (Kort et al., 2014). Patients need to consider costs, stress, time, emotions, and potential inclusion of another individual in the pregnancy process (such as a surrogate). For many patients, the financial costs associated with in vitro fertilization and subsequent embryo cryopreservation are prohibitive (Krychman & Millheiser, 2013). Consideration also needs to be given to the current rate of failure for in vitro fertilization procedures (Loren et al., 2013). Religious and cultural considerations may also influence fertility preservation strategies (Loren et al., 2013).

Younger women with cancer must cope with having cancer at a young age in addition to the infertility that may result from treatment of the malignancy. Women who must undergo a hysterectomy for gynecological cancer must also cope with issues related to being unable to carry a pregnancy (Loren et al., 2013).

ASSESSMENT

Standards of practice include discussions of sexuality as an area of nursing responsibility (Oncology Nursing Society, 2016). Healthcare providers often feel ill-prepared for such discussions and fear opening up a Pandora's box when they do not have enough time to devote to such sensitive issues. They may be uncertain about how to deal with the complex and multifaceted problems of intimacy and relationships for patients diagnosed with cancer.

A comprehensive sexual assessment includes a complete medical and psychosexual history with a physical examination, including a pelvic examination (Dow & Kennedy Sheldon, 2015). This may be obtained by a single healthcare provider or by several healthcare providers as part of a multidisciplinary approach.

One of the most important factors in adjustment after being diagnosed with cancer is the person's feelings about his or her sexuality before cancer (Depke & Onitilo, 2015; Dow & Kennedy Sheldon, 2015). An evaluation of an individual's sexual function should include clarification of the nature of the woman's stated problem(s) or concerns. Assessment includes:

- Frequency of experiencing spontaneous desire for sex

- Ease of feeling subjective pleasure with sexual stimulation

- Signs of physiological arousal, including vaginal expansion

- Amount of vaginal lubrication

- Ability to reach an orgasm

- Types of sexual stimulation that can trigger an orgasm

- Pain in the genital area

The level of sexual functioning before diagnosis and treatment, interest, satisfaction, and importance of sexual functioning in the relationship all influence the patient's potential distress related to current sexual status. Women who are already experiencing sexual difficulties may be especially vulnerable to the effects of treatment (Katz, 2009; Sarfati, Koczwara, & Jackson, 2016).

The patient may or may not have a sexual partner at the time of diagnosis. Sexuality should be taken no less seriously if there is no partner. Treatment still has an impact on self-perception and sexuality. This should be assessed by the healthcare professional (Depke & Onitilo, 2015).

Assessment takes into account the patient-partner relationship – its duration, commitment, and characteristics. This includes a nonjudgmental approach to heterosexual, homosexual, and transgender lifestyles.

Many women fear rejection and abandonment by their partner after the cancer diagnosis. The nurse should inquire about the partner's response to the illness and the patient's concerns about the impact of treatment on the partner and relationship. Partners share many of the same reactions as patients, in that their most significant concerns typically relate to loss and fear of death (Schover et al., 2014). Moreover, the partner's physical, sexual, and emotional health should be considered as part of the ongoing assessment.

Assessment should consider present and past psychosocial functioning, including psychological treatment. The nurse should also review current use of psychotropic medications with respect to impact on sexual function.

Comorbid conditions that increase the risk of sexual dysfunction include diabetes, hypertension, and vascular disease. Smoking and substantial alcohol consumption also have a negative impact on sexual functioning (Sarfati, Koczwara, & Jackson, 2016). Some medications have a negative effect on sexual function, especially antihypertensives and some antidepressants.

Based on an assessment, patient teaching follows. BETTER is an acronym used to outline and organize the approach and actions for patient teaching, and the discussion with the patient and partner. BETTER is defined as follows:

- Bring up topics so the patient knows that sexuality can be discussed.

- Explain concerns about all aspects of the patient's life.

- Tell the patient that sexual dysfunction can occur and that resources are available.

- Timing of sexual issue discussions: Plan whether they will occur during one visit or over many visits.

- Educate patients about adverse effects of treatment.

- Record assessments and interventions.

(Mick, Hughes, & Cohen, 2004)

A common assessment strategy is to move from less sensitive to more sensitive issues (Falk & Dizon, 2013). The following questions are an example of an assessment/discussion strategy.

1. Has your role as a parent, spouse, or intimate friend changed since you were diagnosed with or treated for cancer?

2. Do you feel differently about yourself or your body since you were diagnosed with or treated for cancer?

3. Has your sexual functioning changed (or do you think it will change) as a result of your diagnosis or cancer treatment? If yes, how has it or will it change?

Another method used to organize a sexual assessment and plan for intervention is the PLISSIT model, which represents the levels of permission, limited information, specific suggestion, and intensive therapy (Kaplan & Pacelli, 2011). The PLISSIT model was first proposed by Jack Annon in 1976 (Kaplan & Pacelli, 2011). It provides a hierarchy for intervention with persons experiencing sexual dysfunction. The assumption underlying the PLISSIT model is that there are varying degrees of need for intervention. Most people who are dissatisfied with their sexual function do not need intensive sexual therapy (Pillai-Friedman & Ashline, 2014). The model is primarily intended for use by healthcare professionals who are not trained as sexual therapists, such as nurses. The tone and setting of assessment can be as important as the questions asked, and the goal is to build trust in the patient and protect confidentiality. The nurse should also be aware of verbal and nonverbal communication that can influence data gathered on sexual health, such as self-esteem and body image (Dow & Kennedy Sheldon, 2015). The levels of the PLISSIT model are as follows:

- The first level is *permission,* which involves the practitioner giving the patient permission to feel comfortable about a topic or permission to change her lifestyle or to get medical assistance.

- The second level is *limited information,* wherein the practitioner supplies the patient with limited and specific information on the topics of discussion to learn what sexual topics the patient wishes to discuss, so that information, organizations, and support groups for those specific subjects can be provided.

- The third level is *specific suggestions,* where the practitioner gives the client specific suggestions related to the patient's unique situation and assignments to complete to help the patient address the problem or concern.

- The fourth and final level is *intensive therapy,* in which the practitioner refers the patient to other mental and medical health professionals who can help the client deal with the deeper, underlying issues and concerns being expressed (Annon, 1977; Saboula & Shahin, 2015).

By assessing patients' sexuality, nurses give patients permission to voice their concerns and ask questions about sexual function. When intensive therapy is indicated for those with serious sexual issues, it is conducted by certified sexual therapists (Sanchez Varela et al., 2013).

Sexual assessment ensures that patients receive the care to which they are entitled and provides a baseline of their knowledge and understanding of their disease and treatment side effects; most importantly, it serves as a way for nurses to "give permission" to patients to discuss their concerns about sexuality (Depke & Onitilo, 2015).

Two other communication techniques commonly used when talking about sexuality are unloading and bridge statements (Depke & Onitilo, 2015). Unloading lets patients know that others have similar concerns and that any questions they might have are within the norm. Examples of unloading questions are as follows:

- Many women have concerns about their sexual functioning after being treated for cancer. What are some of your concerns?

- After finishing chemotherapy, some women find they have vaginal dryness when they try to have intercourse. What has your experience been with vaginal dryness since finishing chemotherapy?

(Depke & Onitilo, 2015)

Bridge statements facilitate the transition from easy to more uncomfortable topics, assist in incorporating sensitive topics into interviews, help interviewers gain valuable information, and legitimize inquiries. Examples of bridge statements include the following:

- Many active people like yourself want to continue having a close sexual relationship but don't feel that it's a perfectly normal thing or safe thing to do. How do you feel?

- What has your oncologist told you about the effects of your treatment on having sex?

(Depke & Onitilo, 2015)

INTERVENTIONS

Interventions to address sexual dysfunction are based on correcting the underlying cause whenever possible, such as fatigue or pain. In many cases, when sexual dysfunction is related to treatment, the underlying cause cannot be treated. In this case, healthcare professionals need to implement interventions to enhance sexual health. Table 11-4 shows examples of such interventions. Healthcare providers can help educate couples by offering practical suggestions to overcome changes in responsiveness to sexual stimulation. Couples should allow plenty of time for sexual expression, with sufficient foreplay, to develop the fullest possible sexual arousal.

When patients and their partners find intercourse to be difficult or impossible, it is important for healthcare providers to reassure them that this does not have to be the end of their sex lives. There are many alternative ways for couples to be physically intimate. They can use their hands, mouths, tongues, and lips to receive pleasure and satisfaction. Healthcare providers can also encourage couples to express mutual love and attraction through nonsexual physical affection. Hugging, kissing, and nongenital touching are a few ways for couples to be intimate until they feel ready for sexual activity. Healthcare providers should also encourage couples to share their feelings, concerns, and preferences with each other honestly. Further practices that can help with sexual pleasure include relaxation, dreams, fantasy, deep breathing, and recalling positive experiences in the relationship (Anderson, 2013).

More specific information for the evaluation and treatment of female sexual dysfunction, including painful intercourse (dyspareunia), vaginismus, inhibited orgasm, sexual arousal, and desire disorders, may require a referral to a specialist.

TABLE 11-4: STRATEGIES TO COPE WITH CHANGES IN SEXUALITY

Healthcare professionals can encourage patients to do the following when experiencing changes in sexuality:

- Learn as much as you can about the effects your cancer treatment may have on sexuality. Talk with your doctor, nurse, or other knowledgeable members of the healthcare team. When you know what to expect, it can help how you approach changes and challenges related to sexuality.

- Focus on physical recovery, including diet and physical activities.

- Ask your physician or nurse about maintaining or resuming sexual activity. Include your partner in discussions.

- Discuss fertility and birth control with your physician.

- Report vaginal discharge or bleeding, fever, or pain to your physician or nurse.

- Choose a time for intimacy when you and your partner are rested and free from distractions.

- Create a romantic mood.

- In times of increased fatigue, communicate to your partner to take a more active role in touching.

- If some part of your body is tender or sore, you can guide your partner's touches to create the most pleasure and avoid pain.

- Try different positions until you find one that is more comfortable and less tiring for you.

- Use a water-soluble lubricant if needed.

- Use pain medications, if needed.

- Remember that cancer is not contagious.

- Remember that being intimate will not make the cancer come back or grow.

- Remember that your partner is also affected by your cancer, so talk about both of your feelings and fears.

- Explore different ways of showing love (e.g., hugging and holding, stroking and caressing, and talking).

- If needed, find humor where you can.

Note. Adapted from Anderson, J. L. (2013). Acknowledging female sexual dysfunction in women with cancer. *Clinical Journal of Oncology Nursing, 17*(3), 233-235. doi:10.1188/13.CJON.233-235; Dow, J., & Kennedy Sheldon, L. (2015). Breast cancer survivors and sexuality: A review of the literature concerning sexual functioning, assessment tools, and evidence-based interventions. *Clinical Journal of Oncology Nursing, 19*(4), 456-461. doi:10.1188/15. CJON.456-461; Kaplan, M., & Pacelli, R. (2011). The sexuality discussion: Tools for the oncology nurse. *Clinical Journal of Oncology Nursing, 15*(1), 15-17. doi:10.1188/11.CJON.15-17; Sanchez Varela, V., Zhou, E. S., & Bober, S. L. (2013). Management of sexual problems in cancer patients and survivors. *Current Problems in Cancer, 37*(6), 319-352. doi:10.1016/j.currproblcancer.2013.10.009; and Taylor, S., Harley, C., Absolom, K., Brown, J., & Velikova, G. (2016). Breast cancer, sexuality, and intimacy: Addressing the unmet need. *Breast Journal, 22*(4), 478-479. doi:10.1111/tbj.12614

CASE STUDY 11-1

*C*S *is a 51-year-old female patient who is married, has two adolescent children, and works full time as a professional at an advertising firm. CS prides herself on being fit, trim,* *and attractive despite her busy schedule. She and her spouse have shared a satisfying sexual relationship until this last year when her desire for intimacy really decreased. She attributed the decrease in her sexual desire to symptoms of* *menopause (e.g., always feeling tired) and experiencing rectal pressure and changes in bowel habits. Her husband was concerned for her health, and while supportive, he became distant, frustrated, and then angry about CS's reluctance to obtain care for her bowel symptoms.*

At the urging of her husband, CS eventually scheduled a sick visit appointment with her primary care APRN. After conducting a history and physical examination, the APRN ordered immediate screening with a colonoscopy. CS has no family history of colon cancer and has been otherwise healthy. She started experiencing the menopausal transition with less frequent periods beginning at age 49. CS also had a negative Pap smear and bimanual exam at age 49 years. With confirming pathology of the colonoscopy findings, the APRN referred CS to the major cancer center in the next town for a comprehensive evaluation, including staging. CS did not expect a cancer diagnosis.

CS and her husband learn that the cancer center offers multidisciplinary services, uses one electronic health record (EHR) system for coordination among all providers, and has a strong reputation for communicating with primary care referral sources, home health providers, and other community care services. The center's services include medical oncology, surgery, specialty RNs, APRNs, nurse navigators and care managers, social work and psychology, nutrition, radiology, chaplain, support groups, palliative care, and a holistic center with a myriad of complementary therapies.

During the first surgical planning visit, the details of CS's diagnosis of colorectal cancer are reviewed. The surgeon, surgical team nurse, CS, and her spouse discussed the surgical options, including staging and an abdominal perineal resection. CS was tearful, voicing her fears about surviving and questioning how she would be able to manage her home life

and work with a colostomy. Her husband was present and appeared supportive and sad, holding her hand during the conversation. At this first visit, the nurse was only able to begin the comprehensive assessment, as CS was very overwhelmed and distraught. After listening to CS's immediate concerns, the nurse explained that there was still much time and many steps ahead in developing the treatment plan. The nurse provided support to CS and her husband by reinforcing that the team of providers would be there for them all along the way. The nurse documented CS's extreme distress as well as her spouse's supportive presence in the EHR.

Two days later, CS and her husband returned for a medical oncology session. The medical oncology nurse, who had reviewed the initial visit note, was prepared to spend time with CS and her husband, complete a full patient assessment, and provide support and referrals if needed. During the conversation with the medical oncology nurse, CS was not tearful but her blood pressure was slightly elevated. The nurse also noted that CS was alert and engaged, and her husband expressed relief that the process was moving forward quickly. CS again shared her fears about dying and not being there for her children, adding that she was very afraid of how the treatment was going to affect the way she looked and felt about her body. She then looked at her husband and said, "I handle things better if I have as much information as possible about the problem."

CS began asking the medical oncology nurse questions about which specific changes to expect. The nurse observed that CS's husband appeared uncomfortable and showed facial tension when the nurse responded to CS's inquires about physical changes that were inevitably going to occur. During this interaction, the nurse observed CS's body language, as she seemed to relax in the chair upon hearing what to expect, even though the news was unpleasant. The nurse provided concrete answers that directly addressed CS's inquiries and emphasized what the medical team had already discussed with her regarding an expected positive outcome and the temporary nature of some of the most dramatic changes (i.e., weakness, hair loss, nausea, and fatigue). The permanence of the colostomy was a difficult discussion, but the nurse reassured the couple that while this represented a major life change, many patients adapt successfully with education about self-care techniques and dietary management. She also explained that having a colostomy also requires much communication between couples and often some changes in sexual behavior, but that sexual satisfaction can still be achieved.

As the assessment and conversation progressed, CS shared that her pre-diagnosis extreme fatigue and GI symptoms had negatively affected her sexual relationship with her husband. Using the PLISSIT model to assist the discussion of sexual issues with CS and her husband, the medical oncology nurse helped the couple to feel comfortable in discussing their concerns and receiving the information they need to enjoy ongoing sexual health.

Questions

1. What does the PLISSIT model stand for, and who are the intended users? What is a nurse's goal in applying the PLISSIT model? Which benefits are expected when applying the PLISSIT model to address the sexual health care needs of CS who has colon cancer?

2. Which questions can the nurse use to continue to assess the sexual health care needs of female patients with cancer during follow-up visits?

3. What are some other interview techniques that oncology nurses (RNs and APRNs) can employ during follow-up visits with female cancer patients?

Answers

1. The PLISSIT model is an acronym for four stages of intervention for persons experiencing sexual dysfunction: Permission, Limited Information, Specific Suggestions, and Intensive Therapy. The model is primarily intended for use by healthcare professionals who are not trained as sexual therapists, such as nurses. The tone and setting of conducting the intervention can be as important as the questions asked, and the goal is to build a trusting relationship with the patient while protecting patient confidentiality. Nurses also need to be aware of verbal and nonverbal communication, which can influence the assessment data gathered on sexual health. A supportive partner, a relaxed versus tense posture (e.g., holding hands and using gentle touch) are all observations that assist the nurse in assessing a patient's situation and aligning interventions. Assessment also takes into account the patient-partner relationship, including its duration, commitment, and characteristics.

The assumption underlying the PLISSIT model is that there are varying degrees of need for intervention, and, in this case, the medical oncology nurse can apply the model based on CS and her husband's response to a changing situation and their readiness to seek solutions. The nurse closely observed and documented both the verbal and non-verbal communication of CS and her husband. Initially with surgery and chemotherapy, the change in sexual function and desire for CS and her spouse may be less than desirable. However, with treatment completion, healing, adaptation to having a colostomy, and a return to improved energy levels, CS's sexual desire and function may improve, allowing a new normal to be established for the couple.

2. Some basic questions that the nurse can use for ongoing assessment of sexual function and sexual desire in patients with cancers are:

- Has your role as a parent, spouse, or intimate partner changed since you were diagnosed with or treated for cancer?

- Do you feel differently about yourself or your body since you were diagnosed with or treated for cancer?

- Has your sexual functioning changed (or do you think it will change) as a result of your cancer diagnosis or treatment? If yes, how has it changed, or how do you think it will change?

The nurse can modify these questions for each patient's individual situation. For example, some patients may be more open to talk about intimacy, while others require the development of a trusting relationship over time before they are comfortable. Time, trust, and confidentiality are essential elements needed to foster communication. Standards of practice include discussions of sexuality as an area of nursing responsibility.

3. There are a number of other techniques the RN and APRN can use to assist patients in expressing and seeking help for sexual intimacy issues when they are diagnosed with cancer and undergoing cancer treatment. Two other communication techniques commonly used by nurses when talking about sexuality with patients are unloading and bridge statements. For example, as CS's cancer care evolves, the discussion with the nurse may progress to more detailed or specific questions about sexual behavior, alternative positions, intimacy, desire, and solutions in dealing with the colostomy during intimacy. Unloading lets patients and partners know that others have similar concerns and that any questions they might have are within the norm. Bridge statements facilitate the transition from easy topics to ones that are more uncomfortable and assist in incorporating sensitive topics into interviews. In such situations, the nurse conducting the interview gains valuable information and legitimizes the patient's inquiries.

SUMMARY

Sexuality in a woman's life is important regardless of her age, experience, or status in life. Women with a cancer diagnosis need information about how their cancer and its treatment phases will affect sexuality. Any effort to support the woman with information or tools to optimize functioning should be preceded by a thorough, sensitive assessment.

It is normal for people with cancer to experience decreased libido. Doubts and fears, along with cancer and the side effects associated with cancer treatment, can have a negative impact on a woman's libido and how she perceives sexuality. Concern about health may be much greater than an interest in sex. Once a woman returns to her normal routines or establishes a new normal, interest in sex may begin to return. Patient education before initiating cancer treatment should include a discussion of the impact of the treatment on sexuality. Throughout treatment and during long-term survivorship, women may need assistance and encouragement as they cope with changes in their sexuality related to the cancer treatment.

Above all, support for these issues helps her and her partner cope with changes in the woman's sexuality, changes in sexual functioning, and the impact of cancer on her fertility. When nurses normalize discussion about sexual health and intimacy as part of overall quality-of-life concerns, it becomes easier for patients and healthcare providers to communicate. Nurses can support patients and their partners by personalizing treatment plans, referring the patient to other professionals when appropriate, and engendering hope.

EXAM QUESTIONS

CHAPTER 11
Questions 83–88

Note: Choose the one option that BEST answers each question.

83. When a woman is diagnosed with cancer, factors that can contribute to a lack of sexual desire include

    a. depression and fatigue.

    b. changes in work roles.

    c. support and education.

    d. time and distance.

84. To help a woman with vaginal dryness, the nurse can recommend

    a. use of oil-based lubricants.

    b. use of water-based gel lubricants.

    c. rest.

    d. heat.

85. A physiological sexual dysfunction that occurs after pelvic radiation is

    a. increased vaginal lubrication.

    b. radioactivity of the vagina.

    c. decreased elasticity of the vagina.

    d. decreased risk of vaginal infections.

86. Mrs. G. returns for follow-up after formation of a colostomy for rectal cancer. She asks questions about resuming intercourse. An appropriate suggestion would be

    a. to avoid anal intercourse.

    b. to avoid vaginal intercourse.

    c. to secure the ostomy bag during intercourse.

    d. to avoid face-to-face sexual positions.

87. The first level of assessment (P) in the PLISSIT model conveys the message that

    a. any sexual activity is appropriate.

    b. discussing sexual issues is appropriate.

    c. all women should remain sexually active.

    d. information about sexual function should be referred to a counselor.

88. Interventions with cancer patients to correct sexual dysfunction and restore sexual integrity are based on

    a. correcting the underlying cause.

    b. the patient's prognosis.

    c. the patient's marital status and sexual preference.

    d. the comfort level of the nurse.

REFERENCES

American Cancer Society. (2015). *Breast cancer facts and figures – 2015-2016.* Atlanta, GA: Author.

American Cancer Society. (2016). *Cancer treatment and survivorship facts and figures – 2016-2017.* Atlanta, GA: Author.

Anderson, J. L. (2013). Acknowledging female sexual dysfunction in women with cancer. *Clinical Journal of Oncology Nursing, 17*(3), 233-235. doi:10.1188/13.CJON.233-235

Annon, J. S. (1977). The PLISSIT model: A proposed conceptual scheme for the behavioral treatment of sexual problems. In J. Fisher & H. L. Gochros (Eds.), *Handbook of behavior therapy with sexual problems: General procedures* (Vol. 1, pp. 70-83). New York: Pergamon Press.

Ashraf, A. A., Colakoglu, S., Nguyen, J. T., Anastasopulos, A. J., Ibrahim, A. M., Yueh, J. H., ... Lee, B. T. (2013). Patient involvement in the decision-making process improves satisfaction and quality of life in postmastectomy breast reconstruction. *Journal of Surgical Research, 184*(1), 665-670. doi: 10.1016/j.jss.2013.04.057

Baumgart, J., Nilsson, K., Evers, A. S., Kallak, T. K., & Poromaa, I. S. (2013). Sexual dysfunction in women on adjuvant endocrine therapy after breast cancer. *Menopause, 20*(2), 162-168. doi:10.1097/gme.0b013e31826560da

Boquiren, V. M., Hack, T. F., Thomas, R. L., Towers, A., Kwan, W. B., Tilley, A., ... & Miedema, B. (2016). A longitudinal analysis of chronic arm morbidity following breast cancer surgery. *Breast Cancer Research and Treatment, 157*(3), 413-425. doi:10.1007/s10549-016-3834-8

Brito, L. G., Pouwels, N. S., & Einarsson, J. I. (2014). Sexual function after hysterectomy and myomectomy. *Surgical Technology International, 25,* 191-193.

Carroll, A. J., Baron, S. R., & Carroll, R. A. (2016). Couple-based treatment for sexual problems following breast cancer: A review and synthesis of the literature. *Supportive Care in Cancer, 24*(8), 3651-3659. doi: 10.1007/s00520-016-3218-y

Chesson, H. W., Dunne, E. F., Hariri, S., & Markowitz, L. E. (2014). The estimated lifetime probability of acquiring human papillomavirus in the United States. *Sexually Transmitted Diseases, 41*(11), 660-664. doi:10.1097/olq.0000000000000193

Choi, E. K., Kim, I. R., Chang, O., Kang, D., Nam, S. J., Lee, J. E., ... Cho, J. (2014). Impact of chemotherapy-induced alopecia distress on body image, psychosocial well-being, and depression in breast cancer patients. *Psychooncology, 23*(10), 1103-1110. doi:10.1002/pon.3531

Clayton, A. H., & Harsh, V. (2016). Sexual function across aging. *Current Psychiatry Reports, 18*(3), 28. doi:10.1007/s11920-016-0661-x

Cohen, W. A., Ballard, T. N., Hamill, J. B., Kim, H. M., Chen, X., Klassen, A., ... Pusic, A. L. (2016). Understanding and optimizing the patient experience in breast reconstruction. *Annals of Plastic Surgery, 77*(2), 237-241. doi:10.1097/SAP.0000000000000550

Damast, S., Alektiar, K. M., Goldfarb, S., Eaton, A., Patil, S., Mosenkis, J., ... Basch, E. (2012). Sexual functioning among endometrial cancer patients treated with adjuvant high-dose-rate intra-vaginal radiation therapy. *International Journal of Radiation Oncology Biology Physics, 84*(2), e187-e193. doi:10.1016/j.ijrobp.2012.03.030

Depke, J. L., & Onitilo, A. A. (2015). Sexual health assessment and counseling: Oncology nurses' perceptions, practices, and perceived barriers. *Journal of Community Supportive Oncology, 13*(12), 442-443. doi:10.12788/jcso.0174

Dow, J., & Kennedy Sheldon, L. (2015). Breast cancer survivors and sexuality: A review of the literature concerning sexual functioning, assessment tools, and evidence-based interventions. *Clinical Journal of Oncology Nursing, 19*(4), 456-461. doi:10.1188/15.CJON.456-461

Falk, S. J., & Dizon, D. S. (2013). Sexual dysfunction in women with cancer. *Fertility & Sterility, 100*(4), 916-921. doi:10.1016/j.fertnstert.2013.08.018

Faubion, S. S., Kuhle, C. L., Shuster, L. T., & Rocca, W. A. (2015). Long-term health consequences of premature or early menopause and considerations for management. *Climacteric, 18*(4), 483-491. doi:10.3109/13697137.2015.1020484

Feight, D., Baney, T., Bruce, S., & McQuestion, M. (2011). Putting evidence into practice. *Clinical Journal of Oncology Nursing, 15*(5), 481-492. doi:10.1188/11.CJON.481-492

Fitch, M. I., McAndrew, A., Harris, A., Anderson, J., Kubon, T., & McClennen, J. (2012). Perspectives of women about external breast prostheses. *Canadian Oncology Nursing Journal, 22*(3), 162-174. doi:10.5737/1181912x223162167

Flitcroft, K., Brennan, M., Costa, D., Wong, A., Snook, K., & Spillane, A. (2016). An evaluation of factors affecting preference for immediate, delayed or no breast reconstruction in women with high-risk breast cancer. *Psychooncology, 25,* 1463-1469. doi:10.1002/pon.4087

Fulcher, C. D., Kim, H. J., Smith, P. R., & Sherner, T. L. (2014). Putting evidence into practice: Evidence-based interventions for depression. *Clinical Journal of Oncology Nursing, 18*(Suppl.), 26-37. doi:10.1188/14.CJON.S3.26-37

Goldfarb, S., Mulhall, J., Nelson, C., Kelvin, J., Dickler, M., & Carter, J. (2013). Sexual and reproductive health in cancer survivors. *Seminars in Oncology, 40*(6), 726-744. doi:10.1053/j.seminoncol.2013.09.002

Göttgens, K. W., & Breukink, S. O. (2017). Colorectal and anal cancer. In Y. Reisman & W. L. Gianotten (Eds.), *Cancer, intimacy and sexuality* (pp. 161-165). Cham, Switzerland: Springer International Publishing.

Kaplan, M., & Mahon, S. (2014). Hot flash management: Update of the evidence for patients with cancer. *Clinical Journal of Oncology Nursing, 18*(Suppl.), 59-67. doi:10.1188/14.CJON.S3.59-67

Kaplan, M., & Pacelli, R. (2011). The sexuality discussion: Tools for the oncology nurse. *Clinical Journal of Oncology Nursing, 15*(1), 15-17. doi:10.1188/11.CJON.15-17

Katz, A. (2009). *Woman cancer sex.* Pittsburgh, PA: Hygeia Media.

Kim, M. K., Kim, T., Moon, H. G., Jin, U. S., Kim, K., Kim, J., ... & Minn, K. W. (2015). Effect of cosmetic outcome on quality of life after breast cancer surgery. *European Journal of Surgical Oncology*, *41*(3), 426-432. doi:10.1016/j.ejso.2014.12.002

Koehler, P., & Cornely, O. A. (2016). Contemporary strategies in the prevention and management of fungal infections. *Infectious Disease Clinics of North America, 30*(1), 265-275. doi:10.1016/j.idc.2015.10.003

Koga, C., Akiyoshi, S., Ishida, M., Nakamura, Y., Ohno, S., & Tokunaga, E. (2017). Chemotherapy-induced amenorrhea and the resumption of menstruation in premenopausal women with hormone receptor-positive early breast cancer. *Breast Cancer.* doi:10.1007/s12282-017-0764-1

Konanz, J., Herrle, F., Weiss, C., Post, S., & Kienle, P. (2013). Quality of life of patients after low anterior, intersphincteric, and abdominoperineal resection for rectal cancer – a matched-pair analysis. *International Journal of Colorectal Disease, 28*(5), 679-688. doi:10.1007/s00384-013-1683-z

Kort, J. D., Eisenberg, M. L., Millheiser, L. S., & Westphal, L. M. (2014). Fertility issues in cancer survivorship. *CA: A Cancer Journal for Clinicians, 64*(2), 118-134. doi:10.3322/caac.21205

Krychman, M., & Millheiser, L. S. (2013). Sexual health issues in women with cancer. *The Journal of Sexual Medicine, 10*(S1), 5-15. doi:10.1111/jsm.12034

Liang, Y.-N., & Xu, B. (2015). Factors influencing utilization and satisfaction with external breast prosthesis in patients with mastectomy: A systematic review. *International Journal of Nursing Sciences, 2*(2), 218-224. doi:10.1016/j.ijnss.2015.04.005

Lonnée-Hoffmann, R., & Pinas, I. (2014). Effects of hysterectomy on sexual function. *Current Sexual Health Reports, 6*(4), 244-251. doi:10.1007/s11930-014-0029-3

Loren, A. W., Mangu, P. B., Beck, L. N., Brennan, L., Magdalinski, A. J., Partridge, A. H., ... American Society of Clinical Oncology. (2013). Fertility preservation for patients with cancer: American Society of Clinical Oncology clinical practice guideline update. *Journal of Clinical Oncology, 31*(19), 2500-2510. doi:10.1200/JCO.2013.49.2678

Male, D. A., Fergus, K. D., & Cullen, K. (2016). Sexual identity after breast cancer: Sexuality, body image, and relationship repercussions. *Current Opinion in Supportive and Palliative Care, 10*(1), 66-74. doi:10.1097/SPC.0000000000000184

Marino, J. L., Saunders, C. M., Emery, L. I., Green, H., Doherty, D. A., & Hickey, M. (2014). Nature and severity of menopausal symptoms and their impact on quality of life and sexual function in cancer survivors compared with women without a cancer history. *Menopause, 21*(3), 267-274. doi:10.1097/GME.0b013e3182976f46

Marjoribanks, J., Farquhar, C., Roberts, H., Lethaby, A., & Lee, J. (2017). Long-term hormone therapy for perimenopausal and postmenopausal women. *Cochrane Database of Systematic Reviews, 2017*(1), CD004143. doi:10.1002/14651858.CD004143.pub5

McIntosh, S., Pardoe, H., & Brown, K. (2013). Effect of colorectal cancer surgery on female sexual function: A prospective cohort study. *Gastrointestinal Nursing, 11*(9), 28-35.

Melisko, M. E., & Narus, J. B. (2016). Sexual function in cancer survivors: Updates to the NCCN guidelines for survivorship. *Journal of the National Comprehensive Cancer Network, 14*(Suppl. 5), 685-689.

Mick, J., Hughes, M., & Cohen, M. Z. (2004). Using the BETTER Model to assess sexuality. *Clinical Journal of Oncology Nursing, 8*(1), 84-86. doi:10.1188/04.CJON.84-86

Miles, T., & Johnson, N. (2014). Vaginal dilator therapy for women receiving pelvic radiotherapy. *The Cochrane Database of Systemic Reviews, 2014*(9), CD007291. doi:10.1002/14651858.CD007291.pub3

Minkin, M. J. (2016). Sexual health and relationships after age 60. *Maturitas, 83,* 27-32. doi:10.1016/j.maturitas.2015.10.004

Mitchell, S. A., Hoffman, A. J., Clark, J. C., DeGennaro, R. M., Poirier, P., Robinson, C. B., & Weisbrod, B. L. (2014). Putting evidence into practice: An update of evidence-based interventions for cancer-related fatigue during and following treatment. *Clinical Journal of Oncology Nursing, 18*(Suppl.), 38-58. doi:10.1188/14.CJON.S3.38-58

Moawad, N. S., Santamaria, E., Rhoton-Vlasak, A., & Lightsey, J. L. (2017). Laparoscopic ovarian transposition before pelvic cancer treatment: Ovarian function and fertility preservation. *Journal of Minimally Invasive Gynecology, 24*(1), 28-35. doi:10.1016/j.jmig.2016.08.831

Morris, L., Do, V., Chard, J., & Brand, A. H. (2017). Radiation-induced vaginal stenosis: Current perspectives. *International Journal of Women's Health, 9,* 273-279. doi:10.2147/IJWH.S106796

Oncology Nursing Society. (2016). *Oncology nurse generalist competencies.* Pittsburgh, PA: Author. Retrieved from https://www.ons.org/sites/default/files/Oncology%20Nurse%20Generalist%20Competencies%202016.pdf

Paterson, C. L., Lengacher, C. A., Donovan, K. A., Kip, K. E., & Tofthagen, C. S. (2016). Body image in younger breast cancer survivors: A systematic review. *Cancer Nursing, 39*(1), E39-E58. doi:10.1097/NCC.0000000000000251

Personal Care Products Council Foundation, American Cancer Society, and the Professional Beauty Association. (2016). *Look Good Feel Better program.* Retrieved from http://lookgoodfeelbetter.org/

Pillai-Friedman, S., & Ashline, J. L. (2014). Women, breast cancer survivorship, sexual losses, and disenfranchised grief – A treatment model for clinicians. *Journal of Sexual and Relationship Therapy, 29*(4), 436-453. doi:10.1080/14681994.2014.934340

Rhoten, B. A. (2016). Body image disturbance in adults treated for cancer – A concept analysis. *Journal of Advanced Nursing, 72*(5), 1001-1011. doi:10.1111/jan.12892

Roberts, H., & Hickey, M. (2016). Managing the menopause: An update. *Maturitas, 86,* 53-58. doi:10.1016/j.maturitas.2016.01.007

Saboula, N. E. S., & Shahin, M. A. (2015). Effectiveness of application of PLISSIT counseling model on sexuality for breast cancer's women undergoing treatment. *American Journal of Nursing, 4*(4), 218-230.

Samouei, R., & Valiani, M. (2017). Psychological experiences of women regarding menopause. *International Journal of Educational and Psychological Researches, 3*(1), 1-4.

Sanchez Varela, V., Zhou, E. S., & Bober, S. L. (2013). Management of sexual problems in cancer patients and survivors. *Current Problems in Cancer, 37*(6), 319-352. doi:10.1016/j.currproblcancer.2013.10.009

Sarfati, D., Koczwara, B., & Jackson, C. (2016). The impact of comorbidity on cancer and its treatment. *CA: A Cancer Journal for Clinicians, 66*(4), 337-350. doi:10.3322/caac.21342

Schover, L. R., van der Kaaij, M., van Dorst, E., Creutzberg, C., Huyghe, E., & Kiserud, C. E. (2014). Sexual dysfunction and infertility as late effects of cancer treatment. *European Journal of Cancer Supplements, 12*(1), 41-53. doi:10.1016/j.ejcsup.2014.03.004

Simonelli, C., Eleuteri, S., Petruccelli, F., & Rossi, R. (2014). Female sexual pain disorders: Dyspareunia and vaginismus. *Current Opinion in Psychiatry, 27*(6), 406-412. doi:10.1097/YCO.0000000000000098

Slatman, J., Halsema, A., & Meershoek, A. (2016). Responding to scars after breast surgery. *Qualitative Health Research, 26*(12), 1614-1626. doi:10.1177/1049732315591146

Taylor, S., Harley, C., Absolom, K., Brown, J., & Velikova, G. (2016). Breast cancer, sexuality, and intimacy: Addressing the unmet need. *Breast Journal, 22*(4), 478-479. doi:10.1111/tbj.12614

Tersigni, C., Di Simone, N., Tempestilli, E., Cianfrini, F., Russo, R., Moruzzi, M. C., ... Villa, P. (2015). Non-hormonal treatment of vulvo-vaginal atrophy-related symptoms in post-menopausal women. *Journal of Obstetrics & Gynaecology, 35*(8), 835-838. doi:10.3109/01443615.2015.1014326

Thakar, R. (2015). Is the uterus a sexual organ? Sexual function following hysterectomy. *Sexual Medicine Reviews, 3*(4), 264-278. doi:10.1002/smrj.59

Thorley, J. (2016). HRT for menopause: A delicate balance. *The Lancet: Diabetes & Endocrinology, 4*(1), 25. doi:10.1016/S2213-8587(15)00472-6

Tonorezos, E. S., & Jones, L. W. (2013). Energy balance and metabolism after cancer treatment. *Seminars in Oncology, 40*(6), 745-756. doi:10.1053/j.seminoncol.2013.09.011

Vural, F., Harputlu, D., Karayurt, O., Suler, G., Edeer, A. D., Ucer, C., & Onay, D. C. (2016). The impact of an ostomy on the sexual lives of persons with stomas: A phenomenological study. *Journal of Wound Ostomy & Continence Nursing, 43*(4), 381-384. doi:10.1097/WON.0000000000000236

Welsh, L. C., & Taylor, A. (2014). Impact of pelvic radiotherapy on the female genital tract and fertility preservation measures. *World Journal of Obstetrics and Gynecology, 3*(2), 45-53. doi:10.5317/wjog.v3.i2.45

CHAPTER 12

COMPLEMENTARY AND ALTERNATIVE MEDICINE

LEARNING OUTCOME

After completing this chapter, the learner will be able to identify common complementary and alternative medicine and ways to evaluate their value and effectiveness.

CHAPTER OBJECTIVES

After completing this chapter, the learner will be able to:

1. Describe motivations for women with cancer to include complementary and alternative medicines (CAMs) as a component of their care.

2. Explain the focus of the National Center for Complementary and Integrative Health.

3. Identify selected CAMs used by patients with cancer that have shown efficacy.

4. Describe the role of the nurse in assisting cancer patients with selecting CAMs.

INTRODUCTION

No discussion of cancer in women is complete without addressing the use of complementary and alternative medicines (CAMs) for the side effects associated with a cancer diagnosis and its treatment. Because some CAMs may alter traditional medical treatment,

or their effect is not known, it is critical that the nurse assess the patient regarding her intent to use or her current use of CAMs. The nurse needs to be aware that a patient's practices or beliefs in spirituality can be the foundation or impetus to engage in some CAM modalities.

DEFINITIONS AND TYPES OF COMPLEMENTARY AND ALTERNATIVE MEDICINES

Complementary and alternative medicine (CAM) is the popular term for health and wellness therapies that typically have not been part of conventional or mainstream Western medicine. According to the National Center for Complementary and Integrative Health (NCCIH, 2016), complementary refers to treatments that are used along with conventional or mainstream medicine. Alternative refers to treatments used in place of conventional or mainstream medicine. The NCCIH (2016) also uses the term *integrative health* when incorporating and organizing complementary approaches into mainstream health care.

Table 12-1 shows the five categories of CAMs that women with a diagnosis of cancer might utilize for various symptoms and side effect management. Some CAMs require inter-

TABLE 12-1: CATEGORIES OF COMPLEMENTARY AND ALTERNATIVE MEDICINE THERAPIES

Mind-body practices: Complementary and alternative medicine (CAM) practices based on the belief that the mind is able to affect the body. Some examples of mind-body practices are

- meditation;
- biofeedback;
- hypnosis;
- yoga;
- imagery; and
- art, music, or dance therapy.

Biologically based practices: CAM practices that use natural products, such as dietary supplements and herbal products. Some examples of biologically based practices are

- vitamins,
- herbs,
- foods, and
- special diets.

Manipulative and body-based practices: CAM practices based on working or moving one or more body parts. Some examples of manipulative and body-based practices are

- massage,
- chiropractic care, and
- reflexology.

Energy medicine: CAM practice based on the belief that the body has energy fields that can be used for healing and wellness. Some examples of energy medicine are

- tai chi,
- Reiki, and
- therapeutic touch.

Whole medical systems: CAM practices that consider the mind, body, and spirit. Some examples of whole medical systems are

- ayurvedic medicine,
- Chinese medicine,
- acupuncture,
- homeopathy, and
- naturopathic medicine.

Note. Adapted from Adams, J. (2013). *Primary health care and complementary and integrative medicine: Practice and research.* London: Imperial College Press; Bonacchi, A., Toccafondi, A., Mambrini, A., Cantore, M., Muraca, M. G., Focardi, F., ... Miccinesi, G. (2015). Complementary needs behind complementary therapies in cancer patients. *Psycho-Oncology, 24*(9), 1124-1130. doi:10.1002/pon.3773; Frenkel, M., Sierpina, V., & Sapire, K. (2015). Effects of complementary and integrative medicine on cancer survivorship. *Current Oncology Reports, 17*(5), 445. doi:10.1007/s11912-015-0445-1; National Center for Complementary and Integrative Health. (2016). *Complementary, alternative, or integrative health: What's in a name?* Retrieved from https://nccih.nih.gov/health/integrative-health#term; and Witt, C. M., & Cardoso, M. J. (2016). Complementary and integrative medicine for breast cancer patients – Evidence-based practical recommendations. *The Breast, 28*, 37-44. doi:10.1016/j.breast.2016.04.012

vention from a specialist (such as acupuncture), whereas others can be initiated by the patient (such as an herbal supplement). To date, no CAM has been proved to be universally effective in the treatment of cancer or in the alleviation of the side effects of the disease and treatments, but there is promising research that some CAMs may be a valuable adjunct to treatment (Adams, 2013; NCCIH, 2016).

Women may seek CAMs for the following reasons:

- To cope with the diagnosis

- To reduce stress

- To reduce fatigue

- To provide a sense of control

- To manage side effects of cancer and treatment, such as pain or nausea

Any discussion of CAMs should include the following aspects (Mulkins, McKenzie, Verhoef, Balneaves, & Salamonsen, 2016):

- Potential interactions with treatment or medications

- Explanations of the physiological basis of how specific CAMs might work

- Referrals to reputable CAM providers and practitioners

The challenge for nurses and other healthcare providers is to be supportive of patients who use CAMs while also being appropriate advocates. CAMs can be promoted by charlatans who seek out the vulnerable (Bauml et al., 2015). The obligation of healthcare providers is to help patients sort through information, to support studies that generate documented effectiveness data, and to focus on those options proven to be effective and safe.

Some women with cancer are concerned that their healthcare providers will not approve of the use of CAMs. Communication with a healthcare provider is important to ensure that there are no dangerous interactions between traditional cancer therapies and CAMs (Sohl et al., 2015). Nurses can be instrumental in determining patients' real or intended actions related to the use of CAMs, and they need to incorporate this information during the initial and ongoing assessment process. An environment of open communication will help to prevent complications.

COMPLEMENTARY AND ALTERNATIVE MEDICINE USE IN GENERAL POPULATIONS

The prevalence of CAM use in the general population substantially increased from 1990 to 2005. In December 2015, NCCIH released new findings on Americans' use of CAM. In 2012, an estimated 33.2% of U.S. adults used complementary health approaches, with the most commonly used complementary approach being natural products such as dietary supplements other than vitamins and minerals (Clarke, Black, Stussman, Barnes, & Nahin, 2015). These approaches can be expensive; approximately 59 million Americans spent $14.7 billion out of pocket on visits to complementary practitioners and $12.8 billion on natural products (Clarke et al., 2015). The mind and body approaches most commonly used include yoga, meditation, and massage therapy. The percentage of adults who practice yoga has increased substantially, from 5.1% in 2002 to 6.1% in 2007 and 9.5% in 2012 (Clarke et al., 2015). More than 85% of U.S. adults who practiced yoga perceived reduced stress as a result of this activity (Clarke et al., 2015). People of all backgrounds use CAM, but it is used more by non-Hispanic White than Hispanic White individuals. CAM use among adults is greater among women and those with higher levels of education and higher incomes (Clarke et al., 2015).

CAM users are likely to use more than one CAM therapy in conjunction with conventional medicine. Commonly cited reasons for CAM use include the beliefs that these therapies have the following effects:

• Boost immune function

• Prevent cancer and/or improve quality of life

• Increase the feeling that patients are more in control and play an active role in their own care

• Palliate symptoms of cancer treatment

(Adams, 2013)

Nondisclosure of CAM use by patients with cancer has been well documented, with studies reporting rates from 44% to 77% (Sohl et al., 2015). Reasons given for nondisclosure on the part of patients included "it wasn't important for the doctor to know" and "the doctor never asked." Research also suggests that some patients do not see the potential of CAMs to affect their standard cancer treatment, and some patients do not perceive the therapies they choose to use as being CAMs (especially products marketed as a natural supplement, vitamin, or food product; Sohl et al., 2015). Other possible reasons are feared disinterest or negative response by the healthcare provider and the view that the discussion of CAM is a poor use of time or is inappropriate (Synovitz & Larson, 2013). The reality that patients do not reveal CAM use to the healthcare team is of particular concern because the safety and efficacy of some CAM therapies are not yet fully known (Bonacchi et al., 2015).

NATIONAL CENTER FOR COMPLEMENTARY AND INTEGRATIVE HEALTH

In 1998, the National Institutes of Health established the National Center for Complementary and Alternative Medicine, now known as the NCCIH. The NCCIH conducts basic and clinical research, trains researchers, and educates the public by communicating findings concerning therapeutic and preventive CAMs. NCCIH is the leading U.S. agency for scientific research and reliable information on CAM. Nurses can access the many resources available at the CAM website (http://NCCIH. nih.gov/health/providers) if they have specific questions about a treatment (Giron, Haddad, Lopes de Almeida Rizzi, Nazário, & Facina, 2016). The NCCIH has the following four primary areas of focus:

• Advancing scientific research

• Training CAM researchers

• Disseminating news and information

• Supporting integration of proven CAM therapies

The NCCIH accomplishes its mission by sponsoring and conducting research that uses scientific methods and advanced technologies to study CAM, among other strategies.

Nurses can become familiar with the many reliable resources that are available at the NCCIH website, such as a comprehensive list of CAM therapies that includes a description of each therapy, pictures related to the therapy, the scientific basis of the therapy, and safety considerations. Nurses can also refer patients to this website if they have additional questions.

CANCER PATIENTS AND COMPLEMENTARY AND ALTERNATIVE MEDICINES

The effects of CAM use are subjective, and the perceived benefits of CAM are unique to each individual. The following discussion is not exhaustive and highlights some common CAMs that cancer patients and clinicians report to be reasonably safe and sometimes helpful (Frenkel, Sierpina, & Sapire, 2015).

Acupuncture

Acupuncture is a technique in which the practitioner inserts very thin needles of varying lengths through the client's skin to treat a variety of conditions including pain, fatigue, chemotherapy-induced nausea and vomiting, anxiety, depression, insomnia, and hot flashes (Chon & Lee, 2013).

According to traditional Chinese medicine, qi, which is considered vital energy, flows through the body along a network of paths, called meridians (National Cancer Institute, 2016). Qi can be unblocked by using acupuncture at certain places on the skin, called acupoints. Acupoints are places where the meridians come to the surface of the body. There are more than 360 acupoints on the human body, with specific acupoints for each condition being treated.

When done by a trained professional, acupuncture is generally considered safe (Chon & Lee, 2013). Clients report relatively few complications related to acupuncture; however, there is a risk that acupuncture may be harmful to the patient if the acupuncturist is not well trained (Lau et al., 2016). Although the needles used in traditional needle acupuncture are very fine, they can cause dizziness, fainting, local internal bleeding, nerve damage, and increased pain (see Figures 12-1 and 12-2; Giron et al., 2016; Witt & Cardoso, 2016). The risk of infection is low because acupuncturists in the United States use sterile needles that are discarded after a single use (Chon & Lee, 2013).

Aromatherapy

Aromatherapy is the use of fragrant substances, called essential oils, distilled from plants to alter mood or improve health (National Cancer Institute, 2017). The client either inhales these highly concentrated aromatic substances

FIGURE 12-1: SIZE OF ACUPUNCTURE NEEDLE

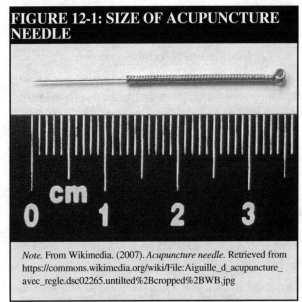

Note. From Wikimedia. (2007). *Acupuncture needle.* Retrieved from https://commons.wikimedia.org/wiki/File:Aiguille_d_acupuncture_avec_regle.dsc02265.untilted%2Bcropped%2BWB.jpg

FIGURE 12-2: LUNG MERIDIAN PRESSURE POINTS

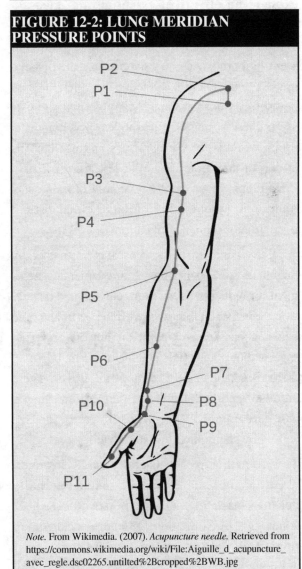

Note. From Wikimedia. (2007). *Acupuncture needle.* Retrieved from https://commons.wikimedia.org/wiki/File:Aiguille_d_acupuncture_avec_regle.dsc02265.untilted%2Bcropped%2BWB.jpg

or the practitioner applies them during massage to the patient's skin (National Cancer Institute, 2017). Practitioners commonly use approximately 40 different essential oils, including lavender, rosemary, eucalyptus, chamomile, marjoram, jasmine, peppermint, lemon, and geranium (Shin et al., 2016).

Research suggests different theories regarding how aromatherapy may work. For example, scent receptors in the nose send chemical messages through the olfactory nerve to the brain's limbic region, influencing emotional responses, heart rate, blood pressure, and respiration (Frenkel et al., 2015); these connections could explain the effects of essential oils' pleasant smells. The effects may partly depend on previous associations of the person with a particular scent. Laboratory studies suggest that the oils can affect organ function, although whether this can be useful is not yet clear. Many aromatherapists are trained as massage therapists, psychologists, social workers, or chiropractors and use the oils as part of their practices (Witt & Cardoso, 2016). Practitioners may use the essential oils one at a time or in combination, through either patient inhalation or topical application.

Early clinical trials suggest that aromatherapy may have some benefit as a complementary treatment for reducing stress, pain, nausea, and depression. Some studies show no difference in outcome between massage with aromatherapy oils and massage without them (Papagiannaki & Shinebourne, 2016; Rankanen, 2016; Shin et al., 2016). There are also reports that inhaled peppermint, ginger, and cardamom oil seem to relieve the nausea caused by chemotherapy and radiation.

Aromatherapy is generally safe. However, essential oils should not be taken internally because many of them are poisonous (Reis & Jones, 2017). Some oils can cause sensitization (allergy to the oil) and may cause irritation if applied undiluted to the skin.

Art Therapy

Art therapy is a CAM that helps people manage physical and emotional problems through the use of creative activities to express emotions (Rankanen, 2016). It provides a way for people to come to terms with emotional conflicts, increase self-awareness, and express unspoken and often unconscious concerns about their illness and their lives. It may include dance and movement, drama, poetry, and photography in addition to the more traditional art methods.

Art therapy programs provide patients with access to the tools they need to produce paintings, drawings, sculptures, and many other types of artwork. Art therapists work with patients individually or in groups (Rankanen, 2016). The role of the art therapist is to help patients express themselves through their creations and to talk to patients about their emotions and concerns as they relate to their art.

Case studies have reported that art therapy benefits patients with both emotional and physical illnesses (Papagiannaki & Shinebourne, 2016). Some of the potential uses of art therapy include reducing anxiety levels, improving recovery times, decreasing hospital stays, improving communication and social function, and facilitating pain control.

Art therapy is considered safe when conducted by a skilled therapist. It may be useful as a complementary therapy to help people with cancer deal with their emotions. Although art therapy may stir up uncomfortable feelings at times, this is part of the healing process (Rankanen, 2016). More information about art therapy is available through the American Art Therapy Association, including how to locate a licensed art therapist (https://arttherapy.org).

Biofeedback

Biofeedback is a treatment method that uses monitoring devices to help people consciously control physical processes, such as heart rate, blood pressure, temperature, sweating, and muscle tension, that are usually controlled automatically (Witt & Cardoso, 2016). By helping a patient change these activities in the body, biofeedback can reduce stress and muscle tension from a number of causes. It can promote relaxation, and because it facilitates a greater awareness of bodily functions, it can help a person regulate or alter other physical functions. Biofeedback is often a matter of trial and error as patients learn to adjust their thinking and connect changes in thought, breathing, posture, and muscle tension with changes in physical functions that are usually controlled unconsciously (Witt & Cardoso, 2016).

Although biofeedback has no direct effect on the development or progress of cancer, it can improve the quality of life for some people with cancer (Adams, 2013). Research has found that biofeedback can be helpful for patients in regaining urinary and bowel continence after surgery (Frenkel et al., 2015). Patients often use biofeedback along with relaxation for the best results (Witt & Cardoso, 2016).

Biofeedback is thought to be a safe technique. It is noninvasive. Biofeedback requires a trained and certified professional to manage equipment, interpret changes, and monitor the patient. Physical therapists often provide this therapy. A typical session takes 30 to 60 minutes (Adams, 2013).

Guided Imagery

Guided imagery involves using one's imagination to create sights, sounds, smells, tastes, or other sensations to create a kind of purposeful daydream. The techniques used in guided imagery can help to reduce stress, anxiety, and depression; manage pain; lower blood pressure; ease some of the side effects of chemo-

therapy; and create feelings of being in control (Burhenn, Olausson, Villegas, & Kravits, 2014).

For people with cancer, guided imagery can relieve nausea and vomiting from chemotherapy, relieve stress associated with having cancer, enhance the immune system, improve weight gain, combat depression, and alleviate pain (Witt & Cardoso, 2016).

Imagery techniques are considered safe, especially when they are provided under the guidance of a trained health professional.

Massage

Massage involves manipulation, rubbing, and kneading of the body's muscle and soft tissue to enhance the function of those tissues and promote relaxation (Lee, Kim, Yeo, Kim, & Lim, 2015). In all forms of massage, therapists use their hands (and sometimes forearms, elbows, and massage tools) to manipulate the body's soft tissue. Massage strokes can vary from light and shallow to firm and deep, and from slow, steady pressure to quick tapping. The choice will depend on the health and needs of the individual and the training and style of the massage therapist. Massage therapy has been shown to reduce pain and anxiety in randomized controlled trials (Lee et al., 2015). It can decrease stress, anxiety, depression, pain, and fatigue in some patients.

Patients should consult with their healthcare provider before undergoing any type of therapy that involves manipulation of joints and muscles; in some situations, patients may require an order to obtain massage therapy based on their condition and the care setting (Karagozoglu & Kahve, 2013). Massage or manipulation of a bone in an area of cancer metastasis could result in a bone fracture (Pirri, 2011). Patients who have had radiation may find even light touch on the treatment area to be uncomfortable. If the woman is receiving radiation treatment, the massage therapist should not use lotion or oil on the areas where radiation is delivered and until skin, if inflamed, heals. Massage is contraindicated in persons with significant risk for a deep vein thrombosis (Shin et al., 2016).

Therapeutic touch, which is also sometimes called healing touch, is a CAM-based energy therapy based on the belief that vital energy flows through the human body (Senthil, Prabha, Jeganathan, D'Souza, & Misri, 2014). This energy is said to be balanced or made stronger by practitioners who pass their hands over, or gently touch, a patient's body (Hammerschlag, Marx, & Aickin, 2014). Nurses can receive additional training on these techniques (Senthil et al., 2014). Therapeutic touch is being studied in patients who are receiving cancer therapy, to determine whether it can improve quality of life, boost the immune system, or reduce side effects (Hammerschlag et al., 2014).

Meditation

Meditation is a mind-body process that uses concentration or reflection to relax the body and calm the mind (Witt & Cardoso, 2016). A person may meditate by choosing a quiet place free from distraction, sitting or resting quietly with eyes closed, mindful of breathing and physical sensations, and being aware of and then letting go of all intruding thoughts. The person may also achieve a relaxed, yet alert state by focusing on a pleasant idea or thought or by chanting a phrase known as a mantra or special sound silently or aloud. The ultimate goal of meditation is to separate oneself mentally from the outside world by suspending the usual stream of consciousness. Some practitioners recommend two 15- to 20-minute sessions a day.

Clinical trials have studied meditation as a way of reducing the effects of stress on both the mind and the body. Research shows that meditation can help reduce anxiety, stress, blood pressure, chronic pain, and insomnia.

Meditation may help with symptoms of anxiety and mood disturbance (Pirri, 2011).

There are a number of different types of meditation. Although step-by-step guides are available, most individuals will benefit from an initial session with a therapist skilled in teaching meditation skills (Frenkel et al., 2015).

Music Therapy

Music therapy is offered by licensed healthcare professionals who use music to promote healing and enhance quality of life. Individuals may use music therapy to encourage emotional expression, promote social interaction, relieve symptoms, and for other purposes (Mahon & Mahon, 2011). Music therapists may use active (such as engaging the patient in singing or playing instruments) or passive (such as playing or singing for the patient) methods, depending on the patient's needs, interests, and abilities. Music therapy can help to reduce pain and relieve chemotherapy-induced nausea and vomiting. It may also relieve stress and provide an overall sense of well-being. Music therapy can lower heart rate, blood pressure, and breathing rate and can improve comfort, relaxation, and pain control (Mahon & Mahon, 2011). Individuals can also use music therapy for distraction.

Music therapists design music sessions for individuals and groups based on their needs and tastes. Some aspects of music therapy include making music, listening to music, writing songs, and talking about lyrics. It may also involve imagery and learning through music (Mahon & Mahon, 2011). Music therapists provide music therapy in different settings, such as hospitals, cancer centers, hospices, at home, or anywhere people can benefit from its calming or stimulating effects. The patient does not need to have any musical ability to benefit from music therapy.

In general, music therapy provided under the care of a professionally trained therapist has a helpful effect and is considered safe when used along with standard treatment. Musical intervention by untrained people can be ineffective or even cause increased stress and discomfort (Bradt, Dileo, Magill, & Teague, 2016). More information about professional licensed musical therapists is available through the American Music Therapy Association (https://www.musictherapy.org).

Tai Chi

Tai chi is an ancient Chinese martial art. It is a mind-body, self-healing system that uses movement, meditation, and breathing to improve health and well-being. Tai chi is useful as a form of exercise that may improve posture, balance, muscle mass and tone, flexibility, stamina, and strength in older adults. Research also recognizes tai chi as a method to reduce stress that can provide the same cardiovascular benefits as moderate exercise, such as lowered heart rate and blood pressure (Chaoul, Milbury, Sood, Prinsloo, & Cohen, 2014).

The slow, graceful movements of tai chi, accompanied by rhythmic breathing, relax the body and the mind. Each form contains between 20 and 100 moves and can require up to 20 minutes to complete the movements, which the individual practices in pairs of opposites; for example, a turn to the left follows a turn to the right. While performing these exercises, the person is urged to pay close attention to her breathing, which is centered in the diaphragm. Tai chi emphasizes technique rather than strength or power, although the slow, precise movements require good muscle control (Witt & Cardoso, 2016).

Tai chi is associated with a sense of improved well-being and increased motivation to continue exercising. Many people like tai chi because it is self-paced, is noncompetitive, and does not require large amounts of space, special equipment, or clothing (Pirri, 2011). Tai chi

is considered to be a relatively safe, moderate physical activity. As with any form of exercise, individuals must consider personal physical limitations, and patients should talk with their healthcare provider before starting any type of therapy that involves movement of joints and muscles.

Yoga

Yoga is a form of nonaerobic exercise that involves a program of precise posture, breathing exercises, and meditation. It is a way of life that combines ethical standards, dietary guidelines, physical movements, and meditation to create a union of mind, body, and spirit (Chaoul et al., 2014).

A typical yoga session lasts between 20 minutes and 1 hour. A yoga session starts with the person sitting in an upright position and performing gentle movements, all of which are done very slowly, while taking slow, deep breaths from the abdomen. Yoga requires several sessions a week for a person to become proficient. Individuals can practice yoga at home without a teacher or in group classes. Many books and DVDs on yoga are also available. Yoga programs are often offered through groups such as the Cancer Support Community (www.cancersupportcommunity.org).

Individuals can use yoga to control physical functions, such as blood pressure, heart rate, breathing, metabolism, body temperature, brain waves, and skin resistance (Pirri, 2011). This can result in improved physical fitness, lower levels of stress, and increased feelings of relaxation and well-being. Some yoga postures are hard to achieve, and damage can occur from overstretching joints and ligaments. Individuals should check with their healthcare provider before initiating a yoga program.

DIETARY SUPPLEMENTS

Many patients consider the use of dietary supplements, such as vitamins, herbs, or any product made from plants, an important part of their cancer treatment. Currently, few governmental standards are in place to control the production and ensure the safety, effectiveness, and quality of dietary supplements; however, the U.S. Food and Drug Administration (FDA) released regulations in 2007 to help improve the safety and consistency of supplements; these guidelines are updated regularly (FDA, 2016).

Dietary supplements have potential risks and side effects, just like any medication. For some supplements, manufacturers provide dosage guidelines. Patients can usually use supplements safely within certain dosage guidelines (Frenkel, 2015). However, unlike drugs, dietary supplements are, in general, self-prescribed with minimal input from healthcare providers. There may not be documented information to support safe use with acceptable risk.

Patients may assume that over-the-counter supplements are safe to take. In fact, large doses of some vitamins or minerals can be dangerous and toxic. Another common misconception is that if the substance is natural, it is safe (Sanders, Moran, Shi, Paul, & Greenlee, 2016).

Many people assume that they can safely take dietary supplements along with any prescription drugs. This also is not true. Manufacturers of herbal supplements do not provide adequate research verifying drug interactions and risks. Most drug companies and producers of herbal supplements do not conduct research on possible drug interactions, so the risks of taking supplements along with many other medications are unknown (Sanders et al., 2016).

In the United States, all over-the-counter and prescription drugs are regulated by the FDA. Because dietary supplements (including all forms of botanicals and vitamins) are not considered drugs, they are not put through the same strict safety and effectiveness requirements that are applied to other drugs (Sanders et al., 2016). Table 12-2 provides guidelines for the selection of dietary supplements.

NON-CAM INTERVENTIONS AS PART OF INTEGRATED CANCER CARE

Psychotherapy, spiritual practices, and support groups can be effective adjuncts to therapy and are often part of integrated cancer care.

Psychotherapy

The term *psychotherapy* encompasses a wide range of approaches designed to help people change their ways of thinking, feeling, or behaving. Psychotherapy can help people, including those with cancer, find the inner strength they need to improve their coping skills, allowing them to more fully enjoy their lives. Individuals can use psychotherapy to help cope with the diagnosis and treatment of cancer and to aid in overcoming depression and anxiety, which are common in people with cancer (Witt & Cardoso, 2016).

Psychotherapy is available in many forms. People may seek individual therapy, where there is a one-on-one relationship with a therapist. Other therapists work with couples or entire families to deal with the impact of the cancer and its diagnosis on those most closely affected. Psychotherapy may also be practiced with groups, in which a number of people meet to discuss common experiences and issues and to learn specific coping techniques (Frenkel et al., 2015).

Psychotherapists vary in their amount of training and experience in dealing with issues that are important for people with cancer.

TABLE 12-2: PATIENT EDUCATION AND GUIDELINES FOR CHOOSING SAFE DIETARY SUPPLEMENT PRODUCTS

- Speak with a healthcare provider about any supplement under consideration. Healthcare providers should evaluate the supplement using information from reputable sources, such as the National Center for Complementary and Integrative Health or the Office of Dietary Supplements of the National Institutes of Health (http://dietary-supplements.info.nih.gov).

- When shopping for supplements, the patient should look for "USP-NF" on the package label. *The United States Pharmacopeia – National Formulary* (USP-NF) is a book of public pharmacology standards. It contains standards for medicines, dosage forms, drug substances, medical devices, and dietary supplements.

- When shopping for a botanical, patients should be sure to find a product that uses only the effective part of the plant. Avoid botanicals that have been made using the entire plant, unless the entire plant is recommended.

- The patient should be taught to consider the name and reputation of the manufacturer or distributor. Is it a nationally known name? Large companies with a reputation to uphold are more likely to manufacture their products under strict, quality-controlled conditions.

- The label should provide a way to contact the company if there are questions or concerns about the product. Reputable manufacturers will provide contact information on the label or packaging of their products.

- Patients should try to avoid mixtures of many different supplements. The more ingredients there are, the greater the chances are of harmful effects.

- Patients should try to avoid supplements priced significantly lower than similar products; they are likely to be of lower quality.

- In particular, patients should be taught to avoid products that claim to be "miracle cures," "breakthroughs," or "new discoveries"; to have benefits but no side effects; or to be based on a "secret ingredient" or method. Such claims are almost always fraudulent, and the product may contain potentially harmful substances or contaminants.

- Patients should be taught to avoid products that claim to be effective treatment for a wide variety of unrelated illnesses. If a supplement claims that it can diagnose, treat, cure, or prevent disease, such as "cures cancer," the product is being sold illegally as a drug.

Note. Adapted from Frenkel, M. (2015). Is there a role for nutritional supplements in cancer care? Challenges and solutions. *Future Oncology,* *11*(6), 901-904. doi:10.2217/fon.14.309; Pirri, C. (2011). Integrating complementary and conventional medicine. *Cancer Forum, 35*(1), 31-39; Sanders, K., Moran, Z., Shi, Z., Paul, R., & Greenlee, H. (2016). Natural products for cancer prevention: Clinical update 2016. *Seminars in Oncology Nursing, 32*(3), 215-240. doi:10.1016/j.soncn.2016.06.001; and Witt, C. M., & Cardoso, M. J. (2016). Complementary and integrative medicine for breast cancer patients – Evidence-based practical recommendations. *The Breast, 28,* 37-44. doi:10.1016/j.breast.2016.04.012

Psychotherapy may be performed by practitioners with a number of different qualifications, including psychologists, marriage and family therapists, licensed clinical social workers, counselors, psychiatric nurses, and psychiatrists (Pirri, 2011). Difficult personal issues that arise or are exposed and expressed when a person engages in psychotherapy can be emotionally upsetting or uncomfortable, and working through these issues is part of the therapy process.

Spirituality

Spirituality is an awareness of something greater than the individual self. People often express spirituality through religion or prayer, although there are many other paths of spiritual pursuit and expression. Studies have found that spirituality and religion are very important to quality of life for some people with cancer. The psychological benefits of praying may include reduction of stress and anxiety, promotion of a more positive outlook, and a strengthening of the will to live (Witt & Cardoso, 2016).

Spirituality has many forms, and individuals can practice spirituality in many ways. Prayer, for example, may be silent or spoken out loud and can be done alone in any setting or in groups. Research has shown that spirituality can improve quality of life in persons with cancer (Whitford & Olver, 2011).

Individuals who are not members of a formal religion can also practice spirituality. Meditation, 12-step work (as practiced in Alcoholics Anonymous and similar groups), and seeking meaning in life all involve spirituality (Bauml et al., 2015). Many medical institutions and practitioners include spirituality and prayer as important components of healing. In addition, hospitals have chapels and contracts with ministers, rabbis, clerics, and voluntary organizations to serve their patients' spiritual needs.

Support Groups

Support groups present information, provide comfort, teach coping skills, help reduce anxiety, and provide a place for people to share common concerns and emotional support; for many patients, they can improve quality of life (Witt & Cardoso, 2016). For many patients and their families, these are an important adjunct to therapy and are discussed in detail in Chapter 13.

COMPLEMENTARY AND ALTERNATIVE MEDICINES AND NURSING ASSESSMENT

CAM availability and use are considerations for nurses caring for cancer patients. Awareness and resource management with regard to reputable CAMs falls within nursing practice. Assessment, education, and advocacy for women with a diagnosis of cancer who are seeking CAMs are actions nurses need to integrate as they deliver care. Advocacy for patients – in the form of helping them evaluate CAMs – becomes an appropriate focus of nurses. The nursing assessment of medical and lifestyle history should include direct questions about CAMs. If a patient uses a CAM therapy or product, the nurse should explore this in more detail, to determine whether it is safe for the individual patient (Witt & Cardoso, 2016). Sharing assessment findings with the healthcare team is essential. Facilitating appropriate referrals when indicated is a key nursing function. CAMs can be a useful adjunct to therapy, but nurses need to emphasize safety in each individual situation.

Table 12-3 provides a list of questions that patients can ask when considering CAMs. With the amount of CAM information and publicity on the Internet, no coaching of patients about CAMs is complete without guidance in reviewing potential treatments (Pirri, 2011).

SUMMARY

The use of CAMs is widespread, especially among women. Although more research is needed across the spectrum of CAMs, some research has shown that CAMs can boost the perceived effectiveness of treatment and enable patients to better deal with adverse treatment

TABLE 12-3: SELECTING A COMPLEMENTARY AND ALTERNATIVE MEDICINE PRACTITIONER

Issues to consider when selecting a complementary and alternative medicine (CAM) practitioner include the following:

- Select a CAM provider with the same care as the selection of any other member of the healthcare team. A patient seeking a CAM practitioner should speak with her healthcare provider(s) or someone knowledgeable about CAM regarding the therapy under consideration. The healthcare provider may be able to make a recommendation for the type of CAM practitioner the patient is seeking.

- Before engaging a CAM practitioner, ask basic questions about his or her credentials and practice. Where did the practitioner receive training? What licenses or certifications does he or she have? How much will the treatment cost? Patients can contact CAM professional organizations to get the names of practitioners who are certified. This means that they have proper training in their fields.

- CAM can be expensive. Check with insurers to determine whether the cost of therapy is covered.

- Make a list of questions to ask at the first visit. Ideally, the patient will bring a friend or family member who can help ask questions and note answers.

- On the first visit, be prepared to answer questions about health history, including injuries, surgeries, and major illnesses, and use of any prescription medicines, vitamins, and other supplements.

- Assess the first visit and decide whether the practitioner is a good fit. Aspects to consider include level of comfort, willingness to answer questions, and reasonableness of the treatment plan.

Note. Adapted from: Mulkins, A. L., McKenzie, E., Verhoef, M. J., Balneaves, L. G., & Salamonsen, A. (2016). From the conventional to the alternative: Exploring patients' pathways of cancer treatment and care. *Journal of Complementary & Integrative Medicine, 13*(1), 51-64. doi:10.1515/jcim-2014-0070; Pirri, C. (2011). Integrating complementary and conventional medicine. *Cancer Forum, 35*(1), 31-39.

effects (Adams, 2013). CAMs can provide physical, emotional, and spiritual methods for mind-body interventions, biologically based treatments, manipulative and body-based treatments, and energy therapies. Oncology nurses and APRNs have experienced the use of CAMs with cancer patients in various practice settings for many years. Many CAM therapies have been available for centuries; more recently, their value in oncology is being recognized (Leggett, Koczwara, & Miller, 2015). Clinicians are still educating themselves about what is needed to assist patients in navigating and selecting the various CAM options. When integrating CAMs into practice, nurses need to help patients assess their safety, reliability, ability to enhance or complement standard treatment protocols, and their real and perceived benefits for quality of life.

EXAM QUESTIONS

CHAPTER 12
Questions 89–94

Note: Choose the one option that BEST answers each question.

89. Women diagnosed with cancer might choose to use complementary and alternative medicine (CAM) cancer treatments because they

    a. offer a sense of control.

    b. are in vogue.

    c. are harmless.

    d. are pure.

90. A reliable source of information about CAM is

    a. patient testimonials.

    b. support groups.

    c. the NCCIH.

    d. books on CAM.

91. One of the four focuses of the National Center for Complementary and Integrative Health (NCCIH) is to

    a. train CAM researchers.

    b. promote the use of CAMs.

    c. discourage the use of CAMs.

    d. review all CAM research protocols.

92. Which CAM therapy has been shown to reduce pain and anxiety in randomized controlled trials?

    a. Antidepressants

    b. Massage

    c. Antiemetics

    d. Pain medications

93. Which CAM therapy is able to lower heart rate, blood pressure, and breathing rate; can improve comfort, relaxation, and pain control; and can be used for distraction?

    a. Paclitaxel therapy

    b. Gamma knife radiation therapy

    c. Sentinel node biopsy

    d. Music therapy

94. Assessment, education, and advocacy for women with a diagnosis of cancer who are seeking CAMs are actions the nurse needs to integrate as care is delivered. Which two key nursing behaviors will help the nurse support the patient?

    a. Selecting a biased approach and referring patients to the Internet

    b. Awareness and resource management

    c. Lack of awareness and making a referral to a social worker

    d. Not disclosing the patient's interest in seeking CAM

REFERENCES

Adams, J. (2013). *Primary health care and complementary and integrative medicine: Practice and research.* London: Imperial College Press.

Bauml, J. M., Chokshi, S., Schapira, M. M., Im, E.-O., Li, S. Q., Langer, C. J., ... Mao, J. J. (2015). Do attitudes and beliefs regarding complementary and alternative medicine impact its use among patients with cancer? A cross-sectional survey. *Cancer, 121*(14), 2431-2438. doi:10.1002/cncr.29173

Bonacchi, A., Toccafondi, A., Mambrini, A., Cantore, M., Muraca, M. G., Focardi, F., ... Miccinesi, G. (2015). Complementary needs behind complementary therapies in cancer patients. *Psycho-Oncology, 24*(9), 1124-1130. doi:10.1002/pon.3773

Bradt, J., Dileo, C., Magill, L., & Teague, A. (2016). Music interventions for improving psychological and physical outcomes in cancer patients. *Cochrane Database of Systematic Reviews, 2016*(8), CD006911. doi:10.1002/14651858.CD006911.pub3

Burhenn, P., Olausson, J., Villegas, G., & Kravits, K. (2014). Guided imagery for pain control. *Clinical Journal of Oncology Nursing, 18*(5), 501-503. doi:10.1188/14.CJON.501-503

Chaoul, A., Milbury, K., Sood, A. K., Prinsloo, S., & Cohen, L. (2014). Mind-body practices in cancer care. *Current Oncology Reports, 16*(12), 417. doi:10.1007/s11912-014-0417-x

Chon, T. Y., & Lee, M. C. (2013). Acupuncture. *Mayo Clinic Proceedings, 88*(10), 1141-1146. doi:10.1016/j.mayocp.2013.06.009

Clarke, T. C., Black, L. I., Stussman, B. J., Barnes, P. M., & Nahin, R. L. (2015). Trends in the use of complementary health approaches among adults: United States, 2002-2012. *National Health Statistics Reports No. 79.* Hyattsville, MD: National Center for Health Statistics. Retrieved from http://www.cdc.gov/nchs/data/nhsr/nhsr079.pdf

Frenkel, M. (2015). Is there a role for nutritional supplements in cancer care? Challenges and solutions. *Future Oncology, 11*(6), 901-904. doi:10.2217/fon.14.309

Frenkel, M., Sierpina, V., & Sapire, K. (2015). Effects of complementary and integrative medicine on cancer survivorship. *Current Oncology Reports, 17*(5), 445. doi:10.1007/s11912-015-0445-1

Giron, P. S., Haddad, C. A. S., Lopes de Almeida Rizzi, S. K., Nazário, A. C. P., & Facina, G. (2016). Effectiveness of acupuncture in rehabilitation of physical and functional disorders of women undergoing breast cancer surgery. *Supportive Care in Cancer, 24*(6), 2491-2496. doi:10.1007/s00520-015-3054-5

Hammerschlag, R., Marx, B. L., & Aickin, M. (2014). Nontouch biofield therapy: A systematic review of human randomized controlled trials reporting use of only nonphysical contact treatment. *Journal of Alternative and Complementary Medicine, 20*(12), 881-892.

Karagozoglu, S., & Kahve, E. (2013). Effects of back massage on chemotherapy-related fatigue and anxiety: Supportive care and therapeutic touch in cancer nursing. *Applied Nursing Research, 26*(4), 210-217. doi:10.1016/j.apnr.2013.07.002

Lau, C. H. Y., Wu, X., Chung, V. C. H., Liu, X., Hui, E. P., Cramer, H., ... Wu, J. C. Y. (2016). Acupuncture and related therapies for symptom management in palliative cancer care: Systematic review and meta-analysis. *Medicine, 95*(9). doi:10.1097/MD.0000000000002901

Lee, S. H., Kim, J. Y., Yeo, S., Kim, S. H., & Lim, S. (2015). Meta-analysis of massage therapy on cancer pain. *Integrative Cancer Therapies, 14*(4), 297-304. doi:10.1177/1534735415572885

Leggett, S., Koczwara, B., & Miller, M. (2015). The impact of complementary and alternative medicines on cancer symptoms, treatment side effects, quality of life, and survival in women with breast cancer – A systematic review. *Nutrition and Cancer, 67*(3), 373-391. doi:10.1080/01635581.2015.1004731

Mahon, E. M., & Mahon, S. M. (2011). Music therapy: A valuable adjunct in the oncology setting. *Clinical Journal of Oncology Nursing, 15*(4), 353-356. doi:10.1188/11.CJON.353-356

Mulkins, A. L., McKenzie, E., Verhoef, M. J., Balneaves, L. G., & Salamonsen, A. (2016). From the conventional to the alternative: Exploring patients' pathways of cancer treatment and care. *Journal of Complementary & Integrative Medicine, 13*(1), 51-64. doi:10.1515/jcim-2014-0070

National Cancer Institute. (2016). *Acupuncture (PDQ®) – Health professional version.* Retrieved from https://www.cancer.gov/about-cancer/treatment/cam/hp/acupuncture-pdq

National Cancer Institute. (2017). *Aromatherapy and essential oils (PDQ®) – Health professional version.* Retrieved from https://www.cancer.gov/about-cancer/treatment/cam/hp/aromatherapy-pdq

National Center for Complementary and Integrative Health. (2016). *Complementary, alternative, or integrative health: What's in a name?* Retrieved from https://nccih.nih.gov/health/integrative-health#term

Papagiannaki, A., & Shinebourne, P. (2016). The contribution of creative art therapies to promoting mental health: Using interpretative phenomenological analysis to study therapists' understandings of working with self-stigmatisation. *Arts in Psychotherapy, 50,* 66-74. doi:10.1016/j.aip.2016.06.007

Pirri, C. (2011). Integrating complementary and conventional medicine. *Cancer Forum, 35*(1), 31-39.

Rankanen, M. (2016). Clients' experiences of the impacts of an experiential art therapy group. *Arts in Psychotherapy, 50,* 101-110. doi:10.1016/j.aip.2016.06.002

Reis, D., & Jones, T. (2017). Aromatherapy: Using essential oils as a supportive therapy. *Clinical Journal of Oncology Nursing, 21*(1), 16-19. doi:10.1188/17.CJON.16-19

Sanders, K., Moran, Z., Shi, Z., Paul, R., & Greenlee, H. (2016). Natural products for cancer prevention: Clinical update 2016. *Seminars in Oncology Nursing, 32*(3), 215-240. doi:10.1016/j.soncn.2016.06.001

Senthil, K. P., Prabha, A., Jeganathan, P. S., D'Souza, C., & Misri, Z. K. (2014). Efficacy of therapeutic touch and reiki therapy for pain relief in disease conditions: A systematic review. *Journal of Psychiatric Nursing, 3*(1), 15.

Shin, E.-S., Seo, K.-H., Lee, S.-H., Jang, J.-E., Jung, Y.-M., Kim, M.-J., & Yeon, J.-Y. (2016). Massage with or without aromatherapy for symptom relief in people with cancer. *Cochrane Database of Systematic Reviews, 2016*(6), CD009873. doi:10.1002/14651858.CD009873.pub3

Sohl, S. J., Borowski, L. A., Kent, E. E., Smith, A. W., Oakley-Girvan, I., Rothman, R. L., & Arora, N. K. (2015). Cancer survivors' disclosure of complementary health approaches to physicians: The role of patient-centered communication. *Cancer, 121*(6), 900-907. doi:10.1002/cncr.29138

Synovitz, L. B., & Larson, K. L. (2013). *Complementary and alternative medicine for health professionals: A holistic approach to consumer health.* Burlington, MA: Jones & Bartlett Learning.

U.S. Food and Drug Administration. (2016). A food labeling: Revision of the nutrition and supplement facts labels. Final Rule, 21 CFR 101. *Federal Register, 81*(103), 33741-33999.

Whitford, H. S., & Olver, I. N. (2011). Prayer as a complementary therapy. *Cancer Forum, 35*(1), 27-30.

Witt, C. M., & Cardoso, M. J. (2016). Complementary and integrative medicine for breast cancer patients – Evidence-based practical recommendations. *The Breast, 28,* 37-44. doi:10.1016/j.breast.2016.04.012

Wikimedia. (2007). *Acupuncture needle.* Retrieved from https://commons.wikimedia.org/wiki/File:Aiguille_d_acupuncture_avec_regle.dsc02265.untilted%2Bcropped%2BWB.jpg

CHAPTER 13

PATIENT EDUCATION CONSIDERATIONS

LEARNING OUTCOME

After completing this chapter, the learner will be able to discuss ways for the nurse and interdisciplinary team to assist patients in evaluating and accessing credible educational resources.

CHAPTER OBJECTIVES

After completing this chapter, the learner will be able to:

1. Describe the nurse's role in patient education.

2. Explain common approaches to providing education and identify barriers to learning.

3. Describe strengths and limitations of Internet resources for patient education.

4. Explain the role of cancer information centers and additional approaches to patient education.

INTRODUCTION

The amount of information available regarding a diagnosis of cancer can be very overwhelming. Websites, books, pamphlets, and help lines are available to provide information regarding diagnosis and treatment options and the use of complementary and alternative treatments. Although many of these resources provide qual-

ity information, both the academic literature and popular press have published numerous warnings regarding a wide range of medical misinformation and misrepresentation (Mazzocut et al., 2016; Sahin & Celikkan, 2012).

IMPORTANCE OF PATIENT EDUCATION

One of the nurse's key education roles throughout the cancer experience trajectory is helping patients identify appropriate sources of information regarding cancer. During the initial assessment, the nurse determines whether the patient wants a large amount of information or, based on the learning and needs assessment of the patient and family members, some combination of information. Some patients seek detailed information, whereas others desire only what is essential to manage their immediate care. Patient-focused care includes both the types and amount of education they receive, with the reassurance that they will have enough information to manage their illness safely and make appropriate decisions. The education process is ongoing and changes over the trajectory of the cancer diagnosis (Rohrmoser, Preisler, Bär, Letsch, & Goerlin, 2017).

Nurses, along with other members of the multidisciplinary team, provide patient education. This is an important and challenging component of practice. The nurse-patient relationship has shifted away from a paternalist approach to one incorporating patients in decision making (Reyna, Nelson, Han, & Pignone, 2015). Professional patient care means providing timely and accurate information so that patients have the knowledge they need and desire to participate in treatment decisions and self-care. Information on cancer can be delivered with written materials, through support groups, via Internet resources, and through cancer information centers.

Assessment

Assessment throughout the cancer trajectory should include a discussion about preferences and methods of education delivery (Salmon & Young, 2017). Choices for patient education can include printed patient materials, government websites and professional medical publications, scientific conferences open to the public and presented by healthcare professionals, as well as telephone and education sessions (Tucker, Martin, & Jones, 2017). Nurses need to be aware that the level of health literacy, readability of information, and cultural relevance may influence patient engagement and the effectiveness of the education process.

Age and generational differences affect information needs and source preferences. Older women with cancer may prefer more passive roles and express less need for information (Tucker et al., 2017). Younger women may have different concerns. For example, younger women with cancer may experience more treatment-related sexual dysfunction and infertility concerns that may not completely resolve; therefore, information on sexuality may be of special interest (Tucker et al., 2017). Approaches cannot be generalized. Getting to know the patient and providing education customized to the patient's stated interest, safety needs, preferred method of delivery, ability to comprehend, and cultural con-

text are factors that influence the outcome of the educational process.

The nurse needs to be aware of barriers to learning and mindful of bias when approaching patients with regard to education methods, health literacy, and communication preferences. Younger women may have a preference for more electronic and web-based forms of education (Salmon & Young, 2017). However, omitting such options to older women may reinforce an ageism stereotype.

Health literacy is the degree to which individuals have the capacity to obtain, process, and understand basic health information and services needed to make appropriate health decisions (Salmon & Young, 2017). Those with lower education levels and limited health literacy may experience barriers to understanding their disease and treatment options (Foste, Idossa, Mau, & Murphy, 2016). Women with higher educational levels have been found to be associated with a more active information-seeking style (Tucker et al., 2017). Information may need to be translated into other languages so the patient can understand the information. When developing an education plan, nurses should not assume the patient is literate in their self-selected primary language. Patients may be conversational but not able to read translated health information. Interpreters or translation lines can help facilitate the exchange of information and feedback.

Regardless of the type of cancer, nurses should focus on eliciting patient preferences, concerns, and needs pertaining to education about treatment plans, screening for second malignancies, survivorship care, and end-of-life care.

Ethnicity, race, and cultural background also influence information-seeking behaviors in women with a cancer diagnosis (Salmon & Young, 2017). Educational approaches may vary from group to group and among individuals within a group. Historically, cultural competence has focused on having healthcare providers learn relevant attitudes, values, beliefs, and behaviors of certain cultural groups including key "dos and don'ts" for each group. A limitation to this approach to clinical cultural competence is that culture is multidimensional and dynamic. Culturally competent clinical practice should focus on communication skills and sensitivity to the needs of individuals (Epner & Baile, 2012). This patient-centered approach relies on identifying and negotiating different styles of communication and learning, decision-making preferences, roles of family, sexual and gender issues, and issues of mistrust, prejudice, and racism.

Information needs, including the type of information sought, vary with the stage of diagnosis and position in the cancer trajectory (Tucker et al., 2017). Nurses need to be aware that an important aspect of cancer care is provision of specific information that is tailored to the specific stage the patient is experiencing along the disease continuum. Communication plans must take into consideration individuals who may be hearing, sight, speech, or intellectually impaired. Specialized approaches need to be developed and implemented to meet the treatment, education, and communication needs of patients who require assistance that goes beyond the exchange of information about their care.

Newly diagnosed patients with cancer often have complex educational and informational needs, and are often challenged when they are expected to choose from a variety of diagnostic, treatment, and symptom management options that were not available previously (Schofield & Chambers, 2015). Diagnostic procedures may include genetic testing, the use of tumor markers, or high-tech imaging to help guide treatment decisions. Complex surgical techniques, novel chemotherapy regimens, targeted therapies, and genetic approaches to treatment are available to patients with cancer. New antiemetics and biologic response modifiers allow for the administration of complicated chemotherapy regimens. Patients may choose to participate in clinical trials or undergo complex treatment regimens that might require innovative nursing interventions and comprehensive education to keep patients on track. Making informed treatment decisions becomes a high priority when so many choices are available (Reyna et al., 2015) and when decisions need to be made as the plan of care evolves. To make an informed choice, the patient and family must have appropriate and adequate education.

Long-term survivors' informational needs relate to their diagnosis, prognosis, and treatment options, including understanding and managing treatment-related toxicities and effects such as psychosocial complications (including anxiety and adjusting to a new self-image; Tucker et al., 2017). In the end-of-life and palliative treatment phase, specific information needs may include late-disease risks, complications of advanced disease, specific palliative care therapies and potential side effects, pain management, skin care, symptom management, and support for family and caregivers.

Presenting Patient Education

Various members of the healthcare team may provide information related to treatment options to patients, family members, and caregivers. Often that information is complex and confusing. In a busy unit, nurses may find it challenging to take the time to teach patients. Education needs to be a priority of the entire oncology team, including all of the nurses who encounter the woman throughout the cancer trajectory (Jenerette & Mayer, 2016). To facilitate patient education, many cancer centers utilize oncology nurse navigators (ONNs) as another resource for patient education and support (McMullen et al., 2016). The Oncology

Nursing Society (ONS) defines an ONN as a registered nurse with oncology-specific clinical knowledge who provides individualized assistance to patients, families, and caregivers to help overcome and navigate healthcare system barriers (ONS, 2015). A major responsibility of ONNs is to use the nursing process to provide education and resources to facilitate informed decision making and timely access to quality health and psychosocial care throughout all phases of the cancer trajectory (ONS, 2015). This definition establishes the importance of ONNs in the coordination of care for individuals affected by cancer. For accreditation by the American College of Surgeons, the healthcare facility must provide some form of nurse navigation (American College of Surgeons, 2016).

Teaching is often less effective with patients who experience high anxiety levels secondary to a cancer diagnosis (Fulcher, Kim, Smith, & Sherner, 2014; Mitchell et al., 2014). If a patient is experiencing significant anxiety or pain, the nurse must address these barriers to learning before delivering an educational message, because the pain or anxiety can greatly limit a patient's ability to participate in and understand educational information and materials. Patient safety may depend on adequate understanding of the side effects of treatment and how to manage side effects at home. Optimal teaching plans ensure that the extent, content, and timing of information given to patients are tailored to meet their needs (Reyna et al., 2015). Patients who have difficulty using standard written materials or those who learn best from auditory or visual information may require innovative and nontraditional teaching methods (Mann, 2011; Howell, Harth, Brown, Bennett, & Boyko, 2017).

Additional Considerations

Creativity and common sense can help with patient education. Directly asking the patient whether certain things or approaches have been effective for learning in the past is often helpful. Guidance the nurse can offer to patients includes, but is not limited to:

- Advise bringing a friend, family member, or spouse to the appointments so they can also hear and reinforce information. If a family member or friend cannot physically be at the appointment, offer the option to call in during the discussion.

- Suggest that the patient bring a notebook where she can keep questions to discuss at upcoming appointments, during phone calls, or when communicating by e-mail.

- Provide a folder where patients can keep all information in one place, including business cards of healthcare providers, patient education pieces, medical reports, and referral information.

- Provide the patient with a phone number and/or e-mail address to connect with the nurse and/or nurse navigator. Emphasize that this is a primary resource for patient information and if the nurse or nurse navigator cannot answer the question, he or she will connect the patient with a healthcare provider who can. Emphasize that the nurse is available and that this is a major focus of nursing. The patient and family should understand that they can contact the nurse between the patient's appointments as questions arise.

WRITTEN MATERIALS

Traditional oncology teaching tools include written booklets and teaching sheets that can be expensive to print, require significant storage space, and need periodic updates. Because of those constraints, educational materials housed in healthcare facilities may be limited, and information about rare cancers or unusual procedures may be difficult to find.

Despite these limitations, there remains a place for printed literature in patient education. Most importantly, it can serve as a reinforcement of information after the patient leaves the medical setting (Mann, 2011; Ryan et al., 2014).

Both complex and easy-to-read booklets are intended to help patients and caregivers communicate with healthcare providers about their treatment and support needs. The easy-to-read booklets often target newly diagnosed patients and individuals with lower reading levels. For such publications to be a useful adjunct to patient education, patients must be able to comprehend the material, which requires varying degrees of health literacy. These types of booklets are readily available from the American Cancer Society (ACS) and the National Cancer Institute.

Approximately one in five Americans is functionally illiterate (Vágvölgyi, Coldea, Dresler, Schrader, & Nuerk, 2016). Research suggests that one in five Americans reads at a fifth-grade level or lower. This is not necessarily a result of learning disorders or low IQ; it is often linked to poverty, unemployment, or advancing age. Persons who are illiterate may be very functional because they have learned to compensate for their lack of reading skills in other ways (Ballard & Hill, 2016). The nurse must consider literacy statistics when developing patient education materials. Health literacy is the degree to which individuals can obtain, process, and understand the basic health information and services they need to make appropriate health decisions. Readers of easy-to-read materials are not limited to those with little education, those who speak English as a second language, and children. Individuals who need easy-to-read materials are found in every race, ethnicity, age, and income group.

The inability to understand simple health information is a common, yet often overlooked limitation in oncology patients. Health literacy describes the capacity to which patients can comprehend and make decisions about their health care. Because health literacy is a difficult concept to measure in clinical practice, the practice of universal precautions for all patient interactions is the standard of care. In the context of health literacy, universal precautions involve the practice of plain language (written and oral) and the application of the teach-back method. With the use of universal precautions techniques and practices, nurses can effectively give patients the information that is critical to their health and wellness (Ballard & Hill, 2016).

Another issue with literacy in oncology patients relates to an increased risk for cognitive dysfunction compared with those who have never had cancer or cancer treatment (Von Ah, Jansen, & Allen, 2014). Cognitive dysfunction is a frequent finding in people with cancer, but it may go unnoticed. Cognitive problems result from many causes, including the direct effects of cancer on the central nervous system, indirect effects of certain cancers, and effects of cancer treatment on the brain. Cognitive dysfunction is often compounded by the mental and emotional aspects of dealing with a cancer diagnosis, including information overload, the stress of living with uncertainty and making treatment decisions, changes in schedule, anxiety, fear, and financial pressures (Von Ah et al., 2014). Ultimately, cognitive dysfunction also affects literacy, especially when providing patient education to individuals who are experiencing disease recurrence, progression of disease, or a second malignancy. Just because they have had treatment in the past does not mean that they understand the current treatment plan. Nurses must ensure that those with cognitive dysfunction receive education that will enable them to make good decisions and safely manage the side effects associated with the chosen regimen (Von Ah et al., 2014).

The nurse should consider the following issues when determining whether a brochure or guide is acceptable for persons with lower health literacy. These concepts also apply when creating printed materials.

Suggestions to improve written materials include (Ballard & Hill, 2016; Foste et al., 2016):

- Keep sentences short.

- Use plain and simple language.

- Eliminate jargon, medical terminology, and acronyms. Define any technical terms that must be included.

- Emphasize only one main objective or focus, not multiple concepts.

- Present information as a conversation. Material is sometimes easier to understand if it is presented this way.

- Ensure that each page flows into the next, and mutually supporting concepts are on the same page spread.

- Provide materials that are at a grade 5 or lower reading level.

- Break up paragraphs into shorter sections with clear subheadings.

- Include illustrations that aid comprehension.

- Avoid using words with more than one meaning.

- Provide only culturally sensitive pieces.

- Make the font large, and there should be a balance of white space and pictures with text. Too much text is overwhelming to persons with lower literacy.

Some patients want more detailed and complex information. This information is available from many agencies, including the National Institutes of Health, the ACS, and the National Comprehensive Cancer Network. Many detailed guides can be accessed and downloaded from the websites of these agencies. Patients may wish to access books and materials typically utilized by healthcare practitioners. In some cases, medical librarians may be able to assist with more intensive searches. Medical librarians are an often overlooked resource in oncology.

The nurse or nurse navigator in a healthcare facility may be instrumental in accessing the librarian and obtaining articles and journal information for specific patients. A reading list can be assembled and available for those who desire more in-depth information and ideally needs to be revised on a routine basis to be current. Cancer information centers also often keep lists of helpful publications and resources.

SUPPORT GROUPS AS AN EDUCATIONAL RESOURCE

Support groups may include education, behavioral training, and group interaction. Many different kinds of support groups are available, and they vary in their structure and activities (Pirri, 2011). Behavioral training can involve muscle relaxation or meditation to reduce stress or the effects of chemotherapy or radiation therapy (Mehta & Roth, 2015). Other groups function as an educational forum for group education. Still others provide a place for persons to share their feelings, concerns, frustrations, and fears. Many support groups combine multiple approaches. Often a facilitator manages or provides direction to discussions and offers other coordination services (Faller, Schuler, Richard, Heckl, Weis, & Küffner, 2013). A benefit of support groups is that most involve little or no cost to the participants (Frenkel, Sierpina, & Sapire, 2015).

Support groups can enhance quality of life for people with cancer by providing information and support to overcome the feelings of aloneness and helplessness that sometimes result from a diagnosis of cancer. Some people with cancer are better able to deal with their disease when supported by others in similar situations (Adams, 2013). Regardless of whether it is the direct purpose of the group, education about cancer and how to manage issues related to cancer occurs in support groups. Some individuals with cancer may find that the support group they have joined does not discuss topics of interest to them. Some people may find a support group upsetting because it stirs up too many uncomfortable feelings or because the leader is not skilled in group facilitation. Information that is shared in some groups may not always be reliable (Witt & Cardoso, 2016). For these reasons, nurses need to understand what goes on in the various groups their patients might participate in, and nurses should provide patients with information on how to select a group that will provide reputable information (Ashing-Giwa et al., 2012).

Some support groups take place on the Internet (Dolce, 2011). This support and education approach has strengths and weaknesses (see Table 13-1). Such groups usually involve interacting with people by sending and receiving messages via computers. These groups vary widely in quality. Some are led by moderators in chat rooms or on e-mail lists, and others are not moderated.

People may find online support groups helpful. For some, it may be comforting to share – through chat rooms, discussion boards, or mailing lists – thoughts and feelings with other people who are facing the same experiences. These groups allow people to connect with others who might otherwise be difficult to reach because of rarity of diagnosis, situation, or geographic location. They also allow individuals to keep their real identity private if they choose.

However, online groups may not be the best sources of health information, especially if they are not monitored by trained professionals or experts. Individuals should discuss any information obtained in an online group with a healthcare provider to determine whether it is accurate and appropriate in their individual situation.

Some support groups are organized according to the cancer type. For example, women with breast cancer may not be as comfortable in a mixed-diagnosis group with men who have lung cancer or other types of cancer. In some circumstances, this type of grouping seems more natural and enables people to address common issues more effectively. Many women prefer to be in groups of individuals of the same sex and with the same tumor types (Ashing-Giwa et al., 2012).

Another way to organize a support group is by the stage of the cancer experience. The issues that arise for a person with a new diagnosis are different from the issues for those who have recurrent cancer. For some, this may be an important distinction in choosing a support group.

Open membership in a group means that members may come and go within the group freely. There is often no requirement to sign up for the group ahead of time and no expectation that a patient will stay in a group over the group's time course. If an individual chooses to attend three meetings and is then unable to attend the next four but wants to return again later, this is acceptable. In an open-membership group, the membership will change with each group meeting. Such groups are a poor choice for persons who are interested in consistent or intimate relationships or friendships, but they are a good choice for persons who are not sure of a group or are not able to commit regularly to sessions.

In a closed group, the group members usually preregister for the group. The group achieves a certain number or mix and is then closed to new members. In a closed group, the members are usually expected to commit

TABLE 13-1: ADVANTAGES AND DISADVANTAGES OF INTERNET-BASED SUPPORT GROUPS

Advantages

- Absence of prejudices that sometimes arise in face-to-face support groups (such as age, gender, dress, or social status)

- Around-the-clock availability

- Reasonable cost

- Ability to read others' comments without responding, until the user is comfortable with the group

- Ability to avoid being seen while affected by chemotherapy or cancer

- No geographical limitations

Disadvantages

- Typically no professional facilitator

- Inability to include/assess nonverbal behavior

- Potential for members to present themselves falsely

- Language that may be offensive

- Lag time between comments/posts

- For some, delay in developing relationships and trust because of online communication only

Note. Adapted from Dolce, M. C. (2011). The Internet as a source of health information: Experiences of cancer survivors and caregivers with healthcare providers. *Oncology Nursing Forum, 38*(3), 353-359. doi:10.1188/11.ONF.353-359; Mann, K. S. (2011). Education and health promotion for new patients with cancer. *Clinical Journal of Oncology Nursing, 15*(1), 55-61. doi:10.1188/11.CJON.55-61

to attending a certain number of sessions. The advantages of this type of group include the consistency of the group members and the ability to get to know one another well and therefore support each other more fully. Sometimes this is just not feasible for cancer patients or their families because of the demands of the illness. Closed groups often have a specific plan of education or topics to be discussed, and there may be progression in the information shared over a set series of meetings.

Most cancer support groups are peer support groups (Mann, 2011). This type of group typically consists of those who have similar experiences. The group may be led by a layperson or health professional. These groups are often cohesive because of members' shared experiences and information. They can provide comfort, companionship, and a safe place to address issues such as fear, guilt, pain, and depression. Not only is the peer network supportive, but it can also be empowering. Laughing about the unique experiences one has as a cancer survivor is best done with others who have similar experiences. Similarity of experiences when shared can be very supportive. Education may be the framework for such groups, followed by a discussion.

An educational intervention group is a group that meets to share information on topics related to cancer. This type of group might include having a medical expert speak on a specific topic, such as infertility, genetics, new research, a specific treatment, or side effects. Following the presentation, the group has a question-and-answer discussion with the expert. This type of group is more focused on medical information but often provides some emotional support in the process of sharing. Sometimes having a concrete topic makes it easier to move into personal discussions with people who otherwise find it difficult to talk about their feelings. Having more information about the disease or treatment can help patients feel more in control.

Telephone support groups and some Internet support groups communicate by telephone, often by conference call (Dolce, 2011). This is helpful for people who are unable or unwilling to participate in face-to-face meetings. These groups can take any form. Some may be educational, whereas others may be focused on stress management. Some may have open membership, and others may be closed to new members. They can be time limited or ongoing. Sometimes participants contact one another in between group sessions and provide individual support. This type of group can be challenging because members are not able to see one another's facial expressions or body language. Careful listening and concentration are required. This may be a good option for someone who is physically immobile yet desires more contact with people. It is important that these groups are affiliated with a reputable organization and hosted by a trained professional (Reyna et al., 2015).

Support groups can be traditional discussions, classes to learn new skills, or exercise/lifestyle classes. All of these formats enable people to share with others and learn new ways to manage their cancer diagnoses and treatments.

There are support groups for children who have parents with a diagnosis of cancer. A support group for children gives them a safe place to verbalize their frustrations and ask questions. It can provide education for children delivered at an age-appropriate level. It is often very therapeutic for children to meet other children whose

parents have cancer. Children can feel isolated if a parent is sick and may think that no one else has the same feelings and worries. Support groups for children should be led by professionals. People such as schoolteachers or guidance counselors, art therapists, music therapists, oncology social workers, and nurses who have experience with children are examples of possible group leaders (Rashi, Wittman, Tsimicalis, & Loiselle, 2015). The professional should be knowledgeable about cancer and the issues it raises for families. Parents can check with resources in their community to find support groups for children whose parents have cancer.

THE INTERNET – AN EDUCATION TOOL

The Internet provides disease reviews, treatment information, clinical trials, the latest research news, decision-making tools, and discussion/support groups, both nationally and internationally (Dolce, 2011; Hesse, Greenberg, & Finney Rutten, 2016).

In a study from the American Association for Cancer Education, the percentage of cancer survivors who reported information seeking on the Internet increased from 66.8% in 2003 to 80.8% in 2013. Cancer information seeking on the Internet was independently associated with age, education, and income. According to one study, Internet information seeking was less likely among older adults, those with less education, and those with lower incomes (Finney Rutten et al., 2015).

Use of the Internet for patient education has some definite advantages, including access to potentially current information 24 hours a day, 7 days a week without having to travel from one's home. Online sources also provide a variety of teaching tools that use audio and video formats, which may be beneficial to people who have limited visual or language skills. The Internet can function as an educational strategy or tool. Some patients feel empowered when they have access to information, and some reports claim that patients cope better and experience less uncertainty when using the Internet as a resource for obtaining health-related materials (Dolce, 2011; Finney Rutten et al., 2016). Online information can be used to reinforce teaching provided in the healthcare setting, at a time of the patient's choosing, and can help patients formulate questions for discussion with the nurse and their care team.

There are clearly disadvantages to using the Internet for patient education. For some patients, the volume of information is excessive and can be overwhelming. Internet searches may not always provide information that is personally relevant or accurate. Although the Internet may be a source of empowerment for patients, it can also overwhelm users because of the sheer amount of information that is available (Salmon & Young, 2017). Issues of trustworthiness and security are also concerns in all cases where online sources provide health-related information.

Accessibility

For many patients, the Internet has become one of the first places to go for important information, including health information that ultimately guides treatment decisions. The Internet provides instant access to almost any topic. Most households have at least one computer or phone with access to the Internet. Others access the Internet at work or in public places such as libraries.

Although the Internet is a potentially powerful tool for the education of patients, its usefulness is still sometimes limited by accessibility factors. Although older adults in the United States are using technology in increasing numbers, they typically report more difficulty than younger people in learning to operate computers

and use the Internet effectively. Many adults may also experience frustration when using the Internet to obtain health information because many online sites require at least a high school level of proficiency in reading (Croyle, 2015).

Nurses can integrate Internet resources into practice by reviewing reputable sites and then incorporating the information into teaching sessions with patients. Computers with Internet access and appropriate links to patient-related material can be provided in clinic waiting rooms. If clinics provide their own websites for patient information, those websites should be user-friendly and easy to navigate (Dolce, 2011). Volunteers with technological savvy could assist patients who wish to access information on clinic computers. Patient education materials, offered on CDs and DVDs, may be alternatives to online resources.

Finding Information Online

Websites can provide basic facts about certain types of cancer, assist in locating the most current clinical trials, and provide information and support in dealing with cancer. It is possible to access research articles, information on doctors and hospitals, cancer treatment guidelines, drug information, and information on complementary and alternative therapies.

Unfortunately, there is also a great deal of inaccurate information posted on the Internet (Dolce, 2011). The Internet is not a peer-reviewed journal, and anyone can post almost anything. The fact that information is posted does not mean it is accurate. Some inaccurate information comes from well-meaning, but misinformed, people. There are also those who purposely try to deceive people, to sell either their ideas or their products. Because of this, it is important to teach patients to consider the credentials and reputation of the person or organization providing the information. Always remember that not all information is good information. There are millions of websites on the Internet. Finding sites that are reliable and accurate and that address an individual's specific concern or question can be more challenging than it appears (see Table 13-2).

Determining Credibility of Online Sources

Cancer information on the Internet originates from many different sources. Many of these sources are people or groups who really want to help others learn more. Many reputable professional organizations provide a wealth of useful and accurate information at no cost via the Internet. A sample of such organizations is listed in Table 13-3.

However, because anyone can post information on the Internet, some people may be passing along information that is incorrect. Unfortunately, some Internet sites are set up to deceive patients (Dolce, 2011). Scam artists and other dishonest people use the Internet because of the low cost and relative anonymity when posting information. Selling a product (bogus or not) over the Internet generally costs much less than opening and running an actual store. The Internet also allows the author of the web page to get information, messages, or products out to people all over the world. All it takes is some computer programming experience and a computer to host the website. The impersonal nature of the web makes it easier to mislead people (Dolce, 2011). Patients should be instructed to exercise caution when obtaining information from the Internet and especially before purchasing medications, supplements, or medical devices online.

One approach to help patients access safe information is to provide them with a list of web addresses to sites that are reputable. Patients can type the web address (also known as the uniform resource locator, or URL) of the exact website and be connected to the site. This approach ensures patients' access to safe information. If the site does not have the information the patient is searching for, this method can be a source of frustration for patients.

The most reliable sources of online health information tend to be government agencies, hospitals, universities, and major public health and health advocacy organizations, such as the ACS, whose information is reviewed by noted experts and updated often. Table 13-4 provides considerations for evaluating online medical resources.

The source of funding for the site should be determined because it can affect the material selected for the site and how it is presented. Government sites end in "gov." Many universities provide reputable information for their patients; these sites frequently end in "edu." If the source is a commercial business, such as an advertiser or provider of a service or product, there may be some bias or prejudice in the information. These sites frequently end in "com." Not-for-profit sites and organizations typically end in "org." Even with nonprofit websites, especially if the site is full of advertisements or is supported or funded by an outside company, it is important for the patient to ask whether the information presented might be biased in some way.

The U.S. Federal Trade Commission (2011) has developed a list of claims that should make an individual suspicious of a website.

- Claims of a "scientific breakthrough," "miraculous cure," "secret ingredient," or "ancient remedy"

- Claims that a product can cure a wide range of illnesses (no single product can do this)

- Case histories of people who have had amazing results (but no clear scientific data)

- Claims that a product is available only from one source (especially if payment must be made in advance)

- Claims of a "money-back" guarantee (Although this may make the product seem risk-free, it is often impossible to get your money back.)

TABLE 13-2: TIPS FOR FINDING ONLINE HEALTH INFORMATION RESOURCES

- Choosing an online health information resource is like choosing a healthcare provider. In most cases, an individual is encouraged to get opinions from several healthcare providers. Therefore, individuals should not rely on just one Internet site for all health information. A good rule of thumb is to find the website of a person, institution, or organization in which the user already has confidence. If possible, the user should seek information from several sources and not rely on a single source of information.

- Trust what is seen or read on the Internet only if the source of the information can be validated. Authors and contributors should always be identified, along with their affiliations and financial interests, if any, in the content. Phone numbers, e-mail addresses, or other contact information should also be provided.

- Question websites that credit themselves as being the sole source of information on a topic and sites that disrespect other sources of knowledge.

- Do not be fooled by a comprehensive list of links. Any website can link to another, and this in no way implies endorsement from either site.

- Find out if the site is professionally managed and reviewed by an editorial board of experts to ensure that the material is both credible and reliable. Sources used to create the content should be clearly referenced and acknowledged.

- Medical knowledge is continually evolving. Make sure that all clinical content includes the date of publication or modification.

- Any and all sponsorship, advertising, underwriting, commercial funding arrangements, or potential conflicts should be clearly stated and separated from the editorial content. A good question to ask is the following: Do the authors have anything to gain from proposing one particular point of view over another?

- Avoid any online physician who proposes to diagnose or treat without a proper physical examination and consultation regarding medical history.

- Read the website's privacy statement and make certain that any personal medical or other information supplied will be kept absolutely confidential.

- Most importantly, use common sense. This includes shopping around, always getting more than one opinion, being suspicious of miracle cures, and always reading the fine print.

Note. Adapted from Ashing-Giwa, K., Tapp, C., Rosales, M., McDowell, K., Martin, V., Santifer, R. H., … Mitchell, E. (2012). Peer-based models of supportive care: the impact of peer support groups in African American breast cancer survivors. *Oncology Nursing Forum, 39*(6), 585-591. doi:10.1188/12.ONF.585-591; Dolce, M. C. (2011). The Internet as a source of health information: Experiences of cancer survivors and caregivers with healthcare providers. *Oncology Nursing Forum, 38*(3), 353-359. doi:10.1188/11.ONF.353-359; Mann, K. S. (2011). Education and health promotion for new patients with cancer. *Clinical Journal of Oncology Nursing, 15*(1), 55-61. doi:10.1188/11.CJON.55-61

- Websites that fail to list the company's name, street address, phone number, and other contact information

Problems in any of these areas should raise a red flag – a warning – to the user that the site may contain information that is not based on careful science and cannot be trusted. This may be especially important when looking at sites that promote complementary or alternative cancer treatments.

Nursing Considerations

Nurses must understand how the Internet has influenced and changed the ways in which patients learn about and cope with their diseases. Nurses are uniquely suited to use online resources to aid in patient education and support. Patients look to nurses for reputable information. If the patient or family does not feel they are getting accurate information, then they will turn to other places such as the Internet, which may lead to inaccurate information (van der Wouden et al., 2016). Nurses need to be aware of and assess

TABLE 13-3: SELECTED CANCER INFORMATION RESOURCES

American Cancer Society: www.cancer.org

Cancer.Net: www.cancer.net/portal/site/patient

Cancer Wise (an online newsletter from the University of Texas, MD Anderson Cancer Center): www.cancerwise.org

Medline Plus: www.nlm.nih.gov/medlineplus/cancers.html

National Cancer Institute (NCI): www.cancer.gov

National Comprehensive Cancer Network (NCCN): www.nccn.org

Centers for Disease Control and Prevention (CDC): www.cdc.gov

Federal Trade Commission (FTC): www.ftc.gov

National Institutes of Health (NIH): www.nih.gov

National Center for Complementary and Alternative Medicine (part of NIH): http://nccam.nih.gov

U.S. Food and Drug Administration (FDA): www.fda.gov

Facing Our Risk Empowered (FORCE): www.facingourrisk.org/index.php

Susan G. Komen for the Cure: ww5.komen.org

Skin Cancer Foundation: www.skincancer.org

American Congress of Obstetricians and Gynecologists: https://www.acog.org

Tobacco-Free Kids: www.tobaccofreekids.org

National Society of Genetic Counselors: www.nsgc.org

Oncology Nursing Society: www.ons.org

American Society of Clinical Oncology: www.asco.org

Cancer Support Community: www.cancersupportcommunity.org

Help Me Understand Genetics: https://ghr.nlm.nih.gov/primer

Note. Western Schools, 2017.

TABLE 13-4: EVALUATING MEDICAL RESOURCES ON THE WEB

- Who runs the site? Investigate whether the site is managed or produced by healthcare professionals, reputable institutions such as academic medical centers, specialty or professional organizations, government agencies, and experts who are knowledgeable about current and effective treatments, trends, and information.

- Who pays for or sponsors the site? Commercial sponsors may be more interested in promoting their product(s) than providing unbiased information.

- What is the purpose of the site? Some sites want to provide education, whereas others may want to promote a product or service.

- Where does the information come from? Information should come from reputable professionals, not just promote patient testimonials or individual opinions.

- What is the basis of the information? The information should not be designed to sway a reader to a product or particular treatment. It should be factual and unbiased. Ideally, additional references or sources of information are included.

- How is the information selected? The information should be reviewed and/or written by healthcare professionals, not individuals or companies promoting a product or service.

- How current is the information? The site should be updated and reviewed regularly because medical information changes frequently. Check for a date of last review and contact information to reach the site.

- How does the site choose links to other sites? The site should provide information to find out more about complicated topics, but these should not link to sites that promote products or are not reviewed by healthcare professionals.

- What information about the user does the site collect, and why? Collecting other data on the site might be for advertising purposes or intended to target the user in other ways. Beware of sites that require memberships or payment unless you are interested in subscribing to a professional journal or organization.

Note. Western Schools, 2017.

whether patients are seeking information through Internet sources. Internet searches can provide information that sparks questions the patient and/or family can discuss with their healthcare team.

Nurses have a role in educating patients that the information found on the Internet should not take the place of medical advice. Any health-related problem should be discussed directly with a healthcare provider (Reyna et al., 2015). This is true for making a diagnosis and for many of the risk-assessment models available online. Even if a risk calculation is made, the risk needs to be interpreted by a medical professional and used to guide screening, prevention, or treatment decisions. Meeting with a healthcare provider who can examine the individual's health history, unique medical situation, and symptoms is still the best method for obtaining accurate information and care recommendations. If the nursing assessment indicates the patient is interested in or is actively accessing the Internet, then the nurse has an opportunity to provide the patient with information about accurate and reputable sites (van der Wouden et al., 2016).

CANCER INFORMATION CENTERS

Many institutions and government agencies provide patient education through cancer information centers. Patients can benefit from this coordinated approach to patient education.

The National Cancer Information Center of the ACS is a nationwide help line that is open 24 hours a day, 7 days a week. It answers calls and e-mails from cancer patients, family members and friends of cancer patients, and others who have questions about cancer-related issues. The database includes information about various types of cancer, cancer treatments, how to manage symptoms, prevention and detection guidelines, and many other topics. Each document in the database has been written and reviewed by a team of medical experts and further reviewed by professional editorial staff to translate any difficult medical terminology. This comprehensive information helps cancer patients better understand their disease and make informed decisions about their care.

Individuals who contact the ACS with more specific medical and cancer-related questions may be referred to oncology nurse information specialists. They provide clinical information, such as information on treatments, side effects of treatments, testing, and disease-related questions. These specialists answer more than 1.6 million calls yearly in more than 200 languages (ACS, 2017).

The National Cancer Institute's Cancer Information Service (CIS) provides current and accurate cancer information to patients, their families, the public, and health professionals. It serves the United States, Puerto Rico, the U.S. Virgin Islands, and the Pacific Islands. The CIS provides personalized, confidential responses to specific questions about cancer. Patients can access this service over the phone or online as follows:

- By telephone: U.S. residents may call the CIS toll-free at 1-800-4-CANCER (1-800-422-6237). Information specialists answer calls Monday through Friday from 9:00 a.m. to 4:30 p.m. local time, in English or Spanish. Callers with TTY equipment may call 1-800-332-8615. Callers also have the option of listening to recorded information about cancer 24 hours a day, 7 days a week.

- Online: Information specialists also offer online assistance in English, Monday through Friday, from 9:00 a.m. to 11:00 p.m. Eastern Time at https://www.cancer.gov.

Many institutions offer cancer information centers, which often operate on a walk-in basis to assist anyone whose life has been affected by cancer. Such centers might serve patients, their families, medical professionals, and others who need current information on cancer prevention; early detection, diagnosis, and treatment; coping; and community resources. Cancer information centers might typically provide the following resources:

- Internet access

- Educational programs

- Literature, videos, CDs, and DVDs

- Book-lending programs

- Smoking cessation programs

- Support groups

- Classes on chemotherapy and other treatments

- Wigs and turbans

- Breast prostheses

- Nutritional supplements

- Personalized one-on-one education and support

ADDITIONAL APPROACHES TO PATIENT EDUCATION

Nurses should not forget that there are other ways to approach and incorporate patient education into their practice. These approaches vary from one institution to another. Nurses need to think about ways to creatively increase patient education opportunities in their work setting.

For example, posters can be effective and inexpensive teaching tools. They can be purchased from commercial agencies and often are available free of charge from organizations such as the ACS. Posters can effectively deliver a simple message.

Bulletin boards are another effective way to deliver information. They can be placed in waiting rooms and examination rooms, and the information can be updated or changed on a regular basis. Bulletin boards are relatively inexpensive and can provide a means to tailor education to a specific population, geographic region, or type of cancer. If a nurse provides the educational material, often a volunteer can creatively construct the bulletin board in a visually appealing way.

Nurses can distribute items that promote a healthy lifestyle. Examples include hats to block ultraviolet light exposure and recipes for healthy food items. Pedometers are often relatively inexpensive and can be used to promote participation in a walking program. When nurses distribute such items, they also need to provide educational messages to promote the proper use of the items.

SUMMARY

Patient education is a key component of nursing practice. Individual patient assessments resulting in education and communication plans that are appropriate for a patient and family are important steps in the nursing process. Traditional forms of patient education, such as individual sessions and review of materials, are effective and can help to build relationships with patients and families. The Internet and the various opportunities it provides patients to obtain information and connect with others is a present and growing modality in cancer care. Nurses need to be aware of and instruct patients on how to access reliable online information, to identify reputable sources, and to use caution before making any cancer care-related purchases.

Organized groups provide support and education. Nurses can be important referral sources who assist patients in the selection of a specific group based on individual patient preferences. Nurses need to consider the environments in which they practice, selecting approaches that maximize educational opportunities to meet the unique needs of the particular populations they serve.

EXAM QUESTIONS

CHAPTER 13
Questions 95–100

Note: Choose the one option that BEST answers each question.

95. The purpose of the educational component of nursing is to help patients acquire the knowledge they need to

    a. comply with physician orders.

    b. learn what health professionals believe they need to know.

    c. have them become experts in a specific treatment.

    d. participate in treatment decisions and self-care.

96. Which of the following situations presents a major barrier to learning that needs to be addressed before beginning any patient education?

    a. The patient is newly diagnosed.

    b. The patient is experiencing pain.

    c. The patient has completed a college degree.

    d. The patient is unable to walk.

97. The nurse must consider literacy statistics when developing patient education materials. Research suggests that one in five Americans reads at or below a

    a. third-grade level.

    b. fifth-grade level.

    c. seventh-grade level.

    d. ninth-grade level.

98. The Internet provides disease reviews, treatment information, clinical trials, the latest research news, decision-making tools, and discussion/support groups that

    a. are expensive to join.

    b. provide the assurance of privacy.

    c. present information that is always accurate.

    d. are both national and international.

99. Patients should be cautious if accessing an Internet healthcare website

    a. with an editorial review board made up of respected physicians and nurses.

    b. that claims that a product is available from only one source.

    c. that was updated in the last 3 days.

    d. that posts affiliations of the editorial review board.

100. Individuals who contact the American Cancer Society with specific medical and cancer-related questions may be referred to oncology nurse information specialists. These specialists provide clinical information such as

    a. information on treatment side effects and testing.

    b. referrals to alternative therapy interest groups.

    c. vitamin product websites.

    d. health magazines.

This concludes the final examination.

Please answer the evaluation questions found on page v of this course book.

REFERENCES

Adams, J. (2013). *Primary health care and complementary and integrative medicine: Practice and research.* London: Imperial College Press.

American Cancer Society. (2017). *Cancer facts and figures – 2017.* Atlanta, GA: Author.

American College of Surgeons. (2016). *Commission on Cancer: Cancer program standards: Ensuring patient-centered care.* Retrieved from https://www.facs.org/quality-programs/cancer/coc/standards

Ashing-Giwa, K., Tapp, C., Rosales, M., McDowell, K., Martin, V., Santifer, R. H., … Mitchell, E. (2012). Peer-based models of supportive care: The impact of peer support groups in African American breast cancer survivors. *Oncology Nursing Forum, 39*(6), 585-591. doi:10.1188/12.ONF.585-591

Ballard, D., & Hill, J. (2016). The nurse's role in health literacy of patients with cancer. *Clinical Journal of Oncology Nursing, 20*(3), 232-234. doi:10.1188/16.CJON.232-234

Croyle, R. T. (2015). Risks and opportunities for psychology's contribution to the war on cancer. *American Psychologist, 70*(2), 221-224. doi:10.1037/a0038869

Dolce, M. C. (2011). The Internet as a source of health information: Experiences of cancer survivors and caregivers with healthcare providers. *Oncology Nursing Forum, 38*(3), 353-359. doi:10.1188/11.ONF.353-359

Epner, D. E., & Baile, W. F. (2012). Patient-centered care: The key to cultural competence. *Annals of Oncology, 23*(Suppl 3), 33-42. doi:10.1093/annonc/mds086

Faller, H., Schuler, M., Richard, M., Heckl, U., Weis, J., & Küffner, R. (2013). Effects of psycho-oncologic interventions on emotional distress and quality of life in adult patients with cancer: Systematic review and meta-analysis. *Journal of Clinical Oncology, 31*(6), 782-793. doi:10.1200/JCO.2011.40.8922

Federal Trade Commission. (2011). *Dietary supplements.* Retrieved from https://www.consumer.ftc.gov/articles/0261-dietary-supplements

Finney Rutten, L. J., Agunwamba, A. A., Wilson, P., Chawla, N., Vieux, S., Blanch-Hartigan, D., … Hesse, B. W. (2016). Cancer-related information seeking among cancer survivors: Trends over a decade (2003-2013). *Journal of Cancer Education, 31,* 348-357. doi:10.1007/s13187-015-0802-7

Foste, J., Idossa, L., Mau, L. W., & Murphy, E. (2016). Applying health literacy principles: Strategies and tools to develop easy-to-read patient education resources. *Clinical Journal of Oncology Nursing, 20*(4), 433-436.

Frenkel, M., Sierpina, V., & Sapire, K. (2015). Effects of complementary and integrative medicine on cancer survivorship. *Current Oncology Reports, 17*(5), 445. doi:10.1007/s11912-015-0445-1

Fulcher, C. D., Kim, H. J., Smith, P. R., & Sherner, T. L. (2014). Putting evidence into practice: Evidence-based interventions for depression. *Clinical Journal of Oncology Nursing, 18*(Suppl), 26-37. doi:10.1188/14. CJON.S3.26-37

Hesse, B. W., Greenberg A. J., & Finney Rutten, L. J. (2016). The role of Internet resources in clinical oncology: Promises and challenges. *Nature Reviews Clinical Oncology, 13*(12), 767-776. doi:10.1038/ nrclinonc.2016.78

Howell, D., Harth, T., Brown, J., Bennett, C., & Boyko, S. (2017). Self-management education interventions for patients with cancer: A systematic review. *Supportive Care in Cancer 25*(4), 1323-1355. doi:10.1007/ s00520-016-3500-z

Jenerette, C. M., & Mayer, D. K. (2016). Patient-provider communication: The rise of patient engagement. *Seminars in Oncology Nursing, 32*(1), 134-137.

Mann, K. S. (2011). Education and health promotion for new patients with cancer. *Clinical Journal of Oncology Nursing, 15*(1), 55-61. doi:10.1188/11.CJON.55-61

Mazzocut, M., Truccolo, I., Antonini, M., Rinaldi, F., Omero, P., Ferrarin, E., … Tasso, C. (2016). Web conversations about complementary and alternative medicines and cancer: Content and sentiment analysis. *Journal of Medical Internet Research, 18*(6), e120. doi:10.2196/jmir.5521

McMullen, L., Banman, T., DeGroot, J. M., Scott, S., Srdanovic, D., & Mackey, H. (2016). Providing novice navigators with a GPS for role development: Oncology nurse navigator competency project. *Clinical Journal of Oncology Nursing, 20*(1), 33-38. doi:10.1188/16.CJON.20-01AP

Mehta, R. D., & Roth, A. J. (2015). Psychiatric considerations in the oncology setting. *CA: A Cancer Journal for Clinicians, 65*(4), 299-314. doi:10.3322/caac.21285

Mitchell, S. A., Hoffman, A. J., Clark, J. C., DeGennaro, R. M., Poirier, P., Robinson, C. B., & Weisbrod, B. L. (2014). Putting evidence into practice: An update of evidence-based interventions for cancer-related fatigue during and following treatment. *Clinical Journal of Oncology Nursing, 18*(Suppl), 38-58. doi:10.1188/14.CJON. S3.38-58

Oncology Nursing Society. (2015). Oncology nurse navigation role and qualifications. *Oncology Nursing Forum, 42*(5), 447-448. doi:10.1188/15.ONF.447-448

Pirri, C. (2011). Integrating complementary and conventional medicine. *Cancer Forum, 35*(1), 31-39.

Rashi, C., Wittman, T., Tsimicalis, A., & Loiselle, C. G. (2015). Balancing illness and parental demands: Coping with cancer while raising minor children. *Oncology Nursing Forum, 42*(4), 337-344. doi:10.1188/15. ONF.337-344

Reyna, V. F., Nelson, W. L., Han, P. K., & Pignone, M. P. (2015). Decision making and cancer. *American Psychologist, 70*(2), 105-118. doi:10.1037/a0036834

Rohrmoser, A., Preisler, M., Bär, K., Letsch, A., & Goerlin, U. (2017). Early integration of palliative/supportive cancer care – healthcare professionals' perspectives on the support needs of cancer patients and their caregivers across the cancer treatment trajectory. *Supportive Care in Cancer, 25*(5), 1621-1627. doi:10.1007/s00520-017-3587-x

Ryan, L., Logsdon, M. C., McGill, S., Stikes, R., Senior, B., Helinger, B., ... Davis, D. W. (2014). Evaluation of printed health education materials for use by low-education families. *Journal of Nursing Scholarship, 46,* 218-228.

Sahin, Y. G., & Celikkan, U. (2012). MEDWISE: An innovative public health information system infrastructure. *Journal of Medical Systems, 36,* 1719-1729. doi:10.1007/s10916-010-9632-7

Salmon, P., and Young, B. (2017). A new paradigm for clinical communication: Critical review of literature in cancer care. *Medical Education, 51,* 258-268. doi:10.1111/medu.13204

Schofield, P., & Chambers, S. (2015). Effective, clinically feasible and sustainable: Key design features of psycho-educational and supportive care interventions to promote individualised self-management in cancer care. *Acta Oncologica, 54*(5), 805-812. doi:10.3109/0284186X.2015.1010016

Tucker, C. A., Martin, M. P., & Jones, R. B. (2017). Health information needs, source preferences and engagement behaviours of women with metastatic breast cancer across the care continuum: Protocol for a scoping review. *British Medical Journal Open, 7,* e013619. doi:10.1136/bmjopen-2016-013619

Vágvölgyi, R., Coldea, A., Dresler, T., Schrader, J., & Nuerk, H. (2016). A review about functional illiteracy: Definition, cognitive, linguistic, and numerical aspects. *Frontiers in Psychology, 7,* 1617. doi:10.3389/fpsyg.2016.01617. Retrieved from http://journal.frontiersin.org.ezp.slu.edu/article/10.3389/fpsyg.2016.01617/full

van der Wouden, C. H., Carere, D. A., Maitland-van der Zee, A. H., Ruffin, M. T., 4th, Roberts, J. S., Green, R. C., & Impact of Personal Genomics Study Group. (2016). Consumer perceptions of interactions with primary care providers after direct-to-consumer personal genomic testing. *Annals of Internal Medicine, 164*(8), 513-522. doi:10.7326/m15-0995

Von Ah, D., Jansen, C. E., & Allen, D. H. (2014). Evidence-based interventions for cancer- and treatment-related cognitive impairment. *Clinical Journal of Oncology Nursing, 18*(6), 17-25. doi:10.1188/14.CJON.S3.17-25

Witt, C. M., & Cardoso, M. J. (2016). Complementary and integrative medicine for breast cancer patients – Evidence-based practical recommendations. *The Breast, 28,* 37-44. doi:10.1016/j.breast.2016.04.012

RESOURCES

CANCER RESOURCES FOR PATIENTS AND THEIR FAMILIES

American Cancer Society
404-320-3333
1-800-227-2345 (1-800-ACS-2345)
http://www.cancer.org

American Cancer Society Supported Programs
Cancer Survivors Network
https://csn.cancer.org/

Cancer*Care*, Inc.
212-712-8080
1-800-813-4673 (1-800-813-HOPE)
212-712-8400 (Administration)
E-mail: info@cancercare.org
http://www.cancercare.org

Cancer Hope Network
1-877-467-3638 (1-877-HOPENET)
(908) 879-6518
E-mail: info@cancerhopenetwork.org
http://www.cancerhopenetwork.org

The Cancer Support Community
1-202-659-9709
1-888-793-9355
E-mail: help@cancersupportcommunity.org
http://www.cancersupportcommunity.org

Colon Cancer Alliance

212-627-7451 (Main office)

1-877-422-2030 (Help line)

E-mail: info@ccalliance.org

http://www.ccalliance.org

Colorectal Cancer Network

301-879-1500

E-mail: ccnetwork@colorectal-cancer.net

http://www.cancernetwork.com/colorectal-cancer

Facing Our Risk of Cancer Empowered

E-mail: info@facingourrisk.org

http://www.facingourrisk.org

Foundation for Women's Cancer (formerly Gynecologic Cancer Foundation)

1-800-444-4441

http://www.foundationforwomenscancer.org/

Look Good Feel Better

http://www.lookgoodfeelbetter.org

Living Beyond Breast Cancer

610-645-4567

1-888-753-5222 (1-888-753-LBBC) (Survivors' Help line)

E-mail: mail@lbbc.org

http://www.lbbc.org

Lung Cancer Alliance

800-298-2436 (US only)

202-463-2080

E-mail: info@lungcanceralliance.org

http://www.lungcanceralliance.org

Melanoma Research Foundation

(800) 673-1290 (Office)

(877) 673-6460 (Patient Help line)

https://www.melanoma.org

National Asian Women's Health Organization
> 415-989-9747
> E-mail: nawho@nawho.org
> http://www.healthywomen.org

National Cervical Cancer Coalition
> 1-800-685-5531
> http://www.nccc-online.org/

National Coalition for Cancer Survivorship
> 301-650-9127
> 1-877-622-7937 (1-877-NCCS-YES)
> E-mail: info@canceradvocacy.org
> http://www.canceradvocacy.org

National Lymphedema Network
> 510-208-3200
> 1-800-541-3259
> E-mail: nln@lymphnet.org
> http://www.lymphnet.org

National Ovarian Cancer Coalition
> 561-393-0005
> 1-888-682-7426 (1-888-OVARIAN)
> E-mail: NOCC@ovarian.org
> http://www.ovarian.org

Ovarian Cancer Research Fund Alliance
> 202-331-1332
> E-mail: info@ocrfa.org
> https://ocrfa.org/

Pancreatic Cancer Action Network
> 301-725-0025
> 1-877-272-6226 (1-877-2-PANCAN)
> E-mail: information@pancan.org
> http://www.pancan.org

R.A. Bloch Cancer Foundation, Inc.

    816-932-8453 (816-WE-BUILD)

    1-800-433-0464

    E-mail: hotline@hrblock.com

    http://www.blochcancer.org

Reach to Recovery

    http://www.cancer.org/treatment/supportprogramsservices/reach-to-recovery

Sisters Network, Inc.

    713-781-0255

    E-mail: sisnet4@aol.com

    http://www.sistersnetworkinc.org

Susan G. Komen for the Cure

    1-877 GO KOMEN (1-877-465-6636)

    E-mail: helpline@komen.org

    http://ww5.komen.org/

United Ostomy Associations of America, Inc.

    949-660-8624

    1-800-826-0826

    E-mail: uoa@deltanet.com

    http://www.ostomy.org/Home.html

SELECTED INTERNET RESOURCES

American Cancer Society

    http://www.cancer.org

American College of Radiology Mammography Accreditation

    http://www.acr.org

American Society of Clinical Oncology

    http://www.asco.org

Bright Pink

    http://www.brightpink.org

Food and Drug Administration Breast Implant Information Line
http://www.fda.gov/ForConsumers/ConsumerUpdates/ucm063728.htm

Foundation for Women's Cancer
http://www.wcn.org

Fox Chase Cancer Center
http://www.fccc.edu

International Society of Nurses in Genetics
http://www.isong.org

Mayo Clinic
http://www.mayoclinic.com

National Cancer Institute of the National Institutes of Health
http://www.cancer.gov

National Center for Complementary and Alternative Medicine
http://nccam.nih.gov

National Coalition for Cancer Survivorship
http://www.canceradvocacy.org

National Comprehensive Cancer Network
http://www.nccn.org

National Institutes of Health
http://www.nih.gov

National Society of Genetic Counselors
http://www.nsgc.org

OncoLink
http://www.oncolink.upenn.edu/

Oncology Nursing Society

http://www.ons.org

Surveillance, Epidemiology, and End Results database

http://seer.cancer.gov

GLOSSARY

3D-CRT: A procedure that uses a computer to create a three-dimensional picture of the tumor. This allows radiation therapists to give the highest possible dose of radiation to the tumor, while sparing the normal tissue as much as possible. Also called three-dimensional conformal radiation therapy and three-dimensional radiation therapy.

absolute risk: Measure of the occurrence of cancer, either incidence (new cases) or mortality (deaths), in the general population.

acupressure: The application of pressure or localized massage to specific sites on the body to control symptoms, such as pain or nausea. Also used to stop bleeding.

acupuncture: The technique of inserting thin needles through the skin at specific points on the body to control pain and other symptoms.

adenocarcinoma: Cancer that begins in cells that line certain internal organs and that have glandular (secretory) properties.

adenoma: A noncancerous tumor.

adjuvant therapy: Treatment given after the primary treatment to increase the chances of a cure. Adjuvant therapy may include chemotherapy, radiation therapy, hormone therapy, or biological therapy.

AJCC staging system: A system developed by the American Joint Committee on Cancer for describing the extent of cancer in a patient's body. The descriptions include TNM: T describes the size of the tumor and if it has invaded nearby tissue, N describes any lymph nodes that are involved, and M describes metastasis (spread of cancer from one body part to another).

alkylating agents: A family of anticancer drugs that interfere with the cell's deoxyribonucleic acid and inhibit cancer cell growth.

alopecia: The lack or loss of hair from areas of the body where hair is usually found. Alopecia can be an adverse effect of some cancer treatments.

alternative medicine: Practices not generally recognized by the medical community as standard or conventional medical approaches and used instead of standard treatments. Alternative medicine includes the taking of dietary supplements, megadose vitamins, and herbal preparations; the drinking of special teas; and practices such as massage therapy, magnet therapy, spiritual healing, and meditation.

anthracycline: A type of antibiotic that comes from certain types of Streptomyces bacteria used to treat many types of cancer. Anthracyclines damage the DNA in cancer cells, causing them to die. Daunorubicin, doxorubicin, and epirubicin are anthracyclines.

antidepressant: A drug used to treat depression.

antiestrogen: A substance that blocks the activity of estrogens, the family of hormones that promote the development and maintenance of female sex characteristics.

419

aromatase inhibition: Prevention of the formation of estradiol, a female hormone, by interfering with an aromatase enzyme. Aromatase inhibition is a type of hormone therapy used in postmenopausal women who have hormone-dependent breast cancer.

attributable risk: Amount of disease within the population that could be prevented by alteration of a risk factor.

axillary dissection: Surgery to remove lymph nodes found in the armpit region. Also called axillary lymph node dissection.

axillary lymph node dissection: Surgery to remove lymph nodes found in the armpit region. Also called axillary dissection.

axillary lymph nodes: Lymph nodes found in the armpit that drain the lymph channels from the breast.

benign proliferative breast disease: A group of noncancerous conditions that may increase the risk of developing breast cancer. Examples include ductal hyperplasia, lobular hyperplasia, and papillomas. Sometimes referred to as fibrocystic change.

biofeedback: A method of learning to voluntarily control certain body functions such as heartbeat, blood pressure, and muscle tension with the help of a special machine. This method can help control pain.

biopsy: The removal of cells or tissues for examination under a microscope. When only a sample of tissue is removed, the procedure is called an incisional biopsy or core biopsy. When an entire lump or suspicious area is removed, the procedure is called an excisional biopsy. When a sample of tissue or fluid is removed with a needle, the procedure is called a needle biopsy or fine needle aspiration.

brachytherapy: A treatment that allows radioactive material – sealed in needles, seeds, wires, or catheters – to be placed in or near a tumor. The treatment is also called internal radiation, implant radiation, or interstitial radiation.

BRCA1: A gene on chromosome 17 that normally helps to suppress cell growth. A person who inherits an altered version of the *BRCA1* gene has a higher risk of getting breast, ovarian, or prostate cancer.

BRCA2: A gene on chromosome 13 that normally helps to suppress cell growth. A person who inherits an altered version of the *BRCA2* gene has a higher risk of getting breast, ovarian, or prostate cancer.

breast cancer in situ: Abnormal cells that are confined to the ducts or lobules in the breast. There are two forms: ductal carcinoma in situ (DCIS) and lobular carcinoma in situ (LCIS).

breast implant: A silicone gel-filled or saline-filled sac placed under the chest muscle to restore breast shape.

breast reconstruction: Surgery to rebuild a breast's shape after a mastectomy.

breast-conserving surgery: An operation to remove the breast cancer, but not the breast itself. Types of breast-conserving surgery include lumpectomy (removal of the lump), quadrantectomy (removal of one-fourth of the breast), and segmental mastectomy (removal of the cancer as well as some of the breast tissue around the tumor and the lining over the chest muscles below the tumor).

c-erbB-2: The gene that controls cell growth by making the human epidermal growth factor receptor 2; also called *HER-2/neu.*

cervical intraepithelial neoplasia (CIN): A general term for the growth of abnormal cells on the surface of the cervix. Numbers from 1 to 3 may be used to describe how much of the cervix contains abnormal cells.

cervix: The lower, narrow end of the uterus that forms a canal between the uterus and vagina.

colon: The long, tubelike organ that is connected to the small intestine and rectum. The colon removes water and some nutrients and electrolytes from digested food. The remaining material, solid waste called stool, moves through the colon to the rectum and leaves the body through the anus. Also called the large intestine.

colon cancer: A disease in which malignant (cancer) cells are found in the tissues of the colon.

colon polyps: Abnormal growths of tissue in the lining of the bowel. Polyps are a risk factor for colon cancer.

colonoscope: A thin, lighted tube used to examine the inside of the colon.

colonoscopy: An examination of the inside of the colon using a thin, lighted tube (called a colonoscope) inserted into the rectum. If abnormal areas are seen, tissue can be removed and examined under a microscope to determine whether disease is present.

colostomy: An opening into the colon from the outside of the body. A colostomy provides a new path for waste material to leave the body after part of the colon has been removed.

complementary and alternative medicine (CAM): Forms of treatment that are used in addition to (complementary) or instead of (alternative) standard treatments. These practices are not considered standard medical approaches. CAM includes dietary supplements, megadose vitamins, herbal preparations, special teas, acupuncture, massage therapy, magnet therapy, spiritual healing, and meditation.

complementary medicine: Practices not generally recognized by the medical community as standard or conventional medical approaches. They are typically used to enhance or complement standard treatments. Complementary medicine includes dietary supplements, megadose vitamins, herbal preparations, special teas, acupuncture, massage therapy, magnet therapy, spiritual healing, and meditation.

complete hysterectomy: Surgery to remove the entire uterus, including the cervix. Sometimes, not all of the cervix is removed. Also called total hysterectomy.

computed tomography (CT) scan: A series of detailed images of areas inside the body taken from different angles; the pictures are created by a computer linked to an X-ray machine. Also called computerized tomography and computerized axial tomography (CAT) scan.

cone biopsy: Surgery to remove a cone-shaped piece of tissue from the cervix and cervical canal. Cone biopsy may be used to diagnose or treat a cervical condition. Also called conization.

corpus: The body of the uterus.

cosmesis: Surgical correction of a disfiguring defect, or the cosmetic improvements made by a surgeon following incisions.

curettage: Removal of tissue with a curette, a spoon-shaped instrument with a sharp edge.

cutaneous breast cancer: Cancer that has spread from the breast to the skin.

cyst: A sac or capsule filled with fluid.

DCIS: Ductal carcinoma in situ. See *ductal carcinoma in situ.*

de novo mutation: An alteration in a gene that is present for the first time in one family member as a result of a mutation in a germ cell (egg or sperm) of one of the parents or in the fertilized egg itself resulting in the first mutation in a family that is passed to other offspring and generations.

diethylstilbestrol (DES): A synthetic hormone that was prescribed from the early 1940s until 1971 to help women with complications of pregnancy. DES has been linked to an increased risk of clear cell carcinoma of the vagina in daughters of women who used DES. DES may also increase the risk of breast cancer in women who used DES.

digital rectal examination (DRE): An examination in which a doctor inserts a lubricated, gloved finger into the rectum to feel for abnormalities.

dilation and curettage (D&C): A minor operation in which the cervix is expanded enough (dilation) to permit the cervical canal and uterine lining to be scraped with a spoon-shaped instrument called a curette (curettage).

ductal carcinoma: The most common type of breast cancer. It begins in the cells that line the milk ducts in the breast.

ductal carcinoma in situ (DCIS): Abnormal cells that involve only the lining of a duct. The cells have not spread outside the duct to other tissues in the breast. Also called intraductal carcinoma.

endocervical curettage: The scraping of the mucous membrane of the cervical canal using a spoon-shaped instrument called a curette.

endometrial: Having to do with the endometrium (the layer of tissue that lines the uterus).

endometrial disorder: Abnormal cell growth in the endometrium (the lining of the uterus).

endometriosis: A benign but often painful condition that can impact fertility. Tissue grows outside the uterus, in the pelvis and abdomen, and may attach to other organs (e.g., ovaries, bowel, or bladder).

endometrium: The layer of tissue that lines the uterus.

endoscope: A thin, lighted tube used to look at tissues inside the body.

epithelial ovarian cancer: Cancer that occurs in the cells lining the ovaries.

epithelium: A thin layer of tissue that covers organs, glands, and other structures within the body.

erbB-2 oncoprotein: Protein that in humans is encoded by the *ERBB2* gene, and it is also frequently called *HER-2* (from human epidermal growth factor receptor 2) or *HER-2/neu*.

estrogen receptor (ER): Protein found on some cancer cells to which estrogen will attach.

estrogen receptor negative (ER−): Breast cancer cells that do not have a protein (receptor molecule) to which estrogen will attach. Breast cancer cells that are ER− do not need the hormone estrogen to grow and usually do not respond to hormone (antiestrogen) therapy that blocks these receptor sites.

estrogen receptor positive (ER+): Breast cancer cells that have a protein (receptor molecule) to which estrogen will attach. Breast cancer cells that are ER+ need the hormone estrogen to grow and will usually respond to hormone (antiestrogen) therapy that blocks these receptor sites.

estrogen replacement therapy (ERT): Hormones (estrogen, progesterone, or both) given to postmenopausal women or to women who have had their ovaries surgically removed. Hormones are given to replace the estrogen no longer produced by the ovaries.

estrogens: A family of hormones that promote the development and maintenance of female sex characteristics.

external-beam radiation: Radiation therapy that uses a machine to aim high-energy rays at the cancer. Also called external radiation.

fallopian tubes: Part of the female reproductive tract. The long, slender tubes through which eggs pass from the ovaries to the uterus during the ovulatory cycle.

familial adenomatous polyposis (FAP): An inherited condition in which numerous polyps (growths that protrude from mucous membranes) form on the inside walls of the colon and rectum. It increases the risk for colon cancer. Also called familial polyposis.

familial polyposis: As described earlier for familial adenomatous polyposis (FAP).

fibroid: A benign smooth muscle tumor, usually in the uterus or gastrointestinal tract. Also called leiomyoma.

FIGO: International Federation of Gynecology and Obstetrics, named from the Fédération Internationale de Gynécologie et d'Obstétrique (FIGO), is a worldwide organization representing obstetricians and gynecologists. This organization publishes staging criteria and evidence-based standards for the treatment of gynecological cancers.

founder effect: The loss of genetic variation that occurs when a new population is established by a very small number of individuals from a larger population and often results in common genetic mutations.

Gail model: A computer program that uses personal and family medical history information to estimate a woman's chance of developing breast cancer.

Gardner syndrome: An autosomal dominant form of polyposis characterized by the presence of multiple polyps in the colon together with tumors outside the colon, including desmoids, osteomas, and epidermoid cysts.

genetic counseling: A communication process between a specially trained health professional and a person concerned about the genetic risk of disease. The person's family and personal medical history may be discussed, and counseling may lead to genetic testing.

genetic testing: Analyzing DNA to look for a genetic alteration that may indicate an increased risk for developing a specific disease or disorder.

gonads: The part of the reproductive system that produces and releases eggs (ovaries) or sperm (testicles/testes).

gynecological: Having to do with the female reproductive tract (including the cervix, endometrium, fallopian tubes, ovaries, uterus, and vagina).

gynecological cancer: Cancer of the female reproductive tract, including the cervix, endometrium, fallopian tubes, ovaries, uterus, and vagina.

gynecological oncologist: A physician who specializes in treating cancers of the female reproductive organs.

gynecologist: A physician who specializes in treating diseases of the female reproductive organs.

HER-2/neu: Human epidermal growth factor receptor 2. The HER-2/neu protein is involved in growth of some cancer cells. Also called c-erbB-2.

hereditary nonpolyposis colon cancer (HNPCC): An inherited disorder in which affected individuals have a higher-than-normal chance of developing colon cancer and certain other types of cancer, usually before 60 years of age. Also called Lynch syndrome.

high-grade squamous intraepithelial lesion (HSIL): A precancerous condition in which the cells of the uterine cervix are moderately or severely abnormal.

hormone receptor: A protein on the surface of a cell that binds to a specific hormone. The hormone causes many changes to take place in the cell.

hormone receptor test: A test to measure the amount of certain proteins, called hormone receptors, in cancer tissue. Hormones can attach to these proteins. A high level of hormone receptors may mean that hormones help the cancer grow.

hormone replacement therapy (HRT) (older term, now called hormone therapy, or HT): Hormones (estrogen, progesterone, or both) given to postmenopausal women or women who have had their ovaries surgically removed, to provide hormones in the absence of the ovaries.

hormone responsive: In oncology, describes cancer that responds to hormone treatment.

hormone therapy: Term applies to treatment that adds, blocks, or removes hormones. For certain conditions (such as diabetes or menopause), hormones are given to adjust low hormone levels. To slow or stop the growth of certain cancers (such as prostate and breast cancer), hormones may be given to block the body's natural hormones. Sometimes surgery is needed to remove the source of hormones. Called hormonal therapy, hormone treatment, or endocrine therapy.

hormones: Chemicals produced by glands in the body and circulated in the bloodstream. Hormones control the actions of certain cells or organs.

hysterectomy: An operation in which the uterus is removed.

IMRT: Intensity-modulated radiation therapy. A type of three-dimensional radiation therapy that uses computer-generated images to show the size and shape of the tumor. Thin beams of radiation of different intensities are aimed at the tumor from many angles. This type of radiation therapy reduces the damage to healthy tissue near the tumor.

incidence: Number of new cancers in a given time period in a specific population.

incision: A cut made in the body to perform surgery.

incisional biopsy: A surgical procedure in which a portion of a lump or suspicious area is removed for diagnosis. The tissue is then examined under a microscope.

infiltrating ductal carcinoma: The most common type of invasive breast cancer. It starts in the cells that line the milk ducts in the breast, grows outside the ducts, and often spreads to the lymph nodes.

inflammatory breast cancer: A type of breast cancer in which the breast looks red and swollen and feels warm. The skin of the breast may also show the pitted appearance called peau d'orange (like the skin of an orange). The redness and warmth occur because the cancer cells block the lymph vessels in the skin.

in situ cancer: Early cancer that has not spread to neighboring tissue.

internal radiation: A procedure in which radioactive material sealed in needles, seeds, wires, or catheters is placed directly into or near a tumor. Also called brachytherapy, implant radiation, or interstitial radiation therapy.

interstitial radiation therapy: A procedure in which radioactive material sealed in needles, seeds, wires, or catheters is placed directly into or near a tumor. Also called brachytherapy, internal radiation, or implant radiation.

intraductal carcinoma: Abnormal cells that involve only the lining of a duct. The cells have not spread outside the duct to other tissues in the breast. Also called ductal carcinoma in situ.

invasive cervical cancer: Cancer that has spread from the surface of the cervix to tissue deeper in the cervix or to other parts of the body.

in vitro: In the laboratory (outside the body). The opposite of in vivo (in the body).

in vivo: In the body. The opposite of in vitro (outside the body or in the laboratory).

jaundice: A condition in which the skin and the whites of the eyes become yellow, urine darkens, and the color of stool becomes lighter than normal. Jaundice occurs when the liver is not working properly or when a bile duct is blocked.

laparoscopy: The insertion of a thin, lighted tube (called a laparoscope) via an incision through the abdominal wall to inspect the inside of the abdomen and remove tissue.

lobular carcinoma in situ (LCIS): Abnormal cells found in the lobules of the breast. This condition seldom becomes invasive cancer; however, having lobular carcinoma in situ increases one's risk of developing breast cancer in either breast.

lumpectomy: Surgery to remove the tumor and a small amount of normal tissue around it.

Lynch syndrome: An inherited disorder in which affected individuals have a higher-than-normal chance of developing colon cancer and certain other types of cancer, usually before 60 years of age. Also known as hereditary nonpolyposis colon cancer (HNPCC).

magnetic resonance imaging (MRI): A procedure in which a magnet linked to a computer is used to create detailed images of areas inside the body. Also called nuclear magnetic resonance imaging.

mammogram: An X-ray of the breast.

mammography: The use of X-rays to create an image of the breast.

medullary breast carcinoma: A rare type of breast cancer that often can be treated successfully. It is marked by lymphocytes (a type of white blood cell) in and around the tumor that can be seen when viewed under a microscope.

microcalcifications: Tiny deposits of calcium in the breast that cannot be felt but can be detected on a mammogram. A cluster of these very small specks of calcium may indicate that cancer is present.

modifiable risk factor: Risk factor for developing malignancy that is under the control of an individual and can be changed by actions such as adding a protective behavior or eliminating a behavior associated with leading to the development of cancer.

modified radical mastectomy: Surgery for breast cancer in which the breast, some of the lymph nodes under the arm, the lining over the chest muscles, and sometimes part of the chest wall muscles are removed.

mortality/mortality rate: Number or rate of people who die of a specific cancer during a defined time period.

needle biopsy: The removal of tissue or fluid with a needle for examination under a microscope. Also called fine needle aspiration.

negative axillary lymph nodes: Lymph nodes in the armpit that are free of cancer.

neoadjuvant therapy: Treatment given before the surgical treatment. Examples of neoadjuvant therapy include chemotherapy, radiation therapy, and hormone therapy. The goal is to shrink the tumor so it can be surgically excised.

node-negative: Cancer that has not spread to the lymph nodes.

node-positive: Cancer that has spread to the lymph nodes.

nodule: A growth or lump that may be cancerous or noncancerous.

nonmodifiable risk factor: A risk factor that cannot be changed or is not under the control of an individual such as increasing age, gender, or genetic makeup.

oophorectomy: Surgery to remove one or both ovaries. It is often done with a laparoscope.

ovarian: Having to do with the ovaries, the female reproductive glands in which the ova (eggs) are formed. The ovaries are located in the pelvis, one on each side of the uterus.

ovarian ablation: Surgery, radiation therapy, or a drug treatment to stop the functioning of the ovaries. Also called ovarian suppression.

ovarian epithelial cancer: Cancer that occurs in the cells lining the ovaries.

ovarian suppression: Surgery, radiation therapy, or a drug treatment to stop the functioning of the ovaries. Also called ovarian ablation.

ovaries: The pair of female reproductive glands in which the ova, or eggs, are formed. The ovaries are located in the pelvis, one on each side of the uterus.

Paget's disease of the nipple: A form of breast cancer in which the tumor grows from ducts beneath the nipple onto the surface of the nipple. Symptoms commonly include itching and burning and an eczema-like condition around the nipple, sometimes accompanied by oozing or bleeding.

Papanicolaou (Pap) test: The collection of cells from the cervix for examination under a microscope. It is used to detect changes that may be cancer or may lead to cancer, and can show noncancerous conditions, such as infection or inflammation. Also called a Pap smear or Pap test. The smear is the actual material obtained from the cervix that is tested in the laboratory to produce a test result.

peau d'orange: A dimpled condition of the skin of the breast, resembling the skin of an orange, sometimes found in inflammatory breast cancer.

positive axillary lymph nodes: Lymph nodes in the area of the armpit (axilla) to which cancer has spread. This spread is determined by surgically removing some of the lymph nodes and examining them under a microscope to see whether cancer cells are present.

preventive mastectomy: Surgery to remove one or both breasts to decrease the risk of developing breast cancer. Also called prophylactic mastectomy.

proband: A person serving as the starting point for the genetic study of a family.

progesterone: A female sex hormone released by the ovaries during every menstrual cycle to prepare the uterus for pregnancy and the breasts for milk production (lactation). In breast cancer, tumor growth may depend on progesterone. If the woman's tumor does rely on progesterone for growth, she is progesterone receptor positive (PR+). If it does not, she is progesterone receptor negative (PR−).

progesterone receptor negative (PR−): In breast cancer, when the woman's tumor growth is not affected by progesterone.

progesterone receptor positive (PR+): In breast cancer, when the woman's tumor growth is affected by progesterone.

prophylactic mastectomy: Surgery to remove one or both breasts to decrease the risk of developing breast cancer. Also called preventive mastectomy.

prophylactic oophorectomy: Surgery intended to reduce the risk of ovarian cancer by removing the ovaries before disease develops.

radiation therapy: The use of high-energy radiation from X-rays, gamma rays, neutrons, and other sources to kill cancer cells and shrink tumors. Radiation may come from a machine outside the body (external-beam radiation therapy) or from materials called radioisotopes. Radioisotopes produce radiation and can be placed in or near the tumor or in the area near cancer cells. This type of radiation treatment is called internal radiation therapy, implant radiation, interstitial radiation, or brachytherapy. Systemic radiation therapy uses a radioactive substance, such as a radiolabeled monoclonal antibody, that circulates throughout the body. Also called radiotherapy, irradiation, and X-ray therapy.

radical mastectomy: Surgery for breast cancer in which the breast, chest muscles, and all of the lymph nodes under the arm are removed. For many years, this was the operation most used, but it is used now only when the tumor has spread to the chest muscles. Also called the Halsted radical mastectomy.

raloxifene: A drug that belongs to the family of drugs called selective estrogen receptor modulators (SERMs) and is used in the prevention of osteoporosis in postmenopausal women. Raloxifene is also being studied as a cancer prevention drug.

reconstructive surgery: Surgery that is done to reshape or rebuild (reconstruct) a part of the body changed by previous surgery.

regional lymph node dissection: A surgical procedure to remove some of the lymph nodes that drain lymph from the area around a tumor. The lymph nodes are then examined under a microscope to determine whether cancer cells have spread to them.

relative risk: Comparison of the incidence or deaths among those with a particular risk factor compared with those without the risk factor.

resection: Removal of tissue or part or all of an organ by surgery.

risk factor: Trait or characteristic that is associated with a statistically significant and an increased likelihood of developing a disease.

salpingo-oophorectomy: Surgical removal of the fallopian tubes and ovaries.

Sanger DNA sequencing: A laboratory method used to determine the sequence of base pairs in a gene.

Schiller test: A test in which iodine is applied to the cervix. The iodine colors healthy cells brown; abnormal cells remain unstained, usually appearing white or yellow.

selective estrogen receptor modulator (SERM): A drug that acts like estrogen on some tissues but blocks the effect of estrogen on other tissues. Tamoxifen and raloxifene are SERMs.

sentinel lymph node: The first lymph node to which cancer is likely to spread from the primary tumor. Cancer cells may appear first in the sentinel node before spreading to other lymph nodes.

sentinel lymph node biopsy: Removal and examination of the sentinel node(s) (the first lymph node(s) to which cancer cells are likely to spread from a primary tumor). To identify the sentinel lymph node(s), the surgeon injects a radioactive substance, blue dye, or both near the tumor. The surgeon then uses a scanner to find the sentinel lymph node(s) containing the radioactive substance or looks for the lymph node(s) stained with dye. The surgeon then removes the sentinel node(s) to check for the presence of cancer cells.

sentinel lymph node mapping: The use of dyes and radioactive substances to identify the first lymph node to which cancer is likely to spread from the primary tumor. Cancer cells may appear first in the sentinel node before spreading to other lymph nodes and other places in the body.

staging: Performing examinations and tests to learn the extent of the cancer within the body, especially whether the disease has spread from the original site to other parts of the body. It is important to know the stage of the disease to plan the best treatment.

tamoxifen: An anticancer drug that belongs to the family of drugs called antiestrogens. Tamoxifen blocks the effects of the hormone estrogen in the body. It is used to prevent or delay the return of breast cancer or to control its spread.

taxane: Chemotherapy agent that blocks cell growth by stopping cell division. Taxanes interfere with microtubules. which are cellular structures that help move chromosomes during mitosis.

total estrogen blockade: Therapy used to eliminate estrogen in the body. This may be done with surgery, radiation therapy, chemotherapy, or a combination of these procedures.

total hysterectomy: Surgical procedure to remove the entire uterus, including the cervix. Sometimes, not all of the cervix is removed. Can be performed through the vagina or through an open incision in the abdomen. Also called complete hysterectomy.

total mastectomy: Removal of the breast. Also called simple mastectomy.

transvaginal ultrasound (TVS): A procedure used to examine the vagina, uterus, fallopian tubes, and bladder. A wandlike or probe instrument is inserted into the vagina, and sound waves bounce off organs inside the pelvic area. These sound waves create echoes, which a computer uses to create an image called a sonogram.

ultrasound: A procedure in which high-energy sound waves (ultrasound) are bounced off internal tissues or organs and make echoes through the use of a noninvasive smooth, handheld transducer that is rolled over the pelvic or abdominal area. The echoes form an image of body tissues called a sonogram. Also called ultrasonography.

vascular endothelial growth factor (VEGF): Substance made by cells that stimulates new blood vessel formation.

INDEX

Page numbers followed by an italicized *f* indicate figures; *t,* tables; and *b,* boxes.